Sex, Love, and Health
in America

Sex, Love, and Health in America

■

Private Choices and Public Policies

EDITED BY
Edward O. Laumann and Robert T. Michael

THE UNIVERSITY OF CHICAGO PRESS
CHICAGO AND LONDON

EDWARD O. LAUMANN is the George Herbert Mead Distinguished Service Professor in the Department of Sociology at the University of Chicago. ROBERT T. MICHAEL is the Eliakim Hastings Moore Distinguished Service Professor in and dean of the Harris Graduate School of Public Policy Studies at the University of Chicago. Both are authors, with John H. Gagnon and Stuart Michaels, of *The Social Organization of Sexuality: Sexual Practices in the United States* (University of Chicago Press, 1994).

The University of Chicago Press, Chicago 60637
The University of Chicago Press, Ltd., London
© 2001 by The University of Chicago
All rights reserved. Published 2000
Printed in the United States of America

09 08 07 06 05 04 03 02 01 00   1 2 3 4 5
ISBN: 0-226-46967-0 (cloth)
ISBN: 0-226- (paper)

Library of Congress Cataloging-in-Publication Data

Sex, love, and health in America : private choices and public policies / edited by Edward O.
    Laumann and Robert T. Michael.
        p. cm.
    Includes bibliographical references and index.
    ISBN 0-226-46967-0 (cloth : alk. paper)
    1. Sex customs—United States.   2. Sexual behavior surveys—United States.   I. Laumann, Edward O.   II. Michael, Robert T.
    HQ18.U5 S482 2001
    306.7'0973—dc21

                                                                    00-042612

CONTENTS

■

Acknowledgments   vii
Abbreviations   x

Introduction: Setting the Scene   1
    EDWARD O. LAUMANN AND ROBERT T. MICHAEL

Part 1: Sex during Adolescence   **39**
1   Teenage Sex and the Sexual Revolution   41
    KARA JOYNER AND EDWARD O. LAUMANN

2   Choices Leading to Teenage Births   72
    ROBERT T. MICHAEL AND KARA JOYNER
    Summary: Part 1, Sex during Adolescence   105

Part 2: Sex during Adulthood   **107**
3   Sexual Expression in America   109
    EDWARD O. LAUMANN AND YOOSIK YOUM

4   Sexual Contact between Children and Adults: A Life-
    Course Perspective   148
    CHRISTOPHER R. BROWNING AND EDWARD O. LAUMANN

5   Race, Gender, and Class in Sexual Scripts   197
    JENNA MAHAY, EDWARD O. LAUMANN, AND
    STUART MICHAELS

6   Emotional and Physical Satisfaction with Sex in Married,
    Cohabiting, and Dating Sexual Unions: Do Men and
    Women Differ?   239
    LINDA J. WAITE AND KARA JOYNER
    Summary: Part 2, Sex during Adulthood   270

Part 3: Sex and Health   **275**

7   Circumcision in the United States: Prevalence,
       Prophylactic Effects, and Sexual Practice   277
           EDWARD O. LAUMANN, CHRISTOPHER M. MASI, AND
           EZRA W. ZUCKERMAN

8   Reported Changes in Sexual Behavior in Response to
       AIDS in the United States   302
           JOEL A. FEINLEIB AND ROBERT T. MICHAEL

9   Racial/Ethnic Group Differences in the Prevalence of
       Sexually Transmitted Diseases in the United States:
       A Network Explanation   327
           EDWARD O. LAUMANN AND YOOSIK YOUM

10   Sexual Dysfunction in the United States: Prevalence and
       Predictors   352
           EDWARD O. LAUMANN, ANTHONY PAIK, AND
           RAYMOND C. ROSEN

11   Abortion Decisions in the United States   377
           ROBERT T. MICHAEL

12   Private Sexual Behavior, Public Opinion, and Public
       Health Policy Related to Sexually Transmitted Diseases:
       A U.S.-British Comparison   439
           ROBERT T. MICHAEL, JANE WADSWORTH,
           JOEL A. FEINLEIB, ANNE M. JOHNSON,
           EDWARD O. LAUMANN, AND KAYE WELLINGS
       Summary: Part 3, Sex and Health   454

       Epilogue   **463**
13   Private Sex and Public Policy   465
           ROBERT T. MICHAEL

       References   493
       List of Contributors   517
       Author Index   519
       Subject Index   525

■

This volume is based on the National Health and Social Life Survey (NHSLS) data set, and we editors were two of the three who crafted and undertook that survey project in 1988. We acknowledge the contribution of our other colleague, John H. Gagnon, who, with us, designed and implemented the survey and placed in the public domain the resulting data set, which has now been used by many other analysts as well. The seven private foundations that funded the survey project deserve our thanks once again. Had they not been willing to take the risk of paying for a survey many believed could not be completed, this book would not have been feasible. They were the Robert Wood Johnson Foundation, the Henry J. Kaiser Family Foundation of Menlo Park, the Rockefeller Foundation, the Andrew Mellon Foundation, the John D. and Catherine T. MacArthur Foundation, the New York Community Trust, and the American Foundation for AIDS Research.

Soon after the publication in 1994 of our two books, *The Social Organization of Sexuality* and *Sex in America,* and the public release of the NHSLS data that autumn, we began further research using those data. That research was supported by the Ford Foundation (grant 940–1417), and we acknowledge that support with gratitude. Additionally, in 1993, the National Institute for Child Health and Human Development (NICHD) awarded us a grant (R01-HD28356) that has also been essential in helping us complete the chapters and sustain our research program on sexual behavior. The NICHD instigated our research on adult sexual behavior with its call for proposals in 1987 and its funding of the design of the study, so we are particularly appreciative of its continued support and encouragement over the years.

As the several chapters in this book were reviewed by workshop audiences, and some have been through reviews and editing at journals, while others have received the benefit of critiques at various scholarly meetings, each chapter will carry its own acknowledgment to those who have helped us improve it. The peer review of this volume by the University of Chicago Press as well as that by the Press editor, Anita Samen, have also improved the work substantially. Throughout the project period, we have benefited from the superb technical and administrative support of Conray Weathers, who has brought years of experience to the preparation of text, tabular, and graphic materials.

A project of this size, complexity, and duration—now over a decade— is beholden to many people at the National Opinion Research Center and on the project staff itself who have contributed in important and often unrecognized ways to the execution of technically sophisticated and challenging features of the study design, data preparation, and the analysis of the NHSLS. Here we can single out for special mention only a few who played critical roles in this final phase of analysis, interpretation, and discussion.

Perhaps our greatest asset was the talented group of graduate students on the project staff who worked together closely, handling the myriad details of data preparation (e.g., cleaning, checking consistency, and constructing variables), analysis, and write-up. Stuart Michaels, a coauthor of chapter 5 in this volume, was the senior student coordinator who worked on the NHSLS prior to the survey and subsequently also oversaw the preparation of the data set for public release. A coauthor of *The Social Organization of Sexuality,* he completed his dissertation (based on the NHSLS data) in 1997 and has for the past several years been a postdoctoral fellow at the Institut National de la Santé et de la Recherche Médicale (INSERM) in Paris, working with the French survey team that conducted the national French survey of sexual practices in 1991 on a comparative study of the U.S. and French data. Christopher Browning began work on the project in 1992 as a junior research assistant, assisted in drafting several chapters in the first volume, completed a dissertation (on adult/child sexuality) using the NHSLS in 1997, and again contributed as the first author for chapter 4 in this book. He recently completed a two-year postdoctoral fellowship in demography at the University of Chicago and is now an assistant professor of sociology at the Ohio State University. Kara Joyner, whose tenure on the project is comparable to Browning's, has coauthored three chapters (chapters 1, 2, and 6), completed a dissertation on a closely related topic (equity and partnership stability), and served two years as a postdoctoral fellow in demography at the University of North Carolina at Chapel Hill; she is now an assistant professor of sociology at McGill University. Ezra Zuckerman, coauthor of the chapter on circumcision, has contributed sophisticated quantitative skills to the project since 1993 and completed a dissertation on an unrelated topic (economic sociology) in 1997; he is now an assistant professor of business strategy at the Stanford University Business School.

Yoosik Youm, Anthony Paik, and Jenna Mahay are currently sociology graduate students and senior research assistants working on the Chicago Health and Social Life Survey project, which has overlapped the NHSLS project since 1995; each has contributed to various chapters in this book. Joel Feinleib, coauthor of the chapter on behavioral changes in sexual behavior in response to AIDS, was a doctoral student in the Irving B. Harris School of Public Policy Studies at the University of Chicago. Christopher Masi, M.D., used his medical expertise to review the voluminous medical literature on circumcision for chapter 7. He is currently in family/adolescent practice in an inner-city African American neighborhood and is pursuing a Ph.D. in social work at the School of Social Service Administration of the University of Chicago.

Professor Linda Waite, a noted demographer of the family and coauthor of chapter 6 (on partnership satisfaction, happiness, and health), has been a valued colleague and adviser on various phases of the study and has served on several doctoral committees supervising dissertations based on the NHSLS data set. Professor Raymond C. Rosen, a clinical psychologist in the Department of Psychiatry at the Robert Wood Johnson Medical College in New Jersey, and coauthor of chapter 10 (on sexual dysfunction), has played an important role in the design and implementation of clinical trials for a variety of medications and devices designed to improve the sexual functioning of both men and women. He is the codirector of the Center for Sex Therapy at Robert Wood Johnson. One of our colleagues, Jane Wadsworth, died in July 1997. Jane had been a principal author of chapter 12, our joint paper comparing sexual practices in Britain and the United States. She had been a leading researcher in England studying sexual behavior and the transmission of sexual disease. Her untimely death took away a dear friend and an influential scholar. She, Anne M. Johnson, M.D., and Kaye Wellings were the principal coinvestigators responsible for the British national survey of sexual practices, conducted in 1991.

Edward O. Laumann and Robert T. Michael

ABBREVIATIONS

∎

SIA   Michael, R. T., J. H. Gagnon, E. O. Laumann, and G. Kolata. 1994. *Sex in America.* Boston: Little, Brown.

SOS   Laumann, E. O., J. H. Gagnon, R. T. Michael, and S. Michaels. 1994. *The social organization of sexuality: Sexual practices in the United States.* Chicago: University of Chicago Press.

■

Setting the Scene

EDWARD O. LAUMANN AND ROBERT T. MICHAEL

O n 6 October 1994, the Thursday morning edition of the *Chicago Trib-une* broke the embargo against prepublication release of the findings from the National Health and Social Life Survey (NHSLS). The official release date for the two books reporting those findings, *Sex in America* (*SIA*)—by Robert T. Michael, John H. Gagnon, Edward O. Laumann, and Gina Kolata—and *The Social Organization of Sexuality* (*SOS*)—by Edward O. Laumann, John H. Gagnon, Robert T. Michael, and Stuart Michaels—was to have been Sunday, 9 October 1994. But the *Tribune* was unwilling to wait when it learned that "20/20" was airing its own report on the findings on Friday, 7 October. Peter Gorner, a *Chicago Tribune* staff writer specializing in science and health topics, had spent weeks working with us on preparing a wonderfully detailed and graphic account of the key findings. He put the "spin" on the story that was widely adopted throughout the country with his headline: "Sex Study Shatters Kinky Assumptions." The same day, the front-page headline of the *New York Daily News* proclaimed: "Marrieds Do It More. New Sex Study Reveals Americans' Co-Habits" (Saltonstall 1994). The *Washington Post* chimed in the following day with "Survey Finds Most Adults Sexually Staid" (Vobejda 1994), while the *New York Times,* also a day late, noted the violation of the embargo agreement but stressed much the same story line (Lewin 1994).

Within several days, nearly every metropolitan newspaper in the United States had major news stories, usually on the front page, reporting highlights of the findings. *Time* (Elmer-Dewitt 1994), *U.S. News and World Report* (Schrof 1994), and *Glamour* (Michael et al. 1994b) had extensive cover stories the following week providing detailed reports and commentaries; television news and talk shows such as "20/20," "Good Morning, America," and "The Phil Donahue Show," National Public Radio shows such as "All Things Considered," "Fresh Aire," and "Talk of the Nation," and myriad local radio and television programs, book reviews, interpretive essays and commentaries, political cartoons, and humorous essays (by Garrison Keillor in *Time* [Oct. 17, 1994] and Anthony Lane in *The New Yorker* [Dec. 19, 1994], among others) appeared with startling frequency in the months that followed. Over the following two years, scores of book reviews in a broad array of professional journals, newspapers, and general purpose and specialty magazines broadened the examination of the findings and the interpretation and critique of the methodology of the NHSLS.

For the most part, the media's treatment of our work was respectful, accepting the study's claim that it was an accurate scientific representation of the broad outlines of sexual practices and beliefs in the adult U.S. population (see, e.g., Robinson 1994; DeLamater 1995). But there were certainly some who harbored major reservations about the validity and accuracy of a survey that rested exclusively on self-reported information about such a socially sensitive topic. Richard C. Lewontin, a noted population geneticist at Harvard, captured this concern with his lead review in the *New York Review of Books,* entitled "Sex, Lies, and Social Science" (1995)—a review that covered both books. The thrust of his review was that, since everyone lies about matters sexual, how can we possibly take anyone's self-report seriously? While this is surely a serious question— and one that deserves an answer—the review itself was unsophisticated, developing its case by relying on literary examples and rhetorical devices rather than criticizing the specific efforts that we reported undertaking to ensure, as far as was possible, reliability. Especially ironic was the accusation that our findings were based on a tissue of pervasive and coherent lies and fabrications about sexual conduct since the portrait we drew was one of a population with quite modest sexual appetites and relatively limited means of sexual expression. Our findings were in stunning contrast to the images of sexual excess or exaggeration that pervade the myriad sex reports appearing over the past forty years, all based on volunteer samples of the sexually interested and active (including, e.g., the Hite, *Playboy,* and Janus Reports, not to mention the original Kinsey Reports themselves). When, and how, had the "lies" that people were "always" telling us stopped being braggadocio and become demure understatement?

From the very outset of our work on the sex survey, we had, of course, been very concerned about the candor of our respondents, and we devoted considerable thought, time, and effort to securing and assessing it. We were quite aware of the many temptations to provide less than full and honest disclosure of one's sexual activities, interests, and beliefs—particularly those that might be socially disapproved. From long experience with professional social surveys, however, we also appreciated that interviews conducted by professional interviewers and supported by an appropriate and compelling rationale can provide sufficiently convincing warrant for people to be truthful about and forthcoming with sensitive information concerning their lives—especially if there is no chance that this information will be shared with significant others in the person's social network (cf. Bradburn and Sudman 1974, chaps. 1–2).

The Social Organization of Sexuality describes in great detail the various measures we took to help respondents understand the need for honesty and frankness, including our elaborate efforts to ensure the privacy and confidentiality of responses through self-administered questionnaires, to help respondents accurately recall events from a long time ago, and to cross-check answers for consistency by formulating different questions on the same topic and asking them at different points in the interview (see *SOS,* esp. chaps. 2, 5 [including apps. 5.1A and 5.2A], 9, 11, and 12 and apps. A and B). After carefully reviewing the results of these extensive efforts to secure forthcoming and honest answers, we concluded that, for the most part, our respondents exhibited a remarkable willingness to share the grim and problematic as well as the happy features of their multifaceted sex lives. To be sure, the data may still err in the direction of underestimating rather than overreporting negative sexual events and experiences (Turner et al. 1998).

Reflecting the willingness of people to share problematic aspects of their sex lives was our finding that about 43 percent of the men and 31 percent of the women reported suffering in the past twelve months from at least one major sexual dysfunction of at least two months' duration (see chaps. 7 and 10 below). There is only a slight age trend in these data; that is, young people—both men and women—reported these symptoms almost as often as did people in their fifties. Yet only one in ten men and one in five women reporting a symptom reported seeking medical help. About one in five women and one in nine men reported having sexual experiences during their childhood with a substantially older person, usually an adult (see chap. 4 below). Most did not tell anyone at the time, and most found the experience to be a negative one. Yet they shared this information with us. Moreover, we can show that those who had such experiences have quite distinctive trajectories in their sexual careers when compared to those who did not report such experiences. Nearly 30 percent of the women reported that their first experience with sexual intercourse was unwanted at the time but consensual. Both men and women reported low rates of abortion up until 1973, when we suddenly observe a sharp rise to a much higher rate. No one reminded respondents that *Roe v. Wade,* the Supreme Court decision affirming the right to an abortion, was rendered in 1973 (see chap. 11 below). This temporal patterning of abortion rates provides remarkably persuasive external validation for the accuracy of respondents' reports about the disposition of their pregnancies over the years.

Perhaps the most frequent public questioning of our results centered on the reported numbers of sex partners over the lifetime. On the one hand, we reported that the median number of partners since age eighteen was two for women and six for men. Many expressed surprise at how low the medians were—but this is hardly consistent with an expectation that men can be expected to exaggerate and women to underreport the number of

partners they have had. In our discussion of these results in chapter 5 of
SOS, we adduce a variety of reasons for believing these numbers to be
reasonably accurate, especially in the lower ranges (see also Morris 1993b;
Wiederman 1997), and several logical possibilities for reconciling the
differences between the reports of men and those of women. In general,
careful analysis of the data on number of partners suggests that the bulk
of the respondents are giving quite accurate counts. Systematic distortion
seems to be concentrated among those who have had very large numbers
of partners and must somehow estimate them, although this practice does
not, of course, affect the median.

The media's reception and the considerable interest in our findings
throughout the nation were gratifying to us. The public acclaim, but not
the public interest in the work, stands in striking contrast to the reception
accorded the Kinsey Reports nearly fifty years before, when the primary
author was personally vilified, the two books, reporting the sexual behavior of males (Kinsey, Pomeroy, and Martin 1948) and females (Kinsey et
al. 1953), were widely denounced as contributing to the moral decay of
the nation, and even advertising for the books was refused by the *New
York Times.* The public interest in the Kinsey books was, if anything,
greater than that which we experienced.

Perhaps the difference in the scientific and media treatment of our
books compared to Kinsey's reveals a greater maturity about human sexuality in the 1990s. If that is the case, that maturity cannot be credited to
social policy designed to promote the study and understanding of sexual
behavior. It may, however, be a by-product of the public exposure to sexual
matters throughout the 1960s and 1970s that both desensitized public discussion and raised many issues of public policy regarding sex.

Perhaps, as well, the difference reflects greater respect for social science
research on important social behavior than existed a half century ago. Our
study used state-of-the-art survey procedures and analytic methods, yet
we broke no new ground. Instead, our contribution was the application of
those respected and useful research methods to the study of adult sexual
behavior, where they had seldom been employed.

Both these explanations of why our study was so much better received
by the general public than Kinsey's are optimistic ones. There were no
corresponding grounds for optimism, however, in the troubled political
history our project had endured when it was under active consideration
for funding by the federal government a few years before (for a brief account, see Laumann, Gagnon, and Michael [1994] and also Ericksen
[1999, esp. chap. 9]). Congressional opponents of the survey had successfully prevented the National Institutes of Health (NIH) from funding the
survey it had itself requested in 1987, despite the perceived urgency of
obtaining information about adult sexual practices for the purpose of de-

signing more effective public health strategies to counter the spread of AIDS. For about three years, beginning in late 1988, political deliberations halted our survey.

The contrast is stark between the political interference or squeamishness of federal government policy makers, on the one hand, and, on the other, the public interest in the study's findings and the public's willingness to be interviewed. Readers will probably not be surprised by these reactions—the sustained political pressure from Capitol Hill on government health agencies not to fund studies of this nature or the seemingly mature and healthy public interest in our findings and the willingness of a probability sample of all adults in the country to cooperate with the lengthy survey that we had crafted—but the disjunction between the two is surely a fascinating reflection of the gap between the interests of our political leaders and those of the body politic (see also Laumann 2000).

Public policy regarding adult sexual behavior has apparently advanced very little in the half century since Kinsey, while social acceptance of the study of sexuality and of diverse forms of sexual behavior has grown substantially. It is to be hoped that, before another decade passes, the political climate will come to reflect the maturity evidenced in the general public's reaction to our two previous books.

The present book is the third to be based on the NHSLS. Because of the unconscionable delay in undertaking the survey (a delay due to political interference), we felt that, once the study had been conducted, we needed to present the findings publicly as expeditiously as possible. Accordingly, only a little more than a year was spent analyzing the data and writing both *The Social Organization of Sexuality,* designed to be a detailed account of our procedures and findings, and *Sex in America,* designed to highlight the most important findings of interest to the general public. The data themselves were also placed in the public domain at the time the books were published so that other researchers could examine them for their own purposes.[1]

This time limitation imposed serious constraints on the depth in which we explored topics in those two books. The present volume contains thirteen essays based on further analysis of the NHSLS data. These have been written mostly by the two of us and our graduate students, who have been essential helpers throughout the project; each essay is separately authored. A few are revisions of articles published in diverse professional journals addressed to disparate professional audiences. The others have not previously been published. We believe that, by publishing these essays together in one place, we can indicate the ways in which they mutually inform one another, emphasizing the underlying integrity of the social organization of sexuality and the manifold ways in which sexuality affects our personal and public lives. These essays demonstrate, we hope, the remarkable richness and range of information to be gleaned from the NHSLS data and the intellectual challenge of studying sexual behavior from a social scientific perspective.

Master Statuses and Master Relationships

One principal way in which the chapters mutually inform one another arises from their consistent use of *master statuses* and *master relationships* as an analytic framework within which to view their various substantive foci. Six *master statuses* receive special attention: *age, gender, marital status, education, race* (and *ethnic background*), and *religious affiliation*. Each of these characteristics or statuses is a basic component of the self-identity of the individuals who possess them, organizing the patterning of social relationships and people's understanding of the social world around them. Of course, many other characteristics also possess these features; however, this basic set is both universally recognized and, in many cases, arguably most salient—hence the term *master statuses*. These three features imply that differences in master statuses are likely to be associated with differences in the scripts to which people are exposed (cf. Gagnon and Simon 1973; chapter 5 below for a detailed exposition and application of their approach), in the types of choices that people perceive as viable as well as the costs and benefits that they associate with these choices, and in the structure of the social networks in which people are embedded. In short, our approach is to focus on differences across the *status groups* defined by the master statuses in sexual behaviors and attitudes in an attempt to infer the existence of different scripts, choices, and network structures.

It is important to note some of the empirical properties of these statuses that determine how they are implicated in specific social processes. For example, these statuses differ in the extent to which they can be recognized socially. Gender is an attribute that cannot escape even the most cursory face-to-face encounter, while religious affiliation is generally a latent characteristic that is more difficult to determine, even for those with whom one interacts a great deal. Also, not all people consider all statuses to be equally important. Thus, someone who is a devout Catholic is likely to take that label more seriously than someone who does not attend church and is Catholic only by default (i.e., having been raised Catholic).

Yet another property of master statuses is that they are not implicated in a homogeneous manner throughout the population. Thus, being Catholic in New England, and probably of Irish or French descent as well, means something different from being Catholic, and of German or Italian descent, in St. Louis; consequently, people expect Catholics in New England to behave differently than do Catholics in St. Louis. Similarly, being a woman means different things in different places and situations; one might expect that a woman college student in New York City has more opportunity than a middle-aged woman living in a small Southern town to pursue a male sex partner actively without being considered deviant. Not only do the meanings attached to specific statuses vary, but, in most cases, a specific status does not operate in isolation. Instead, each individual embodies all these statuses simultaneously and must therefore manage the expectations associated with each of these statuses simultaneously.

Because of these latter two properties—that specific statuses have different meanings in different segments of the population and that they do not operate alone but in concert with each other—we are less interested in differences based on a particular status in isolation and focus instead on the set of social positions consisting of specific combinations of status characteristics. This is especially true with regard to gender: almost all the analyses that we present have been conducted separately for men and women. That is, we allow the associations between the other master statuses and sexual behavior to vary across gender. Not only is sexual activity physiologically different for men and women (see, e.g., Hines and Culotta 1998), but our sexual interactions and our very understanding of sexuality are fundamentally organized around our concept of gender (Ortner and Whitehead 1981). Thus, it seems reasonable to hypothesize that men and women express themselves sexually in fundamentally different ways.

One final property of the master statuses is the inherent complexity in the ways in which they affect sexual activity. An important example concerns gender and age (and perhaps also race). While these statuses possess the three social features described above, they are also associated with biological differences that may have important consequences for sexual expression. Since we were unable to collect any biological data (and since, in many cases, it is unclear what type of biological data would be relevant), we are not able to differentiate analytically between the effects of social factors and those of biological factors. In fact, even with both types of data, it turns out to be quite difficult to separate the two effects (for a discussion of some of the relevant issues, see Udry [1988] and Udry and Campbell [1994]). In some cases, we will indicate where biological effects may be present. Moreover, we hope that the national baselines for behavior established by this study (see chaps. 7–12) will help those investigators researching biologically related topics with clinical or otherwise specially selected samples evaluate the sexual activity of those samples relative to the population as a whole.

Another example of the complexity with which the master statuses affect sexual behavior concerns age. As we have said, an individual's age may be associated with various sexual behaviors as a result of factors related to biological maturity, social expectations concerning what conduct is appropriate at a given age, and various age-related experiences, such as having children, becoming divorced, and entering retirement. This set of factors has become the basis for a new approach to social research called the *life-course perspective,* an approach that is especially useful in studying sexual behavior (cf. Laumann, Gagnon, and Michael 1989a). In addition, however, it is likely that the social environment experienced by an individual during puberty (especially the latter stages involving first sexual experiences) is especially important and that the effects of these experiences will persist throughout the individual's lifetime (for instances of this proposition, see chaps. 1, 2, and 4). Such effects (called *cohort effects* by demographers) are impossible to distinguish from the other type of age effect using cross-sectional data; thus, in interpreting the data, we consider both types when appropriate.

Our strategy of relying on certain individual characteristics as master statuses may be extended by using certain, observable characteristics of sexual *relationships* to identify fundamental differences in the social and behavioral aspects of those relationships. One such characteristic is whether the relationship involves *marriage.* Among nonmarital relationships, we will also want to distinguish between those relationships in which the partners are *living together* and those in which they are not. Both these characteristics—being married and living together—reflect important cultural, legal, and interpersonal distinctions among sexual relationships. In addition, cultural wisdom suggests that there may be a distinction between those nonmarital, noncohabitational relationships that one or both partners have some intention of pursuing further—*long-term relationships*—and those that the partners explicitly view as *short term.* This possibility is evinced by the various labels that people use to describe their own partnerships and those of their acquaintances: *boyfriend/girlfriend, one-night stand,* etc. This third distinction is less objective than the first two and, as such, is more difficult to measure with a survey instrument. For our immediate purposes, we have used the convention of identifying as short-term relationships those that consist of only one or a very few sexual events.

Just like the master statuses discussed above, these *master relationships* can also be part of the participants' self-identities, can affect the participants' locations in the surrounding social network, and can serve to organize people's understandings of the sociosexual world. And, like master statuses, these relationships also vary in the degree to which they are socially visible or, in other words, in the extent to which people other than the partners themselves are aware of the relationship and consider it to be significant. Clearly, marriage is the most socially visible of the four relationship types, short-term relationships the least. Long-term relationships and those in which the partners are living together are in the middle, although it is unclear which is more visible than the other. On the other hand, the mere fact of sharing a household may result in cohabiting relationships being more socially visible than those in which partners do not live together; however, certain long-term partnerships, such as those in which the couple is engaged to be married, are also likely to be quite visible. A related issue that intersects with visibility is the extent to which a relationship is considered to be socially legitimate. This becomes important because relationships not considered legitimate are more likely to be concealed by the partners or ignored by those around them. Thus, a young woman may not tell her family and friends that she is living with her boyfriend in order to avoid criticism or a reputation of being sexually permissive; consequently, her family and friends may underestimate the significance of the relationship.

The significance of a relationship's degree of social visibility is twofold. First, and most obviously, people who are not aware of a particular relationship are unable to comment on its appropriateness or the lack thereof. For example, an interracial couple may choose to tell only their closest friends about their relationship, thus avoiding potential criticism. As a result, the couple also forgoes the potential social support that can facilitate maintaining the relationship. Consistent with this reasoning are a few studies showing that, among dating couples, perceptions of negative third-party reactions are negatively associated with level of romantic involvement and stability of the relationship (Eggert and Parks 1983; Parks and Adelman 1983).

Also important is the fact that social visibility can often be used to predict the degree to which various third parties will be "interested" in the relationship. For example, consider parents whose daughter decides to date a man whom they (and others around them) consider to be in some way inappropriate. Although they may disapprove of the relationship, the parents may tolerate the boyfriend in the interest of maintaining a positive relationship with their daughter. However, if the couple decides to live together, the parents are then forced to speak about and justify the boyfriend in front of family members and friends. Doing so may cause the parents to reevaluate their initial position on the relationship and perhaps to remind or inform their daughter of their disapproval.

In addition to differences in social visibility, our four master relationships can also be differentiated in terms of the motivations that are likely to be attributed to the participants, providing considerable analytic leverage in explaining between whom certain relationships will occur and how those relationships will be conducted. For example, a short-term relationship is likely to result from purely sexual motivations, whereas marriage clearly results from a complex set of motivations, of which sexual interests may be only a small part. On the basis of the theoretical arguments presented above, we expect these differences in motivation to correspond to observable differences in sexual conduct (chaps. 3, 5, 7, and 9, in particular, exploit this interpretation of master relationships).

The Choice versus the Institutional Approach to Public Policy

An important additional objective of this volume is to highlight some of the policy implications of the findings. In this introduction, and in chapter 13 below, we suggest ways in which alternative approaches to public policy lead to different expectations about policy outcomes and the process of constructing policies related to sexuality. We alternately use an economics-inspired "choice" model and a more sociological "institutional" model in these discussions about policy, and we demonstrate how we might interpret and utilize the NHSLS data from each perspective.

Briefly, the choice model starts with individual choices about sexual behavior and explains them as the result of effort to achieve personal satisfaction subject to the limitations of resources, preferences, abilities, etc. as reflected in individual attributes (such as master statuses, family background, income, and beliefs). These choices can include concern for others and can accommodate quite different tastes; they are not assumed to be fully informed or always wise, but they are viewed as purposive and self-satisfying. These private decisions and actions become public matters when they affect others. Their effect can be positive or negative, although most attention focuses on the negative effects, as when one's actions spread a sexually transmitted infection and threaten public health or impose health care costs on others. Public policy surrounding sexual behavior, then, is oriented to finding ways to cause decision makers to take full account of both the social and the private costs and benefits of their decisions and actions. Where a collective choice must be made about a circumstance that must, by definition, be shared—as, for example, with a public good such as the right to an abortion—information about the real or potential costs and benefits of different sexual behaviors and tastes becomes critical in formulating policy. The underlying assumption of the model is that better information about the nature of the sexual choices that individuals make and why they make them (e.g., the selection of partners, the decision to use condoms or birth control) will allow policy makers to create more effective interventions.

The institutional model starts with the claims that sexual problems are socially constructed and that their construction is driven by the struggle among competing stakeholders to win support and resources for their particular definition of problems, causes, and solutions (see Laumann and Knoke 1987, chaps. 1, 4–6, 12, 14). In other words, sexual behaviors or outcomes such as premarital sex or disease become problems only when interested stakeholders define them as such for specific populations (e.g., pregnancy is defined as a public problem for unmarried adolescents, especially those from minority populations, but not for single adult women who are not poor) (cf. Nathanson 1991). In sum, the notion of *costs* itself is a socially constructed category. What are considered the real costs of sexual behavior, and the salience or import of costs associated with sex, will be based on the stakeholders' conceptualizations of sexuality and will be the focus of intense struggle (cf. Shilts 1988; DiMaggio and Powell 1991).

Stakeholders represent several institutional spheres—public health and medicine, social services, religion, politics—and they address sexuality from different normative positions and with different interests and resources. Normative frameworks powerfully shape how stakeholders understand sex, what they define as problems, how they conceptualize their causes and their possible solutions. Clinicians and public health officials tend to view sexuality through the lens of a biomedical understanding of disease, and they treat the symptoms accordingly. Conversely, religious leaders may identify sexual problems as moral failures. Their solution, then, may be, not to provide access to or information about birth control or condoms (the biomedical solution), but instead to urge abstinence or demand that sexual activity be confined to particular types of relationships (e.g., heterosexual marriage) (for an excellent history of public health campaigns in the United States against prostitution and sexually transmitted diseases, see Brandt [1987]). The institutional model claims that public policy surrounding sexuality is the outcome of a contested process in which stakeholders with deeply held and organizationally embedded understandings of sex struggle to win ownership of problem domains and implement their desired solutions. What is defined as a problem may depend on the abilities of different stakeholders to create alliances across institutional boundaries through which they harness the political and financial capital necessary to place issues in the public arena and onto the agenda of gatekeepers (e.g., the media) (cf. Epstein 1996).

The rational choice and the institutional models offer two different perspectives on where the impetus lies for changes in observed behavior over time or across ages, genders, religions, etc. We suggest that, in truth, neither holds a unique purchase on insight about the determinants or consequences of sexual practices and preferences, that rather each contributes to a deeper understanding of this complex domain of human behavior and social policy. Better factual information about sexual behavior is useful from both perspectives, but it is definitive in neither. The choice model typically assumes that new information may alter tastes, or change objectives, or alter the perceived "price" of doing one thing or another, but that new data are then weighed against other considerations in determining any change in behavior (e.g., the information that smoking is unhealthy has influence, certainly, but is not the only consideration in determining whether one smokes). Similarly, the institutional model assumes that providing policy makers with new information about the sexual tastes and proclivities of certain subgroups of the population will not necessarily result in more effective policies or interventions; those policy makers will, however, use the information, fitting it into their operative normative frameworks. More accurate and detailed information about sexual behavior has real value from both perspectives, nevertheless, and misinformation or ignorance about that behavior is harmful in formulating, implementing, or understanding public policy about sex in these or any other perspectives of which we are aware.

Both perspectives can be helpful as we consider public policies aimed at promoting public health and minimizing sexually transmitted infections and sexual abuse of various kinds. The institutional perspective will help scholars and policy makers understand how and why stakeholders understand sexual problems in the ways in which they do, the consequences of taking alternative paths toward defining and resolving problems, and what means might most effectively achieve these objectives. The rational choice model identifies the constraints on the sexual choices that individuals make and on the interventions created by institutional actors. The latter model focuses attention on the costs and benefits to individuals and collectivities associated with sexual behavior, while the former focuses attention on the origin, meaning, and consequences of these costs and benefits. Together, the two perspectives will allow us to explain the processes and potential outcomes of public policy regarding sexual behavior.

In what follows, we first briefly describe the rationale and design of the National Health and Social Life Survey. We then highlight some key findings reported in the first two volumes in order to provide the broader context within which the work in this volume is to be understood. Finally, we preview the remaining essays in this book.

The National Health and Social Life Survey

The prospect for federal government funding of the survey of sexual behavior that we had designed for the NIH ended decisively when, in September 1991, at the behest of Senator Jesse Helms, the U.S. Senate voted sixty-six to thirty-four against funding the survey in favor of a "say-no-to-sex" campaign directed at adolescents (Ericksen 1999, 176–218). It was only as a result of this public act that we were able to secure funding for the survey from eight private foundations, led by the Robert Wood Johnson Foundation and also including the Henry J. Kaiser Family Foundation of Menlo Park, the Rockefeller Foundation, the John D. and Catherine T. MacArthur Foundation, the Andrew Mellon Foundation, the New York

Community Trust, the American Foundation for AIDS Research, and the Ford Foundation.

The National Health and Social Life Survey is a nationally representative probability sample of 1,511 men and 1,921 women between the ages of eighteen and fifty-nine living in households throughout the United States. That subpopulation covers about 97 percent of the population in this age group—roughly 150 million Americans. It excludes people living in group quarters (barracks, college dormitories, and prisons) as well as those who do not know English well enough to be interviewed. The sample includes an oversampling of African Americans ($N = 458$) and Hispanics ($N = 267$). The survey was conducted by the National Opinion Research Center (NORC) at the University of Chicago between February and September 1992 and readied for analysis by March 1993. The sample's response rate was over 79 percent, at the higher end of such rates obtained in national surveys in recent years. Checks against other high-quality samples (e.g., the Census Bureau's Current Population Survey) suggest that the NHSLS succeeded in obtaining a truly representative sample of the population. Each respondent was surveyed in person by experienced interviewers from NORC. Interviews averaged ninety minutes in duration, and both direct questioning by the interviewer and self-administered questionnaires, filled out by the respondent at various points during the interview and given to the interviewer in a sealed envelop (to ensure the confidentiality of the respondent's answers), were employed. Extensive discussion of the sampling design and evaluation of sample and data quality can be found in chapter 2 and appendices A and B of *SOS*.

Our objective in undertaking this project was, and remains, to use social scientific methods and tools to help provide a better understanding of the motivations and consequences of adult sexual behavior and attitudes, thereby improving private decisions and public policy as regards sexual behavior, especially decisions affecting health policy as it is related to sexually transmitted diseases. When we began our work, the number of AIDS cases reported to the Centers for Disease Control and Prevention (CDC) were doubling every ten months or so, and the virus implicated in the spread of the disease had only recently been identified. The three major routes by which the virus was spread had been identified: sexual contact, the sharing of needles during intravenous drug use, and blood transfusion. By far, the most important avenue was sexual contact.

Confronting AIDS, the report of a committee of the Institute of Medicine (1986) chaired by David Baltimore, a Nobel Prize–winning microbiologist, noted the near total absence of reliable and valid information about sexual practices in the United States. The Kinsey Reports on sexual behavior were still being used for projections of sexual patterns in the population. By then some forty years old, the Kinsey estimates were known to be flawed and misleading from the outset because the sampling procedures necessary to draw appropriately representative samples had not been followed by Alfred Kinsey, who was convinced that truly random sampling could not be achieved in a study of sexual practices in the adult population at large. Randomly selected respondents, he believed, would simply refuse to participate in such a study because of the sensitivity of the topic.

From the outset, our research team—Edward O. Laumann, Robert T. Michael, and John H. Gagnon—was committed to designing a comprehensive approach to human sexuality, with special reference to the characterization of sexual partnerships, rather than a narrowly targeted inquiry into the factors directly implicated in the sexual transmission of infection and disease, including HIV/AIDS. In fact, the original request for proposal (RFP) from the National Institute for Child Health and Human Development issued in June 1987 was entitled "Social and Behavioral Aspects of Fertility-Related Behavior" (NICHD-DBS-87–13). It quaintly avoided the term *sex* for the first three pages of the problem statement but clearly required a comprehensive approach to the topic. Only after substantial political opposition to the study surfaced was there pressure from the most senior administrative levels of the NIH to transmute our original response to the RFP into a biomedical disease-prevention-oriented project. At one point, it was stipulated that only those questions could be included in the survey that had a demonstrable capacity to illuminate the vectors by which sexually transmitted diseases could be passed from one person to another. According to such a rule, no questions about masturbation, sexual fantasy, or religious orientation could justifiably be included in the survey. Once it became clear that the federal government would not be funding the study, we were able to revert to the original design, but, because of the expense involved, we found it necessary to reduce the number of persons to be interviewed to a fifth of that suggested in the original proposal (Laumann et al. 1989b). This curtailment in sample size was fateful because it precluded detailed analysis of significant population subgroups, such as persons who have sex with persons of the same gender.

In pursuing a comprehensive approach to human sexuality, we attempted to include some aspects of the following facets: physical states of arousal; more diffuse emotional states of arousal; ideation, thinking, or fantasy about sexual things; experiences of sexual interest or arousal from visual and auditory stimuli; behavioral acts that are explicitly labeled *sexual* or may be ambiguous in meaning, including autoeroticism and masturbation; the search for sex partners; securing access to a sex partner by dating, building social relationships, and so on; partnered sexual activities of various sorts, including vaginal intercourse and anal and oral sex; the social networks that include sex partners and others who hold views on the appropriateness of partner selection, pursuit, and content of behavior; and normative understandings of appropriate and inappropriate sexual activities and partner choice. In an effort to move the survey definition of *sex* away from a male-dominated focus on orgasm, vaginal intercourse, or intromission, we offered the following definition of sexual activity in the survey:

> Now I am going to be asking some questions about your sexual activity during the *last 12 months*. People mean different things by sex or sexual activity, but in answering these questions, we need everyone to use the same definition. Here, by "sex" or "sexual activity", we mean any mutually voluntary activity with another person that involves genital contact and sexual excitement or arousal, that is, feeling really turned on, even if intercourse or orgasm did not occur.
>
> In answering these questions, please include all persons or times in the *last 12 months* where you had direct physical contact with the genitals (the sex organs) of someone else and sexual excitement or arousal occurred. . . . (NHSLS questionnaire, sec. 4 [see *SOS*, 622])

In sum, the two distinctive features of the NHSLS were (1) its commitment to a comprehensive inclusion of sex-related topics and (2) its focus on the sexual partnership as the organizing framework for data collection. Sex-related topics range from early childhood and adolescent experiences to the last time the respondent had sex and include behavioral practices over the life course (e.g., anal, oral, and vaginal intercourse); autoeroticism; physical and emotional satisfaction with sexual partnerships and practices; partner choice and quality and character of sexual relationships; sexual fantasies and ideation; sexual preferences, attitudes, and knowledge; and lifetime and current experiences with sexually transmitted infections and sexual dysfunction. Attention was devoted to the timings of sexual partnerships (marital, cohabiting, and long- and short-term dating relationships) and conceptions resulting in live births, miscarriages or stillbirths, or abortions. We thus avoided an overly medicalized or disease-driven emphasis that focuses attention away from the profound embeddedness and regularity of sexual conduct in people's lives. The survey instrument was designed to elicit a respondent-friendly social narrative of a person's sexual biography and the ways in which it is implicated in his or her life course.

In providing a new perspective with which to understand the many descriptive facts that we report, we focus on sex as a series of ongoing social transactions whose content, pacing, partner choice, and frequency, as well as the physical and emotional satisfaction thereby derived, are determined by the character of the relationship between the sex partners and the social networks in which the sexual partnerships are embedded.

Overview of the Main Findings Reported in *The Social Organization of Sexuality* and *Sex in America*

While we make no attempt to summarize the large number of specific findings about sexual practices and attitudes reported in the two previous books, we characterize here four broad findings and illustrate them with a few details. Our objective is to give the reader who is unfamiliar with the earlier publications some sense of the range and character of those findings as background for the studies reported in this volume.

The first of these broad conclusions is that *the sexual behavior of most adults in the United States is remarkably conventional:* A vast majority of the U.S. population aged eighteen to fifty-nine has only one sex partner within a year. The median number of sex partners since age eighteen is two for women and six for men. Americans do not have sex all that frequently—the average rate is fewer than two times a week—and, when they do have sex, it does not last all that long. A large majority of Americans engage in a limited repertoire of sexual activities, finding many practices unappealing. Yet, despite the modest amount of sex reported, our respondents also reported that they were quite happy with their sex lives and with their lovers.

Table I.1 shows the evidence for each of these assertions, taken from tables in *SOS* or *SIA*. The tables in those books also provide much more detail about each of these topics, and in them one observes that the primary personal characteristics that organize our sex lives are gender, age, and marital status, while there are only modest differences in sexual behavior, overall, when race/ethnicity, educational level, or religious affiliation are taken into account.

Readers sometimes react with surprise or skepticism to this first general conclusion, that adults' sexual conduct is rather conventional, assuming that the survey did not elicit full disclosure of more unusual behavior. Yet, on reflection, one comes to realize that most of our preconceptions about the sexual behavior of the adult population are neither very reliable nor unbiased. The basis for our perceptions of what is typical sexual behavior is not a series of factual reports by scholars or reputable national statistics on sexual behavior compiled by government agencies. Instead, we typically have had two questionable sources for our information about sex: our own social network of friends, family, and acquaintances and the media—television, newspapers and magazines, the movies, and the theater. Without belaboring the point, neither source is particularly unbiased or accurate. Consequently, our preconceptions are not well founded.

Consider for a moment the fact seen in table I.1 that, in the most recent sexual event (meaning the last time the respondent had sex), about one in five women and one in four men said that they had performed oral sex on

Table I.1 Summary Finding That the Sexual Behavior of Most Adults in the United States Is Remarkably Conventional

A. The Vast Majority of the U.S. Population Aged 18–59 Has Only One Sex Partner within a Year

	Number of Sex Partners in the Past 12 Months (%)			
	0	1	2–4	5+
All	11.9	71.1	13.7	3.2
Men	9.9	66.7	18.3	5.1
Women	13.6	74.7	10.0	1.7

Sources: SOS, table 5.1A; *SIA,* table 6. See also *SOS,* chap. 1; or *SIA,* chap. 5.

B. The Median Number of Sex Partners since Age 18 Is 2 for Women and 6 for Men

	Number of Sex Partners since Age 18 (%)						
	0	1	2–4	5–10	11–20	21+	Median
All	2.9	26.1	29.5	21.7	10.6	9.2	3
Men	3.4	19.5	20.9	23.3	16.3	16.6	6
Women	2.5	31.5	36.4	20.4	6.0	3.2	2

Sources: SOS, tables 5.1C, 5.1D; *SIA,* table 6. See also *SOS,* chap. 1; or *SIA,* chap. 5.

C. Americans Have Sex Not All That Frequently—Fewer Than 2 Times a Week, on Average—and for Not All That Long a Duration When They Do Have Sex

	Frequency of Sex in the Past Year (%)				
	Not at All	A Few Times a Year	A Few Times a Month	2–3 Times a Week	4 + Times a Week
Men	9.8	17.6	35.5	29.5	7.7
Women	13.6	16.1	37.2	26.3	6.7

	Duration of Last Sexual Event (%)		
	Less than 15 Minutes	15–60 Minutes	60 or More Minutes
Men	11.0	69.3	19.7
Women	14.7	70.5	14.8

Sources: Frequency: *SOS,* table 3.4. See also *SOS,* chap. 3; and *SIA,* chap. 6. Duration: *SOS,* table 3.5; *SIA,* table 10. See also *SOS,* chap. 3; and *SIA,* chap. 7.

(continued)

Table I.1 (continued)

D. A Large Majority of Americans Do Not Find Many Sex Practices Very Appealing, So They Engage in a Limited Repertoire of Sexual Activities

	% Saying Practice is "Very Appealing"		% Engaged in Practice in Last Event		% Engaged in Practice Ever	
	Men	Women	Men	Women	Men	Women
Vaginal intercourse	83.8	76.8	94.6	95.6	95.0	97.0
Watching partner undress	47.8	26.8				
Receiving oral sex	45.0	28.8	27.5	19.9	78.7	73.1
Giving oral sex	33.5	16.5	26.8	18.8	76.6	67.7
Group sex	13.3	1.1				
Using a dildo or vibrator	4.4	2.9				
Watching others have sex	5.3	1.5				
Same-gender sex	3.2	2.9	2.7[a]	1.3[a]	4.9[b]	4.1[b]
Having sex with a stranger	4.1	.9				
Anal intercourse	2.8	1.0	2.3	1.2	25.6	20.4
Forcing someone to have sex	.3	.2			2.8	1.5
Being forced to have sex	.1	.1			3.9	22.8

Sources: SOS, tables 3.6, 4.2, 8.1, 9.7, 12.5. See also SOS, chaps. 3–4, 8–9, 12; or SIA, chaps. 7, 9.
[a]Last 12 months, not last event.
[b]Since age 18, not ever.

E. Yet, Despite the Modest Amount of Sex, These Same Men and Women Report Themselves to Be Quite Happy with Their Sex Lives and with Their Lovers

	Satisfaction with Sex Life (%)		
	Extremely or Very Happy	Generally Satisfied	Unhappy
All	57.7	29.2	13.1
By number of sex partners in past 12 months:			
0	40.7	35.4	23.9
1	63.4	27.2	9.4
2–4	44.9	32.7	22.4
5+	47.2	37.1	15.7
By frequency of sex in past 12 months:			
None	39.5	36.7	23.8
1–12 times/year	45.6	32.8	21.6
2–3 times/month or once/week	59.2	29.3	11.5
2–3 times/week	69.0	25.1	5.9
4+ times/week	64.5	22.0	13.6

Table I.1 (continued)

		Satisfaction with Lover (%)					
			Partner Made Respondent Feel:				
	Physically Pleased[a]	Emotionally Satisfied[a]	Satisfied	Loved	Thrilled	Wanted	Taken Care Of
Had only 1 partner:							
Spouse	87.4	84.8	97.1	97.5	90.9	92.2	89.9
Cohabitant	84.4	75.6	95.5	95.2	89.6	88.2	84.0
Neither	78.2	71.0	92.9	87.6	90.8	87.1	76.0
Had more than 1 partner:							
Primary:							
Spouse	61.2	56.7	88.1	86.4	77.6	77.6	68.7
Cohabitant	74.5	57.9	90.5	86.2	91.6	85.1	78.7
Neither	77.9	61.7	92.8	83.9	86.6	84.8	72.8
Secondary partner	54.3	33.0	81.6	48.4	75.6	66.7	53.1

Sources: Sex life: *SOS,* table 10.4. See also *SOS,* chap. 10. Lover: *SOS,* tables 10.5; 10.7. See also *SOS,* chap. 10.
[a]Percentage "extremely" or "very" pleased or satisfied.

their partner. Those figures may sound low. But that same table tells us that, among these same respondents, 33.5 percent of the men found it "very appealing" to give oral sex and 28.8 percent of the women found it "very appealing" to get oral sex. So the probability that both members of a randomly paired couple would find that particular practice "very appealing" is only 0.10 (= .288 × .335), and it is not inconsistent with these stated preferences to find that only a quarter of couples reported engaging in oral sex the last time they had sex. (Of course, couples are not likely to be randomly paired, as will be shown below, but neither are they likely to have sorted themselves out—explicitly—in terms of preferences for specific sex practices—that is just not the social scripting that takes place in our society.)

A second observation about this conclusion that a large portion of adults report that they are basically happy with their sex lives and with their lovers—they were not simply being Pollyannas. We also asked a series of questions about seven specific sexual dysfunctions and found that somewhat less than half the women (43 percent), and somewhat fewer men (31 percent), reported at least one of these problems within the past twelve months. In another section of the interview, we asked about sexually transmitted diseases, and, there, about one in six men and women reported having had one of the ten diseases about which we asked explicitly. So respondents were not reluctant to admit to unpleasant aspects of their sexual experiences, including dysfunction and disease. Yet they assessed their sex lives, overall, as quite satisfying and pleasing. That is a more realistic and fundamentally healthy perception of sex than we might have expected. It seems to us to be consistent with the 79 percent survey response rate: it suggests that Americans are less hung up about sex, and less unrealistic about it, than are their political leaders or those who make the decisions in the media and the entertainment industries. In our judgment, the first broad finding suggests that most adults have a pretty sophisticated view of sexual life: there are problems, and it does not mirror the fantasy life portrayed by the entertainment world, but it is, on balance, pretty good. As we put the point in *Sex in America:* "Our findings . . . explode many myths about sex and show a society that is, at heart, very different from the tales we tell ourselves" (p. 13).

The second broad conclusion is that *our sex lives are deeply embedded socially:* We meet our sex partners through our friendship networks. Well over half of adults are introduced to their lovers by someone who knows both partners. Thus, a very large percentage of couples are of the same race/ethnic background, the same education level, the same age, and the same religion. Table I.2 shows a few details, again, drawn from tables in *SOS* and *SIA*.

To understand why this strong sorting of sexual partnerships by social characteristics is useful, think of the delicacy of a sexual encounter itself. The communication is of necessity subtle, with nuances that matter greatly, so the more shared the prior experience is, the less awkward and the more effective those sexual cues and communications are likely to be. In exposing ourselves in a most intimate and vulnerable way in sexual exchange, it is reasonable and self-protective to select as a mate one with whom you share much since doing so is most likely to result in effective communication and a positive outcome.

This social embeddedness of our sex lives has important implications. It means that our social networks can influence the types of partners we select and the sexual behaviors in which we engage; conversely, they can also discourage certain behaviors. Seldom are these social pressures closely linked to what we might consider the powerful, raw sexual satisfaction of the partner or the practice; the point is, rather, encouraging behavior that promotes cohesion within the network itself, not the joys of sex. We are expected to bring our lovers to meet and share outings with our friends, and they, like our lover's friends, help evaluate the new prospective couple, encouraging some and discouraging others, and typically protecting the cohesion of the group. The romantic notion of seeing a stranger across a crowded room and falling in love at first sight has, in reality, a subtext: typically that crowded room is in a school, or at a private party,

Table I.2 Summary Finding That the Sex Lives of Adults in the United States Are Deeply Embedded Socially

A. We Meet Our Sexual Partners through Our Friendship Networks, and Well over Half of Adults Are Introduced to Their Lover by Someone Who Knows Both Partners

| Met Through: | Married (%) | Cohabitating (%) | Other Partnerships Currently Lasting: | |
			More Than 1 Month (%)	Less Than 1 Month (%)
Family member	15	12	8	3
Mutual friends	35	40	36	37
Coworker	6	4	6	3
Classmate/neighbor	7	2	5	6
Self-introduction	32	36	42	47
Other	2	3	1	2
Total	100	100	100	100
% of partnerships	46	12	33	9

Sources: SOS, table 6.1; SIA, fig. 1. See also SOS, chap. 6; and SIA, chap. 4
Note: Percentages do not add to 100 percent because a small number of respondents reported multiple answers.

B. Thus, a Very Large Percentage of Couples Are of the Same Race/Ethnic Background, Same Education Level, Same Age, and Same Religion

| Characteristic | Married (%) | Cohabitating (%) | Other Partnerships Currently Lasting: | |
			More Than 1 Month (%)	Less Than 1 Month (%)
Same race/ethnicity	93	88	89	91
Same age (5-year interval)	78	75	76	83
Same education level (category)	82	87	83	87
Same religious affiliation	72	53	56	60

Sources: SOS, table 6.4; SIA, table 3. See also SOS, chap. 6; and SIA, chap. 3.

attended by others who are demographically or socially much like you. So that stranger is already selected in large measure to be someone about your age, about your education level, and so on (for a discussion of the formation of sexual networks and their epidemiological implications for the spread of infection, see *SOS*, 225–82).

This social embeddedness also requires us to face certain trade-offs and make choices in our sex lives. We cannot have both socially approved monogamous marital sex and a wild, free-spirited, multipartnered sexual exploration on the side. We must choose. For most of our lives, most of us are immersed in social networks that strongly encourage the one and strongly discourage the other behavior. Our sexual choices become one with our economic and social choices about living arrangements—cohabiting and marrying—about parenting, even about careers and location. Choices about sex are not the dissociated, disembodied hedonistic and sensuous affairs of the fantasy world; they are linked, and rather tightly linked by their social embeddedness, to the other domains of our lives. That social embeddedness helps define what we consider pleasurable and satisfying sexually, and it may be why the monogamous, married respondents consistently rate their sex partners higher than others rate theirs. Secondary partners are rated far behind in terms of producing feelings of being loved, wanted, cared for sexually, even thrilled, and just the reverse holds for negative feelings like fear, guilt, anxiety, and sadness (see *SOS,* Table 10.7).

Now take this observation one step further. When the social embeddedness that occurs in our sex lives is accompanied by little or no factual information about sexual behavior generally and only the most scripted and stylized forms of social debate about sexual issues, considerable isolation and segmentation about sexual attitudes results. This leads to rigidity of views and perceptions, to strongly held opinions, reinforced by our social peers and seldom confronting the range of views represented by other groups. Sex is not a topic about which people engage in natural or easy dialogue outside their small social groups. Nor is it a topic about which public policy has encouraged interest or debate since government policy has discouraged collecting or analyzing data on sexual behavior. Consequently, informed social discussion has not taken place until very recently. That is one explanation for why we find in the NHSLS such deeply held and remarkably diverse views about pornography, abortion, nudity, extramarital sex, homosexuality, and on and on.

We find that about 30 percent of those whom we surveyed fall into a category we describe as *reproductive* or traditional in their views about sex—that sex is appropriate only within a formal marriage, that homosexuality and abortion are always wrong, for example. Many opinions are categorical, the behavior in question being declared "always wrong." Another quarter of those surveyed hold what we call the *recreational* view of sex—if it feels good and hurts no one, then it is a good thing. (More men than women fall into this category—33 and 19 percent, respectively.) The other roughly 45 percent fall into what we call a *relational* view of sex— that is, sex should be accompanied by affection or love, but not necessarily formal marriage, and there are no behaviors that are always wrong, but restraint and balance are called for (for a detailed analysis of normative orientations to sexuality, see *SOS,* 509–40; *SIA,* chap. 13).

These three categories—the reproductionists (on one side), the relationalists (in the center), and the recreationalists (at the other end)—all seem to hold to their views quite strongly. They generally see them as conforming to their religious or ethical tenets. Similar views are often also held by their peers and within their social networks, and these opinions are strikingly consistent with their own sexual behavior (as it was reported to us separately in the survey). Consequently, these opinions are not easily swayed; they are largely a part of the person's self-identity. This helps us understand how difficult it may be to reach consensus about the policy issues that surround sex—abortion or homosexuality, for example. It also further persuades us that it is of importance that we study the topic, that we know the range of behavior and judgments, that we engage in the dialogue among social groups, and between lovers for that matter, that can enhance our capacity to understand and thus to respect those diverse views and, where a consensus or common practice is required, to reach some tolerable understanding.

The third important general finding from our study is that *there is a high prevalence of sexually transmitted diseases in the United States and there is strong evidence of what the risk factors are for these diseases:* One in every six men and women in our survey reported having had a sexually transmitted disease at some time in their life. The evidence of risk is compelling: those with more partners are dramatically more likely to have had either a bacterial infection like gonorrhea, syphilis, or chlamydia or an incurable viral infection like herpes, hepatitis B, genital warts, or HIV. And it is clear why: those with more partners are exposed to many more attributes of partners that reflect risk. There is strong evidence as well of behavioral responses to the risks of AIDS.

These rates of having a sexually transmitted disease are high. The pattern of these rates suggests that most adults who have ever had one of these diseases contracted it during their early adulthood, and this reflects the pattern of when during the lifetime they have the most sex partners. Table I.3 shows that, as the number of sex partners increases, so does the likelihood that the respondent has had a sexually transmitted infection. The table also reveals why it is that those with more partners have a higher risk of disease: they are much more likely to have sex with someone whom they do not know well (someone who was a one-time-only partner or a one-night stand) or with someone they knew for only a few hours or days when they first had sex. Presumably, these less-well-known partners are less motivated to protect the partner as well as more likely to have been exposed to a higher risk of disease.

Table I.3 The Prevalence of Sexually Transmitted Diseases in the United States and the Risk Factors for Those Diseases

A. One in Every Six Men and Women Reported Having Had a Sexually Transmitted Disease at Some Time in Their Lives, and the Evidence of Risk Is Compelling: Those with More Partners Are Dramatically More Likely to Have a Bacterial or Viral Infection

Disease	Respondent's Gender* (%)		Respondent's Number of Sex Partners since Age 18 (Cases per 1,000)					
	Male	Female	0	1	2–4	5–10	11–20	21+
Bacterial:								
Gonorrhea	9.0	4.7	0	11	30	83	148	206
Syphilis	.9	.7	0	1	4	13	9	21
Chlamydia	1.9	4.4	0	14	20	44	64	70
NGU[a]	1.9		0	0	4	16	31	62
PID[b]		2.2	0	9	12	40	77	54
Any bacterial	12.1	10.6	0	28	58	150	241	300
Viral:								
Genital warts	3.3	5.9	0	11	37	70	91	98
Herpes	1.2	2.9	0	5	10	19	51	80
Hepatitis	1.3	.9	11	5	5	12	24	25
HIV/AIDS	.2	.1	0	0	0	2	3	7
Any viral	5.4	9.0	11	17	50	98	159	177
Any sexually transmitted infection	15.9	17.8	11	43	104	234	338	404

Sources: SOS, tables 11.3, 11.4. See also SOS, chap. 11; and SIA, chaps. 10–11.
*Includes those with at least one sex partner in their lifetime.
[a]Nongonococcal urethritis.
[b]Pelvic inflammatory disease.

B. And It Is Clear Why: Those with More Partners Are Exposed to Many More Attributes of Partners That Reflect Risk

Attribute of Sex Partners	Number of Partners in the Past 12 Months			Percentage with an STI in the Past 12 Months Whose Partners Did Have This Attribute	Percentage with an STI in the Past 12 Months Whose Partners Did Not Have This Attribute
	1	2	3+		
Any new partner	9.0	63.7	73.8	4.0	1.1
Any one-time partner	1.1	25.2	60.8	5.6	1.3
Any partnership lasting less than 2 months	2.0	38.6	78.8	4.6	1.3
Any partner known for 2 days or fewer	4.0	17.2	30.8	3.1	4.7
Any partner known less than 1 month	22.8	66.4	69.7	7.7	1.7

Table I.3 (continued)

Attribute of Sex Partners	Number of Partners in the Past 12 Months			Percentage with an STI in the Past 12 Months Whose Partners Did Have This Attribute	Percentage with an STI in the Past 12 Months Whose Partners Did Not Have This Attribute
	1	2	3+		
				Not Monogamous	Monogamous
Either/any partner not expected to be monogamous	1.7	13.9	20.2	3.5	1.6
Sum of partner's other partners:				Primary Partner	Secondary Partner
No other partners	95.6	32.6	25.1	1.4	3.6
1 other partner	2.7	26.4	27.2	2.3	5.4
2 other partners	.8	14.5	18.4	3.8	.0
3 other partners	.4	12.0	10.9	7.1	7.5
4+ other partners	.4	14.5	18.4		

Sources: SOS, tables 11.13A, 11.13B, 11.15. See also *SOS,* chap. 11; and *SIA,* chaps. 10–11.

C. There Is Strong Evidence as Well of Behavioral Responses to the Risks of AIDS

	% Ever Tested for HIV/AIDS	% Reporting Having Changed Their Sexual Behavior because of AIDS
Number of sex partners since age 18:		
0	9.4	12.8
1	16.4	9.6
2–4	24.4	24.8
5–10	32.3	39.5
11–20	36.1	47.6
21+	42.0	63.3

Number of sex partners:	% Using Condom during Last Sexual Event Involving Vaginal Intercourse	Share of Cases (%)
1	13.7	84
2	25.8	9
3	36.1	3
4	40.5	2
5+	31.2	3
All categories	16.3	100

Sources: Changed behavior: *SOS,* table 11.29B. Used condom: *SOS,* table 11.18A.

In terms of sexual exclusivity, 96 percent of those who have only one sex partner in the year report that the relationship with that partner is monogamous. But, of those with two partners in the year, only 33 percent report that both of those partners had sexual relations only with them, while more than a quarter report that those two partners themselves had a total of three or more other partners in the year. And, of those who report having three or more partners in the year, more than one-third report that those other partners had three or more additional partners during the year. That is, one's exposure to disease during the year does not increase additively—from one to two to three to four—as one's partners increase. Rather, exposure increases geometrically—from one to four to nine to sixteen. Those who have sex with many people have sex with people who have sex with many other people, too, so the risk of exposure to disease rises dramatically, a fact confirmed, sadly, by the nearly geometric increase in the lifetime prevalence of disease with an increase in the number of lifetime partners and likewise by the increase in the prevalence of disease in the past year with an increase in the number of partners in the past year.

There is some good news in the findings in table I.3 as well. As the number of sex partners rises, so does the use of condoms. There is much purposive behavior seen here. The fact that, overall, only 16 percent of respondents reported using a condom the last time they had sex may not be very impressive, but 84 percent of all those respondents also reported having only one sex partner within the year, and, for the most part, that sex partner was the respondent's spouse. So, for most, the risk of disease is very low, and the correspondingly low rate of condom use seems appropriate. While there is evidence that there exists a small core group of individuals who engage in high-risk behavior without taking any precautions—of the 3 percent who reported having five or more partners, fewer than a third used a condom during the last sexual event—overall, where the risk is greater, greater effort is generally made to protect against that risk. And, as we show in *SOS,* knowledge of effective means of protecting against a sexually transmitted infection—by abstaining from sex, by maintaining a monogamous sexual relationship, or by using condoms—is widespread in the United States.

When asked about the risks of AIDS, 27 percent of our respondents said that they had been tested for HIV, and 30 percent said that they had changed their behavior because of the risks. Again, it is those most at risk who have reported the most behavioral change.

Regarding the spread of AIDS in the United States, in *SOS* we concluded—on the basis of four facts, three of which come directly from the data in the NHSLS—that it is not likely that there will be a major epidemic of AIDS in the general population in the United States. The one fact that comes exclusively from others' research is that the likelihood of,

say, a woman contracting HIV from engaging in unprotected vaginal intercourse with an infected man is 1 in 500. The risk is higher for anal intercourse and lower for transmission from a woman to a man. But the risk
of contracting HIV from one act of unprotected intercourse is relatively
low, compared to the risk of conception if both partners are fertile (about
one in fifty) or the risk of contracting gonorrhea if the man is infected
(one in two). Now, one encounter can spread the HIV virus, and the result
is terrible, so the low odds of contracting the disease should not lessen
one's resolve to take appropriate protective action. But, from a public
health perspective, this is, fortunately, an inefficiently transmitted infection in a healthy population like that of the United States.

Combine the low odds of contracting HIV with three other facts to be
gleaned from our data. First, over 80 percent of adults have only one or
no sex partner in a year's time. Second, adults overwhelmingly have sex
with partners whose social characteristics are very much like their own,
and this effectively segments the population, with the result that relatively
few instances occur of someone from one segment of society having sex
with someone from another. Because of this segmentation and the low
rate of infectivity, in those segments of society in which HIV is not now
prevalent it is not likely to become so. Third, respondents reported an
impressive extent of behavior change, particularly those who are at risk.
In combination, then, these four facts imply that there is not a high likelihood of a major outbreak of AIDS occurring in the general population—
under the conditions specified.

We hasten to add that those conditions may not hold in other societies
or in the United States at some time in the future, and this assessment
should not in any way diminish the commitment to HIV/AIDS research,
or our compassion for those with AIDS, or one's own diligence and resolve to lower the risk of exposure to the disease. It does suggest that
targeting AIDS education efforts at those pockets at highest risk of contracting the disease—the young, the unmarried, and those population
groups known to have a higher prevalence of HIV (the gay population
and intravenous drug users, e.g.)—will have the biggest payoff. Before our
survey and others were conducted, we knew a great deal about the characteristics of the high-risk groups, but what we did not know is how low the
risks are among other groups, and, thus, it would not have been prudent
to target education efforts as narrowly as is now believed to be the best
social policy for the United States.

Outline of the Book

All the chapters in this volume use the data gathered by the NHSLS. This
unifying fact of a shared database provides many opportunities to examine
the interrelatedness of sexual activities and beliefs in particular social con-

texts considered from different points of view. Thus, while each chapter can be read as a freestanding discussion, all the chapters mutually inform and enrich one another, yielding a whole that is greater than the sum of its parts.

Except for this introduction and the final chapter, which addresses public policy regarding sexual behavior, the chapters in this volume are organized into three groupings: chapters 1 and 2 analyze aspects of sexual behavior during adolescence, chapters 3–6 investigate aspects of adult sexual expression, and chapters 7–12 focus on sexual aspects of health. Throughout the volume, the overarching theme is the systematic way in which sexuality is socially organized at different stages of the life cycle and in different historical periods according to the master statuses and master relationships. The NHSLS data provide a powerful lens through which to view many questions about sexual behavior, questions with profound consequences for individuals and society. Many of the findings reported in the chapters to follow were wholly unanticipated by current theory and research because of the pervasive lack of relevant information from large-scale population samples regarding detailed sexual behavior and attitudes.

Sex during Adolescence

Chapter 1, "Teenage Sex and the Sexual Revolution," uses the NHSLS data to examine the effects of such master-status variables as religion and class, period or cohort, family structure, preteen sexual experiences, and other elements of teenagers' transitions to premarital sexual activity. On the basis of logistic discrete-time (annual) hazard methods, results are compared for blacks and whites and women and men who reached age eighteen before and after 1970. Substantial differences are found in the effects of some variables across cohorts of respondents who came of sexual age before or after the sexual revolution (e.g., parents' education and adherence to Catholicism significantly reduced premarital sex among the early but not the later cohorts). Important similarities in effects across the "historical divide" are also discovered (e.g., lack of religious affiliation, preteen sexual experiences, and age at menarche have similarly sized effects across cohorts). The results are discussed for their implications about the so-called sexual revolution of the late 1960s and early 1970s.

Chapter 2, "Choices Leading to Teenage Births," focuses on the sequence of decisions that a young woman (under eighteen) makes leading to a live birth. In particular, she chooses whether to have sex; if she does have sex, she selects some birth control strategy (including none); and, if she becomes pregnant, she decides whether to have an abortion. Of the women in the NHSLS, 46 percent had sex before their eighteenth birthday; of those, 34 percent became pregnant; and, of those, 76 percent had a live birth, 16 percent an abortion, and 8 percent a miscarriage or stillbirth.

The product of those percentages or "risks" is 12 percent, and that is the proportion of these women who had a live birth prior to age eighteen.

The chapter shows the trends in these several rates over the postwar era, documenting the dramatic rise in the numbers of women engaging in sex at earlier ages, but also showing why there has been no corresponding rise in teenage births. The chapter analyzes each of these three conditional choices separately, investigating the effects of personal demographic characteristics on each, and offering a rational choice interpretation of the findings. The results show that some characteristics have a consistent effect on all three choices and that these characteristics, then, have a strong association with whether the woman gives birth before age eighteen. For example, young women with well-educated parents are less likely to begin having sex at an early age, are less likely to become pregnant if they do engage in sex, and are far more likely to have an abortion if they become pregnant. Consequently, these young women are dramatically less likely than others to give birth before age eighteen. Other characteristics appear to be associated with only one of these three choices or to have offsetting effects on two of the choices, and, consequently, these characteristics are not so strongly associated with the likelihood of giving birth before age eighteen.

Sex during Adulthood

Chapter 3, "Sexual Expression in America," explores the correlates of modes of sexual expression, defined as gender-specific configurations of partnered and autoerotic sexual activity, in the past twelve months. First, it is argued that it is desirable to characterize a person's mode of sexual expression in a holistic and multidimensional way, one that brings into focus the multifaceted ways in which an individual can express his or her sexuality and the relative volume or level of his or her sexual activities when compared to others. Using five dimensions of an individual's sexual conduct in the past twelve months, we establish empirically that we can exhaustively classify the modes of sexual expression of men and women in the U.S. population in only a few mutually exclusive categories. In fact, about half of all the adult men and women in the United States can be assigned to a single mode of sexual expression, one that involves monogamous relationships with low levels of sexual activity and excludes autoeroticism and unconventional erotic stimulation. We then explore the subjective, behavioral, health, and social factors that are differentially associated with each of the four modes of sexual expression for men and women, respectively. The approach permits us to characterize the differences in sexual expression and their associated consequences for health and well-being in a highly compact but richly nuanced way.

Chapter 4, "Sexual Contact between Children and Adults: A Life-

Course Perspective," exploits the quality and scope of the NHSLS to adjudicate between two competing models of the long-term effects on women and men of adult-child sexual contact. The psychogenic perspective conceptualizes adult-child sexual contact as a traumatic event generating intense affect that must be resolved. Behaviorally, attempts to deal with the trauma of adult-child sexual contact take opposing forms—some will engage in compulsively sexualized behavior, while others will withdraw from sexual activity. The more severe the sexual contact, the more adverse the long-term effects (including sexual dysfunction and lessened well-being). From an alternative, sociogenic, or life-course, perspective, adult-child sexual contact provides a culturally inappropriate model of sexual behavior that increases the child's likelihood of engaging in an active and risky sexual career in adolescence and adulthood. These behaviors, in turn, create long-term adverse outcomes. While we find evidence of heightened sexual activity in the aftermath of adult-child sex (predicted by both perspectives), we find no evidence of a comparable tendency toward avoidance of sexual activity (predicted by the psychogenic perspective). Moreover, we find little evidence in support of the hypothesis that the severity of the sexual contact increases long-term adverse outcomes. In contrast, we find strong evidence that sexual trajectories account for the association between adult-child sex and adult outcomes. Since the effect of adult/child sexual contact on life-course outcomes differs in important respects by gender, the first part of the chapter is devoted to an analysis of the data on women's and the second to an analysis of the data on men's adult-child and peer-child sexual experiences.

Chapter 5, "Race, Gender, and Class in Sexual Scripts," analyzes racial and ethnic variations in sexual scripts, paying special attention to the role of gender and class within the sexual scripts of racial and ethnic groups. Rather than analyze racial/ethnic differences in isolated sexual practices, as other studies have done, this chapter analyzes a broad range of sexual attitudes, practices, and preferences as they are patterned over the life course as a whole. While sexual scripts have been well theorized in the abstract, less well understood are the specific variations in the sexual scripts of different collectivities, such as racial and ethnic groups in the United States. This chapter theorizes racial/ethnic variations in sexual scripts and then presents an empirical analysis of the similarities and differences in the sexual scripts of racial/ethnic groups using the NHSLS data. Because sexual scripts tend to differ by gender, the sexual scripts for men and women are analyzed separately within each racial/ethnic group.

The NHSLS data set allows analysis of the effects of race/ethnicity, class, religious affiliation, age, and marital status simultaneously on a broad range of sexual attitudes and practices throughout the life course, something that has not been possible in other studies. Using logistic regression, this chapter tests whether race/ethnicity has an independent effect on sexual scripts after controlling for these other master-status characteristics. While the sexual scripts of all racial/ethnic groups share some basic similarities, there are still significant racial/ethnic differences, even after controlling for class and other master-status variables. Gender differences in sexual scripts are observed in all racial/ethnic groups but appear to be sharpest among African Americans.

Chapter 6, "Emotional and Physical Satisfaction with Sex in Married, Cohabiting, and Dating Sexual Unions: Do Men and Women Differ?" takes note of the fact that marriage differs from cohabitation and from dating in terms of the expectations that the partners bring to the relationship. The "coupleness" expected in the relationships tends to differ, with married couples expecting more merging of financial, social, emotional, and work lives than do either cohabiting or dating couples. Marriage itself increases sexual exclusivity and publicly signals a lifetime commitment to the relationship. Cohabiting and dating women are much less likely than married women to be sexually exclusive, having made no public or legal commitment to their partner.

The chapter finds that differences between types of unions in emotional commitment and sexual exclusivity account for the higher levels of emotional satisfaction with sex reported by married men but not married women. Once we take into account characteristics of individuals and unions, we see no differences between men and women in different unions in physical satisfaction with sex. But, even within types of relationships, those men and women who report greater emotional commitment to their partner and more commitment to sexual exclusivity also express greater satisfaction with both the emotional and the physical aspects of sex.

Sex and Health

Chapter 7, "Circumcision in the United States: Prevalence, Prophylactic Effects, and Sexual Practice," observes that, for over forty years, neonatal circumcision has been the most commonly performed surgical procedure in the United States. In this chapter, we review the modern history of the practice, demonstrating that its exceptional popularity in the United States has more to do with the influence of significant social institutions than with the advance of medical science. In addition, we exploit the survey data from the NHSLS to assess the prevalence of circumcision across various social groups as well as various outcomes of circumcision. We find no significant differences between circumcised and uncircumcised men in terms of the likelihood of contracting sexually transmitted infections. However, uncircumcised men appear slightly more likely to experience sexual dysfunctions, especially later in life. Finally, we find that circumcised men engage in a more elaborated set of sexual practices. This pattern differs across ethnic groups, suggesting the influence of social factors. Since the annual cost of neonatal circumcision has been estimated to be between $150 and $270 million and its health consequences are minimal, public debate about its costs and benefits is essential.

Chapter 8, "Reported Changes in Sexual Behavior in Response to AIDS in the United States," notes that the risks of contracting disease through sexual activity have long confronted adults, but not since the advent of penicillin has that risk been so salient to Americans, and not for centuries has it been a fatal risk. In 1992, the NHSLS asked respondents whether they had changed their behavior in any way because of the new, deadly risks associated with exposure to HIV. Some 30 percent of the respondents said that they had changed their behavior in some way because of that risk. This chapter uses previously uncoded verbatim responses to the follow-up question about what changes the respondent made. It documents the nature of those changes and the number of changes made by those who said that they changed their behavior. The chapter also associates those changes with the nature of the sexual behavior of that person in order objectively to assess the extent to which the change effectively lowered the risk of exposure to HIV and other sexually transmitted infections (STIs). In general, the findings in this chapter suggest that, as the riskiness of the sexual behavior increases, so too does the effort made to reduce that risk. A small group of those at highest risk, however, exhibits very little reported behavior change, and this small group constitutes a major public health challenge.

In chapter 9, "Racial/Ethnic Group Differences in the Prevalence of Sexually Transmitted Diseases in the United States: A Network Explanation," we suggest, first, that official statistics on the incidence and prevalence of STIs collected by the Centers for Disease Control and Prevention may be systematically biased in such a way that rates for lower socioeconomic status groups are overestimated and those for upper socioeconomic status groups underestimated. According to the NHSLS data, for example, whites report higher infection rates for viral STIs both at the zeroorder level and when multiple risk factors are taken into account. Second, we show that social and attitudinal factors, such as church attendance, sexual value orientations, frequency of thinking about sex, and fantasy about sex with a stranger, are as stable and consistent predictors of STIs as sexual behavior factors are. In addition, a logistic regression analysis demonstrates that most of these effects are not easily suppressed, even when we control for all the risky behavioral factors. They are thus costeffective and valid predictors for use in monitoring populations at risk of STIs.

Third, in empirically evaluating network-oriented models of epidemiology, we describe mixing matrices that track the different ways in which persons with particular master-status attributes like race or ethnicity choose sex partners from the same or different status categories. Of the three racial/ethnic categories, blacks appear to have the highest levels of assortative mixing, regardless of their level of sexual activity. This stronger preference for racial homophily amplifies infectious spread within the black population. Whites also express strong homophily for their own race, even though the strength of this preference is weaker than it is for blacks. But homophily becomes stronger as one moves toward the core group (i.e., more sexually active people are more race exclusive in sex partner choice). Thus, in terms of the transmission of infection, the two races are somewhat isolated from one another. The bridge between them appears to be provided by Hispanics. In contrast to the pattern for whites, the Hispanics' preference for homophily becomes much weaker as one moves toward the core group. Moreover, the distinctive mixing pattern of the black core group by region can give us a hint about why the Southern region of the United States has the highest rates of infection for syphilis and gonorrhea.

While, given the limitations of the NHSLS sample size and measurement of core group status, these findings about mixing models and their epidemiological implications can be only suggestive, they do indicate the power of empirically estimated models to illuminate nonobvious features of the underlying processes of the spread of STIs as those processes are shaped by the social organization of sexuality.

Chapter 10, "Sexual Dysfunction in the United States: Prevalence and Predictors," explores the remarkably extensive prevalence of sexual dysfunctions in the population at large. While 31 percent of the men and 43 percent of the women reported at least one sexual dysfunction of at least two months' duration in the preceding twelve months, only one in ten men and one in five women reporting a dysfunction, including pain during sex, erectile or lubrication problems, lack of interest in sex, and anxiety about performance, sought professional help. This chapter documents the prevalence of various sexual dysfunctions among adult men and women by selected master statuses. It identifies both physical health–related and psychosocial factors associated with dysfunctions and demonstrates the pervasiveness of dysfunction throughout the life cycle—that is, most dysfunctions are only very modestly associated with age, if at all. Finally, we demonstrate that there is a strong association between sexual dysfunction and impaired quality of life, suggesting that this problem warrants recognition as a significant public health concern.

Chapter 11, "Abortion Decisions in the United States," analyzes the NHSLS information on abortions, as reported by both the women and the men. The analysis is conducted separately for each conception since the factors that influence the decision to have an abortion appear to differ by the circumstances prevailing at the time—the person's marital status and age, the legal status of abortion at the time, and so on. The effects that personal characteristics have on the decision are quite different by the gender of the respondent. A woman whose first pregnancy was at a young age, say, under eighteen, was much more likely to have an abortion if her parents were better educated and less likely if she was black. By looking at abortions conception by conception, the study also shows that those who abort one pregnancy are more likely to abort a second, even though a vast majority of those who have ever had an abortion have had only one.

Chapter 12, "Private Sexual Behavior, Public Opinion, and Public Health Policy Related to Sexually Transmitted Diseases: A U.S.-British Comparison," compares findings from the nationwide surveys of sexual behavior and attitudes in the United States and Great Britain. It documents how similar the sexual behavior of Americans and Britons is, on average. Despite this similarity, the rate of STIs in the United States is roughly twice that in Britain. This chapter suggests a provocative explanation for this paradox of broadly similar sexual behavior and attitudes about sex yet very different experiences with sexually transmitted diseases (STDs). The explanation derives from the observation that, while the centers of the distributions of many sexual behaviors and attitudes (the means or medians) are similar in the United States and the United Kingdom, the dispersion in many of those distributions of behaviors is far greater in the United States. The larger proportions in both the lower and the upper tails of many of these distributions signal the difficulty of mounting an aggressive public health stance against STDs: there are disproportionately more people in the United States who do run the risks in question (one tail of one dimension) and disproportionately more in the United States who have strong opinions that those underlying behaviors are in fact wrong, not merely risky (the other tail of another distribution). These latter individuals oppose public health policies that promote safer sex, which they also consider wrong. The heterogeneity of the U.S. population is itself a substantial obstacle to effective public policy. The more homogeneous, like-minded Britons are, thus, more accepting of the public health initiatives designed to reduce the risk of disease. The chapter suggests that the breadth of views on sexual matters in the United States, so strongly held, may have a high cost, paid in the currency of public health.

The final chapter, "Private Sex and Public Policy," addresses the issue of the public nature of much private sexual behavior. It outlines the issues involved in formulating public policy regarding sexual behavior from the rational choice and institutional perspectives. It then raises and briefly discusses some of the public policy implications to be drawn from each of the chapters in the volume and, with that orientation, provides a summary of the volume's findings.

Appendix—An Aside on Method: Introducing the Logistic

The following chapters use a variety of statistics to make their cases. Most will be familiar to the reader and require no introduction. We do, however, employ logistic analysis quite extensively, and it may be helpful to discuss the technique and the meaning of its characteristic quantities in some detail.

When we consider a relation between a variable (or many variables) and a proportion of people who have done something, it is often the case that we characterize that relation in a particular form called a *logistic*. A typical shape of a logistic relation is seen in figure I.1, where P is the proportion (e.g., the proportion having had a child, or ever been married, or had a sexually transmitted disease, or ever had sexual intercourse), and X might be age, or income, or education level, or race/ethnicity, or some combination of several descriptive variables. A computer program can estimate the relation between P and one or several X's and our interest here is in the interpretation of the coefficients that are calculated. The mathematical statement of a logistic relation between P and X takes the form.

$$P = 1/(1 + e^{-XC}),$$

where each observation or respondent has a value of P and of X, and the computer program calculates the value of the coefficient C. There are, unfortunately, three different ways in which one can report these coefficients, and sometimes one or another is more useful, so we describe all three here.

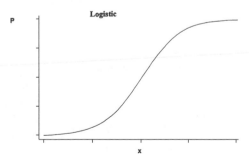

Fig. I.1 A typical shape of a logistic relation, where P is the proportion, and X represents one or more descriptive variables.

To be explicit, let us consider P to be the proportion of respondents who have ever been married and X to be age in years. For a particular data set (the General Social Survey [GSS] for the years 1988–91), we estimate that the logistic on these six thousand observations and the calculated value of C, including an intercept, is $XC = -2.15 + 0.09$ (age). (The standard errors on the intercept and on the age coefficient are 0.12 and 0.003, respectively, with an overall χ^2 [with one degree of freedom] of 1,2443.4. In these data, the mean age is 45.6 years and the mean proportion 0.80.) Now we move to the interpretation of that coefficient of $+0.09$.

The Probability of the Event

For some purposes, it is convenient to think of the proportion as the probability of the event occurring, in this case, the probability of having married by some age. One can show that the change in P for a unit change in X is equal to $C[P(1 - P)]$, evaluated at some level of P such as the mean. Thus, at around the average probability at 0.8, that value is 0.0144 ($= 0.09 \times 0.8 \times 0.2$). Using this value of 0.0144, we would report that the probability of having ever married rises 1.4 percentage points with each year of age around that level. To check this, we compute the probability from the equation at ages thirty-eight, thirty-nine, forty, forty-one, and forty-two, respectively. Those probabilities are 0.793, 0.807, 0.821, 0.834, and 0.847, respectively, so the probability does go up by about 1.4 percentage points with each year of age. (Of course, the amount will be different at much younger and much older ages since the shape of the logistic is not a straight line.)

The Odds Ratio

If we calculate the ratio $P/1 - P$, we obtain the odds of the event happening. We can calculate this odds ratio, 0.80/0.20, and can say that, for the whole data set, the odds are four to one that a person has married. Then it would be reasonable to ask how age affects this odds ratio, and one can show that the change in the odds $P/1 - P$ associated with a one-unit change in X is equal to e^c. Using that formula, we calculate its value, which in this case is 1.094 ($= e^{0.09}$). Here, then, we would report that the odds rise by a factor of 1.09 for each additional year of age. If we compute the odds at ages thirty-eight through forty-two using the values of P listed above, they are 3.83, 4.18, 4.59, 5.02, and 5.54, respectively, or around four to one or five to one at these ages, and we can see that each additional year raises the odds by about 9 percent, or by a factor of 1.09, as the equation suggests. In this case, the increase holds at all ages, which is one reason that this is a convenient way to report the result.

The Log-Odds Ratio

For reasons having more to do with convenience of the computer program than practical application, often one sees results reported as the effect of X on the log-odds ratio, that is, as the effect on the log of the odds. The effect of a unit change in X on the log of the odds is simply the coefficient C, which explains why it is often reported. There is the usefulness here that its sign shows the direction of effect of the variable X on the event, so a negative sign indicates that the event is less likely as the value of X rises, and, for some purposes, that is all that we are interested in. In the case illustrated here, we would report that the effect of age on the log-odds is 0.09, indicating that the proportion rises with age.

Note

1. Copies of the NHSLS data can be obtained from the Interuniversity Consortium for Political and Social Research at the University of Michigan (Ann Arbor) or from Sociometrics Corporation (170 State St., Suite 260, Los Altos CA 94022).

PART ONE

■

Sex during Adolescence

■

CHAPTER ONE

Teenage Sex and the Sexual Revolution

KARA JOYNER AND EDWARD O. LAUMANN

Since the 1970s, research addressing sexual behavior among young people has proliferated, primarily because early sexual activity is considered consequential in both the short and the long term. Individuals who have sex during childhood have been shown to experience any number of negative adult outcomes, such as sexual dysfunction and relationship dissatisfaction (see, e.g., Browne and Finkelhor 1986). Individuals who have sex during adolescence are at risk not only of sexually transmitted infections but of pregnancy as well (Hofferth and Hayes 1987). Some of these costs are borne privately by individuals and their families; others are borne collectively, making the sexual behavior of young people a social policy issue.

Studies of teen sex conducted in the United States since the Second World War typically follow one of two approaches. The first approach considers how the social control exercised by parents and peers on adolescent sexual behavior differs when such factors as historical period, gender, social class, religion, and race are taken into consideration (e.g., Hogan and Kitagawa 1985; Thornton 1993). Studies following this approach link historically and group-based differences in sexual behavior to the fulfillment and timing of work and family roles. The second approach concerns how individual propensities influence sexual behavior (e.g., Udry and Billy 1987). Studies following this approach relate adolescents' motivation and opportunity to have sex to their personal biography, that is, their individual experiences and characteristics.

Generally speaking, studies conducted before the 1970s examine group differences in adolescents' sexual attitudes and behavior using samples of select groups in the population, such as high school students in the Midwest (e.g., Coleman 1966). Contemporary examinations of individual differences in these attitudes and behavior are based on representative samples of individuals, typically females, who came of age in the 1970s and 1980s (e.g., Zelnik and Kantner 1980). Because both types of studies draw their samples from a delimited historical period, we can only speculate whether group membership and personal biography have had the same bearing on adolescent sexual behavior in different periods. Researchers have found noteworthy changes in the effects of variables influencing adolescent sexual behavior within periods as narrow as a decade (see Brewster et al. 1988; Cooksey, Rindfuss, and Guilkey 1996). Changes in the determinants of teen sex over several decades will undoubtedly be even more profound.

Integrating these two traditions of research, we consider how the determinants of adolescent sexual behavior have changed in the United States since the 1940s. We propose that adolescent sexual behavior has become less influenced by membership in broad social groupings and more influenced by personal biography. To compare these influences on teen sex before and after the sexual revolution, we use data from the National Health and Social Life Survey (NHSLS). Our results are based on retrospective accounts of respondents' childhood and adolescent sexual experiences in addition to their group membership and personal biography. We find that, over time, the initiation of intercourse has become somewhat less structured by group membership but not any more influenced by personal biography.

1.1 Background

Both earlier and contemporary perspectives on adolescent sexual behavior share the assumption that adolescents decide whether to engage in intercourse on the basis of the rewards and costs they associate with it (e.g., Duncan and Hoffman 1990; Furstenberg et al. 1987; Leibowitz, Eisen, and Chow 1986). The short-term costs can include the girl's loss of status in the eyes of her partner and peers. The long-term costs essentially involve "derailing" her future in the event that a pregnancy does occur (Anderson 1990). The rewards expected from sex include physical pleasure and emotional satisfaction but also the elevation of a boy's status among select peers.

Studies of teen sex suggest that group members' expected rewards and costs of engaging in different types of sexual behavior are reflected in their norms regarding this behavior (see, e.g., Anderson 1990).[1] Norms are thought to influence adolescent sexual behavior both directly and indirectly. Directly, norms prescribe the appropriate ages at which and the types of relationships in the context of which sexual behavior should take place; indirectly, they specify the appropriate sequencing of family formation with respect to schooling and work (Billy, Brewster, and Grady 1994; Brewster, Billy, and Grady 1993; Hogan 1987). Norms are first inculcated by parents but later weakened as adolescents are exposed to a more permissive peer environment (Coleman 1961; Reiss 1967).

Earlier and contemporary studies alike suggest that the expected rewards and costs of having sex differ by group membership. And they similarly consider adolescents' parents and peers to be particularly salient because they sanction and monitor behavior. But, in contrast to earlier studies, contemporary ones offer a distinctive emphasis on individual characteristics and experiences. They highlight, not only differences between groups, but also differences within groups. Below, we review how studies concerning the influence of group membership and personal biography on adolescent sexual behavior explain these differences. We first review studies that consider the norms of adolescent sexual behavior in the baby boom period. These studies set the foundation for contemporary work.

Group Membership and Teen Sex in Studies of the Baby Boom Era

Earlier and contemporary studies alike suggest that the key to explaining group differences in sexual patterns among young people is understanding group differences in the transition to young adulthood (see Coleman 1961; Reiss 1967; Simon, Berger, and Gagnon 1972). The baby boom era (1946–60) is a period known for its increased fertility but also for its greater emphasis on family roles, especially for women (Davis and van den Oever 1982). During these years, adolescents and parents considered family formation, along with the completion of schooling and entry into the labor force, important milestones on the path to adulthood (for a more general discussion of pathways to adulthood, see Hogan and Kitagawa [1985]).

Parents and adolescents considered dating to be an important practice because it enabled individuals to meet potential marriage partners and to learn gender-appropriate roles and skills valued in marriage (Modell 1988). Adolescents, in particular, considered dating a way in which to affirm their status in the newly emerging youth culture. Studying adolescent values in the late 1950s and early 1960s, Coleman (1961) took adolescents' criteria for being in the "leading crowd" as evidence of this distinct value system. For females, popularity with males was especially critical to status since they did not have the opportunity to "star" in athletics, as did males. While dating could elevate the social status of females in the eyes of their peers, crossing the line between petting and intercourse could jeopardize their status—but, given the prevailing double standard, not that of males (Coleman 1966; Modell 1989; Nathanson 1991).

A number of theorists have linked the double standard to traditional gender role practices, according to which men specialized in market production and women in domestic production. An important by-product of this gendered division of roles was that female adolescents expected to derive their ultimate status from marriage (Coleman 1966; Reiss 1967). Since engaging in intercourse presumably reduced their value on the marriage market, females had a stake in avoiding sex. Even if they were able to conceal their sexuality from parents and peers, the unavailability of effective means of birth control and the illegality of abortion increased their chances of eventually "getting caught" (Rubin 1976, 60). These factors surely amplified the expected costs of having intercourse for adolescent females in the baby boom period.

Adolescents of the baby boom era typically expected to marry on the completion of schooling (Modell 1989; Thornton 1993). Because working-class adolescents' avenue to adulthood was through marriage and work as opposed to higher education, they were more motivated to marry just after high school than were their college-bound peers; it follows that they took dating more seriously. Suggesting that this was the case was the fact that working-class adolescents were found to change partners less frequently and to declare themselves to be in love more often than college-bound youths (Modell 1988). Since the event of pregnancy typically validated or advanced plans to marry, they are thought to have considered intercourse less risky (Rubin 1976).

For Catholics, engaging in intercourse was especially risky in the baby boom period. While Protestant churches reluctantly approved birth control in the 1930s, the Catholic Church continued (and continues) to oppose birth control. Surely this discouraged Catholic adolescents from purchasing contraceptive protection since doing so revealed a premeditated decision to violate the church's teachings. Assuming that they were obedient to church authority (see Greeley 1990), Catholic adolescents were probably less prepared and hence less likely to engage in intercourse than their Protestant counterparts.

During this period, the institution of dating was just as pervasive among black adolescents as it was among white adolescents (Modell 1988). However, the costs of intercourse are presumed to have been lower for blacks. For one thing, a smaller proportion of blacks than whites went to college (see Sweet and Bumpass 1987). In addition, blacks were less able to capitalize on the socioeconomic achievements of their parents than were whites in this period (Blau and Duncan 1967; Hogan and Kitagawa 1985). Finally, the percentage of female-headed families among blacks was double that among whites (Wilson and Neckerman 1987). The greater prevalence of single-parent families among blacks is thought to have made pregnancy seem less stigmatizing for black females than for white females. Reflecting racial differences in the expected costs of sexual intercourse, studies of this time found blacks to be more sexually permissive than whites and the double standard to be less pervasive among blacks than among whites (Coleman 1966; Reiss 1967).

These differences by social class, religion, and race reinforced—and were reinforced by—popular stereotypes about what "good" and "bad" individuals did and did not do. As Nathanson points out, "[Sexuality] has always been attributed to categories of persons located outside the margins of respectable society—immigrants, lower-class women, prostitutes, and blacks" (1991, 217). Adolescents, particularly females, could display their status by behaving accordingly and, at the same time, distance themselves from those outside their own social group (for a more general discussion of the process of social closure, see Parkin 1979).

Personal Biography and Teen Sex in Studies of the Contemporary Era

Contemporary studies stress that, because parents are important role models and agents of social control, their behavior affects the romantic and sexual lives of their children directly. Single mothers themselves are at risk of having intercourse outside marriage; about half of all women who separate have at least one sex partner before they remarry (see *SOS*). In addition, they are thought to establish single motherhood as a viable alternative in their children's minds and not to supervise their children's activities as closely (for more extended considerations of these mechanisms as they are linked to different outcomes, see McLanahan [1985] and Wu and Martinson [1993]). In sum, the experience of living with a single parent reduces the costs that adolescents associate with sexual activity.

Udry and Billy (1987) offer an explanation of why adolescents are tempted to have intercourse in the first place. They argue that pubertal development triggers sexual activity by increasing the levels of those hormones that elevate sexual interest. Furthermore, pubertal development not only increases adolescents' attractiveness to potential sex partners but also signals to the adolescents themselves and to others that they are mature enough for age-graded sexual behavior. The mechanism by which hormones influence sexual activity is biological, while the mechanism by which attractiveness and signaling influence sexual activity is social (Hofferth and Hayes 1987).

Studies are silent with respect to childhood experiences that may influence subsequent sexual activity. Sexual experiences during childhood are thought to create an orientation toward sexuality and to reduce the effectiveness of norms and sanctions discouraging sexual behavior (see chap. 4 below). Suggesting these possibilities, Musick (1993) extensively documents the ways in which abusive sexual experiences shape females' subsequent sexual behavior. She finds that sexual exploitation by older males leads female adolescents to develop a sense of learned helplessness in their relationships with men and also to confuse sex with love.

1.2 Teen Sex before and after the Sexual Revolution

In support of these general notions, several studies find that variables measuring group membership and personal biography do significantly influence the timing of first intercourse (for a thorough review of these studies,

see Miller and Moore [1990]). More recent, representative studies of adolescents support the influence that a number of factors are thought to have
on the expected costs of intercourse, including gender, socioeconomic
background, religion, race, family structure, and age at menarche (e.g.,
Billy, Brewster, and Grady 1994; Brewster, Billy, and Grady 1993; Day
1992; Ku, Sonenstein, and Pleck 1993; Lauritsen 1994). Less representative studies, which examine retrospective reports of childhood events, find
that females sexually abused during childhood begin having intercourse
earlier than their counterparts (see, e.g., Luster and Small 1994; Wyatt
1990). Studies to date have not systematically examined how the effects of
these variables have changed over time.

Nevertheless, a number of researchers note that, in more recent decades,
teenagers, especially females, have become increasingly likely to have sex.
These researchers attribute increases in teen sex to the sexual revolution
that took place in the late 1960s and early 1970s (e.g., Hofferth and Hayes
1987). The sexual revolution received its impetus from broader structural
and ideological changes.

Perhaps the most important exogenous change leading to the sexual
revolution was the development and diffusion of contraceptive technology,
as exemplified by the advent of the pill and the intrauterine device (IUD)
(Michael 1988). This "contraceptive revolution" made having intercourse
outside the context of marriage an acceptable possibility by dramatically
reducing the chances of becoming pregnant (see Westoff and Ryder 1977).
The 1973 Supreme Court decision in *Roe v. Wade,* which legalized abortion, further reduced the costs of having intercourse. Once the cost or risk
of having sex declined, the effectiveness of social controls was seriously
undermined.

Another critical factor considered to have weakened traditional proscriptions on premarital intercourse among young people in more recent
times is the postponement of marriage. In her ethnographic work, Rubin
finds this to be the case for working-class youths. Discussing their logic,
she argues, "If getting married is no longer 'such a big deal,' why wait for
marriage to explore one's sexuality?" (1994, 5). But, were it not for the
contraceptive revolution, this exploration would not be possible.

The weakening of social controls has also been linked to greater individualism. On a macro level, several decades of rising income are thought to
have fostered a greater sense of self-reliance on the part of individuals
(Lesthaeghe 1983; Michael, Fuchs, and Scott 1980). On a micro level, college attendance, female labor force participation, and independent living have been found to have this very same effect, especially for women
(Mason 1974; Spitze 1978; Waite, Goldscheider, and Witsberger 1986).
According to Lesthaeghe (1983), this greater self-reliance increases self-
expression and reduces commitment to the family, religion, and other
sources of authority, allowing individuals themselves to choose what is

best for them. Typically, this means that "feeling good" is a more important basis for decision making than "being good" (Bellah et al. 1985, 78).

While the changes discussed above have encompassed the general population (e.g., Klassen, Williams, and Levitt 1989), they are considered to have been more consequential to the attitudes and behavior of women than to those of men (Goldscheider and Waite 1991). Improvements in contraceptive technology have meant that far greater control of the outcome associated with intercourse is now in the hands of women since the pill, the IUD, and abortion are all female-friendly methods. Increased female labor force participation and an imbalanced sex ratio are thought to have reduced the gains from marriage for women (see, e.g., Becker 1981; Davis and van den Oever 1982; Grossbard-Shechtman 1993; Guttentag and Secord 1983).

A number of studies suggest that, as societal and group levels of permissiveness with respect to intercourse increase, social controls become less effective in deterring young people from acting on their urges. Studying adolescents, Udry and his colleagues (see, e.g., Udry 1988; Udry and Billy 1987) find that, while hormonal levels increase white males' likelihood of initiating intercourse, they fail to influence white females' initiation of intercourse.[2] However, hormonal levels do increase white females' sexual motivation and noncoital behavior. These results suggest that social control inhibits white females from engaging in intercourse. Studying young adults, Reiss (1967) finds that, while social control influences the levels of sexual permissiveness among white women, it has little effect on these levels among black men.

While several studies suggest how the effects of group membership on the likelihood of intercourse have changed since the Second World War, they are less clear about the effects of personal biography. Extrapolating from the proposition outlined above, we hypothesize that, as societal and group levels of permissiveness increase, the effects of variables that we classify as pertaining to personal biography become more critical. Below, we speculate about what these societal changes portend for the relative influence of group membership and personal biography on teen intercourse before and after the sexual revolution. We contrast these two particular periods because they reference strikingly different climates of permissiveness, especially for women.

Social Class. We know from previous studies that working-class adolescents in both periods are more likely to have intercourse than are middle- and upper-class adolescents. Yet we have reason to believe that social class is less critical to intercourse in the later period, basically because sexual and reproductive liberalism have been more strongly embraced by the better-off (Reiss 1967; Luker 1984). As Reiss argues, "The current movement towards permissiveness among the middle and upper social classes seems

to be based differently than it used to. Rather than permissiveness being
the philosophy of a group with less to 'lose,' it is a philosophy of a group
with access to contraceptive controls on pregnancy, ways of combating
venereal diseases, and an intellectualized philosophy of the importance of
ties based on affection and sex, and an integration of this viewpoint with
a generally liberal position" (1967, 55).

Catholicism. The changes among the general population outlined above
have led many churches to modify their traditional stances toward premarital sex. Yet some churches' resistance to change has weakened individuals' commitment to religion. The erosion of religious authority has
been most notable among Catholics. Writing in 1977, Westoff and Ryder
document a "dramatic change in the adherence of Catholic women to their
Church's teaching on birth control" and note that "the blurring of the
difference between Catholics and non-Catholics is most evident among
younger women" (pp. 23, 28).[3] (With respect to differences in contraceptive use according to religion, see also Goldscheider and Mosher [1991].)
Suggesting that this is the case, Catholics' sexual attitudes and behavior
have been shown to have converged with those of Protestants (Greeley
1990; Thornton 1993). On the basis of these findings, we expect Catholicism to be less consequential to sexual behavior in the later period.

Race. We expect the changes outlined above to have narrowed the "permissiveness gap" between white and black adolescents (see Reiss 1967).
Blacks coming of age after the sexual revolution have been better able to
capitalize on the socioeconomic achievements of their parents than have
their predecessors (see Hogan and Kitagawa 1985). Assuming that the
process of status attainment on the part of some groups of blacks has even
converged with that of whites, we expect black adolescents to be more
similar to white adolescents in the later period with respect to having intercourse.

Family Structure. We expect that, in both periods, adolescents living
with a single parent are more likely to have intercourse than their counterparts living with two parents. Yet we have reason to expect that this experience was less critical in the earlier period. Our logic here is that peer group
oversight was more effective then and that the presence of both parents to
reinforce these controls was not as essential (see Modell 1989). Besides,
the broader social climate of that time presumably offered little or no endorsement of single parenthood, reducing its acceptability even among
single parents and their children. Of course, we could make an entirely
different argument for the effect of family structure over time. We could
argue, for instance, that, where societal and group proscriptions against

intercourse are weak, parents' efforts to serve as agents of social control are futile. We could additionally argue that, in this same context, parents who do separate are a less select crowd, making their own behavior less of an issue than would otherwise be the case.

Pubertal Development. The work reported above suggests that pubertal development has a critical effect on adolescent sexual activity, regardless of whether that effect is originally social or biological. But, when the behavior concerned is more strongly proscribed, such as intercourse is, social controls may deter adolescents from acting on their own urges, not to mention those of a partner. Since social controls were undoubtedly stronger in the earlier period, pubertal development certainly had less of an influence then.

Childhood Sexual Contact. We expect childhood sexual contact to increase adolescents' likelihood of having intercourse in both periods. Recall that such an experience may reinforce an orientation toward sexuality or reduce the effectiveness of norms proscribing and sanctions against sexual behavior. We believe that these effects were of lesser magnitude in the earlier period, basically because broader societal norms sent a clearer and stronger message that premarital intercourse was wrong, and thus more effectively deterred adolescents with childhood sexual contact from having intercourse.

On the whole, we expect adolescent sexual behavior to have become less structured by membership in social groups and more influenced by personal biography. Our underlying proposition may also be generalized to additional measures of personal biography. While we do include other factors in our analyses of intercourse, we have focused simply on the factors highlighted in our discussion of previous studies.

1.3 Methods

Sample and Data

We restrict our analyses to individuals in the NHSLS sample whose age at puberty and age at first intercourse are known. The NHSLS is ideal for our purposes, basically because it collected detailed retrospective accounts of childhood and adolescent sexual experience from respondents who reached adolescence at the onset of the baby boom (e.g., those born in 1933) as well as from respondents who came of age well after the sexual revolution (e.g., those born in 1974). This allows us to examine how the effects of factors influencing first intercourse differ over a four-decade period.

Substantive Variables

To determine the age at which individuals first have intercourse, we use responses to a question asked in the main questionnaire: "How old were you the *first* time [after puberty] you had vaginal intercourse with a (. . . male/female)?" (*SOS,* 652). By this point in the questionnaire, interviewers had given respondents an explicit definition of what was meant by this. We remind the reader here that older respondents will be reporting an event that took place decades ago while younger respondents will be reporting an event that may have taken place just a year before.[4] This study focuses simply on the likelihood of intercourse before age eighteen rather than on the likelihood of intercourse at specific ages. To the extent that turning eighteen is associated with such events as reaching legal adulthood and graduating from high school, individuals probably remember fairly well whether they had intercourse before this critical point in their life, even if they cannot recall the exact age.

To measure race, we use a dummy variable indicating whether the respondent is black. For social class, we use a dummy indicating whether either of the respondent's parents finished college. For religion, we use a dummy indicating whether the respondent was raised Catholic. For childhood sexual contact, we use a dummy indicating whether the respondent experienced genital stimulation or insertion (i.e., oral sex, vaginal intercourse, or anal intercourse) before reaching puberty. For pubertal development, we use respondent's age at puberty.[5] And, for family structure, we use a dummy indicating whether the respondent was living with a single parent. But we also include a number of control variables: Hispanic; foreign born; neither parent graduated from high school; fundamentalist Protestant; in the Northeast, South, or West; living with a stepparent; and mother employed.

Note that a number of these variables pertain to respondents' circumstances at age 14. We believe that these variables serve as good proxies for respondents' conditions at all ages of risk. Also keep in mind that we exclude a number of variables from our analyses because they had negligible effects in our models (i.e., number of siblings; had an older sibling; in a rural area, a town, or a big city at age fourteen; and whether the interviewer felt the respondent was being frank).

Analysis Plan

We begin our analysis with a presentation of descriptive statistics for the variables we use in our multivariate analyses. We present separate statistics for respondents born before and after the sexual revolution. This enables us to consider how adolescents' exposure to factors associated with teen sex has changed since the sexual revolution. Next, we present the results for models that estimate the effects of group membership and personal biography on teen sex. In this part of the analysis, we formally test whether the relative influence of group membership and personal biography has changed since the sexual revolution.

For the women in our sample, the likelihood of having intercourse before age eighteen shows a general pattern of increase, which is most pronounced for those born between 1953 and 1957 (the results are shown later). These women, who turned fourteen any time between 1967 and 1971, appear to be the adolescent vanguard of the sexual revolution. Consequently, we define their cohort as the first to reach adolescence after the sexual revolution. To the extent that our break point for historical period is somewhat arbitrary, it may not sufficiently capture the experiences of individuals caught in the midst of social change. Still, we think that dividing our sample accordingly reduces our chances of finding results in our favor by minimizing differences.

1.4 Results

Sample Statistics

Considering the sample means for sexual behavior, group membership, and personal biography, we focus here on differences in the values of the key variables by historical time since dramatic changes have occurred over time. Examining table 1.1, we see that the percentage who had sex before age eighteen is higher for men than for women both before and after the sexual revolution. However, the gender gap here is much bigger before than after the sexual revolution. Among those who came of age before the sexual revolution, 47 percent of men and 31 percent of women had sex before age eighteen. Among those who came of age after the sexual revolution, 60 percent of men and 53 percent of women did so.

With respect to group membership, we find that the percentage of individuals with a parent who completed college has about doubled over time. We also find that there is an increase over time in the proportion Catholic among women. Turning to personal biography, we see that roughly the same percentage of individuals reaching adolescence in different periods report childhood sexual contact. This is interesting, given that the prevalence of intercourse during early adolescence (i.e., before age fifteen) differs considerably by historical period (the results are not shown). The mean age at puberty has also remained pretty much constant. Like having a parent who has completed college, family structure has changed over time for adolescents, but not as considerably. About one-fifth of individuals reaching adolescence before the sexual revolution lived without both biological parents at age fourteen, whereas about one-third of individuals

Table 1.1 Descriptive Statistics: NHSLS Sample Members by Whether They Reached Adolescence before or after the Sexual Revolution

	Mean			
	Before the Sexual Revolution		After the Sexual Revolution	
Panel and Explanatory Variable	Men	Women	Men	Women
Sexual behavior				
Had intercourse before 18	.47	.31	.60	.53
Historical time				
Born 1933–37	.18	.21		
Born 1938–42	.20	.21		
Born 1943–47	.26	.25		
Born 1948–52	.36	.34		
Born 1953–57			.22	.25
Born 1958–62			.26	.27
Born 1963–67			.26	.22
Born 1968–74			.26	.26
Group membership				
Black	.11	.13	.11	.14
Hispanic	.07	.05	.07	.09
Foreign born	.08	.06	.09	.08
Neither parent graduated from high school	.37	.41	.18	.22
Either parent had college degree	.14	.13	.28	.23
Fundamentalist Protestant at 14	.28	.33	.27	.29
Catholic at 14	.31	.26	.31	.33
In the Northeast at 14	.22	.21	.19	.21
In the South at 14	.30	.31	.31	.31
In the West at 14	.12	.16	.18	.15
Personal biography				
Sexual contact before puberty	.12	.14	.11	.15
Age reached puberty	13.07	12.69	13.10	12.70
Living with a single parent at 14	.15	.15	.19	.21
Living with a stepparent at 14	.08	.06	.09	.11
Mother employed when respondent was 14	.40	.44	.54	.54
n	507	675	854	1,057

Note: Analyses exclude respondents from the oversample. Omitted variables include born 1933–37; white, Asian, and Native American; both parents graduated from high school; Protestant and other; in the Midwest at age 14; and living with both biological parents at age 14.

reaching adolescence after the sexual revolution lived without both biological parents at this age.

The patterns outlined above of increase in parents' college attendance, Catholicism, and living without both biological parents among these sample members appear to be consistent with changes among the general population (see, e.g., Roof and McKinney 1987; Sweet and Bumpass 1987). The modal age of menarche among females in our sample—thirteen—is also consistent with estimates in previous studies (see, e.g., the statistical appendixes in Hofferth and Hayes [1987]). To our knowledge, there are no comparable estimates from another nationally representative sample with which we may corroborate our estimates of sexual contact before puberty for men and women or pubertal development for men.

Models

For all our multivariate analyses, we use logistic regression models that estimate the probability of intercourse before age eighteen.[6] We estimate four different models separately for men and women. The first model estimates the effects of historical time, group membership, and personal biography on intercourse. A second model includes interaction terms between group membership and historical period (e.g., reached adolescence after the sexual revolution) to estimate different effects for group membership by historical period. A third model instead includes interaction terms between personal biography and historical period to estimate different effects for personal biography by historical period. Finally, a fourth models adds both sets of interaction terms together.

Estimating this last model is roughly analogous to estimating the first model separately for both historical periods. As evidence of this, coefficients estimated from separate models (not shown) are almost identical to the ones estimated from pooled models. With respect to our theoretical agenda, estimating pooled models allows us to conduct Chow tests and, in so doing, formally test whether the general pattern of effects for group membership and personal biography differs by historical period (see Kennedy 1985, 63).

Table 1.2 displays the logistic regression coefficients, standard errors, and significance levels for logistic regression models that estimate men's likelihood of intercourse before age 18 as a function of independent variables. Because the coefficients themselves are difficult to interpret, we will refer to their respective exponentiated coefficients or "odds ratios" in discussing our results. In interpreting the effects that are displayed, note that coefficients greater than one represent a higher likelihood of intercourse for any given variable and that coefficients less than one signify a lower likelihood. Also, these effects represent the proportion change in odds per unit change in a given independent variable (DeMaris 1992).

Table 1.2 Logistic Regression Estimates of Models Predicting Intercourse before Age 18: Men

Panel and Explanatory Variable	(1)	(2)	(3)	(4)
1. Historical time				
Born 1938–42	−.631*	−.699*	−.643*	−.717*
	(.307)	(.313)	(.310)	(.318)
	[.532]	[.497]	[.526]	[.488]
Born 1943–47	−.016	−.073	−.012	−.064
	(.285)	(.293)	(.287)	(.296)
	[.984]	[.929]	[.988]	[.938]
Born 1948–52	.039	−.033	.033	−.036
	(.272)	(.280)	(.275)	(.285)
	[1.040]	[.968]	[1.033]	[.964]
Born 1953–57	.587*	−.073	−.532	−2.036
	(.272)	(.373)	(1.269)	(1.352)
	[1.798]	[.930]	[.588]	[.131]
Born 1958–62	.379	−.330	−.730	−2.283†
	(.265)	(.372)	(1.263)	(1.348)
	[1.461]	[.719]	[.482]	[.102]
Born 1963–67	.350	−.306	−.748	−2.244†
	(.266)	(.372)	(1.260)	(1.345)
	[1.419]	[.736]	[.473]	[.106]
Born 1968–74	.948***	.283	−.165	−1.683
	(.277)	(.382)	(1.272)	(1.358)
	[2.581]	[1.328]	[.848]	[.186]
2. Group membership				
Black	1.028***	1.097**	1.027***	1.192**
	(.216)	(.352)	(.218)	(.364)
	[2.794]	[2.996]	[2.791]	[3.294]
Hispanic	.617*	.875*	.609*	.868*
	(.265)	(.419)	(.265)	(.427)
	[1.853]	[2.399]	[1.838]	[2.382]
Foreign born	−.573	−.355	−.558*	−.261
	(.233)	(.421)	(.234)	(.427)
	[.564]	[.701]	[.572]	[.77]
Neither parent graduated from high school	.565***	.569*	.570***	.580*
	(.154)	(.221)	(.155)	(.225)
	[1.760]	[1.766]	[1.768]	[1.785]
Either parent had college degree	−.092	−.474	−.091	−.529†
	(.148)	(.302)	(.148)	(.307)
	[.912]	[.623]	[.913]	[.589]
Fundamentalist Protestant at 14	−.208	−.140	−.216	−.183
	(.156)	(.268)	(.157)	(.272)
	[.812]	[.870]	[.806]	[.833]
Catholic at 14	.027	−.608*	.031	−.622*
	(.146)	(.255)	(.147)	(.258)
	[1.027]	[.544]	[1.031]	[.537]
In the Northeast at 14	−.065	−.453	−.070	−.479†
	(.168)	(.279)	(.169)	(.283)
	[.937]	[.636]	[.932]	[.619]

(continued)

Table 1.2 (continued)

Panel and Explanatory Variable	(1)	(2)	(3)	(4)
In the South at 14	.163	−.126	.168	−.110
	(.159)	(.272)	(.159)	(.275)
	[1.177]	[.881]	[1.182]	[.896]
In the West at 14	−.126	−.377	−.129	−.422
	(.184)	(.327)	(.184)	(.334)
	[.882]	[.686]	[.879]	[.656]
3. Personal biography				
Sexual contact before puberty	.258	.300	.343	.383
	(.190)	(.193)	(.301)	(.312)
	[1.294]	[1.35]	[1.409]	[1.466]
Age reached puberty	−.235***	−.241***	−.285***	−.334***
	(.045)	(.046)	(.076)	(.080)
	[.791]	[.786]	[.752]	[.716]
Living with a single parent at 14	.155	.160	−.014	−.059
	(.163)	(.165)	(.276)	(.285)
	[1.168]	[1.173]	[.986]	[.943]
Living with a stepparent at 14	.645**	.627**	.850*	.830*
	(.223)	(.225)	(.368)	(.382)
	[1.907]	[1.871]	[2.340]	[2.292]
Mother employed when	.188	.199†	.131	.138
respondent was 14	(.119)	(.120)	(.195)	(.200)
	[1.207]	[1.221]	[1.140]	[1.148]
4. Group membership after sexual revolution				
Black		−.161		−.304
		(.443)		(.455)
		[.851]		[.738]
Hispanic		−.306		−.299
		(.546)		(.552)
		[.736]		[.742]
Foreign born		−.282		−.387
		(.507)		(.512)
		[.754]		[.679]
Neither parent graduated from high school		−.019		.052
		(.311)		(.315)
		[.981]		[.949]
Either parent had college degree		.466		.534
		(.348)		(.353)
		[1.594]		[1.706]
Fundamentalist Protestant at 14		−.097		−.046
		(.331)		(.334)
		[.908]		[.955]
Catholic at 14		.946**		.959**
		(.315)		(.318)
		[2.576]		[2.608]

(continued)

Table 1.2 (continued)

Panel and Explanatory Variable	(1)	(2)	(3)	(4)
In the Northeast at 14		.705*		.734*
		(.354)		(.357)
		[2.024]		[2.084]
In the South at 14		.464		.451
		(.337)		(.339)
		[1.591]		[1.569]
In the West at 14		.391		.445
		(.395)		(.402)
		[1.479]		[1.561]
5. Personal biography after sexual revolution				
Sexual contact before puberty			−.173	−.185
			(3.87)	(.398)
			[.842]	[.831]
Age reached puberty			.081	.144
			(.094)	(.097)
			[1.085]	[1.155]
Living with a single parent at 14			.265	.341
			(.340)	(.351)
			[1.304]	[1.406]
Living with a stepparent at 14			−.320	−.301
			(.461)	(.472)
			[.726]	[.740]
Mother employed when			.098	.102
respondent was 14			(.244)	(.250)
			[1.103]	[1.107]
Intercept	2.5863***	3.101***	3.264**	4.361***
χ² (df)	148.233	170.545	150.642	174.618
	(22)	(32)	(27)	(37)
n	1361	1361	1361	1361

Note: Standard errors are given in parentheses, odds ratios in brackets.
†$p < .1$.
*$p < .05$.
**$p < .01$.
***$p < .001$.

The first model shown in table 1.2 (col. 1) estimates the effects of historical time, group membership, and personal biography for men in our sample. It is important to note that this model constrains the effects of variables to be the same for men growing up in both historical periods. In this constrained model, the coefficients under the first, second, and third panels (respectively labeled *historical time, group membership,* and *personal biography*) pertain to the *average* effects of variables for men reaching adolescence in both periods.

But recall from the earlier discussion that we expect adolescent sexual behavior to have become less structured by group membership and more influenced by personal biography. The remaining models address this proposition by estimating the effects of group membership and personal biography separately by historical period. The second model (col. 2) constrains the effects of individual time and personal biography to be the same across both periods but allows the effects of group membership to differ. The group membership coefficients under the second panel of this model apply strictly to men reaching adolescence before the sexual revolution. The respective coefficients under the fourth panel (*group membership after sexual revolution*) represent the *net* effects of group membership for men reaching adolescence after the sexual revolution. To obtain the *gross* effects of these variables for men reaching adolescence after the sexual revolution, we add their coefficients under the second panel to their respective coefficients under the fourth panel. To determine whether the net effect of a given coefficient is significant, we examine the significance levels corresponding to the interaction terms.

In contrast, the third model (col. 3) allows only the effects of personal biography to differ by historical period. We interpret this model's coefficients for group membership in the same manner as in the first model. The coefficients for personal biography under the third panel of this model pertain to men reaching adolescence before the revolution. The respective coefficients under the fifth panel (*personal biography after sexual revolution*) represent the net effects of personal biography for men reaching adolescence after the sexual revolution. To determine the gross effects of personal biography for men reaching adolescence after the sexual revolution, we add their respective coefficients under the third and fifth panels. Again, we examine the significance levels corresponding to the interaction terms to determine whether the net effect of a given coefficient is significant.

Finally, the fourth model (col. 4) allows the effects of both group membership and personal biography to differ by historical period. We interpret this model's coefficients for group membership in the same manner as we did with the second model, and we interpret its coefficients for personal biography as we did with the third model.

What these models do not indicate is whether the gross effects of variables are significant for individuals reaching adolescence after the sexual revolution. To determine the significance levels of these variables, we estimate separate equations for individuals reaching adolescence before and after the sexual revolution. We refer to the results of these models in our discussion.

For the sake of example, consider the effect on women of having a parent who has completed college in the first two models shown in table 1.3. In the first model, the coefficient for this variable under the second panel

Table 1.3 Logistic Regression Estimates of Models Predicting Intercourse before Age 18:
Women

Panel and Explanatory Variable	(1)	(2)	(3)	(4)
1. Historical time				
Born 1938–42	.227	.245	.247	.261
	(.273)	(.279)	(.275)	(.280)
	[1.255]	[1.277]	[1.280]	[1.298]
Born 1943–47	.159	.146	.175	.157
	(.262)	(.268)	(.264)	(.270)
	[1.172]	[1.158]	[1.192]	[1.170]
Born 1948–52	.107	.080	.107	.083
	(.249)	(.257)	(.253)	(.259)
	[1.113]	[1.083]	[1.113]	[1.087]
Born 1953–57	.841***	.858*	.236	.298
	(.239)	(.351)	(.918)	(.969)
	[2.318]	[2.359]	[1.266]	[1.347]
Born 1958–62	1.229***	1.242***	.615	.673
	(.238)	(.351)	(.922)	(.974)
	[3.416]	[3.463]	[1.849]	[1.960]
Born 1963–67	1.202***	1.202***	.581	.630
	(.247)	(.356)	(.920)	(.971)
	[3.325]	[3.326]	[1.788]	[1.877]
Born 1968–74	1.646***	1.654***	1.018	1.073
	(.246)	(.353)	(.923)	(.974)
	[5.184]	[5.228]	[2.769]	[2.924]
2. Group membership				
Black	.395*	.046	.402*	.089
	(.172)	(.268)	[.174)	(.275)
	[1.484]	[1.047]	[1.495]	[1.093]
Hispanic	−.354	.464	−.345	.465
	(.228)	(.467)	(.228)	(.471)
	[.702]	[1.590]	[.709]	[1.593]
Foreign born	−.861***	−.149	−.856***	−.103
	(.244)	(.468)	(.244)	(.472)
	[.423]	[.861]	[.425]	[.902]
Neither parent graduated from	.347**	.220	.349**	.227
high school	(.131)	(.193)	(.131)	(.195)
	[1.415]	[1.246]	[1.417]	[1.255]
Either parent had college degree	−.285*	−1.007**	−.274†	−.991**
	(.145)	(.349)	(.146)	(.350)
	[.752]	[.365]	[.760]	[.371]
Fundamentalist Protestant at 14	.387**	.688**	.368**	.667**
	(.141)	(.220)	(.142)	(.222)
	[1.473]	[1.990]	[1.445]	[1.948]
Catholic at 14	−.241†	−.721**	−.247†	−.724**
	(.138)	(.270)	(.138)	(.271)
	[.786]	[.486]	[.781]	[.485]
In the Northeast at 14	.228	.497†	.229	.510†
	(.153)	(.269)	(.154)	(.271)
	[1.256]	[1.643]	[1.257]	[1.666]

(continued)

Table 1.3 (continued)

Panel and Explanatory Variable	(1)	(2)	(3)	(4)
In the South at 14	.237†	.260	.244†	.288
	(.141)	(.246)	(.142)	(.248)
	[1.267]	[1.297]	[1.276]	[1.333]
In the West at 14	.120	.393	.120	.363
	(.170)	(.284)	(.170)	(.288)
	[1.127]	[1.481]	[1.127]	[1.437]
3. Personal biography				
Sexual contact before puberty	.472**	.461**	.757**	.692**
	(.153)	(.155)	(.243)	(.250)
	[1.603]	[1.586]	[2.133]	[1.998]
Age reached puberty	−.162***	−.164***	−.191***	−.190***
	(.034)	(.034)	(.056)	(.057)
	[.850]	[.849]	[.826]	[.827]
Living with a single parent at 14	.632***	.646***	.576*	.546*
	(.144)	(.145)	(.237)	(.242)
	[1.882]	[1.908]	[1.779]	[1.727]
Living with a stepparent at 14	.574**	.587**	.808*	.758*
	(.190)	(.191)	(.357)	(.367)
	[1.776]	[1.798]	[2.244]	[2.134]
Mother employed when respondent was 14	.154	.172	.007	.031
	(.108)	(.109)	(.181)	(.185)
	[1.167]	[1.188]	[1.007]	[1.032]
4. Group membership after sexual revolution				
Black		.591†		.523
		(.349)		(.357)
		[1.805]		[1.687]
Hispanic		−.984†		−.981†
		(.534)		(.538)
		[.374]		[.375]
Foreign born		−.986†		−1.036†
		(.547)		(.551)
		[.373]		[.355]
Neither parent graduated from high school		.207		.195
		(.265)		(.266)
		[1.229]		[1.216]
Either parent had college degree		.876*		.867*
		(.386)		(.388)
		[2.402]		[2.380]
Fundamentalist Protestant at 14		−.525†		−.513†
		(.288)		(.289)
		[.591]		[.599]
Catholic at 14		.629*		.627*
		(.317)		(.318)
		[1.875]		[1.872]
In the Northeast at 14		−.389		−.408
		(.329)		(.331)
		[.678]		[.665]

(continued)

Table 1.3 (continued)

Panel and Explanatory Variable	(1)	(2)	(3)	(4)
In the South at 14		.002		−.032
		(.302)		(.304)
		[1.002]		[.968]
In the West at 14		−.431		−.380
		(.354)		(.358)
		[.650]		[.684]
5. Personal biography after sexual revolution				
Sexual contact before puberty			−.453	−.362
			(.308)	(.317)
			[.636]	[.696]
Age reached puberty			.047	.042
			(.070)	(.071)
			[1.048]	[1.043]
Living with a single parent at 14			.086	.156
			(.294)	(.303)
			[1.090]	[1.168]
Living with a stepparent at 14			−.312	−.225
			(.418)	(.430)
			[.732]	[.798]
Mother employed when			.232	.217
respondent was 14			(.225)	(.229)
			[1.261]	[1.242]
Intercept	.490	.488	.857	.831
χ^2 (df)	291.777	315.874	296.007	318.917
	(22)	(32)	(27)	(37)
n	1732	1732	1732	1732

Note: Standard errors are given in parentheses, odds ratios in brackets.
†$p < .1$.
*$p < .05$.
**$p < .01$.
***$p < .001$.

(−0.285) represents its average effect for women reaching adolescence before and after the sexual revolution. In the second model, the coefficient for having a parent who has completed college in the second panel (−1.007) corresponds strictly to its effect on women reaching adolescence before the sexual revolution. We add this coefficient to the respective coefficient in the fourth panel (0.876) to obtain the coefficient for women reaching adolescence after the sexual revolution (i.e., −1.007 + 0.876 = −0.131). For women reaching adolescence before the sexual revolution, having a parent who has completed college decreases the odds of intercourse by about 64 percent (i.e., $1 - \exp[-1.007]$, or $1 - 0.365$). For women reaching adolescence after the sexual revolution, having a parent who has completed college decreases the odds of intercourse only by about 12 percent (i.e., $1 - \exp[-.0131]$, or $1 - 0.878$).

The significance levels shown in these same panels suggest that, for women reaching adolescence before the sexual revolution, having a parent who has completed college has a significant effect on the likelihood of having intercourse before age eighteen and that, for women reaching adolescence after the sexual revolution, the effect of having a parent who has completed college is significantly different. In a model run separately for women reaching adolescence after the sexual revolution (results not shown), having a parent who has completed college fails to make a significant difference.

To determine whether the overall effects of group membership and personal biography are more or less critical in the later period (i.e., to perform a Chow test), we compare the χ^2 values across the different models. Significant changes in the χ^2 values indicate that the effects of the added set of variables differ by historical period. For example, the addition of interaction terms between group membership and historical time in the second model increases the χ^2 from 291.777 to 315.874 and the degrees of freedom from 22 to 32, suggesting a significant improvement in the fit of the model at the level $p < .01$. In contrast, the addition of interaction terms for personal biography and historical period in the third model increases the χ^2 from 291.777 to 296.007 and the degrees of freedom from 22 to 27. This improvement in the fit of the model fails to reach statistical significance even at the level $p < .10$. Taken together, these changes in model fit suggest that, for women, only the effects of group membership differ significantly by historical period.

Men

In table 1.2 above, the first panel of column 1 shows that historical time does not have a dramatic effect on men's likelihood of having intercourse before age eighteen. As we would expect, men reaching adolescence after the sexual revolution (i.e., those born between 1953 and 1974) have a greater likelihood of having intercourse than the omitted reference group— men born between 1933 and 1937. However, the only men with a significantly higher likelihood of intercourse are those born between 1953 and 1957 and those born between 1968 and 1974. In fact, men from the youngest cohort have 2.5 times the odds of having intercourse as do men from the oldest cohort. Interestingly, men born between 1938 and 1942 are significantly *less* likely to have intercourse than men born between 1933 and

1937. We have no explanation for this effect, which is robust in a variety of our models.

The second panel of column 1 shows that, overall, being black has a highly significant effect on men's likelihood of having intercourse before age eighteen—it almost triples the odds. Having a parent who has completed college and being Catholic fail to influence significantly men's likelihood of having intercourse before age eighteen. The third panel shows that childhood sexual contact and living with a single parent also fail to have significant effects. Reaching puberty at older ages, however, significantly decreases men's likelihood of intercourse. Because this model averages these effects for men growing up in both periods, it is difficult to tell exactly what is going on here.

The second panel of the second column displays the effects of group membership for men who reached adolescence before the sexual revolution. For these men, being black about triples the odds of intercourse before age eighteen, as it does for the entire group. Having a parent who has completed college and being Catholic both have negative effects on the likelihood of intercourse; however, only being Catholic is significant at the level $p < .05$. Men with a parent who completed college have about three-fifths the odds of having intercourse as their counterparts with a parent completing only high school. Men who were raised Catholic have about half the odds of intercourse as men who were not.

Moving to the fourth panel, we see that the effect of being black barely changes over time. While the effect of having a parent who has completed college fails to differ significantly by historical period, it has diminished over time. For men who reached adolescence after the sexual revolution, having a parent who has completed college reduces the odds of intercourse by less than 1 percent. The effect of Catholicism, however, does differ significantly by period. Recall that, for men who reached adolescence before the sexual revolution, being Catholic reduced the odds of having intercourse by half. In contrast, Catholic men who reached adolescence after the sexual revolution have 1.4 times the odds of having intercourse as their counterparts. Results from separate models (not shown) reveal that this last difference fails to reach significance at the level $p < .05$.

We hypothesized that the gap between white and black men would narrow over time. Instead, differences between white and black men have remained about the same. While we anticipated an effect of having a parent who attended college for white males who reached adolescence before the sexual revolution, our finding is foreshadowed by the literature on teen sex. As Reiss points out, the changes introduced by courtship autonomy were more dramatic for females than for males: "The female's change [was] an introduction to the free dating system, whereas the male's adjustment required recognition of a new type of dating partner—a dating partner with a much higher likelihood of ultimately being his mate" (1967, 175).

Evidently, personal biography had some bearing on men who came of age before the sexual revolution. The third panel of the third column shows that, for these men, pubertal development and living with a stepparent have a significant influence on their likelihood of having intercourse before age eighteen. The fifth and last panel of this model suggests that, for men who grew up after the sexual revolution, this very same pattern persists.

It seems peculiar that living with a single parent fails to increase the likelihood of intercourse for men, especially in the period after the sexual revolution. Then again, parents probably exert less control in the first place over their sons' sexuality than over their daughters'. Furthermore, adolescent males living with single mothers may take on several of the responsibilities that a father would ordinarily take on; these responsibilities may preclude them from capitalizing on opportunities to have sex. In contrast, living with a stepparent significantly *increases* the likelihood of intercourse before age eighteen for men in both periods. We did not expect that living with a stepparent would have such an effect, assuming that two parents are better able to monitor an adolescent's sexual behavior than one is.

According to Wu and Martinson, researchers must be careful about the conclusions that they reach on "snapshot" measures of family structure. Basically, they find that, through the mechanisms of socialization and social control, family structure has little effect on premarital births. What is more important is instability and change because "an unstable family environment alters parenting practices and reduces parental control as adults and children adjust to new circumstances and roles following a change in family situation" (1993, 228). It could be the case that living with a stepparent better indexes this instability than does living with a single parent. After all, we know that an adolescent living with a stepparent has experienced not one but two transitions. This might explain our finding that living with a stepparent is more consequential than living with a single parent.

A number of other control variables also have a significant effect on men's likelihood of intercourse before age eighteen. These include being Hispanic, being foreign born, and having neither parent graduate from high school. On average, being Hispanic almost doubles the odds of intercourse, whereas being foreign born almost cuts the odds in half (for similar effects of being foreign born among today's adolescents, see Harris [1998]). Having neither parent complete high school increases the odds of intercourse by three-fourths. None of the effects of these variables change significantly by historical period, with the exception of living in the Northeast. Yet in neither period is the effect of this variable significant (the results are not shown).

The addition of interaction terms between group membership and historical time in the second model increases the χ^2 from 148.233 to 170.545 and the degrees of freedom from 22 to 32, a significant improvement in the fit of the model at the level $p < .05$. The addition of interaction terms between personal biography and historical period in the third model increases the χ^2 from 148.233 to 150.642 and the degrees of freedom from 22 to 27. This improvement in the fit of the model reaches statistical significance at the level $p < .10$. Combined with the results for the individual coefficients, these changes in model fit suggest that, for men, group membership has become less critical but that personal biography has continued to exert the same effect. The lack of change in model fit due to interaction terms between personal biography and historical period is unexpected.

Women

The first panel of the first column of table 1.3 above shows that women's likelihood of having intercourse before age eighteen differs according to when they grew up. In comparison to women born between 1933 and 1937, women born between 1953 and 1974 are significantly more likely to have intercourse before age eighteen. Generally speaking, women who came of age after the sexual revolution are more likely to have intercourse the more recent their birth cohort. For instance, women born between 1953 and 1957 have over twice the odds of having intercourse as women born between 1933 and 1937. In sharp contrast, women born between 1968 and 1974 have over five times the odds of having intercourse as women born between 1933 and 1937. Additional models (not shown) reveal that this trend on the part of women has closed the gender gap. In the light of the structural and ideological trends alluded to earlier, it makes sense that females have "caught up" with males in this arena.

As mentioned above, the model displayed in the first column does not allow the effects of any of the variables to differ by historical period. The second panel of this column shows that being black, having a parent who has completed college, and being Catholic all have effects that are significant and in the expected direction. Being black increases women's likelihood of having intercourse before age eighteen, while having a parent who has completed college and having been raised Catholic both decrease their likelihood. The third panel demonstrates that childhood sexual contact, pubertal development, and living with a single parent additionally have a significant effect on their likelihood of intercourse before age eighteen. Women who have had childhood sexual contact are more likely than those who have not to have intercourse. The older these women were when they reached menarche, the less likely they are to have intercourse. And women living with a single parent at age fourteen are more likely to have intercourse than their counterparts living with both biological parents at this age.

Moving to the second panel of the second column, we first examine the effects of group membership for women who reached adolescence before the sexual revolution. As expected, having a parent who has completed college and being Catholic have significant effects on women's likelihood of intercourse before age eighteen. Women with a parent who has completed college have about one-third the odds of intercourse as women whose parents have only a high school education. And women raised Catholic have about half the odds of intercourse as other women, excluding women raised fundamentalist Protestant.

The fourth panel of the second column shows that the effect of having a parent who has completed college is significantly different for women who reached adolescence after the sexual revolution. This is explicitly demonstrated above in the example of how to interpret these effects. Having a parent who has completed college has a stronger negative effect on intercourse for women reaching adolescence before the sexual revolution than for their counterparts reaching adolescence after the sexual revolution. Consistent with this study's expectations, the effect of being raised Catholic differs significantly by historical time as well. Like having a parent who has completed college, being Catholic has a greater effect on women who came of age before the sexual revolution. Among these women, being Catholic decreases the odds of having intercourse by 50 percent. Among women who came of age after the sexual revolution, being Catholic decreases the odds by less than 10 percent.

We hypothesized that being black would be more critical in the earlier period than in the later. Our results reveal the opposite. Being black only significantly increases the likelihood of intercourse for women born after the sexual revolution (the results are not shown). Although this suggests that being black has become more important over time, this change is significant only at the level $p < .10$. Keep in mind that these analyses already control for variables associated with being black, such as education. In analyses where these variables are excluded, the effect of being black fails to differ at all.

To get a better idea of the changing influence of race, we would have to compare the effect of being black on women with different characteristics in different periods. This would tell us, for example, whether white and black women from more educated backgrounds have the same likelihood of having teen sex before and after the sexual revolution. Regrettably, our sample size precludes us from making this more detailed comparison.

The third panel of the third column suggests that personal biography has an effect on the sexual behavior of women who reached adolescence before the sexual revolution. These women have about double the odds of having intercourse before age eighteen if they experienced childhood sexual contact. Their odds of having intercourse decrease as their age at menarche increases. And they have almost twice the odds of having intercourse if they are living with a single parent at age fourteen.

In contrast to this study's expectations, the fifth and final panel of the third column suggests that, for women who came of age after the revolution, the effects of childhood sexual contact, pubertal development, and living with a single parent fail to differ significantly. This is at odds with this study's expectations. Earlier, we argued that societal proscriptions with respect to premarital sexual behavior were previously more effective in deterring individuals experiencing childhood sexual contact or living with a single parent from having intercourse during adolescence.

With respect to childhood sexual contact, this explanation does not take into account the attributions that individuals may have made for this experience, not to mention the reactions of others following disclosure. Considering these reactions, Morrow and Sorell suggest, "Maternal blaming might seem to cast the victim as rival or whore, increasing the likelihood that she will view herself in this manner and thus assume such a role" (1989, 678). Perhaps reactions and attributions weaken the effect of societal proscriptions in the earlier period. Since our measure of pubertal development is crude, it is probably not worth figuring out why its effect fails to change over time.

Considering the effect of living with a single parent, we pointed out earlier that, where societal proscriptions against intercourse are stronger, parents who do separate are a more select crowd, rendering societal proscriptions less effective. Or it could be the case that single parents are less able to monitor the behavior of their children than are two biological parents in *any* societal context.

Regarding the effects of control variables in the first model, being foreign born, having neither parent graduate from high school, being a fundamentalist, and living with a stepparent at age fourteen all influence the likelihood of intercourse before age eighteen for women. Being foreign born decreases their likelihood of intercourse, whereas having neither parent graduate from high school, being fundamentalist, and living with a stepparent increase their likelihood. The second and third columns reveal no significant change in the effects of these variables.

Previous studies typically distinguish between living with two parents and living with a single parent (a recent exception is Day [1992]). Given the fact that living with a stepparent increases the likelihood of intercourse among both males and females, it is erroneous to combine those living with both biological parents with those living with one biological parent and one stepparent.

We saw earlier that, even though the inclusion of interaction terms between group membership and historical time substantially improves the model fit, the inclusion of these terms between personal biography and historical time fails to make a difference. This same pattern was found among men.

1.5 Discussion

We hypothesize that adolescent sexual behavior has become less influenced by membership in social groups and more influenced by personal biography. However, our multivariate results suggest that our general proposition only partly explains the determinants of teen sex before and after the sexual revolution. Generally speaking, they demonstrate that sexual behavior has become less structured by gender, social class, and religion. At the same time, our results fail to reveal any overarching change with respect to the effects of individual experiences and circumstances over time, such as family structure, childhood sexual contact, and pubertal development.

Even though we were able to predict our basic pattern of results for group membership, we failed to foresee that indicators of personal biography would have such constant effects. Yet we are hesitant about reaching conclusions about the effects of personal biography because our measures are limited.

Of course, we are not able to determine whether these changes reflect processes at the group or individual level. For instance, we do not know whether the effect of parents' education is more of a reflection of how adolescents weigh the costs and benefits of having sex or of norms operant in different groups. Examining trends in group-level processes is further complicated by the fact that the composition and meaning of groups change over time. For example, the foreign born are represented by different countries in different periods of time.

This study finds that, for men and women alike, being foreign born decreases the likelihood of teen sex. An important question is whether this variable influences the costs and benefits that individuals associate with having sex or simply their opportunity to have it. Future studies should take into account the mechanisms by which different variables influence intercourse.

Future surveys covering adolescent sexual behavior will surely profit if they collect information about childhood sexual contact and its circumstances. Of course, researchers may be skeptical about the validity of reports of sexual contact, not to mention reports about sexual activity in general. Surely, efforts to collect such sensitive information will require SAQs (self-administered questionnaires) or audio-CASIs (computer-assisted self-interviews).

Future studies may also benefit from more careful tracking of the effects of variables over time. Owing to sample size limitations, we mainly contrast these processes in two periods, even though the transition is probably more gradual than our depiction of it. Additionally, future studies may benefit by examining whether the effects of these processes differ by the period of adolescence. In analyses not shown, we find that childhood sexual contact increases the likelihood of having intercourse during early and middle adolescence; however, this contact fails to distinguish individuals during later adolescence.

Appendix 1A

Table 1A.1 Logistic Regression Estimates of Models Predicting Intercourse before Age 18: Men

Panel and Explanatory Variable	(1)	(2)	(3)	(4)
1. Historical time				
Born 1938–42	.532*	.497*	.526*	.488*
Born 1943–47	.984	.929	.988	.938
Born 1948–52	1.040	.968	1.033	.964
Born 1953–57	1.798*	.930	.588	.131
Born 1958–62	1.461	.719	.482	.102†
Born 1963–67	1.419	.736	.473	.106†
Born 1968–74	2.581***	1.328	.848	.186
2. Group Membership				
Black	2.794***	2.996**	2.791***	3.294**
Hispanic	1.853*	2.399*	1.838*	2.382*
Foreign born	.564*	.701	.572*	.770
Neither parent graduated from high school	1.760***	1.766*	1.768***	1.785*
Either parent had college degree	.912	.623	.913	.589†
Fundamentalist Protestant at 14	.812	.870	.806	.833
Catholic at 14	1.027	.544*	1.031	.537*
In the Northeast at 14	.937	.636	.932	.619†
In the South at 14	1.177	.881	1.182	.896
In the West at 14	.882	.686	.879	.656
3. Personal biography				
Sexual contact before puberty	1.294	1.350	1.409	1.466
Age reached puberty	.791***	.786***	.752***	.716***
Living with a single parent at 14	1.168	1.173	.986	.943
Living with a stepparent at 14	1.907**	1.871**	2.340*	2.292*
Mother employed when respondent was 14	1.207	1.221†	1.140	1.148

(continued)

Table 1A.1 (continued)

Panel and Explanatory Variable	(1)	(2)	(3)	(4)
4. Group membership after sexual revolution (the gross effects)				
Black		2.550		2.431
Hispanic		1.766		1.768
Foreign born		.529		.523
Neither parent graduated from high school		1.732		1.695
Either parent had college degree		.993		1.005
Fundamentalist Protestant at 14		.789		.795
Catholic at 14		1.403**		1.400**
In the Northeast at 14		1.286*		1.290*
In the South at 14		1.402		1.406
In the West at 14		1.015		1.024
5. Personal biography after sexual revolution (the gross effects)				
Sexual contact before puberty			.842	.831
Age reached puberty			1.085	1.155
Living with a single parent at 14			1.719	1.870
Living with a stepparent at 14			1.050	1.084
Mother employed when respondent was 14			1.340	1.352

Note: Standard errors are given in parentheses.
†$p < .1$.
*$p < .05$.
**$p < .01$.
***$p < .001$.

Table 1A.2 Logistic Regression Estimates of Models Predicting Intercourse before Age 18: Women

Panel and Explanatory Variable	(1)	(2)	(3)	(4)
1. Historical time				
Born 1938–42	1.255	1.277	1.280	1.298
Born 1943–47	1.172	1.158	1.192	1.170
Born 1948–52	1.113	1.083	1.113	1.087
Born 1953–57	2.318***	2.359*	1.266	1.347
Born 1958–62	3.416***	3.463***	1.849	1.960
Born 1963–67	3.325***	3.326***	1.788	1.877
Born 1968–74	5.184***	5.228***	2.769	2.924
2. Group Membership				
Black	1.484*	1.047	1.495*	1.093
Hispanic	.702	1.590	.709	1.593

(continued)

Table 1A.2 (continued)

Panel and Explanatory Variable	(1)	(2)	(3)	(4)
Foreign born	.423***	.861	.425***	.902
Neither parent graduated from high school	1.415**	1.246	1.417**	1.255
Either parent had college degree	.752*	.365**	.760†	.371**
Fundamentalist Protestant at 14	1.473**	1.990**	1.445**	1.948**
Catholic at 14	.786†	.486**	.781†	.485**
In the Northeast at 14	1.256	1.643†	1.257	1.666†
In the South at 14	1.267†	1.297	1.276†	1.333
In the West at 14	1.127	1.481	1.127	1.437
3. Personal biography				
Sexual contact before puberty	1.603**	1.586**	2.133**	1.998**
Age reached puberty	.850***	.849***	.826***	.827***
Living with a single parent at 14	1.882***	1.908***	1.779*	1.727*
Living with a stepparent at 14	1.776**	1.798**	2.244*	2.134*
Mother employed when respondent was 14	1.167	1.188	1.007	1.032
4. Group membership after sexual revolution (the gross effects)				
Black		1.889†		1.844
Hispanic		.594†		.597†
Foreign born		.321†		.320†
Neither parent graduated from high school		1.531		1.525
Either parent had college degree		.878*		.884*
Fundamentalist Protestant at 14		1.177†		1.166†
Catholic at 14		.911*		.908*
In the Northeast at 14		1.113		1.107
In the South at 14		1.299		1.291
In the West at 14		.963		.983
5. Personal biography after sexual revolution (the gross effects)				
Sexual contact before puberty			.636	.696
Age reached puberty			1.048	1.043
Living with a single parent at 14			1.382	1.488
Living with a stepparent at 14			1.046	1.153
Mother employed when respondent was 14			1.512	1.495

Note: Standard errors are given in parentheses.
†$p < .1$.
*$p < .05$.
**$p < .01$.
***$p < .001$.

Notes

We are especially grateful to Robert T. Michael for his extended methodological and substantive suggestions at various stages in the preparation of this chapter. We also wish to acknowledge the helpful comments and support of Avner Ahituv, Shoshana Grossbard-Shechtman, David Ribar, J. Richard Udry, and Linda Waite on an earlier version of this chapter that was presented at the 1995 meeting of the Population Association of America in San Francisco. Additionally, we are indebted to participants at the University of Chicago's Demography Workshop for their helpful suggestions on earlier analyses.

1. For a discussion of how opportunity costs and social norms are linked, see Billy, Brewster, and Grady (1994).

2. These studies measure adolescents' hormonal levels *and* their stage of development using the Tanner scale and are thus able to distinguish between biological and social mechanisms (see also Udry 1990; and Udry and Campbell 1994). As a proxy for pubertal development, most studies use females' age at menarche (e.g., Zabin et al. 1986).

3. Westoff and Ryder use the 1955 and 1960 Growth of American Families Studies and the 1965 and 1970 National Fertility Studies.

4. A study considering the consistency of first intercourse reports finds that about two-thirds of adolescents report different ages of first intercourse from one grade to the next (i.e., ninth to tenth) and that black males are most likely to do this (see Alexander et al. 1993). Still, the vast majority of adolescents report ages within one or two years. For some adolescents, these inconsistencies are due to dishonesty, while, for others, they result from memory error. Memory error, in particular, is thought to increase with the period of recall.

5. To determine age at puberty, the NHSLS survey instrument asks, "How old were you when you reached puberty?" This question is followed by gender-specific prompts. For females, it continues, "By puberty I mean when you had your first menstrual period." For males, it continues, "By puberty I mean when your voice changed or when you began to grow pubic hair" (*SOS,* 649). As can be seen, the females' question is less subject to interpretation than the males'. Offering reassurance that the females' question is relatively straightforward, one study that explores the reporting of menstrual histories shows that about 90 percent of women aged twenty-five to sixty-four correctly recalled their age at menarche within a year (Bean et al. 1979). To the extent that the males' question is so subjective, there could be a tendency for them to associate their physical maturation with their initiation of sexual activity. If this is the case, the results for males with respect to the effects of age at puberty should be considered with caution.

6. We also use event history models that estimate the probability of intercourse before age eighteen as a function of covariates (the results are not shown). These models assume that the effects of covariates on intercourse do not vary with age and therefore estimate proportional hazards for the covariates. Since we know only the age at first intercourse as opposed to the month and year, we use discrete-time event history models that divide the period of risk into yearly intervals. Individuals enter the risk set when they reach puberty and remain in it until they experience intercourse or reach age eighteen. Individuals who experience forced intercourse or who marry remain in the risk set until the age of either experience. To capture the age dependence of intercourse, we include a linear term that specifies the year of risk. The pattern of results for these models is practically identical to those for models that simply predict any intercourse before age eighteen. For the sake of parsimony, we discuss the results for these simpler models.

CHAPTER TWO

■

Choices Leading to Teenage Births

ROBERT T. MICHAEL AND KARA JOYNER

Few social issues today are of greater concern to the public or to social policy makers than teenage childbearing. Among those taking a position on the issue, some are concerned about the healthy development of adolescents and see their early sexual activity and early assumption of the obligations of parenthood as harmful to both the new parent and the infant. Some see the issue in terms of religious beliefs that for young and unmarried boys and girls to engage in sex is wrong and a sign of moral decay. Some are concerned about the right of the young woman to make a decision about the outcome of her pregnancy, especially about abortion. Some focus on the cost to society: the direct cost, incurred immediately of supporting teenagers' children, who disproportionately live in poor families, and the indirect costs incurred later on, as poorly nurtured infants become difficult to educate children and adolescents. And some are most concerned about encouraging responsible behavior on the part of teenage fathers. None, so far as we are aware, argue that teenage childbearing is something that should be encouraged.

Yet teenage childbearing is, and has been for decades, a relatively common event. In the year of our survey, 1992, of the 4,065,000 births recorded in the United States, 518,000 were to women under age twenty.[1] In this chapter, we hope to contribute to a better understanding of teenage childbearing. We suggest that a thoughtful decomposition of the choices leading to that event can help us understand the variation in outcome among young women. We limit ourselves to looking only at the choices surrounding the woman's first pregnancy and only at those first pregnancies that occur before the eigteenth birthday. Despite the relevance of marital status to many of the social concerns about teenage childbearing, we disregard that factor throughout this chapter since it involves a decision that is not directly related to the birth. We investigate the effects of a set of personal characteristics on three distinct choices leading to teenage births, and we consider these choices for women over a relatively broad period of time.

2.1 Decomposing the Risk of Teenage Childbearing

The three choices faced by a young woman that can lead to a birth are depicted in the decision tree shown in figure 2.1. Typically, studies focus on one or another of the decisions or on the composite outcome of a live birth. We explore these three decision points separately and conditionally. The actions or choices that lead to a birth are well known, if seldom described in this context: First is the decision to have sex, without which no birth will result (setting aside, of course, recent in vitro innovations). Second, and conditional on having sex, the individual can engage in several actions that may alter the likelihood of conception. Third, if sexual intercourse results in a conception, there is a subsequent set of actions or choices that can affect the outcome of a live birth.

The probability of a live birth can be thought of, then, as the product of these three distinct choices: to have sex, to control fertility, and to have an abortion. The latter two are conditional on the outcomes of the previous decisions. However, fertility control and the outcome of the conception, even without the consideration of induced abortion, are quintessential stochastic or random processes. A particular choice does not guarantee a particular outcome; the outcome is not deterministic, although both the conception and the birth outcome can be influenced by the individual's behavior.

We focus initially on the mechanics of these three probabilities. Then we return to each and discuss the personal characteristics that we think might influence the three choices. First is the probability of a young woman having sex before her eighteenth birthday, P_s. We assume that the relevant time interval begins at puberty and extends to her eighteenth birthday. Because the age at puberty for women in the United States varies between approximately nine and fifteen years, this "at-risk" period may be as short as three years or as long as nine.[2]

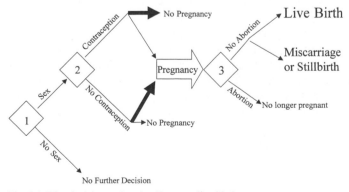

Fig. 2.1 The decision points leading to a live birth.

The second probability is $P_{C|S}$, the likelihood of conception given that sexual intercourse occurs before age eighteen. The key elements in this probability are the risk of conception during a given act of sexual intercourse and the frequency of sex. Expressed most simply, if P_{CA} is the probability of a conception during each act of sex, N is the number of acts of intercourse in the year, and Yr is the number of years from the age at first intercourse to age eighteen, then $P_{C|S}$ is approximated by the product (P_{CA}) (N) (Yr).[3]

The third probability is the likelihood that the pregnancy ends in a live birth, and this, in turn, is affected both by a stochastic process involving spontaneous abortion or miscarriage, reflected by the probability $P_{M|C}$, and by a choice about whether to end the pregnancy by abortion, reflected by the probability $P_{A|C}$. If we think of these two as independent, then the probability of a pregnancy resulting in a live birth is $1 - P_{A|C} - P_{M|C}$.

So the overall probability of a live birth, P_B, can be thought of as the product of these three probabilities. Each of the three reflects a distinct decision point: the decision to have sex, the decision to alter the risk of conception if sexually active, and the decision to abort or to carry the fetus in anticipation of a live birth. These probabilities may not be determined exclusively by those decisions; as mentioned, two of the three involve stochastic processes. The probability of a live birth can be written as

$$P_B = P_S \times P_{CIS} \times (1 - P_{AIC} - P_{MIC}).$$

A few other recent studies have also decomposed the probability of a teenager giving birth. Nathanson and Kim (1989), for example, utilize a framework similar to ours, decomposing the probability of a birth into the same three conditional probabilities of having sex, becoming pregnant, and having a live birth. They focus empirically on two points of time, 1971 and 1979, and they track the change in births to single and to married teenage women separately. They, however, place a major emphasis on marriage and draw attention to the changes in marital and nonmarital teenage behavior.

Akerlof, Yellen, and Katz (1996) also set up a decision tree featuring the three choices of having sex or not, becoming pregnant (using contraception) or not, and having an abortion or not. Their focus is on the strategy for securing a commitment of marriage from the partner in the event of pregnancy, in a game-theoretic context. See also Lundberg and Plotnick (1990), who set up a similar decision tree in their paper on premarital births.

Our interest in this decomposition is to look at the effect of the same, small set of the woman's personal characteristics on each of these three choices in turn and to consider the cumulative effects of those variables on the likelihood of a live birth. Some researchers collapse the separate choices into one, emphasizing the decision about a birth or about having a child and interpreting the intervening decisions about having sex or using contraception as deriving from that major choice. Many economic models of fertility employ that strategy. Some economic models do emphasize joint production in achieving sexual satisfaction while affecting the probability of pregnancy.[4]

We discuss elements of a model that we think useful for the issue under consideration here—choices made by adolescent women.[5] Those elements, of course, would not necessarily apply to the circumstances in which older women make these decisions.[6] For the context of interest to us, we think that it is appropriate to model or analyze each of the three decision points separately and sequentially. This does not imply that the young woman does not anticipate subsequent repercussions, but many young people are quite myopic. So, for those under age eighteen, we suggest that each decision—to begin having sex, to attempt to avoid conception, and to have an abortion if a pregnancy occurs—is made in a separate and sequential manner.

2.2 Three Choices, Three Probabilities

We now return to our discussion of the three decision points and consider the personal characteristics that may be associated with these three choices.

The Decision to Have Sex

Over her lifetime, a woman may decide to have sex for a wide variety of reasons. We are interested here only in the reasons that a young woman who has passed puberty and is under age eighteen might chose to do so. It is an intriguing question whether a teenager who has sex at an early age does so because of the strength of the positive attraction of doing so or because of the weakness of the negative deterrence (in the form of the risk of pregnancy, disease, social disapproval, or conflict with personal ethics or beliefs). Udry and Billy (1987) offer an insightful discussion of the reasons teenagers first engage in sex. Their taxonomy has three forces: (1) motivation, primarily biologically driven (libido); (2) social controls, including restrictions on opportunities and internalized controls imposed by parents, society, or self; and (3) attractiveness, meaning pubertal development and whether the youth is handsome or pretty. They contend that "adolescent coitus [is] the failure of age-graded controls," and they find that there is a gender difference: "In males the hormone effects may overwhelm the social controls" (pp. 841, 852). Udry (1988) further documents the importance of the social controls exerted by friends and parents, studying white boys and girls in the eighth to the tenth grades and measuring coitus, masturbation, and thinking about sex.

Discussing young white women from the National Survey of Family Growth (NSFG)–Cycle III (1982), Brewster, Billy, and Grady (1993) find that sex is more likely at an early age for those women who are behind in school, whose mothers have received less education, and who are living with only one parent as a teenager. We interpret these three variables as reflecting the young woman's career prospects, her aspirations, and her opportunity to have sex, respectively.

There are surely some teenagers who have strong convictions that sex at an early age is inappropriate; for them, the natural positive aspects of experiencing sex are probably outweighed by those convictions, so the likelihood of volitional sex as a teenager is low for them. There are other teenagers for whom long-term career plans or other opportunities imply that the cost of risking an unwanted pregnancy or a disease represents a major deterrent to having sex. For a teenager with either of these motivations, the opportunity to have sex, such as rarely having a parent at home after school hours, would probably have little or no effect on the likelihood of beginning to have sex in the age interval prior to age eighteen. Likewise, there are surely other teenagers who do not hold strong convictions that sex at an early age is inappropriate or who do not have career plans or opportunities that would be dramatically altered by a pregnancy. In addition, there are teenagers for whom, through hormonal or social stimulation, sex has become a major fascination, focus, and personal objective. For a teenager in these latter categories, the opportunity to have sex or the degree of adult supervision and direct control may be a major determining factor of the age at which sexual activity commences.

We suggest five factors that will affect the adolescent woman's decision whether to have sex. They are expressed here as deterrents to sexual activity in each case: (1) a strong conviction that sex is inappropriate at her age; (2) the perception that the opportunity cost of having sex is very high, in terms of risking some other valued life goal; (3) little or no curiosity about sex or little hormonal stimulation to experience sex at that time; (4) greater parental and societal oversight and supervision, with the result that the opportunity to have sex is restricted; and (5) greater social approbation or stigma from any of the consequences of having sex, such as being known to have lost one's virginity, having a baby, or getting a disease. We operationalize these five notions with variables from the NHSLS data set. Before describing these variables, however, we move on to discuss the choice about lowering the probability of getting pregnant given that she has chosen to have sex and the choice about ending the pregnancy by abortion if she becomes pregnant. It is the comparison across these three separate choices that we emphasize in this chapter, so we structure our discussion around them.

The Decision to Avoid Conception

If the woman is sexually active, then she and her partner face the choice of doing something to alter the risk of getting pregnant, which, in the context of adolescent women, means doing something to lower that risk. The possibilities include choosing among particular sexual practices since only one, vaginal intercourse, leads to conception. But the key elements in this decision are probably the frequency with which she has sex (N and Yr in the discussion presented above) and the contraceptive strategy that she and her partners adopt (which affects P_{CA}). If we consider her age at puberty (and thus Yr) to be beyond her control, contraceptive choice and the frequency with which she has sex are her primary means of affecting the probability of becoming pregnant.

Most of the demographic literature emphasizes the birth control decision, while a much smaller body of literature discusses the fact that not all sexually active young couples have sex very often (see Sonenstein, Pleck, and Ku [1989], who present evidence pertaining to boys, Zelnik, Kantner, and Ford [1981], who report a relatively low rate of coital frequency among unmarried adolescent women [an average four-week rate of 2.6 times], and Vinovskis [1988, 148], who points out that unmarried teens are much less active than their married counterparts). The issue of frequency of sex should, we think, be given more attention.

There is, of course, a trade-off between the risk of pregnancy with each act of intercourse and the frequency of intercourse. If we suppose, as is approximately the case, that P_{CA} from unprotected sex by a fecund couple is 0.03, then a woman who has unprotected sex *ten* times has a probability of getting pregnant of approximately 0.26 (= $1 - [1 - 0.03]^{10}$). Alternatively, if that woman uses a birth control method that is 50 percent effective, she could have sex *twenty* times and face that same risk of 0.26 (= $1 - [1 - 0.015]^{19.9}$), or, if she uses a birth control method that is 90 percent effective, she could have sex *one hundred* times and still face that same risk of 0.26 (= $1 - [1 - 0.003]^{100.2}$). Since, as just noted, many sexually active adolescents do not have frequent sex, they may not engage in much effort to lower the probability of pregnancy from a single act of intercourse.

Regarding the decision to practice contraception early in one's sexual career, Mosher and Bachrach (1987) use the NSFG-1982 to document the trends in first premarital contraception over two decades beginning in the early 1960s. (Note that they do not limit their analysis to young women only, so our results may differ since we will be focusing only on behavior prior to age eighteen.) Over those two decades, only about half the women reported using some form of contraception at their first intercourse, but a strong trend is evident, with a much higher proportion doing so by the early 1980s than in the earlier years. The personal characteristics that were found to be associated with a higher rate of use of contraception at first intercourse included being Jewish, living with both parents at age fourteen, having a mother with a higher level of education, being older at the time of that first intercourse, and being white (although the contraceptive method that dominated that race difference was a greater use of withdrawal by whites than blacks).[7]

The Decision to Have an Abortion

If a conception occurs, there is yet another decision—about abortion—that can prevent a live birth. An extensive literature addresses this choice; since chapter 11 of this volume reviews that literature in some detail, we do not do so here.[8] Many of the same personal characteristics or family background factors that influence decisions about beginning to have sex as an adolescent or about using contraceptives to avoid pregnancy would be expected to influence the decision to have an abortion as well. If that characteristic is associated with a desire to avoid having a child, we would expect that desire to affect all three of these decisions since all three influence that outcome. There is, of course, an additional aspect to the abortion decision since one's opinion about the use of abortion may also play an important role.[9]

2.3 Empirical Strategy

We assess the influence of six personal characteristics on the three decision points and the resulting live births to teenage women. The first of these personal characteristics is the woman's reported age at puberty. Udry (1988, 1990) and others have used measures of hormonal activity in youths and found, not surprisingly, that those who have early hormonal activity are more likely also to experience sex at an earlier age. Citing more than a half dozen studies of this issue, Miller and Moore (1990, 1026) summarize, saying, "There is substantial evidence that precocious puberty development is associated with early initiation of sexual activity."

We do not have direct indication of hormonal activity in our data, but we do have a self-report of the woman's age at puberty (measured in years), the variable MATURE in the tables presented below. The older a woman is at puberty, the shorter the time interval the woman is at risk of entering into a sexual relationship prior to age eighteen, so we would expect this variable to be negatively associated with the probability of having sex before age eighteen. The influence of this variable on the probability of getting pregnant given that she is sexually active, however, would not be comparable to its influence on the probability of having sex before age eighteen. There is no reason to expect an effect on P_{CA}, the risk per act of intercourse, but there may be an influence through (N) (Yr), the frequency of sex or the length of time the woman is exposed to the risk of conception before age eighteen. Moreover, there would seem to be no reason to expect an effect on $P_{A|C}$, the probability of having an abortion.

So, if this variable, age at puberty, has an effect on the probability of the woman giving birth before age eighteen, it is most likely to operate through an influence on P_S, and perhaps also through $P_{C|S}$, but not through $P_{A|C}$. This variable illustrates our point that a characteristic may influence one or another of these three decision points but that its cumulative effect on the probability of a live birth may be quite different from its effect on one or more of these intermediate probabilities.

A second personal characteristic that may influence one or more of the three choices is the woman's religious beliefs. Those beliefs may influence her willingness to have sex, thus affecting P_S, affect her choice of birth control or her frequency of having sex, thus affecting $P_{C|S}$, or influence her views about abortion, thus affecting $P_{A|C}$. It is possible that holding a particular religious affiliation would affect all three choices. Those effects could reinforce each other, resulting in a very strong association between that religion and P_B, the probability of a birth before age eighteen. Alternatively, a set of beliefs could have an offsetting effect: say, having no influence on the onset of sex, having a positive influence on the use of birth control, but then having a strong deterrent effect on the choice about abortion. The net or composite effect on P_B might then be very small even though the effect on two of the three components was large. We have information about the religion in which the woman was raised, in terms of mainline Protestantism (the comparison group), fundamentalist Protestantism (FUNDAM), Catholicism (CATH), other religions (OTHER), and no religion (NORELIG).[10] These four variables measure this second personal characteristic included in the statistical analyses reported below.

Family structure is the third personal characteristic that we explore. Our measures of family structure, defined at the time the woman was fourteen, are BIOPAR, a dummy variable indicating that she lived with both her biological parents at age fourteen; STPPAR, a dummy indicating that she lived with a parent and a stepparent at age fourteen (with the comparison group being those who lived with one parent only); and MAWORK, a dummy variable indicating that the girl's mother was employed when she (the respondent) was fourteen.

Family structure may influence the choice about having sex through several mechanisms. If family structure reflects the values the young woman uses to guide her choices, then it may affect her willingness to have sex. If it reflects the degree of parental oversight and supervision to which

she is subjected, it may be associated with the opportunity she has to engage in sex or the extent to which she is occupied with other activities. It
may, instead, proxy the salience with which her mother is a role model,
affecting her interest in exploring sexual relations or some other expression of her maturity. Whatever the effect of family structure on the probability of initiating sex at an early age,[11] it is not evident that this same effect
should be expected on the probability of getting pregnant if she does have
sex or on the probability of having an abortion if she does get pregnant.
The mechanism suggested here regarding parental supervision inhibiting
sexual behavior would not be the same, for example, regarding the decision to have an abortion if pregnant. As reported above, studies using the
NSFG have found that women who reside with both parents at age fourteen are substantially more likely to use contraception the first time they
have intercourse, so they are probably also more likely to do so throughout
their early, premarital sexual career.

Young women who are born outside the United States may have had a
very different personal experience in their youth than native-born women,
so the fourth characteristic that we use is a dummy variable indicating that
the woman was foreign born, FOREIGN. The fact of being foreign born
may be associated with greater difficulty fitting in with teenage peers, or
with having a more closely supervised adolescence, or perhaps with having
come to the US with more intense aspirations for pursuing an education
and a subsequent career. Given any of these arguments, the foreign born
may have a lower probability of early sex. It is unclear why a young woman
who is foreign born would be more or less likely to have a different probability of getting pregnant or of choosing to have an abortion if pregnant.

The opportunity cost of having a baby may differ among young women.
A high opportunity cost would influence a woman's efforts to avoid pregnancy or giving birth. Here, since the opportunity cost of having a baby
is the deterrent to initiating sexual activity, this same argument implies
that the opportunity cost will also encourage efforts to avoid pregnancy if
sex occurs and, additionally, will encourage abortion if a pregnancy does
occur. This fifth personal characteristic, then, is one that may have a cumulative effect across the three choices, and, if so, it would likely have a
particularly strong influence on the probability of having a live birth before age eighteen. We used parents' education level as an indicator of a
young woman's perception that her opportunity cost of having a baby is
high in terms of forgone life goals. We used as our measure of parents'
education the highest grade of schooling attained by either parent and
constructed two dummy variables indicating that a parent had completed
high school (HSPAR) or had attended college (COLPAR), with the comparison group being those women neither of whose parents had completed
high school.[12]

Our sixth personal characteristic is race/ethnicity. Cultures differ in the extent to which social approbation or stigma is attached to having sex and any of its consequences. As we know from other data, African American teenagers have a higher rate of births, so, in their neighborhoods, in their families, and among their peers, the stigma associated with being sexually active or having a baby may be much lower. If so, young African American women may be less concerned about delaying the onset of sexual intercourse, about avoiding a pregnancy, or about carrying a pregnancy to term. We know from other studies that blacks are more likely to begin having sex at an early age and are also less likely to use a contraceptive the first time they have intercourse. These two components may therefore reinforce each other, yielding a higher likelihood that a black woman will have a child before age eighteen. We use two variables in our analysis, BLACK and HISPANIC, dummy variables indicating that the teenager is African American or Hispanic (the comparison group is whites).

These six personal characteristics— age at puberty, religious beliefs, family structure, whether native born, parents' education, and race/ethnicity—are used in our empirical inquiry. The same six are used in our statistical model of each of the three probabilities, P_S, $P_{C|S}$, and $P_{A|C}$. In particular, we want to see whether each variable appears to play the same role in influencing each of these three components of the probability of a live birth. It would be unexpected if they did, but it should be useful to know where each has its influence if there is one.

Since our respondents were age fourteen to seventeen (the age interval of interest) from the late 1940s to the early 1990s, time trends may play an important role. We control for time period in all our statistical models using a series of five-year dummy variables (the comparison time period is 1947–54).[13] One complication of the analysis might be noted here. Very few women report having had an abortion prior to 1973, when the Supreme Court decision in *Roe v. Wade* made the procedure legal throughout the nation. Therefore, in the logistic analysis of the choice about abortion, we restricted the data to women under age forty at the survey date and hence under age twenty-one in 1973. Since the only conceptions being analyzed in this statistical model are those occurring in women under age eighteen, these older women have been removed from the analysis.

2.4 Empirical Results

Summary Statistics

We first summarize the empirical magnitudes of the three separate conditional probabilities and the probability of a birth before age eighteen, and we trace the movement of each of these four probabilities over the past half century, as the NHSLS data permit. As part of the NHSLS interview, respondents were asked several questions about their sexual behavior prior to age eighteen. They were also asked about every pregnancy they had experienced or been responsible for, including its outcome: abortion, miscarriage, stillbirth, or live birth. While both our topic and this data set can be applied to males as well as females, we limit ourselves here to females only. There are 1,748 females in the cross-sectional sample, which we use here exclusively, and, of those, 1,615 (92 percent) have complete and consistent records about their sexual behavior prior to age eighteen and their conceptions over their lifetime.

The accuracy of the survey responses used in this chapter is challenged by two issues. First, questions about sexual activity, intimate relationships, and abortion are inherently private and possibly embarrassing or controversial. This may, of course, discourage respondents from answering wholly and completely truthfully about these matters. However, because of the design of the survey, the public health motivation described to respondents, and the reports of the field interviewers, we are convinced that the quality of the responses is acceptably high.[14]

Second, the women were asked to report on behavior during their adolescence and on their experiences with their first pregnancy, even though many of the women were in their forties or fifties and, for many of them, the time period at issue was therefore many years earlier. The ability to recall events that transpired long ago compromises the quality of responses, of course. However, the nature of the events about which we were asking is very salient, and one is less likely to have eroded memories of an event as important as one's first pregnancy. Furthermore, the internal consistency of the answers provided is impressive and reassuring, and the external validation of some of the patterns seen in these data lends further credibility to these reports about behavior that took place years earlier. Nevertheless, data quality is an issue that prompts some caution in interpreting the results reported below.

We use the women's reports about their life-cycle interval from puberty to age eighteen. Since the women were aged eighteen to fifty-nine at the time of the survey, the life-cycle interval in question is 1947–91, a wonderfully long period during which much change in social demography took place. These data, then, permit us to track some of the important social changes that have occurred over nearly half a century.

Table 2.1 uses the NHSLS data for women. It shows the three probabilities discussed above and the composite probability of a live birth for these women. The first row shows the probabilities for the whole sample of 1,615 women. The subsequent rows show these probabilities separately for women of specified ages in 1992. The top row shows that nearly half the women—44.3 percent—were sexually active before they were eighteen, that exactly one-third of those who were sexually active became pregnant at some

Table 2.1 Decomposing the Probability of a Birth by Age 18, by Age

Age	P_B	=	$P_S \times P_{C|S} \times (1 - P_{A|C} - P_{M|C})$	Period the Cohort Was 14–17
All	.113	=	$.443 \times .335 \times (1 - .167 - .075)$	1947–91
18–24	.129	=	$.631 \times .337 \times (1 - .268 - .125)$	1982–91
25–29	.128	=	$.518 \times .354 \times (1 - .275 - .025)$	1977–84
30–34	.084	=	$.505 \times .268 \times (1 - .270 - .108)$	1972–79
35–39	.096	=	$.444 \times .279 \times (1 - .097 - .129)$	1967–74
40–44	.107	=	$.307 \times .364 \times (1 - .000 - .042)$	1962–69
45–49	.105	=	$.309 \times .383 \times (1 - .056 - .056)$	1957–64
50–54	.161	=	$.323 \times .500 \times (1 - .000 - .000)$	1952–59
55–59	.117	=	$.292 \times .400 \times (1 - .000 - .000)$	1947–54

point before they turned age eighteen, and that about three-quarters of those pregnancies (= $1 - 0.167 - 0.075$) resulted in a live birth. Overall, a little more than one in ten (11.3 percent) of all these women reported having a child before turning age eighteen.

There are several intriguing patterns in the row-by-row comparisons in table 2.1. First, notice that P_B does not change very dramatically over time and has no apparent trend. About 10 percent of women in each time interval over these forty years had a child before turning age eighteen.[15] The absence of a trend in live births to teenagers over this long period, however, belies changes in the other probabilities that offset each other.

By contrast with P_B (the probability of a live birth), the variable P_S (the probability of having sex before age eighteen) has a tremendous trend: it rises from well under one-third for the women who were aged fourteen to seventeen in the interval 1947–54 to nearly two-thirds for the women who were that age in the interval 1982–91. That dramatic increase in the likelihood of a young woman having sex is itself often considered evidence of a sexual revolution beginning in the late 1960s.

However, notice that $P_{C|S}$ (the probability of getting pregnant if a woman does have sex) also has a very strong time pattern, and it goes in the *opposite direction* from the probability of having sex: it falls by nearly half from the cohort aged fourteen to seventeen in the time interval 1952–59 to the cohort who were that age in the time interval 1972–79, owing to improved contraceptive technology, and then rises again somewhat. The abortion probability, $P_{A|C}$, is effectively zero up to the cohort who were aged fourteen to seventeen in the time interval 1967–74 and then rises substantially. The *Roe v. Wade* decision in January 1973 explains this dramatic change in reported abortions in the subsequent time intervals. (This abrupt rise in reported abortions after 1973, with no reference at any time in our survey to the legalization of abortion, is one of the impressive indicators that these women were reporting these facts with considerable accuracy.)[16]

Overall, for each cohort of women, the product of these three probabilities is the probability of a live birth. This is a mechanical or mathematical relation, of course, and, by itself, it does not imply any purposive or strategic behavior. Studying these three separate components, however, reveals a great deal about the choices and behavior of these women, and, overall, these choices determine their fertility behavior in this age interval prior to reaching age eighteen. The stability of that product, P_B, does not hint at the dramatic rise in the incidence of sex, offset by the equally dramatic decline in the conditional probabilities of a pregnancy and of carrying that pregnancy to term. Both the decline in the probability of conception, $P_{C|S}$, and the rise in the sum of abortions and miscarriages, $P_{A|C} + P_{M|C}$, offset the effect on live births of that rise in the incidence of sex among adolescents. Notice, finally, that the group for whom the rate of live births per woman was highest is that aged fifty to fifty-four in 1992. These are the women who were aged fourteen to seventeen during the peak of the baby boom (1952–59). This is yet another indication that these women are reporting accurately.

Multivariate Logistic Regression Analysis

Our statistical model is a standard logistic regression; the dependent variable in each regression is one of the four probabilities discussed above: P_S, the probability of having sex before age eighteen; $P_{C|S}$, the probability of conception given that the woman was sexually active before age eighteen; $P_{A|C}$, the probability that she chose to abort her first pregnancy given that it occurred before age eighteen; and P_B, the probability of a live birth before age eighteen. Table 2.2 shows the mean value for each of the variables used in the empirical analysis reported below. (Those variables not yet defined will be as they are introduced below.)

In each separate logistic regression, a set of eight time dummy variables is included. Table 2.3 shows these four separate models, one each for the four probabilities; the table shows the effect of each variable on the odds ratio and indicates the statistical significance of the coefficient in the logistic regression.

We describe these results beginning with the choice about having sex, P_S, column 2 in table 2.3. The calendar time dummy variables reported in row 1 simply indicate the range in the values of these eight coefficients, and several were statistically significant in this case. In particular, the values of the dummies were 1.21 for 1955–59, 1.20 for 1960–64, 1.18 for 1965–69, 2.29 for 1970–74, 3.39 for 1975–79, 3.30 for 1980–84, 5.07 for 1985–89,

Table 2.2 Summary Statistics of Variables Used in Analyses

Variable	Mean[a]	Variable	Mean
P_B	.113		
P_S	.443	YEAR50	.08
$P_{C|S}$	.335	YEAR55	.08
$P_{A|C}$	.167	YEAR60	.09
$P_{M|C}$	.075	YEAR65	.13
MATURE	12.68	YEAR70	.15
	(1.6)		
NORELIG	.04	YEAR75	.17
FUNDAM	.32	YEAR80	.13
PROTESTANT	.28	YEAR85	.13
CATH	.31	YEAR90	.03
OTHER	.05		
BIOPAR	.73	BC	.31
STPPAR	.08	VI13	.06
MAWORK	.51	VI14	.09
FOREIGN	.07	VI15	.17
BLACK	.13	VI16	.30
HISP	.08	VI17	.37
HSPAR	.68	VIP1	.55
COLLPAR	.19	VIP2	.16
NUMFIRST	17.28	VIP4	.21
	(17.3)		
NUMTOT	30.4	VIP5+	.08
	(53.3)		

[a]The standard deviation is given in parentheses if the variable is not a dummy.

and 4.40 for 1990–92 (the last five values were statistically significant at the level $p < .01$). These results indicate that there were no differences in the base probability for the women from the late 1940s through the 1960s but that, from the 1970s on, the probability of having sex before age eighteen rose dramatically and remained much higher than it had been earlier. Those aged fourteen to seventeen after the mid-1970s were several times more likely to have had sex before age eighteen than were those who passed through that age interval in the early 1950s.[17] This surely constitutes a "revolution" in adolescent sexual behavior, one that has been well documented elsewhere and confirmed here once again. These differences across time were also featured in chapter 1 (see table 1A.2 above).

While the onset of partnered sex is probably not one of the most rational of human activities, even if it is among the most highly anticipated, the arguments presented above are clearly reflected in the coefficients on many of the variables in this model. Those who experienced puberty at a later age are less likely to have had sex by age eighteen, as are those who are

Table 2.3 Logistic Regression on Probability of a birth before Age 18, P_B: Effect on Odds Ratios ($P_B = P_S \times P_{C|S} \times [1 - P_{A|C} - P_{M|C}]$)

	P_B	P_S	$P_{C|S}$	$P_{A|C}$
YEAR 70/90	1.0–1.9	1.2–5.1**	.7–1.8	1.7–1.9
MATURE	.88*	.86**	.95	1.07
NORELIG	1.22	1.56	1.10	1.70
FUNDAM	1.31	1.12	1.11	.42
CATH	.65	.69*	.79	.81
OTHER	.53	.54*	.45	. . .
BIOPAR	.77	.58**	1.04	.42
STPPAR	1.71	1.14	1.75	.66
MAWORK	1.05	1.19	.83	.51
FOREIGN	.42	.40**	.68	.77
BLACK	1.73*	1.62**	1.65*	.40
HISP	1.70	.66	2.32*	.39
HSPAR	.35**	.60**	.43**	4.60**
COLLPAR	.15**	.77	.46**	5.98**
χ^2	157**	236.7**	84.3**	39.6**
	(21)	(21)	(21)	(15)

Note: Degrees of freedom are given in parentheses.
* Statistically significant at the 5 percent level.
** Statistically significant at the 1 percent level.

Catholic, who belong to the 'other' religions,[18] who lived with both biological parents at age fourteen, who are foreign born, and whose parents graduated from high school. Black women were substantially more likely to have sex than whites.[19]

Before we probe the statistical or substantive meaning of this regression model, let us compare these results to the effects of these same six personal characteristics on the other probabilities. Column 3 reports the model estimated on $P_{C|S}$, the probability of getting pregnant given that the young woman is sexually active. Here, none of the time dummy variables is statistically significant, and many fewer of the personal characteristics have a statistically significant coefficient. Both black and Hispanic sexually active women are more likely than their white counterparts to become pregnant, and those women with more educated parents are far less likely to do so. But none of the several other variables exhibits statistical significance. Of those four variables with a statistically significant coefficient, the direction of effect across these first two choices (P_S and $P_{C|S}$) is reinforcing for the blacks compared to the whites and for the women with more educated parents, but, for the Hispanics, the two effects are offsetting. The Hispanic women are less likely than the whites to engage in sex but are more likely to become pregnant if they do so.

Look next at column 4, the model for $P_{A|C}$, the probability of having an abortion if a conception occurs (recall that this model includes only those women under age forty whose adolescence occurred after the national legalization of abortion). With the older women removed, there is no discernible time trend, and none of the several variables have a significant coefficient, except for the very strong effect of parents' education. Age at puberty has no effect, nor does religion, or family structure (as measured here), or being foreign born, or even race/ethnicity. Only the young women with better-educated parents behave systematically differently, and they are far more likely to report having chosen to have an abortion.

Now look at the cumulative effect of those two parents' education variables across columns 2, 3, and 4. Not only are the women with more educated parents much *less likely* to begin having sex before age eighteen, but they are also much *less likely* to get pregnant if they do, and, on top of that, they are several times *more likely* to have an abortion if a pregnancy occurs at that young age. None of the other six personal characteristics have a constantly strong, statistically significant effect across these three distinct decision points. Black women are consistently more likely to have sex, and are more likely to become pregnant if they are sexually active, but, if they do become pregnant, appear to abort the pregnancy at much lower rates, although this latter effect is not statistically significant, even though large in magnitude.

The first column in table 2.3 shows the model estimated on the underlying behavior of interest, P_S, the probability of having a birth before the woman turns eighteen. This model is more commonly estimated, and the previous discussion of the other three models helps us understand it better. Here, in column 1, the absence of a time trend is documented, and only four of the explaining variables have statistical significance. Those women who experienced puberty at a later age are less likely to bear their first child before turning eighteen, and the other three columns clarify that this effect works exclusively through an influence on the likelihood of beginning to have sex at a younger age. It is not related to the risk of pregnancy among those who are sexually active, and it is not related to the choice about abortion.

Black women are much more likely to give birth before turning eighteen, and we see here that the two key factors in terms of the statistical precision with which the coefficients are estimated are the first two choices, although the size of the coefficient on the abortion choice is also quite large and reinforces the other two. As was anticipated by the results in the three separate models, the effect of parents' education level on the probability of giving birth before age eighteen is quite large and very strong. At each decision point along the way, the young women whose parents are better educated choose the outcome less likely to result in a birth at a young age. Religion, family structure, and being foreign born are not statistically related to the probability of giving birth before turning eighteen.

The column-by-column comparison of the effects of each personal characteristic on the three components of the choice to give birth is, we think, most intriguing and informative. A few of the variables—notably parents' education level—have a cumulative effect on that final probability of live birth, while others have an effect on only one of the components or have an offsetting effect on two of the choices, yielding a much smaller overall effect on the probability of a live birth.[20]

Discussion

As a way of calibrating and illustrating the models' capacity to discriminate among women with different characteristics, we have constructed three synthetic cases and have estimated for each of these hypothetical women each of the four probabilities P_S, $P_{C|S}$, $P_{A|C}$, and P_B using the four regressions reported in table 2.3. For convenience of reference, we have given each of the hypothetical women a name: "Tonya" is black, a fundamentalist Protestant; she went through puberty at age twelve; neither of her parents graduated from high school; and she had no father present at age fourteen. "Tammy" is white, a fundamentalist Protestant; she experienced puberty at age thirteen; her parents have a high school education; and she lived in an intact family at age fourteen. "Terri" is white, Catholic; she went through puberty at age fourteen; her parents have a college education; and she too lived in an intact family at age fourteen. Table 2.4 shows the four predicted probabilities for these three hypothetical women,

Table 2.4 Predicted Probabilities Based on the Model in Table 3.3, Three Hypothetical Women, Two Time Periods

Synthetic Case	P_S	$P_{C|S}$	$(1 - P_{A|C} - x)$	P_B
1955				
Tonya	.652	.705	. . .	.450
Tammy	.259	.379	. . .	.100
Terri	.124	.161	. . .	.007
1985				
Tonya	.888	.603	$(1 - .079 - x)$	.432
Tammy	.595	.280	$(1 - .307 - x)$	.094
Terri	.373	.109	$(1 - .846 - x)$	.007

Note: Tonya: black, fundamentalist Protestant, puberty at 12, neither parent graduated high school, no father present. Tammy: white, fundamentalist Protestant, puberty at 13, parents with high school education, intact family. Terri: white, Catholic, puberty at 14, parents with college education, intact family.

and it does so for two separate dates, 1955 and 1985, since some of the behavior exhibits such a strong time trend.

For the 1955 estimates, we see that there are large differences in the predicted probabilities for the three women for both P_S and $P_{C|S}$. Tonya is about five times as likely as Terri to have had sex before turning eighteen, and she is also about four times as likely to have gotten pregnant if she did have sex. So both the model on P_S and that on $P_{C|S}$ do, indeed, discriminate among women according to these six personal characteristics. If we assume no abortions and no miscarriages or stillbirths, then the product $P_S \times P_{C|S}$ is equal to P_B, the probability of a live birth. The probability shown in table 2.4 under P_B is not the product but is instead the prediction from the estimated model in column 1 of table 2.3 above. We see that Tonya has a probability estimated at 45 percent of having given birth by age eighteen while Terri has a probability of less than 1 percent. Each of these is approximately the numeric product of the two predicted components (i.e., for Tonya, $0.652 \times 0.705 = 0.460$). Tonya is more likely both to have sex and to conceive if she does have sex, and the product of the two is a much higher probability of giving birth.

Look next at the predicted probabilities for 1985. The probability of having sex is higher for all three women, and the ratio for Tonya compared to Terri is no longer five to one but only about two to one. The probability of getting pregnant if sexually active is lower now, for all three women. Since the model on $P_{A|C}$ is estimated only for the subset of women under age forty in 1992, there was no estimate of that probability for 1955, but for 1985 we see that Terri has a much higher likelihood of having an abortion than does Tonya.

When the probability of a live birth, P_B, is estimated for each of the three women for 1985, we see no apparent difference between 1955 and 1985, but there remains a very big difference between Tonya and Terri. Ironically, the differences over time in the three components for the women have yielded no apparent difference in the outcome of live birth. Tonya's likelihood of having sex has gone up somewhat, while her likelihood of getting pregnant has gone down somewhat, and, with the modest probability of having an abortion, her probability of giving birth before turning eighteen remains slightly under 50 percent. Terri is much more likely to have sex in 1985, substantially less likely to get pregnant, and dramatically more likely to have an abortion if she does get pregnant, so the probability that she will give birth before turning eighteen is essentially zero. The constancy that the predicted P_B of each of these women displays masks much change in the three choices they make.

To illustrate the responsiveness of these estimated risks, suppose that we switched Tonya's and Terri's predicted probabilities of abortion, 0.079 and 0.846, respectively, while keeping all the other estimated probabilities as they are for 1985. Then Tonya's P_B would fall to 0.02 (instead of 0.432), and Terri's P_B would rise to 0.04 (instead of 0.007). With this one probability reversed, Tonya and Terri's comparative likelihood of giving birth also reverses. Although Tonya would still have a high probability of having sex and a high probability of conceiving, she would not have a higher probability of having a live birth if she had Terri's probability of having an abortion. And, if these respective probabilities were applied to, say, 500 Tonyas and 500 Terris, the expected number of these 1,000 young women who would give birth before turning eighteen would fall from 220, using the probabilities as estimated here, to 30, using this one reversed pair of probabilities. To be clear, this is not something that we advocate, nor is it something that we suggest is feasible. But the calculation serves to illustrate how dramatically different is the experience of the young woman with Tonya's characteristics compared to that of her counterpart with Terri's characteristics.

2.5 Further Exploration and Next Steps

In the preceding two sections, we have focused on four statistical models, using the same six personal characteristics as explanatory variables. We emphasized their reinforcing or offsetting effects on the product of the choices, a live birth before age eighteen. There is value, as well, in exploring the three separate choices somewhat more independently, probing the sensitivity of the results reported in table 2.3 above to modest changes in each of the three models separately. Here, we report a few of these probes.

Probability of Having Sex

Regarding the choice reflected in P_S, the choice of having sex at an early age, we first note two additional empirical points. First, the NHSLS asked respondents *why* they first had sex, and their responses are informative. Of those for whom the act was not forced, 42 percent of the women who were sexually active before age eighteen said that the reason was affection for their partner or an expression of love, while another 6 percent said that it was their wedding night. About 29 percent gave as their explanation for their first sexual experience that they were curious about sex, and another 3 percent listed physical pleasure as the explanation. Another 13 percent responded that peer pressure or partner pressure was their reason. About 3 percent were under the influence of alcohol or drugs, and 3 percent gave a variety of other explanations. While these "reasons" for first having sex are interesting, they do not necessarily map well into the descriptive characteristics used in our analysis. We note them here with the suggestion that there may be value in looking more closely at these reasons, over time, as they correlate with the personal characteristics we use in our analysis.

Second, many of these women who were sexually active before age eighteen had rather little sexual experience in that age interval. Overall, while nearly half the women had sex before age eighteen, more than half of those who did so (55.0 percent) said that they had sex with only one partner by the time of their eighteenth birthday. Some 6.6 percent of the total number of sexually active women said that they had sex only one time with that one partner only, another 11.0 percent said that they had sex no more than ten times and only with that one partner prior to their eighteenth birthday, while another 10.6 percent said that they were still having sex with that first sex partner at the time of the interview. So, while almost half the women said that they had sex before age eighteen, more than four out of five of those who did so reported either that their sexual experience was quite limited (to fewer than ten times total and with one person only) or that their first partnership became a long-term and continuing sexual relationship.

Those women in general had sex infrequently, defying the stereotype of the young woman who begins her sexual career at an early age and thereafter has sex very frequently. For that matter, the woman who has sex at a young age and continues into her mature years still having sex with the same partner also does not fit the stereotype of the promiscuous young woman. This characterization of the early sexual experience of these women is consistent with the findings, referenced earlier, of Sonenstein, Pleck, and Ku (1989) for boys and Zelnik, Kantner, and Ford (1981) for girls.

Turning to a further analytic probe, since the model in column 2 of table 2.3 above controls for time period by the eight time-period dummies, it constrains the coefficients on the covariates to be constant over that whole time period. We have reestimated that model on P_S for three separate age subsets, thus allowing the coefficients on the covariates to vary over time. The subsets are the women aged forty-five to fifty-nine, those aged thirty to forty-four, and those aged eighteen to twenty-nine; these three subsets were in the age range fourteen to seventeen during the years 1947–64, 1962–79, and 1977–91, respectively. A few results from that time-partitioned model, shown in panel A of table 2.5, are noteworthy. The coefficient on MATURE does not change over time. Entering puberty at a later age has the same deterrent effect on the likelihood of having sex before age eighteen for women over this whole forty-year interval, although its statistical significance has grown over time. CATHOLIC, by contrast, is significant only for the oldest group. Its effect is strong for those women who were this age from the late 1940s to the early 1960s: the effect on the odds ratio is 0.47 then, but it declines in value and is not significant in either of the later time periods. The influence of being Catholic on the likelihood of the young woman having sex before age eighteen has disappeared by the time the thirty to forty-four-year-old women were

Table 2.5 Models Estimated for Women in Three Age Categories

	Age		
	18–29	30–44	45–59
	A: Logistic on the Probability of Having Sex, P_S		
Mature	.83**	.89*	.87
Norelig	1.89	1.35	.76
Fundam	.75	1.19	1.52
Cath	.87	.74	.47*
Other	.55	.49	.62
Biopar	.47**	.64	.48*
Stppar	1.33	1.00	1.05
Momwork	1.26	1.39*	.88
Foreign	.19**	.62	.47
Black	2.64**	1.19	1.74
Hisp	.77	.39*	1.87
HSPAR	.43**	.69	.79
COLLPAR	.89	.81	.44
χ^2	67.3**	60.0**	45.4**
	(13)	(13)	(13)
	B: Logistic on the Probability of Conception Given Sex, $P_{C|S}$		
Mature	.88	.92	1.07
Fundam	1.11	1.35	.65
Cath	1.34	.48	.68
Other	.24	.17	.66
Biopar	1.18	1.23	.75
Stppar	2.59*	1.65	.90
Momwork	1.27	.50*	1.13
Foreign	.22	2.46	.28
Black	2.76**	1.24	1.40
Hisp	3.10*	1.00	3.14
HSPAR	.48*	.32**	.48
COLLPAR	.38*	.54	.32
χ^2	42.8**	45.0**	10.0
	(12)	(12)	(12)

Note: Degrees of freedom are given in parentheses.
* Statistically significant at the 5 percent level.
** Statistically significant at the 1 percent level.

of age, that is, by about the mid-1960s. (This finding is consistent with the views of Ryder and Westoff [1971, chap. 8] and Greeley [1994, chap. 2] and is reported as well in chap. 1 in this volume.)

Another personal characteristic appears to have no discernible time trend and is substantial in all three subperiods. It is family structure as measured by the variable BIOPAR, which indicates that the woman grew up in a household with both her natural parents. Those who did so have a lower probability of having sex before age eighteen, and that effect is persistent over time. For the FOREIGN and BLACK variables, the whole effect observed in the model reported in table 2.3 above appears to come from the youngest women, those aged eighteen to twenty-nine. While both variables operate in their respective directions in the earlier time intervals, neither is significant until the most recent interval. The influence of having a parent who completed high school grows from the earliest to the later time interval. It is very strong and statistically significant in the most recent period.

Both the study of the trends over time in the effects of the six personal characteristics and the exploration of a wider array of characteristics is warranted. Many relevant studies can be found in the social demography literature. Some of the time-period differences in effects on the choice to have sex at an early age are explored and interpreted by Joyner and Laumann (chap. 1 in this volume).[21]

The Probability of a Conception

Turning to the second of the choices, $P_{C|S}$, the probability of a pregnancy given sexual activity, we have also run this model for these three time subperiods, as seen in panel B of table 2.5. The four variables that were statistically significant over the whole period seen in column 3 of table 2.3 above were significant only for the youngest subset of women (aged eighteen to twenty-nine), that is, only for those who were in their early adolescence during the period 1977–91. Most of those significant coefficients were in fact stronger for that subset of women than for the whole group of women. For the women who were young adolescents in the interval 1962–79 (age thirty to forty-four), only one of those four coefficients was significant. And, for those who were young adolescents in the earliest time interval, 1947–64 (age forty-five to fifty-nine), the whole regression model failed to have any statistical power, which is to say that none of these six personal characteristics seem to help explain who among those sexually active young women became pregnant in that immediate postwar time interval.

The fact that the sexually active woman's personal characteristics are more important as determinants of $P_{C|S}$ in the recent time period, and are unimportant in the earlier time periods, may be explained by the improvements in contraceptive efficacy that came about with the oral contraceptive and the IUD in the early 1960s. (For a very different explanation, see chap. 1 in this volume.)

Aside from this time-period decomposition, we can also explore more directly two of the mechanisms through which personal characteristics affect $P_{C|S}$—the risk of conception from each act of intercourse and the frequency of intercourse over the several years of the adolescent's sexual life prior to age eighteen. We have a measure, albeit a rather crude one, of each of these mechanisms. It is of interest to use those measures in the statistical model to see if they are in fact associated with the outcome of that sexual experience, as reflected in the probability $P_{C|S}$.

In our data set, we have one direct indicator of birth control behavior that we can use. The respondent was asked, "Did you or your partner use birth control this first time [you had sex]?" (*SOS*, 653). Her answer (yes or no) is the basis of the dummy variable BC (yes is coded 1) that we use here. Of course, this information is not very complete. But those women who did use contraception that first time—31 percent—are more likely to have used contraception throughout their adolescent sexual career than are those women who did not use any contraception that first time.[22] There are studies that suggest that couples have contraceptive strategies, and these are not isolated or random occurrences of use or nonuse. So we think that this simple dummy variable may distinguish one group of women who do use contraception relatively often from another group of women who do not.

Similarly, we can obtain from the NHSLS data a crude measure of the number of acts of sex the woman had prior to age eighteen. For this, we have one direct measure and one indirect indicator. First, our survey asked specifically how many times the respondent had sex with her first sex partner before age eighteen. So for the first partner we have complete coverage, although it may not be wholly accurate. If the respondent had *one* additional sex partner before age eighteen, the same question was asked about that second partner. So, again, we have complete coverage. But, if, instead, she had several other sex partners before age eighteen, she was asked how many of these partners she had sex with only once, two to ten times, or more than ten times. Using this information, we can construct an estimate of the number of sex acts she experienced prior to age eighteen. Certainly, the exact number of sex acts before age eighteen is not accurately measured here since, for many of these women, the time in question was long ago. On the other hand, this is pretty salient information, so, if a respondent had sex only a few times, she may well remember that number or have an estimate of it that is reasonably accurate. If she had sex a couple of dozen times, then her estimate may be in that ballpark; if she had sex several hundred times, she may well be able to inform us of that order of magnitude. So, even if it is not a precise measure, our variable NUMTOT may quite adequately reflect the order of magnitude of the total number of times the respondent had sex before her eighteenth birthday.

We also have two indirect proxies for the number of times a respondent had sex before age eighteen. We know her age at her first intercourse, so we know the total length of time prior to age eighteen over which she had sexual experience. This we measure as a set of three dummy variables, indicating that she began to have sex by age fourteen (VI14), at age fifteen (VI15), or at age sixteen (VI16), with those who began to have sex at age seventeen as the reference group. Second, the woman was asked, "Other than this first person . . . , how many different (. . . males/females) did you have vaginal intercourse with before you were eighteen?" (*SOS,* 655). We construct three dummy variables indicating that the woman had one other partner (hence a total of two) (VIP2), two to five other partners (VIP4), or more than five other partners (VIP5+). Using these six dummies that indicate the age at which she first had sex and the number of partners, we have a reasonable, if indirect, measure of the woman's exposure to the risk of conception.

Table 2.6 shows some general statistics related to these measures of the use of birth control at first intercourse and the frequency of sex. It does so for the whole sample of women and by narrow age groups to reveal the trends in these measures. Notice that the percentage of the women who used birth control the first time they had sex (col. 1) shows no trend until the three youngest age groups, who were age fourteen to seventeen after 1970.[23] Perhaps this increase in usage reflects awareness of the risks of HIV. The second set of columns (cols. 2–5) in table 2.6 shows the frequency distribution of number of times a respondent had sex with her first partner. Interestingly, the younger women are much more likely to have had sex with that partner only once or fewer than ten times, while the older women tended to have sex more often with that first partner or to switch partners less quickly. That same pattern is evident in the third set of columns (cols. 6–7), which indicate the number of additional sex partners the woman said she had before reaching age eighteen. Of those over age fifty, more than 80 percent had no other sex partner than that first one by age eighteen, whereas only about one-third of their younger counterparts report having no other sex partner by age eighteen.

Using the information about frequency of sex with that first partner or with other partners prior to turning eighteen, table 2.6 (col. 8) shows that there is not a dramatic trend over this time period (from about 1945 to about 1991) in the average number of times a woman had sex before her eighteenth birthday. These women report an average of fewer than twenty times with their first partner and about thirty times overall with all partners prior to age eighteen. The median frequency overall is twenty times, and the interquartile range of the total number of times is from twelve to forty times. Looking across the specific age groups in table 2.6 (the rows),

Table 2.6 Use of Contraception and Frequency of Sex before Age 18, by Age

Age	Used Birth Control	Frequency of Sex with First Partner (% Distribution)				Number of Other Partners (% Distribution)		Frequency of Sex with First Partner	Total Frequency of Sex Prior to 18th Birthday			N
		1	2–10	11+	Still With	None	5+		Mean	Median	Q25–Q75[a]	
All	.31	.19	.27	.42	.12	.55	.08	17.3	30.4	20	12–40	1,615
18–24	.40	.25	.33	.34	.08	.34	.13	13.7	39.8	21	12–51	165
25–29	.41	.20	.31	.40	.09	.48	.11	15.3	29.2	20	12–40	113
30–34	.30	.19	.29	.43	.09	.55	.09	16.1	26.1	20	6–32	138
35–39	.23	.16	.24	.46	.14	.63	.04	18.9	25.1	20	12–36	111
40–44	.23	.15	.20	.55	.11	.70	.05	18.6	29.2	20	20–26	66
45–49	.21	.15	.26	.38	.17	.68	.02	20.4	26.1	20	6–40	45
50–54	.25	.10	.15	.40	.32	.88	.05	29.2	35.6	20	20–60	39
55–59	.26	.09	.23	.57	.11	.80	.06	19.7	26.0	20	8–20	35

[a]The frequency observed at the twenty-fifth and seventy-fifth quartiles.

one sees no real trend in frequency of sex prior to age eighteen. The older women report having sex more often with their first partner, while the younger ones have more partners but fewer incidents of intercourse with each. While the risk of pregnancy may not have varied much over this segment of the lifetime, that the younger women had a larger number of partners probably implies a higher risk of disease. We remind the reader that we are not controlling for marital status; we know from demographic trends that the percentage of acts of intercourse occuring outside marriage is probably much higher for younger than for older women.

Returning to the logistic regressions on $P_{C|S}$, table 2.7 shows several models, the first few using the measure of either use of contraception or frequency of sex before age eighteen. The next models use both these measures, and the final model includes these measures and also the six personal characteristics shown in column 3 of table 2.3 above. In every regression shown here, the eight time-trend dummies are included as well.[24]

Each of the variables performs as we would expect. Using some form of birth control on the occasion of the first act of intercourse is associated with a dramatically lower probability of conception across this time span up to age eighteen—it reduces by about half the odds of a conception among these sexually active women, with or without holding constant the number of times the woman has had sex.[25] The number of acts of intercourse raises the probability of a conception in this interval. Beginning sex at an even younger age increases $P_{C|S}$: if the woman begins to have sex at age thirteen, the odds are about twelve times higher that she will conceive before age eighteen! None of these relations is surprising; they are, we suggest, yet another indication of the internal consistency of the NHSLS data set. The effect of VIP2, VIP4, and VIP5+ is puzzling at first glance—it says that a woman is less likely to conceive the more partners she has. The explanation is, we think, that, if a woman has only one or two partners, she may have married and conceived, whereas, if she is sexually active but not married, her motivation to avoid pregnancy may be greater.[26]

For completeness, we have also run two of these models on the probability of pregnancy separately for the three age intervals. These are shown in table 2.7B. Here, another confirmation of the internal consistency of the data set is seen: the birth control variable is not substantial or significant in the model for the women who passed through this age interval before the introduction of the Pill and the IUD, but that variable has become very significant and large in magnitude by the 1980s! The indirect measures of the frequency of sex do not have much time trend to them. The age at which sexual intercourse began has a strong effect throughout, as it should since it reflects greater risk through longer exposure, at any given level of risk per act of intercourse.

Table 2.7 Logistic Models on $P_{C/S}$

A. Including Measures of Birth Control and Frequency of Sex (Time Dummies Included)

Variable	Model 1	Model 2	Model 3	Model 4	Model 5	Model 6
BC	.55**			.56**	.64**	.72
NUMTOT		1.008**		1.007**		
VI13			12.71**		11.55**	10.89**
VI14			4.60**		4.25**	3.59**
VI15			4.86**		4.66**	5.18**
VI16			2.89**		2.77**	3.28**
VIP2			.61		.61	.49*
VIP4			.61*		.59*	.54*
VIP5+			.32**		.30**	.38*
MATURE						1.02
NORELIG						.83
FUNDAM						.99
CATH						.71
OTHER						.33
BIOPAR						1.14
STPPAR						1.60
MAWORK						.82
FOREIGN						.75
BLACK						1.75*
HISP						2.54*
HSPAR						.44**
COLLPAR						.44**
χ^2	25.4**	19.7*	80.1**	29.5**	84.5**	139.5**
	(9)	(9)	(15)	(10)	(16)	(29)

B. Models 1 and 3 from Table 2.7A, for Specified Age Groups

	Age		
	18–29	30–44	45–59
Regression 1			
BC	.38**	.60	1.12
χ^2 (1)	12.7**	2.8	.08
Regression 2			
V14	6.38**	7.39**	3.92*
V15	2.98**	7.04**	6.57**
V16	2.60*	2.32**	4.87**
VIP2	.64	.62	.42
VIP4	.69	.60	.23*
VIP5+	.36*	.35	.34
χ^2	20.4**	33.4**	16.9**
	(6)	(6)	(6)

Note: Degrees of freedom are given in parentheses.
*Statistically significant at the 5 percent level.
**Statistically significant at the 1 percent level.

The only puzzling and somewhat disturbing result is shown in model 6 of table 2.7A. Here, the six personal characteristics are included in the logistic regression along with the two measures of risk, BC, and the indirect measures of the total number of sex acts, proxied by several dummies indicating the age at which sex began and the number of sex partners before age eighteen. The puzzling aspect of this regression is that including these two measures of risk does not substantially influence any of the key coefficients on race/ethnicity or parents' education level. That is, the same results are found here as are reported in column 3 of table 2.3 above, which does not control for whether the woman used birth control the first time she had intercourse or for the extent of her sexual activity prior to age eighteen. This is puzzling since these are exactly the mechanisms through which we expect these personal characteristics to operate. Holding these constant, it is not clear why or how the personal characteristics affect the probability of getting pregnant. One explanation is that these two measures of birth control and frequency are inadequate controls. While they themselves do capture a part of the variance, they do not fully remove the effect, so the race/ethnicity and parents' education variables also capture some of that same effect. Further work on this intriguing finding seems warranted.[27]

The Probability of an Abortion

Finally, regarding the regression model on $P_{A|C}$ here, too, several alternative models were estimated.[28] We also ran the identical logistic regression on the probability of a miscarriage or stillbirth (not shown). There, running the regression as a check only, one would not expect systematic relations. In fact, none of the variables approached statistical significance, and the overall χ^2 statistic on that model was 10.1 with 14 degrees of freedom, badly failing the test of significance and confirming our expectation.

We also ran the combined model on the same group of women, including not only the abortions but also the miscarriages and stillbirths. The result, as we would expect since this dependent variable just includes the stochastic miscarriages or stillbirths, shows every variable except one with a smaller coefficient. The one exception is the single strongest variable in the model in table 2.3 above: if the young woman has a parent with some college education, she faces odds nine times as high that she will have an abortion or have a miscarriage or stillbirth.[29]

Next Steps

There are several extensions or refinements of our analysis that might be undertaken. First, our investigation covers a very long time interval—1947–91—too long, in fact, for estimating coefficients of interest for careful policy analysis and implementation. One would like to know, for example, the coefficient on MAWORK on the probability of sex, or of conception, in the past fifteen years, not the average over the past forty-five years. The refinements discussed above suggest the nature of the modifications, but we have too few observations in the NHSLS to warrant a finely grained and detailed empirical study for a much shorter time period.

Second, we have treated the three choices about sex, risk of conception, and abortion as if they were independent analytically and statistically. These three choices might be nested in a single statistical model to take advantage of gains in statistical efficiency, but we have not pursued this strategy and instead treat the three choices as separate ones. This limitation could be relaxed.

Regarding the second step in the sequence, the conception, we have considered here only the woman's first pregnancy prior to age eighteen. If before her eighteenth birthday she became pregnant again following a fetal loss, she might have given birth as well as had an abortion or miscarriage by that age. We have not considered that circumstance in this analysis as we have considered only the first conception and its resolution. Likewise, we have not included in the analysis any second births or second pregnancies following a live birth before age eighteen. We note, however, that there were only eighteen women who bore a child after terminating their first pregnancy and before their eighteenth birthday.

Also, there are other intervening decisions that we have set aside and not systematically considered, although we have looked into some of them briefly, as mentioned in the notes. The most important of these, probably, is the decision to marry. That commitment has a major influence on the costs and benefits of childbearing, so we would expect a change in the marital status of the woman to influence her choices and behavior regarding both conception and abortion. Other intervening factors include forced sex, same-gender sex, and sex that does not involve vaginal intercourse, each of which can influence the choices that we do discuss here.

Finally, we focus only on women. Neither the choices that we analyze nor the data set that we use imposes that limitation on us. It will be of interest to replicate the study as it applies to men.

Notes

The authors thank Michael Grossman, Edward O. Laumann, and Daniel Trefler for comments on an early draft.

1. Of the 1,225,000 births that year to unmarried women, 365,000, or 30 percent, were to women under age twenty (U.S. Bureau of the Census 1995, table 89, p. 74, and table 94, p. 77). To put a finer point on it, in that year, of all births to women in the age range fifteen to seventeen, 79 percent were to unmarried women (the corresponding proportions of the births in that age range to unmarried white, black, and Hispanic women were, respectively, 71, 96, and 69 percent [Office of the ASPE 1996, table SD4.8, p. 179]).

2. For a woman who experiences puberty at age thirteen, e.g., the probability that she will have sex by her eighteenth birthday is the sum (adjusted) of her annual probability of having sex for each of those five intervening years:

$$P_S = P_{S13} + P_{S14}(1 - P_{S13}) + P_{S15}\Pi(1 - P_{S15-i}) + P_{S16}\Pi(1 - P_{S16-i})$$

$$+ P_{S17}\Pi(1 - P_{S17-i}),$$

where P_{S13} is the probability of first sex during her thirteenth year, P_{S14} is the probability of first sex during her fourteenth year, etc. We know that the hazard rate is not constant over these adolescent years and rises with age. As all the women in our sample are over age eighteen, all have passed through the entire age interval of interest. We will think about the whole time interval as a single, homogeneous period.

3. Of course, P_{CA} may not be constant over this interval, and N also undoubtedly varies year to year, probably increasing with age. But, since we are not using this equation in any formal manner, the simple product conveys our point.

4. See Michael and Willis (1976), Rosenzweig and Schultz (1989), Becker (1991), and, for an excellent recent review, Hotz, Klerman, and Willis (1997). The modeling of the fertility plans for a couple as a sequence of decisions, reacting to the stochastic outcomes of their prior decisions and strategies, was developed by Heckman and Willis (1975). Wolpin (1984) explored that dynamic modeling more fully, including the possible outcome of child mortality.

5. There are a number of excellent discussions of the context in which young men and women make these decisions. See, e.g., Chilman (1980), Udry and Billy (1987), Miller and Moore (1990), and, for a discussion of the historical European context, Hobcraft and Kiernan (1995).

6. A thirty-five-year-old married woman with no children, e.g., does not face the same costs or benefits as does the adolescent virgin woman. The married woman probably does not even consider whether to have sex or not—that decision has long since been made, and she probably has sex with some regularity. For her, the benefits of having a child and the opportunity costs of having it soon may weigh on her mind as she and her husband make decisions about birth control. For the adolescent woman, by contrast, the key decision is more likely to be whether to engage in sex at all and whether her current social relationship with her boyfriend warrants the greater intimacy of a sexual relationship.

7. In a subsequent paper, Mosher and McNally use the later NSFG-1988 data and again document a strong trend that results "entirely from an increase in the use of condoms" (1991, 108). In these data as well, the characteristics associated with greater use of contraception (primarily condoms) at first premarital intercourse were being white, being Jewish, having a mother who completed high school, and being older at the time of that first intercourse.

8. For an introduction to the literature covering the factors that influence a young woman's decisions about abortion, see, e.g., Hayes (1987), Leibowitz, Eisen, and Chow (1986), or Henshaw and Van Vort (1989).

9. For a literate discussion of many of the results of research by social demographers in recent years, see Luker (1996, esp. chap. 6).

10. For a focus on this issue of religion and sexual behavior among adolescents, see Thornton and Camburn (1989). They stress the reciprocal relation between the two and find a greater influence of religion on sexual attitudes than on sexual behavior and of religious participation than religious affiliation. We have only affiliation measured at age fourteen in our study, and we focus exclusively on behavior.

11. Brewster (1994, 416–17), employing a hazard model, finds that living in a nonintact family is associated with a higher probability of sex, while Billy, Brewster, and Grady (1994, 395) find the same using a logistic framework.

12. Miller and Moore (1990, 1028), among many others, note persistent empirical evidence

that parents' education is negatively associated with teenage sexual activity. Brewster (1994) uses NSFG-III data and finds that mother's education has a strong negative relation to early sexual activity among teenage girls.

13. Several studies document the rising trend in early teenage sex. Hofferth (1990), e.g., shows that trend from 1970 to 1985 and notes that sex first occurs usually at one of the partner's homes, suggesting the importance of direct supervision by parents.

14. Before these women were asked about their adolescent sexual experiences, they were questioned in great detail about their most recent sexual event, the facts of their past year's sexual experiences, and their marriage and fertility history and asked to provide a summary of their sex life since age eighteen. These very personal questions about recent experiences called for answers that were easy for respondents to recall and prepared them for the remainder of the interview. When the inquiries about their life prior to age eighteen were finally asked, these women had already been conditioned by many quite intimate and sensitive questions about their behavior.

15. The absence of a big upward trend in this rate may seem suspicious given the publicity in recent years focused on the growing problem of teenagers having children. The level here is not low: one in ten young women has a child before turning eighteen. The teenage fertility rates (births per one thousand women) for the years 1970, 1975, 1980, 1985, and 1990 are 38.8, 36.1, 32.5, 31.0, and 37.5, respectively (Office of the ASPE 1996, 176). So there is no trend in those data either (and note that they include multiple births), whereas our number is not the fertility rate but the percentage of women who had given birth to at least one child by age eighteen. The rate that *has* shot up in recent years is the percentage of all births to *unmarried* teens: for women aged fifteen to seventeen, that percentage rose from 24 in 1960 to 43 in 1970 to 61 in 1980 to 78 in 1990 (Office of the ASPE 1996, 179). This has more to do with declines in marital rates than increases in fertility rates. The NHSLS sample also reveals this same trend. Dividing the women into three groups that were aged thirteen to eighteen in the intervals 1947–64, 1962–79, and 1977–91, the percentage of first births (before the eighteenth birthday) that were out of wedlock rose from 26 to 44 to 68 percent.

16. The reader may notice that the miscarriage rate $P_{M|C}$ also seems to have a time trend. This is not so easily explained.

17. We also ran these eight time dummies alone, i.e., with no other regressors (the regression is not shown), and the trend was not substantially changed by the inclusion of these other covariates.

18. These "other" religions are various Eastern and Middle Eastern religions. The data set is too small to measure their effects separately.

19. Of these 1,615 women, 47 reported that their adolescent sex was forced. As we were modeling or thinking about the decisions that these women make as volitional and strategic, we reran the model in the table excluding these 47 cases, resulting in 42.7 percent sexually active instead of the 44.3 percent reported in the text. The coefficients were changed only very slightly. The odds ratio for Catholic became 0.68 ($p < .01$), somewhat more significant; no other behavioral coefficient had a notable change in magnitude or significance.

20. To illustrate this point, look at the magnitudes of the odds ratios for the two religion variables for fundamentalist Protestants and those with no religious affiliation. Disregarding the statistical significance in order to make our point, of the two variables, those with no religious affiliation are more likely to begin having sex early (an odds ratio of 1.56 vs. 1.12, respectively), but they are less likely to give birth before age eighteen (1.22 vs. to 1.31). The explanation for this seeming inconsistency is found in their respective choices about abortion—the fundamentalists are quite unlikely to abort a pregnancy, while those with no religious affiliation are exceptionally likely to do so (0.42 vs. 1.70).

21. To mention but one fascinating additional factor, Haurin and Mott (1990) exploit the availability of twin pairs in the National Longitudinal Survey of Youth (NLSY) to investigate the influence of an older sibling's sexual behavior on the youth's age at first intercourse.

First, they found that, for whites, the first intercourse occurs at a later age if the mother is college educated, if the youth regularly attends church, and if the youth lived with both parents at age fourteen. These results mirror those reported in our statistical analysis. But, after adding information on the age at which an older sibling first had sex, Haurin and Mott found that, for each year's delay in the onset of sex by the older sibling, there is an associated three- to four-month delay for the younger sibling. The inclusion of the age at which the sibling first had sex, moreover, reduces the direct effect of many of the other background factors, especially that of living with two parents. These results for white males and females, separately, are mirrored by those for black females, but, as is so often the case, none of these same effects seem to exist for black males. As an added complexity, for black females, the family background effects are not attenuated by including the age at which the older sibling first had sex.

22. Kahn, Rindfuss, and Guilkey (1990) use the NSFG-1982 to study adolescent contraception use, and they speak of the "slow pace with which nonusers [the first time] become users" (p. 331).

23. One might have expected the rate of contraceptive usage before age eighteen to rise after the introduction of the Pill and the wider adoption of the IUD in the mid-1960s (i.e., for those aged forty to forty-four in these data), but that is not the case here. It is likely that the fact that those newer and more effective techniques require a physician's prescription greatly inhibited their use at the start of sexual experimentation. The NSFG-1982 data suggest that younger teenagers are more likely to use withdrawal, douche, or rhythm at first intercourse, so there would not be a reason for a noticeable increase in usage of contraception during the 1960s (see Hayes 1987, 48, citing Pratt et al. 1984).

24. The time-trend dummies never have any influence; when run alone, the χ^2 on the set of eight time dummies is not even statistically significant ($\chi^2[8] = 14.8$). There is no time trend to the probability that a sexually active woman becomes pregnant before age eighteen. Now, that may seem wrong or disappointing since the "contraceptive revolution" occurred along the way, but we are conditioning here only on nonvirginity, not (yet) the amount of sex the woman had.

25. Note that we are assuming that women who use some form of birth control the first time they have sex use birth control thereafter with greater regularity than other women do.

26. To investigate this point, we have rerun model 5, table 2.7, adding one additional variable, WED, a dummy defined as one if the woman was married to her partner the first time she had sex. That is, WED identifies the 8.5 percent of the women who said that the first time they had sex was on their wedding night. As expected, that variable is associated with a much higher probability of becoming pregnant before age eighteen—the effect on the odds ratio is 7.36, and the coefficient is statistically significant at .0001. Also, as expected, its inclusion in the regression did diminish the magnitude and significance of VIP2, VIP4, and VIP5+—the magnitudes for these three, to be compared to the magnitudes reported for model 5 of table 2.7, are 0.72, 0.69, and 0.36 (the last is significant at the 1 percent level).

27. Note 26 above introduced the variable WED, indicating that the woman first had sex on her wedding night. Without modeling the dynamics of decisions made throughout adolescence—a strategy we wish to avoid here—we cannot introduce the marital status of the woman as she progresses from prepuberty to age eighteen. This one variable, WED, does permit us to bring into the equation estimating the probability of conception the information that the woman was or was not married as an initial condition for beginning her sexual career. If she was married at the outset, then the costs and the benefits of conceiving may be quite different than if she was unmarried and sexually active. Including this one additional variable in model 6 of table 2.7 above has the following effects: its own coefficient is significant at the .0001 level, and its effect on the odds ratio is 9.68 (the married women are nearly ten times as likely to conceive as the initially unmarried women). The four variables that have statistical significance in model 6 each retain that significance; their magnitudes of

effects in terms of the odds ratio changes very little: BLACK, 2.24 ($p < .01$); HISP, 2.46 ($p < .05$); HSPAR, 0.46 ($p < .01$); COLLPAR, 0.44 ($p < .01$). The only other coefficient that is affected is that on other religion, which becomes slightly significant with an effect on the odds ratio of 0.23 ($p < .05$). The χ^2 on the whole model rises substantially when WED is included; it is 190 ($p < .01$) with 30 degrees of freedom.

28. For example, we reran this model including four additional dummy variables that indicate that the conception occurred at specific ages: thirteen, fourteen, fifteen, or sixteen (the omitted group is age seventeen). Other evidence makes it clear that the proportion of conceptions that end in abortion is much higher at very young ages, so we thought that age might be an important factor here. Those four dummy variables' coefficients did suggest that the probability of an abortion was higher if the woman was younger: e.g., the odds ratio is 5.4 times higher if she is fourteen than if she is seventeen at the time of conception. But none of these four coefficients is statistically significant. Moreover, their inclusion did not have a material effect on the coefficients shown in table 2.3 above.

29. Cooksey (1990) uses NLSY data on adolescent, premarital conceptions and looks at the influence of family background on the decision to end the pregnancy by abortion, or to legitimate it by marriage, or to have the baby out of wedlock. She estimates a multinomial logistic separately by race/ethnicity. Focusing on the choice of interest here, abortion is more likely if the woman's parents' are more highly educated—for all three race/ethnic groups. Cooksey also finds that, if a white woman has many siblings, she is less likely to choose to have an abortion.

■

Sex during Adolescence

Chapters 1 and 2 both focus on the behavior of the National Health and Social Life Survey (NHSLS) respondents when they were adolescents. For the youngest respondents, that was only a very few years ago, but others, obviously, were adolescents many years ago. The passing of time compromises the ability to recall events, but, as these two chapters suggest, the respondents appeared able to provide useful and informative information about events as salient as those under discussion here.

Chapter 1: Teenage Sex and the Sexual Revolution

This chapter focuses on factors that influence whether the NHSLS respondents had sex before age eighteen. The analysis is conducted separately for whites and blacks and for men and women. For these four groups, the proportion who said that they had sex before age eighteen ranged from 42 percent of the white women, to 50 percent of the white men, to 61 percent of the black women, to 77 percent of the black men.

There are several well-documented patterns in adolescents' first sexual experiences, and this study first confirms four of these: (1) There is a strong positive relation between the adolescent's age and the likelihood of beginning to have sex. (2) There is a consistent pattern of boys reporting their first sex at an earlier age than girls. (3) There is also a consistent pattern of blacks reporting an earlier age than whites. (4) There is a strong time trend toward a younger age at first intercourse: those born more recently across the decades 1930–70 report beginning to have sex at an earlier age.

The study then controls for these four well-known factors and investigates a more subtle hypothesis: that several family and personal characteristics may have had a decidedly different influence on the age of first sexual experience before and after the sexual revolution of the late 1960s. The paper suggests that, before that time, group identification—gender, race, religion, social class—working through the influence of family and peer pressure, principally influenced when it was acceptable to begin having sex. So, during the 1940s, the 1950s, and the early 1960s, the young person's classification by race, religion, and social class largely determined the age at which sex was initiated. After the sexual revolution, the influence of these categories faded when compared to personal biographical factors such as age at puberty and whether one had experienced preadolescent sexual abuse. This hypothesis was partially supported by the empirical study.

Chapter 2: Choices Leading to Teenage Births

This chapter decomposes the probability of having given birth by age eighteen into three distinct probabilities: (1) the unconditional probability of having sex before age eighteen; (2) the conditional probability of becoming pregnant before age eighteen; and (3) the conditional probability of having an abortion. As the chapter shows, the product of these three, slightly rearranged, is mathematically the same as the probability of having given birth by that age. So the chapter then investigates the personal socioeconomic factors that affect each of the three decision points separately for the women in the NHSLS.

Along the way, the chapter reports that there was no trend in the probability of having given birth by age eighteen over the past four decades, but this stable probability masks both a big increase in the probability of having sex and a corresponding and offsetting decline in the probability of becoming pregnant among those who were sexually active (reflecting a near doubling of the percentage who reported using birth control) and, after *Roe v. Wade,* a large increase in the probability of having an abortion among those who did become pregnant. An interesting pattern is also described whereby younger adults report having sex a fewer number of times with their first sex partner but having more sex partners before they turned age eighteen, while the older respondents who had sex before age eighteen more often had continued sexual relations with that first partner and had fewer partners by the time they had reached eighteen.

The chapter assesses the effects of six personal characteristics on these three choices. The characteristics are the woman's age at puberty, her religious beliefs, the structure of her family of origin when she was fourteen, her birthplace (native or foreign born), her parents' level of education, and her race/ethnicity. The effects of these six personal characteristics on the three choices that affect the probability of a woman's giving birth before age eighteen vary. Only one of the six—parents' education level—has a consistent and cumulative effect across all three choices, and hence that personal characteristic is strongly negatively associated with the probability of a woman's giving birth before her eighteenth birthday.

■

PART TWO

Sex during Adulthood

CHAPTER THREE

■

Sexual Expression in America

EDWARD O. LAUMANN AND YOOSIK YOUM

I was about 16 and I had this friend—not a boyfriend, a boy friend—and I didn't know what to give him for his birthday, so I gave him a blow job. I wanted to know what it was like; it was just for kicks.
—Twenty-year-old Ellen, a student at the University of Michigan
(Rubin 1990, 14)

It was weird; it was so hard to say no. The guys just took it for granted that you'd go to bed with them and you felt like you had to explain it if you didn't want to. Then if you tried, you couldn't think of a good reason why not to, so you did it.
—Thirty-eight-year-old Paula, a furniture designer in Pittsburgh
(Rubin 1990, 93–94)

Anna and I dated steadily for a year and a half, as I finished high school. I must confess that in hindsight I think I dated her for all of the wrong reasons. We were somewhat friendly with each other, but I do not think I really liked her as a person. . . . I think the reason I dated her was because she was the kind of girl that all of my friends thought they wanted to date. I dated her almost exclusively for social impact.
—Nick, in his forties (Skeen 1991, 33)

I was still acting out when I started having sex. I had a boyfriend, Daniel, who was nineteen. I did not know much about sex. I had never masturbated or anything. I just knew I wanted affection, and sex was what I could give to get it. . . . And we continued to have sex pretty often, but I kept thinking, What is the big deal about this? It meant nothing to me, not bad, not good, but he did stay with me.
—Jennifer, in her forties (Skeen 1991, 81–82)

These comments raise a number of interesting questions about the manifold ways in which people express their sexuality. Social scientists rooted in various disciplines would understand these remarks in distinctly different ways. Anthropologists and sociologists who study culture would ask what sex meant to each person. To Ellen, it might be just recreation or fun; to Paula, who came to sexual maturity at the height of the sexual revolution, it was an act mandated by the emerging norms of sexual liberation; to Nick, it was a means of gaining social recognition from his male peer group; and, to Jennifer, it was a way of getting affection. Psychologists or psychotherapists might focus on the mental problems that explain Jennifer's lack of interest in sex itself. Biologists or sociobiologists might connect the benefits of sex as recreation to the human species in general. Or they might explain Nick's behavior in terms of sexual selection and how that might have contributed to reproductive success among his ancestors. Sociologists who study social structure and the normative order might be interested in each individual's class background (surmising, e.g., that Jennifer has a lower socioeconomic status than Paula has) or in the effects of marriage on socially approved behavior (after Ellen marries, can she give the same present to her male acquaintances?).

At the theoretical level, most observers (e.g., McClelland 1975; Abramson and Pinkerton 1995; Posner 1992; Rossi 1994a; Hill 1997) conceive of *sexuality,* or even the more limited notion *sexual expression,* as an integrated entity that includes all the possible ways in which people can express their sexual interest in physical and emotional gratification, thought and fantasy, and act or deed. Empirical research, however, has typically focused on only one or at most a few aspects of sexuality and their interrelations (e.g., Donnelly 1993; Feldman et al. 1995; Belcastro 1985; Gagnon and Simon 1987). Few researchers have dealt with multiple dimensions at the same time because of the dearth of appropriately comprehensive data on an appropriately drawn sample representative of the sexually mature adult population.

But it is important to know the answers to questions of the following sort if we are to understand an individual's sexual expression and its potential consequences for him or her and for society more generally. First, we should want to know the broad configuration of a person's sexual expression. For example, does Ellen also enjoy masturbation? Does she mind if her boyfriend concurrently has other sex partners? And, if sex is just for fun, how often does she have it? Second, we might ask, Is Ellen's sexual expression (e.g., having several overlapping sex partners who also have other sex partners, engaging in frequent masturbation and partnered sexual activity) a configuration unique to her, or is it a pattern of sexual expression characterizing many people in America? These two sorts of questions have not been asked in the past, not because they are of no consequence, but because the data allowing us to answer them did not exist.

In this chapter, we try to answer these questions using the National Health and Social Life Survey (NHSLS) data, which include wide-ranging information on sexual thought and fantasy, normative orientations and preferences, partnering patterns, sexual activities alone and with partners, and assessments of physical and emotional satisfaction. After an extensive review of the voluminous information we have in hand about various aspects of an individual's sexual expression, we identified five dimensions of his or her sex life in the past twelve months as providing a useful global characterization: (1) number of sex partners in the past twelve months; (2) the primary partner's number of sex partners, identified as such by the respondent; (3) participation in venues that provide erotic stimulation; (4) frequency of masturbation; and (5) frequency of partnered sex.[1] We discuss each of these dimensions in greater detail below, but, for present purposes, we treat each dimension as a dichotomy even though each has, in fact, multiple values across a substantial range. For example, the number of sex partners in the past year can range between none and numbers in excess of fifty. If, however, we dichotomize the five dimensions on some meaningful basis, there are thirty-two permutations or classes (2^5) for each gender. Applying the statistical technique called *latent class analysis* (described below) to the NHSLS data reveals that we require only four of these thirty-two classes of sexual expression for each gender. That is, we can assign the entire adult population of the United States to one of four male or female classes with respect to sexual expression. This is a powerful reduction in the complexity of our characterization of individuals' sexual expression because the small set of latent classes is (as will be shown) remarkably homogeneous internally with respect to how adults conduct their current sex lives. We can then examine the social and personal factors that regulate and shape these classes of sexual expression.

3.1 A Model of the Determinants of Sexual Expression

If we can identify a small set of meaningful modalities in terms of which an individual's sexual expression can be globally characterized, our next step is to sketch a set of factors that might determine a person's mode of sexual expression. Four broad classes of determinants can be identified, as graphically displayed in figure 3.1: (1) individual preferences for particular sexual experiences; (2) state of physical health and physical capacity to engage in particular sexual activities; (3) competence to initiate and main-

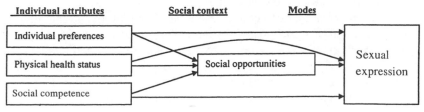

Fig. 3.1 A model of the determinants of sexual expression.

tain social relationships of various sorts; and (4) social opportunities to secure appropriate sex partners.

First, let us consider *individual preferences* for specific sexual activities, including generalized level of sexual interest. Whether one assumes that these preferences and levels of interest are genetically encoded, acquired through social learning, or arise through some combination of the two processes or through some other systematic or random process, we are, for present purposes, treating them as stable attributes of the individual for at least a unit of time, say, the current twelve-month period. While there are many indicators of an individual's subjective preferences in the NHSLS, we focus attention on only a few of them: frequency of thinking about sex and the appeal of having extramarital sex, sex without love, and sex with a stranger. In reviewing the relevant psychological literature on individual differences in sexual interest, drive, or motivation, we were struck by the relative absence of research attention paid to such issues in recent years, especially as they relate to adults (see, e.g., Rossi 1994b; Lancaster 1994; Udry and Campbell 1994; McKinlay and Feldman 1994). Whether one treats sexual interest as rooted in human biology or as an acquired or learned response to one's social and life-course status, it is quite evident that people differ greatly in terms of the centrality of sexual concerns in their daily lives. We attempt to monitor relative levels of sexual interest by the frequency with which an individual engages in sexual fantasies on the assumption that fantasy is more responsive to individual states of being and less constrained by the social realities of partner availability and opportunities to engage in partnered sexual activities. People who think about sex a lot presumably regard it as of much greater importance in their daily activities than those who rarely give it a thought (see, e.g., Hill 1997).

With respect to *physical health,* we are interested in an individual's current health status as it facilitates or constrains his or her capacity to engage in sexual activities of whatever description and level of intensity. Self-reported physical health status and age as a proxy for stage in the physical life cycle are the two indicators used. People with impaired physical or mental health (e.g., erectile or other sexual dysfunctions—see chap. 10 below) may simply not be able to engage in certain patterns of sexual expression, whatever their individual preferences.

Third, individuals' skills at and resources for initiating and maintaining ongoing social relationships of various sorts—what we call *social competence*—vary greatly. Here, we include concrete skills (social communication) as well as resources (time, money and goods, and people-handling skills). Since we did not measure these skills and resources directly, we use an individual's level of education and occupational prestige as proxies for his or her generalized capacity to compete successfully in contemporary society. Highly socially competent people can more easily gain access to potential sex partners and maintain such partnerships over time. Possessing such social competence, however, does not necessarily mean that an individual will, in fact, have multiple partners because being unfaithful to publicly acknowledged partners, such as spouses or cohabitants, is strongly stigmatized.

Finally, our model suggests that these three sets of individual-level attributes jointly affect the *social opportunities* that individuals confront in seeking and maintaining sexual partnerships of particular kinds. Social opportunities also exert independent effects on sexual expression. Social opportunities may be defined in a variety of ways, but always with reference to the variable normative constraints associated with particular social attributes and contexts, such as marital status, mode of meeting potential partners (through one's other social contacts [social network of friends, kin, and acquaintances] or particular social scenes that preselect who is likely to be present [such as bars or private parties]), membership in particular religious communities, sexual identity, urban or rural residence, social class, and racial and ethnic status.

Our analytic strategy, then, is, first, to demonstrate the existence of a limited number of modalities for expressing sexuality and, then, using multinomial logit analysis, to explore how membership in these different modalities is associated with the several sets of determinants discussed above.

3.2 Specifying the Dimensions of Sexual Expression

The NHSLS attempted a comprehensive characterization of the many facets of an individual's sexual expression in the current period and over the life course. Extensive treatments of these facets presented in *The Social Organization of Sexuality* provide us with a strong empirical basis for selecting the best nonredundant "markers," or indicators, for distinctive and only loosely interrelated aspects of an individual's sexual activities in the current year. These extended discussions cover (1) the numbers of sex partners over different time periods (*SOS*, 172–224); (2) the kinds of sexual partnerships (e.g., married, cohabiting, long- or short-term dating) and their social compositional similarities and differences (*SOS*, 225–68); (3) the varieties of sexual behavior, including oral, anal, and vaginal intercourse and autoerotic practices (*SOS*, 77–111), (4) physical and emotional satisfaction with sexual activities (*SOS*, 111–21), and (5) subjective preferences or tastes for particular sexual activities and experiences (*SOS*, 148–71). Nearly every aspect of sexual expression that we examined shared a common feature with respect to its distribution in the population at large: either most people or relatively few people—fewer than 20 percent—

reported doing or enjoying it. Moreover, one can meaningfully classify these features into one of three broad, conceptually distinct categories: (1) sexual partnerships; (2) partnered sexual activities and preferences; and (3) autoerotic activities and preferences.

After detailed exploration of the ways in which the features of sexual expression are related within and across the three categories, we identified five that seemed to tap distinctive and only loosely interrelated aspects of an individual's sexual activities in the current year, thus affording us a global snapshot of a person's sexual conduct. Each of the five dimensions discussed below is measured by one indicator, typically selected from a number of alternatives, that empirically or conceptually can be shown to be the best marker for the dimension in question.

First, let us consider the number of sex partners that the respondent reported having during the past twelve months. No other measure of sexual behavior has been so often studied in recent years, not only because it is a key indicator of risk for sexually transmitted diseases (STDs), but also because it reflects the broad social dimension of sexual behavior in a most succinct way (*SOS,* 172). Although about 17 percent of the population reported two or more partners in the past year and about 11 percent reported having no partner, we divide the population into those who had only one partner in the past year and those who had more than one. Persons without a sex partner in the past year were dropped from this analysis because they lack the opportunity for partnered sexual activities.

Even though the number of sex partners is a crucial dimension of sexual expression, it is insufficient by itself when characterizing the sociosexual network in which the respondent is implicated. We must consider whether the partner has had other sex partners in the same time period as well. Here, again, we consider only two situations: a partner who has no other sex partner than the respondent and a partner who has sex partners in addition to the respondent.

Consider the following situation (depicted in fig. 3.2). If we were to restrict our attention to the number of sex partners reported, we would have no means of distinguishing respondents (egos) in mutually monogamous relationships ($<11>$) from those in primarily monogamous relationships ($<12>$) or of telling respondents in primarily polygamous relationships ($<21>$) from those in mutually polygamous relationships ($<22>$). The sex lives of these four types of people differ significantly, however. Even though egos in mutually monogamous ($<11>$) and primarily monogamous ($<12>$) relationships have only one sex partner, we can easily imagine that their sex lives differ in important ways. The ego in a primarily monogamous relationship ($<12>$) lacks a committed sex partner because that partner's resources (e.g., time, passion, emotional commitment, money) must be divided between two or more partners. We can easily infer

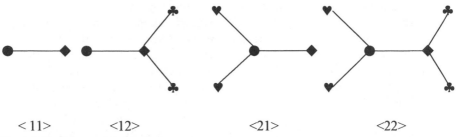

<11>   <12>   <21>   <22>

Fig. 3.2 The four possible forms of sexual networks.
Note: ● = self-ego; ♦ = ego's primary partner; ♥ = ego's nonprimary partners; ♣ = primary partner's other partner than ego. <11> = a mutually monogamous relationship; <12> = a primarily monogamous relationship; <21> = a primarily polygamous relationship; <22> = a mutually polygamous relationship.

The primary partner is identified on the basis of the answer to the question, "Which of the people that you mentioned do you consider to have been your most important or primary sexual partner during the last 12 months?"

that the ego in a mutually monogamous relationship (<11>) might enjoy a less-troubled sex life (enjoying more frequent sex and a greater emotional commitment on the part of his or her partner) than the ego in a primarily monogamous relationship (<12>), other things being equal. We can also expect differences in the sex lives of egos in primarily polygamous relationships (<21>) and those in mutually polygamous relationships (<22>). For example, the ego in a primarily polygamous relationship (<21>) is likely to enjoy more frequent sex and a higher level of emotional commitment than the ego in a mutually polygamous relationship (<22>) does because the former has exclusive access to his or her primary partner but the latter must share his or her partner's attention with others. This may induce feelings of jealousy, guilt, and anger on the part of those partners who lack exclusive access to one person. And the induction of these feelings may differ by gender because of the characteristic differences in normative understandings of sexual scripts by gender.[2]

The discussion presented above suggests that sexual expression is not merely the sum of a person's *individual*-level attributes but is also the product of his or her location in sexual *networks*. Among the five dimensions that we discuss, this dimension is the only one that is not strictly an individual attribute. As we show below, network position is highly consequential in one's sex life.[3]

Frequency of partnered sex in the past twelve months is the third dimension of sexual expression that we consider. This is a central issue in the sexual expression of most people who have only one partner. Here, we distinguish between those who have partnered sex more than once a week and those who have partnered sex once a week or less often.

Engaging in erotic activities other than intercourse is the focus of the fourth dimension of sexual expression. Here, we are attempting to broaden the view of sexual activity to include a person's search for erotic stimulation (within the past twelve months) outside the venue of partnered sexual activities in the conventional sense of vaginal, oral, or anal intercourse or mutual masturbation.[4] These activities need not necessarily include the respondent's sex partner. Again, we divided the respondents into two groups: those who participated in at least one of the activities listed in note 4 in the past year and those who did not participate in any of these activities in the past year.

Finally, we consider autoeroticism, or masturbation, in the past twelve months. We divide the respondents into two groups: those who masturbated at least once in the past year and those who had not. We hope to shed some light on the persistent question about the relationship between the frequency of partnered sex and the frequency of masturbation. Is the latter a substitute for the former? If so, then there must be a negative correlation between the two. Or does masturbation tap a different dimension of sexual expression than partnered sex does? If so, there could be a positive correlation between the two. The fact that several types or modes of sexual expression exist allows us to examine the relation between autoerotic excitement and partnered sex in the larger context of the other dimensions of sexual expression and thereby determine the particular permutations of the five dichotomized dimensions in which the relation is positive, negative, or unrelated.

3.3 Identifying the Latent Classes of Sexual Expression

Performing latent class analyses separately for men and women,[5] we identify a set of only four classes for each gender that can be statistically shown to provide the best fit for the empirically observed permutations of the five dichotomized dimensions of sexual expression described above. It should be recalled that, logically, there are thirty-two permutations of the five dichotomies.

The Four Latent Classes of Sexual Expression for American Men

Table 3.1 indicates the proportion of men from the NHSLS in each latent class and the incidence of each dimension within each class. Class 1 represents a pattern of mutual monogamy (i.e., both the respondent and his sex partner have no other sex partners during the past year) and includes about 50 percent of the total male population. Only 7 percent of the men in this class had more than one partner during the past year, and only 0.7 percent of their primary partners had more than one partner. None of the men in this class seek erotic stimulation in venues other than conventional

Table 3.1 Four Latent Classes of Sexual Expression for American Men (%)

	Comfortable Monogamists (Class 1)	Venturesome Cohabitors (Class 2)	Moderate Polygamists (Class 3)	Enthusiastic Polygamists (Class 4)
Proportions in the population (row percentages)	49	35	1.6	15
Five dimensions of sexual expression:				
Having multiple partners	7	24	100	71
Primary partner has multiple partners	.7	0	100	67
Masturbating	48	73	0	93
Having sex more than once a week	38	52	43	29
Seeking erotic stimulation	0	100	22	77

sexual encounters, and fewer than half engage in masturbation and have partnered sex more than once a week. We call them *comfortable monogamists* because of the generally low volume of sexual activity.[6] In general, we estimate an individual's volume of sexual activity as the summation of his or her positive location on four of the five dimensions. We exclude primary partner having multiple partners from the sum because that dimension refers to the partner's sexual activity rather than the respondent's.

Class 2, which includes about 35 percent of all the men in the NHSLS, characterizes men who themselves have a 0.24 probability of having multiple partners and whose partners have no likelihood of having any other partners—that is, their partners observe strict monogamy (as reported by male respondents). All the men in this class seek erotic stimulation in addition to conventional sexual encounters. The large majority (73 percent) masturbate, and about 52 percent engage in more frequent partnered sexual activities than do the men in the other three classes; that is, they have sex more than once a week. *All* the members of this class seek erotic stimulation in venues outside the conventional sexual encounter itself. We labeled this class *venturesome cohabitors* because monogamous relationships dominate the class and the volume of sexual activity on various dimensions is high.

Only 1.6 percent of American men are found in class 3. All report that they have had multiple sex partners in the past year and that all their primary partners have had multiple partners as well. (In chap. 9 below, we discuss at length how these individuals play a key role in the core group implicated in the maintenance of sexually transmitted diseases in the population at large.) None of these men say that they masturbated in the past year, but they are very likely to seek erotic stimulation in addition to conventional sexual activities and are moderately likely to engage in partnered sex more than once a week. We call this class *moderate polygamists*.

Finally, class 4, some 15 percent of American men, includes those who have a 0.71 probability of having multiple partners and a 0.67 likelihood of their primary partners having multiple partners. They are the most likely to engage in masturbation (virtually all of them masturbate), and they are very likely to seek erotic stimulation in addition to conventional sexual activities. Somewhat ironically, given their high levels of sexual expression on several dimensions, the class has the lowest incidence of partnered sex more than once a week. This class is designated *enthusiastic polygamists.* It is predominantly composed of single men (only 1 percent of the married men fall into this class), split equally between young men who have not yet married and older men who are divorced. The core group that is critically implicated in the maintenance of sexually transmitted diseases in the population at large, as discussed in chapter 9 below, is recruited from this class.

From this quick overview of the four classes of male sexual expression, we can make several important general observations. The first concerns the relation between partnered sex and autoerotic sex. The rank of the four classes with respect to masturbation is enthusiastic polygamists/venturesome cohabitors > comfortable monogamists > moderate polygamists. The ordering of the four classes in terms of partnered sex is moderate polygamists > enthusiastic polygamists > venturesome cohabitors > comfortable monogamists. Except for the venturesome cohabitors, the order is reversed. That is, for three of the four classes, the relation between partnered sex and masturbation is negative: more partnered sex means less masturbation. Venturesome cohabitors, however, are not only most likely to engage in partnered sex more than once a week but also very likely (73 percent) to masturbate. For this class, then, the relation is positive. If we had not divided the men into different unobserved (latent) classes of sexual expression, this positive relation would not have been identified. We observed the same situation in the case of women (see below).

The second general observation relates to the significance of the patterning of sexual networks for sexual expression. Let us consider once again figure 3.2, which depicts the four possible patterns of sexual networks. Here, venturesome cohabitors represent the largest proportion (28 percent) of those involved in primarily polygamous relationships (<21>), while those involved in mutually polygamous relationships (<22>) constitute all those men classified as moderate polygamists and the largest fraction (70 percent) of those classified as enthusiastic polygamists.[7] As predicted (see table 3.1) venturesome cohabitors engage in a high volume of sexual activity across the various dimensions of sexual expression, while those involved in a mutually polygamous relationship (<22>) exhibit only moderate levels of sexual activity (as in the case of those classed as moderate polygamists) or high levels of sexual activity on some dimensions but low levels of partnered sex (as in the case of those classed as enthusiastic polygamists). Had we omitted the dimension identifying a person's position in his or her social network, we might have missed these important differences in sexual expression.

The four classes of sexual expression for American men are graphically illustrated in figure 3.3. The figure is intended to facilitate simultaneous comparisons of the four classes with respect to their relative emphases among the five dimensions of sexual expression. The expanding shaded areas as one moves from class 1 to class 4 suggest the increasing volume of overall sexual expression across the classes.

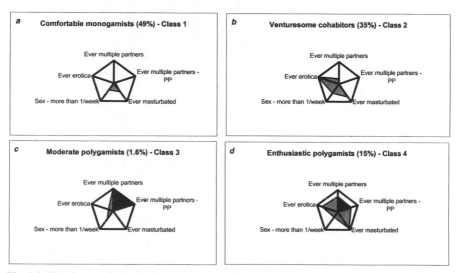

Fig. 3.3 The classes of sexual expression for American men. *a,* Class 1, comfortable monogamists (49 percent). *b,* Class 2, venturesome cohabitors (35 percent). *c,* Class 3, moderate polygamists (1.6 percent). *d,* Class 4, enthusiastic polygamists (15 percent).

Note: Shaded areas represent the total amount of sexual activity. This total is constructed by linking four points along the four dimensions. Each point in each dimension shows the proportion who engaged in each activity. We excluded the dimension *primary partner having multiple partners* from the sum because it refers to the partner's sexual activity rather than the respondent's. The shaded area is also drawn in order to show the proportion whose primary partner had multiple partners.

Ever multiple partners reflects the proportion who had more than one partner last year.

Ever multiple partners–PP shows the percentage who had a primary partner with multiple partners last year.

Ever masturbated reflects the fraction who ever masturbated last year.

Sex–more than 1/week shows the proportion who had sex more than once a week last year.

Ever erotica shows the proportion who ever engaged in erotic stimulation activity last year. Such activity includes buying or renting an X-rated movie, buying any sexually explicit magazines, buying sex toys or dildos, engaging in phone sex, going to a nightclub presenting nude dancers, hiring a prostitute, attending a public gathering in the nude, and having a picture taken in the nude.

The Four Latent Classes of Sexual Expression for American Women

Using latent class analysis, we find that American women can be allocated to one of four classes or modes of sexual expression, although the character of these classes (in terms of size and composition) differs in important respects from those observed for American men. Table 3.2 summarizes their characteristics.[8]

Class 1, by far the most popular class (encompassing 54 percent of American women), includes those women who maintain mutually monogamous relationships with their partners. These women rarely masturbate or seek erotic stimulation outside conventional partnered sexual outlets. They have the lowest incidence of participating in all four of the dimensions of sexual activity. They do, however, engage in moderate levels of partnered sex more than once a week. We call this class *comfortable monogamists;* it corresponds to the class *comfortable monogamists* for men (although, of course, we do not know whether men in this class are married to women in this class because our data come from individuals rather than couples).

Class 2, encompassing 23 percent of American women, includes women who themselves have a 0.16 probability of having multiple partners and whose primary partners have a 0.07 likelihood of having multiple partners. All these women masturbate. They also seek moderate levels of erotic stimulation outside conventional sexual activities. However, they rarely have partnered sex more than once a week. This class is designated *autoerotic singles;* it corresponds roughly to the male *venturesome cohabitors.* However, the correspondence is not perfect because venturesome cohabitors have a higher likelihood of having multiple partners (24 vs. 15 percent) but a lower likelihood of having primary partners who have multiple partners (0 vs. 7 percent). In short, class 2 is more strongly colored by mutually

Table 3.2 Four Latent Classes of Sexual Expression for American Women (%)

	Comfortable Monogamists (Class 1)	Autoerotic Singles (Class 2)	Moderate Polygamists (Class 3)	Enthusiastic Cohabitors (Class 4)
Proportions in the population (row percentages)	54	23	5	18
Five dimensions of sexual expression:				
Having multiple partners	4	16	100	7
Primary partner has multiple partners	5	7	100	2
Masturbating	10	100	47	59
Having sex more than once a week	31	13	25	99
Seeking erotic stimulation	9	37	31	52

monogamous relationships for women than for men. Second, the women in class 2 do not engage in as high a level of sexual activity as the men of class 2 do. In fact, they exhibit the least amount of partnered sex among the four classes but, far and away, the greatest amount of autoerotic activity. We examine the source of this gender difference below.

Class 3, encompassing only 5 percent of American women, includes only those women who are in mutually polygamous relationships with their primary partners—that is, all these women had multiple partners during the past year and reported that their primary partner had multiple partners as well. They exhibit moderate levels of participation in partnered sex more than once a week, masturbation, and erotic stimulation. We call them *moderate polygamists*. This class corresponds fairly closely to class 3 for men except that the women are much more likely to masturbate than the men in class 3 are. This is the class from which the core group discussed in chapter 9 below is recruited.

Class 4, in which 18 percent of American women are found, is unique to women, having no corresponding class among the men. Only 7 percent of the women have multiple partners, and only 2 percent of these women's primary partners are said to have multiple partners. The strong accent is on mutually monogamous relationships, but in the context of high levels of sexual activity. Virtually all the women in this class engage in partnered sex more than once a week. Half of them seek erotic stimulation in addition to conventional sexual outlets (a pattern of behavior that is generally avoided by women), and almost two-thirds masturbate (another behavior generally avoided by women). We call this class *enthusiastic cohabitors*.[9] The women that it encompasses are predominantly cohabitors, split equally between those never married and the divorced, separated, or widowed.

The biggest gender difference in the modes of sexual expression is that women have three monogamous classes while men have only two.[10] Also, as was mentioned above, primarily monogamous relationships ($<12>$) appear to operate somewhat differently according to gender, men engaging in high volumes of sexual activity, but women not doing so.

Again, we can examine the relation between partnered sex and autoerotic sex. The ranking of the classes of female sexual expression in terms of frequency of partnered sex is moderate polygamists > autoerotic singles > enthusiastic cohabitors > comfortable monogamists, and the ordering for masturbation is autoerotic singles > enthusiastic cohabitors > moderate polygamists > comfortable monogamists. Once again, except for one class, enthusiastic cohabitors, these two orderings are the reverse of one another. In this class, the relation is positive. Virtually all the enthusiastic cohabitors engage in partnered sex more than once a week, and they have the second highest incidence of masturbation. The relation is negative for the other three classes.

Table 3.3 Contents of Relationships for Type <21> for Each Gender (Row Percentages)

	Noncohabiting	Cohabiting	Married
Venturesome cohabitors (men)	65	15	20
Autoerotic singles (women)	80	8	13

Note: <21> = primarily polygamous relationship.

In considering the effect of the sexual network on sexual expression among women, refer again to figure 3.2 above. A woman in the class auto-erotic singles, which has the largest proportion of primarily polygamous relationships (<21>), has the lowest incidence of partnered sex more than once a week, while women in the class moderate polygamists, which includes only mutually polygamous relationships (<22>), are ranked third for frequency of partnered sex. This contrasts with our findings for men. These differences in effect of network on sexual expression arise, we expect, from the higher social costs imposed on women who are implicated in networks with multiple partners. Women are much more likely to adhere to traditional normative expectations about sexual activity in committed relationships than are men and are therefore likely to experience greater internal discomfort and feelings of guilt and shame as partnerships involving multiple others unfold. Moreover, the nature of the partnership differs for men and women in the classes venturesome cohabitors and autoerotic singles, respectively. Table 3.3 contrasts the incidence of non-cohabiting, cohabiting, and married partnerships for men and women in these two classes.

Thirty-five percent of men in primarily polygamous relationships who are classed as venturesome cohabitors have stable partnerships (cohabiting or married) with their primary partners, while only 21 percent of women in primarily polygamous relationships are in such stable partnerships. As we shall see, persons in stable partnerships derive greater emotional stability and commitment from their primary partners than do those who are not in coresidential partnerships. We examine additional evidence for some of these speculations below.

Figure 3.4 graphically summarizes the four classes or modes of sexual expression for women, as figure 3.3 above did for the men. Our task now becomes the identification of the factors that predict membership in one or another of the four classes.

3.4 Social, Subjective, and Behavioral Features of the Classes or Modes of Sexual Expression

Recall our discussion of figure 3.1 above depicting several sets of determinants that allocate people to one or another mode of sexual expression.

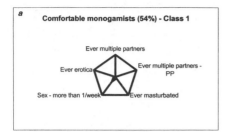
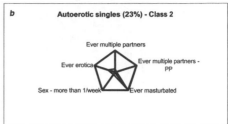
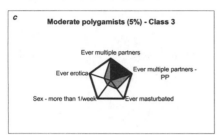
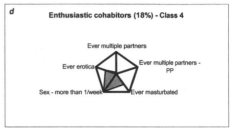

Fig. 3.4 The classes of sexual expression for American women. *a,* Class 1, comfortable monogamists (54 percent). *b,* Class 2, autoerotic singles (23 percent). *c,* Class 3, moderate polygamists (5
percent). *d,* Class 4, enthusiastic cohabitors (18 percent).
Note: See fig. 3.3 above.

Now that we have empirically identified in some detail men's and women's
different modes of sexual expression, we can begin to answer several
broader questions: (1) What type of people are more or less likely to be
allocated to the different modes of sexual expression? (2) Are there distinctive sexual contents, subjective orientations, wants, or desires associated
with each mode? (3) Are there differences in levels of physical and emotional satisfaction, overall happiness, physical health, and sexual dysfunction to be found among the modes of sexual expression? In answering
these questions, we employ several strategies. First, we examine some
simple tabulations relating the individuals' master statuses to specific
modes of sexual expression that permit cross-class comparisons. Since
these master statuses and other variables of interest are often interrelated
in complex ways, we then use a multivariate technique, multinomial logit
analysis, to disentangle their effects on membership in particular classes
of sexual expression.[11]

How Are the Master Statuses Distributed across
Each Mode of Sexual Expression?

Table 3.4 provides a cross-tabulation of six master statuses with the modes
of sexual expression. Close inspection of each panel in the table and, in
particular, comparisons across gender within each master status provide a
rewarding overview of the distribution of sexual expression in terms of the

Table 3.4 Cross-Tabulation of Master Statuses with Modes of Sexual Expression (Row Percentages)

	Men				Women			
	Class 1	Class 2	Class 3	Class 4	Class 1	Class 2	Class 3	Class 4
Age (N = 1,050 men, 1,287 women):								
18–24	36	39	4	20	45	17	14	24
25–29	32	55	1	13	43	24	4	28
30–34	42	46	1	11	42	27	5	26
35–39	53	39	1	6	48	24	6	22
40–44	49	40	2	9	49	34	2	16
45–49	71	22	2	5	56	25	4	16
50–54	78	20	1	1	71	20	2	7
55–59	77	22	0	1	77	17	3	3
Overall	50	38	2	10	50	24	6	20
Marital status: (N = 1,038 men, 1,274 women):								
Never married/not cohabiting	28	40	5	28	39	32	17	12
Never married/cohabiting	23	68	0	9	43	13	5	39
Married	63	36	0	1	56	22	1	21
Divorced, separated, or widowed/not cohabiting	35	33	6	26	39	27	15	19
Divorced, separated, or widowed/cohabiting	52	45	0	3	38	23	8	31
Overall	50	38	2	10	50	24	5	20
Education (N = 1,046 men, 1,280 women):								
Less than high school	59	34	3	4	64	13	8	16
High school graduate	55	32	3	9	58	18	5	19
Some college	46	41	1	12	43	29	7	22
Finished college	42	45	1	13	44	30	4	23
Master's/advanced degree	45	46	0	9	33	42	4	21
Overall	50	39	2	10	50	24	6	20

	Men class 1	Men class 2	Men class 3	Men class 4	Women class 1	Women class 2	Women class 3	Women class 4
Race/ethnicity (N = 1,050 men, 1,287 women):								
White	50	39	1	10	49	26	5	21
Black	56	30	8	6	54	20	10	16
Hispanic	45	43	0	12	56	14	5	25
Overall	50	38	2	10	50	24	6	20
Religion (N = 1,047 men, 1,285 women)								
None	42	43	1	14	32	30	11	27
Type I Protestant[a]	50	42	0	8	49	28	5	18
Type II Protestant[b]	61	28	4	8	58	18	5	19
Catholic	44	45	1	10	48	25	5	22
Others	44	39	0	17	45	27	9	19
Overall	50	38	2	10	50	24	6	20
Residence (N = 1,050 men, 1,287 women):								
Top 12 central cities	49	37	3	10	53	17	7	23
Next 88 central cities	39	43	2	16	43	27	10	20
Suburbs, top 12 central cities	45	41	0	13	48	29	2	21
Suburbs, next 88 central cities	54	39	1	6	47	30	5	18
Other urban areas	47	40	3	10	51	22	5	22
Rural areas	70	27	0	3	60	17	5	17
Overall	50	38	2	10	50	24	6	20

Note: For men, class 1 = comfortable monogamists, class 2 = venturesome cohabitors, class 3 = moderate polygamists, and class 4 = enthusiastic polygamists. For women, class 1 = comfortable monogamists, class 2 = autoerotic singles, class 3 = moderate polygamists, and class 4 = enthusiastic cohabitors.

[a]Type I Protestants are affiliated with mainstream, moderate to liberal Protestant denominations, including Methodists, Presbyterians, Episcopalians, and members of the United Church of Christ. For a fuller description, see *SOS*, 146–47.

[b]Type II Protestants are affiliated with conservative, evangelical, and fundamentalist Protestant denominations, including Baptists and Pentecostals. For a fuller description, see *SOS*, 146–47.

principal social attributes describing the U.S. population. We note here only some of the most significant findings.

Let us first consider the age distribution of the modes of sexual expression. The numbers of both men and women classed as comfortable monogamists steadily increase with age; on the other hand, the number classed as enthusiastic polygamists (men) and enthusiastic cohabitors (women) steadily decreases with age. While men between the ages of twenty-five and thirty-four are most likely to be venturesome cohabitors, women between the ages of forty and forty-four—the cohort that came to sexual maturity during the sexual revolution of the 1960s and early 1970s (for an extended treatment of this period, see chap. 1 above)—are most likely to be autoerotic singles. Men aged eighteen to twenty-four are most likely to be enthusiastic polygamists, while women aged twenty-five to thirty-four are most likely to be enthusiastic cohabitors. While the highest proportion of men up to age thirty-four are venturesome cohabitors, the largest proportion of women across the whole age range (eighteen to fifty-nine) are comfortable monogamists (usually married). There are thus substantively significant gender differences in the age distributions for different modes of sexual expression.

The panel on race/ethnicity reveals some interesting differences among different race and ethnic groups by gender (a topic explored in much greater depth in chap. 5 below). Black men and women are the most likely to be moderate polygamists. This is one source for the characterization of black sexuality as promiscuous, especially for black men. This stereotype is misleading, however, because black men and women are also the most likely to be comfortable monogamists. In sum, black people display polarized behavior: when compared to other racial and ethnic groups, they are found disproportionately in the restrained monogamous and the polygamous modes of sexual expression. Hispanic men are disproportionately concentrated among venturesome cohabitors, while Hispanic women are much less likely to be autoerotic singles, in which primarily polygamous relationships (<21>) are overrepresented.

Religion also makes a difference. Having 'No religious affiliation' sharply increases the odds of being an enthusiastic polygamist or a venturesome cohabitor. Type I Protestants focus on venturesome cohabitation, while type II Protestants are disproportionately concentrated among comfortable monogamists.[12] Catholics follow a pattern similar to that of Hispanics. Rural residence increases the odds of being a comfortable monogamist, and residence in the hundred largest cities (but not in their suburbs) increases the probability of being a moderate polygamist. Since race/ethnicity, religion, and rural/urban residence have complicated interrelations with socioeconomic status, age, and marital status, one must always interpret their effects carefully in the absence of controls. Below, we use an appropriate statistical technique to sort out these effects.

Marriage is associated with lower levels of sexual activity and decreased polygamous behavior for both genders. Noncohabiting (whether never married or divorced, separated, or widowed) and cohabiting partnerships have different consequences for each gender. For men, both noncohabiting and cohabiting relationships decrease the likelihood of being a comfortable monogamist. Only never married/cohabiting relationships, however, sharply increase the probability of being a venturesome cohabitor, a class in which primarily polygamous relationships are overrepresented, while only noncohabiting relationships increase the probability of being in one of the polygamous classes. The contrast with women is striking. Being in a noncohabiting relationship increases the probability of being either a moderate polygamist or an autoerotic single, both classes in which primarily polygamous relationships are overrepresented. Being in a never married/cohabiting relationship, however, substantially decreases the probability of being an autoerotic single.

Let us underscore the significant gender difference here. Never married/cohabiting substantially enhances men's likelihood of being in the class venturesome cohabitors, which contains the highest fraction of primarily polygamous relationships among men and the highest levels of sexual activity in general, while it decreases women's probability of being in the class autoerotic singles, which also contains the highest proportion of primarily polygamous relationships among women. Never-married men seem to utilize cohabitation both to secure primary sex partners and to seek additional sex partners. This latter activity may be interpreted by the men as somewhat more permissible because of the looser obligations with regard to fidelity imposed by cohabitation than by marriage. In sharp contrast to this pattern, women show more commitment and obligation when they are never married and cohabiting.

Table 3.5 clearly demonstrates this point. Note that 32 percent of never married/cohabiting men are in a primarily polygamous relationship (<21>), while only 9 percent of never married/cohabiting women are in such a relationship.

For men, higher education increases the probability of being in the classes venturesome cohabitors and enthusiastic polygamists, while it decreases the odds of being a comfortable monogamist or a moderate polygamist. For women, education increases the odds of being an autoerotic single or a comfortable monogamist. Thus, education increases the likelihood of being in a primarily polygamous relationship (<21>) and the likelihood of experiencing higher levels of sexual activity.

Table 3.5 Partnership Patterns for Each Marital Status (Row Percentages)

	Men				Women			
	<11>	<12>	<21>	<22>	<11>	<12>	<21>	<22>
Never married/noncohabiting	36	9	32	23	51	12	20	17
Never married/cohabiting	60	0	32	9	86	0	9	5
Married	93	.5	5	1	97	1	2	1
Divorced, separated, or widowed/ noncohabiting	34	9	34	23	58	13	14	15
Divorced, separated, or widowed/ cohabiting	88	0	9	3	77	0	15	8

Note: <11> = a mutually monogamous relationship; <12> = a primarily monogamous relationship; <21> = a primarily polygamous relationship; <22> = a mutually polygamous relationship.

Is Distinctive Sexual Content Associated with Particular Modes of Sexual Expression?

Figure 3.5 graphically displays a selection of sexual content that is associated with each of the modes of sexual expression. Such content includes the reasons people have for engaging in sexual activity, the feelings they experience when having sex with a primary partner, and the incidence of oral sex in the past year. Among men, there is an ordering of comfortable monogamists/venturesome cohabitors > moderate and enthusiastic polygamists with respect to the expression of affection as a reason for sexual activity. On the other hand, negative feelings, such as feeling sad, scared, guilty, or anxious when having sex with one's primary partner, occur with the greatest frequency among both classes of polygamists and decline to low levels among the comfortable monogamists. Positive feelings, such as feeling loved or thrilled, are most likely to be experienced by people in monogamous relationships. Polygamous men are the least likely to feel loved. Although it might seem contrary to common sense, monogamous men enjoy feeling thrilled more than polygamous men. Among women, this positive affect ordering is enthusiastic monogamists > comfortable monogamists/autoerotic singles > moderate polygamists. In the case of oral sex, however, the orderings are different for each gender. Venturesome cohabitors and enthusiastic polygamists have the highest incidences of oral sex among men, while enthusiastic monogamists have the highest incidence among women. We include oral sex here as an index of diversity in sexual practice. The incidence of oral sex across modes of sexual expression simply follows the ordering of the volume of sexual activity more generally.

Among men, we can say that venturesome cohabitors and enthusiastic polygamists engage in a high volume and diverse number of sexual activities, while comfortable monogamists and venturesome cohabitors are both more likely to derive good feelings from sex. Thus, venturesome cohabitors enjoy both quantity/diversity and positive feelings about sex, while moderate polygamists lack both quantity/diversity and positive feelings.[13] Among women, enthusiastic monogamists uniquely enjoy the strongest position both with respect to quantity and diversity and with respect to positive subjective qualities.

Are There Differences in Levels of Physical and Emotional Satisfaction Associated with the Modes of Sexual Expression?

Figure 3.6 graphically displays several indicators of physical and emotional satisfaction, general happiness, and sexual dysfunction as they relate to modes of sexual expression by gender. There is a subtle but important change in the ordering of physical and emotional satisfaction and happiness by mode of expression for men. The ordering is comfortable monogamists > venturesome cohabitors/moderate polygamists > enthusiastic polygamists. The classes venturesome cohabitors and enthusiastic polygamists have slipped in the positive rankings (recall that the primary ordering for subjective sexual content was comfortable monogamists > venturesome cohabitors > moderate/enthusiastic polygamists) relative to moderate polygamists. There could be two sources for this important change: emotional problems and stress. The bottom panel of figure 3.6 indicates how frequently a respondent reported that sex was adversely affected by emotional problems or stress. Enthusiastic monogamists (women) and enthusiastic polygamists (men) are the most frequently adversely affected by both of these problems, while men who are moderate polygamists are the least likely to be adversely affected by these issues. Emotional problems and stress must certainly affect the levels of physical and emotional satisfaction. Let us examine these two sources of interference with a person's subjective satisfaction with sex in greater detail.

First, venturesome cohabitors and enthusiastic polygamists (men) are the most likely to report that their sexual activities are adversely affected by emotional problems. None of the moderate polygamists are married or in cohabiting relationships, while most venturesome monogamists and a substantial proportion of enthusiastic polygamists are in cohabiting relationships. Thus, venturesome monogamists and enthusiastic polygamists are likely to confront emotional problems either because their primary partners (spouses or cohabitors) are likely to make difficulties if they discover that their men have other partners or because the nonprimary partners of the men are pressuring the men to make them their primary partners. In contrast to this situation, moderate polygamists are relatively free

Men

Women

a

Reasons for sex (% for "yes")

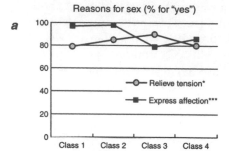

- ○— Relieve tension*
- ■— Express affection***

Reasons for sex (% for "yes")

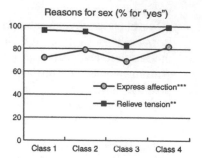

- ○— Express affection***
- ■— Relieve tension**

b

Feelings from having sex with primary partner (% for "yes")

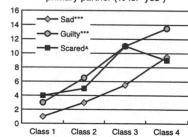

- ◇— Sad***
- ○— Guilty***
- ■— Scared^

Feelings from having sex with primary partner (% for "yes")

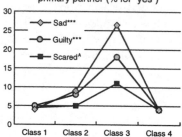

- ◇— Sad***
- ○— Guilty***
- ■— Scared^

c

Feelings from having sex with primary partner (% for "yes")

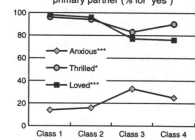

- ◇— Anxious***
- ○— Thrilled*
- ■— Loved***

Feelings from having sex with primary partner (% for "yes")

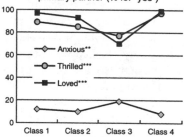

- ◇— Anxious**
- ○— Thrilled***
- ■— Loved***

d

Oral sex (% "ever" last year)

- ■— Ever***

Oral sex (% "ever" last year)

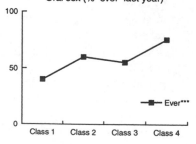

- ■— Ever***

from these emotional problems because they are in mutually polygamous relationships, in which the commitment is not expected to be exclusive. Second, venturesome cohabitors and enthusiastic polygamists are in social situations especially productive of stress. For the most part, they are highly educated and hold white-collar jobs at an age (twenty-five to thirty-four) when the stress of building a career and establishing a family is at a peak.

In contrast to the patterning of the interference with sex of stress or emotional problems, almost every sexual dysfunction follows the order moderate polygamists > enthusiastic polygamists > comfortable monogamist/venturesome cohabitors. Even for the case of lacking interest in sex, comfortable monogamists and venturesome cohabitors are less likely to experience sexual dysfunction. This ordering is consistent with the notion that the lower levels of satisfaction reported by venturesome cohabitors and enthusiastic polygamists result from factors not related to their sex lives.

In the case of women's modes of sexual expression, the ordering of the chances for satisfaction and happiness from high to low is enthusiastic cohabitors > comfortable monogamists > autoerotic singles > moderate polygamists. The ordering for the positive subjective feelings derived from sexual activity is enthusiastic cohabitors > comfortable monogamists/autoerotic cohabitors > moderate polygamists. The ordering for incidence of sexual dysfunctions across modes reverses the order for positive subjective feelings. These orderings are in sharp contrast to those for men and speak to the very real differences between the genders in the ways in which sexual expression is associated with subjective satisfaction and feelings about sexuality.

Two observations about the women's orderings are especially noteworthy. First, the class autoerotic singles has slipped a bit when compared to comfortable monogamists. Second, the autoerotic singles' position is unchanged when compared with moderate polygamists, and this is in

Fig. 3.5 Sexual contact associated with each class of sexual expression. *a,* Reasons for sex (percentage responding yes). *b–c,* Feelings resulting from having sex with the primary partner (percentage responding yes). *d,* Oral sex (percentage reporting ever last year).
Note: For men, class 1 = comfortable monogamists, class 2 = venturesome cohabitors, class 3 = moderate polygamists, and class 4 = enthusiastic polygamists. For women, class 1 = comfortable monogamists, class 2 = autoerotic singles, class 3 = moderate polygamists, and class 4 = enthusiastic cohabitors.
$\wedge p > .1$.
$* p < .1$.
$** p < .05$.
$*** p < .01$.

Men

Physical satisfaction with primary partner

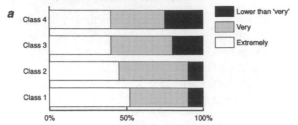

a

Class 4
Class 3
Class 2
Class 1

0%   50%   100%

- Lower than 'very'
- Very
- Extremely

Emotional satisfaction with primary partner

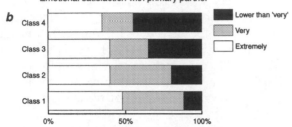

b

Class 4
Class 3
Class 2
Class 1

0%   50%   100%

- Lower than 'very'
- Very
- Extremely

General happiness

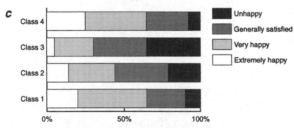

c

Class 4
Class 3
Class 2
Class 1

0%   50%   100%

- Unhappy
- Generally satisfied
- Very happy
- Extremely happy

Sexual dysfunctions: ever (%)

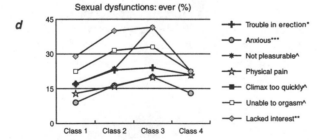

d

45

30

15

0

Class 1   Class 2   Class 3   Class 4

- Trouble in erection*
- Anxious***
- Not pleasurable^
- Physical pain
- Climax too quickly^
- Unable to orgasm^
- Lacked interest**

Sex was affected (% for "yes")

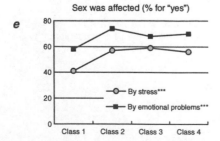

e

80

60

40

20

0

Class 1   Class 2   Class 3   Class 4

- By stress***
- By emotional problems***

Women

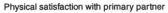

Physical satisfaction with primary partner

a

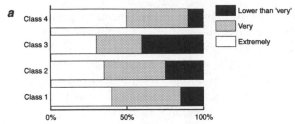

Emotional satisfaction with primary partner

b

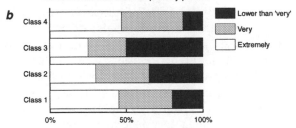

General happiness

c

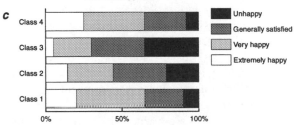

Sexual dysfunctions: ever (%)

d

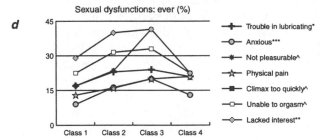

Sex was affected (% for "yes")

e

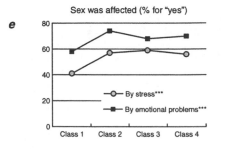

Fig. 3.6 Levels of satisfaction associated with each class of sexual expression. *a,* Physical satisfaction with primary partner. *b,* Emotional satisfaction with primary partner. *c,* General happiness. *d,* Ever sexual dysfunction (percentage). *e,* Sex was affected (percentage responding yes).

Note: For men, class 1 = comfortable monogamists, class 2 = venturesome cohabitors, class 3 = moderate polygamists, and class 4 = enthusiastic polygamists. For women, class 1 = comfortable monogamists, class 2 = autoerotic singles, class 3 = moderate polygamists, and class 4 = enthusiastic cohabitors.

$\wedge\, p > .1$.
$*\, p < .1$.
$**\, p < .05$.
$***\, p < .01$.

sharp contrast to the situation for men. Let us examine the first pattern in greater detail. Women in the class autoerotic singles must address emotional problems arising from having multiple partners, even if their primary partners are monogamous. The incidence of emotional conflict does not appear to be as high as it is in the comparable mode for men, moderate polygamists. Comfortable monogamists simply do not encounter emotional problems arising from conflicting commitments to sex partners. (As fig. 3.6 indicates, the class comfortable monogamists has the lowest incidence of disruption in sexual activity owing to emotional problems.) Second, let us think about the relative position of autoerotic singles in comparison to moderate polygamists. Autoerotic singles do not report emotional problems as often as their male counterparts, venturesome cohabitors. Recall that autoerotic singles are more likely to be noncohabiting, while venturesome cohabitors are especially likely to be cohabiting. Even though autoerotic singles are highly educated and likely to be young, they are less likely to be working. As a result, they report lower levels of interference with sex from work stress than their male counterpart, moderate polygamists (see the last diagram in fig. 3.6).

Before reporting the results of our multinomial logit analysis, we first discuss the effects from the partner side. Since sexual expression is, self-evidently, the result of interaction between the participating partners, it would be quite useful to include the focal person's sex partners' preferences, physical health status, physical availability, and social competence in any model of sexual expression. Unfortunately, such information is hard to get. As a proxy measure for the social opportunity of the partner, we have included information on the means by which the partners became acquainted with one another (e.g., through self-introduction or by being introduced by a third person who knew both partners). We also investigated the relevance of the primary partner's education when compared to the respondent's education. The log-linear analysis indicated that, for either gender, there is no added effect on mode of sexual expression of the relevance of the partners' comparative education levels. We believe that this lack of effect is due to the strong educational homophily that characterizes partner choice (for an extended discussion of educational homophily between sex partners, see chap. 9 below), making it difficult to detect separate effects for partner's education, if there are any.

3.5 Results of the Multinomial-Logit Analysis

We are now ready to examine the data from the vantage point of the model of the determinants of membership in particular modes of sexual expression depicted at the outset of the chapter (see fig. 3.1 above). Tables 3.6 and 3.7 summarize the results of the multinomial logit analysis for men

Table 3.6 Multinomial Logit Models for Modes of Sexual Expression for Men

	Individual Preferences (Pseudo-R^2 = .09)		+ Physical Status (Pseudo-R^2 = .15)		Models + Social Opportunity (Pseudo-R^2 = .5)		+ Social Competence (Pseudo-R^2 = .26)	
	Class 2	Class 4	Class 2	Class 4	Class 2	Class 4	Class 2	Class 4
Background variables (control variables):								
Adult-child sexual contact:								
Ever	1.7**	2.4***	1.8**	2.5***	1.8**	3.1***	1.8**	3.1***
Never	*1.0*	*1.0*	*1.0*	*1.0*	*1.0*	*1.0*	*1.0*	*1.0*
Race/ethnicity:								
White	*1.0*	*1.0*	*1.0*	*1.0*	*1.0*	*1.0*	*1.0*	*1.0*
Black	.7	.4**	.7*	.3**	.7	.2**	.7	.2**
Hispanic	1.2	1.3	1.3	1.3	1.1	.8	1.4	1.3
Individual subjective preferences:								
Attitude toward extramarital sex:								
Wrong	*1.0*	*1.0*	*1.0*	*1.0*	*1.0*	*1.0*	*1.0*	*1.0*
Not wrong	.8	1.4	1.0	2.0**	.9	1.6	.9	1.7
I would not have sex without love:								
Agree	*1.0*	*1.0*	*1.0*	*1.0*	*1.0*	*1.0*	*1.0*	*1.0*
Disagree	.9***	4.6***	2.1***	4.7***	2.0***	2.7***	2.0***	2.9***
Sex with a stranger:								
Appealing	1.9***	1.6*	1.8***	1.5	1.8***	1.5	1.8***	1.4
Not appealing	*1.0*	*1.0*	*1.0*	*1.0*	*1.0*	*1.0*	*1.0*	*1.0*
Thinking about sex:								
Less than every day	.5***	.3***	.6***	.4**	.5***	.3***	.6***	.3***
At least once a day	*1.0*	*1.0*	*1.0*	*1.0*	*1.0*	*1.0*	*1.0*	*1.0*

(continued)

Table 3.6 (continued)

	Individual Preferences (Pseudo-R^2 = .09)		+ Physical Status (Pseudo-R^2 = .15)		+ Social Opportunity (Pseudo-R^2 = .2)		+ Social Competence (Pseudo-R^2 = .26)	
	Class 2	Class 4	Class 2	Class 4	Class 2	Class 4	Class 2	Class 4
Physical status:								
Physical health:								
Excellent			1.0	1.6	1.1	1.9	1.2	2.3
Good			*1.0*	*1.0*	*1.0*	*1.0*	*1.0*	*1.0*
Fair or poor			1.1	**1.7***	1.1	**1.7***	1.0	1.6
Age:								
18–24			.8	1.7	.8	.9	.9	1.2
25–29			**1.6***	1.5	1.5	1.2	1.5	1.3
30–34			*1.0*	*1.0*	*1.0*	*1.0*	*1.0*	*1.0*
35–39			.8	.5	.8	.6	.8	.7
40–44			.8	.6	.9	.9	.8	.9
45–49			**.3***	**.2**	**.3***	.4	**.3**	.4
50–54			**.2***	**.04***	**.2***	**.05**	**.2***	**.04***
55–59			**.2***	**.07**	**.3***	.2	**.3***	.2
Social opportunity:								
Urban:								
Urban					*1.0*	*1.0*	*1.0*	*1.0*
Rural					**.5***	**.3**	**.6**	**.3***
Cohabitation status:								
Never married/noncohabiting					1.3	**36***	1.4	**43***
Never married/cohabiting					**2.5**	**8.3***	**2.8**	**9.7***
Divorced, separated, or widowed/ noncohabiting					1.4	**40.8***	1.4	**44.8***
Divorced, separated, or widowed/ cohabiting					1.1	3.4	1.2	3.6
Married					*1.0*	*1.0*	*1.0*	*1.0*

How one met sex partner:[a]				
Place, socially preselected; person, socially integrated	*1.0*	*1.0*	*1.0*	*1.0*
Place, socially preselected; person, not socially integrated	.8	**2.2****	.8	**2.1****
Place, not socially preselected; person, socially integrated	1.4	**5.1****	1.5	**5.8*****
Place, not socially preselected; person, not socially integrated	.7	1.4	.7	1.3
Current religion:				
No religion	**1.7***	1.5	**1.6***	1.6
Protestant Type I	**2.0*****	1.0	**1.9*****	1.0
Protestant Type II	*1.0*	*1.0*	*1.0*	*1.0*
Catholic	**1.8*****	1.1	**1.7****	1.0
Others	1.7	1.5	1.6	1.4
Social competence:				
Occupational prestige:				
Low			**.7***	**.5***
Middle			*1.0*	*1.0*
High			1.1	.6
Education:				
Less than high school			**.6***	**.2****
High school			**.7****	1.0
More than high school			*1.0*	*1.0*

Note: All values are odds ratios; class/(comfortable monogamists) is the comparison group. Values printed in boldface type are statistically significant at at least the 10 percent level. Italicization indicates baseline category. Pseudo-R^2 = [1 − (log-likelihood of model with variables/log-likelihood of model with only constant)]. Class 2 = venturesome cohabitors; class 4 = enthusiastic polygamists. Subsequent models are better than previous models (nested models) at the 1 percent significance levels (we used log-likelihood values for comparisons). This means that every added set of variables improves the model. [a]Socially preselected places include work, school, church, private parties, and social organizations. Not socially preselected places include personal ads, vacation spots, and bars. Socially integrated people include family, mutual friends, coworkers, classmates, and neighbors. *Not socially integrated person* indicates self-introduction.

*$p < .1$.
**$p < .05$.
***$p < .01$.

Table 3.7 Multinomial Logit Models for Modes of Sexual Expression for Women

| | Models | | | | | | | | | | | |
| | Individual Preferences (Pseudo-R^2 = .07) | | | + Physical Status (Pseudo-R^2 = .1) | | | + Social Opportunity (Pseudo-R^2 = .16) | | | + Social Competence (Pseudo-R^2 = .17) | | |
	Class 2	Class 3	Class 4	Class 2	Class 3	Class 4	Class 2	Class 3	Class 4	Class 2	Class 3	Class 4
Background variables (control variables):												
Adult-child sexual contact:												
Ever	1.7**	2.1**	1.5*	1.6**	2.1**	1.5*	1.7**	2.7**	1.5*	1.7**	2.8***	1.5*
Never	*1.0*	*1.0*	*1.0*	*1.0*	*1.0*	*1.0*	*1.0*	*1.0*	*1.0*	*1.0*	*1.0*	*1.0*
Race/ethnicity:												
White	*1.0*	*1.0*	*1.0*	*1.0*	*1.0*	*1.0*	*1.0*	*1.0*	*1.0*	*1.0*	*1.0*	*1.0*
Black	.6*	2.4**	.7	.6*	2.4**	.7	.7	2.2*	.9	.7	2.1	.9
Hispanic	.5*	1.3	1.3	.5*	1.0	1.1	.5*	1.0	1.1	.6	.9	1.2
Individual subjective preferences:												
Attitude toward extramarital sex:												
Wrong	*1.0*	*1.0*	*1.0*	*1.0*	*1.0*	*1.0*	*1.0*	*1.0*	*1.0*	*1.0*	*1.0*	*1.0*
Not wrong	1.4	2.8**	1.1	1.5	3.4***	1.2	1.3	2.3*	1.2	1.4	2.7**	1.2
I would not have sex without love:												
Agree	*1.0*	*1.0*	*1.0*	*1.0*	*1.0*	*1.0*	*1.0*	*1.0*	*1.0*	*1.0*	*1.0*	*1.0*
Disagree	2.2***	6.9***	2.4***	2.2***	6.7***	2.3***	1.9***	5.6***	2.2***	1.8***	6.0***	2.2***
Sex with a stranger:												
Appealing	7.2***	5.2***	5.3***	7.0***	4.7***	5.1***	7.1***	5.9***	5.0***	7.0***	5.9***	4.9***
Not appealing	*1.0*	*1.0*	*1.0*	*1.0*	*1.0*	*1.0*	*1.0*	*1.0*	*1.0*	*1.0*	*1.0*	*1.0*
Thinking about sex:												
Less than every day	*1.0*	*1.0*	*1.0*	*1.0*	*1.0*	*1.0*	*1.0*	*1.0*	*1.0*	*1.0*	*1.0*	*1.0*
At least once a day	1.2	1.5	2.6***	1.2	1.5	2.5***	1.2	1.2	2.6***	1.2	1.1	2.6***
Physical status:												
Physical health:												
Excellent				.8	.5	1.0	.7	.4	1.0	.8	.4	1.1
Good				*1.0*	*1.0*	*1.0*	*1.0*	*1.0*	*1.0*	*1.0*	*1.0*	*1.0*
Fair or poor				1.1	1.0	1.2	1.1	.9	1.3	.9	.9	1.2

Age:								
18–24	.5**	1.9	1.0	.4***	1.7	1.1	.4**	1.6	1.2
25–29	.9	.7	1.0	.9	1.0	.9	.8	.8	.8
30–34	*1.0*	*1.0*	*1.0*	*1.0*	*1.0*	*1.0*	*1.0*	*1.0*	*1.0*
35–39	.8	1.0	.8	.8	.9	.7	.7	.9	.7
40–44	1.1	.3	.5**	1.1	.3	.5**	1.0	.3	.4***
45–49	.6	.4	.4***	.7	.5	.3***	.7	.4	.3***
50–54	.6	.4	.2***	.6	.5	.2***	.6	.6	.2***
55–59	.4**	.4	.08***	.5*	.7	.08***	.5*	.6	.08***
Social opportunity:									
Urban				*1.0*	*1.0*	*1.0*	*1.0*	*1.0*	*1.0*
Rural				.7	1.8	.7	.9	2.0	.7
Cohabitation status:									
Never married/noncohabiting				2.3***	18.3***	.5**	2.2***	19***	.5**
Never married/cohabiting				.6	1.5	1.3	.8	1.6	1.3
Divorced, separated, or widowed/noncohabiting				1.7**	38***	1.3	1.7***	40.6***	1.4
Divorced, separated, or widowed/cohabiting				1.6	23.1***	2.3**	1.8	22.6***	2.5**
Married				*1.0*	*1.0*	*1.0*	*1.0*	*1.0*	*1.0*
How one met sex partner:[a]									
Place, socially preselected; person, socially integrated				*1.0*	*1.0*	*1.0*	*1.0*	*1.0*	*1.0*
Place, socially preselected; person, not socially integrated				1.3	1.0	1.1	1.3	1.0	1.1
Place, not socially preselected; person, socially integrated				1.6*	1.8	.9	1.6**	1.7	1.0
Place, not socially preselected; person, not socially integrated				1.5	2.3*	.6	1.5	2.3*	.6
Current religion:									
No religion				2.2**	3.5**	2.2**	1.5*	4.4**	2.0**
Protestant Type I				1.8***	1.4	1.3	1.3	1.5	1.2
Protestant Type II				*1.0*	*1.0*	*1.0*	*1.0*	*1.0*	*1.0*
Catholic				1.5	1.7	1.4	1.3	1.7	1.3
Others				1.5	2.2	1.3	1.1	2.2	1.1

(continued)

Table 3.7 (continued)

	Models											
	Individual Preferences (Pseudo-R^2 = .07)			+ Physical Status (Pseudo-R^2 = .1)			+ Social Opportunity (Pseudo-R^2 = .16)			+ Social Competence (Pseudo-R^2 = .17)		
	Class 2	Class 3	Class 4	Class 2	Class 3	Class 4	Class 2	Class 3	Class 4	Class 2	Class 3	Class 4
Social competence:												
Occupational prestige:												
Low										**.7***	.7	.9
Middle										*1.0*	*1.0*	*1.0*
High										1.2	.5	1.3
Education:												
Less than high school										**.5***	1.2	.6
High school										**.5***	.7	.8
More than high school										*1.0*	*1.0*	*1.0*

Note: All values are odds ratios; comfortable monogamists (class 1) is the comparison group. Values printed in boldface type are statistically significant at at least the 10 percent level. Italicization indicates baseline category. Pseudo-R^2 = [1 − (log-likelihood of model with variables/log-likelihood of model with only constant)]. Class 2 = autoerotic singles; class 3 = moderate polygamists; class 4 = enthusiastic cohabitors. Subsequent models are better than previous models (nested models) at the 1 percent significance level (we used log-likelihood values for comparisons). This means that every added set of variables improves the model.

[a]Socially preselected places include work, school, church, private parties, and social organizations. Not socially preselected places include personal ads, vacation spots, and bars. Socially integrated people include family, mutual friends, coworkers, classmates, and neighbors. *Not socially integrated person* indicates self-introduction.

*$p < .1$.
**$p < .05$.
***$p < .01$.

and women, respectively. (The reader will find an exposition of the technique in the technical appendix to the introduction.) We omitted male moderate polygamists in table 3.6 because there were too few of them to sustain statistical analysis. All the cell entries are odds ratios, and comfortable monogamists are the comparison (or baseline) group. For example, the number 1.7 reported in column 1, row 1 of table 3.6 means that the odds of being a venturesome cohabitor as opposed to a comfortable monogamist—that is,

$$\text{prob(venturesome cohabitor)/prob(comfortable monogamist)}$$

—are 1.7 times greater for men who experienced adult-child sexual contact before puberty than for men who did not.

Note, first, that the predictor variables in the stub column of the table are arranged in four blocks of determinants labeled *individual subjective preferences, physical status, social opportunity,* and *social competence.* Blocks are added successively to more inclusive models of the determinants of membership in a particular mode of sexual expression, as indicated in the column headings. For example, columns 3 and 4 report on models for venturesome cohabitors and enthusiastic polygamists, respectively, that include background variables (adult-child sexual contact and race/ethnicity) and individual subjective preferences as well as the two physical status variables, physical health and age.

Second, each successive model significantly improves on the previous model at the .01 level. We can thus be confident that, even after individual preferences and physical health are taken into account, factors relating to social opportunity and social competence make a difference in mode of sexual expression. This result is at least consistent with the many arguments about the social construction of sexuality (Malinowski [1927] 1970, 18; Gagnon and Parker 1995, 15; Laumann and Gagnon 1995, 191). It must be conceded, however, that the individual effects identified as statistically significant do not, for the most part, exert very large effects substantively. Perhaps the most consistent generalized effect appears to be rooted in the multiplicity/singularity of partnership itself.

Third, note that most parameters (odds ratios) do not change as new variables are added. For example, the ratios reported in columns 1, 3, 5, and 7, row 1, of tables 3.6 and 3.7 show that, for both men and women who experienced adult-child sexual contact, the odds of being a venturesome cohabitor as opposed to a comfortable monogamist remain essentially constant.[14] This implies that there is no strong interaction between the four blocks of determinants—each block operates as a set of independent effects. Moreover, it is also worth noting that adult-child sexual contact consistently increases the likelihood of being in class 2 (venturesome cohabitor/autoerotic single), class 3 (moderate polygamist), or class 4 (enthusiastic polygamist/enthusiastic cohabitor) as opposed to class 1 (comfortable monogamist). Fourth, the pseudo-R^2 is much smaller for women than it is for men. This arises mainly from the negligible effects exerted by physical status (especially physical health) and social opportunity. For women, once age is controlled, physical health does not appear to exert any independent effect in determining modes of sexual expression.

Once social opportunity and social competence are taken into account for women, race/ethnicity disappears as a significant factor in predicting mode of sexual expression. Race/ethnicity, however, remains significant for men, even when these other determinants are added to the model. The effect of racial/ethnic differences for women mainly derives from their effect on marital status and education (see table 3.5 above). Black women are more likely to belong to the class moderate polygamists than are women in other racial and ethnic groups because they are more likely never to have been married and not to be cohabiting (31 percent of black women in the sample report never having married and not cohabiting, while only 12 percent of white women do so), and that increases the odds of being a moderate polygamist. Black women are less likely to be in the class autoerotic singles because they are less likely to have no religion or to be affiliated with a Protestant Type I religious denomination (i.e., only 13 percent of black women are nonreligious or belong to Protestant Type I religious denominations, while 40 percent of white women are in one of these two categories), and that increases the odds of being an autoerotic single. Hispanic women are less likely to be autoerotic singles because they are less likely to have more than a high school education (only 40 percent of Hispanic women have more than a high school education, compared to 60 percent of white women).

Black men are less likely to be enthusiastic polygamists than are men of other racial and ethnic groups. In particular, when we control for marital status and the way in which sex partners met, this difference becomes even larger and statistically more significant—a result of the fact that, among those who are not cohabiting (a factor that sharply increases the chance of being an enthusiastic polygamist), only 11 percent of the black men but 30 percent of the white men are enthusiastic polygamists. Instead, black men are more likely to be moderate polygamists than are white men (15 vs. 3 percent, respectively). Thus, black men are more likely to be moderate polygamists when, on the basis of their other characteristics, one would have expected them to be enthusiastic polygamists.

Sexual norms and frequency of thinking about sex exert strong and consistent effects on both genders. A particularly intriguing finding is that thinking about sex is of special significance only for being an enthusiastic cohabitor (among women).

As discussed above, cohabiting (especially among the never married) increases a man's likelihood of being a venturesome monogamist, while not cohabiting increases a woman's likelihood of being an autoerotic single. This accounts for the fact that, among women, autoerotic singles have the lowest rate of partnered sex. It is also interesting to note that cohabiting increases divorced, widowed, or separated women's odds of being enthusiastic monogamists more than being married does. A possible reason for this pattern is that previously married women are more sexually experienced and older (as are their partners), which would operate strongly against a women having multiple sex partners. Attention is drawn to the fact that how sex partners met one another has a strong, persistent effect on membership in particular modes of sexual expression. As one might readily anticipate, if both the places where sex partners met and the people introducing them are associated with low levels of social selectivity, the odds of being a moderate polygamist increase (we cannot confirm this for enthusiastic polygamists, who were dropped from the analysis owing to insufficient numbers).

One of the strong claims of this chapter is that social competence plays a critical role in shaping the modes of sexual expression. People who lack the competence to initiate and sustain ongoing social relationships and to compete successfully for the status achievements that society regards as important will find it difficult to maintain ongoing sexual partnerships as well since these are but special instances of social relationships. Lacking ongoing access to a sex partner necessarily curtails the volume of sexual activity in which one can engage. Although one would like to have direct measures of an individual's social competence, these are lacking in the NHSLS. We must turn to such indirect indicators of an individual's social competence as are provided by the relative prestige of an individual's occupation or socioeconomic status (e.g., earned income) and level of education. As predicted, higher occupational prestige[15] and educational attainment increase the odds of being classed in a mode of sexual expression involving the partner's monogamy and high levels of sexual activity: being a venturesome cohabitor or an enthusiastic polygamist (among men) or an autoerotic single (among women).

3.6 Concluding Remarks

In this chapter, we set for ourselves several ambitious tasks. First, we argue that it is desirable to characterize a person's mode of sexual expression in a holistic and multidimensional way, one that brings into focus the multifaceted ways in which an individual can express sexuality and the relative volume or level of one's sexual activity when compared to that of others. Recognizing that these modes of expression are necessarily gendered, whether because of innate biological differences in sexual function or social and cultural expectations, or some combination of the two, we establish empirically that we can exhaustively classify the modes of sexual expression of men and women in the U.S. population as falling into only a few categories. In fact, about half of all adults in the United States can be assigned to a single mode of sexual expression, one that involves mutually monogamous relationships and low levels of sexual activity and minimizes autoeroticism and unconventional erotic stimulation.

We then explore the subjective, behavioral, and social factors that are differentially associated with each of these modes of sexual expression. The patterns of association provide us with a rich, nuanced sense of the very different life experiences and subjective meanings and emotions that are associated with particular expressive modes. The NHSLS study design, which employs only a cross-sectional sample gathered at one point in time, imposes serious limits on our ability to characterize how people might move in and out of particular modes of sexual expression over the life course. Given the substantial effect of age in sorting people into particular modes of sexual expression, one can reasonably speculate that people do adopt different modes of expression over the life course and that an important topic for future research is the factors implicated in precipitating changes in modes of sexual expression. Turnover tables displaying the probabilities of staying in a particular mode or shifting to another over time would be especially instructive; they would cast light on the dynamics of differential risk taking in which individuals engage when they adopt particular modalities of sexual expression. These risks include exposure to sexually transmitted infections, sexual dysfunctions, and other hazards to health. These turnover tables cannot be calculated, however, without repeated observations over time of the same respondents, so we must await the creation of such longitudinal data.

Appendix 3A

Table 3A.1 Frequency of Partnered Sex and Emotional Satisfaction with a Primary Partner by Position in Sexual Network (%)

	Men		Women	
Relationship	Partnered Sex: Occurring More Than Once a Week[a]	Emotional Satisfaction: Extremely or Very Satisfied[b]	Partnered Sex: Occurring More Than Once a Week[a]	Emotional Satisfaction: Extremely or Very Satisfied[b]
Mutually monogamous	43	88	41	80
Primarily monogamous	21	42	31	46
Primarily polygamous	44	71	33	59
Mutually polygamous	34	59	25	50

[a]P-value from Pearson χ^2 is 0.031 for men and 0.024 for women.
[b]Pearson χ^2 for men and for women both less than 0.001.

Table 3A.2 Proportions of Each Sexual Network Pattern (from Figure 3.2) by Mode of
Sexual Expression among Men (%)

	Relationship			
	Mutually Monogamous	Primarily Monogamous	Primarily Polygamous	Mutually Polygamous
Comfortable monogamists	91	.4	9	0
Venturesome cohabitors	72	0	28	0
Moderate polygamists	0	0	0	100
Enthusiastic polygamists	0	30	0	70

Table 3A.3 Comparison of the Fit of Five Latent Class Models

	df	Pearson χ^2	P-Value	Likelihood Ratio χ^2
2 latent classes	21	122.35	.000	130.65
3 latent classes	15	25	.05	29
4 latent classes	11	8.3	.686	9.15
5 latent classes	8	4.55	.804	4.35
6 latent classes	5	.49	.992	.5

Note: Among the five possible models, the four-class model is the best in terms of reduction of χ^2 with relatively small number of parameters used (even though five or six latent
class models have more reduction in χ^2, the four-class model requires fewer parameters for
almost the same goodness of fit).

Table 3A.4 Proportions of Each Sexual Network Type (from Figure 3.2) by Mode of
Sexual Expression among Women (Row Percentages)

	Relationship			
	Mutually Monogamous	Primarily Monogamous	Primarily Polygamous	Mutually Polygamous
Comfortable monogamists	91	5	4	0
Autoerotic singles	81	6	13	0
Moderate polygamists	0	0	0	100
Enthusiastic polygamists	91	2	7	0

Notes

The authors wish to thank James Davis, Stephen Ellingson, John P. Heinz, Jenna Mahay,
Sarah Hdry, Robert T. Michael, Anthony Paik, and Martha van Haitsma for their helpful
comments.

1. We exclude two groups of people from the analysis. First, we exclude people who had
no sex partner within the last twelve months because the second and fifth dimensions would

not apply to them. Second, we exclude people having sex only with same-gender partners in the past year because we want to focus on the gender differences in sexual expression that are associated with persons having sex with persons of the other gender. There are simply too few cases of same-gender partnering to sustain a statistical analysis comparable to the one we perform here on heterosexual partnering.

2. Appendix table 3A.1 suggests that our propositions are correct. We have set more than once a week as a threshold for frequency of partnered sex on the expectation that only at this higher level would strong competition for division of attention and resources among multiple partners come into play. Note that, in every comparison of mutual monogamy and primary monogamy and of primary polygamy and mutual polygamy for each gender, the network characterized by a greater number of partners shows substantially lower rates of frequency of partnered sexual activity and of positive emotional satisfaction.

3. The number of one's partner's partners also became important in the age of AIDS (Bozon and Leridon 1996, 10) because it plays a critical role in the spread of STDs (for an extensive discussion of this point, see chap. 9 below).

4. The search for other venues for erotic stimulation includes buying or renting X-rated movies, buying any sexually explicit magazine, buying any sex toys or dildos, calling for phone sex, going to a nightclub presenting nude dancers, hiring a prostitute, attending a public gathering in the nude, and having a picture taken in the nude.

5. Latent class analysis is a technique for condensing the information in a large set of qualitative or categorical variables, as we have here; it is analogous to the factor analysis of quantitative variables. In our case, with five dichotomous variables, we have noted that there are thirty-two total possible cells or classes, and the latent class analysis allows us to reduce that number of distinct classes, employing a statistical criterion to decide how many classes are needed. Imagine putting all the men respondents into a single class. That would not be very useful, so we might try two classes to characterize all five of those dichotomies: (1) having more than one sex partner in the past year or not; (2) having partners who have other partners or not; (3) having sex more than once a week or not; (4) participating in one of the list of erotic activities or not; (5) masturbating or not. A two-class scheme would be a lot better than a one-class scheme, and the χ^2 statistic tells us so. We could then try a three-class scheme, a four-class scheme, etc., all the way up to a thirty-two-class scheme, which is a full characterization but one that contains far too many classes to make use of. The statistical criterion that we chose yields a four-class scheme for the men and also a four-class scheme for the women.

Now, these four classes are a statistical sorting and can allocate all the observations into these four classes, but some observations fit very naturally, while others are a bit forced and would be those most likely to be moved if we went to a five-class scheme. Moreover, the four classes have no natural descriptive names, so we give each class a name that we think reflects the nature of that class, judging by the values of the five dichotomies that it partitions.

6. We have tried to label each class using a "typical" member of the class as an exemplar, primarily to facilitate the reader's recall of the underlying pattern of characteristics that define the latent class. Such labeling does oversimplify the underlying empirical reality (i.e., not every member possesses every characteristic defining the latent class), but we found that the use of letters or other arbitrary symbols to refer to the classes made it very difficult for readers to follow the argument. In this case, about two-thirds of the class members are married (see table 3.4 below).

7. For the proportions of each sexual network pattern (from fig. 3.2) by mode of sexual expression among men, see app. table 3A.2.

8. For a comparison of several latent class models, see app. table 3A.3.

Among the five possible models, the 4-class model is the best in terms of reduction of Chi-square and fits the data very well (0.69 p-value).

9. For proportions of each sexual network type (from fig. 3.2) by mode of sexual expression among women, see app. table 3A.4.

10. One cannot directly determine the correspondence in the classes of sexual expression by gender simply by comparing the population distributions by gender. For example, one might ask how men who are polygamous can constitute about 16.6 percent of the male population (1.6 percent are moderate polygamists and 15 percent enthusiastic polygamists) when only 5 percent of the women are found in a mutually polygamous class. To frame the question in this way is misleading, for several reasons. First, that we label a class *polygamous* does not mean that the entire population in that particular class is in a mutually polygamous relationship. For example, among the men who are enthusiastic polygamists, 70 percent are in mutually polygamous relationships (<22>), but 30 percent are in primarily monogamous relationships (<12>). In short, the latent classes do not precisely describe every individual within them. If one calculates the incidence of mutually polygamous relationships using the individual-level data, however, we get the result that those who are polygamous constitute 9 percent of the male population and 6 percent of the female population. Second, we must take into account the population size for each gender. There are about 1.2 times as many women as men in our data set. We thus need to adjust our estimates for women upward to 7.2 percent, which begins to approximate the number of men. Third, there is ambiguity in the label *primary partner* that might engender systematic reporting errors. And, of course, there may be systematic error in reporting because being unfaithful usually meets with social disapproval. In particular, one might expect a gender bias in reporting multiple partners (for an extended discussion of the biases in reporting numbers of sex partners, see *SOS*, chap. 5).

11. To employ this technique, we must assign each respondent to a particular class. In assigning classes, some error is introduced because some people simply do not fit any of the classes. For men, $\lambda = 0.89$, and 94.3 percent of the respondents are correctly allocated. For women, $\lambda = 0.75$, and 88.2 percent are correctly allocated. The latent class analyses thus yield very satisfactory class assignments with high reproducibility of results.

12. Type I Protestants are affiliated with mainstream, moderate to liberal Protestant denominations, including the Methodist, Presbyterian and Episcopalian Churches and the United Church of Christ. Type II Protestants are affiliated with conservative evangelical and fundamentalist Protestant denominations, including the Baptist and Pentecostal Churches. For a fuller description, see *SOS*, 146–47.

13. Feelings derived from sex refer only to sex with one's primary partner in the past year. As a result, the causal direction is unclear under certain circumstances. It is possible, e.g., that a man who is dissatisfied with his primary partner may seek another partner and will thus be classified as being a moderate or an enthusiastic polygamist. As we see below, however, men experiencing sexual dysfunctions, including lacking interest in sex, have high odds for also being moderate or enthusiastic polygamists. This suggests that the causation is operating in both directions.

14. For a detailed analysis, see chap. 5 above.

15. People are assigned to one of three equivalently sized status groups (low, middle, and high) according to their occupational prestige scores.

■

CHAPTER FOUR

Sexual Contact between Children and Adults: A Life-Course Perspective

CHRISTOPHER R. BROWNING AND EDWARD O. LAUMANN

In 1994, Ross Cheit, a professor of public policy at Brown University, publicly revealed that he had been sexually abused by a boys' choir director in San Francisco during the 1960s. The case received a great deal of publicity because of Cheit's willingness to come forward as a victim of abuse and, perhaps more important, because of his claim that the memory of abuse had surfaced only recently, at the age of thirty-six. In the context of increasing popular and academic interest in the possibility that memories of sexual abuse can be repressed, Cheit's story was particularly compelling. Yet the case was also interesting because of a less visible but undeniable fact. Cheit was an award-winning, successful, articulate professional and widely acknowledged as such. Moreover, he was happily married and, by all accounts, mentally healthy. The image of the victim of sexual abuse as emotionally unstable and permanently afflicted by the trauma of abuse was clearly at odds with the picture that Cheit presented (Freyd 1996).

How did Cheit manage to endure the experience of sexual abuse with such apparent success? What sets cases like his apart from those that lead to substantial problems in adulthood? When sexual abuse began receiving more academic attention in the 1970s, researchers were primarily interested in establishing the nature of its effect on subsequent well-being. This largely descriptive research focused on both the severity of negative effects in adulthood and their breadth. Analysis of clinical samples revealed strong and consistent associations between the experience of early sexual contact with an adult and a host of adverse adult outcomes. A secondary and often ignored finding of this descriptive research, however, was the clearly nondeterministic relation between adult-child sex and poor adult adjustment. Individuals who reported early sexual experiences did not inevitably suffer long-term negative effects: some exhibited no discernible effect at all.

This finding has called attention to a critical question: Why do some children who experience sexual abuse suffer a host of negative consequences while others do not? In the absence of measures to prevent the occurrence of child sexual abuse, it is critical for parents, therapists, and policy makers to understand the mechanisms by which such experiences lead to poor adjustment in adolescence and adulthood. Without this knowledge, intervention efforts may be misguided and ineffective.

Increasingly, researchers in the area of child sexual abuse have recognized the importance of developing explanations for the link between early sexual experiences and long-term effects. The dominant theoretical framework to emerge in response to this need can be described as a *psychogenic* perspective on the long-term effects of childhood sexual experiences. This perspective encompasses a number of different approaches, including the posttraumatic stress disorder (PTSD) framework (APA 1994; Briggs and Joyce 1997; Deblinger et al. 1989; McLeer et al. 1988), Lenore Terr's typological trauma theory (Terr 1991), the cognitive-behavioral model (Hoier, Shawbuck, and Pallotta 1992), and elements of David Finkelhor's traumagenic dynamics model (Finkelhor 1988). These theories share a core vision of abusive sexual experiences as variably traumatic events occurring between children and significantly older partners that directly affect long-term well-being through lingering emotional disturbance.

We offer an alternative model to explain the long-term effects of childhood sexual experiences, one that integrates social learning theory (Akers 1973; Bandura 1973; Elliott, Huizinga, and Ageton 1985), social control theory (Hirschi 1969; Sampson and Laub 1993), and concepts taken from the sociology of the life course (Caspi 1987; Elder 1985). In this view, adult-child sex as well as explicitly sexual contacts with peers are understood as early transitions to sociosexual activity. Aspects of this transition induce vulnerability to subsequent experiences that have independent effects on adult well-being. From this perspective, the effects of childhood sexual contacts are indirect. That is, risky behavior patterns established in the *aftermath* of early sex and their unfolding effect over time account for the association between childhood sexual experience and adult mental, sexual, and interpersonal well-being (three of the most commonly affected areas of adult adjustment). In what follows, we describe the psychogenic and life-course perspectives in detail and test their competing claims regarding the effect of childhood sexual experiences.

4.1 The Psychogenic Perspective

The modern history of research on the effect of childhood sexual experiences began with the publication of Freud's essay "The Aetiology of Hysteria" ([1896] 1955). Delivered at the Society for Psychiatry and Neurology in Vienna, "The Aetiology of Hysteria" proved to be one of the most controversial statements of Freud's highly contentious career. The central thesis of the paper was Freud's claim that the roots of hysterical symptomatology could be found in early sexual trauma. In the context of this theory—now known as the *seduction hypothesis* (Gay 1989)—Freud used the term *trauma* with reference to painful or overwhelming stressors that produce an intense emotional response. The quantity of affect produced by the traumatic event cannot be managed by the conscious mind and is repressed. This unresolved affect, however, remains in the unconscious and may periodically be manifest in hysterical symptoms. Freud's advocacy of the seduction hypothesis provoked vociferous criticism among his colleagues in the medical community, and he subsequently abandoned the theory (Masson 1984).

After Freud's retraction, there followed an extended hiatus in research on the effects of childhood sexual experiences, a hiatus that lasted until the topic was rediscovered in the 1960s. Yet the theories that emerged over the next three decades to explain the effects of sexual abuse bore witness to Freud's enduring legacy. In large part, these theories reproduced a basic set of assumptions about the nature of childhood sexual experiences that find their original expression in the seduction hypothesis. The first and most basic claim of the psychogenic perspective is that *trauma* is the central concept to be used to explain the effects of child sexual abuse (typically understood as interaction of a sexual nature between a child and an adult or a significantly older partner). Although conceived in a variety of ways in the psychogenic literature (see "Conceptions of Trauma" below), the notion that the effects of childhood sexual experiences flow from their traumatic character remains unchallenged. A second assumption concerns the pathway through which the trauma of sexual abuse is hypothesized to effect subsequent well-being. The psychogenic perspective views this path as *direct*. That is, the emotional disturbance induced by the trauma of sexual abuse may linger across long stretches of the life course. The effect of abuse at any subsequent period, then, is said to be a manifestation of this emotional disturbance in a relevant life domain. For example, painful memories associated with the event may diminish interest in or provoke anxiety during sex, or residual anger resulting from the experience of abuse may interfere with the capacity to sustain a rewarding intimate relationship in adulthood.

A third assumption of the psychogenic perspective is that abuse leads to opposing sexual behavior strategies. Some victims may withdraw from sexual activity, particularly activities that occurred during the abusive relationship. Others may respond to abuse by engaging in heightened or compulsive levels of sexual activity. The latter response is typically attributed to a "mastery" impulse—some victims may continually reenact the abuse experience in order to gain some measure of control over the emotions and memories associated with it. A fourth assumption concerns the explanation for variation in the long-term outcomes of abusive sexual experiences. In the psychogenic view, childhood sexual experiences fall on a continuum of severity that describes the level of stress induced and predicts the extent to which the child will suffer long-term negative consequences (the dose-response hypothesis) (Rutter 1988). More traumatic events are hypothesized to lead to more acute long-term negative outcomes. The severity of an abusive experience is typically measured by such characteristics of the event as the frequency of sexual contact, the type of sexual activity that occurred, and the relationship of the child to the perpetrator (e.g., whether the perpetrator was related to the child). Finally, the psychogenic perspective, on the whole, implies that childhood sexual contacts with peers or slightly older children are not significant sources of trauma and therefore will not lead to the same symptom profile as early sexual contacts with adults. Indeed, because peer sexual contacts among children are largely absent from the psychogenically oriented theoretical and empirical literature on the effects of early sexual experiences, we use the term *adult-child sexual experiences* interchangeably with the term *sexual abuse* in the review of this literature to follow.

These five assumptions form the core of the psychogenic vision of childhood sexual experiences and their consequences. Despite their commonalities, however, the major psychogenic theories of the effects of childhood sexual experience do vary in their conceptualization of trauma and the constellation of symptoms for which they seek to account. Traumatic scenarios can be organized by cross-classifying two dimensions (see table 4.1): the active or passive orientation of the victim and the assumed positive or negative nature of the stimuli. To these dimensions, we add the relevant relationship between the actor and the stimuli, yielding four scenarios: (1) the presentation of negative stimuli (e.g., painful or overwhelming experiences of sexual intrusion); (2) the removal of positively valued stimuli (e.g., betrayal by a parent, in the case of incest); (3) blocked escape from negative stimuli (e.g., thwarted efforts to avoid repeated sexually abusive episodes); and (4) blocked acquisition of positive stimuli (e.g., the

Table 4.1 Trauma-Producing Scenarios

	Victim Orientation	
Stimuli	Passive	Active
Negative	Presentation of noxious stimuli (the seduction hypothesis, PTSD [Freud 1896; Hoier, Shawbuck, and Pallotta 1992; Green 1993])	Blocked escape from negative stimuli (anticipatory dissociation [Terr 1991])
Positive	Removal of valued stimuli (betrayal trauma [Freyd 1996])	Blocked achievement of valued stimuli (strain theory [Merton 1938])

classic conception of delinquency-producing strain offered by Robert Merton [1938]). The first three scenarios capture major tendencies in the theoretical literature on the effects of adult-child sexual experiences.

Conceptions of Trauma

By far the most popular conception of the effects of adult-child sexual contact envisions the experience as the presentation of noxious stimuli to a child. In this view, adult-child sex is seen as a painful or an overwhelming event that produces adverse emotional responses. This perspective is represented both by Freud's early seduction theory and by the more recent widespread application of the PTSD framework to the case of sexual abuse (APA 1994; Horowitz 1976; Janoff-Bulman 1985; Pynoos and Eth 1985). Rooted in a psychoanalytic conception of trauma (Freud 1920), the PTSD model suggests that the experience of stress during sexual contact with an adult generates powerful psychic energy (memories and affect associated with the event) that, if unresolved, leads to adverse mental health outcomes (Gelinas 1983). Thus, negative outcomes in adulthood are "symptoms" of a lingering psychic disorder, the etiology of which is traced directly to the original sexual experience.

By implication, the PTSD framework suggests that the degree of traumatic stress experienced during the abusive relationship is the factor that best accounts for variation in the long-term adverse effects of sexual abuse. More stressful events will induce more subsequent emotional disturbance and an increased likelihood of exhibiting PTSD symptomatology. Advocates of the PTSD perspective have operationalized the level of trauma experienced by examining such characteristics of the event as the frequency and type (e.g., penetrative vs. nonpenetrative sex acts) of sexual contact that occurred (Briggs and Joyce 1997) and whether force was involved (Urquiza and Capra 1990).

The hypothesized response to sexual stimuli resulting from the trauma of adult-child sex is polarized in the PTSD framework. On the one hand, PTSD typically involves the adoption of avoidance strategies designed to structure all reminders of the traumatic incident out of daily experience (APA 1994). An alternative response, however, involves confronting stimuli associated with the traumatic experience in order to achieve mastery over the event (Horowitz 1976). The PTSD perspective, then, suggests a polarized response pattern, with adverse reactions to sexual trauma taking the form of withdrawal from sexual activity (and the specific sex acts associated with the sexual trauma) *or* compulsive sexual behavior (Green 1992, 1993).

Some or all of the assumptions embedded in the PTSD model—the centrality of trauma, the direct effect of emotional disturbance on subsequent well-being, the dose-response hypothesis, and the assumption of a bipolar behavioral orientation—are reproduced in other "noxious stimuli" models of the long-term effects of sexual abuse (Hoier, Shawbuck, and Pallotta 1992) as well as in models that posit alternative trauma-generating scenarios. For instance, the notion of trauma as the removal of positive stimuli finds expression in perspectives that emphasize betrayal as the consequential component of adult-child sex (Freyd 1996). From this point of view, the trauma of abuse results from the child's recognition that a valued caretaker is exploiting the child's trust. The key event characteristic predicting subsequent adjustment is the relationship of the child to the perpetrator. Betrayal by adults to whom the child is more attached (dose) is hypothesized to lead to more severe long-term effects (response).

Trauma stemming from the failure to escape negative stimuli has been emphasized by Terr (1991), who suggests that chronic exposure to stressful events creates a sense of anticipation and a recognition that the child has little control over the occurrence of the stressor. The hypothesized consequences of this type of trauma include denial, psychic numbing, dissociation, and rage.

Finally, one of the more popular psychogenic theories—Finkelhor's traumagenic dynamics framework—integrates all three of the trauma-generating scenarios in an alternative model of the long-term effects of sexual abuse. An additional contribution of the model is its recognition that effects may stem from processes subsequent to the actual sexual contact, including the stigmatization that may result from the intervention of authorities and maladaptive patterns of sexual behavior ("traumatic sexualization"). Unfortunately, Finkelhor does not extend the traumagenic dynamics framework far enough in this theoretical direction. The notion of trauma remains an essential element of Finkelhor's model—as in the PTSD framework—as does the dose-response hypothesis (Browne and Finkelhor 1986). Subsequent experiences, including behavior patterns developed during adolescence and young adulthood that are related to early childhood sexual activity, are not taken into account.

By failing to locate early sexual experiences within an unfolding life course, Finkelhor is constrained to explain the wide-ranging consequences of adult-child sex as direct effects of one or another traumagenic dynamic—often resulting in awkward causal linkages. Moreover, as do proponents of the PTSD framework, Finkelhor hypothesizes a tendency either to avoid sexual stimuli or to experience heightened sexual interest and activity (reproducing the hypothesis of a polarized pattern of behavioral responses to adult-child sex) (Finkelhor 1988).

Shortcomings of the Psychogenic Perspective

The popularity of the psychogenic perspective may reflect the nature of the collective response to sexual abuse. The notion of trauma as emotional shock at the experience of sexual victimization mirrors our own collective outrage and revulsion at the phenomenon of the sexual exploitation of children. Yet evidence suggests that the experience of sexual abuse rarely fits the imagery of the trauma concept. Most childhood sexual experiences involve the subtle manipulation of the child over time by partners familiar to him or her rather than abrupt and forceful violation.

Moreover, as a theory of abuse effects, the psychogenic perspective suffers from a number of critical shortcomings. First, the emphasis on withdrawal from sexual activity as an outcome of sexual abuse, particularly in its PTSD formulation, runs counter to the increasing evidence of heightened and accelerated sexual behavior in the aftermath of abuse. Indeed, "sexualized behavior" is one of the most consistently observed short-term outcomes of sexual abuse, while evidence of a corresponding sexual avoidance tendency is limited. Although most psychogenically based theories of the effects of abuse suggest that sexual behavior will be either avoidant or heightened in response to abuse, the former is typically emphasized and more consistent with the basic assumptions of the trauma model.

Second, although empirical research has documented a tendency for sexual abuse to lead to a diverse set of problem behaviors in adolescence— including precocious sexual activity, drug use, delinquency, and running away from home—the explanation for this generalized response is poorly developed in the psychogenic perspective. Nearly every variety of problem behavior in adolescence can be conceptualized in the psychogenic perspective as a "coping" response. Thus, drug use is an effort to self-medicate, while delinquency is a manifestation of a tendency to act out in response to abuse. Unfortunately, the coping response model cannot provide a theoretical basis on which to expect one type of outcome over another. Thus, the psychogenic perspective offers only weak predictive capacity in explaining the range of adolescent problem behaviors associated with sexual abuse.

Third, the psychogenic perspective's assumption of a direct effect of sexual abuse on long-term well-being forces the perspective to link the emotional disturbance of abuse with outcomes across the life course. Yet the mechanisms that serve to maintain affective disturbance over such long periods of time are not clearly specified in the psychogenic perspective. How is it that the emotional effect of abuse is so resiliently maintained, even decades after the event occurred? Often, an unacknowledged psychoanalytically informed model of consciousness underlies the claim that long-term effects are anchored in intrapsychic processes. The life-course approach, considered in more detail below, explains the wide-ranging effects of childhood sexual experiences by exploring their effect on subsequent life trajectories rather than forcing an artificial linkage between an induced psychic condition and multiple, diverse, and temporally distant outcomes.

4.2 A Life-Course Perspective on the Effects of Childhood Sexual Experiences

Although sociologists have been largely silent on the topic of sexual abuse, they have developed a sophisticated research program to explain many of those behaviors with which sexual abuse is often associated. Most notably, the tradition of criminological research in sociology has, for many decades, concentrated on unearthing the etiology of adolescent delinquency and related problem behaviors. The theoretical perspective developed below brings general theories of adolescent problem behavior to bear on the processes that link sexual abuse with these and other outcomes.

Specifically, we dynamically integrate two major theories of delinquency, social learning and social control theory, using concepts from the sociology of the life course—a developing framework for the analysis of life paths through social structure. The theory posits a characteristic behavioral pathway in the aftermath of early sexual experiences from age-inappropriate sexualized behavior to resulting conflict with the social environment. In some cases, this dynamic process may lead to an active and risky sexual trajectory—and its attendant consequences—as well as a diversification of problem behavior as critical social bonds are threatened.

Learning and control processes account for different aspects of subsequent behavioral pathways in the life-course theory. In its typical criminological formulation, the learning perspective suggests that delinquency is the result of imitation and reinforcement of such behaviors through associations with delinquent individuals. In turn, the nature and extent of these associations will best predict delinquent outcomes (Akers 1973; Bandura 1973; Elliott, Huizinga, and Ageton 1985). Sources of reinforcement include the social rewards of participating in peer-group-supported delinquent activities as well as the intrinsic rewards of specific criminal behaviors (Wood et al. 1997). Reinforced behaviors, however, are always concrete—that is, participating in a rewarding burglary should increase the likelihood of future participation in *burglary* but not necessarily homicide. Unless all delinquent peer groups model deviant activities indiscriminately, the social learning perspective implies some degree of "specialization" in delinquent behavior.

The social control perspective suggests that delinquency is a result of attenuated ties to conventional persons and institutions (Hirschi 1969; Kornhauser 1978). Social control is achieved through effective socialization (development of the internal capacity to regulate action [Gottfredson and Hirschi 1990]) and the establishment of strong social bonds that enforce conformity to mainstream norms (Sampson and Laub 1993). In the absence of adequate controls, individuals are "free" to pursue short-term gratification resulting in a pattern of generalized deviance (Hirschi and Gottfredson 1994).

Childhood Sexual Experiences in the Short Term

The life-course approach developed in *Trauma or Transition* (Browning 1997) suggests that early sexual experiences must be contextualized in an unfolding life history in order to understand their effect across time. In essence, the life-course perspective suggests that the long-term effects of early sexual experiences stem from the nature of the sexual socialization that occurs during these relationships. First, early sexual experiences (focusing on those involving physical contact) reinforce particular sexual behaviors and "scripts" for sexual interaction. Second, as formative sexual socialization experiences, they typically fail to produce adaptive internal control over sexual impulses.

Sources of reinforcement include the nonsexual rewards for which sexual activity may be exchanged, including social approval (Finkelhor 1988), as well as the incipient sexual arousal experienced. These sources of reinforcement may affect the child's overall level of sexual interest. Moreover, reinforcement may extend to modes of interaction and specific behaviors as well as overall levels of sexual interest. Having few if any alternative sources of knowledge regarding sexuality, children who participate in early sexual relationships assimilate a model or script of sexual interaction on which future relationships are based (Gagnon and Simon 1973; Wyatt, Newcomb, and Riederle 1993). Elements of this model include, for instance, concrete sexual behaviors and sequences of acts constituting sexual interaction and same-gender sexuality (if the partner is of the same sex).

Early sexual activity, however, activates sexual impulses and interests without also providing the capacity to manage or regulate them. The early timing of reinforced sexual activity, combined with poorly developed sexual impulse controls, leads to developmentally inappropriate sexual behavior. Indeed, as noted earlier, the most consistently documented short-term effect of sexual abuse is heightened or age-inappropriate sexual behavior (Beitchman et al. 1991; Knutson 1995; Urquiza and Capra 1990). Accordingly, the life-course perspective points to "sexualization"—the discrepancy between sexual impulses and self-regulatory capacities—as the critical link between childhood sexual experiences and long-term adverse outcomes. Thus, in contrast to the notion of trauma, the life-course concept *transition* is employed to understand the effect of childhood sexual contacts. Aspects of this transition lead to a *unidirectional* increase in the level of sexual behavior. This expectation contrasts with the psychogenic hypothesis of a *bidirectional* effect on subsequent behavior.

It should be stated that *Trauma or Transition* (Browning 1997) does not argue that childhood sexual experiences are experienced as positive by the child involved. Indeed, short-term traumatic symptoms have been documented in some children who experienced early sexual contact. Gomes-Schwartz, Horowitz, and Cardarelli (1990), however, found that these symptoms tend to diminish over time. Sexualized behavior, on the other hand, appears to be a more enduring effect of early sexual experiences. The sexualization of the child induces vulnerability to subsequent experiences that are independently associated with long-term adverse outcomes. The long-term effects of childhood sexual experiences, then, are anchored in ensuing behavioral orientations rather than enduring emotional unrest.

Continuity and Cumulative Risk: Early Sexual Experiences in the Intermediate and Long Term

Precocious and heightened sexual interest in children constitutes a risk factor for subsequent maladaptive behavioral patterns. These behaviors, in turn, may serve as risk factors—in gender-specific ways—for still other negative outcomes. In this sense, the long-term effects of early sexual experiences are a result of the progressive accumulation and diversification of risk over time and should be understood as *indirect* (Finkelhor 1995; Finkelhor and Kendall-Tackett 1997; Rutter et al. 1994). This runs counter to the psychogenic expectation of a direct effect of abuse-related trauma on subsequent well-being.

First, heightened levels of interest in sexual activity and a willingness to act on that interest may lead to more rapid entry into sexual partnerships. For women, early adolescent intercourse is associated with multiple sex partners as well as pregnancy and childbirth during the teenage years (Roosa 1997). Higher numbers of sex partners increase the likelihood that a sexual encounter will be unwanted or forced and place individuals (of both genders) at increased risk of contracting a sexually transmitted disease (STD) (*SOS*, chap. 10). The latter, in turn, may affect subsequent sexual functioning. The tendency to enter sexual relationships more rapidly may account for a substantial proportion of the increase in number of sex partners observed among those who have early sexual experiences. Even if partnership duration were unaffected by early sexual experiences, the reduction in the length of the gap between partners would lead to an overall increase in the number of lifetime partners reported.

Second, rapid entry into sexual partnerships can escalate relationship intimacy. To the extent that individuals who enter sexual relationships more rapidly have, on average, less information about their nonsexual interpersonal compatibility, these relationships will tend to be less satisfying overall and shorter. Indeed, short-term partnerships (one month or less) are more likely than more stable relationships to have occurred between individuals who knew each other for shorter periods of time prior to sexual involvement (*SOS*, 1994). Men, in particular, derive significant benefits from stable intimate relationships (Gove 1972, 1973; Ross, Mirowsky, and Goldsteen 1990; chap. 6 below). Those who have early sexual experiences, however, are less likely to enjoy these benefits.

For men, the introduction of same-gender sexual scripts is also an important potential source of long-term effects for those who experience early sexual contact. Since a majority of adult-child sexual experiences occur with males (compared with a minority of peer sexual contacts), a possible effect of this experience may be sexual preference conflicts stemming from erotic impulses toward both genders. Long-term sexual adjustment problems may result from efforts to reconcile both same- and opposite-sex desire in a culture that emphasizes strict, bipolar categories of sexual orientation—particularly for men (Bem 1996). According to the expectations of this hypothesis, the problematic category—for men who experience early same-gender sexual contact—would be reported attraction to *both* sexes, not to one exclusively.

Social Control Implications of Early Sexual Experiences

The social learning component of the life-course approach allows us to explain the consistent pattern of increase in the level of sexual activity among those who experience childhood sexual contact. Understanding how active and risky sexual trajectories cumulatively affect well-being, we can begin to track the life paths and mechanisms through which childhood sexual experiences progressively curtail adult well-being. However, the social learning element of the model alone cannot account for the pattern of generalized problem behavior exhibited by those who report early sexual experiences, particularly boys. We address this issue by conceptualizing the effect of patterns of sexual activity established in the aftermath of childhood sexual experiences on the strength and effectiveness of informal social controls.

Sexualized behavior in the aftermath of childhood sexual experiences may lead to conflicts with parents, teachers, or peers, resulting in "child effects" on the likelihood of negative environmental responses (Lytton 1990). In one sample of abused children, Gomes-Schwartz et al. (1990) found that conflict between abused children and parents *worsened* between an initial postabuse evaluation and an eighteen-month follow-up interview, while, as noted earlier, affective disturbance declined over the same period. Consistent with social control theory, the diminished effectiveness of important informal sources of social control will result in a reduction in the incentive to avoid a range of deviant behaviors, including delinquency, drug use, and other analogous behaviors. This behavioral orientation may have consequences for long-term well-being, affecting the odds of marriage for men (Sampson and Laub 1993; Laub and Sampson 1993) and, in turn, adequate physical health (Ross, Mirowsky, and Goldsteen 1990; Umberson 1987), as well as successful educational and occupational outcomes (Caspi, Elder, and Bem 1987; Sampson and Laub 1993; Laub and Sampson 1993). Thus, the life-course perspective offers an explanation of variation in the experience of long-term effects that focuses on the extent to which life trajectories expose children to adversity.

4.3 Hypotheses

In the psychogenic perspective, efforts to resolve the emotional disturbance stemming from early sexual experiences take opposing forms—either compulsive sexual activity or avoidance of sexual stimuli. The life-course perspective, however, emphasizes the process of sexualization that produces a unidirectional tendency toward increased sexual activity in adolescence and adulthood. Hypotheses 1A and 1B state the competing psychogenic and life-course expectations regarding behavioral outcomes, respectively:

> HYPOTHESIS 1A. Adult-child sexual contact has a polarizing effect on subsequent sexual activity. That is, compared to no childhood sexual contact, adult-child sex (but not peer sexual contact) leads to heightened levels of subsequent sexual activity for some who experience it and *reduced* levels of sexual activity for others. Polarized behavioral orientations extend to specific acts experienced during early sexual activity—for example, those who experienced early oral sex will have polarized orientations toward this activity in adulthood.

> HYPOTHESIS 1B. Adult-child sexual contact *and* peer sexual contact have a unidirectional (positive) effect on subsequent levels of sexual activity and the recurrence of event-specific sexual activities in adulthood.

The life-course perspective suggests that heightened interest in sexual activity reinforced during early experiences may extend to concrete acts and characteristics of the childhood sexual relationship. This specialization in aspects of the early sexual event may be manifest in an increased likelihood of engaging in these behaviors later in life:

> HYPOTHESIS 2. Early childhood sexual experiences lead to specialization in characteristics of the early sexual contact. These include specific sexual activities (e.g., oral sex) as well as relationship characteristics (whether the partner was of the same gender).

Finally, the two perspectives differ with respect to their explanations for why some children are more adversely affected in adulthood than others.

The psychogenic explanation emphasizes the degree of trauma experienced during the sexual contact. More traumatic contacts are hypothesized to generate more intense psychic disturbance and more severe long-term consequences. Hypothesis 3A considers the association between the severity of the early sexual event and subsequent well-being (or the dose-response hypothesis):

> Hypothesis 3A. The likelihood of experiencing long-term effects from childhood sexual experiences (in the form of low overall well-being, relationship dissatisfaction, and sexual dysfunction) is dependent on the severity of the sexual contact. Adult-child sexual contacts will be associated with greater long-term negative effects than will peer sexual contacts.

The life-course perspective focuses attention on the *extent* to which childhood sexual contacts produce maladaptive cognitive models of sexuality, encourage risky sexual activity, and lead to associated problem behaviors in adolescence and early adulthood that diminish long-term prospects. Hypothesis 3B states the life-course expectation that subsequent life events mediate the effect of early sexual experiences on long-term well-being:

> Hypothesis 3B. Life trajectories established in the aftermath of childhood sexual experiences mediate the effect of early sex on adult well-being. Controlling for unstable or risky sexual trajectories and their consequences (including teen childbirth, STDs, and forced sex for women and generalized deviance, STDs, poor health, and the exclusivity of sex partner preferences for men), we should find no differences between those who report adult-child sexual contact, those who report peer sexual contact, and those who had no childhood sexual experiences in their likelihood of reporting the long-term effects noted above.

4.4 Data and Measures

Conducted in 1992, the National Health and Social Life Survey (NHSLS) is currently the only national probability sample to combine information on childhood sexual experiences with detailed accounts of the respondent's subsequent sexual history and current sexual practices. The richness of the NHSLS thus offers a unique opportunity to contextualize early sexual experiences within a life history. Indeed, the tendency of previous studies to ignore experiences occurring in the aftermath of adult-child sex may derive from the limited quality of the available data.

The retrospective nature of the NHSLS data on early sexual experiences, however, renders it vulnerable to three primary error-generating mechanisms: memory repression ("motivated" forgetting), memory failure ("conventional" forgetting), and refusal (or misrepresentation). The psychoanalytic concept of repression posits a psychodynamic process by which the memory of highly emotionally charged or traumatic events is transferred from the conscious to the unconscious mind. In this view, traumatic childhood sexual experiences are not forgotten in the conventional sense. Rather, while memory of the trauma is not available to the conscious mind, it is expressed in hysterical symptoms (Freud [1896] 1955; Freyd 1996). Bias due to memory repression would result in underreporting of those experiences that were most traumatic—and possible underestimation of the long-term negative effect of childhood sexual experiences.

Memory loss may also be a function of conventional processes of forgetting. The details of early childhood events can be difficult to remember, especially for older respondents, some of whom are recounting an event that took place forty to fifty years ago. Memories of early sexual experiences may also be subject to revision over time, as the meaning of the event changes within an evolving personal biography. Finally, a respondent may not disclose the event (or part of the event) to an interviewer because of the perceived social stigma that may accompany such a revelation.

Ultimately, we cannot know the extent to which particular sources of measurement error affect estimates of the prevalence or effects of early sexual experiences taken from the NHSLS data. However, an analysis of *partial* patterns of nonresponse in the NHSLS data (i.e., the tendency not to report components of an early sexual experience) does not provide evidence that events typically thought to be more traumatic (incestuous, repeated, penetrative, etc.) are associated with "partial amnesia" (Browning 1997).

Evidence that nonresponse may be a significant source of error, however, does exist. Some researchers have gathered evidence designed to measure the tendency not to report early sexual experiences. Williams (1994) identified a sample of women who had documented histories of sexual abuse during childhood by reviewing hospital records of all sexual abuse victims examined between April 1973 and June 1975. Williams contacted a total of 129 women some seventeen years later (when the women were between ages eighteen and thirty-one) in order to estimate the reporting rate of abusive childhood sexual experiences in adulthood. When asked about childhood sexual experiences, 38 percent of the sample of adult women did not report the "index" (or documented) abuse experience.[1]

The implications of measurement error in data on early sexual experiences differ, however, depending on the question addressed. Estimates of the *prevalence* of early sexual contacts, for instance, will clearly be biased downward if significant proportions of individuals do not recall or report such experiences. On the other hand, parameter estimates describing the long-term *effects* of early sexual experiences will be biased only if the proportion of respondents who disclose early sexual experiences is systematically different from that who had early sexual experiences but do not report them. That is, an analysis of long-term effects may be immune to bias generated by reporting failure. An interesting finding from Williams's study relevant to this issue is the degree of similarity between women who did and women who did not report the index sexual abuse. No statistically significant differences were found between the two groups with respect to the proportions reporting other sexual assaults (in addition to the index abuse), the experience of abortion, prostitution, or having a sexually transmitted disease (one summary variable indicating any of the three outcomes), alcohol or drug problems, or having a close friend or family member who was killed. Moreover, the two groups were remarkably similar with respect to characteristics of the event, including the use of physical force, the occurrence of penetrative sexual activity, and genital trauma.[2] The two groups, then, did not vary on a variety of important measures of subsequent behavior and well-being and differed only marginally with respect to characteristics of the event. Although Williams's findings call into question the accuracy of prevalence estimates drawn from self-reported data, they do not offer evidence that an analysis of long-term effects will be subject to significant error. Unfortunately, similar investigations of retrospective reporting of early sexual contacts among men have not been undertaken.

Acknowledging the potential for measurement error, the NHSLS took a number of steps to promote accuracy and candor in respondents' reports of their early sexual experiences. First, questions regarding early sexual experiences were not asked until well into the interview. Inquiries into childhood, adolescent, and forced sexual experiences were placed in section 8 of a ten-section questionnaire. At this stage of the interview, respondents had already discussed intimate details of their sex lives, reducing the marginal social cost of further revelations. Second, while memory problems are difficult to surmount, the survey avoided unduly taxing or ambiguous questions concerning the details of the event. Evidence also exists that respondents were generally willing to discuss sensitive issues relating to sexuality. Nearly 80 percent of the initial sample responded to the survey—a high response rate even for surveys not oriented toward sensitive behavior. Despite the retrospective nature of the reports and the inevitably lower-bound estimates derived from them, the accuracy of the data gathered in the NHSLS, particularly for an analysis of early sexual experience effects, should be considered exceptionally high.

Construction of Early Sexual Contact Variables

The NHSLS asked respondents (face to face) whether they had been touched sexually before puberty or the age of twelve or thirteen. If a positive response was given, the respondent was asked a number of questions about the experience, including the age of the respondent and the partner when the sexual contact began and ended, what happened sexually (specific acts), the frequency of contact, the relationship of the respondent to the partner, and whether the respondent experienced sexual contact with anyone else during childhood. If the respondent was touched by more than one person, comparable summary information was requested regarding those experiences.[3] Adult-child sexual contact was defined as any genital fondling or oral, vaginal, or anal sex before age fourteen with a partner who was at least four years older than the respondent and no younger than age fourteen. By this definition, 12 percent of women and 6 percent of men reported experiencing sexual contact with an adult during childhood.

Childhood sexual experiences were also partitioned on the basis of the severity of the event. Early sexual experiences were assigned a severity score based on the number of the following characteristics reported: (1) the type of sexual contact that occurred: oral, vaginal, or anal sex versus only fondling of the genitals; (2) whether the partner was a father/stepfather (for women) or relative/stepfather (for men); (3) the number of times sexual contact occurred: many times versus a few times or only once; (4) the number of individuals with whom contact occurred: two or more versus one; and (5) the age of the respondent when the sexual contact began: nine or younger versus ten to thirteen.[4]

We also constructed a variable indicating whether the respondent reported experiencing childhood sexual contact with a peer but not with an adult. Respondents were coded as having experienced *peer* or *mildly asymmetrical* contact if they reported being touched sexually only by another child under age fourteen while also a child. These events were distinguished exclusively by the age of the parties involved, not by any other aspect of the sexual contact. By this definition, 4 percent of men and 1 percent of women reported a sexual experience with another peer during childhood. While, at first glance, this proportion appears low, it should be emphasized that the wording of the filter question " . . . did anyone touch you sexually?" (*SOS*, 650) was intended to capture events in which a partner or partners engaged in overtly sexual behavior with the respondent during childhood. It is reasonable to expect that a relatively small number of respondents would have experienced explicitly sexual contact initiated by another child age thirteen or under. Moreover, respondents who reported sexual contacts with peers *and* adults were not included in these proportions (4 percent of women and 9 percent of men reported any peer sexual contact). Unfortunately, because of the low number of women who reported only peer sexual contacts, analysis of this experience independent from that of adult-child sexual contact was not feasible for this group. Consequently, only peer sexual contacts reported by men were analyzed. Finally, variables measuring the occurrence of oral sex during the early event (occurrence vs. nonoccurrence) and the gender of the sex partner (at least one male partner vs. no male partners during childhood) were constructed.

Dependent Measures

Sexual Behavior Measures. A set of items measuring patterns of sexual activity in the aftermath of early sex were constructed to test the hypothesis of a bipolar versus a unidirectional behavioral response to early sexual experiences. Three category outcome variables were constructed, measuring age at first intercourse (nineteen or over/never, sixteen to eighteen, or younger than sixteen), number of sex partners in the last year (zero, one, and two or more), number of partners in the last five years (zero or one, two to three, and four or more), and number of partners since age eighteen (women: zero to two, three to six, and seven or more; men: zero to two, three to eight, and nine or more).[5] Measures of the tendency to engage in oral sex (both passive and active) with a primary partner in the last year (never, sometimes/rarely, always/usually) were also constructed.

Well-being. A second set of outcomes attempts to assess the respondent's well-being both generally and with respect to current intimate relationships. The overall measure of well-being was based on an item inquiring into the general level of happiness the respondent experienced in the last year. The item asks the respondent, "Generally, how happy have you been with your personal life during the past 12 months? Have you been . . . Extremely happy, . . . Very happy most of the time, . . . Generally satisfied, pleased, . . . Sometimes fairly unhappy, or . . . Unhappy most of the time?" (*SOS,* 659). The well-being measure collapses the two categories at the low end of the happiness scale owing to small numbers of cases. The measure of relationship satisfaction was constructed on the basis of responses to a question asking how emotionally satisfied the respondent felt with his or her current or "primary" partner in the last year. The respondent was asked, "How emotionally satisfying did you find your relationship with (PARTNER) to be, extremely satisfying, very satisfying, moderately satisfying, slightly satisfying, or not at all satisfying?" (*SOS,* 627). Again, the two low-satisfaction categories were collapsed. For both outcomes, higher categories represent lesser well-being.

Sexual Dysfunction.   The NHSLS asked a number of questions designed to tap the respondent's level of dysfunction along both physical and emotional dimensions of sexual adjustment (for an extended analysis of these data, see chap. 10 below). A latent class analysis (LCA) of a subset of these items identified typical categories of sexual dysfunction.[6] The content of the latent class solutions is consistent with clinical descriptions of typical constellations of symptoms and their associated features, if not precisely correspondent with specific sexual disorders. Precise correspondence, however, may be unlikely in a description of the actual experience of dysfunction. Clinical diagnosis of sexual dysfunction isolates phases of the sexual response cycle and assesses the level of disturbance therein. Accordingly, disorders associated with each phase have been identified—disorders of the *desire* phase (e.g., hypoactive sexual desire disorder, sexual aversion disorder), the *excitement* phase (e.g., female sexual arousal disorder, male erectile disorder), and the *orgasm* phase (orgasmic disorder). A separate condition describes the experience of pain during intercourse (dyspareunia). Clearly, however, disturbances in one phase of the sexual response cycle may lead to, or interact with, problems in other phases. For example, difficulties experiencing orgasm may diminish interest in sexual activity, and the experience of pain may affect all phases of the sexual response cycle (APA 1994; Wincze and Carey 1991).

For women, the four-class solution proved to be the most efficient balance between parsimony and goodness of fit. The analysis yielded a class characterized by little or no dysfunction, a class characterized by a lack of interest in sex and some problems with orgasm (sexual *desire* dysfunction), a class reporting little decrease in level of sexual interest but experiencing problems with lubrication and pain during intercourse (sexual *response* dysfunction), and, finally, a highly dysfunctional class characterized by both physical problems (pain, poor lubrication) and emotional problems (stress and emotions interfering with sex) during sexual activity (high dysfunction).

For men, the best-fitting latent class solution produced three classes— one characterized by little or no sexual dysfunction, a second characterized by a high probability of anxiety interfering with sexual activity, and a third, highly dysfunctional class (including problems achieving erection, adverse emotional responses to sexuality, and diminished pleasure).

Independent Measures

Covariates included in the analyses were designed to capture background factors that are potentially associated with the occurrence of early sexual contacts as well as sexually active careers and subsequent well-being. These include race (black, Hispanic vs. white), cohort (1943–52, 1953–62,

1963–72 vs. 1933–42), mother's education (some high school, finished high school vs. less than high school), mother's work status when the respondent was age fourteen (working vs. not working), family structure at age fourteen (intact vs. nonintact), the respondent's number of siblings, and the type of place in which the respondent was living at age fourteen (rural, small town, medium-sized city/suburb, or large city).

Intervening Measures

For women, we focused on the intervening effect of four sexual trajectory variables: the occurrence of childbirth at age eighteen or younger, the number of sex partners after age eighteen (zero to one, two to ten, eleven to twenty, or twenty-one or more), the lifetime occurrence of a sexually transmitted disease, and the occurrence of forced sex after childhood (never, once, or more than once). For men, four categories of measures were tested for the extent to which they mediate the long-term effect of childhood sexual experiences: (1) two measures of adolescent deviance: an item indicating whether the respondent had ever spent at least one night in jail[7] and a dichotomous item measuring whether the respondent left home before age eighteen; (2) two variables measuring the stability and consequences of the respondent's sexual trajectory: a dichotomous item measuring whether the respondent reported sex with a stranger to be very or somewhat appealing versus not or not at all appealing[8] and a measure of the experience of STD-related symptoms in the last twelve months (including painful or difficult urination, painful intercourse, lesions or sores in the genital area, or intense chronic itching of genital area);[9] and (3) marital status (whether the respondent was currently married) and physical health status (whether the respondent self-reported fair or poor health in the last twelve months).

Finally, a measure of the exclusivity of sexual preference with regard to the gender of the respondent's sex partners was constructed. The base category for the variable is exclusive opposite-sex attraction. Categories 2 and 3 represent sexual attraction toward both sexes and exclusive *same-gender* sexual attraction, respectively. This variable was constructed out of two items: one measuring the respondent's reported attraction to only women, mostly women, both women and men, mostly men, or only men and another asking the respondent whether he found having sex with someone of the same sex very appealing, somewhat appealing, not appealing, or not at all appealing. The advantage of the latter construction of the response categories was that it allowed the respondent to mark a negative category but to indicate some distance from the extreme negative category. This is where we might expect men who are experiencing some conflict about their sexual preference to fall. Thus, those men who reported attraction to the opposite sex *as well as* any attraction to members of the same sex *or* who marked any category of appeal for same-sex sexual activity other than the extreme category (not at all) were coded as having nonexclusive sexual preference with regard to gender of partner.

Tables 4.2A/4.2B and 4.3A/4.3B provide univariate descriptive statistics for variables in the analysis and bivariate associations between childhood sexual experience and subsequent outcomes, respectively. Tables 4.3A/

Table 4.2A Definitions, Means, and Standard Deviations for Background Variables in the Analysis (Women)

Variables	Mean	S.D.	N
Background characteristics			
Race			1,921
White	.697	.460	
Black	.178	.383	
Hispanic	.096	.294	
Cohort			1,919
1933–42	.160	.367	
1943–52	.221	.415	
1953–62	.324	.468	
1963–74	.295	.456	
Mother's education			1,921
Less than high school	.210	.408	
High school	.168	.374	
More than high school	.568	.495	
Missing	.054	.225	
Mother worked for pay when respondent was 14			1,914
Yes	.466	.499	
No	.507	.500	
Missing	.027	.161	
Family structure at age 14			1,920
Respondent lived with both own parents	.714	.452	
Type of place respondent lived in at age 14			1,912
Rural	.194	.396	
Small town	.343	.475	
Medium-size city/suburb	.283	.451	
Large city	.180	.385	
Number of siblings	3.806	2.978	1,914
Type of childhood sexual interaction			1,664
None	.869	.338	
Peer	.010	.069	
Adult-child	.126	.332	

Note: Univariate statistics for background variables are calculated including the oversample of blacks and Hispanics ($N = 3,432$). Childhood sexual interaction statistics are calculated using only the cross section.

Table 4.2B Definitions, Means, and Standard Deviations for Background Variables in the Analysis (Men)

Variables	Mean	S.D.	N
Background characteristics			
Race			1,509
White	.738	.440	
Black	.138	.345	
Hispanic	.091	.287	
Cohort			1,508
1933–42	.141	.348	
1943–52	.227	.419	
1953–62	.306	.461	
1963–74	.326	.469	
Mother's education			1,511
Less than high school	.179	.384	
High school	.143	.350	
More than high school	.625	.484	
Missing	.052	.223	
Mother worked for pay when respondent was 14			1,511
Yes	.483	.500	
No	.473	.499	
Missing	.044	.204	
Family structure at age 14			1,508
Respondent lived with both own parents	.733	.443	
Type of place respondent lived in at age 14			1,506
Rural	.218	.413	
Small town	.307	.462	
Medium-size city/suburb	.298	.458	
Large city	.176	.381	
Number of siblings	3.721	3.182	1,503
Type of childhood sexual interaction			1,411
None	.899	.302	
Peer	.038	.190	
Adult-child	.064	.244	

Note: Univariate statistics for background variables are calculated including the oversample of blacks and Hispanics ($N = 3,432$). Childhood sexual interaction statistics are calculated using only the cross section.

4.3B support the findings of previous research that adverse outcomes in adulthood are more likely given an adult-child sexual experience but are by no means inevitable. For women, adult-child sexual contact is associated at the bivariate level with all three of the adverse outcomes considered. Compared with those who reported no childhood sexual interactions, women who experienced adult-child sex reported slightly elevated rates of sexual desire dysfunction (21 vs. 17 percent) and sexual response

Table 4.3A Definitions, Means, Standard Deviations, and Bivariate Associations with Childhood Sexual Experience for Sexual Behavior, Intervening, and Adult Well-Being Variables in the Analysis (Women)

Variables	Univariate Statistics		Childhood Sexual Contact		N
	Mean	S.D.	None	Adult-Child	
Sexual behavior outcomes					
Time of first intercourse					1,716
19 or older	.378	.485	.399	.250	
16–18	.484	.500	.475	.531	
Under 16	.137	.344	.126	.219	
Number of partners since age 18					1,647
0–2	.507	.500	.541	.364	
3–8	.310	.463	.308	.308	
9 or more	.182	.386	.154	.328	
Number of partners in last 5 years					1,664
0–1	.680	.466	.694	.627	
2–3	.196	.397	.198	.182	
4 or more	.123	.328	.108	.191	
Number of partners in last year					1,743
0	.136	.343	.139	.110	
1	.747	.435	.757	.719	
2 or more	.117	.322	.104	.171	
Passive oral sex with partner in last year					1,464
Frequently	.145	.353	.141	.159	
Occasionally	.520	.500	.507	.577	
Never	.334	.472	.352	.264	
Active oral sex with partner in last year					1,463
Frequently	.124	.329	.114	.148	
Occasionally	.524	.500	.513	.582	
Never	.352	.478	.373	.269	
Intervening variables					
Childbirth before age 19	.236	.425	.210	.281	1,744
Number of sex partners since age 18					1,647
0 or 1	.345	.476	.371	.237	
2–10	.563	.496	.560	.535	
11–20	.060	.237	.046	.147	
20 or more	.032	.176	.023	.081	
STD in lifetime	.177	.382	.155	.304	1,693
Coerced sexual experience					1,725
Never forced after childhood	.850	.357	.879	.655	
Forced once after age 13	.109	.312	.092	.218	
Forced more than once after age 13	.041	.199	.029	.126	

(continued)

Table 4.3A (continued)

Variables	Univariate Statistics		Childhood Sexual Contact		
	Mean	S.D.	None	Adult-Child	N
Adult well-being					
Latent sexual dysfunction classes					1,599
Low dysfunction	.690	.462	.712	.555	
Sexual desire dysfunction	.175	.380	.171	.205	
Sexual response dysfunction	.067	.250	.063	.095	
High dysfunction	.068	.252	.054	.145	
Overall well-being					1,741
Extremely happy	.164	.371	.169	.139	
Very happy	.407	.491	.428	.325	
Generally satisfied	.290	.454	.278	.349	
Unhappy	.139	.346	.125	.187	
Emotional satisfaction in relationship					1,482
Extremely satisfied	.385	.487	.394	.342	
Very satisfied	.377	.485	.389	.304	
Moderately satisfied	.166	.372	.153	.239	
Slightly/not satisfied	.071	.258	.065	.114	

Note: Univariate descriptive statistics and *N*'s are calculated using only the cross section (*N* = 3,159).

dysfunction (10 vs. 6 percent) and significantly elevated rates of high dysfunction (15 vs. 5 percent). The well-being measures indicate a similar pattern of association. Of women who reported adult-child sex, 19 percent (vs. 13 percent of those reporting no childhood sexual interaction) reported low levels of happiness in the last year, and 35 percent (vs. 22 percent) reported moderate or lower levels of relationship satisfaction.

Perhaps the most striking pattern revealed in table 4.3B (men) is the consistently comparable elevations in tendency to experience both heightened sexual behavior and adverse adult outcomes among men who report sexual contact with a peer during childhood but not with an adult and those who reported adult-child sex. While roughly 11 percent of those men who reported no childhood sexual interaction reported low levels of happiness, 22 percent of those who reported adult-child sex and 16 percent of those who experienced peer sexual contact did so. Similarly, 19 percent of men who reported no childhood sexual interaction said that they were moderately or less satisfied with the current relationship, while 33 and 35 percent of those who reported adult-child and peer sexual contact, respectively, reported lower emotional satisfaction with their primary partner in the last year. Finally, one in ten of those who reported no early

Table 4.3B Definitions, Means, Standard Deviations, and Bivariate Associations with Childhood Sexual Experience for Sexual Behavior, Intervening, and Adult Well-Being Variables in the Analysis (Men)

Variables	Univariate Statistics		Childhood Sexual Contact			
	Mean	S.D.	None	Adult-Child	Peer	N
Sexual behavior outcomes						
Time of first intercourse						1,349
19 or older	.321	.467	.328	.324	.220	
16–18	.453	.498	.458	.338	.439	
Under 16	.226	.418	.215	.338	.342	
Number of partners since age 18						1,339
0–2	.320	.467	.350	.182	.106	
3–8	.309	.462	.317	.260	.213	
9 or more	.371	.483	.333	.558	.681	
Number of partners in last 5 years						1,329
0–1	.529	.499	.555	.405	.292	
2–3	.214	.410	.216	.215	.229	
4 or more	.257	.437	.230	.380	.479	
Number of partners in last year						1,406
0	.099	.298	.977	.159	.100	
1	.667	.471	.698	.463	.500	
2 or more	.234	.423	.204	.378	.400	
Passive oral sex with partner in last year						1,230
Frequently	.189	.391	.180	.284	.233	
Occasionally	.507	.500	.505	.493	.512	
Never	.304	.460	.315	.224	.256	
Active oral sex with partner in last year						1,228
Frequently	.207	.405	.193	.269	.326	
Occasionally	.496	.500	.494	.522	.512	
Never	.297	.297	.313	.209	.163	
Intervening variables						
Left home at 17 or younger	.195	.396	.180	.317	.320	1,408
Spent at least one night in jail	.229	.421	.208	.366	.360	1,407
Fair or poor health last year	.099	.298	.092	.110	.200	1,408
Currently married	.519	.500	.539	.407	.280	1,394
STD symptoms last year	.093	.291	.079	.173	.265	1,386
Find anonymous sex appealing	.312	.464	.289	.390	.540	1,402
Exclusivity of sexual preference						1,399
Attracted only to women	.878	.328	.898	.695	.820	
Attracted to both genders	.099	.298	.086	.232	.120	
Attracted only to men	.024	.152	.017	.073	.060	
Adult well-being						
Latent sexual dysfunction classes						1,341
Low dysfunction	.775	.418	.796	.641	.652	
Anxiety interfered with sex	.107	.309	.102	.167	.174	
High dysfunction	.119	.323	.102	.192	.174	

(continued)

Table 4.3B (continued)

| | Univariate Statistics | | Childhood Sexual Contact | | | |
Variables	Mean	S.D.	None	Adult-Child	Peer	N
Overall well-being						1,407
Extremely happy	.178	.383	.187	.122	.120	
Very happy	.407	.491	.426	.281	.240	
Generally satisfied	.294	.456	.280	.378	.480	
Unhappy	.122	.327	.107	.220	.160	
Emotional satisfaction in relationship						1,245
Extremely satisfied	.414	.493	.429	.328	.326	
Very satisfied	.379	.485	.385	.343	.326	
Moderately satisfied	.161	.367	.143	.254	.302	
Slightly/not satisfied	.046	.209	.043	.075	.047	

Note: Univariate descriptive statistics and *N*'s are calculated using only the cross section (*N* = 3,159).

sexual contact reported anxiety interfering with sexual activity, and the same proportion reported high dysfunction in the last year. Roughly 18 percent of those who experienced both peer and adult-child sexual contact reported sexually related anxiety in the last year, and comparable proportions reported high dysfunction. We examine multivariate patterns of association between childhood sexual experiences and subsequent outcomes in the analyses to follow.

4.5 Analyses and Results

In order to adjudicate between the psychogenic hypothesis that adult-child sexual contact has a polarizing effect on sexual behavior outcomes (hypothesis 1A) and the life-course expectation of a unidirectional positive effect of both peer and adult-child sexual experiences on subsequent sexual behavior (hypothesis 1B), we examined the effect of early sex on four trichotomous outcome variables measuring the extent of sexual activity during specific phases of the respondent's life course and two measures of the frequency of oral sex in the last year. We predicted the latter two outcomes using a measure of whether the respondent reported the occurrence of oral sex during childhood, a childhood sexual event without oral sex, or no childhood sexual interaction.

Multinomial logit analyses were performed decomposing the coefficients measuring the effect of childhood sexual experiences into linear and quadratic components. The linear component measures the extent to which peer or adult-child sexual contact increases the odds of falling in

the higher categories (representing more sexually active or precocious behavior) of each outcome when compared with children who report no
childhood sexual contact. The quadratic effect measures the extent to
which these experiences increase the odds of falling into each of the two
extreme categories (compared with the middle category).[10] Table 4.4 presents the results of likelihood ratio χ^2 comparisons of models fitting only
the linear effect of childhood sexual experiences with models including
only background characteristics (col. 1) and of models fitting both the
linear and the quadratic effects of childhood sexual contacts with models
fitting only the linear effects (col. 2). The life-course perspective predicts
significant improvements in fit with the inclusion of linear effects alone
(but not quadratic effects), while significant improvements in model fit
with the inclusion of quadratic terms conform to the expectations of the
psychogenic perspective.

Consistent with the expectations of the life-course perspective, including the linear effects of adult-child sex (or the occurrence of early sexual
events without and with oral sex), for women, resulted in significant improvements in model fit for all measures except the frequency of passive
oral sex last year. All coefficients were positively associated with the behavioral outcomes. Including quadratic effects, moreover, did not improve
the fit of the model for any of the outcomes considered. For men, including the linear effects of both peer and adult-child sexual contact resulted
in significant improvements in model fit for models of number of sex partners since age eighteen, in the last five years, and in the last year. Linear
effects of childhood sexual experiences with and without the occurrence
of oral sex improved the fit of models of both measures of frequency of
oral sex in the last year. The linear effects of peer sexual contacts were
positive and significant for all four sex partner outcomes, while adult-child
sex was positively and significantly associated with number of partners
since age eighteen and in the last five years. The occurrence of childhood
sexual contacts without and with oral sex was significantly and positively
associated with the occurrence of both passive and active oral sex in the
last year.

In contrast to the expectations of the psychogenic perspective, fitting
the quadratic term did not result in significant improvements in fit for
models of age at first intercourse, number of sex partners since age eighteen, number of sex partners in the last five years, or frequency of passive
or active oral sex last year, for men. Only in the case of number of sex
partners in the last year did the quadratic term result in a significant
change in likelihood ratio χ^2. Yet an analysis of coefficients for adult-child
and peer sexual contacts indicated that both have significant quadratic
effects on number of sex partners last year. This finding suggests that polarized sexual activity in the last year may be more a function of an un-

Table 4.4 Likelihood Ratio χ^2 Comparison for Multinomial Logit Models of Sexual Behavior Outcomes

Construction of Child Sex Parameter and Behavioral Outcome	Likelihood Ratio χ^2 Comparison[a]	
	$\Delta\chi^2$: Model 2 vs. Model 1	$\Delta\chi^2$: Model 3 vs. Model 2
Women		
Adult-child vs. no child sex:		
Age at first intercourse (< 16, 16–18, 19+/never)	25.10**	.00
Number of partners since 18 (0–2, 3–8, 9+)	49.79**	3.08
Number of partners in last 5 years (0–1, 2–4, 5+)	12.35**	2.45
Number of partners last year (0, 1, 2+)	15.23**	3.45
Childhood oral sex, childhood sex without oral sex, vs. no child sex:		
Active oral sex last year (frequently, occasionally, never)	11.01**	1.77
Passive oral sex last year (frequently, occasionally, never)	3.63	2.30
Men		
Adult-child vs. no child sex:		
Age at first intercourse (< 16, 16–18, 19+/never)	3.49	2.66
Number of partners since 18 (0–2, 3–8, 9+)	38.57**	.60
Number of partners in last 5 years (0–1, 2–4, 5+)	17.80**	.05
Number of partners last year (0, 1, 2+)	6.15*	7.29*
Childhood oral sex, childhood sex without oral sex, vs. no child sex:		
Active oral sex last year (frequently, occasionally, never)	9.07*	2.48
Passive oral sex last year (frequently, occasionally, never)	10.83**	.89

Note: Model 1: Sexual behavior outcome regressed on background factors only (see below). Model 2: Sexual behavior outcome regressed on background factors and linear effects of childhood sexual experience. Model 3: Sexual behavior outcome regressed on background factors and both linear and quadratic effects of childhood sexual experience.
[a]Likelihood ratio χ^2 comparisons tests are conducted on 1 degree of freedom for women and 2 degrees of freedom for men (since effects of both peer and adult-child sex are included in models 2 and 3). The models control for race (white, black, Hispanic), cohort (1933–42, 1943–52, 1953–62, 1963–74), mother's education (less than high school, high school, more than high school), mother's work status (working for pay when respondent was 14 or not), family structure at age 14 (intact vs. nonintact), the type of place respondent lived at age 14 (rural, small town, medium-sized city/suburb, or large city), and respondent's number of siblings.
*$p < .05$ (two-tailed tests).
**$p < .01$ (two-tailed tests).

stable sexual career rather than opposing strategies to cope with lingering emotional disturbance. Over the life course, sexual careers marked by less relationship stability and a tendency to avoid marriage may lead to both an increasingly intermittent pattern of sexual partnering and higher probabilities of having multiple partners simultaneously. Measured over a relatively short time span, then, these men are more likely to appear sexually inactive *or* highly sexually active. In conformity with the expectations of the life-course perspective, linear effects of early sexual experience were strong and positive, resulting in consistent improvements in goodness of fit across outcomes.

We next considered hypothesis 2—the extent to which individuals specialize in sexual behaviors and relationship characteristics specific to the early sexual contact. Tables 4.5A and 4.5B report the results of analyses examining this tendency through modeling the effect of the reported occurrence of oral and same-gender sex during early sexual contact on their occurrence or appeal in adulthood.[11] In order to isolate the effect of the specific characteristic itself on subsequent orientations most effectively, we compared early sexual experiences where the event occurred both to other cases of early sexual contact as well as to those reporting no early sex (the omitted category). For men, the magnitude of the effect of events in which the behavior did occur is considerably larger than the effect of events in which it did not for the frequent occurrence of oral sex last year and the appeal of same-gender sex. For women, this pattern holds for all three outcomes (active and passive oral sex and same-gender sex).

Because of the paucity of measures of both deviance and parental and other informal attachments during youth, the effect of early sexual experience on the manifestation of diversity in deviant behavior could not be considered as effectively with the NHSLS. The life-course perspective suggests that the generalization of deviant behavior in adolescence is an indirect effect of attenuation of critical social bonds in the aftermath of early sex, not an expression of the emotional disturbance or strain induced by traumatic childhood sexual contact. Although the specific mechanism linking early sex with measures of deviance could not be tested using the NHSLS, models predicting ever having spent a night in jail and leaving home early (analyses not presented), for men, indicate that both adult-child and peer sexual contact are associated with these events (at comparable magnitudes and levels of significance). This finding warrants examination of the potential mediating effect of deviance on long-term well-being.

In contrast to the life-course focus on the events that may mediate the effect of early sex, the psychogenic perspective points to the severity of the childhood sexual experience as the key variable accounting for differ-

Table 4.5A Adult Oral Sex Activity and Appeal of Same-Gender Sex by Childhood
Occurrence and Background Characteristics (Logistic Regression Models) (Women)

Characteristics of Sexual Contact (vs. No Child Sexual Contact)	Frequent Occurrence of Active Oral Sex (Last Year)	Frequent Occurrence of Passive Oral Sex (Last Year)	Appeal of Same-Gender Sex
Oral sex:			
Did not occur	.328	.055	. . .
	(.206)	(.205)	
Occurred	1.169*	1.096*	. . .
	(.475)	(.460)	
Same-gender sex:			
Did not occur	. . .	. . .	1.090**
			(.236)
Occurred	. . .	. . .	2.237**
			(.450)
Total N	1,582	1,583	1,891

Note: Coefficients are log-odds ratios. Numbers in parentheses are standard errors. The
models control for race (white, black, Hispanic), cohort (1933–42, 1943–52, 1953–62,
1963–74), mother's education (less than high school, high school, more than high school),
mother's work status (working for pay when respondent was 14 or not), family structure
at age 14 (intact vs. nonintact), the type of place respondent lived at age 14 (rural, small
town, medium-sized city/suburb, or large city), and respondent's number of siblings.
*$p < .05$ (two-tailed test).
**$p < .01$ (two-tailed test).

ences in adult well-being. To examine this dose-response hypothesis (3A),
a cumulative measure of event severity (the number of severe characteristics reported by the respondent, ranging from zero to five) was included
in a multinomial logit model predicting sexual dysfunction latent class
membership and two ordered logit models predicting the four-category
well-being and relationship-satisfaction measures (see tables 4.6A and
4.6B).[12] For both genders, the cumulative severity measure was not a significant predictor of sexual dysfunction in the multinomial logit model,
nor was it in either of the ordered logit models predicting levels of well-
being and emotional satisfaction with the primary partner. The results
of these analyses are not consistent with the psychogenic hypothesis that
severity of early sexual experience accounts for variation in adult well-
being.[13]

Finally, tables 4.7A/4.7B and 4.8A/4.8B report the results of multinomial logit and ordered logit models measuring the effects of both peer and
adult-child sexual contact as well as the intervening variables described
above on the three measures of adult adjustment.[14] For each outcome considered, an initial model is fit examining the effect of childhood sexual
experience controlling for background factors (col. 1 under each outcome

Table 4.5B Adult Oral Sex Activity and Appeal of Same-Gender Sex by Childhood Occurrence and Background Characteristics (Logistic Regression Models) (Men)

Characteristics of Sexual Contact (vs. No Child Sexual Contact)	Frequent Occurrence of Active Oral Sex (Last Year)	Frequent Occurrence of Passive Oral Sex (Last Year)	Appeal of Same-Gender Sex
Oral sex:			
Did not occur	.242	.357	. . .
	(.202)	(.201)	
Occurred	1.365**	.349	. . .
	(.366)	(.419)	
Same-gender sex:			
Did not occur	. . .	. . .	−.570
			(.296)
Occurred	. . .	. . .	1.267**
			(.255)
Total N	1,304	1,306	1,496

Note: Coefficients are log-odds ratios. Numbers in parentheses are standard errors. The models control for race (white, black, Hispanic), cohort (1933–42, 1943–52, 1953–62, 1963–74), mother's education (less than high school, high school, more than high school), mother's work status (working for pay when respondent was 14 or not), family structure at age 14 (intact vs. nonintact), the type of place respondent lived at age 14 (rural, small town, medium-sized city/suburb, or large city), and respondent's number of siblings.
*$p < .05$ (two-tailed test).
**$p < .01$ (two-tailed test).

heading). For women, adult-child sex is associated with overall well-being and relationship satisfaction as well as all three sexual dysfunction latent classes. For men, adult-child sex is also associated with all the adult adjustment variables. Moreover, consistent with the life-course perspective, peer sexual contacts were associated with both adult overall well-being and high sexual dysfunction, although the coefficients predicting emotional satisfaction and anxiety during sexual activity did not reach conventional levels of significance. These results also run counter to the psychogenic assumption that those who experience sexual contacts with age peers will not manifest similar adult outcomes.

Analyses examining the life-course explanation of variation in the long-term effects of childhood sexual experience are presented in columns 2 and 3 of tables 4.7A/4.7B and 4.8A/4.8B. Models under columns 2 and 3 add in intervening variables in order to examine their mediating effect on the outcome considered. For women, model 2 adds in measures of the occurrence of teen childbirth and number of sex partners since age eighteen, and model 3 adds the occurrence of sexually transmitted disease and forced sex. For men, model 2 adds in measures of leaving home early and delinquency, and model 3 adds marital and health status as well as sexual

Table 4.6A Adult Outcomes by Severity of Childhood Sexual Experiences and Background Characteristics (Multinomial and Ordered Logit Models) (Women)

Independent Variables	Sexual Dysfunction			Well-Being	
	Sexual Desire Dysfunction	Sexual Response Dysfunction	High Sexual Dysfunction	Low Overall Well-Being	Low Satisfaction with Partner
Number of severe characteristics	−.118	.143	.251	−.011	.043
	(.171)	(.217)	(.183)	(.110)	(.118)
Total *N*	. . .	. . .	202	212	186

Note: Sample restricted to those respondents reporting childhood sexual contact. Coefficients are log-odds ratios. Numbers in parentheses are standard errors. The models control for race (white, black, Hispanic), cohort (1933–42, 1943–52, 1953–62, 1963–74), mother's education (less than high school, high school, more than high school), mother's work status (working for pay when respondent was 14 or not), family structure at age 14 (intact vs. nonintact), the type of place respondent lived at age 14 (rural, small town, medium-sized city/suburb, or large city), and respondent's number of siblings.
$p < .05$ (two-tailed test).
$p < .01$ (two-tailed test).

Table 4.6B Adult Outcomes by Severity of Childhood Sexual Experience and Background Characteristics (Multinomial and Ordered Logit Models) (Men)

Independent Variables	Sexual Dysfunction		Well-Being	
	Anxiety Interfered with Sex	High Sexual Dysfunction	Low Overall Well-Being	Low Satisfaction with Partner
Number of severe characteristics	.381	.006	.142	.038
	(.235)	(.200)	(.127)	(.139)
Total *N*	. . .	165	173	149

Note: Sample restricted to those respondents reporting childhood sexual contact. Coefficients are log-odds ratios. Numbers in parentheses are standard errors. The models control for race (white, black, Hispanic), cohort (1933–42, 1943–52, 1953–62, 1963–74), mother's education (less than high school, high school, more than high school), mother's work status (working for pay when respondent was 14 or not), family structure at age 14 (intact vs. nonintact), the type of place respondent lived at age 14 (rural, small town, medium-sized city/suburb, or large city), and respondent's number of siblings.
$p < .05$ (two-tailed test).
$p < .01$ (two-tailed test).

Table 4.7A Adult Well-Being by Childhood Sexual Experience, Intervening Sexual Trajectory, and Background Characteristics (Ordered Logit Models) (Women)

| | Well-Being Last Year | | | | | |
| | Low Overall Well-Being | | | Low Satisfaction with Partner | | |
Independent Variables	(1)	(2)	(3)	(1)	(2)	(3)
Childhood sexual experience:						
Adult-child	.423**	.272	.202	.469**	.315	.245
	(.146)	(.149)	(.153)	(.160)	(.163)	(.167)
Sexual career:						
Childbirth before 19	...	.220	.212	...	.152	.158
		(.128)	(.129)		(.138)	(.136)
2–10 sex partners since 18	...	.406**	.355**	...	.475**	.430**
		(.105)	(.107)		(.117)	(.119)
11–20 sex partners since 18	...	.839**	.724**	...	1.136**	1.009**
		(.211)	(.220)		(.238)	(.247)
21 or more sex partners since 18	...	1.303**	1.129**	...	1.515**	1.303**
		(.311)	(.324)		(.336)	(.350)
Adverse events:						
Had at least one STD	...	...	.145	...	...	.127
			(.137)			(.148)
Forced sex once after age 13	...	...	.251	...	...	.165
			(.162)			(.173)
Forced sex more than once after age 13	...	...	.338	...	...	.500
			(.256)			(.269)

(continued)

Table 4.7A (continued)

	Well-Being Last Year					
	Low Overall Well-Being			Low Satisfaction with Partner		
Independent Variables	(1)	(2)	(3)	(1)	(2)	(3)
Threshold parameter estimates:						
θ_1	−1.695	−1.347	−1.343	−.807	−.453	−.448
θ_2	.294	.671	.679	.850	1.246	1.255
θ_3	1.916	2.325	2.338	2.288	2.713	2.727
Log-likelihood	−1,899.1	−1,880.7	−1,878.1	−1,537.9	−1,517.0	−1,514.5
df	16	20	23	16	20	23
N	1,493	1,493	1,493	1,274	1,274	1,274

Note: Coefficients are log-odds ratios. Numbers in parentheses are standard errors. The models control for race (white, black, Hispanic), cohort (1933–42, 1943–52, 1953–62, 1963–74), mother's education (less than high school, high school, more than high school), mother's work status (working for pay when respondent was 14 or not), family structure at age 14 (intact vs. nonintact), the type of place respondent lived at age 14 (rural, small town, medium-sized city/suburb, or large city), and respondent's number of siblings.

*$p < .05$ (two-tailed test).

**$p < .01$ (two-tailed test).

Table 4.7B Adult Well-Being by Childhood Sexual Experience, Intervening Sexual Trajectory, and Background Characteristics (Ordered Logit Models) (Men)

	Well-Being Last Year					
	Low Overall Well-Being			Low Satisfaction with Primary Partner		
Independent Variables	(1)	(2)	(3)	(1)	(2)	(3)
Childhood sexual experience:						
Peer	.650*	.543*	.015	.542	.457	.040
	(.259)	(.261)	(.270)	(.284)	(.287)	(.294)
Adult-child	.841**	.755**	.557*	.623**	.543*	.425
	(.212)	(.214)	(.220)	(.238)	(.241)	(.247)
Generalized deviance:						
Spent a night in jail	...	.488**	.334	...	.479**	.329*
		(.125)	(.127)		(.131)	(.134)
Left home at 17 or younger	...	.222	.223	...	.160	.149
		(.133)	(.134)		(.141)	(.142)
Marital/health status and sexual trajectory:						
Currently married	...	...	-.869**	...	...	-.983**
			(.117)			(.128)
Poor health	...	...	.786**	...	...	.208
			(.183)			(.207)
STD symptomatology	...	...	.499**	...	...	.054
			(.183)			(.203)
Anonymous sex appealing	...	...	.425**	...	...	.596**
			(.114)			(.121)

(continued)

Table 4.7B (continued)

	Well-Being Last Year					
	Low Overall Well-Being			Low Satisfaction with Primary Partner		
Independent Variables	(1)	(2)	(3)	(1)	(2)	(3)
Sexual preference exclusivity:						
Attracted to both genders	...	...	.167	...	...	.304
			(.169)			(.186)
Attracted to men only	...	...	.643	...	...	-.187
			(.337)			(.418)
Threshold parameter estimates:						
θ_1	-1.732	-1.615	-2.099	.312	.457	-.235
θ_2	.203	.339	-.038	2.044	2.205	1.627
θ_3	1.963	2.119	1.860	3.797	3.969	3.455
Log-likelihood	-1,678.3	-1,668.6	-1,612.6	-1,366.4	-1,358.6	-1,310.3
df	17	19	25	17	19	25
N	1,330	1,330	1,330	1,188	1,188	1,188

Note: Coefficients are log-odds ratios. Numbers in parentheses are standard errors. The models control for race (white, black, Hispanic), cohort (1933–42, 1943–52, 1953–62, 1963–74), mother's education (less than high school, high school, more than high school), mother's work status (working for pay when respondent was 14 or not), family structure at age 14 (intact vs. nonintact), the type of place respondent lived at age 14 (rural, small town, medium-sized city/suburb, or large city), and respondent's number of siblings.

*p < .05 (two-tailed test).

**p < .01 (two-tailed test).

Table 4.8A Adult Sexual Adjustment by Childhood Sexual Experience, Intervening Sexual Trajectory, and Background Characteristics (Multinomial Logit Models) (Women)

Independent Variables	Type of Sexual Dysfunction in Last Year								
	Sexual Desire			Response			High		
	(1)	(2)	(3)	(1)	(2)	(3)	(1)	(2)	(3)
Childhood sexual experience:									
Adult-child	.455*	.406	.310	.741*	.789**	.499*	.874**	.875**	.747**
	(.219)	(.225)	(.230)	(.293)	(.300)	(.313)	(.259)	(.267)	(.274)
Sexual career:									
Childbirth before	—	−.338	−.342	—	−.812	−.839*	—	−.163	−.183
age 19		(.237)	(.239)		(.421)	(.427)		(.296)	(.299)
2–10 sex partners	—	.282	.189	—	.146	−.099	—	.723**	.623*
since 18		(.175)	(.180)		(.246)	(.259)		(.253)	(.258)
11–20 sex partners	—	.749*	.474	—	−.014	−.593	—	.692	.434
since 18		(.298)	(.315)		(.517)	(.551)		(.450)	(.469)
21 or more sex	—	.521	.067	—	.327	−.664	—	.303	−.107
partners since 18		(.416)	(.448)		(.580)	(.655)		(.661)	(.687)
Adverse events:									
Had at least one STD	—	—	.372	—	—	.397	—	—	.277
			(.198)			(.301)			(.265)
Forced sex once after	—	—	.203	—	—	.888**	—	—	.438
age 13			(.244)			(.322)			(.300)
Forced sex more than	—	—	.822*	—	—	1.808	—	—	.860
once after age 13			(.351)			(.420)			(.420)
Log-likelihood	—	—	—	—	—	—	−1250.2	1234.6	1224.3
df	—	—	—	—	—	—	21	33	42
N	—	—	—	—	—	—	1381	1381	1381

Note: Coefficients are log-odds ratios. Numbers in parentheses are standard errors. The models control for race (white, black, Hispanic), cohort (1933–42, 1943–52, 1953–62, 1963–74), mother's education (less than high school, high school, more than high school), mother's work status (working for pay when respondent was 14 or not), family structure at age 14 (intact vs. nonintact), the type of place respondent lived at age 14 (rural, small town, medium-sized city/suburb, or large city), and respondent's number of siblings.

*p < .05 (two-tailed test).
**p < .01 (two-tailed test).

trajectory measures (experience of STD-related symptoms, the appeal of anonymous sex, and exclusivity of sexual preference).

Considering women, in each reduced model (as noted), adult-child sexual contact is significantly associated with the outcome considered. Women who experienced adult-child sexual contact were (exp{0.423} =) 1.5 times as likely as women who reported no childhood sexual interaction to report low overall well-being and (exp{0.469} =) 1.6 times as likely to report low satisfaction with their partner. Women who ex-

Table 4.8B Adult Sexual Adjustment by Childhood Sexual Experience, Intervening Sexual Trajectory, and Background Characteristics (Multinomial Logit Models) (Men)

| | Sexual Dysfunction Latent Class | | | | | |
| | Anxiety Interfered with Sexual Activity | | | High Sexual Dysfunction | | |
Independent Variables	(1)	(2)	(3)	(1)	(2)	(3)
Childhood sexual experience:						
Peer	.719	.630	.592	.829*	.316	.288
	(.415)	(.428)	(.170)	(.401)	(.421)	(.421)
Adult-child	.673*	.616	.464	.688*	.505	.435
	(.335)	(.339)	(.347)	(.328)	(.339)	(.341)
Marital/health status and sexual trajectory:						
Currently married	...	−.132	−.078	...	−.414*	−.390
		(.206)	(.209)		(.208)	(.209)
Poor health	...	.185	.173	...	1.160**	1.159**
		(.342)	(.341)		(.257)	(.257)

	(1)	(2)	(3)	(4)
STD symptomatology	.578* (.291)	.543 (.293)	.782** (.280)	.777** (.281)
Anonymous sex appealing	−.156 (.214)	−.152 (.215)	.693** (.196)	.692** (.197)
Sexual preference exclusivity:				
Attracted to both genders	...	.719** (.263)	...	.576* (.284)
Attracted to men only	...	.887 (.509)	...	.241 (.671)
Log-likelihood	−829.6		−815.0	−799.9
df	34		40	46
N	1,284		1,284	1,284

Note: Coefficients are log-odds ratios. Numbers in parentheses are standard errors. The models control for race (white, black, Hispanic), cohort (1933–42, 1943–52, 1953–62, 1963–74), mother's education (less than high school, high school, more than high school), mother's work status (working for pay when respondent was 14 or not), family structure at age 14 (intact vs. nonintact), the type of place respondent lived at age 14 (rural, small town, medium-sized city/suburb, or large city), and respondent's number of siblings.

*p < .05 (two-tailed test).

**p < .01 (two-tailed test).

perienced adult-child sex were also 1.6, 2.1, and 2.4 times as likely to
report sexual desire dysfunction, sexual response dysfunction, and high
dysfunction, respectively. For every outcome except high dysfunction and level of sexual elaboration, the introduction of the sexual trajectory variables renders the adult-child sexual contact coefficient insignificant at the .05 level, indicating that the effects of adult-child sex
on adult outcomes are largely indirect, mediated through sexual trajectories.

The associations between adult-child sexual contact and measures of
well-being in the last year (table 4.7A) were primarily mediated by sexual
career variables. The strong association between adult-child sexual contact
and overall well-being present in model 1 was rendered insignificant in
model 2 with the introduction of the number of sex partners since age
eighteen. The introduction of the adverse sexual experience variables in
model 3 did not result in a significant increase in log-likelihood.

Sexual career variables also mediated the effect of adult-child sexual
contact on relationship satisfaction in the last year. Echoing the pattern
found for overall well-being, the introduction of the sexual career variables
in model 2 resulted in an insignificant adult-child sexual contact coefficient. While teen childbirth was not associated with relationship satisfaction, number of lifetime sex partners had strong associations with this outcome. Again, the introduction of the adverse sexual experience variables
in model 3 did not result in a significant increase in the log-likelihood.

Referring to table 4.8A, both sexual career and intervening adverse experience variables were significant predictors of current levels of reported
sexual dysfunction. Women who reported higher numbers of lifetime sex
partners (two to ten and eleven to twenty—although not the highest category, twenty-one or more) were more likely to report sexual desire dysfunction compared with respondents who had no partners or only one.
These associations, however, were attenuated with the introduction of the
adverse sexual experience variables. The effect of number of partners on
this form of dysfunction appears, in part, to be a function of the relationship between number of partners and the occurrence of forced sex after
childhood. Those women who reported having been forced to have sex
more than once since childhood were 2.3 times as likely to report sexual
desire dysfunction in adulthood.

Intervening experiences of forced sex also mediated the association between adult-child sex and sexual response dysfunction. The association
found in model 1 remained significant when sexual career variables were
added in model 2 but disappeared with the introduction of adverse sexual
experience variables in model 3. Women who reported a single incident of
forced sex after childhood were 2.6 times as likely to report sexual response dysfunction in adulthood, while women who experienced multiple

occurrences of forced sex after childhood were over 6 times as likely to do so when compared with women who were never forced to have sex. Only the association between adult-child sex and high dysfunction remained with the introduction of the sexual career variables, but this declined somewhat with the addition of the adverse sexual experience variables in model 3.

For men, coefficients describing the association between both peer and adult-child sexual contact and low overall well-being in adulthood are significant in model 1. For those who experienced adult-child sex, the odds of reporting low overall well-being are ($\exp\{0.841\}$ =) 2.3 times higher than the odds for those who experienced no childhood sexual contact. Similarly, the odds for those who report peer sexual contacts are ($\exp\{0.650\}$ =) 1.9 times higher than the odds for those who report no childhood sexual contacts. The introduction of measures of deviance (specifically jail time, which is associated with low overall well-being in adulthood) in model 2 results in modest reductions in the size of the coefficients for childhood sexual experiences. However, marital and health status, STD symptoms, and the appeal of anonymous sex are all associated with adult overall well-being and result in a dramatic drop in the magnitude and significance of the coefficient for peer sexual contacts and a further and more marked reduction (by comparison to model 2) in that of the adult-child coefficient (although it remains significant at the .05 level). Controlling for subsequent trajectories, the odds of reporting low overall well-being for men who report adult-child sex are 1.7 times higher than the odds for those who did not report a childhood sexual experience. The coefficient for peer sexual contacts is negligible and nonsignificant in model 3.

The mediating effect of subsequent trajectories can also be seen in the analyses of the association between childhood sexual experience and low emotional satisfaction with the respondent's primary partner in the last year. In model 1, the odds of falling in a given category of low emotional satisfaction or lower for those who report adult-child sexual experience are 54 percent of those for respondents reporting no childhood sexual contact. Again, the experience of jail time results in a modest reduction in the size of the coefficient for adult-child sex, but, with the introduction of marital status and the appeal of anonymous sex in model 3, subsequent trajectory controls result in a 40 percent reduction in the magnitude of the coefficient (vs. model 1) and render it nonsignificant (at the .05 level). The importance of marital status and the appeal of short-term sexual partnering as mechanisms linking early sexual contact with adult relationship satisfaction conforms with the expectations of the life-course perspective. Early sexual experience may result in the assimilation of models or scripts of sexual interaction that do not facilitate the development of stable intimate relationships. The durability of relationships may be of central importance to men. Evidence suggests that the benefits of stable relationships may not be apparent in the short term but are a cumulative and increasing function of the amount of time men spend in these relationships (Laub, Nagin, and Sampson 1998). Although it is not clear from the model whether the effect of marriage is state dependent or the result of heterogeneity in the tendency to marry, these results, nevertheless, point to the potential importance of sexual and marital trajectories in mediating the effects of childhood sexual experiences on adult well-being.

Further evidence suggesting the importance of intervening trajectories was provided in the analysis of the association between childhood sexual experience and sexual dysfunction. Table 4.8B reports the results of multinomial logit models assessing the association between peer and adult-child sexual contact and membership in the two sexual dysfunction latent classes (compared with the low dysfunction class). Model 2 adds measures of marital and health status, STD symptoms, and the appeal of anonymous sex,[15] while model 3 adds sexual preference exclusivity. In model 1, adult-child sexual contact was associated with anxiety during sexual activity at the conventional level of significance (96 percent increase in odds over those reporting no childhood sexual contact), while both adult-child and peer sexual contacts were associated with high sexual dysfunction (99 and 130 percent increases in odds, respectively).

With regard to the experience of anxiety during sexual activity, the introduction of marital status, physical health, and sexual trajectory variables modestly reduced the magnitude and the significance ($p > .05$) of the coefficient for adult-child sex. The significant effect of STD symptoms suggests that indications of a sexually transmitted disease may contribute to anxiety about the ability to perform sexually, the potential for passing the STD to a partner, or the partner's reaction to external symptoms, among other potential sources of anxiety. Model 3 introduces sexual preference exclusivity, which results in a further 30 percent reduction in the magnitude of the coefficient. Although the effect of exclusive same-sex orientation is relatively large in magnitude, it does not achieve the conventional level of significance. Interestingly, the effect of reported attraction to both sexes is both highly significant and relatively large in magnitude (a 100 percent increase in the odds of anxiety interfering with sexual activity over respondents who reported no childhood sexual contact). Accompanying changes in the size of the adult-child sex coefficient suggest that this category of early sexual experience (which is more likely to involve an older male) may reinforce same-gender sexual activity and subsequently produce conflict over sexual preference in some individuals, with lasting implications for sexual adjustment.

Finally, the significant associations between both peer and adult-child sexual contacts with high sexual dysfunction were reduced (substantially so in the case of peer contacts) and rendered nonsignificant ($p > .05$) in model 2. All four of the intervening variables included in model 2—marital and health status,[16] STD symptoms, and the appeal of anonymous sex—were associated with high dysfunction. The reduction in the magnitude and significance of the adult-child and peer sexual contact coefficients indicates that active sexual trajectories and their consequences may lead to higher rates of both physical problems during sexual activity (poor overall health and STD symptoms may increase the likelihood of erection difficulties or diminished pleasure) and emotional problems and anxiety associated with sexual activity. Although it is possible that sexual dysfunction precipitates a less-stable sexual trajectory, participation in heightened levels of sexual activity begins at relatively early stages of the life course for men who experience early sexual contact, indicating that patterns of interaction are established prior to, and may contribute to, the onset of adult sexual adjustment problems.

Model 3 adds the measure of sexual preference exclusivity. Again, only attraction to both genders had a significant effect on the likelihood of high sexual dysfunction. The coefficient for adult-child sex was only modestly reduced, but the pattern of significance for this item and the consistent sensitivity of the adult-child contact effect to its inclusion is suggestive of a potentially important mediating mechanism. Indeed, the extent to which the relatively limited number of intervening trajectories variables account for the association between childhood sexual experience and both adult well-being measures and sexual dysfunction suggests that the life-course hypothesis that the long-term effects of childhood sex are largely indirect merits further exploration.

4.6 Discussion

The preeminent position of trauma-based conceptions of the long-term effects of early sexual experience has remained largely unchallenged. Although the notion of trauma is multivocal in the psychogenic literature, it anchors the vast majority of research attempting to account for the association between childhood sex and subsequent well-being. Yet the key theoretical claims and expectations uniting psychogenic theories of the long-term effect of childhood sex received little support in analyses of a large, nationally representative sample of U.S. adults.

First, the prediction that adult-child sex leads to a withdrawal from sexual activity received no support in the analysis of women and held for men only in the case of the number of sex partners in the last year. Yet, in contrast to the expectations of the psychogenic perspective, the effect of adult-child sex on measures of sexual behavior over longer periods of the life course (last five years and since age eighteen) indicates that these experiences heighten levels of sexual activity for men but do not result in sexual withdrawal. If the effect on diminished sexual activity in the last year were indicative of a larger pattern of avoidance rather than variability due to less-stable sexual trajectories, this effect should be *more* pronounced (not disappear) when longer periods of the life course are considered.

The assumption that adult-child sex leads to sexual withdrawal as well as heightened levels of sexual activity is one of the most well established of the psychogenic perspective. In fact, sexual withdrawal may occur during isolated phases of the life course in the context of (or in response to) an overall pattern of heightened sexual activity. The therapeutic focus on sexual withdrawal, exemplified in the emphasis placed on this behavioral response in the PTSD framework, may be a function of the tendency among those who have experienced early sexual activity to seek clinical guidance during periods of diminished sexual activity. Thus, *intra*individual rates of sexual activity may, indeed, be more variable among those who experienced childhood sexual contact. The likelihood that this response is based on lingering trauma, however, has not been adequately theorized in the psychogenic framework, nor is this interpretation supported in the NHSLS data. The comparable tendency among those who report peer sexual contact to experience short-term dips in sexual activity suggests that an alternative mechanism is at work.

The trauma-based sexual withdrawal hypothesis extends to specific elements of adult-child sexual experience as well. Noxious stimuli models of the effects of early sex often invoke a traumatic learning model to predict that activities associated with adult-child sexual events will provoke an avoidance response. Yet the association between the early experience of oral sex (the only specific activity on which the NHSLS had adequate information and cases for analysis) and subsequent patterns of participation in that activity is exclusively positive. No tendency subsequently to avoid this activity (given its childhood occurrence) could be discerned for either gender.

Indeed, the evidence suggests that childhood sexual contact tends to result in reinforcement of sexual activity generally as well as acts and relationship characteristics specific to the early sexual event. This conclusion was supported not only by the association between oral sex during childhood and its occurrence in adulthood but also by the association between same-gender sexual activity during childhood and its subsequent appeal. This level of specificity in the linkage between early sexual activity and subsequent patterns of sexual activity and interest is surprising, given the amount of time elapsed between childhood and administration of the survey. The finding regarding same-gender activity, however, should be interpreted with considerable caution. The suggestion of a causal link between early same-gender sex and its later appeal should not be understood as a general theory of homosexual behavior. Nor should it be taken as evidence that every such experience will have a causal effect. Indeed, in some cases, the causal process may be reversed. To the extent that same-gender sexual preference is biologically based or established at a developmentally early stage, some same-gender childhood sexual experiences may occur as a result of a selection process. Nevertheless, patterns of sexual activity in the aftermath of early sex support the life-course hypothesis that childhood sexual contact models and reinforces sexual activity in general and patterns of interaction specific to the childhood event.

The analysis of the relation between event severity and long-term adverse outcomes also ran counter to the expectations of the psychogenic perspective. A cumulative measure of the severity of the sexual contact was not associated with long-term well-being. A notable finding in this regard was the pattern of association between peer sexual contact and adult adjustment for men. Peer contacts were associated—at magnitudes and significance levels comparable to adult-child sexual contacts—with overall well-being and sexual adjustment during adulthood. These results call into question the psychogenic explanation for variation in the long-term effects of childhood sexual contact. The age of the sex partner involved is, perhaps, the key dimension on which trauma is measured in the psychogenic perspective—indicated by the tendency to omit consideration of peer sexual contacts altogether in most psychogenically oriented empirical investigations of childhood sexual experience.

The association of peer sexual contact with adult outcomes, however, is consistent with the expectations of the life-course perspective. Sexualization may result from a salient sexual contact with another child, particularly if the relationship involves asymmetry with respect to sexual knowledge or experience. Indeed, children who initiate peer sexual contact may disproportionately have experienced introductions to sexuality through adult-child contacts. Respondents who reported adult-child sexual contact were significantly more likely also to report a peer sexual contact,[17] suggesting that early sexual practice may diffuse through networks of children tied to those who have experienced sexual contact with an adult. Moreover, of those men who reported a peer contact, half reported more than one such experience during childhood. The diffusion of sexual practices through peer networks may promote a social context in which continuity in sexual behavior patterns is maintained and reinforced.

The analysis of the mediating effects of subsequent trajectories offered evidence of the importance of behavioral adaptations to childhood sexual experiences in predicting long-term adjustment. For women, controlling for subsequent sexual careers and adverse sexual events rendered the association between adult-child sex and all measures of adult adjustment (except high dysfunction) insignificant. Instability in sexual careers was an important mediator of the effect of adult-child sex on overall and relationship satisfaction, while forced sex was a particularly important mediator of the effect of adult-child sex on subsequent sexual functioning.

For men, controlling for subjective orientations toward sexual partnering, symptoms of STDs, and marital and health status resulted in consistent and, in some cases, substantial reductions in the magnitude and significance of coefficients describing the effect of peer and adult-child sex on measures of adult adjustment. The effect of adult-child sex on adult sexual dysfunction was mediated, in part, by reported attraction to both genders, indicating that the conflict potentially accompanying such ambiguity may influence sexual adjustment—particularly the interference of anxiety with sexual activity. The overall pattern of mediation points to the potential importance of life paths through adolescence and early adulthood in explaining the long-term effect of early sexual experience.

It is important to acknowledge that a number of explanations exist for the relation between childhood sexual contacts and adult outcomes. For instance, the occurrence of childhood sexual experiences may be an expression of a social context fostering such activity through low levels of parental supervision or control. Antecedent contextual or familial factors can increase the likelihood of both early sexual experiences and developmental patterns that diminish long-term well-being. In this case, the relation between childhood sexual events and the intervening and adult outcomes considered would be spurious—a particularly important caveat when considering the strong associations between peer sexual contacts and adult well-being.

Another explanation for the patterns observed posits some individual-level characteristic that accounts for both the propensity to engage in childhood sexual activity and the outcomes observed. Gottfredson and Hirschi's (1986) implicit suggestion that "self-control" accounts for the association between early sexual activity and adolescent "illicit" sexual activity and nonsexual deviance is a well-known example of such a trait-based model. The findings of these analyses, however, call into question Gottfredson and Hirschi's general theory in at least two ways. First, it seems unlikely that self-control explains the *occurrence* of early sexual activity, particularly sexual contact with adults. Sexual encounters that involve relatively sophisticated behaviors are not likely to be initiated by otherwise sexually inexperienced children. Second, a self-control hypothesis cannot account for the clear tendency to specialize in forms of sexual behavior specific to the early sexual experience. In contrast to the expectations of the general theory of crime, these findings suggest that early sexual experiences do influence subsequent levels of sexual activity and may have independent effects on the likelihood of nonsexual deviance as well.

4.7 Conclusion

Certainly, no definitive claims about the causal linkage between childhood sexual contact and subsequent outcomes can be made on the basis of retrospective data without more adequate controls. Ideally, childhood sexual experience should be studied through prospective, longitudinal data-collection efforts with more subtle and precise individual and family context measures. Unfortunately, collecting data on sexual experiences during childhood poses difficult ethical and measurement problems. Given the potential limitations of the data, the results of the analyses presented nevertheless suggest some tentative conclusions to guide further research.

First, overreliance on the concept of trauma to account for the range of long-term effects of childhood sexual contacts has obscured the cumulative effect of these experiences. Childhood sexual experience should be understood as embedded in dynamically unfolding lives. Research efforts that seek to track the consequences of early sexual events through behavioral pathways may prove more fruitful than the continued and restrictive focus on the severity and nature of event-specific trauma. Second, and relatedly, shifting attention away from the direct effects of variably traumatic early sexual experiences to the consequences of behavioral patterns in their aftermath motivates a search for the determinants of entry into risky trajectories. More subtle attention to the processes that link early sexual contact with sexualized and maladaptive behavior patterns may enhance our understanding of the mechanisms that induce children to embark on risky and consequential sexual trajectories in adolescence and adulthood.

Future research may also illuminate the consequences of early sexualized behavior for the effectiveness of informal social controls and the potential for a wider range of problem behavior to result as a function of this intervening attenuation of critical social bonds. Hypotheses about the specific mechanism linking childhood sexual experience with nonsexual deviance must remain speculative, however, until more data on the short-term social and familial consequences of early sex are available.

Finally, the perspective developed here points to the potential efficacy of protective as opposed to palliative intervention strategies. Trauma-based conceptions of the long-term effects of early sex often imply a certain degree of inevitability with regard to negative adult outcomes. Highly traumatic events, in this view, doom a child to lingering psychic pain. If the long-term effects of early sexual experience are cumulative, however, a better understanding of "turning points" away from risky trajectories may aid in the development of mechanisms to shield at-risk young people from the adverse experiences to which they are vulnerable.

Notes

The authors are grateful for the financial support of the Ford Foundation (grant 940–1417-2). Christopher R. Browning was supported by a National Institute for Child Health and Human Development predoctoral training grant (T32-HD-07302). An early version of this chapter was presented at the meeting of the American Academy for the Advancement of Science, Atlanta, February 1995. This chapter is a revision and expansion of an article in the *American Sociological Review* (Browning and Laumann 1997), with a substantial discussion of men's experience with adult-child sexual contact added. The analysis of the men's experiences was one focus of Browning's (1997) *Trauma or Transition.* Preliminary analyses of these data were presented in *SOS,* chap. 9.

1. Similarly, Loftus, Polonsky, and Fullilove (1994) found that 31 percent of a sample of 105 women reported partial amnesia or periods of total loss of memory of the abuse (19 percent). Briere and Conte (1993) found that nearly six in ten of a sample of 450 men and women being treated for sexual abuse reported that they had forgotten the experience at some point before age eighteen. Herman and Schatzow (1987) found that 28 percent of their sample of fifty-three sexually abused women organized into therapy groups for incest survivors reported "severe memory deficits" (involving substantial loss of childhood memories or recent retrieval of sexual abuse memories in the context of therapy). Another 36 percent exhibited "mild/moderate" memory deficits.

2. The two groups differed only with respect to the respondent's relationship to the perpetrator and her age at the time of the abuse incident. While cases in which the index abuse was not reported were more likely to involve a blood relative, the victims in these cases were also younger at the time of the abuse, suggesting that reporting failure may have been due to conventional forgetting processes.

3. In cases where the respondent was touched by more than one person, however, the summary method of data collection rendered any clear connection between reported descriptions of the aggregated experiences and characteristics of the persons who touched the respondent impossible. In these cases, then, the occurrence of isolated characteristics (say, the experience of oral sex) during the respondent's childhood could be confirmed, but this information could not be linked with a specific partner. This data constraint clearly limits our knowledge of the experiences of respondents with multiple sexual contacts during childhood. For the vast majority of the cases involved, however, the construction of the variable employed ensures that relatively advanced sexual contact occurred with at least one substantially older individual. In some cases, the respondent reported sexual contact both with an adolescent or adult (at least fourteen years of age) as well as with another child (thirteen years old or younger). Since the percentage of cases involving older partners that did *not* involve at least fondling of the genitals was nominal, we included these cases despite ambiguity regarding the content of the sexual interactions. Because a small number of respondents reported that they reached puberty at ages well into adolescence (fifteen, sixteen, seventeen), some sexual experiences that began after the respondent had reached age thirteen were reported. These cases were excluded.

4. Determination of the cut point for age was based on previous research by Russell (1986), who identified age nine as the critical point before which the probability of long-term effects was elevated. Freud suggested that sexual trauma before, but not after, age nine would generate later hysterical symptomatology (Freud [1896] 1995).

5. Cut points for the numbers of partners in each category were determined by selecting the number of partners roughly corresponding to the thirty-third and sixty-sixth percentiles of the distribution, except in cases where the distribution was heavily skewed (e.g., partners in the last year and the last five years). A number of alternative specifications of the outcome variables were tested; the results did not alter the conclusions of the analysis.

6. LCA is the categorical data analogue of factor analysis (which is used for continuous variables). It provides a method of identifying a set of mutually exclusive latent classes that account for the association among a set of categorical variables. LCA arrives at a solution of T latent classes such that the observed variables, controlling for the latent variable, are independent (i.e., LCA maximizes *local independence* among a set of observed categorical variables).

The general form of the model is as follows:

$$\Pi_{ij...mt}^{AB..EX} = \Pi_{it}^{\bar{A}X} \times \Pi_{jt}^{\bar{B}X} \times \cdots \times \Pi_{mt}^{\bar{E}X} \times \Pi_{t}^{X},$$

where $\pi_{ij,\ldots,m}^{AB,\ldots,EX}$ is the probability that a randomly selected case will fall in cell $i, j, \ldots m, t$, π_i^{AX} is the conditional probability of being at level i of variable A for a case in class t of latent variable (X) (and so on for each observed variable), and π_t^X is the probability of a randomly selected case being at level t of latent variable X (McCutcheon 1987). Using Clogg's MLLSA (maximum likelihood latent structure analysis) program, Browning fit the two- and three-class solutions for men. The three-class solution most efficiently balanced goodness of fit and parsimony ($G^2 = 5.689$ on twelve degrees of freedom—a significant improvement in model fit over the two-class solution). Chapter 10 below, devoted to an analysis of sexual dysfunctions, presents somewhat different, but closely related, results from a latent class analysis.

7. This, of course, measures the occurrence of delinquent events that resulted in official intervention.

8. Since men, in general, are more likely to report multiple partners across the life course, the number of sex partners may not effectively identify those men most at risk of engaging in sexual behavior with adverse consequences. The subjective appeal of anonymous sex is highly correlated with high levels of sexual activity but may also, and more parsimoniously, capture a tendency to engage in a higher-risk, less-stable pattern of sexual partnering for men.

9. Symptom measures more accurately describe the current effect of sexually transmitted infection and do not require the respondent to have been diagnosed by a doctor or have knowledge of the effects associated with a given infection (as do specific STD measures). Men, in general, have less direct contact with medical professionals regarding reproductive health issues and may be less likely to have knowledge regarding, or be willing to admit having, a sexually transmitted disease.

10. In this case, because there are only three outcomes, the model with both linear and quadratic effects is equivalent to the unconstrained multinomial logit model.

11. Because same-gender sexual behavior was so rare in the male population, we used a measure of the subjective appeal of this activity.

12. The ordered logit model is a proportional odds model. The model assumes that a variable's effect on the odds of a response equal to or below a given category of the dependent variable is the same for all such categories. Given an ordinal dependent variable with J categories, a vector of ordered logit coefficients b, and a vector of characteristics x_i (and k independent variables), $\exp\{b_k\}$ is the change in odds of being in category j or below corresponding to a unit change in x_{ik}. Threshold parameters q_j describe the baseline log odds of falling in a given category or below, and $\exp\{q_j\}$ should be interpreted as the log odds of falling in category j or below for persons in the omitted category.

13. Each of the severe characteristics was considered individually in models predicting adult outcomes as well. The coefficients for more and less severe events for each characteristic were roughly equivalent in the majority of the cases. Indeed, the number of models in which the coefficient for less severe cases achieved significance while the coefficient for more severe cases *did not* exceeded the number in which the reverse result was obtained.

14. Likelihood ratio χ^2 comparisons of ordered and multinomial logit models of both overall well-being and relationship-satisfaction measures indicate that the latter do not result in significant improvements in goodness of fit over the ordered logit model.

15. Since no obvious theoretical justification for including measures of deviance to predict these outcomes was apparent, these items were dropped from the analysis of adult sexual dysfunction.

16. In order to ensure that the results of the analysis were not driven by the health status item (which conceivably could be measuring sexual dysfunction as well), the health item was removed from the analysis. Removing the health item results in no change in the magnitude or the significance of the adult-child sexual contact coefficient in model 3.

17. Of men who reported adult-child sexual contact, 16 percent reported a peer sexual contact as well, compared with 8 percent of men who did not report an adult-child sexual contact. Comparable proportions for women were 6 and 3 percent, respectively. Respondents who report adult-child sexual contacts are undoubtedly also more willing to acknowledge the occurrence of a peer sexual contact—nevertheless, the strength of the association between the two events warrants further attention.

■

CHAPTER FIVE

Race, Gender, and Class in Sexual Scripts

JENNA MAHAY, EDWARD O. LAUMANN, AND STUART MICHAELS

While sexuality is popularly described in highly individualistic terms, this chapter examines the ways in which sexual norms, practices, and preferences are shaped by race, gender, and class. Many scholars have already documented group differences in specific sexual behaviors, such as age at first sex, use of condoms, and number of partners. This chapter examines the broader sexual scripts in which these specific acts are embedded and how race, gender, and class intersect to shape those scripts.

A middle-aged, working-class African American man explains what he sees as racial differences in sexual scripts:

> When it comes to woman and man relationships, white people have a tendency to be too damn intellectual. Now that is not one of the true prerequisites of making love. It's the emotion, the passion. You don't have time to ask a woman what kind of degree she has. You see what I'm saying? (quoted in Duneier 1992, 44)

A white woman describes how gender shapes the way she approaches sex with her partner:

> It is sort of an issue that I don't initiate sex. I would always wait for him. And finally he said, "Look, I'm not going to initiate sex all the time," and I would give him the argument: "Oh, men say they want women to initiate sex, but really when it happens they're, like, 'I have a headache tonight, honey.' " So in my mind there was a reason not to initiate it because it threatened him. (quoted in Blumstein and Schwartz 1983, 212)

An African American woman discusses how class plays a part in who she believes is a suitable partner:

> It is difficult to find a person that one is truly compatible with, and that's especially true for a highly educated woman whose expectations often differ from those of most women and are not always consistent with the *eligible pool* [similar status] of men, who seem to have some preference for "traditional" women. (quoted in Staples 1981, 83)

Race, gender, and class, however, do not operate independently in forming sexual scripts; they "intersect" (cf. Connell 1995; Spelman 1988; Scott

1988; Hooks 1990; Butler 1990; and Nagel 1999). In the third quote presented above, for example, ideas of who is a suitable partner and of the difficulties the woman has in finding one have to do not only with class but with race and gender as well. Unfortunately, until recently, there has been an absence of data allowing simultaneous comparisons by race/ethnicity, gender, and class on the broad range of sexual attitudes, practices, and preferences that make up sexual scripts. This chapter uses the rich descriptive resources of the National Health and Social Life Survey (NHSLS) to overcome this limitation. We first develop a theoretical perspective on the systematic variations in the sexual scripts adopted by persons with particular status attributes. We then analyze the similarities and differences in the sexual scripts of racial/ethnic groups and the gender and class variations within those groups.

5.1 Theorizing Variations in Sexual Scripts

Sexual scripts operate at three levels: the cultural, the interpersonal, and the intrapsychic (Simon and Gagnon 1987b). *Cultural scenarios* are the societal norms and narratives that provide guidelines for sexual conduct, thereby broadly indicating appropriate partners and sex acts, where and when to perform those acts, and even what emotions and feelings are appropriate. These scenarios are sufficiently abstract and generalized, however, that their specific application in particular contexts may be unclear. Thus, actors engaged in sexual interactions create *interpersonal scripts* that translate abstract cultural scenarios into scripts appropriate to particular situations. Interpersonal scripts, then, are the strategies for carrying out an individual's own sexual wishes with regard to the actual or anticipated responses of another person. While interpersonal scripts can be seen as "sexual dialogues" with others, *intrapsychic scripts* are sexual dialogues with the self. The intrapsychic script is a person's sexual fantasies, the sequence of acts, postures, objects, and gestures that elicit and sustain sexual arousal (Simon and Gagnon 1987b). Intrapsychic scripts should be seen, not merely as expressions of an individual's biologically generated appetites or drives, but rather as inextricably linked to what that person has learned to mean or understand as *being sexual.*

In the United States, cultural scenarios frequently stipulate that people of races or ethnicities different from one's own are inappropriate for sexual partnerships. In addition, because sex partners are generally chosen from a circumscribed group of people who are met through mutual friends, at work, or in neighborhood activities, the high level of racial segregation in these areas of social life also results in choosing others from the same racial/ethnic group. Indeed, as was reported in *The Social Organization of Sexuality,* 93 percent of those who were married in the last ten years chose marriage partners of the same race or ethnicity. Even among those who had had a very short-term sexual relationship, 91 percent chose partners of the same race or ethnicity. In short, *SOS* (p. 255) reported that racial homophily was higher than all the other types of homophily, including age, education, and religious affiliation.

Because sexual partnering is so highly segregated racially, we would expect different sexual scripts to develop within these segregated subpopulations with their distinctive age, class, religious, and marital compositions. Sexual scripting creates and stages a drama wherein the roles take on meaning in relation to the enactment of related roles and the specific cast of actors (Simon and Gagnon 1987a, 1987b). Thus, we would expect different dramas and roles to be staged when distinctive and segregated casts of actors perform them. Because sexual scripts are *socially* produced, individuals must call on shared meanings and expectations to produce them. Thus, we would expect an independent effect of race/ethnicity after controlling for age, religion, class, and marital status.

In addition to race, gender centrally organizes sexual scripting. Most sexual scripts involve gendered roles, where certain sexual practices take on meaning as either masculine or feminine in relation to the enactment of particular roles by the "appropriate" sex. Cultural scenarios, interpersonal scripts, and intrapsychic scripts all involve assumptions about gender differences in sexuality. For example, at the level of the cultural scenario, the social norm may be that boys are expected to have sex before marriage but that girls are not. At the level of the interpersonal script, it may be that men are generally more aggressive in initiating sexual encounters and that women are more passive sexually. At the intrapsychic level, men and women may find different sexual practices appealing or have different kinds of sexual fantasies. As sexual scripts vary between racial/ethnic groups, so will the gender roles and expectations regarding men's and women's sexual behavior.

Finally, many have speculated on the relation between race and class in sexual behavior, but the data limitations of previous studies have precluded an evaluation of their relative importance. This chapter examines the effects of race and class separately, to test whether racial/ethnic differences in sexual behavior can, in fact, be explained by class alone, after taking into account gender, marital status, age, religion, and family composition.

5.2 Other Studies of Race, Gender, and Class in Sexual Behavior

Racial/Ethnic Differences in Sexual Behavior

Social scientists have long studied race and ethnicity in American society and its effect on attitudes and social life (cf. Jaynes and Williams 1989), but only limited attention has been paid to sexual practices. While some ethnographic studies of particular racial/ethnic communities have included information on their sexual attitudes and practices, this qualitative information does not readily lend itself to comparisons across groups. Quantitative studies, on the other hand, have made such comparisons but have been restricted only to adolescent sexual practices or a very limited range of adult sexual practices. One more comprehensive analysis (Weinberg and Williams 1988) identified interesting differences across racial and class groupings but was based on different samples drawn at different times and different geographic locations. What has been lacking are data from representative samples of the major racial/ethnic groups collected at the same time and covering a wide range of sexual behaviors.

It is clear from the literature that the sexual practices and attitudes of different racial/ethnic groups must be analyzed in relation to each other because sexual relations within racial/ethnic groups are often affected and defined by the race relations between groups (Spelman 1988, 106). For example, in his ethnography of middle-aged working-class African American men in Chicago, Duneier (1992, 41) found his informants to be very aware of the stereotype of themselves as sexual exploiters, an image they self-consciously tried to live down. But Bowser (1994, 143–44) claims that the hypersexuality attributed to African Americans by whites has been incorporated into the self-identity of younger African Americans, motivating them to become experienced as soon as possible and to prove to themselves and their partners that they are sexually superior. In addition, the influence of race relations on specific sexual practices is shown by Sterk-Elifson's (1994, 112) finding that many African Americans considered birth control, masturbation, and anal and oral sex evils that white people invented.

Only a very limited range of sexual experiences has been studied in existing quantitative work on racial/ethnic differences in sexual practices, however. Many studies focus on age at first intercourse, condom use, and teenage pregnancy and thus are concerned mainly with adolescent sexuality (see, e.g., Udry and Billy 1987; Hogan and Kitagawa 1985; Duncan and Hoffman 1991; E. Anderson 1991; Furstenberg et al. 1987; Zelnik, Kantner, and Ford 1981; Pleck, Sonenstein, and Ku 1991; Finkel and Finkel 1981; Lauritsen 1994; Brewster 1994). There have been several national surveys of the sexual behavior of adolescents, such as John Kantner and Melvin Zelnik's 1971 and 1976 National Surveys of Young Women and the 1979 National Survey of Young Men and Women. Sonenstein has more recently conducted the 1988 and 1990 National Surveys of Adolescent Males. Adolescent sexuality, of course, only initiates the sexual life course. The NHSLS allows us a comprehensive view of it.

While numerous studies have been conducted on specific sexual practices (e.g., sexual debut and condom use), we know much less about the prevalence and meanings given to such sexual practices as masturbation, oral sex, anal sex, and same-gender sexual activity. The General Social Survey (GSS) has included only a limited number of questions about sexual behavior in its national surveys, and the 1990 National AIDS Behavioral Surveys asked detailed questions about vaginal and anal intercourse only of respondents who reported an HIV risk factor. Moreover, sexual behavior cannot be understood apart from the attitudes that give insight into the meaning of various sexual activities for their practitioners. Several studies have examined racial differences in sexual attitudes, but with somewhat contradictory results (Furstenberg et al. 1987; Staples 1978; Rodman 1971; Smith 1994; Klassen, Williams, and Levitt 1989; Timberlake and Carpenter 1990). The NHSLS provides a much more comprehensive and detailed picture of people's sexual activities, preferences, and attitudes than has previously been available.

Gender Differences in Sexual Practices

Most sexual practices are highly gendered, meaning that certain sexual practices, such as engaging in a high frequency of sex and having multiple sex partners, are identified as masculine, others, such as waiting until marriage to have sex, as feminine. Many studies of sexual behavior, however, study only one gender (see, e.g., Hogan and Kitagawa 1985; Bowser 1994; Sterk-Elifson 1994; Gilmore, DeLamater, and Wagstaft 1996; Duneier 1992; Ku, Sonenstcin, and Pleck 1993; Brewster 1994). This makes it very difficult to compare the experiences and sexual roles of men and women in relation to each other within and across racial and ethnic groups.

Several studies of gender differences in sexuality have been conducted within specific racial/ethnic and class groups. For example, Anderson (1990) found that adolescent African American men and women living in the ghetto have sharply contrasting orientations toward sexuality. Anderson captures these differences in describing the "game" of men and the "dream" of women. Men see women as objects of a sexual game to be won as trophies for their own personal aggrandizement; sex is used as an important means of enhancing their social status among their male peers. Women, on the other hand, dream of having a boyfriend, a fiancé, or a husband and the fairy-tale prospect of living happily ever after with one's children in a nice house in a good neighborhood: the dream of a middle-class lifestyle and the nuclear family. The reality of inner-city African American men's poor employment prospects means that this dream is not likely to be realized (Anderson 1993, 80).

Gender roles also have an important but different effect on sexual behavior among Latinos (see, e.g., Marín 1996). Women cannot be sexual if they want to be considered "good," resulting in the feelings of discomfort about sex commonly reported by Latino women. At the same time, men are expected to be passionate and to have a constant sexual desire that, once ignited, is beyond their control. For a Latino man, sexual conquest is a proof of masculinity. Because men generally have more status and power than women in Latino culture, women are at a disadvantage in dealing with coercion by men.

Similarly, in her ethnography of a Mexican American community in Chicago, Horowitz (1983, 59) found masculinity to be defined by independence, personal strength, control, domination, and sexual aggressiveness. The ideal of femininity is virginity or faithfulness, domesticity, and dependence. The norms requiring virginity for women and encouraging men to seduce women create an ongoing tension between the sexes. In Mexican culture, men are allowed to have multiple sex partners, while women are required to be faithful. The honor of a man is besmirched if his wife is unfaithful or his daughter loses her virginity before marriage. A close watch is kept and tight control exercised over daughters and wives by their male kin. Horowitz notes that, while the sexual norms are very strict for young women, they are frequently transgressed. When two adolescents have intercourse, the man's status goes up, the woman's down: "She is dishonored and her value is decreased in the eyes of the young men" (p. 117). When a young woman does engage in premarital intercourse, her sexuality is more accepted if it is seen as "bounded." For example, a young woman may account for her actions by saying that she was in love with her boyfriend and gave in to his sexual demands in a moment of passion. This is more acceptable not only because this account denies any prior intention of having sex but also because, when a young woman is in love, she is expected to give in to her boyfriend's sexual demands since femininity requires submission (Horowitz 1983, 123, 125).

Among mainly middle-class whites, Blumstein and Schwartz (1983, 324) found that gender also affects what a person desires in a relationship and how he or she behaves in one. Men are expected to be more aggressive sexually and are thought to be more lustful than women, while women are supposed to be more passive. Women often feel restrained and not in control of their own experiences, and men often feel pressured to perform. This may explain why about one-third of the women in the NHSLS reported a lack of interest in sex for at least several months or more in the past twelve months, while nearly 30 percent of the men complained that they had anxiety about their sexual performance for several months or more in the past twelve months (see chap. 10 below on sexual dysfunction).

While the literature has clearly documented significant gender differences in sexual scripts within racial/ethnic groups, studies typically treat only a single racial or ethnic group and fail directly to compare gender differences *across* racial and ethnic groups. Some authors have speculated that gender differences in sexual practices are smaller for African Americans than for whites. Coleman (1966) suggested that this was because African American women's status does not depend as much on finding a good husband as does that of white women. African American women therefore do not have to treat their sexuality as a commodity that must be protected in order to be exchanged. Similarly, Bowser (1994) argues that African American gender differences in sexual practices are smaller because it is more acceptable for African American women to engage in casual sex. Bowser found that young African American men assume that African American women are, like the men themselves, having sex before marriage and having multiple sex partners. Sterk-Elifson (1994, 115–16) found that many young African American women felt pressured to have sex because they feared that their partners would leave them if they did not. They felt that their boyfriends had more bargaining power because there were always other women willing to date them.

In their statistical analysis of a racially mixed sample, however, Weinberg and Williams (1988, 213) found, to the contrary, that male-female differences in sexual practices were substantially larger among African Americans than among whites. Compared to African American women, African American men have first intercourse at a much younger age, have a higher frequency of premarital sexual activity, and have more sex partners. Weinberg and Williams suggest that this is because African American men are in a social milieu that is sexually permissive and in which sexual opportunities are relatively available, while white men are more constrained by their cultural environment because white women are traditionally regarded as a protected class and not readily available for sexual conquest. These conclusions, however, were based on data collected only through 1970 and may not accurately represent the situation for women and men who came of age after the sexual revolution of the late 1960s and early 1970s.

The Effect of Education on Sexual Practices

Studying racial/ethnic differences in sexual scripts is difficult because race and ethnicity are themselves highly correlated with educational attainment. Findings regarding the relative effect of education versus race on sexual practices have been contradictory. Numerous studies have shown that class has an effect on age at first intercourse (Hogan and Kitagawa 1985; Hollingshead 1949; Kinsey, Pomeroy, and Martin 1948; Sterk-Elifson 1994). In an early sociological community study, Hollingshead (1949) found that class was a major factor in shaping white adolescents' sexual practices. Hollingshead found that adolescents in the lower classes tended to begin having sexual intercourse at an earlier age than those in the working or middle classes. A lower-class boy achieved status if he had sex with a girl on their first date. These lower-class boys "on the prowl" liked to boast that they could " 'get what they can, where they can, as soon as they can, and as cheap as they can' " (p. 421). Lower-class boys generally saw girls as having the same passions as themselves, passions that contradicted the dominant community mores. Most of the lower-class couples in Hollingshead's study did not use contraception, and there was a very high rate of pregnancy before marriage. While going steady, the couple engaged in sexual activity in parked cars in order to escape their parents' surveillance. A lower-class couple tended to marry just a short time (a few months) after "going steady." However, Hollingshead has little to say about the sexual behavior of middle- and upper-class adolescents since his data on sexual practices primarily came from lower-class boys and girls.

In a more recent analysis comparing two different studies, Weinberg and Williams (1980) found that class, as measured by education level, is still important among males in predicting the onset of sexual activity and the incidence and frequency of such sexual behaviors as masturbation and oral sex during adolescence. For females, class was negatively related to early sexual activity and positively related to good feelings about first sexual experiences.

While these studies focused mainly on whites, the increasing polarization of the African American population by socioeconomic class (Wilson 1978) suggests that class may have an even greater effect on African Americans' sexual behavior. Hogan and Kitagawa (1985) examined the linkages between social status, family structures, and neighborhood characteristics as they affected fertility patterns among Chicago's adolescent African American women in 1979. They found that social class was a significant factor, inversely related to teenage pregnancy.

Anderson (1993, 93) also discusses the effect of class on African Americans, specifically adolescents' sense of opportunity and the future. Anderson argues that black ghetto sexual behaviors and values are a result of the "economic noose" in the ghetto—the structural conditions that allow girls to conclude that they have no future to derail by having a baby and boys to conclude that they will be unable to become economically self-reliant and support a family. The same strains are not experienced by middle-class blacks. In addition, middle-class youths have a much higher level of practical education about birth control and sexuality in general. E. Anderson (1991) also discusses how class background and being raised with a sense of opportunity keep adolescent females out of the street culture of sex by leading them to adopt an outlook that "places them in a world beyond their immediate circumstances" (p. 398).

Several other studies of African American premarital parenthood have found that group differences reflect variations in group access to channels of privilege and influence and are responses to broader changes in the society, such as changes in the structure of opportunity for the disadvantaged. For example, Wilson (1987, 91) found that the percentages of out-of-wedlock births can be directly tied to the labor market status of African American men. Similarly, Duncan and Hoffman (1991) found that women with the least to lose were most likely to have a child as a teenager and thus that the deteriorating opportunities for women in the ghetto are crucial to understanding the high rate of teenage pregnancy.

Other studies, however, have shown that sexual relationships are still sharply organized around racial and ethnic categories. Indeed, chapter 6 of *SOS* found a higher degree of race than class homophily (as measured by education) in sexual partnerships. Weinberg and Williams (1988) concluded that cultural differences between races override differences in social class, finding that the effects of race were still prominent even after class was taken into account. Weinberg and Williams found that, regardless of class status, African Americans were more likely to engage in premarital sex earlier and more frequently than whites. African American men had a greater number of partners, and African Americans in general were more liberal and accepting of sex, pursued it more, and reported fewer problems with it. They found no support for Kinsey's hypothesis that these differences are explained by social class. Weinberg and Williams (1988, 213–14) argued that their finding that social class is not a complete explanatory factor for racial differences in sexual behavior is due to a distinct subculture created by African Americans as a result of their specific historical and social circumstances, which have given particular meaning to sexuality for them. In addition, the continuing segregation of blacks and whites regardless of social class has sustained these cultural patterns.

Measuring Class

Likewise, Furstenberg et al. (1987) conclude that African Americans have sex earlier than whites because of racial differences in attitudes and norms regarding sexual behavior and that this is particularly true for African Americans in highly segregated schools. They found that African Americans are more likely to expect parenthood before or at the same time as marriage and that they are more likely to report having peers who are sexually active. These studies lead one to expect that race will have a larger effect on sexual scripts than class, given that distinctive sexual scripts will develop in racially segregated populations.

One difficulty in comparing the effects of race/ethnicity and class is that, while *race* and *ethnicity* are reasonably well defined, socially sanctioned categories, *class* is less easily defined and measured. Social scientists have long debated how to define and measure *class*, and many different theories and operationalizations have been set forth. Previous studies of sexuality that have focused simply on age at first sex, number of partners, and condom use have defined *class* as the potential for upward mobility and thus have used complex composite measures that take into account parents' education, occupation, family income, and labor force experience (cf. Hogan and Kitagawa 1985). However, the concept of class most pertinent to our analysis of broader sexual scripts is that of groups of individuals who share a "style of life," social positions that are characterized by value orientations, attitudes, behavior, and conventions, as in the Weberian concept of status. As Bourdieu (1984) states, as a result of the internalization of class position, members of the same class tend to have similar tastes, which generate a particular kind of lifestyle. Taste is a unitary set of distinctive preferences that express a certain symbolic logic, through such things as language, clothing, and the body. Thus, each dimension of lifestyle, including the sexual, expresses a similar logic. Education has often been thought to be a better measure of this conception of class than occupation or income since cultural capital has a greater influence on one's values and beliefs than does economic capital (Mayer 1997; DiMaggio 1994; Weinberg and Williams 1980, 1988). Thus, although it is not a perfect measure, we use respondent's education as a simple measure of class and the potential for upward mobility and a factor that largely defines the pool of potential sex partners from which one will choose. We have broken education into three categories: no high school degree, high school degree, and more than high school degree (which includes vocational degree, some college, college degree, and advanced degrees). We grouped those with vocational degrees and some college with those who had a college or an advanced degree because, in general, they are more similar to the latter than to the high school graduates.

Racial/Ethnic Categories

There are definitional issues related to ethnicity that also require careful consideration. First, race and ethnicity are not mutually exclusive. In the NHSLS questionnaire, we attempted to collect this information independently. However, some respondents, primarily Hispanics, do not consider themselves white or black, selecting the category *other* on the question about race, and, when queried, specify their race as Hispanic or a close equivalent. For this reason, in following what is the standard practice in reporting census data, we start by dividing the population into Hispanic and non-Hispanic, then break the latter into racial categories: white, black, Asian/Pacific Islander, or Native American (the smaller racial groups are excluded from the analysis). However, the Hispanic group does not form a single homogeneous entity in terms of either race or national origin. It is therefore problematic to treat Hispanics as a single category when comparing them to blacks and whites. One solution is to break them into smaller, more homogeneous groupings. Since Mexican Americans constitute the majority of Hispanics in the United States, we analyze them as a separate group. Unfortunately, no other Hispanic subgroups in our sample are large enough to analyze separately. Therefore, we have created the category *other Hispanic* for all the other Hispanic groups, including Puerto Ricans and Cubans.

Second, the fact that Hispanics are very heterogeneous reminds us that whites also have many ethnic origins. According to the GSS (1988–94), no more than 20 percent of whites in the United States under sixty years of age came from any one country of origin. The most common white family origin is Germany (18 percent), followed by England (12 percent) and Ireland (11 percent). Smaller percentages report family origins in Italy (5 percent), Scotland (3 percent), and Poland (3 percent). Reflecting this diversity in countries of origin is the religious heterogeneity among whites. Whites reporting a religious affiliation in the NHSLS were evenly divided among Catholics, mainline Protestants, and fundamentalist Protestants. Because of insufficient cases to sustain a statistical analysis of white ethnic groups separately, we must ignore the ethnic differences within the white population that surely exert some influence on sexual scripts.

5.3 Understanding Racial/Ethnic Differences

As discussed at length in *SOS,* master statuses other than ethnicity and race can account for considerable variation in sexuality. These statuses characterize members of racial/ethnic groups and affect the nature of the sexual scripts that they follow. Thus, we first give a brief description of the age, religion, education, and marital status composition of the four racial and ethnic groups to be treated in this chapter.

Whites

The whites have, on the average, more school years completed when compared to the other three racial and ethnic groups. Only about 11 percent of the whites in our sample did not finish a high school degree, while over 60 percent had at least some college or vocational training. They were also somewhat older than the other groups that we discuss. About 40 percent of the whites were between forty and fifty-nine years of age. Whites were very heterogeneous in terms of religious affiliation, almost evenly divided among Catholicism, mainline Protestantism, and evangelical and fundamentalist Protestantism, with about 12 percent reporting no religious affiliation.[1] About 55 percent of the men and 59 percent of the women were married at the time of the survey. The white profile is generally older, married, and college educated, but religion is mixed.

African Americans

Compared to the whites in our sample, African Americans had a lower level of educational achievement. About 22 percent of the African Americans had not finished high school, twice the percentage of whites, and only about 40 percent had at least some college or vocational school. African Americans had an age composition similar to that of whites, with about 36 percent between forty and fifty-nine years of age. A much lower percentage of African Americans than whites were currently married. Only 39 percent of the men and 36 percent of the women were married at the time of the interview. The vast majority, 64 percent of the men and 75 percent of the women, were affiliated with more conservative Protestant denominations, such as the Baptist and Pentecostal Churches. The African American profile is thus typified by older, moderately educated, and unmarried conservative Protestants.

Mexican Americans

Of our four racial and ethnic groups, Mexican Americans had the lowest level of educational attainment. Almost 38 percent had not completed high school. Mexican Americans in our sample also tended to be much younger than representatives of the other groups. Almost 80 percent of the Mexican American women were between eighteen and forty, and 45 percent were between eighteen and twenty-nine. Almost 70 percent of Mexican American men were between eighteen and forty years of age, and 49 percent were between eighteen and twenty-nine. Despite their younger ages, however, the proportion married was similar to the proportion of whites married, with 50 percent of the men and 57 percent of the women married at the time of the interview. The vast majority of Mexican Americans in our sample were Catholic, 75 percent of the men and 67 percent of the women. Mexican Americans were concentrated in the Southwest. The Mexican American profile is one of young, less-educated, strongly Catholic married couples.

Other Hispanics

The other Hispanics, consisting mainly of Cubans and Puerto Ricans, were somewhat more educated than the Mexican Americans. More of the other Hispanics than the Mexican Americans had completed college (23 percent of the men and 16 percent of the women). The other Hispanics also tended to be older than the Mexican Americans, with only 26 percent of the men and 37 percent of the women aged eighteen to twenty-nine. The largest cohort of the other Hispanics was between the ages of thirty and thirty-nine. In terms of marital status, the other Hispanics were similar to both Mexican Americans and whites, with 53 percent of the men and 55 percent of the women married at the time of the interview. And, like the Mexican Americans, the majority of the other Hispanics, 78 percent of the men and 61 percent of the women, were Catholic. About 25 percent of both the Mexican American and the other Hispanic women reported affiliation with a conservative Protestant denomination, such as the Pentecostal Church.

In summary, when examining racial and ethnic differences in sexual scripts, we must recognize that racial and ethnic groups are also marked by other master-status variables, such as age, education, marital status, and religious affiliation. Whites tend to be older, better educated, and married and to have heterogeneous religious affiliations. African Americans, on the other hand, tend to have the same age distribution as whites but are less well educated, more often affiliated with a conservative Protestant denomination, and less likely to be married. Mexican Americans tend to be much younger than African Americans and whites and less educated, but the majority are married and Catholic. The other Hispanics fall in between the African Americans and the Mexican Americans in terms of age and education but are similar to Mexican Americans in their high rate of marriage and their Catholicism.

5.4 Data and Methods

Our statistical analysis compares sexual scripts across races and ethnicities, taking into account the effects of class, religious affiliation, age, marital status, and family background. The data for this analysis come from the NHSLS, including the oversamples of African Americans and Hispanics that will permit more detailed statistical investigation of these subpopulations.

To study cultural scenarios, we analyze the responses to the NHSLS questions regarding sexual attitudes. These questions ask respondents whether they think that certain sexual practices are wrong, and the answers to these questions thus form a picture of the social guidelines and norms surrounding sexual behavior. Second, we examine interpersonal scripts by analyzing the responses to the NHSLS questions regarding the sexual practices in which the respondents have engaged, both in their lifetime and in their last sexual event. Third, to study intrapsychic scripts or individual fantasies and desires, we analyze the responses to the NHSLS questions regarding which sexual practices the respondent finds appealing.

5.5 Definition of Variables

Master Statuses

Age is divided into four cohorts: eighteen to twenty-nine, thirty to thirty-nine, forty to forty-nine, and fifty to fifty-nine. The oldest cohort reached adolescence well before the sexual revolution; the youngest cohort came of age after the AIDS epidemic began (1981). Unfortunately, age confounds two analytic issues that cannot be disentangled with cross-sectional data: (1) the physical and physiological processes of maturation and aging and (2) period effects on a cohort, whose members share specific historical experiences, such as wars, depressions, or periods of prosperity, that shape their expectations about having families, sexual experimentation, and so on.

There are four categories of religious affiliation: no religious affiliation, mainline Protestant, evangelical Protestant, and Catholic. Mainline Protestant mainly includes such Protestant denominations as the Episcopalians, Lutherans, Presbyterians, and Methodists. Evangelical Protestant includes the Baptists and Pentecostals and other fundamentalist sectarian churches. (For a more detailed description of the construction of this variable, see *SOS,* app. 3.1A.)

Respondent's marital status was treated differently for different dependent variables. When the dependent variable pertained to sexual activities performed over the lifetime, such as whether the respondent had ever experienced fellatio, marital status distinguished between the ever married and the never married. When the dependent variable referred to sexual activities in the past twelve months, marital status distinguished the currently married from the not currently married.

Family composition was determined from the question, "Were you living with both your own mother and father when you were 14?" (if no: "With whom were you living around that time?") (*SOS,* 610). Three categories were identified: (1) lived with both biological parents; (2) lived with a parent and a stepparent; and (3) lived with a single parent.[2]

Measures of Cultural Scenarios

Aspects of sexual cultural scenarios were measured by the respondents' attitudes toward certain sexual practices. These attitudes concern the age at which the respondent believes sex is appropriate, the appropriate relationship to one's sex partner, the feelings one is supposed to have for one's sex partner, the sexual acts deemed appropriate in a sexual encounter, and the appropriate gender of a sex partner. *SOS* reported a cluster analysis of nine attitudes that identified three broad normative orientations toward sexuality: traditional, relational, and recreational. For the analytic purposes of this chapter, we selected several items to tap each of these three orientations.

Strongly disapproving attitudes toward premarital sex and teenage sex as well as agreement with the statement that religious beliefs shape the respondent's sexual behavior are used to indicate support for the traditional cultural scenario that regards reproduction as the sole purpose of sex, which should take place only within marriage. This orientation is rooted in religious convictions, with the Roman Catholic and more conservative Protestant churches being strong advocates of these ideas. Respondents were asked, "If a man and a woman have sex relations before marriage, do you think it is always wrong, almost always wrong, wrong only sometimes, or not wrong at all?" and, "What if they are in their teens, say 14–16 years old? In that case, do you think sex relations before marriage are always wrong, almost always wrong, wrong only sometimes, or not wrong at all?" (*SOS,* 666). Those who answered always wrong or almost always wrong to these questions were coded as having a traditional cultural scenario. In addition, respondents were asked to respond to the statement, "My religious beliefs have shaped and guided my sexual behavior" (*SOS,* 667). Those who responded strongly agree or agree were coded as having a traditional cultural scenario.

A relational orientation toward sexuality was identified by agreement with the statement, "I would not have sex with someone unless I was in love with them" (*SOS,* 667). Those who answered strongly agree or agree were coded as holding a cultural scenario in which sex should take place in an intimate, loving relationship (thus, a relational cultural scenario allows for premarital sex, but only within a loving relationship).

A recreational cultural scenario is one in which attitudes toward sexual practices do not relate directly either to procreation or to the intimacy of the relationship. This was measured by asking respondents whether they agreed with the statement, "Any kind of sexual activity between adults is okay as long as both persons freely agree to it" (*SOS,* 667). Again, those who answered strongly agree or agree were coded as holding a recreational attitude toward sexuality. This item was used because it was thought to measure a modern, pleasure-centered view of sex, where sex is considered a good in itself as long as it does not hurt anyone.

Finally, respondents' attitudes toward homosexuality are often quite distinct from any of their attitudes toward other sexual matters, and we thus analyze this issue separately. We distinguished between those who regarded homosexual activity as always or almost always wrong and those who said that it was wrong only sometimes or not wrong at all.

Measures of Interpersonal Scripts

For measures of interpersonal scripts, we examined the respondent's actual sexual practices, including both adolescent and adult sexual experiences. Interpersonal scripts can be divided, like cultural scenarios, into three categories: traditional, relational, and recreational.

Two central aspects of interpersonal scripts are the age at the time of first sexual intercourse and the relationship to one's first sex partner. Respondents were asked, "How old were you the *first* time you had vaginal intercourse with a (. . . male/female)?" (*SOS,* 652). It was specified that the interviewer was asking only about the first intercourse after puberty, not about childhood sexual experiences before puberty. We coded those who had sex before age sixteen as having an early initiation into sexual activity and thus have a less traditional interpersonal script. Respondents were then asked, "What was your relationship to this person [i.e., the person with whom respondent had first vaginal intercourse]?" (*SOS,* 652). Those who were married to their first sex partner at the time they had their first sex can be seen as being traditional on this measure. Those who reported that they were in love with their first sex partner (but not necessarily married) were considered to be more relational in their sexual practices than people who reported that they were not in love with their first sex partner. People who reported their first sex as being with someone with whom they were not in love were considered more recreational in their sexual practices.

Another aspect of interpersonal scripts concerns the reasons people report for having decided to have sex for the first time. First, we asked whether this first sexual intercourse was "something you wanted to happen at the time? . . . something you went along with, but did not want to happen? . . . [or] something that you were forced to do against your will?" (*SOS,* 652). This is an important question because it indicates the power the respondent had in negotiating the sexual interaction, a significant part of an interpersonal script and something that helps put the answers in context. For those whose first sex was wanted, the interviewer continued: "There are many different reasons why people go along with having vaginal intercourse for the first time. . . . What was the main reason you decided to go along with having sexual intercourse this first time?" (*SOS,* 653). The answers fell mainly into four categories: affection for partner, curious/ready for sex, physical pleasure, and wedding night. Those who reported having their first sex because it was their wedding night were considered more traditional in their interpersonal scripts. Having first sex because of affection for one's partner indicated a relational script, while having it because of curiosity/readiness or for physical pleasure indicated a more recreational script. We also asked respondents how many sex partners they had had in the past twelve months. Those who reported having three or more partners in the last year were considered more recreational in their sexual practices.

Finally, we asked about the sexual acts occurring in sexual encounters. To determine whether respondents had ever had fellatio or cunnilingus, they were asked, "Have you ever performed oral sex on a [opposite sex: man/woman]?" and, "Has a [opposite sex: man/woman] ever performed oral sex on you?" Regarding heterosexual anal sex, we asked, "Have you ever had anal sex with a [opposite sex: man/woman]?" (*SOS*, 673, 675). The sexual acts in which people engage are not readily associated with particular normative orientations, but they do seem to indicate conventional interpersonal scripts (never having experienced oral or anal sex) as opposed to elaborated interpersonal scripts (ever having experienced oral or anal sex). (For related discussions of these topics, see chap. 1 and 2 above.)

Measures of Intrapsychic Scripts

The respondent's own sexual preferences will serve as measures of his or her intrapsychic scripts. Respondents were asked whether they found certain sex acts, such as vaginal intercourse, watching their partner undress, a partner performing oral sex on them, or performing oral sex on a partner, very appealing, somewhat appealing, not appealing, or not at all appealing. We simply dichotomized the responses into the categories appealing and not appealing. Answers to these questions are best regarded as reflecting either conventional or elaborated intrapsychic scripts. Those who found only vaginal intercourse appealing, a substantial majority of the NHSLS respondents, will be treated as being more conventional in their intrapsychic scripts, while those who find any other sexual act appealing will be regarded as having more elaborated intrapsychic scripts.

5.6 Analyses and Results

For each of the three levels of sexual scripts, we first present cross-tabulations by race/ethnicity and gender so that the actual prevalence of sexual attitudes, practices, and preferences can be examined. We then present the logistic regression models that we ran for men and women separately, and we include in these models the other master statuses. These models do not include interaction terms between race and class because those interactions were not significant for any of the measures of sexual scripts we analyzed, for either men or women.

Table 5.1 below presents the cross-tabulations of attitudes by race/ethnicity and gender so that the actual prevalence of each attitude can be examined. Table 5.2 below presents the logistic regressions on the attitude

variables with respect to the master statuses, for men and women separately. Tables 5.3 and 5.4 below, which follow the same format as tables 5.1
and 5.2, turn attention to interpersonal scripting, that is, sexual practices.
Finally, tables 5.5 and 5.6 below examine intrapsychic scripts (personal
sexual preferences).

Race, Gender, and Class in Sexual Cultural Scenarios

Table 5.1 nicely documents the similarities and differences in cultural scenarios among the racial/ethnic groups. The apparent agreement among
racial/ethnic groups on many aspects of cultural scenarios is perhaps the
most striking feature of the table. Overall, the majority of both men and
women in all the racial/ethnic groups considered do not believe that premarital sex is wrong but do believe that teenage sex (between the ages of
fourteen and sixteen years) is wrong. The majority also agree that any
sexual activity between two consenting adults is OK. Finally, the majority
believe that homosexual activity is wrong.

Relative to one another, however, there are some interesting racial/eth-
nic differences in sexual attitudes that deserve further investigation. Even
after controlling for the other master statuses, the attitudes of Mexican
Americans and African American women are more traditional where sex
is concerned, while whites are less traditional, and African American men
are the least traditional of all.

More specifically, as shown in table 5.2, Mexican Americans are more
than twice as likely as whites to regard premarital sex as wrong when we
control for the other master statuses. Mexican American women are also
three times more likely than white women to believe that teenage sex is
wrong, and Mexican American men are more than twice as likely as white
men to believe that religion shapes their sexual behavior. Thus, Mexican
Americans are more likely than whites to embrace traditional sexual attitudes. Mexican American women are also over three times more likely
than white women to report that homosexual activity is wrong.

In comparison to Mexican Americans, who hold mostly traditional attitudes, whites are more secular and less traditional. For example, whites
are less likely than Mexican Americans to report that religion shapes their
sexual behavior. Whites are also less likely than Mexican Americans to
regard premarital sex as wrong. In addition, whites, and particularly white
women, are much more liberal in their attitudes toward homosexual activity. While the vast majority of whites believe that teenage sex is wrong,
white women are less likely than Mexican American women to believe
this, particularly after taking into account the other master statuses.

The attitudes of African Americans are similar to those of whites on
several issues, such as premarital sex and teenage sex. However, gender

Table 5.1 Racial/Ethnic and Gender Differences in Sexual Attitudes (Percentage Distributions)

	Traditional			Relational: Would Have Sex Only if in Love (% Agree)	Recreational: Any Sex Is OK with Consent (% Agree)	Homosexual: Homosexual Activity (% Wrong)
	Premarital Sex (% Wrong)	Teenage Sex (% Wrong)	Religion Shapes My Sexual Behavior (% Agree)			
White:						
Male	21.6	73.5	44.4	53.1	73.2	71.4
Female	30.3	84.6	56.6	76.4	74.0	63.2
Gender difference	$p < .01$	$p < .01$	$p < .01$	$p < .01$	N.S.	$p < .01$
N	2,440	2,439	2,440	2,434	2,443	2,413
African American:						
Male	25.5	67.6	49.5	43.3	74.4	82.4
Female	38.3	83.2	69.2	77.0	80.1	83.2
Gender difference	$p < .01$	$p < .01$	$p < .01$	$p < .01$	N.S.	N.S.
N	545	546	549	547	549	538
Mexican American:						
Male	27.7	75.9	51.8	56.6	81.9	84.2
Female	41.8	92.4	60.9	78.3	84.6	85.4
Gender difference	N.S.	$p < .01$	N.S.	$p < .01$	N.S.	N.S.
N	174	175	175	175	174	171
Other Hispanic:						
Male	29.8	70.2	44.7	63.8	89.4	70.2
Female	33.3	84.0	63.0	80.3	79.0	71.4
Gender difference	N.S.	N.S.	$p < .05$	$p < .05$	N.S.	N.S.
N	128	128	128	128	128	124
Racial/ethnic difference						
Males	N.S.	N.S.	N.S.	$p < .05$	$p < .05$	$p < .01$
Females	$p < .01$	N.S.	$p < .01$	N.S.	$p < .05$	$p < .01$

Note: N.S. = not significant.

Table 5.2 Racial/Ethnic Differences in Sexual Attitudes (Odds Ratios)

| | Premarital Sex Is Wrong | | | |
| | Men | | Women | |
	Model 1	Model 2	Model 1	Model 2
Race (white):				
African American	1.4†	.9	1.5**	.9
Mexican American	1.4	2.6**	1.8*	2.7***
Other Hispanic	1.4	2.3*	1.1	1.5
Degree (less than high school):				
High school degree		.9		1.1
At least some college		.8		1.1
Age (50–59):				
40–49		.6*		.4***
30–39		.4***		.4***
18–29		.3***		.2***
Religion (none):				
Type I Protestant		2.0*		2.1**
Type II Protestant		8.3***		6.2***
Catholic		1.5		1.7†
Marital status (never married):				
Married		1.6*		1.2
Divorced/separated/widowed		.5*		1.0
Family composition at 14 (2 parents):				
Stepparent		.3**		.9
Single parent		1.1		.9
Pseudo-R^2		.16		.11
N		1,277		1,640

| | Would Have Sex Only if In Love | | | |
| | Men | | Women | |
	Model 1	Model 2	Model 1	Model 2
Race (white:)				
African American	.7*	.7*	1.0	1.0
Mexican American	1.2	1.3	1.3	1.3
Other Hispanic	1.6	1.8	1.1	1.2
Degree (less than high school):				
High school degree		1.0		.8
At least some college		.8		.8
Age (50–59):				
40–49		1.0		.4***
30–39		.8		.4***
18–29		1.1		.4***
Religion (none):				
Type I Protestant		1.6*		1.6*
Type II Protestant		2.2***		2.3***
Catholic		1.5*		1.7*
Marital status (never married):				
Married		2.4***		2.2***
Divorced/separated/widowed		.9		1.1
Family composition at 14 (2 parents):				
Stepparent		.6*		.9
Single parent		.9		1.0
Pseudo-R^2		.06		.05
N		1,271		1,642

Teenage Sex Is Wrong / Religion Shapes My Sexual Behavior

	Teenage Sex Is Wrong				Religion Shapes My Sexual Behavior			
	Men		Women		Men		Women	
	Model 1	Model 2	Model 1	Model 2	Model 1	Model 2	Model 1	Model 2
	.7†	.7	.9	.8	1.3	1.1	1.7***	1.8***
	1.1	1.3	2.2†	3.0*	1.3	2.1**	1.4	1.6†
	.6	.7	1.0	1.2	1.0	1.3	1.2	1.6†
		1.1		1.6*		1.0		.9
		1.1		1.5#		1.6*		1.0
		.8		.4*		.7		.5***
		.5*		.4**		.5**		.4***
		.5**		.2***		.4***		.2***
		1.4		1.6†		3.1***		4.8***
		2.0***		3.2***		6.5***		9.1***
		1.6*		1.8*		2.8***		5.3***
		2.4***		1.6**		1.5**		2.1***
		2.4***		1.3		.7		1.2
		.7†		1.4		.3***		1.0
		.8		.9		1.0		.7*
		.08		.09		.11		.13
	1,273		1,644		1,275		1,646	

Any Sex Is OK with Consent / Homosexual Activity Is Wrong

	Any Sex Is OK with Consent				Homosexual Activity Is Wrong			
	Men		Women		Men		Women	
	Model 1	Model 2	Model 1	Model 2	Model 1	Model 2	Model 1	Model 2
	1.0	1.1	1.6**	1.8**	1.7*	1.3	2.5***	1.3
	1.5	1.0	2.2*	1.7	2.4*	2.0†	3.3***	3.1**
	4.6*	3.7*	1.5	1.2	.8	.7	1.3	1.6
		.9		1.0		.5*		.7
		.5**		.6*		.3***		.3***
		2.0***		1.2		.8		.7†
		1.9**		1.6**		.7		.6*
		2.8***		1.8**		1.0		.6*
		.6†		.6*		2.1***		2.9***
		.3***		.3***		6.1***		9.3***
		.7#		.7		2.4***		2.0**
		.6**		.7*		2.4***		1.3†
		1.2		1.1		1.8*		1.0
		1.1		1.0		.6*		.9
		1.0		1.3		1.0		1.0
		.08		.05		.12		.15
	1,277		1,647		1,266		1,614	

Note: The control group is given in parentheses in the stub column.
†$p < .10$, *$p < .05$, **$p < .01$, ***$p < .001$.

differences between African American men and women are so large that
it is difficult to analyze them together. The attitudes of African American
women are more traditional than those of whites in some respects, while
those of African American men are not. For example, after controlling for
other master-status characteristics, African American women are almost
twice as likely as white women to say that their religion shapes their sexual
behavior. They are also slightly more likely than white women to regard
premarital sex as wrong, although this result is reduced to nonsignificance
when other master statuses are taken into account. Although the attitudes
of African American men are also very similar to those of white men
where sex is concerned, African American men are significantly less likely
than men of other racial/ethnic groups to say that they would have sex
only if they were in love. African American men, in short, hold less relational attitudes than men and women of other racial/ethnic groups.

While the racial/ethnic differences are significant, gender plays the central role in shaping sexual attitudes. In fact, attitudes toward teenage sex,
one's relationship to one's sex partner, and religious beliefs guiding sexual
behavior differ more by gender than by race or ethnicity. More women
than men in all racial/ethnic groups regard premarital and teenage sex as
wrong and assert that their religious beliefs shape their sexual behavior
and that they would not have sex unless they were in love. This may reflect
the sexual double standard that places more restrictions on women's sexuality than on men's. As mentioned above, the gender gap appears largest
among African Americans. While 77 percent of African American women
say that they would have sex only if they were in love, only 43 percent of
African American men agree. And, while 69 percent of African American
women say that their religious beliefs shape their sexual behavior, only 50
percent of African American men say this. Surely, this large gap affects the
negotiation of interpersonal scripts. The gender gap in attitudes toward
premarital sex and teenage sex is also large for Mexican Americans. However, there are no significant gender differences in attitudes toward recreational sexual activity and homosexuality, with the exception of white
men's and women's attitudes toward homosexuality.

What are the effects of class and other master-status variables on sexual
attitudes? Education, age, religion, marital status, and family composition
during adolescence do not diminish racial/ethnic differences in the attitudes toward premarital sex, teenage sex, religious influence on sexual behavior, and having sex only if in love. The one exception is that African
American women do not differ from whites in regarding premarital sex as
wrong once the other master statuses are taken into account. More generally, we observed no interaction effects between race and class for either
men or women.

In most cases, when we control for these other social factors, racial/

ethnic differences are even stronger. For example, only after controlling for these other master statuses are Mexican American men more than twice as likely as white men to regard premarital sex as wrong and to say that their religious beliefs shape their sexual behavior. Differences for Mexican American and other Hispanic women (compared to white women) in the influence of religion on sexual behavior also approach significance once these other social factors are taken into account. While controlling for these other master statuses does not diminish racial/ethnic differences, it is clear that some of these other variables do have significant independent effects, creating variation within racial/ethnic groups. Education, for example, has an effect on women's attitudes toward teenage sex; women with a college education are more likely to regard teenage sex as wrong. For men, education has an effect on men's reporting that their religious beliefs shape their sexual behavior. In the end, however, these attitudes are still largely organized around racial/ethnic lines, with variations according to age and religion.

Other sexual attitudes, however, appear to be more a function of class than of race/ethnicity. Attitudes about recreational sexual and homosexual activity are strongly affected by education. Controlling for education does diminish racial/ethnic differences in attitudes toward homosexual activity and other sexual practices between adults. Those with at least some college are significantly less likely to believe that homosexual activity is wrong. After controlling for education, age, religion, marital status, and family composition, there are no significant racial/ethnic differences among men in attitudes toward homosexuality. The difference in attitudes toward homosexuality between African American women and white women is diminished, although the difference between Mexican American women and white women is only slightly reduced, suggesting perhaps either that homosexuality is understood differently among Mexican Americans (see Carrier 1995) or that there is a particular proscription against homosexuality in Mexican American culture.

Education also has a significant effect on whether the respondent believes that any sexual activity between two consenting adults is OK. Among both men and women, those with at least some college are about half as likely as those who did not finish high school to believe that any sexual activity between two consenting adults is OK. Controlling for these other variables, the difference between Mexican American women and white women is reduced to nonsignificance, but the difference between African American women and white women remains.

In conclusion, education has the strongest effect on attitudes toward recreational sexual practices and homosexuality, at times causing racial/ethnic differences to disappear. This suggests that these attitudes are more related to class and other social characteristics, such as age and religious affiliation, than racial/ethnic group affiliation. However, for other sexual attitudes, racial/ethnic differences largely remain, or become even stronger, after controlling for education and these other social characteristics. Thus, attitudes toward premarital and teenage sex, religious influence on sexual behavior, and having sex only if in love vary more by race and ethnicity than by class.

Race, Class, and Gender in Interpersonal Scripts

Now that we have a picture of the role of race, gender, and class in sexual cultural scenarios, how do these relate to interpersonal scripts or actual sexual practices? Recall that interpersonal scripts refer to the ways in which cultural scenarios are used and adapted to fit specific situations, representing the actor's response to the external world. We first briefly summarize the racial/ethnic similarities and differences in sexual practices and then examine the effects of class and other master statuses on these sexual practices.

Table 5.3 shows us that, just as in the case of cultural scenarios, racial/ethnic groups share basic interpersonal scripts. For example, the majority of men and women in all racial/ethnic groups have had premarital sex. The majority of men and women also report that their first sex was something they wanted to do at the time. In terms of current sexual practices, the majority of people had fewer than three sex partners in the past year and had sex once a week or more in the past twelve months.

Despite these basic similarities among racial/ethnic groups, it is clear that significant differences also exist among the racial/ethnic groups in almost all aspects of interpersonal scripts examined here. For example, even after controlling for other master statuses, whites have sex later in adolescence but engage in more elaborated sexual practices, including oral and anal sex, as adults. Mexican Americans' adolescent sexual behavior is similar to that of whites, but the former are much less likely to engage in oral sex as adults. African Americans have had sex earlier, and have a much higher rate of premarital sex, but are still very conventional in terms of adult sexual practices, being much less likely to engage in oral and anal sex.

When we compare actual sexual practices to the cultural scenarios of the racial/ethnic groups, we find that these two levels of sexual scripts do not always coincide. For example, while Mexican Americans have more traditional attitudes than whites toward premarital sex and teenage sex, their sexual practices are little different from those of whites. And, while African American women hold more traditional sexual attitudes than white women, their actual sexual practices are less traditional. While African American men hold attitudes similar to those of men in other racial/

Table 5.3 Racial/Ethnic and Gender Differences in Sexual Practices (Percentage Distributions)

	Premarital Sex	Teenage Sex (under 16)	In Love with First Sex Partner	First Sex Wanted			Reasons for First Sex (If Wanted)			
				Wanted	Not Wanted	Forced	Affection	Wedding Night	Curiosity/ Readiness	Physical Pleasure
White:										
Male	88.7	21.8	42.3	92.2	7.5	.3	26.1	8.1	53.9	11.9
Female	77.1	13.2	74.8	73.6	22.7	3.8	49.9	22.7	24.7	2.6
Gender difference	$p < .01$	$p < .01$	$p < .01$	$p < .01$			$p < .01$			
N	2,329	2,431	2,329	2,344			1,780			
African American:										
Male	97.5	50.5	33.3	89.5	8.5	2.0	24.5	.6	61.4	13.5
Female	92.5	24.3	69.8	58.9	36.0	5.1	52.6	7.4	34.3	5.7
Gender difference	$p < .05$	$p < .01$	$p < .01$	$p < .01$			$p < .01$			
N	529	547	529	530			338			
Mexican American:										
Male	90.7	30.5	42.7	92.3	7.7	.0	27.4	1.6	50.0	21.0
Female	78.1	19.8	84.2	65.5	29.9	4.6	54.4	21.7	23.9	.0
Gender difference	$p < .05$	N.S.	$p < .01$	$p < .01$			$p < .01$			
N	157	173	157	165			108			
Other Hispanic:										
Male	88.9	38.3	48.9	93.3	6.7	.0	29.3	7.3	43.9	19.5
Female	62.0	16.1	89.9	73.8	23.8	2.5	61.8	21.8	14.6	1.8
Gender difference	$p < .01$	$p < .01$	$p < .01$	$p < .05$			$p < .01$			
N	124	128	124	125			96			
Racial/ethnic difference:										
Males	$p < .01$	$p < .01$	N.S.	N.S.			$p < .01$			
Females	$p < .01$	$p < .01$	$p < .01$	$p < .01$			$p < .01$			

(continued)

Table 5.3 (continued)

	Number of Partners in Last 12 Months		Frequency of Sex in Last 12 Months			Fellatio		Cunnilingus		Anal Sex	
	0–2	3+	None	3 Times/Month	1/Week+	Last Event[a]	Ever	Last Event[a]	Ever	Last Event[a]	Ever
White:											
Male	89.6	10.4	9.7	33.5	56.8	29.5	81.4	29.2	81.7	2.4	25.8
Female	96.0	4.0	12.8	34.1	53.1	21.4	75.3	21.6	78.9	1.2	23.2
Gender difference	p < .01		p < .05			p < .01		p < .01		p < .05	
N	2,352		2,330			1,978	2,330	1,981	2,330	1,982	2,320
African American:											
Male	78.2	21.8	8.3	38.1	53.6	18.6	66.3	17.3	50.5	3.6	23.4
Female	91.7	8.3	17.0	35.3	47.7	9.5	34.4	13.7	48.9	1.5	9.6
Gender difference	p < .01		p < .05			p < .01		N.S.		N.S.	p < .01
N	517		517			429	513	430	513	430	510
Mexican American:											
Male	90.0	10.0	7.7	33.3	59.0	21.7	64.9	23.3	64.9	3.2	31.1
Female	94.4	5.6	7.8	25.6	66.7	16.5	55.8	19.0	61.6	1.3	19.8
Gender difference	N.S.		N.S.			N.S.		N.S.		N.S.	
N	170		168			139	160	139	160	138	160
Other Hispanic:											
Male	88.9	11.1	8.9	24.4	66.7	35.0	83.7	27.5	79.1	7.7	41.9
Female	94.7	5.3	15.8	30.3	54.0	18.2	61.3	22.7	64.0	.0	13.3
Gender difference	N.S.		N.S.			N.S.	p < .05	N.S.		p < .05	p < .01
N	121		121			106	118	106	118	104	118
Racial/ethnic difference:											
Males	p < .01		N.S.			p < .05	p < .01	p < .05	p < .01	N.S.	N.S.
Females	p < .05		p < .05			p < .01	p < .01	p < .05	p < .01	N.S.	p < .01

Note: N.S. = not significant.

[a]Last event variables include only those who had sex more than once with their most recent partner.

ethnic groups regarding premarital sex and teenage sex, they are much less traditional and relational in practice. These disjunctures between the cultural scenario and the interpersonal script suggest that the situational contexts of sexual encounters for racial/ethnic groups are different, leading to differences in the ways in which those cultural scenarios are used. Let us first look in greater detail at adolescent interpersonal scripts and then turn to those of adults.

Adolescent Interpersonal Scripts

Whites are slightly more conventional than other racial/ethnic groups in terms of their early sexual experiences. While the vast majority of whites have had premarital sex, most did not have sex until after they were sixteen. About three-fourths of white women were in love with their first sex partner and reported wanting their first sex at the time. There is a significant gender difference, however, in that only 42 percent of white men reported being in love with their first sex partner. In addition, most white men report wanting their first sex out of curiosity/readiness, while most white women report wanting their first sex because of affection for their partner.

Despite the fact that Mexican Americans have more traditional attitudes than whites, there is no significant difference between the two groups in the proportion who have had teenage sex or premarital sex. Over 90 percent of the men and about 80 percent of Mexican American women had premarital sex, and about 30 percent of the men and 20 percent of the women had sex before they were sixteen. Mexican American women are twice as likely as white women, however, to report being in love with their first sex partner, after controlling for the other master statuses. The higher percentage of Mexican American women who report being in love with their first sex partner is consistent with the feminine ideal in the Mexican American community that makes premarital sex more acceptable for a woman if it is done out of love for her boyfriend (Horowitz 1983). Despite the fact that a higher proportion of Mexican American women report being in love with their first sex partner, almost 30 percent of Mexican American women also report that their first sex was something they went along with but did not want. This, too, may reflect the Mexican American feminine ideal that requires submission to the sexual demands of a boyfriend, particularly when in love. In addition, wanting or intending to have sex transgresses the feminine ideal of passivity and bounded sexuality (Horowitz 1983).

Although the attitudes of African Americans toward premarital sex and teenage sex are not significantly different from those of whites, African Americans do have higher rates of premarital and teenage sex and are less likely than whites to be in love with their first sex partner, even after controlling for the other master statuses. Almost 98 percent of African American men and 93 percent of African American women had premarital sex. African Americans also had a higher rate of teenage sex, with 51 percent of African American men and 24 percent of African American women having sex before they were sixteen. African American women are also the least likely to report that their first sex was wanted at the time even after controlling for other master statuses.

Differences in interpersonal scripts among racial/ethnic groups, despite similarities in cultural scenarios, may be the result of the different situational contexts in which the cultural scenario is used. For example, barriers to their economic success may help explain why African American men have sex before they are sixteen more often than do men in other racial/ethnic groups (despite shared attitudes about teenage sex). In a situation where economic opportunities are blocked, sex during early adolescence is likely to have meaning beyond the sexual, affirming identity as a socially competent, high-status person (Simon and Gagnon 1987b, 58). While this may be true for male adolescents in all racial/ethnic groups, the need for status affirmation may be greater for African American males, for whom other means of obtaining status and affirming identity are blocked (Anderson 1990; Bowser 1994; Hannerz 1969). Indeed, as noted before, twice as many African American men as white men have no high school degree, an indicator of limited later socioeconomic success. However, even after controlling for education, African American men are still three times more likely than white men to have had sex before they were sixteen. In short, blocked opportunities, as measured by education at least, cannot account for all the effects of race on early sexual intercourse.

While having sex early may be a way for African American adolescent males to affirm their status, the literature does not offer the same explanation with regard to African American women. For some African American women, early sex may instead be something that they go along with because they have no future to derail (Anderson 1993). First, African American women are significantly more likely than white women to report that their first sex was something that they went along with but did not want to happen. This may be a result of the very different cultural scenarios with which African American men and women approach the sexual encounter, as discussed above. Second, as shown in table 5.4, education (a measure of future opportunities) has a very strong effect on age at first sex for women at both the high school and the college level. For women, then, the racial/ethnic differences in the percentage having sex before age sixteen disappear when we control for education and the other master statuses.

Gender differences in the percentage actually having sex before age sixteen reflect the differences in attitudes toward teenage sex that are part of the cultural scenarios discussed above. A significantly lower percentage of women than men had premarital and teenage sex in most racial/ethnic groups. Women are also more likely than men to be in love with their first sex partner and to have sex because of affection for their partner. In all racial/ethnic groups, however, women are significantly less likely than men to report that their first sex was wanted.

Adult Interpersonal Scripts

We now turn to an examination of sexual practices occurring in the past twelve months. Compared to other racial/ethnic groups, whites have lower numbers of sex partners but much greater elaboration in sexual practices. The vast majority of whites (90 percent of the men and 96 percent of the women) have fewer than three sex partners in the past twelve months, and most whites have sex once a week or more. About three-fourths of whites have engaged in oral sex, with 30 percent of the men and 21 percent of the women having experienced fellatio in the last event and similar percentages having experienced cunnilingus.

Mexican Americans' number of partners in the last twelve months is very similar to that of whites. As shown in table 5.4, there is also no significant difference in the frequency of partnered sex. However, Mexican Americans are more conventional with regard to other sexual practices, being less than half as likely as whites to engage in oral sex, even after controlling for the other master statuses.

African American men and women are more likely than those in other racial/ethnic groups to have three or more partners in the last twelve months, although, for women, this difference disappears after controlling for other master statuses. Despite the fact that a higher proportion of African American men have three or more sex partners in the past twelve months, there is no significant racial/ethnic difference in the frequency of partnered sex. In terms of other sexual practices, African Americans are more conventional than whites, with African American women being 0.2 times as likely as white women to have ever performed fellatio and African American men and women both being 0.3 times as likely as whites ever to have experienced cunnilingus. African American women are also significantly less likely than white women to have had anal sex, although there is no racial difference among men.

As can be seen in table 5.4, all the differences in specific sex acts remain after we control for the other master statuses. In other words, perhaps owing to the racial/ethnic segregation of sexual partnering, the predominant sexual scripts of these racial/ethnic groups are used by members of those groups irrespective of their other master statuses, giving racial/ethnic group affiliation an independent effect. On the other hand, the other

Table 5.4 Racial/Ethnic Differences in Sexual Practices (Odds Ratios)

| | Married to First Sex Partner | | | |
| | Men | | Women | |
	Model 1	Model 2	Model 1	Model 2
Race (white):				
African American	.2**	.1***	.3***	.2***
Mexican American	.8	1.5	1.0	1.8†
Other Hispanic	1.1	1.8	2.1**	4.1***
Degree (less than high school):				
High school degree		.9		.9
At least some college		1.2		.9
Age (50–59):				
40–49		.5**		.3***
30–39		.3***		.1***
18–29		.2***		.1***
Religion raised in (none):				
Type I Protestant		1.0		2.0
Type II Protestant		3.7*		4.4**
Catholic		1.1		1.9
Family composition at 14 (2 parents):				
Stepparent		.3*		.7
Single parent		.7		.4***
Pseudo-R^2		.13		.19
N		1,230		1,602

Had First Sex before 16

	Men		Women		Men		Women	
	Model 1	Model 2	Model 1	Model 2	Model 1	Model 2	Model 1	Model 2
Race (white):								
African American	3.6***	3.0***	2.2***	1.4	.7*	.6*	.8†	.7*
Mexican American	1.5†	1.2	1.7†	1.2	1.1	1.0	1.8†	2.1*
Other Hispanic	2.7**	2.3*	1.4	1.1	1.4	1.3	3.0**	3.7**
Degree (less than high school):								
High school degree		.8		.4***		.7*		1.0
At least some college		.6*		.3***		.7*		.8
Age (50–59):								
40–49		1.1		1.1		.9		.5**
30–39		1.1		1.9*		.7		.3***
18–29		1.3		3.8***		.7†		.2***
Religion raised in (none):								
Type I Protestant		.7		.5*		.9		1.9*
Type II Protestant		.8		.5*		1.1		2.5**
Catholic		.8		.4***		1.0		1.8*
Family composition at 14 (2 parents):								
Stepparent		2.2***		2.3***		.6*		.9
Single parent		1.7**		1.9***		.9		.8
Pseudo-R^2		.06		.13		.01		.06
N		1,294		1,673		1,230		1,602

(continued)

Table 5.4 (continued)

	First Sex Not Wanted				Had First Sex because of Affection for Partner/Wedding Night			
	Men		Women		Men		Women	
	Model 1	Model 2	Model 1	Model 2	Model 1	Model 2	Model 1	Model 2
Race (white:)								
African American	1.4	1.4	1.8***	1.7***	.7*	.6**	.5***	.5***
Mexican American	1.1	1.0	1.4	1.3	.7	.7	.9	1.1
Other Hispanic	1.0	.8	1.0	1.1	1.4	1.3	1.8	2.1*
Degree (less than high school):								
High school degree		1.2		1.0		.9		1.2
At least some college		1.5		.9		1.0		1.0
Age (50–59):								
40–49		1.5		1.3		1.0		.6*
30–39		1.2		1.7**		.8		.4***
18–29		1.5		1.5*		.7†		.3***
Religion raised in (none):								
Type I Protestant		2.0		1.0		1.1		2.0*
Type II Protestant		2.6		.9		1.9†		3.0***
Catholic		3.2		.8		1.5		2.0*
Family composition at 14 (2 parents):								
Stepparent		1.4		1.5*		.6*		1.1
Single parent		1.4		1.0		1.1		.6**
Pseudo-R^2		.02		.02		.02		.06
N		1,237		1,623		1,126		1,113

Had Sex Once a Week or More in Last 12 Months

3 or More Partners in Last 12 Months

	Men		Women		Men		Women	
	Model 1	Model 2	Model 1	Model 2	Model 1	Model 2	Model 1	Model 2
Race (white):								
African American	.9	1.0	.8†	.9	2.1**	2.0**	2.3**	1.4
Mexican American	1.1	1.0	1.5†	1.3	.8	.6	.9	.9
Other Hispanic	1.6	1.8	1.1	1.0	1.2	1.0	1.4	1.4
Degree (less than high school):								
High school degree		1.3		1.3		.7		.8
At least some college		1.2		1.0		1.3		.6
Age (50–59):								
40–49		1.4		2.4***		1.9		5.7
30–39		1.9***		3.8***		3.1*		13.9*
18–29		3.2***		6.7***		3.9**		17.9**
Current religion raised in (none):								
Type I Protestant		1.1		.8		1.4		.7
Type II Protestant		1.2		1.0		1.1		.5†
Catholic		1.3		.8		1.4		.3**
Marital status (not currently married):								
Currently married		3.5***		3.5***		.1***		.1***
Pseudo-R^2		.07		.10		.18		.21
N		1,263		1,645		1,274		1,657

Note: The control group is given in parentheses in the stub column.

†$p < .10$.
*$p < .05$.
**$p < .01$.
***$p < .001$.

230 J. Mahay, E. Laumann, and S. Michaels

master statuses are related to internal variations in the selection of sexual scripts within particular racial/ethnic groups. For example, people with some college education are much more likely to have elaborated sexual practices and preferences than are less-educated people within the same racial/ethnic group. Again, there were no significant interaction effects between race and class for any measures of interpersonal scripts. The interaction terms were thus not included in the models presented here.

Race, Class, and Gender in Intrapsychic Scripts

Let us now turn to racial/ethnic similarities and differences in individuals' sexual desires and fantasies, key elements of the intrapsychic sexual script. We find that the intrapsychic scripts of racial/ethnic groups generally coincide with their interpersonal scripts. For example, chapter 4 of *SOS* found that, as with their interpersonal scripts, whites had more elaborated intrapsychic scripts than African Americans and Mexican Americans when one counted the number of sexual techniques, such as oral or anal sex and manual stimulation, that respondents found very appealing. White men had the highest mean number of *very appealing* responses, 2.6. African American men had a significantly lower mean number of *very appealing* responses, 2.47, and Hispanic men had an even lower mean number, 2.38. Women in all the racial/ethnic groups had lower mean numbers of *very appealing* responses than men, but they also differed significantly between racial and ethnic groups. White women reported a mean of 1.68 techniques to be very appealing, which was close to Hispanic women's mean of 1.65. African American women, however, found a mean of only 1.48 techniques very appealing. In general, African Americans and Hispanics find fewer sexual techniques very appealing.

The first column in table 5.5 shows the percentage finding each of the three most common sexual practices appealing, while the second column shows the percentage who reported engaging in this sexual practice in the last sexual event. The third column presents the percentage of those who both found a practice appealing and reported that it happened in the last event. Finally, the fourth column presents the expected percentage of "matching," that is, of two randomly paired people both finding the practice appealing.[3]

Vaginal intercourse enjoys almost universal appeal and constitutes a part of the vast majority of people's intrapsychic scripts in all the racial/ethnic groups. However, there are some racial/ethnic variations among women in the appeal of vaginal intercourse. Other Hispanic women are significantly less likely than women of the other racial/ethnic groups analyzed here to find vaginal intercourse very or somewhat appealing. However, there were no racial or gender differences in whether vaginal inter-

Table 5.5 Racial/Ethnic Differences in Sexual Preferences and Last Event Activities (Percentage Distributions)

	Vaginal Intercourse				Fellatio				Cunnilingus			
	Appealing (1)	Happened in Last Event[a] (2)	% (1) + (2)	% Expected Matching	Appealing (1)	Happened in Last Event[a] (2)	% (1) + (2)	% Expected Matching	Appealing (1)	Happened in Last Event[a] (2)	% (1) + (2)	% Expected Matching
White:												
Male	95.8	94.4	94.5	92	82.3	29.5	34.3	53	77.0	29.2	35.6	58
Female	95.9	95.1	95.1		55.3	21.4	33.5		64.8	21.6	30.5	
Gender difference	N.S.	N.S.	N.S.		$p < .01$	$p < .01$	N.S.		$p < .01$	$p < .01$	$p < .05$	
N	2,428	1,916			2,420	1,978			2,422	1,981		
African American:												
Male	94.7	95.8	95.7	88	54.9	18.6	31.6	39	41.8	17.3	34.7	52
Female	92.3	97.3	98.8		25.3	9.5	27.5		40.1	13.7	28.7	
Gender difference	N.S.	N.S.	$p < .05$		$p < .01$	$p < .01$	N.S.		N.S.	N.S.	N.S.	
N	544	423			546	429			545	430		
Mexican American:												
Male	91.6	96.7	96.5	87	68.3	21.7	32.5	49	54.3	23.3	37.8	51
Female	94.5	96.0	98.6		46.2	16.5	28.6		62.6	19.0	27.3	
Gender difference	N.S.	N.S.	N.S.		$p < .01$	N.S.	N.S.		N.S.	N.S.	N.S.	
N	174	136			173	139			172	139		
Other Hispanic:												
Male	93.6	97.3	97.3	84	76.6	35.0	43.8	48	70.2	27.5	35.5	52
Female	88.9	93.9	93.3		46.9	18.2	34.3		54.3	22.7	31.7	
Gender difference	N.S.	N.S.	N.S.		$p < .01$	N.S.	N.S.		N.S.	N.S.	N.S.	
N	128	102			128	106			128	106		
Racial/ethnic difference:												
Males	N.S.	N.S.	N.S.		$p < .01$	$p < .05$	N.S.		$p < .01$	$p < .05$	N.S.	
Females	$p < .01$	N.S.	$p < .05$		$p < .01$	$p < .01$	N.S.		$p < .01$	$p < .05$	N.S.	

[a]Last event variables include only those who had sex more than once with their most recent partner. N.S. = not significant.

course occurred in the last event. When we look at the percentage of people who both find vaginal intercourse appealing and actually had vaginal intercourse in the last event, we find that African American and Mexican American women who find vaginal intercourse appealing are more likely than white women or other Hispanic women to have had vaginal intercourse in the last event.

While vaginal intercourse is almost universally appealing, the appeal of oral sex varies greatly by race and ethnicity. While the vast majority of white men (82 percent) find fellatio appealing, a substantially lower proportion of African American men (55 percent) find it appealing. Mexican American and the other Hispanic men find fellatio appealing more often than African American men do but still less often than white men do. Similarly, while 55 percent of white women find fellatio appealing, only 25 percent of African American women do. It is apparent that there are also significant gender differences in the percentage finding fellatio appealing in all racial/ethnic groups. For example, among African Americans, more than twice as many men as women find fellatio appealing. Thus, the probability that a man and a woman would match in their preference for fellatio, assuming random partnering within racial/ethnic groups, is much lower for African Americans (39 percent) than it is for whites (53 percent).

The appeal of cunnilingus also varied widely among racial/ethnic groups. A much higher percentage of white men (77 percent) than African American men (42 percent) reported that they found cunnilingus appealing. Likewise, a higher percentage of white women (65 percent) than African American women (40 percent) found cunnilingus appealing. Again, Mexican Americans and the other Hispanics are between African Americans and whites in the percentage finding cunnilingus appealing. However, unlike for fellatio, there is no significant gender difference in the proportion finding cunnilingus appealing, except among whites. There is also a significant difference between white men and white women in the percentage who both find cunnilingus appealing and reported that it occurred in the last sexual event: a higher percentage of white men than white women who find cunnilingus appealing reported that it occurred in the last event.

Table 5.6 shows that, when we control for education and other master statuses, racial/ethnic differences in the proportion finding oral sex appealing remain. While education does have a significant effect on preferences for cunnilingus and fellatio, as it does for the actual practice of these acts, the racial/ethnic differences are not diminished. As in the other analyses, we did run a model that included the interaction term between race and class but found no significant interaction effect for any of the sexual preferences examined here.

Thus, while vaginal intercourse is part of the intrapsychic scripts of all four racial/ethnic groups, whites include fellatio and cunnilingus to a larger degree in their intrapsychic scripts, while Mexican Americans and other Hispanics include these sexual practices to a lesser extent. African Americans are the least likely to include fellatio and cunnilingus in their intrapsychic scripts.

5.7 Summary: Racial/Ethnic Similarities and Differences in Sexual Scripts

First, we found that racial and ethnic groups share many aspects of their sexual scripts. The majority of people in all racial/ethnic groups, for example, believe that teenage sex and same-gender sex are wrong and report that they would not have sex unless they were in love. In terms of sexual practices, most people have had premarital sex but waited until they were at least sixteen to have sexual intercourse, have fewer than three sex partners in the last twelve months, and have sex once a week or more. In intrapsychic scripts, vaginal intercourse is found to be almost universally appealing, but only smaller pluralities find most other sexual practices appealing.

However, even after controlling for other master-status variables, there are still significant racial/ethnic variations in these aspects of sexual scripts and even larger differences in the practices of other sexual activities, such as oral sex. Because race and ethnicity are highly correlated with other master statuses, different sexual scripts develop within these sexually segregated racial/ethnic groups. These sexual scripts become the norm for those in racial/ethnic groups and are used even by members of those groups who differ on other master statuses. Thus, we get an independent effect for racial and ethnic group affiliation after controlling for the other master statuses. Below, we summarize the predominant sexual scripts for whites, African Americans, and Mexican Americans.

Secular Cultural Scenario, Relational-Elaborated Interpersonal Scripts

White men's and women's cultural scenarios do not fit neatly into any of the broad normative orientations. While these men and women are similar to the other racial/ethnic groups with respect to recreational and relational attitudes, they are less likely to say that their religious beliefs shape their sexual behavior or that premarital sex is wrong, and they are more liberal in their attitudes toward homosexuality. Although there are significant gender differences among whites, white women still hold attitudes that are less traditional (and more secular) than those of women in the other racial/ethnic groups, particularly Mexican American women.

Regarding interpersonal scripts, whites can best be described as relational-elaborated. While the overwhelming majority of whites had premarital sex and thus cannot be considered traditional in that respect, they are more likely than African Americans to say that they were in love with

Table 5.6 Racial/Ethnic Differences in Sexual Preferences (Odds Ratios)

| | Vaginal Intercourse | | | |
| | Men | | Women | |
	Model 1	Model 2	Model 1	Model 2
Race (white):				
African American	.9	1.2	.5**	.7
Mexican American	.4†	.6	.6	.7
Other Hispanic	.6	.8	.3**	.3**
Degree (less than high school):				
High school degree		2.1*		1.7†
At least some college		3.3***		3.3***
Age (50–59):				
40–49		1.1		1.8†
30–39		1.1		2.6**
18–29		1.3		2.2*
Religion (none):				
Type I Protestant		1.6		.6
Type II Protestant		1.8		.8
Catholic		1.8		.8
Marital status (never married):				
Married		4.0***		5.6***
Pseudo-R^2		.08		.13
N		1,325		1,710

†$p < .10$.
*$p < .05$.
**$p < .01$.
***$p < .001$.

their first sex partner, indicating a more relational orientation. Whites are also much more likely than the other racial/ethnic groups to engage in elaborated sexual behavior, such as oral and anal sex. One hypothesis is that the more elaborated and less procreation-oriented sexual script of whites is due to a weakening of religious influence on sexual attitudes and practices. A lower proportion of whites than of the other racial/ethnic groups assert that their religious beliefs shape and guide their sexual behavior in every age cohort younger than fifty to fifty-nine, even after the other master statuses are taken into account. Evidence that religion is linked to less elaborated sexual practices is found in the fact that respondents who agree that their religious beliefs shape and guide their sexual behavior are less than half as likely to have ever engaged in fellatio or cunnilingus.

Fellatio				Cunnilingus			
Men		Women		Men		Women	
Model 1	Model 2	Model 1	Model 2	Model 1	Model 2	Model 1	Model 2
.3***	.3***	.3***	.3***	.2***	.2***	.4***	.4***
.4***	.4**	.7†	.7	.3***	.3***	.9	.9
.8	.8	.8	.7	.7	.7	.7	.6*
	1.8**		1.9***		1.9**		2.0***
	3.5***		2.9***		2.9***		2.7***
	3.0***		3.0***		2.9***		2.6***
	5.2***		5.3***		4.3***		4.8***
	5.8***		5.2***		4.2***		4.9***
	.8		.5**		.9		.5**
	.4**		.4***		.5**		.5***
	1.0		.5**		1.2		.5**
	1.1		1.2		1.3†		1.0
	.16		.13		.14		.12
	1,321		1,706		1,321		1,706

Gendered Cultural Scenario, Recreational-Conventional Interpersonal Scripts

Characterizing the cultural scenarios of African Americans as a whole is difficult because men and women embrace such different sexual scripts. African American women hold more traditional and relational attitudes toward premarital sex, homosexuality, teenage sex, the influence of religion on sexual behavior, and having sex only if in love than African American men. They are much less likely to describe their first sexual experience as wanted at the time than women in any other group.

Regarding interpersonal scripts, African Americans are typically recreational-conventional in orientation. They are more likely than the other groups to report that they were not in love with their first sex partner, that they had their first sex because of curiosity/readiness or physical pleasure, and that they had three or more partners in the past year. At the same time, they are much more conventional than whites in what they do in sexual encounters, being much less likely to engage in oral or anal sex.

One explanation for the more conventional features of African Americans' sexual scripts is the legacy of fundamentalist and evangelical Protestantism. About 64 percent of African American men and 75 percent of African American women are affiliated with conservative Protestant churches, and similar proportions were raised in such churches. This is over twice, and sometimes more than three times, the rate of affiliation for any of the other racial/ethnic groups. African Americans, particularly women, are especially likely to say that their religious beliefs shape and guide their sexual behavior. Support for the hypothesis that conventional sexual practices arc the result of conservative religious affiliation is found in the fact that whites affiliated with fundamentalist and evangelical Protestant churches are also much less likely to have had experience with oral or anal sex. More research is surely needed to clarify how recreational scripts came to dominate the orientations of African American men.

Traditional Cultural Scenario, Relational-Conventional Interpersonal Scripts

Mexican Americans' cultural scenarios are traditional in orientation with respect to attitudes toward premarital sex, homosexuality, religious influences on sexual behavior (for men), and attitudes toward teenage sex (for women).

Regarding interpersonal scripts, Mexican Americans are relational-conventional. They cannot be considered traditional because the vast majority have engaged in premarital sex. They are, however, relational in their interpersonal scripts because Mexican American women are twice as likely as white women to report that they were in love with their first sex partner, after controlling for the other master statuses. Mexican Americans are also less likely than African Americans to have had three or more partners in the last year. In terms of specific sex acts, Mexican Americans are more conventional than whites in that they are less likely to engage in fellatio or cunnilingus.

Mexican Americans' traditionalism in sexual scripts may be rooted in their Catholicism, which emphasizes procreational sexual practices within the context of marriage. Three-fourths of Mexican American men and two-thirds of Mexican American women are Catholic. Over 50 percent of Mexican American men and over 60 percent of Mexican American women report that their religious beliefs shape and guide their sexual behavior.

Although Mexican American women overwhelmingly reported being in love with their first sex partner, a fairly high percentage (30 percent) also reported that their first sex was something they went along with but did not want. This paradox may be a result of the fact that premarital sex is considered more acceptable in the Mexican American community if it is not something the woman wants but rather something that is done out of love for and feminine submission to her boyfriend (Horowitz 1983).

Elaboration of Sexual Script by Class, Age, Religious Affiliation, and Marital Status

Master statuses other than race and ethnicity also exert significant effects on sexual attitudes, preferences, and practices. The younger age cohorts are less traditional in their attitudes and more likely to have sex earlier, to have more sex partners, to have sex more frequently, and to engage in oral sex. The college educated are also significantly more likely to engage in cunnilingus and fellatio, to find those practices appealing, and to express more liberal views toward homosexuality. Those who are conservative Protestants are less likely to engage in or find oral sex appealing and more likely to regard teenage sex, premarital sex, and homosexual activity as wrong. Married people, compared to the never married, are more likely to regard premarital sex and teenage sex as wrong. They report fewer sex partners but have partnered sex more frequently.

5.8 Conclusion

While racial/ethnic groups share basic similarities in their sexual scripts, important differences remain even after one takes the effects of education, religion, age, and marital status into account. We hypothesize that the racial/ethnic segregation of sexual partnering results in sexual scripts that are particularized to each group. When a specific sexual script becomes the norm in a group, it may be used by other members of the group regardless of their other master statuses. Because the script is *socially* produced, individuals must call on shared meanings and expectations in order to enact them. Further research must be conducted if we are to understand how actual networks and social contexts of sexual partnering facilitate the development and transmission of sexual scripts.

The sexual scripts approach also revealed the complex patterns in which specific sexual practices are embedded. For example, while African Americans may be less traditional in their age at and the context of first intercourse, they are actually more traditional in their actual sexual practices in adulthood. We also found contradictions between the cultural scenarios and the interpersonal scripts of some groups. These disjunctures highlight the different contexts in which these generally shared cultural narratives are applied in actual situations. Along these lines, some have argued that the racial/ethnic differences in sexual behavior are really an effect of class locations. But we found that, although education does have a significant effect on many sexual behaviors, race/ethnicity retains an independent effect.

Finally, we found that, for many aspects of sexual scripts, gender differences are more substantial than racial/ethnic differences. And, where the gender differences in cultural scenarios were the greatest, so were the number of women who reported that their first sex was something that they went along with but did not want. Gender is thus an integral part of sexual scripts, with profound consequences for men's and women's sexual experiences.

Notes

The authors thank Anthony Paik, Martha Van Haitsma, and Yoosik Youm for helpful comments.

1. A small percentage of our sample reported other religious affiliations, such as Muslim. For the purposes of our analysis, these were not included.

2. Those raised without either parent were not included in this analysis.

3. An analysis of the expected matching on a given sexual preference was conducted in chap. 4 of *SOS*. Here, we conduct this analysis separately for the four racial/ethnic groups. In order to calculate the probability of agreement, or match, with respect to a specific sexual preference, we sum the products of the proportions of men and women who prefer a practice and the product of the proportions of men and women who do not find that practice appealing. If P equals the percentage of men who prefer a given sexual practice and Q equals the percentage of women who prefer a given sexual practice, then, assuming random mating with regard to preferences, the expected percentage of matched couples is given by

$$PQ + (1 - P)(1 - Q) = 1 - P - Q + PQ.$$

■

Emotional and Physical Satisfaction with Sex in Married, Cohabiting, and Dating Sexual Unions: Do Men and Women Differ?

LINDA J. WAITE AND KARA JOYNER

The sexual revolution of the mid- to late 1960s marked a change in sexual practices, increasing both the amount of sexual activity outside of marriage and the number of partners people have over their lifetimes. The opening shot in this revolution may have been the introduction and dissemination of the Pill, but the legalization of abortion in 1972 and the women's movement were both allies in the war. Other dramatic social changes occurred in this period, both contributing to and propelled by changes in sexual behavior. The proportion of young adults who were never married increased as age at marriage rose. Divorce rates rose dramatically beginning in about 1960, and the divorced remarried less quickly (Cherlin 1992). Attitudes have tracked these changes in behavior; American adults have become more tolerant of both nonmarriage (i.e., never being married) and divorce (Thornton 1989) and more accepting of premarital sexual relations (Smith 1994).

Currently, more adults are unmarried than at any time since 1950 (Waite 1995). About three-quarters of unmarried men and about two-thirds of unmarried women engage in some form of partnered sexual activity during the course of a year (see *SOS*). A growing number of the sexually active single live with a partner in a socially recognized type of union that we have come to call *cohabitation*. In the early 1990s, almost one-quarter of single adults in their mid-twenties were cohabiting, with smaller but substantial proportions at increasingly older ages (Waite 1995).

The married and cohabiting and many of the sexually active single share an important characteristic—they are in "sexually-based primary relationships" (Scanzoni et al. 1989). Do these relationships differ in terms of the emotional satisfaction and physical pleasure derived from sex that they provide to those in them? In table 3.7 of *SOS*, higher levels of emotional and physical satisfaction with sex were reported for married than for cohabiting or single people. But that table reports only the percentage of respondents in each group who are extremely satisfied with sex, without consideration of the characteristics of the individual or the union that might account for these differences.

This chapter examines the emotional satisfaction and physical pleasure of sexually active men and women aged eighteen to fifty-nine who are married, cohabiting, and in sexually active dating partnerships. We present a conceptual framework of characteristics of different types of sexual relationships and their effect on men's and women's sexual satisfaction within them. We derive a series of hypotheses from this framework and test them using data from the 1992 National Health and Social Life Survey (NHSLS). Our findings suggest that differences between types of unions in terms of emotional commitment and sexual exclusivity account for all the higher levels of emotional satisfaction with sex of married men but not of married women. Once we take into account characteristics of individuals and unions, we see no differences between either men or women in different unions in physical satisfaction with sex. But, even within types of relationships, men and women who report greater emotional commitment to their partner and more commitment to sexual exclusivity also express greater satisfaction with both the emotional and the physical aspects of sex.

6.1 Theoretical Perspectives on Sexual Satisfaction

Previous theories of sexuality suggest that individuals evaluate sexual relationships on the basis of biological, individual, and social factors; these factors structure both the preferences and the behavior of individuals in these relationships. Perspectives on evolutionary biology argue that men and women are "hardwired" differently, in ways that affect their feelings about physical and emotional involvement and, to a lesser extent, their involvement itself. Rational choice perspectives stress that the resources and investments of individuals determine their goals with respect to sexual involvement and their ability to achieve those goals.

Evolutionary biology perspectives suggest that men and women differ in optimal sexual and reproductive strategies (Buss 1994; Feingold 1992; Symons 1979; Townsend 1995). According to these perspectives, the fact that men can have many children without investing much in any of them makes their optimal reproductive strategy fathering children with a number of women. The fact that women can have relatively few children over their reproductive lives and must invest a great deal in each one pushes them toward a stable, long-term relationship with a man who will support her and her children. Men optimize their reproductive potential by mating with women who show signs of sexual exclusivity, which ensures them of their paternity. Women optimize this potential by mating with men who show signs of emotional involvement; such involvement on the part of men proves their willingness to invest (Buunk, Angleitner, and Buss 1996).

These perspectives suggest that evolutionary differences manifest themselves more in sexual feelings than in sexual behavior since behavior is more strongly influenced by social practices (Posner 1992; Singer 1985). Considering emotional responses, women search for signals of a long-term commitment and are dissatisfied in its absence, whereas men's relatively short-term, physical orientation to sex makes a long-term commitment unimportant for their satisfaction with it (Buss 1994; DeLamater 1987; Townsend 1995). Furthermore, men are more likely than women to become distressed in response to a partners' physical involvement with someone else, whereas women are more likely than men to become distressed in response to a partner's emotional involvement with someone else (Buunk 1996). Regarding physical responses, men are aroused by a range of stimuli, such as visual cues, whereas women are aroused under securely partnered conditions, such as a committed relationship (Knoth, Boyd, and Singer 1988).

These perspectives further suggest that the magnitude of these responses differs according to socialization and social practices (Buunk, Angleitner, and Buss 1996). For instance, in cultures where women are less dependent on men for their resources, they become less jealous in response to a partner's extradyadic emotional involvement. To explain differences in emotional satisfaction and physical pleasure, then, we must understand social arrangements and their effect on men's and women's preferences for emotional and physical involvement.

Rational choice perspectives specifically consider how individuals' resources and investments organize their sexual goals in contemporary society. Offering such a perspective, *SOS* argues that finding a partner and negotiating a sexual relationship require such resources as time, money, and social capital. Since the process of securing new partners is costly, it makes better sense for individuals to gratify their emotional and physical needs in a long-term relationship than to keep switching partners. Besides, individuals have an incentive to invest in skills that enhance the enjoyment of sex with a particular partner. Sex with the partner who knows what one likes and how to provide it is more satisfying than sex with a partner who lacks such skills.

A disadvantage of "partner-specific" investments is that they lack portability. For instance, the skills developed to please one partner may not work with another partner. In contrast, investments in such things as earning power may be useful with any partner. Because the utility of partner-pleasing investments is circumscribed, individuals are ill advised to make these investments if they do not expect the relationship to last. Women are considered to invest more than men in partner-pleasing skills, such as understanding the needs of a partner and attending to them (England and Farkas 1986).

6.2 Conceptual Framework and Hypotheses

To understand how men and women evaluate their emotional satisfaction and physical pleasure in marriage, cohabitation, and dating relationships, we need to understand their expectations and behavior in these relationships and how these are related to their preferences. It could be argued that individuals choose between these different types of relationships on the basis of their preferences. Yet relationships involve two individuals who may differ in terms of what they want from it. For example, partners in cohabitation frequently bring different levels of commitment to the relationship, with different expectations for its future (Bumpass, Sweet, and Cherlin 1991). This suggests that the expectations and behavior in any type of relationship may be the result of cooperation and compromise (see *SOS*).

We argue that couples who are married, couples who are living together but not married, and sexually active couples who are neither married nor living together bring different expectations about sex to their relationship and engage in different sexual behavior. In particular, the institutions involved carry with them the framework within which couples negotiate the details of their sex lives. The experience of individuals and couples may depend on the type of union, to the extent that unions differ in important ways. We argue that marriage, cohabitation, and what we call *dating* here differ, as institutions, on three key dimensions: (1) the time horizon expected for the relationship; (2) the level of emotional investment in the relationship; and (3) sexual exclusivity in the relationship. The importance of each of these dimensions may differ for men and women, as we discuss below.

Marriage as a social institution offers guidelines with respect to sexual conduct, among other things. Historically, the institution of marriage has implied a long-term contract between the partners and sexual exclusivity, as expressed in marriage vows in many religions. More recently, this institution has also emphasized an emotional bond between partners (Bernard 1972). Both cohabitation and dating are less institutionalized than marriage, in that the "rules" governing each are less clear-cut and require more negotiation by the individual parties. This very lack of institutionalization may make these types of unions more heterogeneous than marriage.

The institution of marriage socially and legally binds the partners to a lifetime commitment—barring divorce. Because they expect to stay together, married couples have substantial incentives to develop what economists refer to as *marital-specific capital*. This includes learning skills that make this particular marriage better but are generally less useful (England and Farkas 1986). As mentioned earlier, learning to please a partner sexually is one such skill. The long-term contract implicit in marriage also facilitates emotional investment in the relationship, which should increase emotional satisfaction and physical pleasure. The wife or husband who knows what a spouse wants sexually is also highly motivated to provide it because the emotional investment in the relationship makes satisfying him or her important in and of itself. Posner (1992, 112) argues that the emotional investment in companionate marriage makes extramarital sex "an inferior substitute for marital sex . . . or a more costly one."

Although cohabitation and marriage both offer sexual access, they differ in important ways. Cohabitation carries no explicit commitment to stay together for the long term. The fact that cohabiting partners have not married signals both to each other and to those around them a lower level of commitment to each other and to the relationship—at least by one of the partners. It follows that cohabitation is characterized by less investment in the relationship than marriage, both emotionally and in terms of developing partner-specific skills. Although the vast majority of individuals who are cohabiting expect the relationship to be sexually exclusive (see *SOS*), women in cohabiting relationships are substantially less likely than married women to have had a sexually exclusive relationship with their partner (Forste and Tanfer 1996). Cohabitation, then, is characterized not only by a lack of investment but also by divestment. Cohabitation as an institution, albeit one that is incompletely institutionalized, appears to require less from those who enter it than marriage (Thomson and Colella 1992).

Single individuals in an ongoing sexual partnership are probably more heterogeneous than either the married or the cohabiting. Some are engaged or dating someone about whom they are serious. Some are seeing a number of people. Some are in the very early stages of a relationship that may become serious or end quickly. Our guess is that single men and women have, on average, a shorter expected length of relationship, less emotional investment, and less sexual exclusivity than either the married or the cohabiting.

We hypothesize that a long time horizon, emotional investment, and sexual exclusivity all increase the emotional satisfaction and physical pleasure derived from sex. We expect that, within different types of unions, women and men most committed to their partner and those who are sexually exclusive will show the highest levels of emotional satisfaction and physical pleasure. Evolutionary perspectives suggest that the expected length of the relationship and emotional investment will be less important for men than they are for women. They additionally suggest that the sexual exclusivity of the female partner will be more critical than that of the male partner. At the same time, these perspectives suggest that the magnitude of these differences is variable.

We also hypothesize that the expectations and behavior inherent in marriage will increase the emotional satisfaction and physical pleasure that women derive from sex. To the extent that men and women benefit from an extended time horizon, emotional investment, and sexual exclusivity, we expect that—as others have found—the married will report higher levels of satisfaction than either the cohabiting or the single. As suggested above, we expect that married women will benefit more from these things than married men. We test these hypotheses directly, using measures of attitudes, expectations, and behavior on these dimensions.

6.3 Data

Data for these analyses come from the NHSLS. The survey contains information about respondents' emotional satisfaction, physical pleasure, background characteristics, and sexual behavior, attitudes, and tastes.

We compare those who are married with those who are living with someone in a sexual relationship and with those who are not living with a partner. We begin with those in an ongoing sexual relationship, which includes virtually all the currently married and cohabiting individuals. For single individuals, we define an ongoing sexual relationship as one in which the respondent has had sex with the partner at least once and expects to have sex with this partner again. We exclude sample members with a partner of the same sex because the sample contains too few of them to examine processes in their relationships separately. We examine only reports of satisfaction with sex with the primary partner, assumed in the NHSLS to be the spouse if married or the cohabiting partner if cohabiting. Single individuals with more than one partner were asked to consider their most important partner the primary one.

Measures of Sexual Satisfaction. Respondents to the NHSLS were asked, "How physically pleasurable did you find your relationship with (PARTNER) to be: extremely pleasurable, very pleasurable, moderately pleasurable, slightly pleasurable, or not at all pleasurable?" "How emotionally satisfying did you find your relationship with (PARTNER) to be, extremely satisfying, very satisfying, moderately satisfying, slightly satisfying, or not at all satisfying?" Since these questions followed immediately after a question that asked, "Now I would like to ask you how sex with (PARTNER) made you feel," (*SOS*, 627), it was clear that these questions referred to sex in the relationship.

Sexual Activity. A number of scholars link sexual satisfaction to quantity and quality of sexual activity (e.g., Edwards and Booth 1994; Sprecher and McKinney 1993). Our models include objective indicators of this activity. We include both the number of times in the past month the respondent had sex with his or her husband/wife or cohabiting or dating partner, the frequency of orgasm for the respondent during sex with this partner, and the frequency of orgasm for the partner. Values on both indicators of quality range from always to never.

Emotional Investment.   We measure the level of emotional investment in a number of ways. First, we include the extent to which respondents agreed with the statement, "I would not have sex with someone unless I was in love them" (*SOS,* 667). We argue that those who strongly agree with this statement invest more emotionally in their relationships than those who do not strongly agree. Respondents were also asked to give their reasons for having sex with their partner in the last year. We consider those who gave "to express love or affection" as one of the reasons also to be more invested emotionally. Respondents were also asked the extent to which they agreed with the statement, "I try to make sure that my partner has an orgasm when we have sex" (*SOS,* 667). We interpret a response of "strongly agree" as a measure of investment in the sexual satisfaction of one's partner. Respondents were also asked to rate "having sex with someone you don't personally know" (*SOS,* 648) anywhere from very appealing to not at all appealing. Although an individual may not act on his or her feelings, we expect that those to whom sex with strangers is somewhat or very appealing feel less need for emotional investment than those to whom this activity is not appealing.

Sexual Exclusivity.   The NHSLS obtained a number of measures of sexual exclusivity that we use here. These measures include both attitudes and behaviors. Respondents were asked, "What is your opinion about a married person having sexual relations with someone other than the marriage partner—is it always wrong, almost always wrong, sometimes wrong, or not wrong at all?" (*SOS,* 666). We interpret the belief that extramarital sex is always wrong as an indicator of a commitment to sexual exclusivity, at least within marriage. Respondents were also asked to rate "having sex with more than one person at the same time" (*SOS,* 648) from very appealing to not at all appealing. Although an individual may not act on his or her feelings, we argue that those to whom group sex is appealing are less attracted to sexual exclusivity than those to whom this activity is not appealing. We also measure sexual exclusivity directly. We code as not exclusive those who reported that in the past year they had sexual relations with another partner while with their primary partner as well as those who report that their partner had another partner. Finally, the frequency with which an individual masturbated in the last year reflects use of a sexual outlet independent of the partnership. Those who are willing and able to masturbate are less dependent on their partner for sexual activity than are others. *SOS* (p. 83) concluded that "the frequency of masturbation has no set quantitative relation to other partnered sexual activities."

Time Horizon. The NHSLS did not ask married and cohabiting individuals their views about the stability of their relationship, evidently presuming that these men and women saw their relationships as stable. But it did obtain this information for single men and women, asking those in an ongoing sexual relationship how much longer they expected the relationship to last. Responses to this question could range from "a few more days" to "a lifetime."

Other Variables. Our models of the emotional satisfaction and physical pleasure derived from sex include a number of variables in addition to those listed above. We include these variables primarily as controls. Our models include demographic and background characteristics of respondents that might affect these outcomes. They also include age, race, duration of the relationship, health, education, religion and religious participation, presence of young children, employment status, and hours spent performing housework and paid work (*SOS;* see also Call et al. 1995). Finally, they include a variable indicating the presence of the partner at the interview to take into account correlated response bias (see Aquilino 1993).

6.4 Methods

Table 6.1 presents definitions of the variables in the analysis and gives means and standard deviations for each, separately for men and women. The first two rows of the table contain this information for the two dependent variables, the emotional satisfaction and physical pleasure derived from sex in the relationship. Appendix tables 6A.1 and 6A.2 show the mean values for sexual practices, emotional investment, and sexual exclusivity by union status for men and women, respectively.

For both emotional satisfaction and physical pleasure, we present a series of models, estimated separately for men and women (see tables 6.2–6.5 below). All models presented include the entire set of demographic and background variables listed in table 6. 1. Model 1 (col. 1) includes, in addition, two indicator variables for union status, defined as married or single, with cohabitors constituting the reference category. This model tells us whether married men and women report deriving greater emotional and physical satisfaction from sex than do those in cohabiting and dating unions, once we take into account their other characteristics. We do not present the coefficients for the demographic and background variables, but these results are available on request.

Table 6.1 Descriptive Statistics: NHSLS Sample Members in an Ongoing Relationship

Variable	Men (N = 974)		Women (N = 1,221)	
	Mean	S.D.	Mean	S.D.
Measures of sexual satisfaction				
Emotional satisfaction in current relationship (1 = slightly, 4 = extremely)	3.30	.75	3.18	.84
Physical pleasure in current relationship (1 = slightly; 4 = extremely)	3.37	.72	3.26	.76
Demographic variables				
Age 25–29 (age 18–24 reference group)	.15	.36	.14	.35
Age 30–39	.32	.46	.33	.47
Age 40–49	.24	.43	.23	.42
Age 50–59	.16	.37	.14	.34
Black (white/other reference group)	.10	.31	.12	.33
Hispanic	.07	.25	.07	.26
Excellent health	.46	.50	.43	.50
Education in years	13.74	2.45	13.45	2.27
No religion (Protestant/other reference group)	.13	.33	.08	.28
Fundamentalist Protestant	.29	.45	.34	.47
Catholic	.29	.45	.28	.44
Attends church weekly	.22	.41	.29	.45
Child under 6 present in household	.21	.41	.25	.43
Works part-time (nonemployed reference group)	.11	.31	.22	.40
Works full-time	.74	.42	.46	.49
Hours spent in housework	7.92	9.40	16.18	14.84
Hours spent in paid work and housework	45.99	20.52	41.43	20.53
Duration of relationship in months	132.41	122.26	141.21	122.33
Partner present during interview	.09	.29	.08	.27
Single (cohabiting reference group)	.22	.41	.19	.40
Married	.69	.46	.71	.46
Sexual practices				
Monthly frequency of sex	4.90	3.99	4.83	3.98
Frequency of orgasm for respondent (1 = never; 5 = always)	4.66	.68	3.90	.96
Frequency of orgasm for partner (1 = never; 5 = always)	4.16	.86	4.74	.54
Emotional investment				
Strongly agrees that does not have sex unless in love	.21	.41	.42	.49

(continued)

Table 6.1 (continued)

Variable	Men ($N = 974$)		Women ($N = 1{,}221$)	
	Mean	S.D.	Mean	S.D.
Had sex to express love	.97	.18	.96	.19
Strongly agrees that tries to make partner have an orgasm	.41	.49	.35	.47
Finds sex with a stranger appealing	.31	.46	.09	.29
Sexual exclusivity				
Believes affairs are always wrong	.73	.44	.81	.39
Finds sex with more than one person at a time appealing	.43	.49	.08	.27
Days a year masturbates	3.69	10.09	.33	16.79
Respondent had another sex partner in the last year	.12	.32	.05	.21
Partner had another sex partner in the last year	.03	.16	.03	.18
Time horizon (less than a year reference group)[a]				
Expects relationship to last several days	.33	.47	.29	.45
Expects relationship to last a lifetime	.33	.47	.46	.50

[a]For single men and women, $N = 212$, 238, respectively.

Model 2 (col. 2) adds measures of the couple's sexual practices to model 1. These include the monthly frequency of sex and the frequency of orgasm for the respondent and the partner. Model 3 (col. 3) adds to model 1 our measures of emotional investment, including agreement that one would not have sex with someone unless one were in love with that person, having had sex the last time to express love, always trying to make sure that one's partner has an orgasm, and the extent to which the respondent finds sex with a stranger appealing. Model 4 (col. 4) consists of our measures of sexual exclusivity, including the belief that extramarital affairs are always wrong, finding sex with more than one person appealing, frequency of masturbation, and reports that either the respondent or the partner had a sexual relationship with someone else during the past year. Model 5 (col. 5) includes all three sets of variables: sexual practices, emotional investment, and sexual exclusivity.

To assess the effect of union status on the emotional satisfaction and physical pleasure derived from sex, we compare the coefficients for married and single across the five models described above. This allows us to test the hypotheses presented earlier, trace the effect of each of the types of variables on the outcomes of interest, and examine how those variables mediate the effect of union status on sexual satisfaction. We formally test whether the effects of union status, emotional investment, sexual exclusivity, and time horizon on satisfaction differ by gender.

Our outcomes of interest, emotional satisfaction and physical pleasure with one's primary partner, were measured using responses to a question that asked how physically pleasurable (emotionally satisfying) the respondent found sex with the partner: extremely pleasurable (satisfying), very pleasurable, moderately pleasurable, slightly pleasurable, or not at all pleasurable. The underlying construct, sexual satisfaction, is continuous, at least theoretically, but measured in discrete categories. These categories are ordered from lower to higher satisfaction, but the distance between, say, extremely pleasurable and moderately pleasurable need not be the same as the distance between, say, slightly pleasurable and not at all pleasurable. In this situation, appropriate methods must take into account the ordered categories and the potentially variable distance between them.

We estimate all models with ordered logistic regression. The dependent variable consists of J ordered categories, represented by the integers 1, 2, ..., J. The jth cumulative odds is the probability of giving a response in category j or lower, as opposed to giving a response in the category $j + 1$ or higher. The log of this odds is the jth cumulative logit, which we can model as a linear function of the predictors. If β is the vector of the ordered-logit regression coefficients, then $\exp\{-\beta_K\}$ is the odds ratio or the proportionate change in the odds of being in category j or less that is produced by a one unit increase in x_{ik}, the kth explanatory variable. A positive regression coefficient means that an increase in the value of the explanatory variable is expected to raise a respondent's reported satisfaction with sex. We can also interpret the coefficients in terms of relative odds. A predictor variable with a positive sign can be interpreted as reducing the odds of being in a given satisfaction category or a lower one (DeMaris 1992).

Responses to the questions about sexual satisfaction are skewed toward higher, more satisfied categories. Arminger (1995) recommends that an adequate number of the sample be in each category of the dependent variable in order to avoid numerical instability of the parameter estimates. If this is not the case, one can combine categories to achieve this distribution. We have combined the two lowest categories, not at all satisfied and slightly satisfied, which gives us approximately 1 percent of the men and 4 percent of the women in the least emotionally satisfied category and 1 percent of the men and 3 percent of the women in the least physically pleased category. The resulting measures contain four categories, ranging from extremely satisfied to slightly satisfied, with higher scores indicating greater satisfaction.

6.5 Results

Table 6.1 above reveals that men and women derive, on average, very high levels of emotional satisfaction and physical pleasure from sex within their relationship, with men displaying higher levels on both counts. It also suggests that, on a number of counts, men display lower levels of emotional investment and sexual exclusivity than women. Men are less likely than women strongly to believe that they would not have sex unless they were in love and that affairs are always wrong. Moreover, men are more likely than women to find the idea of sex with a stranger or group sex appealing. Finally, men are more likely to masturbate or to conduct multiple sexual relationships simultaneously. Other items reveal less difference by gender. Most men and women have sex in their primary relationship to express love. And only a handful of men and women report having an unfaithful partner. Interestingly, men are more likely than women strongly to agree that they try to make their partner have an orgasm. This difference probably stems from the fact that women's orgasms are more difficult to achieve than men's.

On the whole, these results suggest that men's and women's sexual beliefs, fantasies, and behaviors differ. They also suggest that, within gender, sexual beliefs, fantasies, and behaviors differ from person to person. For instance, roughly one-fifth of women feel that having an affair is reasonable, and about two-fifths of them feel this way about having sex without love. Clearly, some women fit the evolutionary profile of men, and some men fit the evolutionary profile of women. Next, we consider the effect of these differences.

Emotional Satisfaction with Sex

Tables 6.2 and 6.3 present the results from models of emotional satisfaction for men and women, respectively. Model 1, which includes only demographic variables and dummy variables for union status, shows no significant differences in emotional satisfaction between cohabiting men and their single and married counterparts. Model 1 also shows sizable and significant differences between cohabiting and married women. The odds that married women report any given level of emotional satisfaction or higher are (exp{0.520} =) 1.68, or almost 70 percent greater than those for cohabiting women (the omitted category). Single women do not differ from cohabiting women in terms of their emotional satisfaction with sex.

Model 2, which adds the couple's sexual practices, shows that these practices are related to reports of emotional satisfaction for both men and women. One more sexual contact per month is associated with an increase in the odds of reporting emotional satisfaction in any particular level or

Table 6.2 Estimates of Ordered Logit Models of Emotional Satisfaction in Current Relationship: Men

Explanatory Variables (with Demographic Ones)	(1)	(2)	(3)	(4)	(5)
Marriage, cohabitation, and single living					
Single	−.380	−.104	−.252	−.296	.101
	(.246)	(.252)	(.249)	(.254)	(.262)
Married	.304	.451†	.236	.154	.268
	(.261)	(.264)	(.264)	(.267)	(.271)
Sexual practices					
Monthly frequency of sex		.066***			.067***
		(.017)			(.018)
Frequency of orgasm for respondent		−.220[c]			−.154[d]
		(.102)			(.104)
Frequency of orgasm for partner		.448***,[b]			.434***,[b]
		(.080)			(.083)
Emotional investment					
No sex unless in love			.409*		.310†
			(.172)		(.179)
Had sex to express love			2.243***		1.983***
			(.349)		(.357)
Tries to make partner have an orgasm			.168[b]		.001[b]
			(.134)		(.143)
Finds sex with a stranger appealing			−.573***,[c]		−.310*,[c]
			(.141)		(.157)

(continued)

Table 6.2 (continued)

Explanatory Variables (with Demographic Ones)	(1)	(2)	(3)	(4)	(5)
Sexual exclusivity					
Believes affairs are always wrong				.423**	.333*
				(.150)	(.154)
Sex with more than one person appealing				-.412**,[a]	-.391*
				(.142)	(.156)
Logged days a year masturbates				-.079**	-.069*
				(.031)	(.031)
Respondent had another sex partner				-.466*,[a]	-.472*
				(.225)	(.230)
Partner had another sex partner				-1.293**	-1.079**
				(.397)	(.407)
-2 log-likelihood (*df*)	1,981.4	1,936.3	1,916.4	1,923.5	1,838.3
	(22)	(25)	(26)	(27)	(34)
N	974	974	974	974	974

Note: Except where indicated, standard errors are given in parentheses.

[†]$p < .1$.
[*]$p < .05$.
[**]$p < .01$.
[***]$p < .001$.
[a]$p < .1$ (by gender).
[b]$p < .05$ (by gender).
[c]$p < .01$ (by gender).
[d]$p < .001$ (by gender).

Table 6.3 Estimates of Ordered Logit Models of Emotional Satisfaction in Current Relationship: Women

Explanatory Variables (with Demographic Ones)	(1)	(2)	(3)	(4)	(5)
Marriage, cohabitation, and single living					
Single	-.180	.010	-.239	-.035	.097
	(.215)	(.221)	(.217)	(.218)	(.227)
Married	.520*	.566**	.423*	.435*	.422†
	(.211)	(.216)	(.213)	(.213)	(.220)
Sexual practices					
Monthly frequency of sex		.091***,d			.090***
		(.015)			(.016)
Frequency of orgasm for respondent		.442***,b			.417***,d
		(.060)			(.062)
Frequency of orgasm for partner		.159b			.109b
		(.103)			(.105)
Emotional investment					
No sex unless in love			.389***		.222†
			(.118)		(.121)
Had sex to express love			1.756***		1.635***
			(.286)		(.293)
Tries to make partner have an orgasm			.533***,b		.470***,b
			(.123)		(.128)
Finds sex with a stranger appealing			.015c		.264c
			(.194)		(.207)

(continued)

Table 6.3 (continued)

Explanatory Variables (with Demographic Ones)	(1)	(2)	(3)	(4)	(5)
Sexual exclusivity					
Believes affairs are always wrong				.343*	.323*
				(.144)	(.147)
Sex with more than one person appealing				−.001[a]	−.257
				(.210)	(.221)
Logged days a year masturbates				−.070***	−.081***
				(.021)	(.022)
Respondent had another sex partner				−.976***,[a]	−.839**
				(.287)	(.293)
Partner had another sex partner				−.567†	−.632†
				(.328)	(.335)
−2 log-likelihood (*df*)	2,754.9	2,645.4	2,685.7	2,708.9	2,546.2
	(22)	(25)	(26)	(27)	(34)
N	1,221	1,221	1,221	1,221	1,221

Note: Except where indicated, standard errors are given in parentheses.

†$p < .1$.
*$p < .05$.
**$p < .01$.
***$p < .001$.

[a]$p < .1$ (by gender).
[b]$p < .05$ (by gender).
[c]$p < .01$ (by gender).
[d]$p < .001$ (by gender).

higher of 10 percent for women and 7 percent for men (exp{0.091} = 1.095 and exp{0.066} = 1.068, respectively). Note the importance of the frequency of the woman's orgasm for the emotional satisfaction of both sexes and the similarity of the coefficients for the frequency of the woman's orgasm in equations for men's and women's emotional satisfaction. For men, the odds of being in a particular category of emotional satisfaction are almost 60 percent higher for those whose wife, girlfriend, or cohabiting partner has orgasms usually rather than sometimes (or any other movement from one category to the next higher category). For women, a one-unit increase in the frequency of own orgasm is associated with odds this much higher. Whether a man usually has an orgasm matters not at all for a woman's emotional satisfaction with sex and has a modest negative relationship with the man's emotional satisfaction. Clearly, both partners are most emotionally satisfied when the woman frequently has orgasms during sex. The means reported in table 6.1 above give us some insight into this relationship; most men always have orgasms during sex, according to reports, whereas women's orgasms occur less frequently.

This model additionally reveals that differences in these practices between married, cohabiting, and single respondents were hiding differences in their emotional satisfaction with sex. When we take a couple's sexual practices into account, single men and women do not differ from the cohabiting in terms of their level of emotional satisfaction with sex, as in the simpler model. However, the coefficient for those who are married becomes larger for both men and women and reaches statistical significance for men (at the .05 level using a one-tailed test). For married men, the odds of being in any given satisfaction category or higher are (exp{0.451} =) 1.57, or almost 60 percent higher than those of cohabiting men (the omitted category). For women, taking a couple's sexual practices into account raises their advantage in emotional satisfaction from odds of 1.68 to odds of 1.76, compared to cohabiting women.

This increase in the coefficient for married couples is due to the inclusion of information about sexual frequency. As can be seen in appendix tables 6A.1 and 6A.2, the married have sex less often than do the cohabiting, yet more frequent sex increases emotional satisfaction. When we take this suppressor effect into account, the gap between the married and the cohabiting in emotional satisfaction actually increases.

Emotional Investment and Emotional Satisfaction with Sex

Model 3 allows us to test the hypothesis that emotional satisfaction with sex increases with emotional investment. Two of the indicators of emotional investment are significantly related to emotional satisfaction for both men and women at about the same level. Men and women who strongly agreed that they would not have sex with someone unless they were in love have odds of being in any particular category of emotional satisfaction or higher about 50 percent greater than those who do not strongly agree with this statement (exp{0.409} = 1.51 and exp{0.389} = 1.48, respectively). An even stronger relationship with emotional satisfaction with sex exists for our second indicator of emotional investment, having sex to express love. Men who reported that they had sex to express love had odds of being in any particular category of emotional satisfaction or higher 9.5 times greater than those of men who did not give this reason (exp{2.243} = 9.42). For women, the odds are 5.8 times greater for those who had sex the last time to express love (exp{1.756} = 5.79). The other indicators of emotional investment differ for men and women. Women who say that they strongly agree that they try to make sure that their husband, boyfriend, or cohabiting partner has an orgasm report higher levels of emotional satisfaction. No effect appears for men. And men who do not say that they find sex with a stranger appealing are more emotionally satisfied. No effect appears for women, perhaps because anonymous sex figures much less prominently in the fantasies of women than of men (see *SOS*).

Model 3 shows that taking our measures of emotional investment into account reduces the size of the coefficient for married for both men and women. This means that the married are more emotionally satisfied with sex than the cohabiting partly because they are more emotionally invested. Net of their emotional investment, married women remain more emotionally satisfied than cohabiting or single women, but married men do not differ significantly from cohabiting or single men in this model.

Sexual Exclusivity and Emotional Satisfaction with Sex

Model 4 allows us to test our hypothesis that emotional satisfaction with sex increases with sexual exclusivity. We find evidence in support of this hypothesis for both men and women for both attitudinal and behavioral measures of sexual exclusivity. Both men and women who believe that affairs are always wrong report greater emotional satisfaction with sex. Men who disapprove of extramarital affairs show odds of being in any particular category of emotional satisfaction or higher that are 53 percent greater than those of men who do not disapprove of affairs as strongly (exp{0.423} = 1.53). For women, the comparable figure is 41 percent greater odds (exp{0.343} = 1.41). Our second attitudinal indicator, finding group sex appealing, is similar in its effects to the appeal of sex with a stranger—this measure has a strong effect for men and no effect for women. Table 6.1 above shows that group sex holds substantial appeal for men (43 percent find the prospect appealing) and very little appeal for women (only 8 percent find the prospect appealing). The results of model

4 indicate that men who find sex with several people at a time appealing show odds of being in any particular category of emotional satisfaction or higher that are 34 percent lower than those of men who do not find this activity appealing ($\exp\{-0.412\} = 0.66$). Regardless of whether men act on their tastes, the nearly half of all men who are attracted to nonexclusive sex report less emotional satisfaction in their primary sexual relationship than the slight majority of men who are not.

Our behavioral measures of sexual exclusivity also show the expected relationship with emotional satisfaction with sex for both men and women. In all cases, the more exclusive the sexual relationship, the greater the emotional satisfaction reported. We see that, the more frequently men and women masturbate, the lower their emotional satisfaction with sex. And both men and women who say that they had another partner in the past year—in addition to their (marriage, cohabiting, or dating) primary partner—are less emotionally satisfied, as are those whose partner had another partner.

Men and women seem to react differently to extradyadic sex—both their own and their partner's. Men who say that they had another sex partner show odds of being in any particular category of emotional satisfaction that are only 63 percent of the odds ($\exp\{-0.466\} = .63$) of men who did not, as the results of model 4 show. But, if they report that their wife or girlfriend had another sex partner, this lowers their odds to 27 percent ($\exp\{-1.293\} = 0.27$) of those of men who reported that their partner had no other partner. We might conclude that one's own affairs reduce emotional satisfaction less than one's partner's, except that both men and women seem to react more strongly to the woman's secondary sexual relationship than to the man's. So men react more strongly to a wife's or a girlfriend's affair than to their own, and women react more strongly to their own affair than to that of a husband or a boyfriend.

The perspectives on male-female differences in sexual strategies and responses from evolutionary biology suggest that men are more willing than women to have multiple sex partners themselves but are more sexually possessive of their partners than women are (Buss 1994). Our results suggest that this is the case. As the tables show, these measures of sexual exclusivity differ significantly by gender only at the level $p < .10$, so our evidence is subtle.

Of course, we cannot tell from these results the extent to which each of these behaviors results from or leads to lower satisfaction, only that they are related. An individual might turn to masturbation or to another partner as a result of discontentment. Or, as we argued, willingness to masturbate makes partners less dependent on each other for sexual satisfaction and may reduce willingness to compromise and negotiate to achieve agreement about a joint sex life. In a similar sense, an affair begun for reasons other than dissatisfaction may have reduced emotional satisfaction, but one could argue that those who were dissatisfied initially may have sought out or at least been open to another partner.

If we argue that initial unhappiness led to the affair, we must explain why the relationship is so much stronger for women than for men and why men's affairs seem either to cause less emotional dissatisfaction with sex or to result less directly from dissatisfaction than do women's. Keep in mind that the men and women who tell us that their husband, wife, boyfriend, or girlfriend had another sex partner have a number of distinctive characteristics. They know about the other relationship, and they remain in the marriage or partnership in spite of this knowledge. We do not hear from those who do not know about a partner's affair or from those whose relationship ended because an affair was discovered.

Our final model of emotional satisfaction with sex, model 5, includes all three sets of measures at the same time. We point out only that holding constant the other sets of measures changes each of the others very little and leaves our substantive conclusions unaltered. Note that, even when we include measures of sexual activity, emotional investment, and sexual exclusivity together, married women are significantly more likely than cohabiting women to report emotional satisfaction with sex at any particular level or higher and that single women do not differ from cohabiting women in their reports of emotional satisfaction (using a one-tailed test). Keep in mind that we have not taken into account time horizon and that the married presumably have a more extended time horizon than the cohabiting. This could explain why they are more emotionally satisfied. Union status has no effect on emotional satisfaction for men in this most complete model. This makes sense, given the fact that union status is less consequential for them in the other models.

Physical Pleasure from Sex

Tables 6.4 and 6.5 present results for physical pleasure for the same five models examined for emotional satisfaction. These tables show some of the same relationships that we saw for emotional satisfaction, with some important differences. First, we see no effect of union status on physical pleasure in any of the models for either men or women. Married, cohabiting, and single men do not differ noticeably in terms of their levels of physical pleasure, nor do these same groups of women. As we saw for emotional satisfaction, physical pleasure is strongly and positively related to the frequency of sex and to the frequency of orgasm for the female partner. Thus, the finding in SOS of greater physical satisfaction for married (and cohabiting) men and women than for others appears due to differences in their demographic and background characteristics.

Table 6.4 Estimates of Ordered Logit Models of Physical Pleasure in Current Relationship: Men

Explanatory Variables (with Demographic Ones)	(1)	(2)	(3)	(4)	(5)
Marriage, cohabitation, and single living					
Single	−.339	−.072	−.252	−.343	.015
	(.250)	(.259)	(.254)	(.257)	(.270)
Married	.119	.279	.016	−.024	.067
	(.265)	(.271)	(.269)	(.269)	(.278)
Sexual practices					
Monthly frequency of sex		.081***			.083***
		(.018)			(.018)
Frequency of orgasm for respondent		.042[d]			.078[d]
		(.101)			(.103)
Frequency of orgasm for partner		.559***,[b]			.531***,[b]
		(.082)			(.084)
Emotional investment					
No sex unless in love			.122		.156
			(.172)		(.181)
Had sex to express love			2.000***		1.828***
			(.348)		(.355)
Tries to make partner have an orgasm			.384**		.106
			(.136)		(.145)
Finds sex with a stranger appealing			−.628***,[d]		−.478**,[c]
			(.143)		(.160)

(continued)

Table 6.4 (continued)

Explanatory Variables (with Demographic Ones)	(1)	(2)	(3)	(4)	(5)
Sexual exclusivity					
Believes affairs are always wrong				.384*,a	.301†
				(.151)	(.157)
Sex with more than one person appealing				-.153	-.121
				(.142)	(.159)
Logged days a year masturbates				-.074*	-.062†
				(.031)	(.032)
Respondent had another sex partner				-.207a	-.170
				(.227)	(.235)
Partner had another sex partner				-.129	.081
				(.400)	(.419)
-2 log-likelihood (*df*)	1898.2	1819.8	1841.5	1876.4	1760.7
	(22)	(25)	(26)	(27)	(34)
N	974	974	974	974	974

Note: Except where indicated, standard errors are given in parentheses.

†*p* < .1.
**p* < .05.
***p* < .01.
****p* <.001.
a*p* < .1 (by gender).
b*p* < .05 (by gender).
c*p* < .01. (by gender).
d*p* < .001 (by gender).

Table 6.5 Estimates of Ordered Logit Models of Physical Pleasure in Current Relationship: Women

Explanatory Variables (with Demographic Ones)	(1)	(2)	(3)	(4)	(5)
Marriage, cohabitation, and single living					
Single	-.095	.169	-.166	.045	.224
	(.220)	(.232)	(.223)	(.224)	(.238)
Married	.216	.259	.114	.183	.141
	(.215)	(.224)	(.217)	(.217)	(.228)
Sexual practices					
Monthly frequency of sex		.104***			.100***
		(.016)			(.016)
Frequency of orgasm for respondent		.671***,d			.655***,d
		(.064)			(.065)
Frequency of orgasm for partner		.220*,b			.176[b]
		(.106)			(.108)
Emotional investment					
No sex unless in love			.308		.155
			(.119)		(.125)
Had sex to express love			2.149***		1.963***
			(.292)		(.302)
Tries to make partner have an orgasm			.527***,d		.394**,c
			(.124)		(.131)
Finds sex with a stranger appealing			.158		.276
			(.198)		(.215)

(continued)

Table 6.5 (continued)

Explanatory Variables (with Demographic Ones)	(1)	(2)	(3)	(4)	(5)
Sexual exclusivity					
Believes affairs are always wrong				.067[a]	.053
				(.147)	(.152)
Sex with more than one person appealing				.194	-.089
				(.215)	(.230)
Logged days a year masturbates				.039†	-.051*
				(.021)	(.023)
Respondent had another sex partner				-.834**,[a]	-.716*
				(.294)	(.304)
Partner had another sex partner				-.690*	-.751*
				(.334)	(.345)
−2 log-likelihood (*df*)	2,560.5	2,376.0	2,486.5	2,538.2	2,300.5
	(22)	(25)	(26)	(27)	(34)
N	1,221	1,221	1,221	1,221	1,221

Note: Except where indicated, standard errors are given in parentheses.

†*p* < .1.
*p < .05.
**p < .01.
***p < .001.

[a]*p* < .1 (by gender).
[b]*p* < .05 (by gender).
[c]*p* < .01. (by gender).
[d]*p* < .001 (by gender).

Emotional Investment and Physical Pleasure

Emotional investment forms an important component of physical pleasure; men and women who say that one of the reasons they had sex the last time was to express love for their partner are substantially more pleased than others. For men, the odds of being in any given category of physical pleasure or higher are 7.4 times as high if they gave this reason as they were for men who did not (exp{2.0} = 7.39). For women, the odds are 8.6 times greater for those who had sex to express love (exp{2.149} = 8.57). For both men and women, this is the strongest relationship in the model of physical pleasure. Both men and women who say that they try to make sure that their partner has an orgasm during sex report higher levels of physical pleasure themselves. Men who are attracted to the idea of sex with a stranger report significantly lower levels of physical pleasure, but this measure fails to distinguish among the women. Men and women differ significantly in the effect of finding sex with a stranger appealing.

Sexual Exclusivity and Physical Pleasure

Neither of our two measures of attitudes toward some aspect of sexual exclusivity—holding the belief that affairs are always wrong and finding group sex appealing—shows any relationship with physical pleasure for women, and only beliefs about affairs shows any effect for men. Our behavioral measures of sexual exclusivity show a somewhat different pattern. We see that women who had another sex partner themselves and women whose husband or boyfriend did report deriving less physical pleasure from sex than do others. But affairs by either the man or his partner show no relationship with his physical pleasure. Although we see an effect of these measures for women and not for men, the coefficients do not differ significantly for the sexes. We see a modest relation between frequency of masturbation and physical pleasure for both men and women, a relation that changes sign or becomes marginally significant with the addition of other sets of measures in model 5.

The importance of nonexclusivity for women's physical pleasure and the unimportance of it for men's does not follow from the predictions of evolutionary biology. This perspective points to sexual jealousy on the part of men as an effective reproductive strategy. But we see no evidence of sexual jealousy in the results for men's physical pleasure, although we did see this for emotional satisfaction. We also see no evidence here that women are tolerant of their partner's other women, although we did see this for emotional satisfaction. Note that the coefficient for partner had another sex partner in the equation for emotional satisfaction for women is significant only at the level .1.

Taken as a whole, our results support the hypothesis that both physical and emotional dimensions of sexual satisfaction increase with emotional investment and sexual exclusivity. This leaves the question of whether these dimensions depend on time horizon as well.

Emotional Satisfaction and Physical Pleasure

Time Horizon.   Recall that we have direct measures of the time horizon expected for the relationship only for those who are not married or cohabiting. Table 6.6 presents results from a series of models of emotional satisfaction and physical pleasure for single men and women in ongoing sexual partnerships. These models include the demographic variables listed in table 6.1 above in addition to the measures of time horizon.

These results show that, for men, the emotional satisfaction and physical pleasure derived from sex are both higher for those who expect their current relationship to last at least several years than for those who expect their relationship to end sooner and higher still for those expecting it to last a lifetime. However, for women, we see no significant effects of expecting the relationship to last several years on either physical pleasure or emotional satisfaction, although both are quite highly related to expecting a lifetime relationship. For men and women alike, physical pleasure ap-

Table 6.6 Estimates of Ordered Logit Models of Sexual Satisfaction in Current Relationship: Single Men and Women

Explanatory Variables (with Demographic Ones)	Emotional Satisfaction		Physical Pleasure	
	Men	Women	Men	Women
Time horizon				
Expects relationship to last several years	1.180**	.556	.646†.ᵃ	−.262ᵃ
	(.362)	(.343)	(.356)	(.347)
Expects relationship to last a lifetime	2.464***	2.013***	1.315***	.929**
	(.399)	(.346)	(.366)	(.336)
−2 log-likelihood (*df*)	413.4	516.0	419.5	485.6
	(22)	(22)	(22)	(22)
N	212	238	212	238

Note: Except where indicated, standard errors are given in parentheses.
†$p < .1$.
*$p < .05$.
**$p < .01$.
***$p < .001$.
ᵃ$p < .1$ (by gender).
ᵇ$p < .05$ (by gender).
ᶜ$p < .01$. (by gender).
ᵈ$p < .001$ (by gender).

pears less responsive to time horizon. Men and women differ significantly in the effect on physical pleasure of expecting the relationship to last several years.

These results suggest that women require a longer minimum commitment than do men to consider a relationship permanent enough. Women tend to be satisfied with nothing less than a lifetime commitment, whereas men make less of a distinction between a relationship that they expect to last several years and one that they expect to last a lifetime. Our results show, however, that single men who have made a lifetime commitment to their partner and consider her committed as well report substantially higher levels of emotional satisfaction and physical pleasure with that woman. It is, of course, impossible to say whether satisfaction with sex leads to long-term commitment, or visa versa.

6.6 Conclusion

A higher proportion of married than cohabiting or single men and women report being extremely emotionally satisfied with sex, according to *SOS*. It was shown there that about the same proportion of cohabiting as married men and women say that they found sex with their partner to be extremely pleasurable physically, but single people reported lower levels of physical satisfaction with sex. Do the characteristics of married versus cohabiting or single people account for these differences?

We find that the answer to this question depends on the dimension of sexual satisfaction one examines. It also depends on whether one is talking about men or women. Married *women* are more emotionally satisfied with sex—even after one takes into account their demographic and background characteristics—than cohabiting or single women. The greater emotional satisfaction with sex of married men, reported in *SOS,* disappears when one holds constant their characteristics. So the answer to the question posed above, whether the characteristics of married versus cohabiting versus single people account for the differences in their satisfaction with sex, is yes for men and no for women.

Interestingly, differences in sexual practices seem to be masking the relation between marriage and emotional satisfaction for men because a significant positive relation appears when we hold constant frequency of sex and frequency of orgasm for the respondent and his partner. So, when we compare married, cohabiting, and single men with the same sexual practices and demographic characteristics, we find that married men report greater emotional satisfaction with sex. Apparently, married men get more emotional satisfaction from each sexual encounter than do men in other sexual unions. We can look further at the specific processes through which this connection occurs.

For men, marriage and emotional satisfaction seem to be connected through the greater emotional investment of those who are married in their wife than of those who are cohabiting or single in their girlfriend. We can see some of these differences in appendix table 6A.2, which shows means for measures of emotional investment and sexual exclusivity by type of union. This table shows that, on average, married men are more emotionally invested in their sexual relationship than cohabiting or single men on two of the four measures—saying that they would not have sex unless in love and finding sex with a stranger relatively unappealing—and about as invested as indexed by the other two measures. Married men are also more committed to sexual exclusivity, on average, than cohabiting or single men. So, when we hold constant emotional investment in one's partner, the greater emotional satisfaction of married men disappears. The same thing happens when we hold constant sexual exclusivity—the positive coefficient for married disappears for men.

The situation for women is quite different. Married women report getting greater emotional satisfaction from sex than do cohabiting or single women, and this difference persists no matter what other characteristics (theirs or those of the union) we control. Demographic and background characteristics do not account for the greater emotional satisfaction of married women, nor do our measures of sexual practices, emotional investment, or sexual exclusivity. Something *else* about marriage must be responsible.

We hypothesized that, even *within* unions of a particular type, sexual satisfaction would be more common in certain situations than in others. We argued that the emotional satisfaction and physical pleasure derived from sex in relationships increase with sexual exclusivity, with emotional investment in the relationship, and with a long time horizon for the relationship. Emotional investment in the relationship should increase incentives to please one's partner since one gets direct satisfaction from pleasing a loved one. Sexually exclusive relationships also facilitate emotional investment in a particular relationship and specialization in that partner, both of which should be associated with sexual satisfaction. The longer one expects to remain in a sexual relationship, the more incentive one has to make emotional investments.

The physical pleasure and emotional satisfaction of both men and women with sex are both higher for those whose attitudes indicate the importance of emotional investment in their relationships. Those who use sex as a way of expressing their love for their partner report higher levels of both emotional satisfaction and physical pleasure from sex than others. Those who see love as an essential precondition to sex are more emotionally satisfied than others. Both men and women who expressed attitudes and behavior opposed to extradyadic sex show more emotional satisfaction. Among the single, the emotional satisfaction and physical pleasure of both men and women is highest for those expecting the relationship to last a lifetime.

The evolutionary biology perspective suggests that men and women tend to evaluate sexual satisfaction differently, with emotional investment more important to women. We found modest evidence of differences of this type; men who find the prospect of sex with a stranger appealing report less physical pleasure from sex than do men who do not. But the evolutionary perspective (Townsend 1995) suggests that emotional commitment is more important to women's satisfaction with sex, and we found no differences in the effect, and none of our other measures of emotional investment show the expected pattern.

We examined whether the high levels of emotional investment and sexual exclusivity that characterize marriage would account for the greater emotional satisfaction and physical pleasure of the married, especially for women. Although emotional investment and sexual exclusivity increase sexual satisfaction, they explain only a fraction of the difference between married and cohabiting women in terms of emotional satisfaction. But marriage itself carries a long-term commitment both to the partner and to the relationship. It also carries very strong requirements for sexual exclusivity and reinforces them religiously, normatively, and legally. It makes sense that the very persistent effect for women of just being married, over and above the effect of emotional commitment and sexual exclusivity as we measure them, reflects these features of marriage as an institution. If this is so, it suggests that commitment from their partner *is* more important for women than for men and that women respond quite strongly to the most binding and public pledge of commitment.

It is important to note that, for men and women alike, union status and time horizon are more strongly tied to emotional satisfaction than they are to physical pleasure with sex. In contrast, sexual practices have the same effect on emotional satisfaction as they do on physical pleasure. More frequent sex in the relationship and more frequent orgasm for the female partner strongly increase emotional satisfaction and physical pleasure. Were it not for the fact that the cohabiting have sex more often than the married, their levels of emotional satisfaction would be significantly lower than those of the married.

Although the results that we present here are partly consistent with our conceptual framework, we must view them as suggestive and preliminary. The NHSLS is a cross-sectional data set, so information on both the outcomes we examine was measured at the same time as the characteristics and attitudes that we use to predict these outcomes. We suspect that reverse causality may be at work—at least to some extent—in the relationship between frequency of masturbation and satisfaction, for example, with those who have become unhappy or dissatisfied turning to masturbation. The same causal path from dissatisfaction to experience with a secondary sex partner seems likely, although we would guess that not even those involved know which led to which. We feel that we are on firmer ground with attitudes that measure long-run or permanent tastes or values like the appeal of sex with a stranger or the belief that affairs are always wrong.

Panel data containing measures of attitudes, values, the sexual experience and characteristics of the partner and partnership, and initial satisfaction, together with information on sexual satisfaction measured at a later point, would allow us to see whether an expected long time horizon, emotional investment, and sexual exclusivity at the earlier point are related to satisfaction later. Of course, such an analysis would have to deal with attrition from the sample of couples of the most dissatisfied and least sexually exclusive, leaving the more satisfied and monogamous to be analyzed.

Appendix 6A

Table 6A.1 Descriptive Statistics by Type of Relationship: NHSLS Men

Variable	Married ($N = 670$)		Cohabiting ($N = 92$)		Single ($N = 212$)	
	Mean	S.D.	Mean	S.D.	Mean	S.D.
Measures of sexual satisfaction						
Emotional satisfaction in current relationship	3.36	.72	3.29	.70	3.15	.85
Physical pleasure in current relationship	3.40	.71	3.40	.66	3.28	.76
Sexual practices						
Monthly frequency of sex	4.79	3.69	6.72	4.57	4.45	4.40
Frequency of orgasm for respondent	4.67	.67	4.65	.72	4.62	.70
Frequency of orgasm for partner	4.14	.87	4.34	.73	4.14	.88
Emotional investment						
No sex unless in love	.26	.43	.15	.36	.09	.29
Had sex to express love	.98	.13	.97	.18	.92	.28
Tries to make partner have an orgasm	.40	.49	.43	.49	.41	.49
Finds sex with a stranger appealing	.27	.44	.41	.50	.40	.49
Sexual exclusivity						
Believes affairs are always wrong	.75	.43	.64	.48	.69	.46
Sex with more than one person appealing	.38	.49	.54	.50	.51	.50
Days a year masturbates	2.94	9.17	6.83	10.86	5.84	11.76
Respondent had another sex partner	.04	.20	.16	.36	.37	.46
Partner had another sex partner	.01	.10	.02	.15	.08	.27

Table 6A.2 Descriptive Statistics by Type of Relationship: NHSLS Women

Variable	Married (N = 864)		Cohabiting (N = 119)		Single (N = 238)	
	Mean	S.D.	Mean	S.D.	Mean	S.D.
Measures of sexual satisfaction						
Emotional satisfaction in current relationship	3.22	.81	3.08	.96	3.10	.89
Physical pleasure in current relationship	3.25	.75	3.29	.77	3.29	.80
Sexual practices						
Monthly frequency of sex	4.71	3.67	6.74	4.67	4.32	4.43
Frequency of orgasm for respondent	3.95	.92	3.79	.94	3.76	1.13
Frequency of orgasm for partner	4.76	.51	4.74	.51	4.66	.66
Emotional investment						
No sex unless in love	.46	.50	.30	.46	.33	.47
Had sex to express love	.96	.19	.94	.24	.97	.16
Tries to make partner have an orgasm	.36	.48	.30	.46	.33	.47
Finds sex with a stranger appealing	.09	.28	.11	.31	.09	.28
Sexual exclusivity						
Believes affairs are always wrong	.84	.37	.77	.42	.75	.43
Sex with more than one person appealing	.08	.26	.09	.29	.10	.30
Days a year masturbates	.27	14.26	.55	23.20	.56	22.66
Respondent had another sex partner	.01	.11	.08	.26	.17	.37
Partner had another sex partner	.02	.12	.02	.13	.11	.31

Note

This research was supported by a grant from the Center for Population Research, National Institute of Child Health and Human Development (P50 HD12639), to the Rand Corp. The authors thank participants at the Demography Workshops at both Pennsylvania State University and the University of Chicago for helpful comments.

■

Sex during Adulthood

Chapter 3: Sexual Expression in America

This chapter addresses a very broad issue: how might we describe the nature of and the variation in adults' sexual interests and activities? The chapter selects five rather different aspects of sexual behavior, partitions each into two categories indicating very little or relatively much of this behavior, and then looks at the patterns of the number of people who fall into each of the possible combinations. It concludes that adults are not distributed uniformly among all the possible combinations but rather are concentrated in a very few combinations (called *modes of sexual expression*) characterized by the number of sex partners and the amount of sexual activity engaged in. These combinations differ for men and women, but four or five combinations do capture nearly all observed patterns, which is an intriguing finding, the implications of which have not been explored.

The five aspects of behavior, measured as dichotomies, are the number of sex partners in the past twelve months (one partner or two or more partners); the number of sex partners of one's own sex partners, as estimated by the respondent (one's partner[s] had no other partners or had one or more other partners); buying erotic products (such as X-rated movies or magazines), paying for sex, engaging in activities like nude photography, or attending nightclubs with nude dancers (doing none or any of these items); masturbation (never in the past year or more than that); and frequency of sex (no more than once per week or more than once per week).

The many possible combinations of these five behaviors reduce statistically to only four groupings for men and four for women. The proportions of men and women in each of the resulting groups are as follows: monogamous with low levels of sexual activity, 49 percent of men and 54 percent of women; monogamous with high levels of sexual activity, 18 percent of women; mixed (monogamous and polygamous) with high to modest levels of sexual activity, 35 percent of men and 23 percent of women; polygamous with medium levels of sexual activity, 2 percent of men and 5 percent of women; and polygamous with high levels of sexual activity, 15 percent of men.

These lifestyle choices are then studied with regard to factors that influence their choices. The categories of determinants are (a) individual preferences for particular sex experiences as self-reported, (b) the person's health status, (c) measures of social competence, and (d) measures of social opportunities. The chapter investigates the importance of these factors as determinants of the lifestyle choice of the adult. We do not provide a detailed summary of the findings. Instead, we note the "ambitious tasks" undertaken in this essay and suggest that the chapter's importance is in setting an agenda for investigating two important issues: first, a manageable way of describing the variety of sexual orientations and lifestyles that adults have and, second, the personal and social circumstances that influence or are correlated with those choices. That is a large agenda, one that calls for much additional investigation. It is one that should be considered by theorists and empiricists alike; it is potentially a key organizing agenda for social research that can provide a more complete understanding of adult sexual behavior.

Chapter 4: Sexual Contact between Children and Adults: A Life-Course Perspective

The question addressed in this chapter is why adult-child sexual relations have long-term negative consequences for those children. Stipulating that these experiences are bad and inappropriate, the chapter tries to identify the process through which that linkage from the experience to later sexual behavior takes place. Two theories are proposed and tested with the National Health and Social Life Survey (NHSLS) data, which contain substantial detail about these preadolescent events, albeit reported retrospectively by adult respondents. (The main survey question asked whether the respondent had been touched sexually before puberty/age twelve or thirteen. If so, some details about the ages of the youth and the other person, the frequency and nature of these events, and the relationship between the two people were obtained.)

The first theory is a psychological one; it interprets the event as a trauma leading to later psychic disorders, disorders manifested in one of several ways. The other theory is a sociological one; it holds that the event, in effect, jump-starts the youth on a life-course transition to sexual activity at a very early age and provides access to sexuality without also cultivating the emotional and cognitive skills to manage it. Both theories predict an early onset of sexual behavior, greater instability of sexual partnering, dysfunction, and greater risk of disease. They see the event as eroticizing and thus as encouraging sexual experimentation at an earlier age than otherwise. The trauma model implies that the effect depends on the severity of the experience and that later sexual behavior will be heightened for some and avoided by others. The trajectory theory implies that the effects can be mediated by subsequent practices.

The findings are interpreted as supporting the trajectory model rather than the trauma model since the influence of the event(s) on the person's later well-being appears to depend on the "sexual pathway" subsequently taken. Those who avoid more active and riskier sex lives are significantly less likely to report adverse outcomes later in life.

In the study, only relatively serious adult-child sexual touching is considered—genital fondling and oral, vaginal, or anal sex with a person who was four or more years older than the child and age fourteen or older at the time. It is sobering to note that, among the women in the survey, 12 percent reported such an experience. The evidence of its influence on those women was also sobering: those who had experienced adult-child sex were more than twice as likely to report early onset of sex in adolescence, more than three times as likely to have ten or more partners since age eighteen, and 1.6 times as likely to have had a sexually transmitted disease.

The study also found that a larger proportion of boys' preadolescent sex involved same-age and same-gender partners. Since the analysis distinguished between contacts that were between peers and contacts that were between an adult and the child, it allowed testing to see whether that difference had a lasting effect on the boys. The finding is that the two types of early contact do not have dramatically different associations with adverse adult outcomes. However, there were some distinctions, including a larger effect on physical dysfunction (difficulty having erections and finding no pleasure in sex) if the contact had been with a peer but greater affective disturbance (performance anxiety, guilt, and emotional interference with sex) if the contact had been with an adult.

Chapter 5: Race, Gender, and Class in Sexual Scripts

In this essentially descriptive chapter, the differences in sexual attitudes, practices, and preferences by race/ethnicity, gender, and other social categories are explored. "Sexual scripts," that is, communications and interpretations of social and sexual actions, are used to make sense of the many similarities and differences observed. The statistical analyses are conducted separately by gender, while the racial (white-black) and ethnic (white–Mexican American and white–other Hispanic) differences are considered with and without controls for education level, age, religion, marital status, and family composition during adolescence.

The many patterns reported in the chapter make summary difficult. Regarding the sexual attitudes investigated, for example, there are important differences by gender within each racial/ethnic group, and, similarly, there are large differences by race/ethnicity within each gender. An even larger portion of the comparisons of actual sexual behavior differ by gender and by race/ethnicity. Only two sexual preferences are investigated, the appeal of vaginal intercourse and the appeal of oral sex. Interestingly, there were practically no differences in the appeal of vaginal intercourse among men and women or among different racial/ethnic groups. Men of all racial/ethnic groups find fellatio more appealing than do women, while the only gender difference for cunnilingus occurred among whites, men finding it more appealing than do women.

Chapter 6: Emotional and Physical Satisfaction with Sex in Married, Cohabiting, and Dating Sexual Unions: Do Men and Women Differ?

This chapter distinguishes among three levels of commitment and stability in sexual partnerships—formal marriage, cohabitation, and informal dating—and conjectures that these levels will be positively associated with reports of both physical and emotional satisfaction. The NHSLS asked how physically pleasurable and emotionally satisfying respondents found their relationship with their primary sex partner. These are the questions on which this chapter focuses.

The analytic strategy first determines the simple relation between partnership status and the measures of physical and emotional satisfaction. Then measures of sexual attitude and behavior, commitment, and sexual exclusivity are added to the model to observe whether they are the mechanisms through which partnership status affects satisfaction. For the men, the three partnership statuses—marriage, cohabitation, and single living—show no statistically different levels of emotional satisfaction or physical pleasure when demographic controls are included. The additional variables measuring sexual practices and attitudes are correlated with the satisfaction levels of the men, but these practices and attitudes do not diminish or enhance the relation between partnership status and satisfaction. For women, by contrast, emotional satisfaction does show a difference by partnership status, and that difference is modified, but not eliminated, by the inclusion of these other direct descriptions of sexual practices and attitudes. The offered interpretation is that, for men, the sexual component of partnership status is paramount but that, for women, the partnership status has influence independent of sexual behavior.

For the separate analysis of emotional satisfaction with one's primary sex partner, the results are broadly similar: those who are married report higher rates of satisfaction, but, for both men and women, this relation becomes insignificant statistically when the components of sexual attitudes, commitment, and exclusivity are introduced into the equation. This suggests that satisfaction with the sexual partnership increases as the emotional commitment increases and as the exclusivity of the sexual relationship increases.

As the chapter stresses, these correlations are only suggestive of causal linkages since the important factor—the duration of the partnership—is not controlled for. The success of a partnership in promoting physical or emotional satisfaction is expected to be correlated with its duration, so respondents who are in longer-lasting partnerships—and these are overwhelmingly those in formal marriages—are likely to report themselves as more satisfied.

PART THREE

■

Sex and Health

■

Circumcision in the United States: Prevalence, Prophylactic Effects, and Sexual Practice

EDWARD O. LAUMANN, CHRISTOPHER M. MASI, AND EZRA W. ZUCKERMAN

Neonatal circumcision, a procedure whose medical value remains subject to heated debate, has been the most commonly performed operation in the United States for over forty years. The National Center for Health Statistics reports that about 60 percent of all male infants born in this country in 1996 were circumcised. This contrasts starkly with other Western societies, in which circumcision is much less common. Recent debates, both scientific and political, further attest to the contested nature and ambiguous standing of the procedure. While clinical studies of a wide variety of outcomes of neonatal circumcision abound, the debate between advocates and opponents of the procedure continues as each side appeals to divergent sets of criteria for determining its value. This chapter will review the history of circumcision in the United States, illustrating how the practice and the nature of the debate surrounding it assumed unique characteristics in this country. We then exploit data from the NHSLS to examine the effect of circumcision on a wide range of medical and sexual experiences in a manner not possible using conventional clinical studies.

7.1 Background

An Ancient Practice

Circumcision has been performed as a religious rite for thousands of years. Judaism and Islam both base their continued practice of circumcision on the biblical covenant between God and Abraham and his son Ishmael (Gen. 26:7–27). Several sources document the presence of the practice in ancient Egypt and Greece as well. The tomb of Ankh-Maho and the Egyptian Book of the Dead both indicate that circumcision was practiced in ancient Egypt (cf. Kaplan 1977; Weiss and Weiss 1994). Pythagoras reportedly submitted to circumcision (ca. 530 B.C.) in order to gain access to Egyptian temples (Montague 1973). The Greek historian Heroditus discussed the hygienic basis of circumcision among Egyptians.

In addition, cultures on virtually every continent have performed the rite for centuries (Wallerstein 1980). While the justification for the practice in premodern times was largely religious or cultic, hygienic explanations were also advanced (Snowman 1971). In addition, various rationales related circumcision to sexual practice. In A.D. 1194, the scholar and physician Moses Maimonides extolled circumcision as a means of moderating sexual excess (Maimonides 1904). By contrast, in historical Indonesia and Polynesia, circumcision was performed to facilitate coitus (Kaplan 1977).

A Uniquely American Experience

The American experience with circumcision has been unique among industrialized nations. Nonreligious circumcision first gained popularity in the United States in the 1870s because it was believed to promote hygiene and limit nonnormative sexual practices (Kaplan 1977). Indeed, while other English-speaking societies, including England, Canada, Australia, and New Zealand, adopted the practice at the turn of the century, only the United States continues to have high rates of nonreligious circumcision today.

Since its introduction in the United States, neonatal circumcision has depended on a changing mix of scientific, cultural, and institutional supports. The spreading popularity of circumcision reflected its consonance with Victorian sensibilities. In particular, late nineteenth-century American and English documents suggest that circumcision was performed to prevent syphilis and gonorrhea and to curb masturbation (Wallerstein 1980). The appeal of circumcision as a remedy for sexually transmitted diseases continued for some time as a result of the high morbidity associated with these ailments and the ineffectiveness of existing medical remedies.

The history of circumcision in the United States presents a telling contrast to that in other English-speaking countries. In the United States, the medical establishment wholeheartedly embraced neonatal circumcision in the 1940s and 1950s, and the procedure became routine for the growing number of newborns born in hospitals. In contrast to those in America, circumcision rates in other English-speaking countries plateaued in the middle of this century and then declined. British circumcision rates increased from the turn of the century until approximately 1950, then dropped off precipitously. By 1989, the national rate for circumcision among boys had decreased to 7 percent (Gordon and Collin 1993). Circumcision rates in Australia and Canada followed a similar, albeit less dramatic, pattern to that in Britain. While circumcision became common practice in these nations in the middle part of the century, rates in these countries began to decline in the mid-1960s, and, by the mid-1970s, rates were under 50 percent (Wirth 1978).

There appear to be several reasons for the different histories of circumcision in the United States compared to other countries. In the United States, medical research reinforced Victorian-era claims regarding this procedure, helping push circumcision rates still higher. Two studies in particular made a great impression on medical practitioners and the lay public. In 1947, Dr. Eugene A. Hand studied American soldiers in World War II and found that Jews and circumcised Christians had lower rates of sexually transmitted disease than uncircumcised Christians and blacks (Hand 1949; Hand and Nelson 1951). That same year, Plaut and Kohn-Speyer (1947) reported in *Science* the carcinogenic action of smegma in laboratory mice. These studies gained considerable publicity, as they fostered the notion that circumcision protected against both sexually transmitted disease and certain forms of cancer. Although American health insurance programs did not reimburse for circumcision in the 1940s and early 1950s, most middle-class parents paid for the procedure because of its reported medical benefits (Schoen 1990). Infant boys of lower socioeconomic backgrounds were frequently not circumcised during this period because their parents either were unaware of its reported benefits or could not afford the operation. Further, such infants were less likely to be born in hospitals, where physicians typically encouraged circumcision in newborn boys. By the late 1950s, many health insurance and welfare programs began to reimburse for the practice, pushing neonatal circumcision rates to a historical high of 85 percent for white newborns in the mid-1960s.

As American medical authorities and insurance programs encouraged increasing circumcision rates in the United States, corresponding British institutions effected an abrupt decline in the prevalence of the practice in Britain. A different body of research apparently influenced British physicians. In particular, a study by Dr. Douglas Gairdner (1949) in the *British Medical Journal* challenged many of the claims previously made about the value of circumcision. He concluded that circumcision was unnecessary and perhaps harmful. One year after the publication of this study, England's newly formed National Health Service decided not to pay for newborn circumcision (Wallerstein 1980). As a result, British circumcision rates commenced an immediate and rapid decline to their current low level.

The national health services of Australia and Canada continued to pay for circumcision through the mid-1970s. Nevertheless, circumcision rates began to decline in these countries in the late 1960s and early 1970s as a result of questions raised by the medical community and activist groups.

Thus, we see contrasting experiences with neonatal circumcision across English-speaking countries. Circumcision rates in each country were driven principally by the vagaries of particular institutional regimes either favoring or discouraging the practice as well as the preferences of medical establishments for particular studies among a body of largely inconclusive scientific research. Rather than being driven by clear-cut scientific evidence, the prevalence of the ancient rite of circumcision in modern societies reflects the shifting influence of contingent historical and institutional forces.

Status of the Current Debate

The existing American consensus as to the value of neonatal circumcision began to break down in the late 1960s and early 1970s, although less markedly than in Canada or Australia. It was during this period that the medical community began to raise questions regarding the medical risks associated with circumcision as well as the claim that the procedure prevents disease. The most significant indicator of institutional change occurred when, in 1971 and 1975, the American Academy of Pediatrics (AAP) Task Force on Circumcision concluded that valid medical indications for routine neonatal circumcision did not exist (CFN 1975). The AAP counseled that the decision to perform this procedure, formerly a choice about which parents deferred to the authority of physicians, be made by parents who have been apprised of its risks. In 1983, the AAP reaffirmed this position with the American College of Obstetricians and Gynecologists. These pronouncements were associated with a small but steady decline in circumcision rates in the United States, as documented by the National Center for Health Statistics (NCHS) Hospital Discharge Survey (see fig. 7.1). This decline was most dramatic in the West.

Numerous recent studies have attempted to assess the value of neonatal circumcision. Several have found that the procedure has positive effects. For example, an association has been found between circumcision and lower rates of urinary tract infections in infancy (Wiswell, Smith, and Bass 1985; Herzog 1989) as well as lower rates of certain sexually transmitted diseases (STDs) (Parker et al. 1983; Task Force on Circumcision 1989). Male satisfaction has also been debated. Some believe that circumcision reduces male sensitivity and coital enjoyment, while others argue that circumcision may afford greater ejaculatory control (Morgan 1967; Burger and Guthrie 1974). Masters and Johnson (1966) reported no clinically significant difference in the tactile sensitivity of the glans. More recent reports suggest that the sensitivity of the circumcised glans may in fact be reduced (Preston 1970; Cleary and Kohl 1979). Such claims of reduced sexual satisfaction for circumcised men have spurred a significant movement against the circumcision of infants and the reversing of circumcision in adult men (Schmiedeskamp 1999). A technique of uncircumcising has even been introduced (Goodwin 1990). Nevertheless, little consensus exists regarding the role of the foreskin in sexual performance and satisfaction.

As a result of these and other findings, the 1989 AAP Task Force on

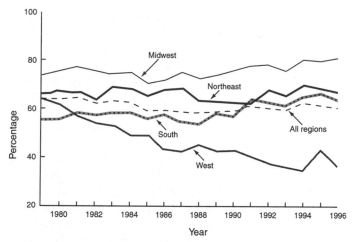

Fig. 7.1 Recent circumcision rates by region.
Source: National Center for Health Statistics data for 1998.

Circumcision changed its position somewhat and acknowledged that circumcision has potential medical benefits that must be weighed against its
risks. The task force based the change in its recommendation on developments in three principal areas of medical research. These included studies
indicating that circumcised male infants have lower incidence of urinary
tract infections, that circumcised men had lower risk of contracting certain
STDs, and that such sexually transmitted diseases were related to cancer
of the penis and cervix (Masi 1995). As shown in figure 7.1, reports of
these findings have been accompanied by an increase in recent circumcision rates in all regions of the United States except the West.

In 1999, the AAP issued yet another report reevaluating the medical
arguments for circumcision. The Task Force on Circumcision found that
data on STDs in general are conflicting, that, although circumcision does
seem to lower the rate of HIV infection, behavioral risk factors are far
more important. The task force also concluded that neonatal circumcision
does decrease the incidence of urinary tract infections in infancy and of
penile cancer in adulthood but that the number of males affected is small.
On the basis of these findings, the AAP reversed its neutral stance on
newborn circumcision, stating that evidence of medical benefits from the
procedure is not sufficient to recommend the routine circumcision of
newborns.

7.2 The Contribution of the NHSLS

Because of the mixed findings, the value of neonatal circumcision remains
difficult to establish. For every research report purporting to demonstrate

the value of circumcision, there exists another demonstrating the absence of any benefit. Further limiting the utility of such debates is the fact that studies arguing either for or against circumcision typically appeal to criteria that are so different as to defy clear comparison. For instance, while advocates of neonatal circumcision point to its role in the reduction of penile cancer in adults, opponents of the procedure direct attention to the infant himself, arguing that the complications associated with the operation pose considerable threats. In addition, the populations under study in research on circumcision vary greatly—from laboratory animals to human cultures that do not necessarily practice circumcision to a wide variety of special populations (e.g., those who attend STD clinics; military conscripts).[1] Such studies are often subject to methodological doubt because they "select on the dependent variable" that circumcision status is supposed to explain or they select study populations that may not be generalizable to the full range of races, social classes, and sexual activities. Thus, the current state of the scientific research on the value of neonatal circumcision lends itself easily to heated political debate with no clear resolution—or any clear criteria for reaching such a resolution—in sight.

The present study attempts to shed light on the debate surrounding circumcision by exploiting the unique features of the National Health and Social Life Survey (NHSLS).[2] Among other things, participants were queried about their education, religion, occupation, and race as well as about their STD experience, sexual practices, and subjective preferences for particular sexual practices. In addition, men were asked whether they were circumcised.[3]

The NHSLS data contain two principal features that make it a unique tool for examining issues related to the value of circumcision. First, respondents constitute a probability sample of the U.S. population. While previous studies were limited in their ability to generalize beyond the clinical populations from which their subjects were typically drawn, NHSLS respondents represent the full range of Americans. Second, rather than being geared to the study of one particular question, the NHSLS questionnaire represents a broadly based effort to chart a wide variety of sexual and health-related experiences and attitudes. Whereas typical assessments of the value of circumcision focus on one of the many purported outcomes of the procedure, the virtue of the present analysis lies in the fact that we may assess the effect of circumcision on an extensive series of possible correlates in the context of a single study population. Similarly, as the NHSLS data contain extensive background information on respondents, they afford the possibility of controlling for various confounding influences that may lurk beneath the surface of many clinical studies.

Our plan of analysis proceeds in three parts. First, we describe the prevalence of circumcision in the NHSLS sample. Beyond limited records on historical circumcision rates, very little is known regarding how the practice is distributed across various groups and strata of Americans. Thus, we exploit the NHSLS data by presenting a first look at circumcision rates across racial, educational, geographic, and religious groups. Second, we illustrate how the NHSLS data speak to current debates regarding the effect of neonatal circumcision on outcomes such as sexually transmitted diseases and sexual dysfunctions. Finally, we present intriguing results indicating significant differences between circumcised and uncircumcised men in terms of their sexual practices and attitudes.

7.3 Methods

A respondent's circumcision status was ascertained by asking whether he was circumcised. He was not asked, however, whether the procedure was performed at birth or later in life. Experience with sexually transmitted diseases was measured by asking the respondent whether he had ever been told by a doctor that he had any of a specified list of such diseases, which were identified by their medical names as well as by vernacular terms (e.g., *gonorrhea, clap,* or *drip*) (for an extended discussion of the data on sexually transmitted diseases, see *SOS,* chap. 11; and chap. 9 below). Experience of sexual dysfunction was ascertained with the question, "Sometimes people go through periods in which they are not interested in sex or are having trouble achieving sexual gratification. I have just a few questions about whether you have experienced this in the past 12 months. During the last 12 months has there ever been a period of several months or more when you . . . ?" (*SOS,* 660). This question was asked regarding a series of sexual dysfunctions ranging from the inability to climax to a lack of interest in sex (for an extended discussion of sexual dysfunction, see chap. 10 below). Respondents were also asked about their engagement in various sexual practices. Lifetime experience of a series of partnered behaviors was ascertained by asking whether they had ever engaged in various sex acts. Respondents were also asked to describe the frequency with which they masturbated on a ten-point scale ranging from never to every day. Finally, respondents were asked how appealing they found a range of sexual practices, including vaginal intercourse, oral, anal, and same-gender sex, and sex under threat of force. Each practice was assessed on a four-point scale ranging from very appealing to not at all appealing (see *SOS,* chap. 4).

We employed a series of univariate and multivariable analyses to chart the distribution of circumcision and examine its effects. In assessing the prevalence of circumcision within various social groups, we performed multiple logistic regression of group membership on circumcision status and calculated adjusted odds ratios that reflected the odds of being circumcised for group members relative to all others in the sample. In addition, we examined how such differences have changed over time by repeating the analyses within three broad age cohorts.

In assessing the effect of circumcision on the contraction of STDs and susceptibility to sexual dysfunction, we performed a series of two-tailed t-tests to uncover significant differences between circumcised and uncircumcised men across a wide array of related outcomes. Next, we estimated logistic equations for each of the STDs and dysfunctions on circumcision status and a series of control variables. These factors included number of lifetime sex partners; education; race/ethnicity; religion; nativity; residence in urban, suburban, or rural areas; a seven-point scale indicating how liberal/conservative were the respondent's sexual attitudes; and the respondent's age. Net of these controls, we calculated adjusted odds ratios for the odds of having the various STDs and dysfunctions for circumcised relative to uncircumcised respondents. Finally, we repeated these comparisons within categories of a critical third variable—for STDs, the number of lifetime sex partners reported by the respondent; for sexual dysfunction, the respondent's age.

We conducted similar analyses to assess the association between circumcision status and various sexual practices and subjective preferences for particular practices. We performed logistic regression to assess this association with the respondent's lifetime experience with various practices and with subjective preferences. As it is an ordinal variable, we employed ordered logit to analyze the association between circumcision status and the respondent's masturbation experience. In addition, we repeated this analysis as a logistic regression with a critical cutoff point, masturbating at least once a month, as the dependent variable. As results from this analysis matched that from the ordered logit, we present the logistic regression results to afford comparability with the other analyses conducted. In all the models of sexual practices and subjective preferences, we controlled for the same factors listed above.[4] In addition, we repeated the analyses for each of the three major ethnic groups featured in the survey, whites, blacks, and Hispanics. All analyses were performed using *Stata* version 4.0.

7.4 Results

Prevalence of Circumcision

Since the age range of men participating in the NHSLS was eighteen to fifty-nine, estimates of the prevalence of neonatal circumcision can be calculated for the years 1933–74. As shown in figure 7.2, the steady increase in circumcision rates among respondents during much of this period reflects the increase identified by other investigators (Herzog 1989). The pro-

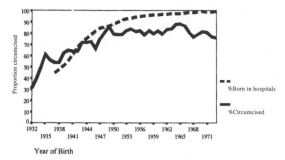

Fig. 7.2 Rates of male circumcision (three-year moving average) and hospital birth in the United States, 1933–71. *Sources:* Male circumcision: NHSLS. Hospital birth: National Center for Health Statistics data for 1998.

portion of newborns who were circumcised reached 80 percent in the years after World War II and climaxed in the mid-1960s. This rise mirrors the increasing prevalence of hospital births. In addition, a slight decline in the proportion circumcised occurred in the last years covered by the survey, about the time when the medical establishment began to question the value of routine neonatal circumcision.[5] Overall, 77 percent of the 1,284 American-born men surveyed in the main NHSLS sample were circumcised, compared with 42 percent of the 115 foreign-born men.

Table 7.1 analyzes circumcision rates for religious, racial, and socioeconomic groupings of American-born respondents. We see that differences in circumcision rates across religious groups are not great. As may be expected, Jewish men report the highest proportion circumcised. However, given the small number of Jews surveyed in the NHSLS, this does not result in a significant adjusted odds ratio. Mainline Protestants (including, e.g., Methodists, Presbyterians, Lutherans, and Episcopalians) are somewhat more likely than conservative Protestants (including, e.g., Baptists and Pentecostals) to be circumcised.[6] However, as indicated by the insignificant adjusted odds ratio, this difference disappears when race is controlled. Indeed, the predominant pattern is one of high circumcision rates for all major American religious groups.

Differences in circumcision levels across racial and ethnic groups are more revealing. In particular, whites are considerably more likely to be circumcised than are blacks or Hispanics (81 percent vs. 65 percent and 54 percent). These differences remain significant when other variables are controlled. Net of these factors, the odds of a black being circumcised are roughly half (95 percent confidence interval (CI): 0.4–0.85) those of whites; the odds for Hispanics are about one-third (95 percent CI: 0.26–0.44) those of whites. Looking across the table, we see that there has been

Table 7.1 Circumcision Rates across Social Groups by Cohort: American-Born Men

Predictor Variable	All Men					Born 1933–47					Born 1947–62					Born 1963–73				
	% Circumcised	N	Adjusted Odds Ratio and 95% CI[a]			% Circumcised	N	Adjusted Odds Ratio and 95% CI[a]			% Circumcised	N	Adjusted Odds Ratio and 95% CI[a]			% Circumcised	N	Adjusted Odds Ratio and 95% CI[a]		
Religion																				
No religion	.80	179		R		.71	28		R		.82	77		R		.82	73		R	
Mainline Protestant	.82	301	.78	1.24	1.98	.64	85	.37	.88	2.09	.87	143	.88	1.83	3.79	.93	73	.69	1.73	4.34
Conservative Protestant	.71	394	.65	.81	1.00	.53	101	.51	.78	1.20	.76	164	.58	1.14	2.21	.81	129	.42	.86	1.76
Catholic	.79	324	.91	1.16	1.47	.68	80	.50	1.19	2.83	.84	150	.74	1.53	3.17	.80	94	.48	1.03	2.21
Jewish	.96	25	...	...	...	...	...	...	...	...	...	...	...	...	...	...	...	...	...	...
Ethnicity[b]																				
White	.81	1067		R		.65	251		R		.86	478		R		.86	332		R	
Black	.65	189	.40	.58	.85	.49	46	.31	.63	1.29	.64	89	.21	.37	.65	.76	58	.30	.62	1.27
Hispanic	.54	90	.26	.34	.44	.35	23	.17	.38	.85	.61	31	.10	.15	.22	.56	36	.10	.21	.46
Mother's education																				
Less than high school	.62	372		R		.52	142		R		.68	153		R		.66	76		R	
High school graduate	.84	538	1.90	2.56	3.46	.69	107	1.30	2.17	3.62	.89	264	1.66	2.78	4.64	.84	167	.68	1.48	3.21
Some college	.84	167	2.15	2.72	3.47	.57	21	.48	1.12	2.60	.93	72	1.90	4.62	11.71	.84	74	.87	1.86	3.96
College graduate	.87	148	2.25	2.93	3.81	.82	22	1.13	3.06	8.32	.81	58	1.14	1.74	2.39	.94	68	1.54	4.07	10.72
N		1,369					358					653					488			

Source: NHSLS.

Note: R = reference category. Ellipses points indicate 20 cases or fewer.

[a]Estimated ratio of odds of being circumcised for members of the specified group to odds for reference group. The middle number represents the estimate; the numbers on the left and right reflect the left and right boundaries of a 95 percent confidence interval (CI) around that estimate. Derived from logistic regression model performed on all American-born respondents. The model includes all predictor variables as well as controls for residence in rural, suburban, or urban areas.

[b]Asians and Indians were also included in the full model but are excluded here because they represent too few cases for reliable results.

some convergence in circumcision rates for the three groups across cohorts, although differences among groups have persisted.

Circumcision rates vary significantly by the level of education attained by a respondent's mother. The critical break occurred between respondents whose mothers did and did not earn a high school diploma. While 62 percent of respondents whose mothers did not finish high school were circumcised, the rate for all other respondents varied from 84 percent to 87 percent. These differences remained significant when other factors were controlled. Net of such factors, the odds of being circumcised for respondents whose mothers earned at least a high school diploma were about 2.5 times (95 percent CI: 1.9–3.8) those of those whose mothers were less educated. This discrepancy appeared to be narrowing in more recent cohorts. Among the youngest group of respondents, only those whose mothers had finished college displayed a significantly higher circumcision rate than those whose mothers had not earned a high school diploma.

Sexually Transmitted Diseases

Table 7.2 compares the incidence of various STDs reported by circumcised and uncircumcised respondents. Note that, in this and subsequent tables, circumcision status serves as an independent variable rather than a dependent variable. Dependent variables are listed in the stub columns of these tables.

Several instructive features of the data presented in table 7.2 deserve attention. First, circumcision status does not appear to lower the likelihood of contracting an STD. Rather, the opposite pattern holds. Circumcised men were slightly more likely to have had both a bacterial and a viral STD in their lifetime. While these differences are not statistically significant, they do not lend support to the thesis that circumcision helps prevent the contraction of STDs. Indeed, for chlamydia, the difference between circumcised and uncircumcised men is quite large. While 26 of 1,033 circumcised men had contracted chlamydia in their lifetime, *none* of the 353 uncircumcised men reported having had it.

Looking across table 7.2, we see a marked increase in the experience of STDs as the number of partners increases. The small, insignificant tendency for circumcised men to contract STDs at higher rates appeared for each category of sexual experience. In addition, contraction of bacterial STDs occurred at a significantly higher rate for men who have had more than twenty sex partners in their lifetimes. Among circumcised men with such a sexual background, the odds of contracting a bacterial STD are estimated at 2.88 times those for uncircumcised men. While this difference is significant, its exact size is difficult to establish, as indicated by the wide confidence interval (95 percent CI: 1.03–8.03). Note as well that this

Table 7.2 Lifetime Experience of STDs by Circumcision Status and Number of Sex Partners

Criterion Variable	All Men Mean Comparison C	UC	All Men Adjusted Odds Ratio and 95% CI[a]			1–4 Partners, Lifetime Mean Comparison C	UC	1–4 Partners Adjusted Odds Ratio and 95% CI[a]			5–20 Partners, Lifetime Mean Comparison C	UC	5–20 Partners Adjusted Odds Ratio and 95% CI[a]			21+ Partners, Lifetime Mean Comparison C	UC	21+ Partners Adjusted Odds Ratio and 95% CI[a]		
Gonorrhea	94.7	104.8	.79	1.42	2.56	22.1	20.4	.25	2.22	19.77	108.4	143.9	.38	.79	1.62	237.3	196.4	.96	3.26	11.11
Syphilis	9.3	10.8	.41	2.14	11.30	2.5	6.8	. . .			9.9	7.6	.07	.77	8.87	28.2	.0	. . .		
Chlamydia	25.1**	.0	. . .			7.4	.0	. . .			32.2	.0	. . .			56.5	.0	. . .		
Nongonococcal urethritis	24.4	19.1	.43	1.33	4.09	2.5	6.8	. . .			27.2	23.1	.20	1.17	6.93	74.3	56.6	.27	1.53	8.76
All bacterial	129.9	112.9	.94	1.61	2.78	29.5	20.4	.35	2.46	17.3	157.6	151.5	.50	.99	1.94	316.4	232.1	1.03	2.88	8.03
Herpes	14.9	8.1	.23	1.18	5.94	2.5	.0	. . .			9.9	15.5	. . .			62.1	17.9	.12	1.27	12.95
Hepatitis	24.2	24.4	.43	1.22	3.46	14.6	13.7	.19	1.53	12.36	32.1	15.3	.30	1.50	7.42	28.2	72.7	.00	.04	2.59
HIV	1.9	5.4	. . .			.0	6.8	. . .			2.5	7.8	. . .			5.7	.0	. . .		
All viral	35.3	32.3	.52	1.30	3.22	17.2	13.7	.19	1.35	9.57	32.0	30.3	.36	1.84	9.51	90.4	89.3	.15	.70	3.24
N	1,449		1,118			554		449			538		444			233		190		

Source: NHSLS.

Note: C = circumcised. UC = uncircumcised. Ellipses points indicate unstable estimate.

[a]Estimated ratio of odds of experiencing the specified STD for circumcised men relative to odds for uncircumcised men. The middle number represents the estimate; the numbers on the left and right reflect the left and right boundaries of a 95 percent confidence interval (CI) around that estimate. Derived from logistic regression model performed in which experience of the STD is the dependent variable and independent variables, in addition to circumcision status, include ethnicity, religion, residence in rural, suburban, or urban areas, education, and, in models for all men, number of sex partners.

**$p \leq .05$ t-test for difference between circumcised and uncircumcised men.

difference is driven largely by the differential rates of contraction of gonorrhea (see chap. 9 below).

Sexual Dysfunction

While some difficulties, such as experiencing pain during sex, were quite rare, table 7.3 demonstrates that sexual dysfunction is a relatively common event for American men. Approximately 45 percent of both circumcised and uncircumcised men experienced at least one of these dysfunctions in the year prior to the survey. In addition, the data indicate a slight tendency for such dysfunctions to plague uncircumcised men. When all age groups are considered, almost every dysfunction is slightly more common among men who have not been circumcised. In particular, the likelihood of having difficulty achieving or maintaining an erection is significantly lower for circumcised men. When other factors are considered, the difference in the odds of experiencing this dysfunction for circumcised men is significantly less than that for uncircumcised men (estimate = 0.66 odds ratio), but only at the 0.07 level (95 percent CI: 0.42–1.03).

Significant differences are more prominent when we examine the association between sexual dysfunction and circumcision status within age cohorts. Looking across table 7.3, we see that, while there appears to be little relation between circumcision status and sexual dysfunction for the two younger cohorts, the association is quite strong for the oldest group of respondents. Of the seven sexual dysfunctions considered, uncircumcised older men were more likely to experience every one of these difficulties than were their circumcised peers. Three of these differences are statistically significant even in the presence of controls. The odds of a circumcised man of this age experiencing anxiety about his performance were approximately half those of his uncircumcised peers (95 percent CI: 0.22–0.95); the odds of a member of the former group having difficulty achieving or maintaining an erection are about 0.40 those of the latter group (95 percent CI: 0.16–0.77). Overall, the odds that a circumcised man of the oldest cohort experienced sexual dysfunction were 0.48 that of uncircumcised men of the same age group (95 percent CI: 0.28–0.79). Thus, while circumcised men did not generally appear to experience different rates of sexual dysfunction, older circumcised men did display lower levels of dysfunction.

Sexual Practice

As evidenced in table 7.4, NHSLS data indicate that circumcised men engage in a somewhat more elaborated set of sexual practices than do men who are not circumcised. Circumcised men engaged in each of the practices examined—lifetime experience of various forms of oral and anal sex

Table 7.3 Sexual Dysfunction in Past Year by Circumcision Status and Age

Criterion Variable	All Men					Ages 18–29					Ages 30–44					Ages 45–59				
	Mean Comparison		Adjusted Odds Ratio and 95% CI[a]			Mean Comparison		Adjusted Odds Ratio and 95% CI[a]			Mean Comparison		Adjusted Odds Ratio and 95% CI[a]			Mean Comparison		Adjusted Odds Ratio and 95% CI[a]		
	C	UC				C	UC				C	UC				C	UC			
Lacked interest in sex	.15	.17	.71	1.04	1.53	.14	.15	.62	1.39	3.13	.16	.12	.79	1.59	3.20	.14	.23	.27	.52	1.02
Unable to ejaculate	.08	.10	.64	1.05	1.72	.06	.09	.25	.58	1.82	.09	.05	.76	1.86	4.54	.09	.16	.30	.70	1.22
Ejaculated prematurely	.28	.31	.64	.87	1.18	.29	.27	.54	1.00	1.84	.29	.28	.68	1.17	2.00	.25*	.37	.34	.59	1.03
Experience pain during sex	.03	.03	.49	1.14	2.68	.04	.04	.22	.93	3.94	.03	.01	…	…	…	.02	.05	.25	1.49	9.04
Did not enjoy sex	.08	.09	.46	.76	1.26	.10	.07	.39	1.04	2.77	.08	.08	.44	1.09	2.69	.05	.10	.11	.33	.97
Was anxious about performance	.17	.18	.60	.87	1.27	.20	.15	.62	1.35	2.94	.18	.17	.55	1.05	2.00	.13*	.22	.22	.50	.95
Had trouble achieving/maintaining erection	.10*	.17	.42	.66	1.03	.07	.09	.30	.85	2.44	.10	.07	.53	1.28	3.11	.13**	.29	.16	.38	.77
Any dysfunction	.43	.48	.64	.85	1.13	.47	.46	.57	.99	1.72	.44	.39	.81	1.33	2.18	.40**	.58	.28	.47	.79
N	1,221	1,203				378	399				586	519				340	285			

Source: NHSLS.

Note: C = circumcised. UC = uncircumcised. Ellipses points indicate unstable estimate.

[a] Estimated ratio of odds of experiencing the specified dysfunction for circumcised men relative to odds for uncircumcised men. The middle number represents the estimate; the numbers on the left and right reflect the left and right boundaries of a 95% confidence interval (CI) around that estimate. Derived from logistic regression model performed in which experience of the dysfunction is the dependent variable and independent variables, in addition to circumcision status, include number of sex partners, religion, residence in rural, suburban, or urban areas, education, and, in models for all men, ethnicity.

* $p \leq .10$ t-test for difference between circumcised and uncircumcised men.
** $p \leq .05$ t-test for difference between circumcised and uncircumcised men.

Table 7.4 Sexual Practice by Circumcision Status, Ethnicity, and Control Factors

Criterion Variable	All Men					Whites					Blacks				
	Mean Comparison		Adjusted Odds Ratio and 95% CI[a]			Mean Comparison		Adjusted Odds Ratio and 95% CI[a]			Mean Comparison		Adjusted Odds Ratio and 95% CI[a]		
	C	UC				C	UC				C	UC			
Lifetime experience															
Active heterosexual oral sex	.80**	.65	.97	1.37	1.92	.84**	.73	1.04	1.57	2.37	.52	.47	.40	.96	2.28
Passive heterosexual oral sex	.81**	.61	.96	1.36	1.93	.84**	.73	1.04	1.57	2.38	.71**	.57	.56	1.38	3.37
Active homosexual oral sex	.05	.02	.85	2.15	5.42	.06	.03	.73	2.22	6.74	.03	.03	...	...	...
Passive homosexual oral sex	.08	.06	.85	1.59	2.96	.09	.06	.73	1.88	6.74	.06	.08	...	...	...
Heterosexual anal intercourse	.27	.23	.56	.80	1.14	.27	.22	.45	.69	1.06	.24	.22	.40	1.16	3.38
Experience in past year															
Masturbation ≥ 1/ Month	.47**	.34	1.04	1.40	1.89	.50**	.34	1.24	1.76	2.51	.27	.28	.35	.92	2.39
N	1,404	1,143				1,046	903				190	126			

Source: NHSLS.

[a]Estimated ratio of odds of experiencing the specified sexual practice for circumcised men relative to odds for uncircumcised men. The middle number represents the estimate; the numbers on the left and right reflect the left and right boundaries of a 95% confidence interval (CI) around that estimate. Derived from logistic regression model performed in which experience of the sexual practice is the dependent variable and independent variables, in addition to circumcision status, include number of sex partners, religion, residence in rural, suburban, or urban areas, education, and, in models for all men, ethnicity.

*p ≤ .05 *t*-test for difference between circumcised and uncircumcised men.

**p ≤ .05.

and masturbation frequency in the past year—at higher rates than did uncircumcised men. The difference between circumcised and uncircumcised men was greatest for masturbation—ironically, a practice that circumcision was once thought to limit. Forty-seven percent of circumcised men reported masturbating at least once a month, whereas only 34 percent of their uncircumcised peers did. This difference remains significant even when various attitudinal and demographic factors are controlled. The odds of a circumcised man masturbating at least once a month are estimated at 1.4 (95 percent CI: 1.04–1.89) those for uncircumcised men. In terms of lifetime sexual experience, the greatest differences occurred for heterosexual oral sex. In models with controls, circumcision status was associated with active heterosexual oral sex with a probability of insignificance of 0.07 (estimate of odds ratio: 1.37; 95 percent CI: 0.97–1.92) and with passive heterosexual oral sex with a probability of insignificance of 0.08 (estimate of odds ratio: 1.36; 95 percent CI: 0.96–1.93).

The association between circumcision status and the various sexual practices exhibited interesting differences across ethnic groups. Looking across the table, we see that, while circumcised men of all three ethnic groups tended to engage in a more elaborated set of sexual practices, this was less true of blacks and Hispanics. For white men, the difference between circumcised and uncircumcised men was stark. Circumcised white men exhibited a greater likelihood of experiencing each of the various practices. In particular, the estimated ratio of the odds of masturbating at least once a month for circumcised men was 1.76 that for uncircumcised men (95 percent CI: 1.24–2.51). The adjusted odds ratios for both forms of heterosexual oral sex were significant as well. These associations were less consistent for blacks and Hispanics. While circumcised Hispanic men did masturbate at a slightly higher rate than their uncircumcised peers, no such difference appeared for blacks. Similarly, while circumcised black men exhibited a greater tendency to engage in passive oral sex than did uncircumcised black men (this difference was insignificant when other factors were controlled), the reverse was true among Hispanic men. Thus, while circumcision status appeared to be significantly linked with a higher likelihood of engaging in various sexual practices, this applied mostly to whites and considerably less to blacks and Hispanics.

Appeal of Sexual Practices

The NHSLS survey asked respondents to rate their preference for a wide range of sexual practices on a scale ranging from very appealing to not very appealing. As with the practices discussed above, we explored the association between circumcision status and the full range of sexual preferences (*SOS,* chap. 4). The findings are very suggestive. When simple zero-order relations are considered, circumcised men expressed a greater preference for every form of sexual behavior but one—the appeal of forcing someone to have sex. These associations were especially high for vaginal intercourse, use of a dildo, active anal intercourse with a woman, performing oral sex on a woman, and receiving oral sex from a woman. The effect of circumcision status on these preferences remained significant even when those control variables considered in tables 7.3 and 7.4 were introduced. The diversity of behaviors to which circumcision status appears to be related challenges facile interpretations of these findings. However, it is noteworthy that the strongest of these effects concerns that of preference for fellatio. Thus, we present the results for this variable, keeping in mind the larger set of findings.

Regression models presented in table 7.5 consider the effect of circumcision status on how appealing a respondent finds receiving oral sex from a woman. The dependent variable is measured as a four-point scale ranging from not very appealing (1) to very appealing (4).[7] The control variables considered in previous analyses are included again. In addition, we consider the effect of circumcision status on preference for fellatio in the context of two additional independent variables. These include a broad, attitudinal variable that categorizes respondents on a seven-point scale ranging from traditional to libertarian attitudes toward sexuality (SOS, chap. 14) as well as a variable indicating whether respondents had ever experienced fellatio. The latter variable should clearly have a strong association with preference for fellatio. The two variables have a somewhat ambiguous causal relation.[8] Nevertheless, we include having experienced fellatio as a control variable as a means of testing whether circumcision status may have an effect even when it is considered.

The results indicate that circumcision status does indeed have a powerful effect on preference for fellatio. The zero-order coefficient for circumcision status, which indicates a 0.5 increase in the four-point fellatio preference scale, is highly significant—more than eight times its standard error. Further, when each set of controls is added, this effect diminishes in strength but remains significant. The third model underlines the strength of the effect. That circumcision status affects a respondent's preference for fellatio even when his lifetime experience of fellatio is taken into account testifies to the robustness of the finding. Clearly, circumcised men are significantly more likely to prefer fellatio than are uncircumcised men.

As before, this pattern is most evident among whites. We see from the second, third, and fourth sets of columns that, even when lifetime experience of fellatio is included as a predictor of having a preference for fellatio, circumcised white men are significantly more likely to express a preference for fellatio than are their uncircumcised counterparts. Black and Hispanic men, by contrast, do not exhibit this pattern to any appreciable extent.[9]

Table 7.5 Regression Models of Appeal of Fellatio on Circumcision Status

	All Groups								Whites			
	β	(SE_B)	β	(SE_B)	β	(SE_P)	β	(SE_B)	β	(SE_B)	β	(SE_P)
Circumcised	.51**	(.06)	.02**	(.07)	.12**	(.06)	.51**	(.07)	.33**	(.08)	.19**	(.07)
Age			−.22**	(.00)	−.02**	(.00)			−.02**	(.00)	−.02**	(.00)
Education			.14**	(.02)	.09**	(.00)			.12**	(.03)	.08**	(.00)
American born	.02		−.15	(.11)	−.09	(.11)	.03		.14	(.15)	.01	
Urbanism[b]												
CC12			.45**	(.13)	.38**	(.12)			.39**	(.16)	.38**	(.15)
CC100			.25**	(.11)	.03	(.10)			.18	(.12)	.03	(.11)
SUB12			.19	(.12)	−.04	(.11)			.04	(.13)	−.17	(.12)
SUB100			.23**	(.11)	.06	(.10)			.12	(.11)	−.00	(.10)
OTHURB			.12	(.09)	−.03	(.08)			.05	(.09)	−.06	(.08)
Ethnicity[c]												
White			.56**	(.16)	.33**	(.15)						
Black			−.05	(.17)	−.17	(.16)						
Hispanic			.38**	(.18)	.20	(.17)						
Cluster Membership					.06**	(.01)					.07**	(.01)
Lifetime Fellatio					1.19**	(.10)					1.03**	(.07)
Constant	2.69**	(.06)	2.70**	(.26)	4.31**	(.26)	2.22**	(.07)	3.14**	(.23)	4.31**	(.24)
R^2	.04		.14		.38		.04		.11		.31	
N	1,384		1,375		1,178		1,082		1,076		930	

Blacks[a] Hispanics[a]

	Blacks[a]						Hispanics[a]					
	β	(SE_B)	β	(SE_B)	β	(SE_P)	β	(SE_B)	β	(SE_B)	β	(SE_P)
Circumcised	.16	(.18)	-.13**	(.18)	-.67*	(.41)			-.06	(.20)	.38**	(.15)
Age			-.03**	(.01)	-.05**	(.02)			-.01	(.00)	.00	(.01)
Education			.26**	(.08)	.03				.23**	(.08)	.01	
American born		(.19)	-.55*	(.31)	-.58	(.59)			-.40*	(.21)	-.30**	(.17)
Urbanism[b]												
CC12			.69**	(.32)	.49	(.35)			1.17**	(.92)	1.52**	
CC100			.51	(.32)	-.02	(.37)			.96*	(.53)	1.06**	
SUB12			.73*	(.39)	.10	(.42)			1.26**	(.55)	1.05**	
SUB100			.40	(.40)	.23	(.43)			1.66**	(.54)	1.40**	
OTHURB			.38	(.31)	.06	(.35)			.84*	(.50)	.92*	
Ethnicity[c]												
White												
Black												
Hispanic												
Cluster Membership					.01	(.04)					-.05	(.04)
Lifetime					1.50**	(.21)					2.12**	(.17)
Fellatio												
Constant	2.40**	(.14)	3.08**	(.57)	5.63**	(.79)	2.79**	(.13)	2.30**	(.64)	4.43	(.58)
R^2	.00		.15		.41		.02		.20		.78	
N	206		202		129		131		131		78	

Source: NHSLS.

[a] The minority oversample is included in these models.

[b] Variables indicate whether respondent lives in the central city of the 12 largest metropolitan areas (CC12), the central city of the largest 100 acres (CC100), the suburbs of these areas (SUB100), or in some other urban area (OTHURB). Respondents living in rural areas serve as the reference category.

[c] Asians and Indians serve as the reference category.

*p ≤ .10.

**p ≤ .05.

That is, while circumcised men express a greater preference for fellatio, this general pattern obscures the fact that this association holds only within one ethnic group.

7.5 Discussion

The United States is set apart from the rest of the Western world by its high rates of neonatal circumcision. Nevertheless, medical research on the topic has generated an ambiguous set of results regarding the effect of circumcision status on the lives of men. As a result, rhetoric has reached a fever pitch as each side of the debate appeals to divergent criteria to make its case.

Our analysis of the NHSLS furnishes needed information that should be useful in such decision-making processes. We examined the prevalence of circumcision among American men as well as its effect on sexually transmitted diseases, sexual functioning, and sexual practice and preferences. Each of these areas generated noteworthy findings.

Prevalence

With respect to prevalence, we demonstrated that circumcision rates are highest among whites and better-educated respondents and that Americans of various religions do not display significantly different rates. The latter fact illustrates the unique cultural status enjoyed by circumcision in the United States. While circumcision has been employed as a religious marker in other Western societies, it has clearly lost such an association in America. American religious organizations have never strongly objected to the circumcision of its members, having instead deferred to medical authority on the subject.

Several factors may account for differential rates of circumcision across ethnic groups. First, as race is associated with socioeconomic differences between Americans, these differences may reflect the greater tendency for middle-class parents to have their sons circumcised. Similarly, blacks and Hispanics are concentrated in such regions as the South or the Southwest, where circumcision is less prevalent. However, the fact that differences in circumcision rates remain significant when region and class are controlled suggests that the various racial groups may have different preferences for circumcision. Members of groups among whom circumcision is less common may avoid circumcising their sons so that a sense of shared physical appearance is retained. Indeed, a recent study revealed that such social considerations typically outweigh medical issues in determining parents' circumcision decisions (Brown and Brown 1987).

As with race, differences among socioeconomic groupings may result from a differential likelihood of being born in a hospital. However, this difference remained salient even in later periods, when hospital births were virtually universal. Thus, it again appears likely that significant social variation exists in the preference for and acceptance of circumcision. Better-educated parents, who are more likely to be exposed to the prevailing scientific wisdom favoring circumcision and to be exposed to significant social pressure to conform to this wisdom, are more likely to have their sons circumcised than less well-educated parents.

In sum, we see that, just as significant social institutions have played critical roles in the propagation of neonatal circumcision in the United States, the practice spread and persisted differentially across social groups. In contrast to societies in which circumcision has indicated religious or cultic difference, the popularity of circumcision in the United States in the twentieth century clearly reflects social distinctions that are salient in contemporary society. Those social groups that had the education and the cultural affinity to follow the recommendations of medical and state authorities adopted circumcision, while those groups that maintained a more distant relationship to such institutions did not embrace the practice to a comparable degree.

Note that these results should be treated with some caution when applied to rates of neonatal circumcision. NHSLS respondents were asked whether they were circumcised but not if the procedure was performed at birth or later in life. Given the rarity with which older boys and men undergo circumcision[10] and the match of our data with existing records on neonatal circumcision, we feel that it is reasonable to assume that different rates across social groups reflect differential experience at birth. Note that this assumption is not necessary for examining the association between circumcision status and various outcomes. In such cases, the procedure must only have been performed before the outcome in question. A second source of ambiguity concerns the accuracy of respondents' reports of their circumcision status. Research from the 1950s (Lilienfeld and Graham 1958) and on adolescents in the 1980s (Schlossberger, Turner, and Irwin 1991) suggests that up to a third of men may not know their circumcision status. While we have no means of independently verifying respondents' reports, we control for education in all our models, a variable that should significantly affect knowledge of circumcision status.

STDs

With respect to STDs, we found no evidence of a prophylactic role for circumcision and a slight tendency in the opposite direction (for a current review of the extant literature that broadly substantiates this finding, see Van Howe [1999]). Indeed, the absence of a foreskin was significantly associated with contraction of bacterial STDs among men who have had many sex partners in their lifetimes. These results suggest that a reexamination of the prevailing wisdom regarding the prophylactic effect of circumcision is in order. While circumcision may have an effect that was not picked up in the NHSLS data, it seems unlikely that this effect is great enough to justify the claims made by those who base their support for widespread circumcision on it.

Several cautions apply to these findings, however. The NHSLS self-reports of STD contraction were almost certainly underreports because respondents may not have known they had an STD if they were asymptomatic and/or never diagnosed or may not have understood the diagnosis. Moreover, given the social stigma associated with having STDs, some respondents may have been reluctant to report having had such a condition. Considerable effort was expended in minimizing underreporting by devising an interview protocol that gave a maximum sense of privacy and confidentiality, that persuaded the respondent of the need for full disclosure for public health reasons, and that provided memory aids to facilitate respondent recall. Even if these procedures were especially effective—and we think that they were—we must still acknowledge that the self-reports understate the incidence of STDs to a substantial but unknown extent. In addition, there may have been systematic biases in underreporting related to particular attributes of respondents. In particular, we might expect better-educated people to be more knowledgeable about disease labels than less well-educated people. By contrast, however, better-educated persons may be more sensitive to the social stigma associated with having an STD. Controlling for education in the various models helped but probably did not fully redress these issues.

Results may also have been affected by the possibility that some respondents did not know whether they had been circumcised. If one assumes that respondents were more likely to say that they were circumcised (i.e., the default answer is to give an affirmative response to any question) and that the same people report higher levels of STDs, this may account for any association found. While we feel that such distortions are small, it is worth reiterating that the principal result of our analysis is that no discernible differences in STD experience can be found to distinguish circumcised and uncircumcised men.

Sexual Dysfunctions

NHSLS data suggest a benefit of circumcision with respect to sexual dysfunction. Circumcised men were slightly less likely than those who had not been circumcised to experience various sexual difficulties. This difference was significant among the oldest age group. Interestingly, this age group presents the best test for establishing differences between circumcised and uncircumcised men as it contains comparable numbers of both. It would seem, then, that the NHSLS data supply some support for those who see circumcision as promoting healthy sexual behavior. This appears most true for older men. While there may be many sources for this relation, it is possible that the association between frequency of masturbation and circumcision status (discussed below) provides a clue. If older men require more direct stimulation to function sexually, men who incorporate masturbation in their sexual scripts (Gagnon and Simon 1973; SOS, chap. 1) may be better able to adapt sexually as they age. Clearly, such reasoning must remain speculative until further research is performed.

Sexual Practice

Our findings regarding sexual practice pose the greatest challenge for future research. NHSLS results reveal a clear pattern in that circumcised men report a more highly elaborated set of sexual practices. In particular, the association between circumcision status and frequency of masturbation was quite strong. Similar results, at a somewhat weaker level, occurred for heterosexual oral sex. These results escape easy interpretation. Certainly, they cast doubt on the Victorian-era notion that circumcision reduces the urge to masturbate.

While we do not wish to push speculation too far, differences in the association between circumcision status and sexual practice across ethnic groups suggest that cultural, rather than physiological, forces may be responsible. In particular, our results may reflect attitudes regarding the cultural acceptability of the uncircumcised penis. Note that the association of circumcision with experience of sexual practices is weakest among ethnic minorities, for whom circumcision is less prevalent. Among whites, by contrast, uncircumcised men are relatively uncommon. A consequence of this may be that a certain stigma is attached to the uncircumcised penis in the white population. If the uncircumcised penis assumes somewhat negative cultural associations among whites, this may lead uncircumcised white men to engage in a somewhat less elaborated set of sexual practices. In particular, such acts that involve direct stimulation of the uncircumcised penis should hold the least appeal.[11]

Preferences for Sexual Practices

The demonstration of systematic associations between circumcision status and subjective preferences for particular sexual practices within particular cultural/racial groups, notably for fellatio but also for a wider range of practices among circumcised white men, poses an unexpected but important challenge. What are we to make of the apparent differences in subjective preferences among white men with respect to "what turns them on" that appear to be a function of their circumcision status when no such relation (or at least a much more modest one) is observed for black or Hispanic men? We have found nothing in the extant literature, or even the popular literature devoted to coaching people in seeking sexual pleasure or advocating pro or con stances regarding circumcision as it relates to adult sexual pleasure, that anticipates these apparently culturally specific patterns. If anything, the literature is inclined to rest its arguments on unsubstantiated but universalistic biological claims of the relative sensitivity of circumcised and uncircumcised penises in conferring or hindering sexual pleasure, with the balance of opinion in favor of the greater sensitivity of the uncircumcised penis because it is natural. Few indeed, at least in the Western tradition, have ever advocated circumcision as an obvious means for enhancing sexual pleasure. Our results suggest that there is a powerful interaction of the physical and biological with the social and cultural and that we need to design an innovative research program that can help us understand their interplay.

7.6 Conclusion

While the NHSLS results do not lend clear support to either side of the circumcision debate, they make a significant contribution to our knowledge regarding the potential risks and benefits of circumcision. In addition to documenting the prevalence of circumcision across various social groups, we have discovered that circumcision provides no discernible prophylactic benefit and may in fact increase the likelihood of contracting an STD, that circumcised men (especially older men) have a slightly lower risk of experiencing sexual dysfunction, and that circumcised men displayed higher rates of experience of various sexual practices. The last association was especially true for white men where masturbation and heterosexual oral sex were concerned. While evidence regarding STD experience contributes to ongoing debates, our results concerning sexual dysfunction, sexual practice, and subjective sexual preferences represent largely unprecedented effects. These findings suggest the need for further research, which should further aid parents in weighing the benefits and risks of having their sons circumcised.

Notes

The authors acknowledge the following people for their helpful comments and suggestions: Anne E. Laumann, William Parish, Nancy Roizen, Sevgi Aral, and Robert Rosenfield. The chapter is an expanded version of an article appearing in the *Journal of the American Medical Association* (277, no. 13 [1997]: 1052–57). The interested reader will find a microcosm of the controversy surrounding circumcision among medical professionals in the commentary that appeared in response to that article (*Journal of the American Medical Association,* 278, no. 3 [1997] 201–3). For another version of the chapter, providing additional information on the surgical procedures used in circumcision, recent evidence of changes in prevalence of circumcision by region, the debate over the pain and suffering occasioned by the procedure, and the social movements arising recently to oppose male circumcision, see Laumann (1999).

1. For a detailed discussion of the various medical issues surrounding neonatal circumcision, see Masi (1995).

2. Recall that the 3,432 persons sampled in the NHSLS include an oversample of blacks and Hispanics. To ensure comparability across major racial and ethnic groups, except when otherwise specified the following analyses use only data from the main sample.

3. It is important to note that respondents were asked whether they were circumcised but not whether the procedure was performed at birth or later in life. In the following discussion, we treat these responses as reflecting neonatal circumcision only. Given that circumcision is rarely performed on adults and the match of our data with existing records on neonatal circumcision, we feel that this is a reasonable assumption. But we have only indirect evidence that circumcision is only relatively rarely performed on adults. The National Hospital Discharge Survey (Graves 1995) for 1993, e.g., estimates that there were twenty-five thousand circumcisions performed that year, exclusive of newborns. About eighteen thousand were of males under age fifteen. Assuming a roughly similar annual number of such operations over the forty years covered in our sample population, and even assuming substantially higher numbers in the earliest years, when circumcision was less common, it is apparent that only a very small percentage of the roughly 100 million circumcised males in the United States today could have been circumcised after age fifteen.

4. However, we exclude number of lifetime sex partners, a variable that is confounded with the tendency to engage in various practices. When this variable is included as a regressor, results for masturbation remain significant, and findings regarding heterosexual oral sex weaken somewhat.

5. To complete the picture of the pattern of circumcision rates to the present day, fig. 7.1 presents the rates by regions in the United States from 1980 through 1996.

6. For the rationale underlying and details of coding the religious groups, see SOS, 146–47. On the coding of types of Protestantism, see the notes to table 3.4 above. See also the note to table 1.1 above.

7. Once again, as the dependent variable is ordinal, we estimated ordinal logit models that are more appropriate for such analyses but present the more familiar regression results. Findings from the two sets of models did not differ significantly.

8. While preferences may usually be considered to precede action, the action in question may have occurred at any time in a respondent's life, while the attitude in question is expressed at the time of the survey.

9. It is likely that the significant effect of circumcision status displayed in the last model for Hispanics reflects the instability of estimates for models with such few cases.

10. See n. 3 above.

11. Note that, because female NHSLS respondents were not asked whether their male partners were circumcised, it is impossible to evaluate whether women with uncircumcised partners are less willing to engage in direct stimulation of their partners' penis.

■

CHAPTER EIGHT

Reported Changes in Sexual Behavior in Response to AIDS in the United States

JOEL A. FEINLEIB AND ROBERT T. MICHAEL

The study of health behavior meant to prevent sexually transmitted diseases, including HIV/AIDS, has been difficult despite acute public interest in the subject. Both public health and public education policy should be informed about the self-limiting efforts made by the population to stem the spread of these diseases. Although there have been many studies of sexual behavior among members of specific, high-risk subgroups of the population, detailed data allowing the analysis of sexual practices across the whole adult population have only recently become available (see Billy et al. 1993; also *SOS*).

Data that are representative of the whole population, as distinct from the high-risk groups, and encompass sexual practices and risk-taking or risk-avoiding behavior are important both for epidemiologists plotting the future course of HIV and for physicians and public health practitioners devising empirically valid and appropriate prevention measures for all their patients. The present study offers new information on this point, describing the extent of reported sexual behavior change in response to AIDS for the U.S. population in the early 1990s.

Several models of the psychosocial process of behavior change have been developed and applied to AIDS-related risk reduction (Bandura 1977; Janz and Becker 1984; Fishbein and Middlestadt 1989; Catania, Kegels, and Coates 1990; Prochaska et al. 1994). Studies of individual responses to the threat of HIV/AIDS have found substantial evidence of behavior change in samples of various high-risk groups (e.g., men who have sex with men, intravenous drug users, STD [sexually transmitted disease] clinic patients) while recognizing the difficulty of maintaining such changes over time (Becker and Joseph 1988; Fisher and Fisher 1992). While these studies have generated valuable information about the usefulness of the various models of behavior change and the effectiveness of targeted interventions based on those models (Kelly et al. 1993; Choi and Coates 1994; Wingood and DiClemente 1996), they tell us very little about the extent of sexual behavior change in the whole adult population or about the propensity of a broad cross section of adults to adopt risk-reduction strategies for fear of contracting HIV/AIDS. The degree of this response is important in understanding the prevention of HIV/AIDS and much more prevalent sexually transmitted diseases such as gonorrhea and chlamydia.

Only a few studies have examined the extent of behavior change using data representative of the U.S. adult population. Some, examining specific behaviors over time (e.g., condom use and sex partners), have shown modest or few changes in behavior because of AIDS (Catania et al. 1992; Catania et al. 1995; Ahituv, Hotz, and Philipson 1996). Despite the advantage of using longitudinal data, these studies contain only limited information on sexual practices and disregard many possible dimensions of risk-reducing behavior. Other studies contain broader measures of behavior change but are limited in geographic or demographic scope (Kanouse et al. 1991; Mosher and Pratt 1993; Catania et al. 1994).

Using the National Health and Social Life Survey (NHSLS) data, this study examines individuals' own descriptions of their behavioral response to the risks of AIDS in the context of very detailed and extensive measures of sexual practices and partnering patterns. This chapter is organized around three main questions: (1) What types of changes in sexual behavior do U.S. adults report having made in response to AIDS? (2) Who is most likely to report having changed his or her sexual behavior? (3) How are reported risk-reduction strategies reflected in recent sexual practices and in the acquisition of sexually transmitted diseases?

The answers to these questions should help reveal the responsiveness of the general public to widespread AIDS prevention messages (Davis 1991; Johnson 1992) and thereby provide guidance about how general prevention messages can be tailored to specific individuals. The data used in this study, however, do not permit us to address many of the details of the behavior change process described in the literature, such as the specific motivations for and barriers to effecting change (Catania, Kegels, and Coates 1990; Kaeming and Bootzin 1990). Nor do we attempt to model the epidemiological implications of the adoption of specific risk-reduction strategies explored in other recent studies (Pinkerton and Abramson 1993; Morris and Dean 1994; Blower, Griensven, and Kaplan 1995). Instead, we emphasize findings applicable to the whole adult population that should be generally relevant for clinicians and other prevention specialists.

8.1 Methods

The NHSLS includes an extensive series of questions about current and lifetime patterns of sexual partnering and practices that were asked throughout the survey in a variety of contexts and in several formats (including both interviewer-administered and self-administered questions). The NHSLS asked respondents directly, "Have you made any kind of changes in your sexual behavior because of AIDS?" and, if so, "What have you changed?" (*SOS,* 664). There were no defined response categories, and all types of changes mentioned by NHSLS respondents were recorded verbatim. The responses were coded into fourteen detailed and six condensed categories (discussed in detail below).[1] These categories of behavior change are the basis of the univariate comparisons and multivariate logistical regression analyses reported below on the unweighted cross section of 3,159 NHSLS respondents (11 cases are missing for the variable of interest, so the analysis is based on 3,148 individuals).

Cross-sectional data are limited in what they reveal about the dynamic of behavior change over time. Furthermore, self-reported data on behavior change are subject to various forms of recall bias and may be exaggerated when the change itself is considered to be socially desirable by the interviewer or the respondent (Ross 1989; Jaccard 1995). For these reasons, we consider our estimates of reported change in sexual behavior to be an optimistic assessment of true changes in behavior in the U.S. adult population up to 1992. Mitigating against this bias in the direction of exaggeration, however, is the apparent willingness of NHSLS respondents to be truthful as reflected in higher reported levels of socially undesirable aspects of sexual behavior than found in other surveys (Miller 1995). In addition, studies of drug users have shown retrospective self-reported behavior change to be comparable to prospective reports (McElrath et al. 1994) and also to be related to lower actual incidence of HIV infection (Des Jarlais et al. 1996).

8.2 Results

What Types of Changes are Reported?

NHSLS respondents reported making a variety of changes in their sexual behavior because of AIDS. Fourteen categories of change are shown in descending order of frequency in panel A of table 8.1; these are further condensed into six categories in panel B. Nearly 30 percent of all respondents reported making some change in their behavior because of AIDS. The most frequently cited responses (see col. 1) include using condoms more frequently (9 percent), sticking to one partner or practicing monogamy (8 percent), selecting partners more carefully (4 percent), getting to know partners better before sex (4 percent), having fewer partners (3 percent), and abstaining from sex altogether (3 percent). Columns 2–4 show the percentages for three subgroups, respectively: those who report any change; those who report one change only; and those who report more than one change. The categories are not mutually exclusive since individu-

Table 8.1 Reported Changes in Behavior because of AIDS (Column Percentages)

		Those Reporting Any Change		
Behavior Changes	Entire Sample (1)	Any Changes (2)	1 Change (3)	2 + Changes (4)
A. Detailed categories:				
Any change	29	100	66	34
N	3,148	926	580	303[a]
Use condoms more frequently	9	32	23	54
Stick to 1 partner/monogamy	8	27	30	25
Select partner(s) more carefully	4	15	9	28
Get to know partner(s)	4	13	5	29
Have fewer partners	3	11	5	25
Not having sex/abstaining	3	11	13	9
Attitude about sex	3	9	7	15
More careful	2	6	4	10
Uncoded	1	5	. . .	. . .
Have sex less often	1	4	1	9
Get tested	0	3	0	7
Avoid certain practices	0	3	0	7
Other	0	2	2	2
Avoid situations/places	0	2	0	4
Drug use	< 1	< 1	< 1	1
B. Condensed categories:				
Any change	29	100	66	34
N	3,148	926	580[a]	303[a]
Fewer partners	12	41	37	55
Use condoms more frequently	9	32	23	54
Partner selection/knowledge	7	25	14	52
Attitude about sex/state of mind	4	14	11	24
Not having sex/abstaining	3	11	13	9
Miscellaneous	2	8	4	16
Uncoded	1	5	. . .	. . .

Note: Columns 1, 2, and 4 do not sum to total because respondent can mention more than one type of change.
[a]Uncoded changes not included in denominator when calculating percentages.

als could indicate as many types of change as they wanted, so the percentages can sum to more than 1.0. Of those who said that they had changed their sexual behavior, most (66 percent) mentioned only one change, while an additional 27 percent mentioned two changes, and 7 percent mentioned more than two changes.

The NHSLS survey instrument recorded reported behavior changes verbatim and did not use a finite set of predefined categories. Analysis of the actual responses reveals how closed-form questioning could conceal the diversity in the expression, perception, meaning, and implication of the behavioral changes that respondents described. (Examples of verbatim responses can be found in app. 8A.) For example, there are several interpretations of responses categorized as "not having sex/abstaining." Some say that they are abstaining temporarily, taking a hiatus from what may be a very active sex life. Others indicate that they have given up sex entirely, but this may also be related to their health, to their age, or to diminished opportunities in the sexual marketplace. Still others indicate that they are delaying initiation into sexual activity or have stopped having sex until they find a permanent partner.

Consider the response "stick to one partner/monogamy"; the respondent's own language illustrates that there are numerous meaningful distinctions within this category. For some, monogamy means returning to the exclusivity of a relationship and no longer engaging in extrarelational affairs. Others indicated that, while they might have been receptive or inclined to have additional partners, fear of AIDS discouraged them. Still others may mean having one partner at a time when they say that they are "sticking to one partner," so this statement may, in their minds, be consistent with having several partners within a year or so.

Several categories of change probably would have been overlooked had the responses not been collected verbatim. A few respondents indicated that they were avoiding certain places where the opportunity to meet risky partners would be greater, such as singles bars. Others indicated that, because of AIDS, they had lost interest in sex or were much less inclined to accept the advances of potential partners. A significant number indicated that they changed their state of mind in some way: some were being "more careful" or "cautious"; others said that they were "more aware" or "scared" without specifying what that meant. Some of these responses may be indicative of the cognitive and motivational precursors to behavioral change described in most psychosocial models of risk-reduction behavior. Furthermore, some of the changes are of little or no value (such as "watch who I drink after" and "very careful using public bathrooms"), and dichotomous questions may more likely include these false positive responses.

Who Reports Behavior Changes?

Table 8.2 shows the proportion of respondents who report any and each of five condensed categories of behavior change, by various sociodemographic characteristics and by numbers of recent sex partners. Males, younger adults, blacks, unmarried adults, and those living in cities are

Table 8.2 Percentage Distribution of Reported Changes in Behavior, by Selected Characteristics (Row Percentages)

Selected Characteristics of Respondents	N (1)	Any Change (2)	No Sex/ Abstaining (3)	Partner Reduction (4)	Partner Selection (5)	Condom Use (6)	Attitude/ State of Mind (7)
			Condensed Categories of Behavior Change[a]				
Gender:							
Male	1,406	35	2	14	10	12	5
Female	1,742	25	4	10	5	7	4
Age:							
18–24	501	43	3	16	11	17	6
25–29	457	36	2	16	10	12	6
30–39	984	32	4	14	8	10	5
40–49	720	23	4	9	6	6	3
50–59	481	14	3	5	4	2	1
Race/ethnicity:							
White	2,407	26	3	10	7	8	4
Black	402	45	4	22	10	15	6
Hispanic	235	37	4	14	10	10	7
Other	104	27	2	13	4	6	5
Current marital status:							
Single, not cohabiting	1,250	51	8	16	14	18	9
Cohabiting	227	40	< 1	22	11	11	3
Married	1,651	11	< 1	8	2	2	1
Place of residence:							
Top 100 central cities	692	40	5	17	10	15	4
Suburban/other urban	2,105	28	3	11	7	8	5
Rural	351	18	2	7	3	6	1
Sex partners in past 5 years:							
0 in lifetime	82	12	8	0	2	0	2
1 in lifetime	554	7	2	2	0	2	0
0 in past 5 years (> 1 in lifetime)	103	29	18	6	3	3	3
1 in past 5 years (> 1 in lifetime)	1,127	14	2	6	2	3	3
2–4 in past 5 years	767	48	3	22	13	16	8
5–10 in past 5 years	261	68	3	28	23	27	7
11 or more in past 5 years	131	74	3	27	24	35	8

[a]Row percentages sum to more than "Any Change" because categories may overlap.

more likely to have changed their behavior because of HIV/AIDS. The bottom panel of table 8.2 shows these responses by the reported number of sex partners over the past five years; this panel exhibits by far the most striking differences in the changed sexual behavior. Among those who have had only one sex partner in their lifetime, only 7 percent reported making any change in their behavior because of AIDS. By contrast, 68 percent of those with five to ten partners and 74 percent of those with eleven or more partners in the past five years reported making a change in their sexual behavior.

Table 8.3 reports multivariate logistic regression results predicting the probability of reporting any type of behavior change (a) for the whole NHSLS sample, (b) for subsamples who are not married, and (c) for subsamples who have had five or more sex partners in the past five years. For each of the three samples, two regression models are estimated, one with only demographic correlates and a second with both demographic and past sexual exposure correlates.

Model 1 (all adults, no sexual exposure covariates) confirms the patterns seen in the cross-tabulations of table 8.2 above. Males, unmarried persons, and nonwhites are most likely to change their behavior, while those over age forty and those living in rural areas are least likely to change. (The coefficients reported in table 8.3 show the effect of each variable on the odds ratio; e.g., the coefficient 1.63 for males means that the odds that a man will change his behavior are more than one and a half times as high— 1.63 times as high—as those that a woman will change her behavior, holding the other covariates constant.) The sexual exposure covariates are introduced in model 2, reported in comparison to those with one partner in the past five years and more than one partner in the lifetime. Those with one partner in their lifetime are less likely to change their behavior (the odds are only 0.44 as high), while those with five to ten sex partners in the past five years are far more likely to change their behavior (their odds are nearly six times as high), and those with more than ten sex partners in the past five years have odds of changing their behavior nearly nine times as high as those in the comparison group. When we control for number of sex partners, the effects of most of the demographic variables are significantly attenuated (i.e., compare their effects in models 1 and 2). This makes much sense: the reason that young, unmarried males change their behavior is that they are more likely to have many partners, to engage in more risky behavior, and thus to have greater reason to change their behavior. The pattern seen in these estimated models (table 8.3) suggests purposive behavior: those most at risk respond most to that risk.

Models 3 and 4 include only the unmarried men and women, and, for this subset, the influence of each demographic covariate is lessened, especially in model 4, where the number of sex partners is further controlled.

Table 8.3 Predictors of Any Reported Behavior Change (Logistic Regression: Point Estimates of Odds Ratios)

Explanatory Variables	Whole Sample				Unmarried Only				5+ Partners			
	(1)	p	(2)	p	(3)	p	(4)	p	(5)	p	(6)	p
Male	1.63	.00	1.25	.03	1.44	.00	1.11	.41	.63	.08	.57	.04
Female	1.00		1.00		1.00		1.00		1.00		1.00	
18–24	.82	.14	.65	.00	.68	.01	.59	.00	.26	.00	.24	.00
25–29	.98	.89	.76	.07	.84	.32	.67	.04	.43	.02	.38	.01
30–39	1.00		1.00		1.00		1.00		1.00		1.00	
40–49	.62	.00	.68	.01	.58	.00	.64	.01	.50	.12	.49	.11
50–59	.35	.00	.51	.00	.33	.00	.50	.00	.32	.17	.37	.24
White	1.00		1.00		1.00		1.00		1.00		1.00	
Black	1.90	.00	1.81	.00	1.65	.00	1.62	.00	1.43	.31	1.38	.37
Hispanic	1.45	.03	1.69	.01	1.62	.03	1.78	.01	.92	.85	1.00	.99
Other race/ethnicity	.90	.68	1.35	.27	.76	.38	1.16	.67	.27	.15	.25	.12
Unmarried, noncohabiting	7.36	.00	4.86	.00	1.00		1.00		3.33	.00	3.51	.00
Unmarried, cohabiting	4.54	.00	2.60	.00	.62	.00	.55	.00	1.81	.15	1.86	.13
Married	1.00		1.00		na		na		1.00		1.00	
Largest 100 central cities	1.27	.03	1.21	.11	1.13	.36	1.08	.60	1.13	.67	1.13	.67
Suburban/other urban	1.00		1.00		1.00		1.00		1.00		1.00	
Rural	.59	.00	.64	.01	.64	.02	.73	.13	.49	.01	.48	.14

(continued)

Table 8.3 (continued)

Explanatory Variables	Whole Sample				Unmarried Only				5+ Partners			
	(1)	p	(2)	p	(3)	p	(4)	p	(5)	p	(6)	p
0 partners ever	...		0.29	.00	...		.25	.00	...		...	
1 partner ever	...		.44	.00	...		.56	.03	...		...	
0 partners in past 5 years (> 1 in lifetime)	...		1.19	.49	...		.94	.81	...		...	
1 partner in past 5 years (> 1 in lifetime)	...		1.00		...		1.00		...		...	
2–4 partners in past 5 years	...		3.15	.00	...		2.49	.00	...		...	
5–10 partners in past 5 years	...		5.81	.00	...		4.60	.00	...		1.00	
11 or more partners in past 5 years	...		8.85	.00	...		7.97	.00	...		1.85	.02
N	3,005		3,005		1,406		1,406		389		389	
χ^2	688		1006		84		274		45		51	
$p > \chi^2$	.00		.00		0		0		0		0	
Log-likelihood	−1470		−1311		−933		−837		−214		−212	
Pseudo-R^2	.19		.28		.04		.14		.10		.11	

Note: Comparison group has odds ratio = 1.00.

Models 5 and 6 include only the 389 adults with five or more sex partners (those most at risk of disease), and there again we see that several of the demographic covariates have no remaining statistical significance—gender, race/ethnicity, and city size. Controlling for the number of sex partners, those with more than ten partners still have dramatically higher odds of changing their behavior than do those with five to ten partners. For the subset of adults in models 5 and 6, men are actually less likely to report changing their sexual behavior than are women, and the youngest adults are also less likely to report any change.

Additional logistic regression models, using the identical set of correlates as in table 8.3, were estimated for each of the six types of change listed in panel B of table 8.1 above. (Results are not shown here.) Among the demographic correlates, men were only half as likely as women to report abstaining but were nearly twice as likely to report that they were trying to select their partners more carefully. Blacks were two times more likely to report reducing their number of sex partners, but there were no other statistically significant differences by race/ethnicity. Singles were much more likely to report all types of changes than were married persons (i.e., the odds ratios are on the order of four times higher for the unmarried).

As in the models shown in table 8.3, for these six specific changes as well the number of partners in the past five years is the most important predictor of behavioral change. Those with many partners have odds that are more than three times as high as those with few partners of reporting reducing their number of partners (although the more partners one has had, the less likely one is to report sticking to just one), selecting partners more carefully, getting to know partners better, and using condoms. Those with no partners in the past five years are far more likely to report abstaining, while the number of partners has no statistically significant effect on reports of a change in attitude or state of mind.

Table 8.4 documents the discriminating effect of these statistical models, by illustrating how the demographic covariates and the number of sex partners affect the probability of reported change in sexual behavior. Here, we arbitrarily define five synthetic individuals in terms of the characteristics shown in table 8.4A and then calculate the probability that a person with those characteristics will change behavior. Each row of table 8.4B shows the predicted probability of any behavior change for one of these synthetic persons; column 1 does not control for number of sex partners, while columns 2–6 vary the number of sex partners. Table 8.4C shows the predicted probability of any change and of specific changes.

Consider case 1. Table 8.4A describes her as a twenty-year-old, unmarried, white female who lives in a rural community. Column 1 of table 8.4B indicates that a woman with these characteristics is predicted by model 1

Table 8.4 Predicted Probability of Change for Simulated Cases
A. Characteristics for Simulated Cases

	Gender	Age	Race	Marital Status	Residence
Case 1	Female	20	White	Unmarried	Rural
Case 2	Female	30	Black	Cohabiting	Central city
Case 3	Female	50	White	Married	Suburban
Case 4	Male	18	Black	Unmarried	Central city
Case 5	Male	38	Hispanic	Married	Central city

B. Predicted Probability of Any Change by Numbers of Partners

			Number of Partners		
	Any[a] (1)	0 Ever (2)	1 Ever (3)	1 in Past 5 Years (4)	2–4 in Past 5 Years (5)	11+ in Past 5 Years (6)
Case 1	.31	.06	.09	.18	.40	.66
Case 2	.58	.15	.21	.38	.66	.84
Case 3	.04	.02	.02	.05	.15	.33
Case 4	.75	.21	.29	.48	.74	.89
Case 5	.28	.07	.11	.22	.46	.71

[a]Probabilities derived from model that does not control for number of partners.

C. Predicted Probabilities of Various Behavior Changes

			Types of Behavior Changes			
Number of Sex Partners	Any Change (1)	Abstain[a] (2)	Partner Reduction (3)	Partner Selection (4)	Condom Use (5)	Attitude (6)
Case 1, no partners in lifetime	.06	.08	.01	.00	.04	.00
Case 2, 8 partners in past 5 years	.78	.06	.52	.21	.29	.03
Case 3, 1 partner in lifetime	.02	.04	.01	.00	.00	.00
Case 4, 12 partners in past 5 years	.89	.02	.40	.29	.58	.10
Case 5, 1 partner in past 5 years	.22	.13	.10	.02	.03	.03

Note: Probabilities pertain to specified number of partners for each case as described in table 8.4A.
[a]Sets values for marital status of all simulated cases to unmarried.

to have a 31 percent chance of reporting a change in her sexual behavior. If she has had no partners in her lifetime, model 2 predicts that the likelihood that she reports a change is very low, 6 percent, but that it rises monotonically with each increase in the number of her past partners to a probability of 66 percent if she has had eleven or more partners in the past five years (col. 6). Table 8.4C shows her propensity for various types of change, assuming that she had no partners in her lifetime. Although her overall propensity for any change is very low, she is most likely to report abstaining (8 percent).

Contrast this hypothetical individual with case 4, an eighteen-year-old, unmarried, black male living in the central city. Table 8.4B indicates that he is predicted to have a 75 percent chance of reporting a change in his sexual behavior, estimated from model 1, which does not control for number of partners. If he had never had any partners, he would still have a 21 percent chance of reporting change (col. 2), and that propensity rises very quickly with each level of sexual exposure to almost 90 percent if we assume that he has had over eleven partners (col. 6). Assuming that he has had twelve partners within the past five years, table 8.4C indicates that he is very unlikely to abstain (2 percent), but likely to report reducing his number of partners (40 percent) and selecting his partners more carefully (29 percent), and most likely to report using condoms more often (58 percent).

Two general findings here deserve emphasis. First, the probability of reporting a change in sexual behavior increases dramatically with the number of recent sex partners. Second, there is substantial variation in the adaptive strategy reported by different people. For example, case 1 (the young, unmarried woman) is most likely to report abstinence if any change is made; the sexually active young, unmarried, black, urban man (case 4) is most likely to report using condoms more often; the sexually experienced, black, urban woman age thirty (case 2) shows a much higher propensity for reducing her number of partners rather than using condoms; while the monogamous, fifty-year-old, suburban, white woman (case 3) reports little propensity to change her behavior at all.

Are the Reported Behavior Changes Reflected in Current Sexual Practices and in the Incidence of Diseases?

Table 8.5 addresses the question of whether the reports of changed sexual behavior because of AIDS are in fact reflected in sexual behavior and the associated risks. The rows of panels A–D distinguish, respectively, four measures of risky sexual behavior: the number of sex partners in the past twelve months; the use of condoms the last time heterosexual intercourse was engaged in (within the past twelve months only); whether any of those partners was not well known or was a "casual partner"; and whether the respondent had contracted any of nine sexually transmitted infections (gonorrhea, chlamydia, syphilis, pelvic inflammatory disease [women only], nongonococcal urethritis [men only], genital herpes, genital warts, hepatitis B, and HIV) in the past twelve months. Each column shows the percentage of individuals engaging in that behavior: column 1 shows those

Table 8.5 Percentage Distribution of Selected Risky Sexual Behaviors in Past 12 Months, by Type of Behavior Change

Measures of Sexual Behavior in Past 12 Months (by Number of Sex Partners)	Categories of Reported Behavior Change			
	No Changes (1)	Stick to 1/ Monogamy (2)	Use Condoms (3)	Partner Selection/ Knowledge (4)
A. Numbers of sex partners (column percentages):				
0 partners	12	2	6	8
1 partner	81	76	36	42
2 partners	4	13	21	21
3 or more partners	3	10	37	29
N	2,220	249	293	235
B. Used a condom in the last sex event:				
Total (cell percentages)	13	13	51	22
N	1,688	214	195	166
C. Any casual partners:				
Total (cell percentages)	2	3	19	15
N	2,114	240	278	225
D. Contracted an STD in the past 12 months (cell percentages):				
Total	1	5	6	2
N	2,161	244	287	231
1 partner in the past 12 months	1	3	2	1
N	1,758	189	110	96
2 partners in the past 12 months	3	10	5	0
N	78	31	58	48
3+ partners in the past 12 months	3	a	10	4
N	60	20	98	67

[a]Cell size fewer than 30.

who reported making no change in their behavior because of AIDS, column 2 those who reported sticking to one partner/monogamy, column 3 those who reported using condoms more frequently, and column 4 those who reported selecting their partners more carefully or getting to know them better before having sex.

In general, there is a high degree of consistency between the types of changes reported and the level of recent risky behaviors. Of those who reported sticking to one partner or practicing monogamy, 76 percent reported having only one sex partner in the past twelve months (col. 2, panel A). Individuals who reported using condoms more frequently because of

AIDS did in fact also report relatively high rates of condom use the last time they had sex (col. 3, panel B): over 50 percent used condoms in the last sex event, compared to 13 percent of those who reported making no changes in their behavior. This pattern holds as well when controlling for number of partners or for partnership status (i.e., single, cohabiting, married) or when measuring frequency of condom use over the whole period of a sexual relationship in the past twelve months. In analyses not shown in table 8.5, we find, for example, that, among married persons who reported more frequent use of condoms, 39 percent used a condom during the last act of intercourse, compared to only 10 percent of married persons who reported no change in their sexual behavior.

The consistency is less clear for those who reported selecting their partners more carefully or getting to know their partners better before having sex. Overall, 15 percent of them have had a casual partner in the past year (col. 4, panel C), which is far more than the percentage of those who have not changed their behavior but slightly less than those using condoms more frequently. In further tabulations, we find that, among persons with three or more partners in the past year who report choosing partners more carefully, 29 percent had a casual partner, compared to 47 percent of persons with three or more partners who did not report any change in their behavior. So there is some indication of movement in the direction that is reported.

Table 8.5 also reveals the recent level of risky sexual behaviors that are not part of the particular risk-reduction strategy mentioned by the respondent (i.e., the off-diagonal elements in the matrix in table 8.5). Those respondents who are trying to avoid AIDS by sticking to one partner, for example, nevertheless face risk because they do not use condoms very often (col. 2, panel B). By contrast, they avoid additional risk by having very few casual partners (col. 2, panel C). Individuals who attempt to reduce their risk of contracting AIDS by increasing their use of condoms expose themselves to risk by having many recent partners (37 percent had three or more partners in the past twelve months [col. 3, panel B]) and by having casual partners (col. 3, panel C). Those who seek to reduce their risk by choosing partners more carefully or getting to know their partners better nevertheless face considerable risk by having many partners (29 percent had three or more partners in the past twelve months [col. 4, panel A]) and by not using condoms very often (col. 4, panel B).

One key measure of risk exposure in the past twelve months is seen in panel D, which gives the percentage of respondents contracting a sexually transmitted disease, shown by the numbers of sex partners during the same period. Only 1 percent of those who reported no behavior change contracted an STD (col. 1, panel D), suggesting that they did, indeed, face slight risk and had little incentive to change their behavior. However, of those who had even two or more sex partners, the percentage contracting an STD within the past twelve months was 3 percent. Similarly, 5 percent of those who reported sticking to one partner contracted an STD, and this included 3 percent of those who indeed had only one partner but as many as 10 percent of those who had two partners. Six percent of those using condoms more frequently because of AIDS nevertheless had an STD during the year, and, again, they were disproportionately those who had more sex partners. Only 2 percent of respondents who said they choose their partners more carefully contracted an STD, and that rate was only slightly higher for those with more partners.

8.3 Discussion

The tabular and multivariate analyses in this chapter describe how adults in the general public characterize their behavioral response to the risk of AIDS as it has become a part of their lives over the past decade. Here, we summarize what that analysis tells us and reflect on those findings.

Before offering that summary, we note again that the data here are self-reports of behavior change and so may be somewhat inflated as compared to actual behavior change because of either recall bias or exaggeration. As we have analyzed respondents' answers to a wide variety of questions about their sex lives, we have been impressed by the internal consistency of reports about various subtle sexual behaviors, and we have reached the conclusion that respondents did in fact attempt to provide accurate and complete information throughout the long interview. Yet both the inclination to elicit a positive response from the interviewer by giving an answer that may make a favorable impression and the inclination to interpret one's own behavior in the best possible light may have caused some overstatement of reported change in sexual behavior because of AIDS.

Two collateral facts provide some further reassurance on this point. First, the respondents in this survey did in fact report quite high rates of other personal sexual behavior that is not socially attractive, for example, incidence of sexual dysfunction (see chap. 10 below), sexually transmitted infections (see chap. 11 of *SOS*), abortions (see chap. 11 below), and extramarital sex (see chap. 5 of *SOS*). These responses seem inconsistent with a respondent bias toward impressing the interviewer or with a reluctance to reveal socially undesirable behavior. Second, the reported changes in sexual behavior map quite well onto the independently reported actual sexual behavior as shown in table 8.5 above. Nonetheless, it is prudent to consider these reports as an optimistic assessment of true changes in behavior.

Turning to our summary, we have three quite straightforward findings and three more complicated ones. First, about 30 percent of all the adults surveyed reported changing their behavior because of AIDS. As table 8.1 above and the description of actual responses indicate, the changes that were reported were many and varied in nature. The changes most frequently mentioned were reduction in number of partners, more frequent use of condoms, and more careful selection of partners. The verbatim responses to the survey's open-ended question reveal a wide range of meaning behind any abbreviated description, and many of these shades of meaning are obscured in closed-form survey questions that restrict the answers to a few set categories of response. But the first important finding here is that a sizable proportion of all adults in the United States report that they have made a variety of changes in their sexual behavior in response to the risks of HIV/AIDS.

Second, almost all the respondents described changes that could be considered strategically appropriate, informed, and potentially effective methods of reducing the risk of contracting AIDS as well as other STDs. Only 11 of the nearly 1,040 respondents who described some change in sexual behavior clearly misunderstood the nature of AIDS transmission or what actions were effective in preventing that transmission. The most frequent types of changes mentioned are precisely the types of risk-reduction strategies that public health officials have been promoting. The wide range of behavior changes actually reflects the wide range of respondents' sexual circumstances.

Probably the most important finding of this study is that individuals with the greatest exposure to risk are precisely those most likely to report adopting risk-reduction strategies. Over the past decade, many people have come to understand which of their activities and practices expose them to the risk of HIV/AIDS, and that information apparently has caused many to change their behavior in an attempt to limit their exposure to that risk.

We note that this finding is broadly consistent with results from other studies based on probability samples, particularly with regard to the range and relative frequency of mentioned changes. Reduction in number of partners, more careful selection of partners, and increased condom use are the types of change most frequently reported by adults (Kanouse et al. 1991; Mosher and Pratt 1993; Johnson et al. 1994). Further, the propensity to report changes in behavior rises dramatically with an individual's number of past sex partners (Mosher and Pratt 1993; Johnson et al. 1994). In addition, several studies using data from repeated cross sections, from longitudinal surveys, and on actual condom sales provide evidence confirming the increased use of condoms throughout the late 1980s and into the early 1990s. Increased use of condoms was most common among those with more risky partners (Catania et al. 1995) and among those living in states with higher prevalence rates of AIDS (Ahituv, Hotz, and

Philipson 1996). There is little direct evidence in these other studies that individuals have reduced their number of sex partners. Our data suggest that individuals tend to recognize when they are at risk and that, if they choose to reduce their exposure, they are likely to choose a potentially effective strategy.

Third, there is a broad consistency between survey respondents' statements that they changed their behavior because of the risk of HIV/AIDS and their descriptions of their actual sexual behavior, as seen in table 8.5 above. Individuals who report making a particular change do in fact appear to have implemented that change in their current behavior, as reported in the interview at some distance from the statement that they had changed their behavior because of the risks involved. This suggests that their statements about the changes they have made do have validity in terms of consistency with reported behavior.

Fourth, a nontrivial proportion of those reporting any behavior change (14 percent) indicated only that they had changed their attitudes about sex without any clear indication of how their actual behavior may have been altered. One may be inclined to disregard these less tangible changes, but, as we discuss below, we think that that may be a mistake.

Fifth, there is evidence in these data that some types of behavior change complement each other and that other types are incompatible. For example, only 11 percent of respondents who reported sticking to just one partner also reported increasing their use of condoms as well. It may be difficult to increase condom use in a relationship that is assumed by at least one partner to be monogamous. In contrast, condom use and being more selective in acquiring sex partners were far more compatible: 25 percent of those who reported increasing their use of condoms also mentioned selecting their partners more carefully. A person who expects or intends to have several sex partners may find it relatively easy to introduce the subject of using a condom and to investigate more closely each potential partner's sexual history than does a person who expects to have, or is thought to be having, a mutually exclusive sexual relationship.

Sixth, table 8.5 also suggests a complicating factor: many adults report that they engage in a single risk-reduction strategy, one that, although appropriate for their sexual lifestyle, fails to limit other sources of risk exposure. Those sticking to just one partner, for example, have low rates of condom use, and, consequently, their reports of STDs suggest that they still face a nontrivial probability of contracting a disease. Likewise, those reporting more frequent condom use tend to have many partners and have a high probability of encountering a casual partner, and, consequently, they too still have a relatively high probability of contracting an STD. Those who report more careful selection of partners nonetheless tend to have many partners and not very high rates of condom use, so they too face considerable risk, even though the strategy that they adopted is somewhat effective in reducing their risk of infection.

On the basis of these six findings, several implications warrant emphasis. First, the strategic nature of the changes reported by adults suggests the purposiveness of their actions. As the adult population has become aware of the risks of HIV/AIDS, behavior has been altered in ways that lower those risks. The basic economic model of human action rests on the premise that observed behavior can be understood as rational action, or at least as purposive behavior in the face of incomplete information or knowledge. While one may not expect sexual behavior to reflect this purposiveness as clearly as, say, the decision to purchase an automobile or to hold assets in some stock equity, the general behavior reportedly made in response to the changed risks faced after the advent of AIDS in the early 1980s shows how widespread is that tendency to act self-beneficially. To a social scientist interested in using that rational actor model to attempt to understand behavior, this evidence of purpose and strategy is reassuring and enabling. To a public health official who may hope to affect behavior by providing information about risks and about effective strategies for reducing those risks, this evidence is also empowering.

The implications of our findings for advice giving is the second of our reflections. There are many contexts in which we adults offer advice: as parents to our children, as professional counselors to our clients, as physicians to our patients, as public health officials to the community at large, and of course as friend to friend. The second finding listed above suggests that most behavioral changes take place at the margin of one's sexual lifestyle, that a wholesale restructuring of that lifestyle does not take place. Accordingly, the advice that we give is likely to be more effective if it is targeted to a modest or marginal change in the person's existing lifestyle, rather than an admonition to "just say no" or "always use a condom."

The findings suggest that there are subtle differences in the meaning of such terms as *abstinence* and *monogamy* that are important when designing public health messages and prevention programs or when strategies for reducing the disease risks from sexual behavior are discussed by physicians, counselors, parents, or friends. These dialogues with an adviser will be more successful if they are placed in context with some straightforward details about the sexual circumstances of the advisee's lifestyle and with questioning that is open-ended enough for clarity about just what is meant by the terms expressed.

Too often in discussions of a sexual nature, much is left implicit because of an element of embarrassment. Since, in general, people do not have much experience discussing their own sexual behavior, oblique and casual references are used. But the statement that a person takes "care in selecting partners," for example, may have very different meanings in different contexts, and, if the adviser is to understand the risks and advise about risk reduction, these oblique comments must be explored and clarified. An adolescent may be reluctant to inform parents about his or her sexual experience or expectations, so parents may offer advice about precautions in several hypothetical cases, thereby providing the relevant information.

Trying to persuade a young, single adult who has already become sexually active to avoid sex until marriage, for example, may be ineffective; it may be far easier to convince that person to use condoms or to get to know his or her partner better as a way of assessing the risks to be encountered. Young adults who have not yet initiated sexual activity, however, may be much more prone to listen to the case for abstinence, and married or cohabiting adults may be most receptive to advice that reinforces the desirability of monogamy.

The point is that the same advice given to two different people will probably not have the same effect. Someone who prefers having multiple sex partners may not be receptive to advice that he limit himself to one, and someone considering entering into an exclusive relationship may not be receptive to advice that she insist her partner use a condom. An understanding of a person's sexual circumstances allows an adviser—a physician, a counselor, a parent—to better assess the margin at which a suggested change in behavior will be adopted. The evidence from the NHSLS suggests that people are in general able to distinguish which strategies will be most effective given their sexual circumstances and will usually act accordingly once apprised thereof. That is why we think that counsel is most effectively given if the counselor first ascertains an individual's sexual circumstances. By suggesting specific, marginally improving strategies rather than generic risk-reducing ones, the counselor is far more likely to be effective.

Moreover, our findings suggest that, in 1992, the adult population understood the importance of attempting to reduce the risks of contracting HIV/AIDS, so public health messages targeting these adults should focus on information about what the magnitude of the risk is and what strategies most effectively reduce risk given the person's sexual behavior. Advice about how to achieve the objective, rather than admonitions about why it is important to attempt to reduce risk, appears to be more useful for the adults represented in our survey. We add, however, that younger people, those who did not experience the advent of AIDS in the early 1980s and who therefore have not internalized the fear that older people know, may in fact need to be informed as to why behavior change is so important before they will accept specific suggestions. We cannot speak to this point directly since our sample included only adults age eighteen and over in 1992. Neither do our conclusions here pertain to any population except that of the United States.

Regarding our finding that many adults reported changing their attitude about sex rather than changing their behavior per se, these changes in state of mind may reflect cognitive processes that necessarily precede changes in self-protective behavior (Cleary 1987; Aggleton et al. 1994; Catania, Kegels, and Coates 1990; Prochaska et al. 1994). They may accompany a real reduction in behavior that involves risk. For example, the decisions not to begin sexual activity and not to have an extrarelational affair are potentially very important strategies for reducing risk. It can be as important for a person not to do something more risky as for that person to do something less risky. In assessing the population's response to the risk of HIV/AIDS, one should not focus exclusively on actual behavior change or disregard reported changes in attitude, sexual receptivity, or expectations. These may be important components of the full story.

Another implication of the findings reported here is how complex the effort to reduce the risk of disease is. While most of the strategies reported by our respondents do in fact have merit as ways of reducing risk, few are wholly effective. Abstinence is, mutual monogamy is, having sex only with healthy partners would be if that were feasible, condom usage is relatively effective, and so forth. But, as we emphasized above, the use of one strategy, such as reducing the number of partners or increasing the frequency with which a condom is used, does not wholly eliminate risk, as evinced by the incidence of STDs among those who adopted such strategies. The risk of contracting AIDS or other STDs is not wholly eliminated just because one somewhat effective strategy is adopted or because a very effective strategy is adopted part of the time or for a period of time, as the bottom panel of table 8.5 above shows. For example, among those whose strategy to reduce the risk of disease is to use condoms more often, the probability of contracting an STD still rises sharply with number of sex partners: from 2 percent for those with only one partner, to 5 percent for those with three partners, to 10 percent for those with three or more partners. A similar pattern is observed for those who reported an intention to stick to one partner (although sometimes that means having only one at a time). In short, while methods are effective in *reducing* risk, most cannot *eliminate* that risk.

This caution in recommending which strategies are in fact most effective highlights a particularly vexing dilemma, one revealed by table 8.5. Using STD rates as proxies for the level of risk exposure, it would appear that sticking to one partner and increasing condom use are less effective than selecting partners more carefully. But public health officials have often stressed that it is not possible to distinguish on sight whether a potential partner is infected with HIV or some other STD. They have been very reluctant to advocate more careful selection of partners as a sufficient prevention strategy. However, avoiding those who belong to high-prevalence groups can be an effective strategy, especially when the infection is highly concentrated either geographically or among people who engage in specific types of behavior (Hearst and Hulley 1988). The problem, of course, is screening potential partners successfully.

The relatively high levels of STDs among those who are sticking to just one partner and those using condoms more frequently may result from their being situated in sexual networks among which the prevalence of STDs is relatively high. Those who report selecting their partners more carefully would appear to have chosen their partners from sexual networks in which the prevalence of STDs is relatively low. This has an important implication for organized prevention efforts since it is apparently easier to get people to change their behavior than it is to get them to change their social networks. This suggests that research efforts should be directed at figuring out just how potential sex partners are selected and how more careful selection of partners can be implemented as a practical risk-reduction strategy.

Finally, the message here is a mixed one regarding the current risk-management stance of the American adult population. The evidence presented in this study suggests that, because of the fear of contracting AIDS, a significant percentage of American adults have changed their sexual behavior. They have done so primarily in ways that have the potential to reduce significantly their risk of contracting HIV or other more prevalent STDs. The apparently disappointing percentage who have changed behavior—30 percent—becomes less disappointing when one sees that a majority of adults report being in a mutually monogamous relationship and thus not exposed to much risk. For them, no change in behavior is called for. Moreover, those whose past behavior, if continued, would expose them to the greatest risk of sexually transmitted infections are precisely those most likely to have changed. That is the good news, together with the generally low numbers of people having multiple partners (see *SOS;* and *SIA*). Additionally, model 1 of table 8.3 above suggests that those who are most likely to have reported a change are, indeed, those whose behavior is most risky—the young, single men who live in large cities.

However, a significant fraction—25–30 percent—of those with the greatest exposure to risk report making no change in their behavior. Even if their risk of contracting HIV/AIDS were small, the likelihood of contracting some other STD remains quite large. As model 6 shows, of those with five or more sex partners in the past, men are only about half as likely as women to report any change in behavior, and young adults are only about one-quarter or one-third as likely to report changing behavior as are others reporting large numbers of partners. Thus, there is a group that faces very high risks and reports making no change in behavior in response to the risk of HIV/AIDS or other STDs. Reaching this group constitutes the major challenge for public health officials and private physicians. While there are grounds for optimism in the effective and strategic responses to the risks of disease reported by many adults in this survey, there are also grounds for serious concern.

Appendix 8A Examples of Verbatim Responses by Assigned Category

Not Having Sex/Abstaining

Abstinence.
I have not had sex since 1987.
Have decided no more sex till I find the person I want to marry.
Become somewhat celibate.
My thoughts of trying it [sex] were terminated.

Partner Reduction

STICK TO ONE PARTNER/MONOGAMY

Monogamous.
Staying with one person; only one partner at a time.
Staying with my wife only.
Only one sex partner—don't fool around anymore.
Instead of having more than one partner now only have one.
That's why I decided to get married and settle down with Pat.
More motivation to remain monogamous and work through problems with partner.
Just exclusive long-term sexual relationships.
Trying to have more of a monogamous life; I've limited my partners.
Even though I've been tempted to have an affair, I wouldn't risk it.

HAVE FEWER PARTNERS

Reduce the number of sex partners.
Not being as promiscuous as I used to be.
Drastically reduce anonymous sex, same-sex partners.
Cut back having sex with various partners; use condoms more.
Don't sleep around as much; chose my partners carefully.

AVOID SITUATION/PLACES

Try to avoid going to bars and night clubs; use condoms now.
Dating; I don't; I'm very skeptical; I just don't date.
Don't try to go out and meet girls.

HAVE SEX LESS OFTEN

I probably don't have sex as often as I would.

Diminished frequency of sex; more selective of partners; more use of condoms.

Less than I use to, you know; don't have sex as often.

Partner Selection/Knowledge

SELECT PARTNER(S) MORE CAREFULLY

I would never be involved with someone who had "been around" a lot.

Avoid partners who are promiscuous/runarounds.

Very selective; extra means of interviewing them; what they value; number of partners.

I don't pick up anyone from bars.

GET TO KNOW PARTNER(S)

I would not sleep with anyone I did not know very well for a long time.

We've discussed throughly—we have had no other sex partners in life.

No more one-night stands.

Ask about sex partner's history of sexual activity; cut down on partners.

Going to make sure to get to know them; make sure tested before sex.

Just don't have casual sex.

Telling my partners that I want to know about any additional sex partners.

Use Condoms More Frequently

I always wear a condom.

Use a condom all the time unless we have been checked together.

I probably say sometimes use condom.

Starting using condoms more often.

I was making sure that all partners used condoms except for yesterday.

Just become more careful; use condoms if I didn't know partner well.

When I have sex outside my marriage, I wear a condom.

I made my partner wear a condom.

Using a condom; not being quite as promiscuous.

I don't have any type of unprotected sex with people I don't know.

Would use a condom if I had sex today.

Attitude about Sex/State of Mind

MORE CAREFUL

I've been overanxious, and basically just being cautious.
I'm more careful.
You have to be extremely careful who you sleep with.
A lot more cautious about getting involved in a sexual relationship.

ATTITUDE ABOUT SEX

My attitude toward [sex] in general; not being wild; I think twice about it.
A lack of interest; it's no fun anymore.
My whole life-style; that would include sex, my personal life, my social life.
More aware that there are possibilities I could get it from someone.
Have decided I needed to find someone I could love the rest of my life.
Being aware of the dangers.
Uninterested in pursuing female partners.
My attitude about free sex.
Cold toward men; do not believe what they say; do not date much.

Miscellaneous

AVOID CERTAIN PRACTICES

No anal intercourse; no anal stimulation or intercourse.
No sharing of body fluids; using condoms, dental dams; increase masturbation.
No oral sex.

DRUG USE

I don't shoot up now; I never knew if the needle was clean.

TESTING

I've been tested; I get tested every month; don't date more than one person.

Mistaken/Described Change Has No Preventive Efficacy

Very careful using public bathrooms.
I always put a seat protection on public toilets when we go out.
Watch who I drink after.
I use a diaphram as a birth control, and I use a jelly with spermicide.

Notes

The authors thank Norman M. Bradburn for helpful comments. This chapter is a somewhat modified version of Feinleib and Michael (1998).

1. This material from the survey has not previously been analyzed and is not available on the public use data files; it has been accessed and coded for this chapter by Joel A. Feinleib.

■

CHAPTER NINE

Racial/Ethnic Group Differences in the Prevalence of Sexually Transmitted Diseases in the United States: A Network Explanation

EDWARD O. LAUMANN AND YOOSIK YOUM

9.1 A Persistent Puzzle

African Americans have substantially higher rates of sexually transmitted diseases (STDs) than do other ethnic and racial groups in the United States (cf. *SOS,* table 11.8, fig. 11.1; Aral 1996; CDC 1996; Louis and Aral 1996; Nakashima et al. 1996; Philipson and Posner 1993). Hispanics also manifest higher rates of primary and secondary syphilis and HIV, although not as disproportionately as African Americans (Sabogal, Faigeles, and Catania 1993). Both groups are overrepresented among new HIV cases (Institute of Medicine 1997). These differentials in rates among racial and ethnic groups are graphically displayed in figures 9.1 and 9.2.

There is some debate about why such dramatic differences should be observed. In a report published in 1996, the Centers for Disease Control and Prevention (CDC) observed: "There are no known biological reasons to explain why racial or ethnic factors alone should alter the risk for STDs. Rather, race and ethnicity in the United States are markers that correlate with other more fundamental determinants of health status such as poverty, access to quality health care, health care seeking behavior, illicit drug use and living in communities with high prevalence of STDs." This explanation is problematic, however, because Hispanics and blacks are quite comparable in terms of their relative poverty, their lack of access to quality health care, and the other disadvantages associated with minority status in the United States, yet the Hispanics look very much like the whites in terms of their rates for gonorrhea and syphilis. We must look elsewhere for a convincing explanation.

Three limitations of the most commonly used methods for collecting and analyzing data on STDs have made it difficult to account for these discrepancies. The first two limitations are inherent in the way in which the data have been collected, and the last derives from the analytic approaches that are conventionally used. First, the most commonly used

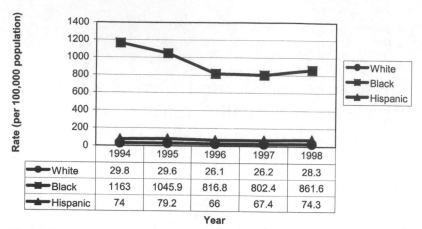

Fig. 9.1 Rates of gonorrhea by race and ethnicity, United States, 1994–98.
Source: CDC 1998, Section 12, table 12B.
Note: Georgia did not report gonorrhea statistics in 1994.

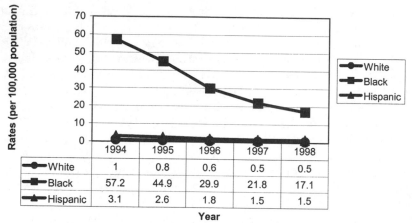

Fig. 9.2 Rates of primary and secondary syphilis by race and ethnicity, United States, 1994–98.
Source: CDC 1998, Section 12, table 12B.

data-collecting methods, usually case based rather than person based—including the contact-tracing method (Garnett and Anderson 1993), residential area studies (Rothenberg 1983; et al. 1996), and the CDC reports (e.g., CDC 1996), based primarily on passive surveillance reports from diverse institutions—have serious weaknesses, especially with respect to their systematic bias against the inclusion of cases from people of higher socioeconomic status. In order to ensure privacy, people of higher socioeconomic status often turn to private doctors, who are likely to place a lower priority on reporting STDs to government agencies (see *SOS*). Thus, their prevalence rates are underestimated (Aral and Holmes 1990; CDC 1997). Studies have found that private physicians may report only 3–60 percent of the gonorrhea cases that they treat, while the majority of cases reported in the national surveillance system come from public providers (Anderson, McCormick, and Fichtner 1994). For a recent example, according to a 1995 cross-sectional survey of residents in Chicago and Cook County, over 62 percent of the self-reported cases of STDs in that twelve-month period were diagnosed and treated by private doctors and only 5.2 percent in publicly funded STD clinics, yet 60–80 percent of the STD cases reported to the CDC from Chicago in that year were reported by the publicly funded STD clinics (Harris School of Public Policy Studies 1995).

Second, most of the data about STDs include information only about infected people. Using data lacking relevant information about the noninfected makes it impossible to examine several critical questions. For example, do the infected have more sexual partners than the noninfected? Do African Americans have higher infection rates, even after controlling for the differential numbers of partners across ethnic or racial groups? In principle, researchers have lacked appropriate tools to examine in detail the causes of the higher infection rates, say, among African Americans or young men. They can only speculate whether those higher rates are related to urban settings, poverty, etc. (Aral 1996; CDC 1996).

The third limitation arises from deficiencies in the analytic approach conventionally employed. Most studies of the incidence or prevalence of STDs focus on attributes of individuals, such as number of partners, use of prostitutes, or frequency of condom use—sometimes called *individual-level risk factors*. Such an approach fails to recognize two fundamental network aspects of STD dynamics. The first concerns the potential infection status of the partners (or *second-order network connectivity*). For example, person A may have a higher likelihood of being infected than person B, despite both having had the same number of sex partners, because person A's sex partners have had more sex partners than person B's sex partners have. In determining who is more vulnerable to infection, then, we must consider not only an individual's risk factors but also the risk factors contributed by the other partners constituting the sexual network. In other words, the selection of sex partners is a critical part of the risk equation. The second network feature critical to STD dynamics concerns the existence of bridges between socially distinct subpopulations. Even though person A may have a higher probability of being infected than person B, person B can be a much more efficient (powerful) transmitter of infection if he or she has sex partners in socially distinct subpopulations, thereby providing a specific link or bridge for infection to spread between the two subpopulations. In this case, without person B being infected, it is impossible for the one group to transmit infection to the other.

In 1978, a much-cited article on the dynamics and control of the transmission of gonorrhea by Yorke, Hethcote, and Nold introduced the concept of the *core group*. While the concept had certain tractable mathematical features for use in epidemiological modeling, it essentially postulated, to quote John Potterat (1992, 16), the existence of "groups of people whose sexual and health behaviors are such that micro-organisms find many opportunities for sustained transmission. These are referred to as core groups. They are small, stable and composed of a sufficient number of infected persons who successfully transmit their infection to others so that STI (sexually transmitted infection) perpetuation is assured. Core groups are also viewed as the fountainhead of STI cases outside of core populations (peripheral cases). A corollary is that if core group transmitters could be kept from infection, STIs would die out." In a recent follow-up article, Garnett and Anderson (1993, 189) too speak of "the notion of a core group of people who change sexual partners frequently" as an important concept in the study of the spread and persistence of sexually transmitted infections. These authors then comment on the many practical problems surrounding the measurement of networks of sexual contacts. They note, in particular, the difficulty of tracing the networks of sexual contacts reported by an initial sample of respondents. Use of a core group definition based on residential area (i.e., spatial location) (e.g., Rothenberg 1983; Potterat et al. 1985) or contact tracing of patients at STI clinics can be a practical strategy for approximating measurement of the initial idea; but the results are, of course, at best proxies, with unknown and very likely systematic distortions obscuring the underlying process.

Judith Wasserheit (1995) recently commented that the term *core group* has spawned both tremendous excitement and substantial frustration—the latter because of the limited consensus on definition (see also May, Anderson, and Blow 1989; Thomas and Tucker 1996). In the following, we hope, first, to clarify some of the issues involved in operationalizing the concept by exploiting the rich variety of information on sexual behavior and sexual networks provided in the National Health and Social Life Survey (NHSLS) and, second, to examine the utility of the NHSLS in accounting for the differential distribution of STDs in the population at large.

This chapter, thus, has two principal objectives. First, we attempt to identify determinants of STD transmission in terms of a broad array of social, attitudinal, and behavioral features of individuals and their sexual networks. Second, based on these analyses, we provide an empirical definition of *core groups* and examine how core groups' roles can differ across racial groups in terms of transmission dynamics. This last analysis can give us some hints about why African Americans have higher infection rates for most bacterial STDs, even after we control for all the other relevant risk factors.[1]

Our approach is distinguished from other discussions of STDs in two broad respects. First, as in the discussion of STDs in chapter 11 of *SOS*, we include a broad spectrum of STDs concurrently in the analysis rather than focusing on specific infectious diseases, such as syphilis or gonorrhea, because our database permits the inclusion of a range of diseases and because many specific STDs are too rare in the population at large to sustain sophisticated analysis separately. This strategy rests on the facts that many STDs share common epidemiological features and that many STDs reinforce each other as cofactors (e.g., chancroid, syphilis, and HSV [herpes simplex virus] are causes of genital ulcer disease, which is associated with increased risk of HIV transmission [Aral and Holmes 1991, 65, 67]). Second, we focus more on the *sociological* elements involved in identifying core groups and exploring their role in STD transmission than on the biological factors of transmission. In sum, we try to address the data limitations noted above by using the NHSLS, a national probability-based sample that is person based rather than case based and includes both infected and noninfected individuals in an unbiased selection process, and by adopting a network analytic strategy.

9.2 Some Methodological Considerations

Measures

LOGISTIC REGRESSION

After excluding the oversamples of African Americans and Hispanics, we constructed a set of independent and dependent variables as described in table 9.1. People who had never had a sex partner were omitted because many of the risk factors affecting them are undefined. Three dependent variables are constructed on the basis of responses to the question, "There are several diseases or infections that can be transmitted during sex. These are sometimes called venereal diseases or VD. We will be using the term *sexually transmitted diseases* or STDs to refer to them." After giving the respondent a hand card listing each STD, sometimes including vernacular terms (e.g., *clap* or *drip* for gonorrhea), interviewers asked, "As I read each STD, tell me whether you have *ever* been told by a doctor that you had it" (*SOS*, 662). Variables for each STD are coded as 1 for ever infected and 0 for never infected.

Table 9.2 and panel A of table I.3 above give the reader some appreciation of the differentials in STD prevalence by gender and number of sex partners since age eighteen (for greater detail about specific diseases by

Table 9.1 Variable Measures

Variable	Description	Mean	S.D.	N
Dependent variables				
Any STDs	Any STDs, including bacterial and viral	.18	.39	2,878
Bacterial STDs	Gonorrhea, syphilis, chlamydia, nongonococcal urethritis (men), pelvic inflammatory disease (women)	.11	.32	2,896
Viral STDs	Genital warts, herpes, hepatitis, HIV/AIDS	.08	.27	2,929
Independent variables				
Number of partners[a]	Five categories	10.75	40.50	2,933
Female	Female = 1, male = 0	.56	.50	2,963
Big city[b]	Big city = 1, others = 0	.22	.41	2,963
Pay for sex	Ever = 1, never = 0	.09	.29	2,745
Being paid for sex	Ever = 1, never = 0	.03	.18	2,732
Anal sex	Ever = 1, never = 0	.25	.44	2,766
Never married	Ever = 1, never = 0	.26	.44	2,926
Military service	Ever = 1, never = 0	.14	.34	2,962
Drug injection[c]	Ever = 1, never = 0	.02	.15	2,742
Group sex	Ever = 1, never = 0	.09	.29	2,787
Concurrent partners[d]	Ever = 1, never = 0	.29	.45	2,963
Prepubertal intercourse[e]	Ever = 1, never = 0	.03	.16	2,958
Age	Continuous variable	36.79	10.86	2,963
Racial/ethnic groups[f]	White = 1, African American = 2, Hispanic = 3			2,963
Education	Five categories[g]			2,945
Church attendance[h]	Almost weekly = 1, sometimes = 2, rarely = 3			2,956
Thinking of sex	Three categories[i]			2,952
Sexual value orientation	Four categories[j]			2,824

Note: All variables are for lifetime duration except big city, education, church attendance, thinking of sex, and sexual value orientation, which refer to current status.

[a] One partner (26 percent), two to four (30 percent), five to ten (23 percent), eleven to twenty (11 percent), and more than twenty (10 percent). We excluded the people who have no partner at all in the logistic regression.

[b] *Big city* is defined as either the central city of the 12 largest standard metropolitan statistical areas (SMSAs) or the central city of the 100 largest SMSAs.

[c] The question is, "Have you ever injected drugs, that is taken drugs using a needle, that weren't prescribed by a doctor?" (*SOS,* 674, 677).

[d] Having several sex partners in a given time period.

[e] We defined *pubertal age* as the age at which the first menstrual period occurred (for females) or the age at which the voice changed or pubic hair appeared (for males). If respondents did not remember this age, we used 12 or 13 years of age.

[f] White (79 percent), African American (13 percent), and Hispanic (8 percent).

[g] Less than high school (14 percent), high school (29 percent), vocational school or 2-year degree (33 percent), finished college (17 percent), and Master's or advanced degree (7 percent).

[h] Frequency of attending religious services. Almost weekly = weekly or nearly every week, sometimes = several times a year to 2 or 3 times a month, rarely = never or at most about once or twice a year. Almost weekly (29 percent), sometimes (32 percent), and rarely (40 percent).

[i] How often do you think about sex? Never or less than once a month (8 percent), a few times a month/year (56 percent), and every day or several times a day (36 percent).

[j] Most conservative (6 percent), conservative (50 percent), liberal (42 percent), and most liberal (2 percent). These are the rounded averages of answers to nine questions about sexual values. These include premarital sex, teen sex, extramarital sex, same-gender sex, laws against pornography, sex without love, abortion, consensual sex (any kind of sexual activity between adults is OK as long as both persons freely agree to it), and religion-guided sexual behavior (my religious beliefs have shaped and guided my sexual behavior). For details, see *SOS,* chap. 14.

Table 9.2 The Likelihood of Ever Having Had a Sexually Transmitted Infection by Number of Sex Partners since Age 18, by Gender

Number of Partners	% Ever Had an STI		% of Adult Population Aged 18–59[a]
	Men	Women	
1	3	5	26
2–4	6	13	30
5–10	14	33	22
11–20	27	48	11
21+	37	55	9

Source: SOS, 179, 387.
[a]The remaining 3 percent had no sex partners.

age, gender, and number of sex partners and by race/ethnicity, see *SOS,* chap. 11). A substantial majority of the respondents reported having had only a moderate number of sex partners in their lifetime or in the recent past, and more than 80 percent claimed that they had never had an STD. As the table readily discloses, for example, almost 80 percent of the adult population between eighteen and fifty-nine years of age reported having ten or fewer sex partners since age eighteen. The likelihood of reporting having had an STD begins to increase rapidly when respondents report five or more sex partners in their lifetime; indeed, there is more than a fourfold increase in the likelihood of reporting an STD for those having eleven or more partners in their lifetime when compared to those with four or fewer partners since age eighteen.[2] Also to be gleaned from inspection of table 9.2 is the fact that, for each level of risk (as indexed by the number of sex partners), women have roughly twice the likelihood of reporting an STD when compared to men. Since we know from human biology that women are more susceptible to sexually transmitted infection than are men, we should expect women to report having more STDs than men at every given level of risk (see Aral and Guinau 1984; and *SOS,* 384–89, 391–96).

NETWORK ANALYSIS

In order to examine the network effects, we constructed a contact matrix (who partners with whom) to reveal the network patterns between different population subgroups. First, we omitted from the data set that was used in the logistic regression analysis the people who had only same-gender sex during the past twelve months. We excluded them, not because they are an unimportant factor in understanding STD transmission dynamics, but because our mathematical model requires the assumption that only people engaging in opposite-gender sex are included.

Second, we divided the entire sample into three groups according to their level of sexual activity: (1) *peripherals* are those who have had only one sex partner in the past twelve months and who are therefore believed to be safe from infection; (2) *adjacents* are those who have had two or three sex partners in the same period; and (3) *core group members* are those who have had at least four sex partners in the same twelve-month period and are therefore considered to be primarily responsible for the existence of sexually transmitted diseases in the population over time. Definitions in mathematical epidemiology have distinguished between core and noncore members of a population only on the basis of their epidemiological function in maintaining STDs (Yorke, Hethcote, and Nold 1978; Jacquez, Simon, and Koopman 1995). Prior empirical definitions (e.g., Garnett and Anderson 1993; Rothenberg 1983) have distinguished among cores, adjacents, and peripherals on the basis of geographic areas treated as proxy indicators for the underlying constructs. Our distinctions are operationalizations of these theoretical constructs and empirical proxies based on individual-level data. We specified the sexual-activity groups within each of the three racial/ethnic groups to obtain a contact matrix between nine subgroups. Table 9.3 presents this contact matrix. (See app. 10.A for the technical details about constructing this table from the raw data using certain assumptions.)

Table 9.3 Contact Matrix (Number of Partnerships for the Last Twelve Months)

	WP	WA	WC	AP	AA	AC	HP	HA	HC
WP	1,463.02								
WA	78.44	199.99							
WC	37.39	160.65	175.98						
AP	12.25	1.53	.86	172.16					
AA	.48	3.01	2.16	18.93	67.02				
AC	1.19	5.61	3.91	16.64	59.88	44.93			
HP	33.75	1.91	2.07	2.24	.39	.93	82.32		
HA	3.96	4.75	8.25	.14	1.00	3.66	4.86	9.67	
HC	.29	4.73	7.79	.23	2.59	4.32	3.14	13.80	10.41

Note: This table shows the estimated number of partnerships between persons in row (chooser) and column (chosen) groups, calculated according to the procedures described in app. 9.A. Since the estimated number of contacts for an ordered row/column combination is the same as for its reversed order, the matrix is symmetrical, and the upper-right-hand entries can thus be omitted to avoid redundancy.
WP = white periphery, WA = white adjacent, WC = white core, AP = African American periphery, AA = African American adjacent, AC = African American core, HP = Hispanic periphery, HA = Hispanic adjacent, HC = Hispanic core.

Analyses

LOGISTIC REGRESSION

Rather than trying to identify the minimum number of significant individual-level factors needed to predict infection status, we used the backward stepwise selection method, a more exploratory procedure that focuses on revealing possible significant factors, rather than the forward selection method, which is less likely to uncover relations. The backward stepwise procedure starts with all the variables in the model. At each successive step, each variable is evaluated for entry or removal. This process continues until no variables meet entry or removal criteria. We adopted the less stringent criterion of a 20 percent significance level for entry or removal in order not to dismiss potentially significant factors. Logistic regressions for each dependent variable (any STDs, bacterial STDs, and viral STDs) were computed (for details, see the appendix to the introduction and Menard 1995).

The individual-level risk factors included in the logistic regression described in table 9.5 below are each, considered by themselves, significantly predictive of the respondent having had an STD at some point in his or her life or having been a member of a core group. We have already discussed gender and number of lifetime sex partners as they pertain to these issues. The currently married enjoy a reduced likelihood of being in the core or having contracted an STD, while cohabitors (who tend to be more heavily focused on sexual concerns and needs than noncohabitors in long-term dating relationships) are more likely to report getting an STD. Most noteworthy for our purposes is the fact that educational attainment is strongly and positively associated with lifetime core membership and somewhat less strongly associated with contracting an STD. This observation is in sharp contradiction with the usual inference from the literature on STDs that implies their prevalence especially among the poor and dispossessed. This conflicting finding probably arises from the likely biases in the CDC case-based methods discussed above in reporting STDs.

Residence in a large city (one with a population over 250,000), a history of service in the military, and having multiple sex partners simultaneously are positively associated with being in the core and having an STD (the latter quite dramatically so), while regular church attendance is negatively associated with these outcomes. There is a powerful association between ever drinking before or during a sexual event in the past year and being a member of the core group. Other behavioral and historical concomitants of reporting an STD and being a core group member include having a sexual experience with an adult when a child—an especially powerful predictor (see chap. 4 above)—and having experience with oral or anal sex.

People who reported never having experienced oral sex had practically no likelihood of being a member of the lifetime core group. Choosing same-gender or bisexual partners (for men only) and ever being paid for sex also have strong correlations with being a core member and reporting an STD.

Finally, we need to consider attitudinal and fantasy predictors of core group membership and having had an STD. Normative orientation divides the respondents into four subgroups that differ along a continuum from sexual conservatism to sexual libertarianism (for an extended discussion of this attitude scale, see *SOS,* chap. 14); here, we simply use average scores for nine items. Respondents who were strongly libertarian in their sexual views were much more likely to report STDs and be a core group member. Respondents were classified according to their answers to the following self-administered question: "On the average, how often do you think about sex? less than once a month . . . one to a few times a month . . . one to a few times a week . . . everyday . . . several times a day . . . I never think about sex" (*SOS,* 647). Thinking frequently about sex proves to be a very powerful predictor of membership in the core and having an STD, even net of all the other predictors! Finally, having fantasies about having sex with a stranger is a strong predictor of core membership.

LOG-LINEAR ANALYSIS FOR INTRARACIAL NETWORK EFFECT

We explore two kinds of network effects. One comes from the sexual network patterns *inside* each racial/ethnic group, and the other comes from the sexual network patterns *between* racial/ethnic groups. The first effect (the intraracial effect) can be revealed by examining how sexual matches between the three sexual activity groups within each racial group differ across these racial/ethnic groups.

Log-linear analysis was used to estimate the population parameters of odds ratios reflecting racial/ethnic differences in these matches. To find the log-linear model that best fits the data displayed in table 9.3, we examined twelve possible models. The results are given in table 9.4. The analysis assumes that each instance of partner choice is an independent event. This is, however, clearly not the case for persons who report multiple partners because their choices, being made by the same persons, are dependent. Given the low average number of partners for most of the population, however, this problem may not be a serious one (see Morris 1993a).

Log-linear analysis is similar to multidimensional scaling in statistics and diverse measures of clique detection in network analysis. There are, however, important differences. First, the log-linear analysis has a substantively meaningful built-in measure of relation, the odds ratio. Second, those odds ratios come from a log-linear model that passes a goodness-of-fit test to check whether it actually fits the data. Third, they are derived from parameter estimates, not just from sample statistics.

Table 9.4 Possible Log-Linear Models for the Contact Matrix

Models	Log-Likelihood χ^2	Pearson χ^2	df^a	p-Value
Independence[b]	4,878.3	7,839.9	36	.0
Quasi-independence[c]	1,242.9	1,754.3	27	.0
1-dimensional RC[d]	1,104.3	3,141.8	28	.0
2-dimensional RC[e]	236.8	285.9	21	.0
3-dimensional RC	8.3	7.8	15	.932
4-dimensional RC[f]	2.0	2.0	10	.996
5-dimensional RC	.8	.7	6	.994
6-dimensional RC	.2	.2	3	.978
1-dimensional quasi-RC	298.6	361.1	19	.0
2-dimensional quasi-RC	95.8	127.5	12	.0
3-dimensional quasi-RC	2.4	2.2	6	.9
4-dimensional quasi-RC	.0	.0	1	1.0

Note: RC = row-column effect model.
[a]Degrees of freedom are corrected from those suggested in the standard statistical packages (SPSS and CDAS) to reflect the fact that the data set and models are in fact symmetrical.
[b]The independence model assumes independence (no relation) between rows and columns in the contact matrix. People choose partners regardless of race/ethnicity and activity level (periphery, adjacent, and core)—i.e., random mixing. Observing an almost zero p-value for this model tells us that this assumption is wrong.
[c]*Quasi-* means that diagonal cells are dropped in the model. The quasi-independence model thus assumes independence between rows and columns except for the diagonal cells. This model is true if random mixing happens except in the diagonal cells (self-selection). Again, the very small p-value tells us that this model does not fit the data (contact matrix).
[d]The one-dimensional RC model assumes that the log odds ratio of i vs. j is equal to $(\mu_i - \mu_j)^2$, where μ_i and μ_j are the parameters for i and j, respectively. Thus, the log odds ratio depends only on one pair of (one-dimensional) parameters for row (μ_i) and column (μ_j), (RC).
[e]The two-dimensional RC model assumes that the log odds ratio of i vs. j equals $(\mu_{i1} - \mu_{j1})^2$ + $(\mu_{i2} - \mu_j^2)^2$. Thus, the log odds ratio depends only on two pairs of row and column parameters.
[f]Even though the four-dimensional RC model has the best goodness of fit (the highest p-value), the three-dimensional RC model is the better model since it requires fewer parameters for estimation (more degrees of freedom) for almost the same goodness of fit. The best model is determined by comparing two models by a χ^2 significance test using log-likelihood χ^2 and degrees of freedom for all possible pairs of models.

A SIMULATION FOR THE INTERRACIAL NETWORK EFFECT

In addition to the intraracial network effect noted above, we also found an interracial network effect. This comes from the sexual matching patterns between racial/ethnic groups rather than the patterns within racial/ethnic groups. What happens if there are more (or fewer) sexual partnerships between Hispanic core and African American core members? Does this change the infection rates for African Americans, Hispanics, and whites?

We examined this question by simulating different matching patterns between the racial/ethnic groups.

In order to capture the pure interracial network effect, we must separate this effect from all the other confounding and intermingled effects. Two effects are especially worth discussing. First, we must take into account the differential initial infection rates for each group (e.g., 4 percent of the whites and 5 percent of the Hispanics have ever been infected with gonorrhea, but 24 percent of the African Americans have been so infected, according to the NHSLS). Second, we must equalize the number of partners among groups because we know that this risk factor strongly affects infection rates as well. For example, the fact that the African American core group has a higher mean number of partners than the other racial/ethnic core groups contributes to the higher infection rate for African Americans.

A series of manipulations of the contact matrix reveals the effects of different matching patterns on the infection rates for each racial/ethnic group, with all the other confounding effects (including the two discussed above) removed (see app. 9.B). The result is the pure network effect regardless of, say, initial infection rates, number of sex partners, age at initial intercourse, and so on.

9.3 Results

Logistic Regressions for Risk Factors

Table 9.5 summarizes the logistic regression analyses produced by the backward selection method (Menard 1995) for the people who have had at least one sex partner in their lifetime. The table reports only the statistically significant odds ratios, indicating that the row variables were significantly associated with the respondents' reports of an STD (as indicated by the column head). If there is no entry in a row/column intersection, then the factor in question has no significant relation to having an STD when all the factors in the list are taken into account.

Let us direct attention to two highly salient points. First, the logistic regressions tell us that African Americans have far higher rates of bacterial diseases, but far lower rates of viral infections, than do whites. A higher infection rate of viral STDs for whites is readily evident in our data at the zero-order level (8.4 percent for whites, 5.4 percent for African Americans, and 4 percent for Hispanics). This finding must be interpreted cautiously, as we indicate in section 9.4 below.

Second, even after controlling for all the appropriate risk factors, African Americans have the highest infection rate for bacterial diseases. They are five times more likely to be infected than whites or Hispanics after controlling all the individual-level risk factors.

Table 9.5 Logistic Regressions for STDs Ever in Lifetime

	Any	Bacterial	Viral
Number of partners	[a]	[a]	[a]
1	.53	.67	.37
2–4	1.00	1.00	1.00
5–10	3.23	3.50	2.08
11–20	5.37	6.05	3.14
More than 20	6.70	6.90	3.65
Female	3.44	3.0	4.30
Ethnic	[a]	[a]	[a]
African American	2.15	4.8	.55
Hispanic	.68	1.04[b]	.55
White	1.00	1.00	1.00
Big city	1.27	1.27	
Pay for sex	2.54	2.54	1.55
Being paid for sex		1.45	
Anal	1.32	1.26	1.40
Never married			
Military service		1.46	
Drug injection	1.66	1.82	1.72
Group sex			
Concurrent partners	1.22		1.65
Prepubertal sex			
Age	1.64	2.16	
(Age) × (age)	(1.00)−	(1.00)−	
Education			[a]
Less than high school			1.01[b]
High school graduate			.74
Vocational school or 2-year degree			1.00
Finished college, 4–5-year degree			1.27[b]
Master's degree or advanced			1.79
Church attendance	[a]	[a]	[a]
Almost always	.59	.55	.72
Sometimes	.81	.85[b]	.57
Rarely	1.00	1.00	1.00
Thinking of sex			[a]
Never or less than a month		.67[b]	
Few times a month/week		1.00	
Every day or several times a day		1.28	
Sexual value orientation			
Most conservative			
Conservative			
Liberal			
Most liberal			
Total number of cases	2,402	2,417	2,444
STD (%)	18.3	11.3	7.9
Pseudo-R^2	.18	.21	.15

Note: This table differs from table 4 in Laumann and Youm (1999) in that we now treat number of partners as a set of discrete, ordered categories rather than a continuous variable. As a result, the odds ratios reported here differ in minor ways from those in the original table, but these differences are so minor that they do not affect the overall interpretation of results. Robert T. Michael has correctly suggested that, because it results in a small but significant odds ratio, the treatment of the numbers of partners as a continuous variable might mislead the reader to underestimate its significance in accounting for an individual's relative risk for STDs.

All values are odds ratios ($\alpha = 0.2$). Reference categories are italicized. "(1.00)−" indicates that the rounded odds ratio is 1.00 but that the actual odds ratio is less than 1.

[a] These are significant, but a single odds ratio cannot be calculated. Instead, each category has an odds ratio.

[b] Not significantly different from the reference category at $\alpha = 0.2$ even though the category as a whole is significant at $\alpha = 0.2$.

Log-Linear Analysis for the Intraracial Network Effect

Table 9.4 above allows us to identify the three-dimensional RC (row/column) model as the best model with a high goodness of fit ($p = .93$). The three-dimensional RC model for symmetrical data can be represented as follows:

$$\ln(F_{ij}) = \gamma + \gamma_i + \gamma_j + \sum_{k=1}^{3} \phi_k \mu_{ik} \mu_{jk},$$

where F_{ij} is an expected frequency for the cell of the contact matrix ($i = 1, 2, 3, \ldots, 9$, and $j = 1, 2, 3, \ldots, 9$) in table 9.3 above. So the log-odds ratio of i versus j becomes

$$\ln(\vartheta) = \ln\left(\frac{F_{ii}F_{jj}}{F_{ij}F_{ji}}\right) = \sum_{k=1}^{3} \phi_k(\mu_{ik} - \mu_{jk})^2.$$

The odds ratio is obtained by taking the exponential of this value.

On the basis of this best-fitting log-linear model, table 9.6 presents the odds ratios between the nine subgroups. It reveals that there is a huge racial/ethnic difference in the odds ratios for the periphery and the core group. In the African American population, there are many more sexual matches between periphery and core. Peripheral African Americans are

Table 9.6 Odds Ratios between Nine Subgroups

	WP	WA	WC	AP	AA	AC	HP	HA	HC
WP									
WA	47.8								
WC	180.4	1.3							
AP	1,751.7	9,365.0	75,280.4						
AA	278,951.1	1,543.4	2,644.0	34.2					
AC	41,459.2	369.4	528.3	32.5	1.1				
HP	103.4	4,986.2	4,446.4	2,889.3	32,945.3	4,660.0			
HA	2,281.1	80.1	26.2	17,493.3	325.5	66.0	29.8		
HC	18,005.7	144.2	39.3	32,880.7	154.5	38.1	134.6	1.2	

Note: This table displays the odds ratios between row (chooser) and column (chosen) groups. For example, look at the odds ratio between WC and WP. White core members are 180 times more likely to have white core partners than they are to have white periphery partners. Or, in the case of HP and WA, Hispanic peripherals are 4,986 times more likely to have Hispanic periphery partners than white adjacent partners. Since the odds ratio for an ordered row/column combination is the same as for its reversed order, the matrix is symmetrical, and the upper-right-hand entries can thus be omitted to avoid redundancy. Diagonal cells odds ratios are also omitted because they are undefined.
WP = white periphery, WA = white adjacent, WC = white core, AP = African American periphery, AA = African American adjacent, AC = African American core, HP = Hispanic periphery, HA = Hispanic adjacent, HC = Hispanic core.

only thirty-three times more likely to have peripheral African American rather than core African American sex partners, whereas peripheral whites are 180 times more likely to have peripheral white rather than core white sex partners. This is an intraracial network effect in the sense that the network effect comes only from the network patterns between different activity groups inside each racial/ethnic group. However, there is another network effect working purely between racial/ethnic groups.

A Simulation of the Interracial Network Effect

Using a simulation strategy, we can derive estimates of the relative infection prevalence for each racial/ethnic group. Relative infection prevalence is calculated by dividing the proportion of infected people in a particular group by the proportion of that group in the population as a whole. For example, if the relative infection prevalence for whites is less than 1, that means that whites are less infected with respect to their population size. Figure 9.3 shows the relative infection prevalence for each racial/ethnic group.

In figure 9.3, the z-axis represents relative infection prevalence, the x-axis shows the number of contacts between the African American core and the Hispanic core, and the y-axis represents the number of contacts between the white core and the Hispanic core. The intersection of the x and y coordinates at level 3 depicts the actual (current) matching patterns, according to our data. Values larger than 3 mean that there are more contacts between the African American core and the Hispanic core (with respect to the x-axis) or between the white core and the Hispanic core (with respect to the y-axis). A unit increase means a 1.5 percent increase.

9.4 Discussion

Before discussing our findings, we should note several important limitations in the data generated by the NHSLS. First, self-reports of STD status are subject to underreporting biases arising from personal concerns about social stigmatization, failures of recall (especially for disease episodes more remote in time), and even lack of knowledge (the respondent may have had a particular sexually transmitted infection while remaining clinically asymptomatic, or the infection may never have been diagnosed). Considerable effort was expended to minimize underreporting by devising an interview protocol that gave a maximum sense of privacy and confidentiality, persuaded the respondent of the necessity of full disclosure for public health reasons, and provided memory aids to facilitate recall. Even if these procedures were especially effective—and we believe that they were—we must still acknowledge that the self-reports understate the prev-

Relative infection prevalence for whites

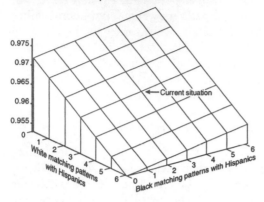

Relative infection prevalence for blacks

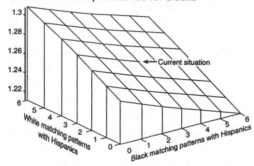

Relative infection prevalence for Hispanics

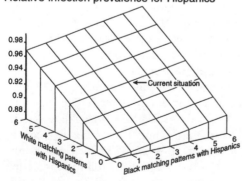

Fig. 9.3 Relative prevalence of infection.
Note: For each x and y-axis, the current matching amount is located at 3. A figure larger than 3 indicates more matches with the Hispanic core group than with the current matching amount. A figure smaller than 3 indicates fewer matches with the Hispanic core group than with the current matching amount. The z-axis represents relative infection prevalence.

alence of STDs to a substantial but unknown extent, as shown in a comparison study of self-reported survey data with surveillance data (Anderson, McCormick, and Fichtner 1994).

Second, there may be systematic biases in underreporting related to particular attributes of the respondents. For example, we might expect better-educated people to be more knowledgeable about and comfortable with disease labels and to be able to recall them more accurately than less well-educated persons, who may have less facility in and familiarity with discussing such matters. Countering this advantage in knowledge and recall, however, may be a greater sensitivity of better-educated persons aspiring to middle-class standing to the social stigma associated with reporting a sexually transmitted infection.

Third, in order to construct the contact matrix, we estimated each partner's activity level by averaging two partners' reported number of partners. We did not have complete information about all the partners' partnering activity because, owing to time limitations, direct questions were not asked about all the partners reported by the respondent in the past year, only about two. Moreover, in relying entirely on the respondent's report of his or her own number of partners and his or her report of the partner's or partners' other partners, we necessarily introduce an unknown level of inaccuracy in estimating the contact matrix.

Logistic Regressions for Risk Factors

First, we found that whites are more likely to be infected with viral STDs. This pattern contrasts sharply with the image of STD prevalence suggested by figures reported by the CDC, which imply a higher prevalence of certain viral diseases among lower socioeconomic groups (cf. CDC 1996; Philipson and Posner 1993; Aral and Holmes 1990). This result implies the possibility of systematic bias in the data reported to the CDC. There are, however, several other possible interpretations.

First, given that tests for viral STDs tend to be more costly than tests for bacterial STDs and that viral STDs are less likely to remain asymptomatic than bacterial STDs, we should expect some bias in the likelihood of diagnosing viral STDs in the direction of persons of higher socioeconomic status. If this were the case, self-reported data would indicate that whites have a higher infection rate, but, in fact, African Americans may have the higher rate. One study using nationally based biomarker data from the National Health and Nutrition Surveys (Fleming et al. 1997), for example, has shown that African Americans are more likely to be infected by herpes simplex virus type 2.

Second, this racial/ethnic difference might arise from African Americans engaging in more risky sex (e.g., having a new partner or a one-time-

Table 9.7 Mean Frequency of Unprotected Sexual Events (No Condom Used) with
Someone Other Than a Spouse or a Cohabitant

	White	African American	Hispanic
Peripheral	8.6	12.5	5.8
	(39.3)	(43.4)	(25.9)
Adjacent	54.7	34.4	27.6
	(102.2)	(71.3)	(66.2)
Core	57.3	19.6	59.1
	(112.3)	(48.3)	(153.7)

Note: Standard deviations are given in parentheses.

only partner). We did not include a sex-without-condom variable in the logistic regression because of the lack of relevant data. As table 9.7 shows, however, we observe no racial/ethnic difference in this variable at least for the past twelve months.

Third, a number of variables in the logistic regression are highly associated with reporting an STD but are not conventionally interpreted as STD risk factors—for example, gender, having concurrent partners, educational attainment, church attendance, and thinking about sex. In other words, how can one explain how thinking about sex frequently or being a college graduate might itself increase the probability of being infected with an STD? Our basic conjecture is that people with a higher probability of being infected in these non–risk factor categories have partners who are more sexually active than are the sex partners of the people in the lower non–risk factor categories. For example, the reason that women have higher odds of being infected than men with the same number of partners is that, in general, women's male partners have higher numbers of partners than men's female partners do. It is thus possible that women have a higher infection rate than men with the same number of sex partners. (This gender difference is also surely rooted in biological considerations as well, such as the differential duration of exposure to the pathogen in question [see Jones and Wasserheit 1991].) In the next section, we examine the case for race/ethnicity.

Log-Linear Analysis for the Intraracial Network Effect

Here, we have one clear explanation for why African Americans have higher infection rates, even after controlling for most risk factors. We found that, even though peripheral African Americans have, by definition, only one partner, the chance that that partner is in the core group is five times higher (180/33) that it is for peripheral whites' partners and four times higher (133/33) that it is for peripheral Hispanics' partners. Therefore, even after controlling for number of partners as a major risk factor, African Americans necessarily have higher infection rates than whites or Hispanics. Among African Americans, then, infections are not limited to the core but overflow to the periphery owing to this strong dissortative mating pattern. This is apparent if we consider the fact that infection is concentrated in the core, a powerful transmitter because of the high rate at which its members acquire new partners. This can be seen as a special case of the general proposition that a high number of sexual linkages between subgroups will lead to extensive dissemination of infection throughout the population rather than confining infection within the subgroups. This proposition has been tested and supported by many papers (cf. Wasserheit and Aral 1996; Rothenberg, Potterat, and Woodhouse 1996; Rothenberg and Potterat 1988).

There is a trade-off here. If the outflow becomes too high, the African American core cannot maintain STDs over time because the transmission power of their partners (i.e., the partners' number of partners) is too weak (the amount of second-order transmission is too low). The current amount of outflow from the African American core, however, is not sufficiently large to eliminate its role as a core group. We can confirm this proposition by testing whether the African American core is actually functioning as a core group in the sense that its members are the primary actors sustaining disease transmission. If we calculate the basic reproduction rates of gonorrhea as an example, with appropriate parameters concerning transmission probabilities and recovery rates, following the case in Garnett and Anderson (1993), we find that the core groups in our analysis are real cores in the sense that their basic reproduction rates are all greater than one and the basic reproduction rate for the whole population is also greater than one, according to the model proposed by Jacquez, Simon, and Koopman (1995).

A Simulation for the Interracial Network Effect

Another reason why African Americans have a higher infection rate can be found in the interracial effect. Figure 9.3 shows that, as interracial contact between the African American core and the Hispanic core increases, the relative infection prevalence of the African American population decreases, given the white matching pattern. Also, more contacts between the white core and the Hispanic core increase the relative infection prevalence for African Americans, given the African American matching pattern. In general, if a given non-Hispanic group has more sexual matches with a Hispanic group, its infection rate decreases, while the other two racial groups' infection rates increase. We can interpret this result as follows: More matches with Hispanics provide an efficient way of transmitting infections to the other racial/ethnic groups. If a group has fewer matches with the Hispanic core, then that group becomes more segregated from the other racial/ethnic groups, and this increases the infection rate for that group and decreases the infection rate for the other groups. Otherwise, if there are more matches, the group has an effective channel through which to relay infection to the other racial/ethnic groups.

Whites have relatively more sexual contacts with Hispanics than do African Americans, as can be observed in table 9.6 above. (That is, every odds ratio between whites and Hispanics is smaller than or almost equal to the corresponding one between African Americans and Hispanics. Note that these odds ratios are obtained after controlling population size.) This network pattern makes the white infection rate low and the African American infection rate high. Once infected, whites can spread infection to the other racial/ethnic groups more effectively than African Americans can. This is why the relative infection prevalence of the African Americans is 1.26 while it is only 0.97 for the whites for the current matching pattern where Hispanics are closer to whites. Thus, the likelihood of African Americans having a sexually transmitted infection is 1.3 ($\cong$ 1.26/0.97) times greater than it is for whites, owing to this factor alone.

In summary, relatively high numbers of sexual contacts between the African American core and the African American periphery (dissortative mating within the African American population) have a network effect that makes infections overflow into the entire African American population from the African American core—that is, an *intraracial network effect*. At the same time, African Americans are somewhat distant from the other racial/ethnic groups (assortative mating of African Americans in the whole population), so infections stay inside the African American population—that is, an *interracial effect*.

9.5 Conclusion

With respect to our most important results, we found, first, that, in addition to the usual behavioral risk factors, one can identify a variety of social and attitudinal items that provide stable and consistent predictors of STD prevalence and incidence, items that could be usefully combined with the STD surveillance system to provide more comprehensive, effective, and targeted intervention strategies for population subgroups at risk. Second, we demonstrated the critical role that social network patterns play in accounting for the known differentials in rates of infection across racial/ethnic groups. In particular, we found that the relatively high number of sexual contacts between the African American core and its periphery facilitates the spread of infection into the entire African American population: the so-called intraracial network effect. These infections remain inside the

African American population because African Americans are highly segregated from the other racial/ethnic groups: the so-called interracial network effect. These network effects cannot be detected in regressions that include only individual-level risk factors.

Appendix 9A Constructing the Contact Matrix

First, we construct the contact matrix for the past twelve months for each gender from the raw data, as in table 9A.1. These two matrices lack one critical piece of information. Neither includes any information about the level of sexual activity for partners. We do not know, for example, how

Table 9A.1 Contact Matrices for the Past Twelve Months

Matrix A. Male respondents to female partners (row to column): number of partnerships

	White	African American	Hispanic
Peripheral			
White	659	3	9
African American	10	55	0
Hispanic	15	0	34
Adjacent			
White	261	2	6
African American	2	68	3
Hispanic	20	0	22
Core			
White	287	0	10
African American	14	133	12
Hispanic	15	1	6

Matrix B. Female respondents to male partners (row to column): number of partnerships

	White	African American	Hispanic
Peripheral			
White	882	12	16
African American	1	135	4
Hispanic	33	1	56
Adjacent			
White	182	9	5
African American	0	60	0
Hispanic	3	1	15
Core			
White	121	9	1
African American	0	44	0
Hispanic	2	9	13

many partnerships were formed between, say, white core members and white adjacent members. To remedy this deficiency, we constructed two mixing matrices that show the percentages of partnerships across activity-level subgroups.

Unfortunately we do not have complete information about the partners' level of sexual activity because, due to time limitations, direct questions were not asked about all partners reported by the respondent in the past year, but only about the primary and secondary partner. Averaging these two partners' reported number of partners, excluding the respondent, we assigned all the partners to the periphery if the average was zero, to the adjacent sub-population if the average was between zero and two (including two), and to the core if the average was greater than two. Even though this assumption seems strong, the resultant tables are consistent with James Koopman's observation of a campus contact matrix (from a personal communication with Koopman).

Second, we can now construct the mixing matrix in table 9A.2 using this assumption.

Third, we integrated matrix A from table 9A.1 and matrix C from table 9A.2 into one matrix. We assumed the row percentages in C applicable to each cell in A, regardless of the partners' race/ethnicity. Thus, among 659 white female partners of white peripheral male respondents, 95% are peripheral. Also, among the 9 Hispanic female partners of the white peripheral male respondents, 95% are peripheral. We thus constructed a 9-by-9 matrix (matrix M) representing contacts from men to women. In the same way, we computed another 9-by-9 matrix from B and D representing contacts from women to men (matrix F).

Fourth, the two matrices (M and F) must, in principle, give us the same information. For example, if there are 100 partnerships between the white male core and the white female periphery, then there must also be 100 partnerships between the white female periphery and the white male core. What discrepancies we observe arise from sampling variability. We propose to resolve these discrepancies by averaging the male-to-female and female-to-male estimates in order to obtain a single contact matrix. We thus computed the final 9-by-9 symmetric contact matrix (matrix C) by using the equation $C = 1/2 \left[(M + F) + (M + F)' \right]$.

Appendix 9B A Simulation of Different Matching Patterns Between Racial/Ethnic Groups

Our goal in this simulation is to show the effects of different matching patterns between racial/ethnic groups, with the two effects (the differential initial infection rates and the different numbers of partners for each subgroup) removed from the pure interracial network effect. First, we trans-

Table 9A.2 Mixing Matrices

	Peripheral	Adjacent	Core
	Matrix C. Male respondents to female partners (row to column): row %		
WP	95.22	2.69	2.09
WA	25.28	45.35	29.37
WC	8.75	47.47	43.77
AP	93.85	3.08	3.08
AA	24.66	53.42	21.92
AC	14.89	56.03	29.08
HP	93.88	0	6.12
HA	35.71	16.67	47.62
HC	0	34.78	65.22

	Peripheral	Adjacent	Core
	Matrix D. Female respondents to male partners (row to column): row %		
WP	94.73	3.29	1.98
WA	24.26	44.85	30.88
WC	15.23	43.15	41.62
AP	89.29	7.14	3.57
AA	16.28	51.16	32.56
AC	22.58	50	27.42
HP	90	3.33	6.67
HA	0	40	60
HC	3.57	46.43	50

Note: WP: white periphery, WA: white adjacent, WC: white core, AP: African American periphery, AA: African American adjacent, AC: African American core, HP: Hispanic periphery, HA: Hispanic adjacent, HC: Hispanic core.

form the matrix C (table 9A.2) into the transformation matrix T by equation (1).

(1)
$$T = \left[C_{ij} / \sum_{j=1}^{9} C_{ij} \right]'$$

Thus equation (1) constructs T as a transposed matrix of the row stochastic matrix of C. Then, every one of the nine groups has the same number of partners because of the 'row stochastic' procedure, and the transformation matrix T becomes the mixing matrix from column to row.

Using T, we can calculate each group's proportion of infecteds at time 2 from each group's proportion of infecteds at time 1. (The sum of the each group's proportions must be one.) Equation (2) shows this relation, where r_1 and r_2 are column vectors representing each group's proportion of infecteds at time 1 and time 2, respectively.

(2) $$Tr_1 = r_2$$

Also, since T is a "regular" matrix, it must have a "stable" proportion for each group that does not change over time. The following equation shows the relationship between T and the "stable" proportion for each group, s (where s is a column vector representing each group's stable proportion of infecteds).

(3) $$Ts = s$$

One of the useful properties of s is that it does not depend on the initial r_1. So we also eliminate the differential initial infection rates for each group. We can solve s from equation (3) and the following equation (4).

(4) $$\sum_{i=1}^{9} s_i = 1$$

After getting s, we divides s into three parts according to the following equation (5).

(5) $$\sum_{i=1}^{3} s_i = y_1, \quad \sum_{i=4}^{6} s_i = y_2, \quad \sum_{i=7}^{9} s_i = y_3$$

Using this equation, we get y_1, y_2, and y_3 for each racial/ethnic group, representing each racial/ethnic group's proportion of infecteds. So if $y_1 = 0.6$, then 60 percent of the infected are whites. If we standardize these with regard to each racial/ethnic group's population size, we finally get z_1, z_2, and z_3 for each racial/ethnic group. This is done by the following equation (6) (each denominator is each group's proportion of the whole population represented in the contact matrix C).

(6) $$z_1 = y_2/0.7966, \quad z_2 = y_2/0.1277, \quad z_3 = y_3/0.0756$$

If z_1 is less than one, it means that the white community has an underrepresented number of infecteds; and if it is greater than one, it means there is an overrepresentation of infecteds for whites. We call these the "relative infection prevalence."

We calculated a series of z_1, z_2, and z_3 from a simulation that changes the two matching patterns simultaneously to see what the effects of these changing matching patterns on the infection rates are. First, there is a change in the amount of contacts between the African American core and the Hispanic core. This means there is a change in $T_{6,9}$ and $T_{9,9}$ (We assume the same amount of change in $T_{6,6}$ and $T_{9,9}$ so that the sum of each column will be one.) Second, the amount of contacts between the white core and the Hispanic core ($T_{3,9}$ and $T_{9,3}$) are also changed at the same time. (For the same reason, this entails the same amount of change in $T_{3,3}$ and $T_{9,9}$.)

Now we can estimate the differential "relative infection prevalence" for each group based on a set of different matching patterns. These results do not depend on the initial infection rates or the numbers of partners for each subgroup.

Notes

A version of this chapter was originally presented at a plenary session of the Conference on the Social Determinants of Sexually Transmitted Diseases held at the University of Alabama, Birmingham, 26 May 1996, and subsequently revised. We especially thank James Koopman, Alberto Palloni, John Potterat, Kazuo Yamaguchi, Dingxin Zhao, and the anonymous reviewers for *Sexually Transmitted Diseases,* where parts of this chapter were published (see Laumann and Youm 1999), for their many helpful comments and suggestions. We make particular note of the indebtedness of this chapter to chap. 11 of *SOS,* which was written by Robert T. Michael, with the assistance of Joel A. Feinleib.

1. A different explanation, not based on networks but highly complementary, is found in the analysis of STDs in chap. 11 of *SOS.* There, the much higher rate of bacterial infection for blacks is documented and discussed (pp. 337–39). The differential rates for blacks (higher for bacterial and lower for viral infections) are shown to persist when several personal characteristics, lifetime sexual practices, and number of partners are controlled (fig. 11.1). In chap. 11 of *SOS,* the risks of disease are shown to be related to what that chapter describes as "risky partners" (measured by familiarity and exclusivity with partners) and "risky practices" (use of condoms and use of drugs and alcohol with sex). Blacks are shown to have less exclusive partnerships, to be far less likely to expect sexual exclusivity (table 11.12), and to be more likely to have had a new partner, a one-time-only partner, and very short-term partnerships (table 11.11). However, that chapter also points out that blacks are somewhat more likely to report always using a condom with a secondary partner (table 11.20) and more likely to have reported a changed sexual behavior because of the risks of AIDS (table 11.29A). The multivariate analyses indicate that these differences in condom use and changed sexual behavior for blacks also persist when several personal characteristics and sexual practices are held constant (fig. 11.3).

2. Entirely consistent with the overall impression that the population in general has had only a modest number of sex partners over the course of a lifetime is the fact (not reported in table 9.2) that 83 percent of the respondents reported that they had had only one sex partner or none in the past twelve months. Only 17 percent reported two or more partners in the past twelve months, and more than half reported only two partners. Slightly more than 5 percent reported five or more partners in the past year, and this high level was strongly associated with age. While 8.6 percent of the eighteen- to twenty-four-years-olds said that they had five or more partners last year, this percentage rapidly declined to 2.4 among the thirty-five to thirty-nine-year-olds and 0.4 among the fifty-five to fifty-nine-year-olds. Again, we remind the reader that people are likely to underreport number of partners for the same reasons that they might underreport having had a STD. People who are married or cohabiting and thus in presumably sexually exclusive relationships might be reluctant to disclose that they had sex partners in addition to their primary partners. We have subjected our information on partnerships to a variety of consistency checks and have been reassured that people were for the most part being candid and forthcoming about their sexual activities, even those that were likely to be subject to social disapproval. (For a detailed examination of the reports of number of sex partners in the NHSLS, see *SOS,* 172–224.)

CHAPTER TEN

■

Sexual Dysfunction in the United States: Prevalence and Predictors

EDWARD O. LAUMANN, ANTHONY PAIK, AND RAYMOND C. ROSEN

Unlike many aspects of social life, the sociological significance of sexual dysfunction is not transparent. Labor unrest, unions, and workplace organization all have unquestioned status as objects of sociological investigation, presumably because of their close links with industrialization and other aspects of modernization. Research on social stress, a topic not entirely dissimilar from sexual dysfunction, is recognized as legitimate social inquiry, and its heritage can be traced to none other than Emile Durkheim's *Suicide* (1951).[1] In contrast, a sociologist studying sexual problems is likely to encounter quizzical expressions from his or her peers, as if they recognize the subject as "dirty work," an activity counter to the more heroic conceptions of the discipline (Hughes 1994).

A partial explanation for the marginal status of sexual dysfunction as a subject of study is that the study of human sexuality in general is relatively neglected in sociology. A central idea promoted by *The Social Organization of Sexuality* is the fact that sexual activity is a form of social action that is shaped by social structure. In the United States and Western Europe, a more secular orientation toward sexual life has supplanted traditional conceptions, replacing distinctions between good and evil, virtue and sin, the spiritual and the animal, with physical and mental health (Laumann and Gagnon 1995). While the idea of religious *suffering* is sociologically relevant, the concepts of health and illness in developed nations are often taken for granted and seen primarily as organic. However, the increasing prominence of sexual expression and sexual health in public life forces the issue that this area of social life should also be desacralized.

A primary reason why the health-illness complex is frequently ignored in sociology is because medical professionals have long established themselves as arbiters of what is healthy and what is diseased. This fact has spawned a number of studies that assess the historical role that medical professionals played in "constructing" sexual dysfunction (Boyle 1994; Morrow 1994). In general, the constructivist approach focuses on the cultural concept of sexual dysfunction and its relation to institutionalized power, medicine being the exemplar. The goal of these studies is to illustrate the manner in which the categories *normal* and *abnormal* sexual functioning have been constructed. An unfortunate by-product of this approach, however, is that positivistic approaches to illness, especially epidemiological studies, have been undermined. This is unfortunate since, as Abbott (1990) has noted, the objectification of this cultural concept through institutionalization permits a positivistic approach to this issue. More important, the constructivist approach narrowly conceptualizes health and illness as an elite construction (i.e., the medical community). An important consequence of this conceptual winnowing is that the health-illness complex is separated from the interactive foundations of social action.

Talcott Parsons has proposed an analytic definition of the health-illness complex that is tied to an individual's capacity for social action. He defines *health* as a teleonomic capacity "to maintain a favorable, self-regulated state that is a prerequisite of the effective performance of an indefinitely wide range of functions both within the system and in relation to its environments" (Parsons 1978a, 69).[2] Illness is obviously the impairment of this teleonomic capacity, a state in which the afflicted individual must access conditions outside the range of voluntary action in order to get well. Parsons's perspective emphasizes that health should be seen as an "interaction medium," one in which expectations exist that individuals will manifest a determinable level of health as defined by the relevant community. Note that this perspective integrates the role that medicine plays by treating institutional forces as just one part of the community in which social control is exerted. The interaction medium of health, however, is stressed since it provides the basis for the institutionalization of the sick and the therapeutic roles (Parsons 1978b).

Following Parsons, the term *sexual dysfunction* covers a class of impairments related to sexual health.[3] If sexual activity is a form of social action, then sexual health and sexual dysfunction are integral parts of the interactive medium. Since sexual activity is generally considered private behavior, the social control of sexual dysfunction is exerted primarily through the forms of sexual expression (see chap. 3 above). However, increased awareness of sexual health issues is now more common owing to the release of Viagra. Medical professionals are now playing a more active role in defining sexual health and dysfunction. This increased politicization of sexual health means that basic information about the dimensions of sexual dysfunction is increasingly essential. In this chapter, we adopt a *social epidemiological* approach to sexual dysfunction, investigating the effect of social conditions on the occurrence of these problems. The key result of this research is to highlight the differential effects of sexual expression and experience on sexual health. Within this framework, master statuses serve as indicators that capture important features of sexual expression. We also identify important life events related to the production of sexual dysfunction. This approach allows us to identify structural situations, which tend to be concentrated within particular social groups, that make people more vulnerable to these problems.

10.1 The Epidemiology of Sexual Dysfunctions

Sexual dysfunctions are characterized by disturbances in sexual desire and in the psychophysiological changes associated with the sexual response cycle in men and women (APA 1994 [DSM-IV]). Despite increasing demand for clinical services and the potential effect of these disorders on interpersonal relationships and quality of life (Morokoff and Gillilland 1993; Fugl-Meyer et al. 1997), epidemiological data are relatively scant. On the basis of the few available community studies, it appears that sexual dysfunctions are highly prevalent in both sexes, occurring in 10–52 percent of men and 25–63 percent of women (Frank, Anderson, and Rubinstein 1978; Rosen et al. 1993; Spector and Carey 1990). Data from the Massachusetts Male Aging Study (MMAS) (Feldman et al. 1994) showed that about 35 percent of men aged forty to seventy had moderate to complete erectile dysfunction, which was strongly related to age, health status, and emotional well-being. Erectile dysfunction has been described as an important public health problem by an NIH Consensus Development Panel on Impotence (1993), which identified an urgent need for population-based data concerning the prevalence, determinants, and consequences of this disorder. Even less is known about the epidemiology of female sexual dysfunction.

Professional and public interest in sexual dysfunction has recently been sparked by developments in several areas. First, major advances have occurred in our understanding of the neurovascular mechanisms of sexual response in men and women (Rajfer et al. 1992; Burnett 1995; Park et al. 1997). Several new classes of drugs have been identified that offer significant therapeutic potential for the treatment of male erectile disorder (Boolell, Gepi-Attee, and Allen 1996; Heaton et al. 1995; Morales et al. 1995), while other agents have been proposed for sexual desire and orgasm disorders (Rosen and Ashton 1993; Segraves et al. 1993). Should these drugs become available, the number of patients seeking professional help for these problems could increase dramatically. Epidemiological data would be of obvious value in developing appropriate service delivery and resource allocation models. Additionally, changing cultural attitudes and demographic shifts in the population have highlighted the pervasiveness of sexual concerns in all ethnic and age groups.

The present study addresses these issues by analyzing data on sexual dysfunction from the National Health and Social Life Survey (NHSLS). Sampling, data collection, and response analysis were all conducted under highly controlled conditions. This unique data source provides extensive information on key aspects of sexual behavior, including sexual problems and dysfunction, health and lifestyle variables, and sociocultural predictors. Prior analyses of sexual dysfunction, utilizing NHSLS data, are limited, presenting basic prevalence rates across demographic characteristics and indicators of overall health and well-being (*SOS*, 368–74). The present study, in contrast, employs multivariate techniques in order to estimate the relative risk of sexual dysfunction for each demographic characteristic as well as for key risk factors. Our study proceeds as follows. First, we establish prevalence and relative risk rates by demographic characteristics for major symptoms associated with sexual dysfunction. Second, we model risk factors, including health and lifestyle, social status, and sexual experience variables, in order to investigate categories and predictors of sexual dysfunction. A latent class analysis is used to identify patterns of symptom reporting, indicating relations between symptoms and broader categories of sexual dysfunction as well as associations with specific predictors. Finally, we analyze how the experience of sexual dysfunction is linked to specific, quality-of-life outcomes, such as personal and relationship satisfaction.

10.2 Methods

Sexual dysfunction was indexed in the NHSLS according to seven dichotomous response items, each measuring presence or absence of a critical symptom or problem during the past twelve months (*SOS*, 660). Response items included (1) lacking desire for sex; (2) arousal difficulties (i.e., erection problems [men] and lubrication difficulties [women]); (3) inability to achieve climax or ejaculation; (4) anxiety about sexual performance; (5) climaxing or ejaculating too rapidly; (6) physical pain during intercourse; and (7) not finding sex pleasurable. Information about the last three items was obtained only from respondents who were sexually active during the prior twelve-month period. Taken together, these items cover the major problem areas addressed in the DSM-IV classification of sexual dysfunction. Self-reports about sexual dysfunction, especially in face-to-face interviews, are subject to underreporting biases arising from personal concerns about social stigmatization. Moreover, there may be systematic biases in underreporting related to particular attributes of the respondents. For example, older or less-educated women or younger Hispanic men might be more reluctant to report sexual problems (see chap. 5 above). Lack of privacy during interviews could also result in underreporting. However, analyses (not reported here) indicate that reporting bias that can be attributed to lack of privacy is negligible in the NHSLS data (*SOS,* 564–70).

A latent class analysis (LCA) was used to evaluate the syndromal clustering of individual sexual symptoms. LCA is a statistical method well suited for grouping categorical data into latent classes (Clogg 1995; McCutcheon 1987). It is well established in sociological research (Birkelund, Goodman, and Rose 1996; Browning and Laumann 1997; Hogan, Eggebeen, and Clogg 1993; Silverstein and Bengston 1997), but it also has a number of medical applications, such as evaluating diagnostic systems (e.g., Uebersax and Grove 1990; Young 1983; Young, Tanner, and Meltzer 1982) and generating epidemiological estimates using symptom data (Eaton et al. 1989; Kohlman and Formann 1997). LCA tests whether a latent variable, specified as a set of mutually exclusive classes, accounts for observed covariation among manifest, categorical variables. A more detailed discussion of this methodology is presented in appendix 10.A. Since diagnostic criteria for sexual dysfunctions involve a complex of symptoms, we used LCA to group symptoms into categories. These categories, then, represent a typology of sexual dysfunctions found in the U.S. population, indicating both prevalence and symptomatology.

We analyzed only those respondents reporting at least one sex partner in the prior twelve-month period. Respondents who were sexually inactive during this period were excluded. This exclusion may limit our results because excluded respondents may have avoided sex because of sexual problems. However, this exclusion was necessary to ensure that each respondent provide information about all the symptom items since information about three items was requested only of sexually active respondents. In all, 139 men and 238 women were excluded on this basis. Excluded men were more likely to be single and have lower levels of education. We expect that this will bias our estimates of the prevalence of sexual dysfunction downward since sexually inactive men generally reported higher rates of symptoms. Excluded women tended to be older and single. The exclusion of these women is likely to bias our estimates of the prevalence of sexual dysfunction upward given that these women tended to report lower rates.

Our analyses utilized logistic and multinomial logistic regression. In order to assess the prevalence of symptoms across demographic characteristics, we performed logistic regressions for each symptom (for an introduction to logistic regression, see the appendix to the introduction). This operation produced adjusted odds ratios, which indicate the odds that members of a given social group (e.g., those who have never married) reported the symptom relative to a reference group (e.g., those who are currently married) while controlling for other demographic characteristics. Demographic characteristics included respondent's age, marital status, educational attainment level, and race/ethnicity. Next, while controlling for these characteristics, we estimated adjusted odds ratios, using multinomial logistic regressions for three sets of risk factors, each modeled separately in a nonnested manner. Risk factors associated with health and lifestyle included alcohol consumption, prior contraction of sexually transmitted diseases (STDs), presence of urinary tract symptoms, circumcision, health status, and experience of emotional or stress problems. Social status variables included change in income level and normative orientation, indexed by how liberal or conservative respondents' attitudes were toward sex. Risk factors associated with sexual experience included number of lifetime sex partners, frequency of partnered sex, how often the respondent thinks about sex, frequency of masturbation, same-gender sexual contact, and experience with potentially traumatic events, such as adult-child sexual contact, forced sexual contact, sexual harassment, and abortion. Finally, we conducted a set of logistic regressions that used the categories of sexual dysfunction as predictor variables. These models measured the association between the experience of dysfunction and quality-of-life concomitants, which included personal and relationship satisfaction. We stress that concomitant outcomes cannot be causally linked to sexual dysfunction. LCAs were performed using maximum-likelihood latent structure analysis (MLLSA) (Clogg 1995). All logistic regressions utilized *Stata,* version 5.0 (1997). Information regarding variable construction is presented in appendix 10.B.

10.3 Results

Prevalence of Sexual Problems

Use of the NHSLS data allows us to calculate national prevalence estimates of sexual problems for adult women and men. While NHSLS data on critical symptoms do not constitute a clinical definition of sexual dysfunction, they do provide important information about the extent and differential distribution of sexual dysfunction among the U.S. population. Table 10.1 analyzes the prevalence of sexual problems across selected demographic characteristics. For women, the prevalence of sexual problems tends to decrease with increasing age, except for those who report trouble lubricating. Older women (aged fifty to fifty-nine) are roughly half as likely to report nonpleasurable sex (95 percent confidence interval [CI]: 0.3–0.8) and sexual anxiety (95 percent CI: 0.2–0.8) and only a third as likely to report pain during sex (95 percent CI: 0.2–0.6), compared to the youngest age cohort. For men, increasing age is positively associated with experience of erection problems and lacking desire for sex. The oldest cohort of men (aged fifty to fifty-nine) is more than three times as likely to experience erection problems (95 percent CI: 1.8–7.0) and to report low desire

Table 10.1 Prevalence of Dysfunction Items by Demographic Characteristics (Adjusted Odds Ratios)

Predictors	Lacked Interest in Sex			Unable to Orgasm			Experienced Pain during Sex			Sex Not Pleasurable			Anxious about Performance			Trouble Lubricating		
	N	%	Adjusted OR (95% CI)	N	%	Adjusted OR (95% CI)	N	%	Adjusted OR (95% CI)	N	%	Adjusted OR (95% CI)	N	%	Adjusted OR (95% CI)	N	%	Adjusted OR (95% CI)
Female respondents	1,486			1,477			1,479			1,479			1,482			1,475		
Age:																		
18–29	154	32	Referent	125	26	Referent	99	21	Referent	129	27	Referent	78	16	Referent	92	19	Referent
30–39	161	32	1.05 (.78–1.41)	140	28	1.25 (.91–1.72)	73	15	.63* (.44–.91)	118	24	.80 (.58–1.11)	57	11	.71 (.47–1.08)	91	18	.84 (.59–1.20)
40–49	101	30	1.02 (.73–1.44)	72	22	.91 (.63–1.32)	42	13	.55* (.36–.85)	55	17	.52* (.35–.77)	36	11	.73 (.46–1.18)	69	21	.97
50–59	53	27	.78 (.52–1.18)	43	23	.92 (.60–1.44)	16	8	.31* (.17–.56)	33	17	.53* (.33–.84)	12	6	.40* (.20–.79)	52	27	1.40 (.91–2.15)
Marital status:																		
Currently married	264	29	Referent	199	22	Referent	132	14	Referent	188	21	Referent	86	9	Referent	196	22	Referent
Never married	108	35	1.15 (.83–1.59)	92	30	1.45* (1.03–2.05)	53	17	.85 (.56–1.27)	79	25	.92 (.65–131)	55	18	1.57* (1.02–2.42)	54	17	.82 (.56–1.21)
Divorced/ separated/ widowed	91	34	1.25 (.93–1.69)	85	32	1.68* (1.23–2.29)	43	16	1.14 (.77–1.68)	66	25	1.24 (.89–1.74)	39	15	1.59* (1.05–2.41)	51	19	.93 (.66–1.33)
Education:																		
Less than high school	85	42	Referent	67	34	Referent	36	18	Referent	57	28	Referent	37	18	Referent	31	15	Referent
High school graduate	149	33	.70* (.49–1.00)	129	29	.79 (.55–1.15)	77	17	.95 (.61–1.51)	102	23	.81 (.55–1.20)	54	12	.66† (.41–1.06)	91	20	1.28 (.81–2.02)
Some college	153	30	.63* (.44–.90)	122	24	.62* (.42–.90)	81	16	.85 (.54–1.34)	115	23	.78 (.52–1.15)	59	12	.57* (.35–.92)	108	21	1.45 (.92–2.30)
College graduate	80	24	.52* (.34–.78)	59	18	.47* (.30–.73)	34	10	.55* (.32–.95)	59	18	.67† (.43–1.06)	32	10	.56* (.32–.98)	72	22	1.49 (.91–2.45)

	Lacked Interest in Sex			Unable to Orgasm			Climax too Early			Sex Not Pleasurable			Anxious about Performance			Trouble Maintaining/ Achieving an Erection		
Race/ethnicity:																		
White	324	29	Referent	275	24	Referent	178	16	Referent	235	21	Referent	125	11	Referent	253	22	Referent
Black	90	44	1.67* (1.16–2.40)	64	32	1.12 (.76–1.65)	27	13	.61† (.37–1.02)	66	32	1.42† (.96–2.11)	33	16	1.18 (.71–1.95)	30	15	.63† (.40–1.02)
Hispanic	35	30	.90 (.57–1.40)	25	22	.69 (.42–1.13)	16	14	.64 (.36–1.15)	23	20	.72 (.43–1.21)	14	12	.86 (.45–1.65)	13	12	.51* (.27–.94)
Other	20	42	1.62 (.86–3.05)	16	34	1.41 (.72–2.78)	9	19	.83 (.36–1.95)	11	23	.77 (.36–1.65)	11	23	1.68 (.76–3.72)	8	17	.57 (.24–1.38)
Male respondents	1,249			1,246			1,243			1,246			1,247			1,244		
Age:																		
18–29	56	14	Referent	28	7	Referent	121	30	Referent	39	10	Referent	77	19	Referent	30	7	Referent
30–39	52	13	1.52† (.95–2.42)	28	7	1.31 (.71–2.40)	122	32	1.01 (.72–1.42)	30	8	.95 (.54–1.69)	65	17	.98 (.65–1.48)	35	9	1.46 (.84–2.57)
40–49	45	15	2.11* (1.23–3.64)	26	9	1.79† (.90–3.55)	83	28	.88 (.60–1.30)	25	9	1.04 (.54–2.01)	55	19	1.09 (.68–1.75)	31	11	1.84† (.97–3.47)
50–59	30	17	2.95* (1.60–5.44)	15	9	1.74 (.79–3.83)	55	31	.95 (.61–1.49)	10	6	.73 (.31–1.69)	25	14	.87 (.49–1.54)	31	18	3.59* (1.84–7.00)
Marital status:																		
Currently married	77	11	Referent	49	7	Referent	214	30	Referent	41	6	Referent	98	14	Referent	65	9	Referent
Never married	71	19	2.75* (1.74–4.36)	31	8	1.55 (.86–2.79)	111	29	.95 (.68–1.33)	40	11	1.80* (1.02–3.18)	78	21	1.71* (1.14–2.56)	37	10	1.73* (1.00–2.97)
Divorced/ separated/ widowed	31	18	1.69† (1.05–2.73)	15	9	1.29 (.69–2.39)	54	32	1.12 (.77–1.62)	21	13	2.27* (1.27–4.04)	45	26	2.29* (1.51–3.48)	24	14	1.61† (.96–2.71)

(continued)

Table 10.1 (continued)

Predictors	Lacked Interest in Sex			Unable to Orgasm			Climax too Early			Sex Not Pleasurable			Anxious about Performance			Trouble Maintaining/Achieving and Erection		
	N	%	Adjusted OR (95% CI)	N	%	Adjusted OR (95% CI)	N	%	Adjusted OR (95% CI)	N	%	Adjusted OR (95% CI)	N	%	Adjusted OR (95% CI)	N	%	Adjusted OR (95% CI)
Education:																		
Less than high school	30	19	Referent	18	11	Referent	61	38	Referent	22	14	Referent	37	23	Referent	21	13	Referent
High school graduate	42	12	.61† (.35–1.05)	25	7	.62 (.31–1.21)	125	35	.91 (.61–1.35)	21	6	.35* (.17–.68)	65	18	.68 (.42–1.10)	32	9	.64 (.34–1.18)
Some college	65	16	.88 (.53–1.47)	32	8	.68 (.35–1.30)	106	26	.58* (.39–.87)	39	9	.59† (.32–1.08)	77	19	.70 (.44–1.13)	43	10	.76 (.42–1.38)
College graduate	44	14	.71 (.40–1.24)	22	7	.55† (.27–1.12)	87	27	.65* (.42–1.00)	21	6	.44* (.22–.88)	41	13	.49* (.28–.83)	31	10	.66 (.35–1.26)
Race/ethnicity:																		
White	134	14	Referent	68	7	Referent	290	29	Referent	70	7	Referent	173	18	Referent	98	10	Referent
Black	27	19	1.13 (.67–1.90)	13	9	1.14 (.57–2.26)	49	34	1.14 (.75–1.72)	23	16	2.33* (1.29–4.20)	35	24	1.22 (.76–1.95)	19	13	1.21 (.67–2.17)
Hispanic	12	13	.94 (.47–1.86)	8	9	1.24 (.54–2.83)	25	27	.78 (.46–1.31)	7	8	.95 (.40–2.29)	5	5	.24* (.09–.61)	5	5	.53 (.20–1.39)
Other	10	24	2.02† (.94–4.32)	8	19	2.83* (1.24–6.50)	17	40	1.63 (.86–3.09)	4	9	1.29 (.44–3.82)	9	21	1.33 (.61–2.90)	5	12	1.17 (.44–3.12)

Source: NHSLS.

Note: Estimated ratio of odds of reporting a given symptom for members of the specified group to odds for reference group. Derived from logistic regression models performed on respondents with at least one partner during the 12-month period prior to the survey. The model includes all predictor variables as well as controls for religious affiliation and residence in rural, suburban, or urban areas. OR indicates odds ratios, CI confidence interval.

†$p \leq .10$.

*$p \leq .05$.

(95 percent CI: 1.6–5.4), compared to men aged eighteen to twenty-nine. Overall, older men are more likely to suffer from impairments of sexual response, while younger women are less likely to report pleasurable sexual experiences.

The prevalence of sexual problems also varies significantly across marital status. Premarital and postmarital (divorced, widowed, or separated) statuses are associated with elevated risk of experience of sexual problems. Unmarried women are roughly one and a half times more likely than married women to have climax problems (95 percent CI: 1.0–2.1 and 1.2–2.3, respectively) and sexual anxiety (95 percent CI: 1.0–2.4 and 1.1–2.4, respectively). Similarly, unmarried men report significantly higher rates of most symptoms of sexual dysfunction than married men. Never-married men are 2.75 times more likely to report low desire (95 percent CI: 1.7–4.4) and 1.75 times more likely to report erection problems (95 percent CI: 1.0–3.0). Formerly married men show similar contrasts with married men. Thus, married women and men clearly have a lower risk of experiencing such sexual symptoms than their unmarried counterparts.

High educational attainment is negatively associated with experience of sexual problems among both women and men. These differences are especially marked between women without high school diplomas and those with college degrees. Controlling for other demographic characteristics, female college graduates are half as likely to experience low desire (95 percent CI: 0.3–0.8), problems achieving orgasm (95 percent CI: 0.3–0.7), pain during sex (95 percent CI: 0.3–1.0), and sexual anxiety (95 percent CI: 0.3–1.0) as women with high school diplomas. In comparison to men without high school diplomas, male college graduates are only two-thirds as likely to report climaxing too early (95 percent CI: 0.4–1.0) and half as likely to report nonpleasurable sex (95 percent CI: 0.2–0.9) and sexual anxiety (95 percent CI: 0.3–0.8). Overall, women and men with lower educational attainment report less pleasurable sexual experience and suffer from raised levels of sexual anxiety.

The association between race/ethnicity and sexual problems is more variable. Black women tend to have higher rates of low desire and displeasure, while white women are more likely to experience pain during sex. Hispanic women, in contrast, consistently report lower rates of sexual problems. Differences between men are not as marked but generally consistent with those shown by women. Indeed, while the effects of race and ethnicity are fairly modest, minority status appears to have a consistently positive association with sexual problems for blacks and a negative association for Hispanics, across gender and type of sexual problem. Finally, in analyses not shown, we observed no significant association between religious affiliation and the differential likelihood of reporting sexual dysfunctions.

Latent Class Analysis

The results of LCA, discussed in appendix 10.A, allow for analyzing risk factors and quality-of-life concomitants in relation to categories of sexual dysfunction rather than individual symptoms. Analyses presented in tables 10.2 and 10.3 below utilize the results of LCA instead of individual symptoms. These results indicate that the clustering of symptoms can be represented by four categories for women as well as for men. LCA also estimates the size of each class as a proportion of the total sample, a result corresponding to the prevalence of categories of sexual dysfunction in the U.S. population. Finally, LCA identifies each class's symptomatology, indicating the likelihood that respondents in that class will exhibit a given symptom, thus providing researchers with information about what elements characterize each category. Although not equivalent to clinical diagnosis, this approach offers a statistical representation of sexual dysfunction.

For women, the four categories identified by LCA roughly correspond to major disorders of sexual dysfunction as outlined by DSM-IV. These include an unaffected group (58 percent prevalence), a low-desire category (22 percent prevalence), a category for arousal problems (14 percent prevalence), and a group experiencing pain during sex (7 percent prevalence). Similarly, a large proportion of men (70 percent prevalence) are unaffected. The remaining categories consist of problems with premature ejaculation (21 percent prevalence), erectile dysfunction (5 percent prevalence), and low desire (5 percent). Overall, the results of LCA show that the total prevalence of sexual dysfunction is higher for women than for men (43 percent vs. 31 percent).

Risk Factors

Table 10.2 presents multinomial logistic regressions on categories of sexual dysfunction. Adjusted odds ratios indicate the relative risk of experiencing a given category of sexual dysfunction versus reporting no problems for each risk factor, while controlling for other characteristics. With regard to health and lifestyle risk factors, women and men who experience emotional or stress-related problems are more likely to be in all the categories of sexual dysfunction. Having these problems significantly increases the odds of low desire (odds ratio 2.7 for women and 3.2 for men) and arousal/ erectile disorder (odd ratio 4.7 for women and 3.6 for men). In contrast, health problems affect women and men differently. Men with poor health have elevated risk for all categories of sexual dysfunction, whereas this factor is associated only with pain during sex for women. The presence of urinary tract symptoms appears to affect sexual function only (e.g.,

Table 10.2 Latent Classes of Sexual Dysfunction by Risk Factors (Adjusted Odds Ratios [95% CI])

Predictors	Low Desire	Arousal Disorder	Sexual Pain
Female respondents			
Health/lifestyle (*N*) = 1,381):			
Drinks alcohol daily	.46	.87	.58
	(.15–1.39)	(.24–3.21)	(.07–4.66)
STD ever	1.44*	1.45†	1.23
	(1.02–2.03)	(.95–2.23)	(.65–2.33)
Urinary tract symptom	1.19	4.02*	7.61*
	(.89–1.59)	(2.75–5.89)	(4.06–14.26)
Poor/fair health	1.44†	1.61†	3.35*
	(.94–2.20)	(.94–2.73)	(1.70–6.63)
Emotional problems/stress	2.70*	4.65*	1.82*
	(2.04–3.58)	(3.22–6.71)	(1.05–3.13)
Social status (*N*) = 1,460):			
Household income (1988–91):			
1%–20% increase	Referent	Referent	Referent
0%–20% decrease	1.12	.88	1.02
	(.84–1.51)	(.60–1.30)	(.57–1.83)
> 20% decrease	1.66*	1.58†	2.22*
	(1.12–2.47)	(.99–2.54)	(1.13–4.36)
Liberal attitudes about sex	1.25	1.36†	.83
	(.95–1.66)	(.96–1.94)	(.48–1.43)
Sexual experience (*N*) = 1,248):			
5 or more lifetime partners	.98	1.29	1.25
	(.68–1.41)	(.84–1.98)	(.66–2.36)
Sex frequency ≤ monthly	2.29*	2.28*	.94
	(1.57–3.32)	(1.43–3.63)	(.41–2.12)
Thinks about sex < weekly	2.37*	1.47†	1.35
	(1.74–3.25)	(.98–2.21)	(.73–2.48)
Masturbation ≥ monthly	1.10	1.41	1.36
	(.75–1.60)	(.90–2.20)	(.71–2.58)
Any same-sex activity ever	.93	.47	1.16
	(.43–2.01)	(.17–1.33)	(.35–3.81)
Had an abortion ever	1.34	1.22	1.01
	(.91–1.97)	(.77–1.92)	(.51–2.01)
Sexually harassed ever	1.17	1.44†	1.64†
	(.85–1.61)	(.98–2.12)	(.93–2.89)
Sexually touched before puberty	1.16	1.73*	1.13
	(.77–1.75)	(1.11–2.71)	(.56–2.28)
Forced by a man ever	1.45†	2.01*	1.05
	(.98–2.12)	(1.31–3.07)	(.53–2.08)

(continued)

Table 10.2 (continued)

Male respondents	Premature Ejaculation	Erectile Dysfunction	Low Desire
Health/lifestyle (N) = 1,202):			
Drinks alcohol daily	.79	1.63	2.24†
	(.36–1.69)	(.61–4.34)	(.89–5.64)
STD ever	1.10	1.29	1.05
	(.70–1.73)	(.64–2.59)	(.51–2.15)
Urinary tract symptom	1.67†	3.13*	1.68
	(.95–2.93)	(1.48–6.63)	(.71–3.97)
Poor/fair health	2.35*	2.82*	3.07*
	(1.40–3.95)	(1.26–6.33)	(1.38–6.81)
Circumcised	.87	1.30	1.64
	(.58–1.31)	(.63–2.70)	(.75–3.58)
Emotional problems/stress	2.25*	3.56*	3.20*
	(1.58–3.20)	(2.00–6.34)	(1.81–5.67)
Social status (N) = 1,232):			
Household income (1988–91)			
1%–20% increase	Referent	Referent	Referent
0%–20% decrease	1.09	1.49	1.23
	(.74–1.61)	(.79–2.82)	(.65–2.34)
> 20% decrease	1.41	2.11*	1.38
	(.87–2.29)	(1.01–4.38)	(.62–3.07)
Liberal attitudes about sex	1.72*	1.33	1.07
	(1.17–2.53)	(.72–2.46)	(.57–2.00)
Sexual experience (N) = 1,039):			
5 or more lifetime partners	.96	1.02	1.26
	(.64–1.45)	(.50–2.05)	(.61–2.60)
Sex frequency ≤ monthly	.94	1.20	1.57
	(.58–1.52)	(.55–2.63)	(.79–3.12)
Thinks about sex < weekly	.99	.77	3.63*
	(.49–2.02)	(.25–2.42)	(1.57–8.40)
Masturbation ≥ monthly	1.09	.66	1.72
	(.73–1.64)	(.33–1.33)	(.86–3.42)
Any same sex activity ever	2.11*	.72	2.51*
	(1.15–3.86)	(.23–2.33)	(1.10–5.74)
Partner had an abortion ever	1.83*	.63	1.98†
	(1.15–2.90)	(.24–1.61)	(.92–4.23)
Forced a woman ever	1.74	3.52*	.49
	(.70–4.30)	(1.03–11.98)	(.06–4.08)
Sexually harassed ever	1.43†	1.27	1.31
	(.97–2.11)	(.66–2.47)	(.69–2.48)
Sexually touched before puberty	1.80*	3.13*	2.23*
	(1.12–2.90)	(1.49–6.59)	(1.10–4.56)

Source: NHSLS.
Note: Estimated ratio of odds of membership in a given latent class for members of the specified group to odds for reference group in the default latent class of having no problems. Derived from multinomial logistic regression models performed on respondents with at least one partner during the 12-month period prior to the survey. Three models were run separately for each gender (health and lifestyle, social status, and sexual experience). Predictor variables, in addition to those listed for health, lifestyle, and sexual history, included age, marital status, education, race and ethnicity, religion, and place of residence. OR indicates odds ratios, CI confidence interval.
†$p \le .10$.
*$p \le .05$.

arousal and pain disorders for women; erectile dysfunction for men). Having an STD in the past results in increased odds of low desire for women (odds ratio 1.4) but does not appear to increase the risk of sexual dysfunction for men. Finally, moderate to high alcohol consumption and circumcision generally do not result in increased odds of experiencing sexual dysfunction.

Social status variables, which measure an individual's socioeconomic and normative position relative to other persons, assess how sociocultural position affects sexual function. Deterioration in economic position, indexed by falling household income between 1988 and 1991, is generally associated with a modest increase in risk for all categories of sexual dysfunction for women but only for erectile dysfunction for men. Women whose household income declined more than 20 percent are one and a half times more likely to experience low desire (95 percent CI: 1.1–2.5) and arousal disorder (95 percent CI: 1.0–2.5) and two times more likely to experience pain during sex (95 percent CI: 1.1–4.4), compared to those who had increases in household income. Men suffering similar economic declines are more than two times as likely to experience erectile dysfunction (95 percent CI: 1.0–4.4). Normative orientation does not appear to have any effect on sexual dysfunction for women; men with liberal sexual attitudes, in contrast, are approximately 1.75 times more likely to experience premature ejaculation (95 percent CI: 1.2–2.5).

Finally, various aspects of sexual experience result in an increased risk of sexual dysfunction. Sexual history, indicated by having more than five lifetime partners and by masturbation practices, does not increase relative risk for either women or men. Women with low sexual activity or interests, however, have elevated risk for low desire and arousal disorders. Men do not exhibit similar associations. The effect of potentially traumatic sexual events is markedly different for women and men. Women reporting any same-sex activity are not at higher risk for sexual dysfunction, while men reporting any same-sex activity are more than two times more likely to experience premature ejaculation (95 percent CI: 1.2–3.9) and low desire (95 percent CI: 1.1–5.7). A similar pattern is evident for abortion. Arousal disorder appears to be highly associated in women with the experience of sexual victimization through adult-child contact or forced sexual contact. Similarly, male victims of adult-child sexual contact are three times more likely to experience erectile dysfunction (95 percent CI: 1.5–6.6) and approximately two times more likely to experience premature ejaculation (95 percent CI: 1.2–2.9) and low desire (95 percent CI: 1.1–4.6). Finally, men who have sexually assaulted women are 3.5 times more likely to report erectile dysfunction (95 percent CI: 1.0–12-.0). Indeed, traumatic sexual acts continue to exert profound effects on sexual functioning, some effects lasting many years beyond the occurrence of the original event (for an extended discussion of these effects, see chap. 4 above).

Table 10.3 Quality-of-Life Concomitants by the Latent Classes of Sexual Dysfunction Satisfaction with Primary Partner and Happiness

Latent Class	N	Low Physical Satisfaction Adjusted OR (95% CI)	N	Low Emotional Satisfaction Adjusted OR (95% CI)	N	Low General Happiness Adjusted OR (95% CI)
Women	1,441		1,442		1,462	
No problems		Referent		Referent		Referent
Low desire		4.31*		3.52*		2.61*
		(3.04–6.11)		(2.59–4.78)		(1.76–3.88)
Arousal disorder		7.04*		4.28*		5.17*
		(4.71–10.53)		(2.96–6.20)		(3.36–7.95)
Sexual pain		2.39*		1.96*		2.62*
		(1.21–4.74)		(1.08–3.57)		(1.31–5.23)
Men	1,218		1,219		1,238	
No problems		Referent		Referent		Referent
Premature ejaculation		.79		.97		1.28
		(.47–1.32)		(.63–1.48)		(.75–2.18)
Erectile dysfunction		4.38*		2.40*		2.48*
		(2.46–7.82)		(1.33–4.33)		(1.22–5.05)
Low desire		3.14*		1.57		2.61*
		(1.74–5.69)		(.85–2.90)		(1.28–5.31)

Source: NHSLS.
Note: Estimated ratio of odds of respondents of each latent class having negative concomitant outcomes. Derived from logistic regression models performed on respondents with at least one partner during the 12-month period prior to the survey. The dependent variables are the concomitant outcomes, and the predictor variables, modeled simultaneously, include latent classes as well as controls for age, marital status, education, race and ethnicity, religion, and place of residence. OR indicates odds ratios, CI confidence interval.
*$p \leq .05$

Quality-of-Life Concomitants

The experience of sexual dysfunction is highly associated with a number of negative outcomes in personal and relationship satisfaction. Table 10.3 highlights the associations of categories of sexual dysfunction with emotional and physical satisfaction with sex partners and with general happiness. However, no causal order should be assumed since quality-of-life indicators are concomitant outcomes of sexual dysfunction. For women, all categories of sexual dysfunction—low desire, arousal disorder, pain during sex—have strong positive associations with low physical and emotional satisfaction and low happiness. Similarly, men with erectile dysfunction and low desire experience diminished quality of life, but those with premature ejaculation are not affected. In short, experience of sexual dysfunction is generally associated with poor quality of life; however, these negative outcomes appear to be more extensive and possibly more severe for women than for men.

In an examination of help-seeking behavior (the analysis is not shown here), we found that roughly 10 and 20 percent of these afflicted men and women, respectively, sought medical consultation for their sexual problems. Contrary to the actual prevalence of sexual problems, the demographic groups least likely to suffer sexual problems tend to utilize medical help more often. Women seeking medical assistance are older, married, educated, and white. For example, 25 percent of female college graduates seek help, in comparison to only 14 percent of women without high school degrees. Black (95 percent CI: 0.2–0.7) and Hispanic (95 percent CI: 0.1–0.9) women are only a third as likely to seek medical help as are white women. Although the analyses for men produced few significant differences, their pattern of help-seeking behavior were similar to women's. Thus, for both women and men, it appears that population subgroups who have a greater prevalence of sexual problems tend to seek medical assistance at lower rates net of other factors.

10.4 Comments

Demographic factors such as age are strongly predictive of sexual difficulties, particularly erectile dysfunction. Sexual problems are most common among young women and older men. Several factors may explain these differential rates. Since young women are more likely to be single, their sexual activities involve higher numbers of partners as well as periodic spells of sexual inactivity. This instability, coupled with inexperience, generates stressful sexual encounters, providing the basis for pain and anxiety. Young men are not similarly affected. Older men are more likely to have trouble achieving or maintaining an erection and to lack interest in sex. Low sexual interest and erection problems are age-dependent disorders, possibly resulting from physiological changes associated with the aging process. Indeed, our results are consistent with those generated by the MMAS, which determined that 9.6 percent of the sample suffered from complete impotence and showed a strong age association increasing from 5 to 15 percent between subject ages of forty and seventy years (Feldman et al. 1994).

Other factors such as poor health and lifestyle are differentially predictive across demographic groups. While not being married is associated with lower overall well-being, part of the higher risk of sexual dysfunction probably stems from differences in sexual lifestyles. Marriage tends to embed sexual relationships in a positive normative environment in the context of which each partner can make substantial relationship-specific investments. These investments come in the form of stable sexual experiences as well as shared management of personal lifestyles. Similarly, the elevated risks associated with low educational attainment and minority status attest to the fact that better-educated individuals are healthier and have lifestyles that are physically and emotionally less stressful. In short, the higher prevalence of sexual problems among young women, the unmarried, the less educated, and minorities indicates that factors intrinsic to the structure of sexual experience and relationships are pertinent. In order to understand the factors that predispose individuals to sexual dysfunction, we now turn our attention to the analysis of risk factors.

The NHSLS data indicate that emotional and stress-related problems among women and men generate elevated risk of experiencing sexual difficulties in all phases of the sexual response cycle. While we caution that the causal order of this relation is uncertain, these results suggest that psychosocial disturbances affect sexual functioning. This does not imply that the effect of poor health is negligible; in fact, the opposite is demonstrated since age, health problems, and urinary tract infections result in elevated risk of experiencing sexual dysfunction. Rather, both physiological status and psychological status are independent factors that affect sexual functioning.

Given the salience of emotional distress for sexual dysfunction, we examine two underlying sources of psychosocial stress: social status and sexual trauma. The NHSLS data clearly suggest that deteriorating social position has a negative effect on sexual functioning. Deterioration in economic position induces higher levels of stress, which in turn affects sexual functioning, a result more pervasive for women than for men. Future research should be directed toward mapping the social distribution of emotional distress.

With respect to possibly traumatic sexual experiences, our findings are complex, and they show distinct gender differences, but they provide clear evidence that these experiences are sources of psychosocial stress. First, we find that the effect of same-sex activity is relevant for men but not for women. The source of this difference may be rooted in the subjective meaning of these sex acts, where many male encounters involve adult-child contact. We should note that these results assess the effect of historical instances of same-sex activity, not the relation between homosexuality and sexual problems. Similarly, indicators for sexual victimization show strong effects in both genders. For women, adult-child contact or forced sex, both generally perpetrated by men, results in increased risk of experiencing arousal disorders. These results support the view that sexual traumas induce lasting psychosocial disturbances, disturbances that ultimately affect sexual functioning (Browning and Laumann 1997; see also chap. 4 above). Similarly, men who were touched sexually before puberty also are more likely to experience all categories of sexual dysfunction. In short, both female and male victims of unwanted sexual contact exhibit long-term changes in sexual functioning.

While the causal relation between quality-of-life concomitants and sexual dysfunction also remains to be investigated, the strong associations observed in the NHSLS data suggest that sexual dysfunction is a largely uninvestigated yet significant public health problem. We should note, however, that 21 percent of men experience premature ejaculation, a type of sexual dysfunction that is not associated with decreases in quality of life. Consequently, while 31 percent of men experience some form of sexual dysfunction, only 10 percent of men are afflicted with a type of sexual dysfunction that is associated with negative concomitants. Recent advances in therapy for erectile dysfunction may increase quality of life for some men. However, since low well-being is strongly associated with female sexual problems, researchers should focus on identifying the consequences of these problems as well as developing appropriate therapies. Given the low rates of medical utilization among the affected population, service delivery efforts should be augmented to target high-risk populations.

10.5 Conclusion

This report provides the first population-based assessment of sexual dysfunction in the half century since Kinsey (Kinsey, Pomeroy, and Martin 1948; Kinsey et al. 1953; Gebhard and Johnson 1979). The results from the NHSLS indicate that sexual problems are widespread in society— roughly 43 percent of women and 31 percent of men report confronting such problems in the past year, their prevalence influenced by both health-related and psychosocial factors. The role of the latter implies that stress-inducing events, the result of either individual or social sources, can affect sexual functioning in both men and women. Differing patterns of sexual dysfunction were observed across gender, age, and demographic groups, highlighting the need for further research on etiological mechanisms. With the strong association between sexual dysfunction and impaired quality of life, this problem warrants recognition as a significant public health concern.

Appendix 10A Latent Class Analysis

This appendix provides a brief overview of LCA, its application to NHSLS symptom data, and the results of our analysis. Our information regarding LCA is abridged and focuses on its applicability to sexual dysfunctions. For an in-depth description of latent class models, see Clogg (1995) or McCutcheon (1987).

The Latent Class Model

The latent class model (LCM) is a statistical method that tests whether a set of mutually exclusive latent classes accounts for observed association in a cross-classification of manifest, categorical variables. A central assumption in the LCM is *local independence.* In short, this assumption means that a *T*-class solution should explain all the associations between the manifest variables, making them statistically independent of one another. Let the variables *A, B, . . . , E* denote observed, categorical variables that take the values *i, j, . . . , m,* respectively, and let the variable *X* denote a *T*-class latent variable. The general form of the latent class model states:

$$\prod{}_{ij...mt}^{AB...EX} = \prod{}_{it}^{\bar{A}X} x \ \prod{}_{jt}^{\bar{B}X} x \ ... \ x \ \prod{}_{mt}^{\bar{E}X} \ x \ \prod{}_{t}^{X},$$

where the left term indicates the probability that a randomly selected case will be located in the *i, j, . . . , m* cell for the *t*th latent class. The final term indicates the probability that an individual will be in class *t* of latent variable *X.* And the remaining terms denote the probabilities that an individual in class *t* of latent variable *X* will be located at level *i, j, . . . , m* of variables *A, B, . . . , E,* respectively (McCutcheon 1987).

A number of researchers have noted the utility of LCA in medical diagnosis. Applications of LCA have focused on rater agreement on diagnostic criteria (Uebersax and Grove 1990; Young 1983; Young et al. 1982), validation of diagnostic indicators (Clogg 1995; Rindskopf and Rindskopf 1985), and the generation of epidemiological estimates using symptom data (Eaton et al. 1989; Kohlman and Formann 1997).

Results of LCA

Table 10A.1 shows latent class and conditional probabilities for the best-fitting models, which, respectively, indicate the prevalence of a category of sexual dysfunction and the likelihood that a class member will exhibit a given symptom.

The procedures used to generate our final latent class models consisted of three stages: (1) selection and cross-classification of manifest variables; (2) generation of best-fitting models; and (3) assignment of individual cases to latent classes. For both women and men, we used six manifest, dichotomous variables, which generated a corresponding cross-classification table with (2^6 =) 64 cells. The mean frequency of women per cell is 23.2, of men 19.7. For each sex, we excluded one symptom variable: orgasm too early for women and pain with sex for men. This is justified on the basis of partly theoretical and partly empirical grounds. Both these symptoms are the least prevalent for the respective gender and are not considered to be critical symptoms of sexual dysfunction. Moreover, if we included these

Table 10A.1 Latent Classes and Conditional Probabilities of Sexual Dysfunction

Women	No Problems	Low Desire	Arousal Disorder	Sexual Pain
Latent class probability	.58	.22	.14	.07
Conditional probabilities of symptoms:				
Lacked interest	.04	.74	.83	.19
Unable to orgasm	.05	.49	.84	.04
Pain during sex	.03	.07	.56	.63
Sex not pleasurable	.01	.38	.80	.36
Anxious about performance	.04	.12	.40	.29
Trouble lubricating	.08	.16	.63	.50

Men	No Problems	Premature Ejaculation	Erectile Dysfunction	Low Desire
Latent class probability	.70	.21	.05	.05
Conditional probabilities of symptoms:				
Lacked interest	.04	.16	.64	1.00
Unable to orgasm	.00	.10	.71	.37
Climax too early	.16	.68	.60	.38
Sex not pleasurable	.00	.17	.51	.41
Anxious about performance	.03	.49	.75	.31
Trouble maintaining erection	.01	.24	.97	.00

Source: NHSLS.
Note: LCA excluded the climax-too-early item for women and the pain item for men in order to avoid sparse data problems.

variables in our analysis, it would have dropped our mean frequency per cell counts to 11.6 for women and 9.8 for men. Using all seven symptoms caused a number of cells with a frequency of 0, thus generating sparse-data problems in our analysis. One important implication of this strategy is that women and men are not completely comparable since they match on only five of the six indicators.

Next, we generated a series of models for women and men. Typically, goodness-of-fit tests utilize degrees-of-freedom calculations that are reclaimed when conditional probabilities are found to be zero or one (McCutcheon 1987; Birkelund, Goodman, and Rose 1996). However, while this is a convenient strategy, it is not, strictly speaking, correct (Heinen 1996). Instead, we performed goodness-of-fit tests that did not reclaim degrees of freedom (Yamaguchi 1998). As shown in table 10A.2, the best-fitting model for women was the four-class model. Although the five-class model misallocated fewer cases (2.6 vs. 3.4 percent), it is not as parsimonious, so we decided to go with the four-class model. The best-fitting model for men was also a four-class solution. Here, the five-class solution did

Table 10A.2 Fit Statistics for Latent Class Models of Female Dysfunction

Number of Latent Classes	Likelihood Ratio χ^2	df	p-value	Index of Dissimilarity
One-class model	1,256.44			
Two-class model	145.79	50	.000	.079
Three-class model	92.23	43	.000	.059
Four-class model	45.76	36	.128	.034
Five-class model	34.89	29	.208	.026
Four vs. five	10.87	7	.144	.008

Table 10A.3 Fit Statistics for Latent Class Models of Male Dysfunction

Number of Latent Classes	Likelihood Ratio χ^2	df	p-value	Index of Dissimilarity
One-class model	771.36			
Two-class model	114.17	50	.000	.066
Three-class model	76.42	43	.001	.045
Four-class model	42.09	36	.224	.032
Five-class model	31.53	29	.341	.032
Four vs. five	10.57	7	.159	.000

not have any advantages over the four class, and the latter was the most parsimonious model. Table 10A.3 shows these results. Finally, in assigning individual cases to the latent classes, the procedure correctly allocated 84.8 percent of the women and 87.1 percent of the men.

Appendix 10B Description of Variables

The variables used in this chapter were constructed using answers provided by respondents to the questions presented in this appendix. For further information about the questionnaire, see *SOS*.

Demographic Characteristics

Age.   We grouped age into ten-year intervals, except for the youngest group, which was expanded to include respondents under twenty.

Marital Status.   We grouped respondents who were, at the time of the survey, divorced, separated from their spouse, or widowed.

Education.   "What was the highest grade or year of schooling you completed?" (*SOS,* 609). The possible answers include: "8th grade or less," "some high school," "finished high school or equivalent," "vocational/ trade/business school," "some college or 2-year degree," "finished college, 4 to 5-year degree," "master's degree or equivalent," and "other advanced degree." We collapsed "8th grade or less" with "some high school" and "vocational/trade/business school" with "some college or 2-year degree" and combined all respondents with at least a four-year college degree.

Race/Ethnicity. Respondents who identified themselves as Hispanic were coded with this ethnicity rather than with a racial category. Asian/Pacific Islanders, native Alaskans/Native Americans, and others were grouped into a single category called *other.*

Religion. The *primary* components of our religious classification are as follows. Mainline Protestants consist of Methodists, Presbyterians, Lutherans, and Episcopalians. Conservative Protestants include Baptists, Pentecostals, and a number of smaller denominations. Other includes Jews, the Greek Orthodox, Muslims, Hindus, other Eastern religions, small Protestant groups, and other religions.

Stress Factors

Drinks Alcohol Daily. "During the past 12 months, about how regularly did you drink alcoholic beverages?" (*SOS,* 660). Possible responses include "daily," "several times a week," "several times a month," "once a month or less," and "not at all." We contrasted those answering "daily" against all the other categories.

STD Ever. "There are several diseases or infections that can be transmitted during sex. These are sometimes called venereal diseases or VD. We will be using the term *sexually transmitted diseases* or STD's to refer to them. . . . As I read each STD, tell me whether you have *ever* been told by a doctor that you had it" (yes/no) (*SOS,* 662). If respondents answered yes to any of the following diseases, they were coded as having an STD ever: gonorrhea, syphilis, herpes, chlamydia, genital warts, hepatitis, AIDS/ HIV, pelvic inflammatory disease (women only), nongonococcal urethritis (men only), and any other STD.

Urinary Tract Symptom. "During the past 12 months, have you ever experienced any of the following symptoms" (yes/no) (*SOS,* 663). If respondents answered "yes" to any of the following: painful or difficult urination, painful intercourse, lesions or sores in the genital area, intense chronic itching of genital area, and vaginal discharge (women only), they were coded as having urinary tract symptoms.

Poor/Fair Health. "In general, would you say your health is . . . " (*SOS,* 659). Possible responses include "excellent," "good," "fair," and "poor." We created a dichotomous variable, grouping "fair" with "poor" and "excellent" with "good."

Circumcised. "Are you circumcised?" (yes/no) (*SOS,* 659).

Emotional Problems/Stress. This dichotomous variable was constructed from two questions. "During the past 12 months, how much of the time have emotional problems interfered with your sexual activities?" and, "During the past 12 months, how much of the time has stress or pressures in your life interfered with your sexual activities?" (*SOS,* 660). Possible answers for both questions include "all of the time," "most of the time," "some of the time," "a little of the time," and "none of the time." If respondents answered "all of time," "most of the time," or "some of the time" to either question, we indicated that the respondent suffered from emotional or stress-related problems.

Household Income. "Compare your *total household income* from all sources in 1991 with your *total household income* four years ago (in 1988)" (*SOS,* 614). Possible answers include "risen a lot (e.g. by 20% or more)," "risen somewhat," "remained about the same," "fallen somewhat," and "fallen a lot (e.g. by 20% or more)." We grouped "risen a lot (e.g. by 20% or more)" with "risen somewhat" and "remained about the same" with "fallen somewhat."

Liberal Attitudes toward Sex. Respondents were asked whether they "strongly agree," "agree," "disagree," or "strongly disagree" with three statements: "Any kind of sexual activity between adults is okay as long as both persons freely agree to it," "I would not have sex with someone unless I was in love with them," and "My religious beliefs have shaped and guided my sexual behavior" (*SOS,* 667). The responses of to the first question were reversed, and then all three were averaged. We then dichotomized the average response.

Five or More Lifetime Partners. For the variable PART18, see *SOS*.

Sex Frequency Less than Monthly. "During the last 12 months, . . . about how often did you have sex?" (*SOS,* 625). Responses include "not at all," "once or twice," "about once a month," "two or three times a month," "about once a week," "two or three times a week," and "four or more times a week." We dichotomized this variable by grouping "not at all" and "once or twice" with "about once a month" and then collapsed the remaining categories.

Thinks about Sex Less Than Weekly. "On the average, how often do you think about sex?" (*SOS,* 647). Possible answers include "I never think about sex," "less than once a month," "one to a few times a month," "one to a few times a week," "every day," and "several times a day." We grouped "I never think about sex," "less than once a month," and "one to a few times a month" and collapsed the remaining categories.

Masturbation More Than Monthly. "On average, in the past 12 months how often did you masturbate?" (*SOS,* 672). Possible answers include "more than once a day," "every day," "several times a week," "once a week," "2–3 times a month," "once a month," "every other month," "3–5 times a year," "1–2 times a year," and "0 times this year." We grouped "every other month," "3–5 times a year," "1–2 times a year," and "0 times this year" and then collapsed the remaining categories.

Any Same-Sex Activity Ever. Male respondents were considered ever to have experienced same-sex activity if they answered yes to any of the following questions: "Have you ever performed oral sex on a man?" "Has a man ever performed oral sex on you?" "Have you ever had anal intercourse with a man where you were the inserting partner?" "Have you ever had anal intercourse with a man where you were the receiving partner?" and, "Have you ever done anything else sexual with a man?" (yes/no) (*SOS,* 676). Female respondents were considered ever to have experienced same-sex activity if they answered yes to any of the following questions: "Have you ever performed oral sex on another woman?" "Has another woman ever performed oral sex on you?" and, "Have you ever done anything else sexual with another woman?" (yes/no) (*SOS,* 674).

Abortion Ever. Women were asked, "Have you ever had an abortion?" (yes/no) (*SOS,* 674). Men were asked, "Have you ever had a sexual partner who became pregnant by you and ended that pregnancy by an abortion?" (yes/no) (*SOS,* 676).

Sexually Harassed Ever. "Sometimes at work, women (men) find themselves the object of sexual advances, propositions, or unwanted sexual discussions from co-workers or supervisors. The advances sometimes involve physical contact and sometimes just involve sexual conversations. Has this ever happened to you?" (yes/no) (*SOS,* 675, 677).

Forced a Woman Ever.   "Have you ever forced a (another) woman to do something sexual that she did not want to do?" (yes/no) (*SOS,* 675, 674).

Forced by a Man Ever.   "Have you ever been forced by a man to do something that you did not want to do?" (yes/no) (*SOS,* 673, 676).

Sexually Touched before Puberty.   "Before you were [age of puberty or, if respondent does not know, twelve or thirteen years old] did anyone touch you sexually?" (yes/no) (*SOS,* 650).

Quality-of-life Concomitants

Low Physical Satisfaction.   "How physically pleasurable did you find your relationship with (PARTNER) to be?" (*SOS,* 629). Possible answers include "extremely," "very," "moderately," "slightly," and "not at all." We dichotomized this variable by grouping "extremely" and "very" and collapsing the remaining variables.

Low Emotional Satisfaction.   "How emotionally satisfying did you find your relationship with (PARTNER) to be?" (*SOS,* 629). Possible answers include "extremely," "very," "moderately," "slightly," and "not at all." We dichotomized this variable by grouping "extremely" and "very" and collapsing the remaining variables.

Low General Happiness.   "Generally, how happy have you been with your personal life during the past 12 months?" (*SOS,* 659). Possible answers include "extremely happy," "very happy most of the time," "generally satisfied, pleased," "sometimes fairly unhappy," and "unhappy most of the time." We grouped "sometimes fairly unhappy" with "unhappy most of the time" and collapsed the remaining categories.

Notes

This chapter is based on Lauman, Paik, and Rosen (1999). We express our appreciation of the helpful comments of George Rhodes.

1. Lin and Ensel (1989) noted the close connection between *Suicide* and current research on social stress.

2. *Teleonymy* is defined as "the capacity of an organism, or its propensity, to undertake successful goal-oriented courses of behavior" (Parsons 1978a, 68).

3. Sexual dysfunction does not constitute all possible impairments of sexual health. These sexual problems are generally problems of *performance,* not *deviance.* Performance-related problems generally distinguish between underperformance and normal function. Deviant problems are unacceptable sexual behaviors, those that violate societal definitions of appropriate sexual conduct (e.g., paraphilia). The distinction made here is analytic, although some researchers have attempted to link these concepts (e.g., Browning and Laumann 1997). Finally, there is little conceptual development of the idea of overperformance.

■

CHAPTER ELEVEN

Abortion Decisions in the United States

ROBERT T. MICHAEL

By the time the National Health and Social Life Survey (NHSLS) was conducted in 1992, the nation was completing its second decade of experience with legal abortion as mandated in *Roe v. Wade,* and the adults who were interviewed had ranged in age up to forty at the time that decision was handed down (22 January 1973). The oldest had completed or nearly completed their fertility prior to that date; the youngest experienced puberty well afterward. This survey, then, provides an interesting window onto the patterns of usage of abortion as a means of controlling fertility over the first two decades following its national legalization.

While a large literature on abortion exists, little has been written on the concerns of this chapter: a description of the pregnancy-by-pregnancy incidence of abortion; a general description of how abortions fit into the larger pattern of fertility control in the United States; an analysis of who does and who does not choose to have an abortion; and an analysis of whether those who do so are then more or less likely to do so with a subsequent pregnancy.

Because of the political sensitivity of the subject of abortion, because of the breadth of the existing literature, and particularly because there is a branch of that literature that questions the usefulness of the research strategy adopted here, this chapter indulges in a longer preamble than is usual. After some dozen pages, the chapter addresses conceptually the issue of what motivates a pregnant woman to have an abortion and proceeds to describe the personal characteristics that are associated with that choice, using a multivariate statistical model and the NHSLS data. The statistical analysis is undertaken pregnancy by pregnancy, for the woman's first three pregnancies. Since the NHSLS also asked men about the outcomes of any pregnancies for which they were responsible, the same analysis is performed, separately, on the men's data.

To summarize the findings briefly, I interpret the statistical models as revealing a substantial amount of purposive or strategic behavior, with those for whom the birth is most costly or will most likely disrupt their life plans far more likely to choose to have an abortion. The broad outlines of these patterns persist across the first three pregnancies and are found, broadly, in the reports by both the women and the men.

11.1 Background

Much of the literature on abortion addresses its ethical nature, its legal status, and, more recently, the rationale for and influence of government funding of abortions for those with low incomes. This chapter does not address any of these important issues directly. As Tribe (1990, 27) argues, much of the current debate about abortion in the United States is posed as "an insoluble conflict between two fundamental values: the right of a fetus to live and the right of a woman to determine her own fate." If this is so, neither facts nor theories about behavior are likely to influence that debate. Yet Tribe also argues that to frame the debate in these terms is "peculiar to late-twentieth-century America. Far from being inevitable outgrowths of the natural order of things, these competing values are socially constructed." For example, in the late eighteenth and early nineteenth centuries, the debates over the propriety of abortion apparently centered on the illicit sex that necessitated it as most abortions were performed on single women wishing to conceal the fact that they had been sexually active. If the current debate is understood to be political and social at its core rather than religious or ethical, then there is a role for research of the nature undertaken here.

Like other recent books on abortion, Tribe's addresses the issue of a "compromise" or a solution to the current impasse over abortion. He focuses on strategic solutions since only at the margins and in the details can any compromise or consensus be found if the issue of abortion involves "fundamental" rights that are not easily modified. Tribe's suggestions include possible limitations on abortions that might meet with acceptance, as, for instance, a limit on abortion in the third trimester, a limit on the reasons for permitting abortion, or some specifics about the amount of and conditions for government funding of abortion. Other suggestions focus on strategies that complement abortion, such as access to birth control methods or encouragement to utilize them with more consistency. In the context of this search for "compromises" that might facilitate a consensus on abortion policy, it may be of considerable value to describe, nonjudgmentally, how legal abortions are being used in the United States and what role they play in the birth control strategies utilized by different segments of the population. This is the objective of this chapter.

There are three strands of thought regarding abortion to which this chapter is closely related. These are (1) the focus on public opinion regarding abortion, (2) studies of the determinants of the choice to have an abortion, and (3) the quality of information about abortion to be obtained from survey data. I consider each in turn.

The Literature on Public Opinion about Abortion

Public opinion about abortion in the United States is characterized by two striking features. First, the nation is deeply divided over the issue. As Smith puts it, "The majority of Americans do not believe that either the woman or the fetus has an absolute right, but instead see a need to balance these competing rights" (1995, 2). Smith's General Social Survey (GSS) annually asks a random sample of Americans their opinion about abortion, and Smith characterizes the 1994 data as 38 percent prochoice, 7 percent prolife, and 55 percent holding an intermediate position (i.e., answering yes to some and no to other questions about abortion under different circumstances). Gallup survey data also track opinions and reveal that the acceptability of abortion depends largely on how far the pregnancy has advanced. For example, in a recent, typical year, 32 percent favored legal abortion under any circumstances during the first trimester, 14 percent in the second trimester, and only 9 percent in the third trimester (see Smith 1995).

The second striking feature is that there has not been a dramatic trend or shift in opinion regarding abortion since the mid-1970s. In the 1960s, there had been a notable increase in the prochoice sentiment, leading up to *Roe v. Wade,* but the several annual surveys that track opinion about abortion have consistently shown few systematic trends in the past two decades, despite all the attention the issue has received. (See Smith [1990, 1995], Rodman [1987], who summarizes the attitudes recorded in several polls and surveys up to the late 1980s, and Craig and O'Brien [1993], who track trends by social characteristics over the past two decades.) The split in opinion in our nation on the broad social policy issue of the appropriateness of abortion remains wide and divisive.

Several studies describe the characteristics of those who hold one or another opinion about abortion. Rodman concludes that "men's attitudes are more favorable to abortion" and that "Catholics are slightly less favorable toward abortion than non-Catholics, ... but the differences are small" (1987, 138). (For an intra-Catholic analysis of attitudes, see Welch, Leege, and Cavendish [1995].) Lynxwiler and Gay (1994, 77) provide an extensive review of evidence about difference of opinion by education level, urbanization, income, and occupation and find that black and white women of childbearing age do not differ in their support for legal abortion when control valuables are included (see also Walzer 1994).

The Literature on the Determinants of Abortion

The second relevant strand of the literature studies determinants of the choice to have an abortion. This literature is most closely related to the spirit of the analysis in this chapter, although one of its most important foci—evidence of the effect of abortion funding and access that differs by geographic area—is a topic that our data cannot address. (To be wholly confident about protecting the privacy of the NHSLS respondents, we adopted the procedure of eliminating any reference to the respondent's location almost immediately on completion of the interview, so we have no information on state of residence. For details and a defense of this practice, see *SOS.*) One of the early studies of this type was conducted by Leibowitz, Eisen, and Chow, who employed an economic-choice framework to examine pregnancy outcome decisions made by teenage girls in Ventura County, California, in the early 1970s. While abortion was legal in California throughout this period, attitudes toward abortion were somewhat less favorable than they are today, and the social welfare supports were substantially different. Leibowitz, Eisen, and Chow (1986, 73) found evidence that "girls who reported better high school grades were more likely to choose abortion" and that Mexican Americans were less likely to do so. Although both public funding and welfare support have changed considerably since that time, their study showed the usefulness of investigating the abortion choice within an economic choice framework. In another important early study, one using time-series data, Trussell et al. (1980) documented the fact that the ending of Medicaid funding for abortion in Ohio and Georgia was associated with a substantial decrease in the number of abortions performed in those states.

Medoff (1988), among others in the late 1980s, employed a state-level strategy to estimate price and income elasticities of the demand for abortion, controlling for a few demographic characteristics of each state. He reports a price elasticity of -0.81 and an income elasticity of 0.79, and he estimates that "forbidding all Medicaid-financed abortions would . . . have resulted in . . . a 17.5 percent drop in the 1980 abortion rate" (p. 358), pointing out that this implies about 262,000 fewer abortions that year. A more recent and more extensive study of the effect of Medicaid funding of abortion using state-level data—Blank, George, and London (1996)— reinforces Medoff's finding. Blank, George, and London suggest that "19–25% of the abortions among low-income women that are publicly funded do not take place after funding is eliminated" (p. 513). Thus, there is a growing body of evidence of price sensitivity on the part of lower-income women.

Another dimension of price—mandatory waiting periods prior to receiving an abortion—is explored by Joyce, Henshaw, and Skatrud (1997), who find that it, too, affects the rate of abortion, especially if the regulations necessitate two separate visits to the abortion provider. These authors compare abortion behavior in Mississippi before and after a mandatory waiting period became effective in 1992, controlling for the time trend by holding constant the pattern of behavior in two other states. They found a clear decline in the abortion rate in the year following the implementation of the new law, with about the same rate of decline for teenagers and adults. They also found that "the Mississippi law was associated with a substantive and statistically significant increase in abortion delay" and "a rise in the absolute number of second trimester abortions in spite of the decline in total abortions," which, they note, implies that "the law has increased the average costs per abortion in Mississippi since second trimester procedures are more expensive than first trimester abortions" (p. 657).

In a most interesting analysis of New York City Department of Health data on abortions and live births, Joyce (1988) looked at pregnancy outcomes for teenagers in New York in 1984. He found strong effects of marital status, age, previous experience of an abortion, and race: unmarried women, younger (i.e., under sixteen) women, those who had previously had an abortion, and those who had previously experienced a greater number of pregnancies (again, within the teenage years only) were more likely to have an abortion. Whites had the highest rates of abortion, followed by blacks, and the lowest rates were recorded by Puerto Ricans; the rates were also higher for those covered by Medicaid.

Another strand of literature on abortion choice is represented by Joyce and Kaestner (1996), which examines the indirect effect on choosing abortion when Medicaid coverage of prenatal and pediatric health care is extended to those whose income had previously been somewhat above the income-eligibility level for these services. Using vital statistics data for three states, South Carolina, Tennessee, and Virginia, during a time period (1986–91) when Medicaid eligibility was progressively extended to women whose income was above 50 percent but below 185 percent of their poverty threshold level, they conclude that this extended medical care coverage was associated with a 2–5 percentage point reduction in abortion for whites but no corresponding reduction for blacks.

In a thoughtful summary of recent literature on the abortion choice as it is influenced by the welfare "reforms" of the mid-1990s, Klerman (1998) concludes that "the literature does find significant effects of Medicaid funding on abortions (in the expected direction). There is some controversy about whether those effects are causal. At this point, a causal interpretation seems appropriate. Whether there is an effect on births remains an open question" (p. 129).

There is a closely related literature on the choice of abortion written by noneconomists who use different terminology and a different analytic approach.[1] It provides important insight about why women have abortions and about the magnitude of differences by race, marital status, education, and other characteristics. Stevans, Register, and Sessions (1992) use the National Longitudinal Survey of Youth (NLSY) data for three survey years, 1983–85, for their analysis of some 1,867 pregnancies and their outcomes reported by the women in that sample (thus covering the ages of about eighteen to twenty-seven). The analysis includes a wide range of covariates in a multivariate logistic model. Their findings were that those women who were more likely to abort were more educated, had greater employment experience and income, or were still in school, unmarried, not black, and living in the Northeast or West regions. Other factors, such as religion and urbanization, did not show high statistical significance.

Trent and Powell-Griner (1991) study differences in the characteristics of women who have abortions using an important and underutilized data source. They combine three vital statistics files from the National Center for Health Statistics (NCHS) for 1980 on "induced terminations of pregnancy (abortion), fetal deaths and live births." The live birth and miscarriage data exist for all fifty states, but the abortion reporting areas cover only twelve states, representing "about 25% of the total US induced abortions reported to CDC" (p. 1125). Their analysis is conducted separately for women under and over age twenty and is limited to only eight of those states plus New York City since they wanted information on a set of other variables (race, marital status, education, age, etc.) and these were, apparently, not available for the other states or New York State. This is nonetheless a very large data set including about 386,000 live births and miscarriages and 124,000 abortions for women over age twenty and about 73,000 births and miscarriages and 45,000 abortions for teenagers.

One interesting finding from Trent and Powell-Griner's multivariate loglinear model is that, while among both whites and blacks married women have much lower abortion rates than unmarried women, there is an interaction with race. For the unmarried, the abortion rate is higher for whites, but, for the married, it is higher for blacks. The differences are dramatic: the abortion rate estimated for married black women was 21 percent, for unmarried black women 55 percent, for married white women 8 percent, and for unmarried white women 64 percent.[2] They also find an interaction between race and parity: "Whites with no live births are much more likely than blacks to abort a pregnancy even after accounting for such factors as age and marital status" (1991, 1131), while, among those who have given birth one, two, or three or more times, already, blacks have a higher likelihood of abortion (both with and without controlling for other factors in the model). Education level is associated with a higher likelihood of abortion, and this relation is very strong for the zero-parity women. The abortion rate is higher for those over age thirty-five than for those twenty to twenty-five.

Trent and Powell-Griner also conduct a separate analysis for women under age twenty. For these teenagers' pregnancies, the same race–marital status interaction is found, and again the abortion rate is much higher among the unmarried who had not given birth before but not among the married or the unmarried who had previously given birth. Abortions were more likely to occur among those who had completed high school and much more likely to occur among those under age fifteen; the rate fell monotonically from age fifteen through age nineteen.

Murry (1995) used data from the 1988 National Survey of Family Growth (NSFG-1988) on African American and Hispanic women aged fifteen to twenty-one who were unmarried and sexually active. A discriminant function analysis was conducted separately for the two racial/ethnic groups. Among African American women, abortion was associated with higher educational attainment, age, and religious affiliation, among other factors; among Hispanic women, age, disclosing the pregnancy to their mother, receiving pregnancy education at home, and church attendance were factors that were associated with abortion.

Data Quality

The third focus of the relevant literature assesses the quality of survey data on abortions. An important paper in this regard is Jones and Forrest (1992), in which the reported abortions in three surveys, the NSFG, the National Survey of Young Women (NSYW), and the NLSY, are compared to Alan Guttmacher Institute (AGI) numbers estimated "from compilations of data submitted to . . . AGI by abortion providers" in certain locations. These AGI numbers—accurately described by Jones and Forrest as "widely accepted as the best available estimates of the incidence of abortion in the United States" (p. 114)—are assumed in their paper to be the benchmark against which the survey data should be compared.

For the NSFG, conducted in 1976, 1982, and 1988, the conclusion is that reported abortions constitute only 45, 48, and 35 percent, respectively, of the abortions that actually occurred. The Self-Administered Questionnaire (SAQ) used in the NSFG-1988 led to a higher rate of reported abortion and an estimated level of reporting of 71 percent, up from 39 percent in the main survey for the same women. Jones and Forrest conclude that "neither the incidence of abortion nor the trend in the number of abortions can be inferred from the [main] NSFG data" (1992, 117).

For the NSYW data on women aged fifteen to nineteen in 1976 and 1979, the conclusion again is that only 59 and 42 percent, respectively, of the actual abortions occurring in those two years among comparable women were reported. For the NLSY data on women aged fourteen to twenty-one in 1979 and covering their reported abortion behavior up through the 1986 survey, including the SAQ used in 1984, the assessment is that only 40 percent of abortions were reported (Jones and Forrest 1992, 121). A roughly similar number was reported by Mott (1983) for these women when they were aged fifteen to nineteen. Jones and Forrest's findings indicate that the reports are far less complete for unmarried women and that the percentages also differ by race: 45 percent for whites, 37 percent for blacks, and 19 percent for the small sample of Hispanics.

Jones and Forrest (1992) concluded that "the reporting of abortion is highly deficient in all of the surveys examined here" (p. 122). Largely because of that conclusion, endorsed by others (e.g., see Bachrach and Baldwin 1991), relatively few papers analyzing survey data on abortion have been published.

This then raises the question of whether is it appropriate to use the NHSLS survey data on abortion behavior. Appendix 11A addresses that issue, and, here, I summarize the points made there. A side-by-side comparison of the NHSLS and AGI abortion rates (see app. table 11A.1) shows that the NHSLS rates are substantially lower, especially for nonwhites, reflecting the discrepancy reported in Jones and Forrest (1992) for other surveys.

Consider briefly the NHSLS survey data and the AGI data separately as sources of information about abortions. In the NHSLS, questions about abortion were asked in the context of a survey that was well motivated, confidential, and focused on intimate sexual behavior. The specific question about abortion came at the end of a sequence of questions regarding every pregnancy the woman had ever had (or the partner of the male respondent had ever had). The abortion data exhibit certain patterns that one would expect to find if they are accurate. Moreover, fewer NHSLS respondents reported an abortion than reported several other socially stigmatized or undesirable sexually related behaviors and experiences, including sexual dysfunction, sexually transmitted disease, and forced sex. That fact implies, I contend, that respondents were not reluctant to report unpleasant or undesirable sexual events in the context of this survey, suggesting that the information that they supplied about abortion is not likely to be systematically biased downward.[3]

Additionally, appendix 11A points out the high rate of consistent answers about abortions in the face-to-face and self-administered portions of the NHSLS, in contrast to the higher rates found in self-administered portions of other surveys. I consider this similarity an additional indication that respondents were in fact motivated to provide our interviewers with accurate information, whether about abortion or about other aspects of their sexual behavior.

Consider the accuracy of the AGI estimates of the total number of abortions performed in the United States. The number rests on reports from many institutional sources that vary in terms of their response rates and the completeness of their answers. Some categories of respondents, such as small medical facilities, exhibit response rates of only about 50 percent, despite AGI's best efforts to obtain complete and accurate reports. The estimated total number of abortions may in fact be an overestimate since AGI attempts to compensate for these incomplete reports by using estimates from informants who probably favor abortion. Since there is no way to measure the accuracy of the AGI estimate and neither the AGI survey response rate nor its supplemental information justifies a high degree of confidence, I suggest that the AGI estimates should not be assumed to be correct. Instead, those estimates should be considered but one relatively good estimate of the number of abortions performed in the United States.

A recent example of excessive reliance on the AGI number of abortions is seen in Fu et al. (1998), which assesses the 1995 NSFG abortion reports. Fu et al. take the AGI abortion numbers to be "the abortions that actually occurred in the United States among women aged 15–44" (p. 129). They mention no reservations whatever about using these AGI numbers as the standard of comparison, despite mentioning in passing that, for years in which no direct data existed, they "derived estimates through interpolations or projection." Again, these AGI estimates may be the best we have, but I find it both troubling and unconvincing that the organization collects, interpolates, or projects these "actual" occurrences of abortions in the United States, then publishes its findings comparing its numbers to other sources of data in its own journal, and summarily rejects all survey data as not usable. Fu et al. conclude, "Underreporting of induced abortions has rendered surveys such as the NSFG virtually unusable for description of analysis of unintended pregnancy and induced abortions" (p. 132). This conclusion seems excessive to me, yet I alert the reader that others who have compared survey data to the AGI figures undoubtedly consider the data that I use in this chapter to be badly flawed.

Even if the AGI estimates of the total number of abortions were flawless, they are only counts of the number of abortions in a time period and are not linked to the characteristics of the women involved. Consequently, the AGI estimates cannot be used directly to conduct research on individual pregnancy outcomes or abortion decisions. The combined AGI–Centers for Disease Control (CDC) effort does display the distribution of abortions by women's characteristics (age, race, marital status, etc.), but the CDC distributions also rely on partial information. Thus, these estimated distributions should also be considered only one useful estimate. It is not evident why they should be assumed to be the standard against which all other estimates are to be judged, given the large portion of the nation, including the state of California, that is not included in the data on which these distributions are based. Additionally, since these AGI-CDC estimates are not derived from individual data records that also report other characteristics of the women concerned, they, too, cannot be used for more complex statistical analyses.

My conclusion is that information about abortions from survey data should not be disregarded simply because surveys imply lower rates of abortion than the AGI-CDC estimates. Surveys may underreport abortions, and caution in interpreting results based on survey data is warranted. But AGI-CDC estimates are based on an institutional survey that has poor response rates, and those response rates are perhaps biased upward by the nature of that reporting. The fact that the AGI number is a higher estimate than any other seems to be accepted by many as evidence of its superior accuracy, but that does not follow logically, and it may not be correct. The fact that surveys may logically undercount abortions does not imply that the AGI estimates are correct or that well-crafted surveys should be disregarded.

The AGI-CDC estimates may well currently be our best point estimates of abortion levels and trends in the United States. Yet they are not so flawless that discrepancies found between them and survey data should lead researchers to discard the survey data. The discrepancy should instead prompt caution in interpreting patterns found in various data sets; the discrepancies are not necessarily evidence of systematic bias in the survey data. Recognizing that no existing data set is flawless and that far more research is required before we can have great confidence in our measures of abortion seems to me to be the correct position currently. To imply that one source of data preempts others, and to hold that one source above question, seems to undercut our incentives to obtain better data.

Definitional Boundaries between Spontaneous and Induced Abortions

Another issue has to do with the interpretation of the boundary between abortion and other terminations of a pregnancy. The definitional boundary, like the demographic and economic factors that are associated with the abortion choice, needs to be explored, debated, and better understood. There is a potential difficulty distinguishing between an induced abortion and a spontaneous abortion or miscarriage. It is not generally emphasized in policy discussions about abortion that the rate of natural fetal loss through miscarriage may be quite high. In a recent survey of the clinical evidence regarding the epidemiology of spontaneous abortions, Alberman (1992) suggests that spontaneous abortions occur at quite high rates at very early gestational age, that is, "loss rates between conception and implantation of 50%," a figure based on observations in a 1973 study on preimplantation ova retrieved at hysterectomy. She notes that "more recent data from IVF [in vitro fertilization] studies support the evidence for losses of this order of magnitude." She reports that loss rates are "approximately 30% . . . between implantation and the fetal stage of pregnancy" and that, "overall, 50% of conceptions are lost and that once the pregnancy is clinically recognizable about 12% are subsequently lost" (p. 11).[4]

Alberman also notes the difficulty of measuring the rate of spontaneous abortions, commenting on the relevance of information coming from health care professionals, hospitals, and women respondents. She suggests that there are differences in reported rates of spontaneous abortion by the background of the women affected, with those who have a medical background recalling more such events than those who do not and with mothers who are planning to conceive being much more likely to recognize the loss of an early pregnancy, etc. This raises the issue of whether there is not an important margin for error in reporting what might be an abortion or a miscarriage or a stillbirth. The viability and medical condition of the fetus, the motivation of the woman, the cost and payment implications of considering the event one or another, and the common practice or perception of the medical personnel or the facility involved may result in much ambiguity or inconsistency about the matter. These differences may also help reconcile the differences reported by women and by medical institutions once that difference is interpreted as something to be investigated instead of privileging the one answer as the truth and the other as unusable.

Moreover, because the data used in many demographic or social science studies feature abortion information provided by abortion service providers and from vital statistics reports of live births, there are no miscarriages included. Consequently, we are not used to thinking of abortions as a fraction of all conceptions or about miscarriages as another outcome of conception, but these are relevant and appropriate ways of thinking of them, from many perspectives. This is an additional reason why survey data of the type reported here have considerable value. As is often the case, no single way of studying an issue wholly dominates other ways, and we benefit from viewing the issue from many different perspectives and with many different types of acceptably accurate data.

To summarize my judgment, while admitting to some personal stake in defense of the NHSLS data as well as other survey data, I have seen no reason not to proceed with my effort to analyze the NHSLS abortion data, albeit with more than the usual caution about data quality, acknowledging the challenging difficulties presented by personal reports that include the boundary definitions between induced and spontaneous abortions. I include this extensive discussion of data quality to alert the reader that other knowledgeable researchers disagree with me about the usefulness of our data and to provide some background information on the basis of which readers can make their own assessment.

Previously Reported Abortion Findings from the NHSLS

As described at length in *SOS* (sec. 12.3, pp. 455–65), there are a total of 7,309 conceptions reported by all respondents in the NHSLS, or 6,608 by those in the cross-sectional sample featured in chapter 12, and the outcomes of these conceptions were described in several ways there. I summarize here the main findings. Of all the conceptions reported by men and women in the cross-sectional sample, 10 percent ended in abortion. As stressed in *SOS,* however, many of those conceptions occurred well before 1973, when abortion became legal throughout the nation, so this overall percentage is of little interest since it combines experiences before and after *Roe v. Wade.* When the abortion rate as a percentage of conceptions is tracked by calendar year, the NHSLS data reveal a dramatic increase in that rate around 1973: only 1 or 2 percent of conceptions prior to that date ended in abortion, but after that date about 14 percent of all conceptions were aborted, as reported by both men and women.

Chapter 12 of *SOS* reported that there is a dramatic U-shaped relation between age and the incidence of abortion, with the rate far higher at younger ages and again at ages over thirty-five for women and over forty for men and much lower during the principal childbearing ages of twenty through the mid-thirties. There is, similarly, a pronounced U shape to the pattern of abortion by the number of the conception, with high rates for the first conception and particularly high rates for the fifth and sixth or more conception and much lower rates for the second, third, and fourth conceptions. Finally, *SOS* pointed out that, of the women who had had at least one abortion, 72 percent had one only, an additional 19 percent had two, 7 percent had three, 1 percent had four, and less than 1 percent had five or more; there was a similar pattern revealed in the men's reports of the partner's abortions. Thus, very few adults seem to use abortion routinely as part of their fertility control strategy. Instead, about three-quarters of those who have ever used abortion have used it only once in their lifetime. Finally, chapter 12 of *SOS* reported that the rate of abortion and the rate of miscarriage reported by the NHSLS sample are nearly the same, overall.[5]

11.2 The Decision to Have an Abortion

Probably no one sets out to have an abortion; no one becomes pregnant in order to undergo this uncomfortable, expensive, and potentially dangerous and emotionally draining procedure. Throughout the extensive literature debating the issue, one does not encounter the argument that this event is a healthy, pleasant, or attractive one that a woman might wish to experience purposely. Instead, an abortion is a corrective strategy, an action taken because it is considered less unattractive than the alternative of carrying the fetus to term. At best, an abortion solves a problem; it removes an unattractive eventuality. It is not a good thing per se.

In analyzing who is more or less likely to choose to have an abortion, I think that it is useful to distinguish two continua and to consider where along each a person lies. First, consider continuum C, which reflects the decision maker's circumstances (the decision maker may be the pregnant woman alone or the woman and her partner or some other person or set of people, including society at large). At one end, say, the left end, is the circumstance that can be described as a reaction of pleasure and joy about the pregnancy. The pregnancy may have been sought or desired, or it may not have been planned but nonetheless have been met with a positive sense of expectation about the birth of the child. At the other end of that continuum is the circumstance in which that pregnancy is a disappointment or major problem, for whatever reason. Naturally, all else equal, the further the decision maker is to the right on continuum C, the greater is the likelihood that an abortion is chosen as the preferred strategy in the event of a pregnancy.

Next, consider continuum O. It is a continuum reflecting the decision maker's opinion about abortion. At the left end of this continuum is the person who holds the opinion that an abortion is always inappropriate or that it is unethical or sinful. At the other end is the person holding the opinion that an abortion is an appropriate and useful option.

Clearly, those decision makers near the left end of either of these continua are unlikely to chose to have an abortion, while those near the right end of *both* these continua are quite likely to chose to have an abortion if a pregnancy occurs. Continuum C may be transitory, with the current circumstance playing an important role in the decision maker's location along that continuum, while continuum O may be more permanent in nature, reflecting opinions that evolve from early childhood and are relatively immutable over time. Interestingly, much of the public discourse and social policy regarding abortion in the United States involves arguments about one or the other of these continua, but usually not both in combination. The debate about opinions and attitudes regarding abortion seems isolated from discussions about the behavior that is linked with abortion. One reason for this partitioning in empirical analyses is that few data sets contain information about both opinion and behavior. The NHSLS does include both.

The Circumstances Affecting the Choice

What then are some of the characteristics of the decision makers that are likely to influence their the location along continuum C? While some decision makers may well make lifetime decisions regarding abortion, typically the decision whether to have an abortion is made in the context of each pregnancy separately, so it is important to analyze that decision conception by conception, which is feasible with the NHSLS, which asked about the outcome of each conception.

The first characteristic considered is *parity,* which identifies how many times a woman has conceived. (Throughout this discussion, I refer to the decision maker as the pregnant woman, but others may also play a decision-making role.) The first pregnancy is different from all others. It is more likely to be unplanned or unanticipated, especially if it occurs at a young age.[6] If the first pregnancy is more likely to be unplanned or unwanted, that circumstance implies location further toward the right end of continuum C and implies that the likelihood of choosing an abortion is higher for that first pregnancy.

Regarding second and subsequent pregnancies, the outcome of earlier pregnancies probably affects the abortion decision. If we are interested in predicting whether a woman will choose to end subsequent pregnancies (as distinct from understanding why she chooses to do so), prior behavior will be an important factor. The probability is lower that a second pregnancy is unintended, which implies that the likelihood of abortion will in general be lower. If the first pregnancy resulted in a live birth, the marginal cost of the second birth is lower, so, unless the woman has achieved her desired fertility level, at the second pregnancy she will be located further to the left along continuum C. Thus, the chance that the second pregnancy will be aborted is probably lower. On the other hand, if the first pregnancy ended in abortion, that fact may imply that the cost of an abortion to her is lower, and evidently she is not unwilling to have an abortion. So, wherever a woman is located along continuum C in terms of the desirability of that subsequent pregnancy, she will be expected to be more likely to choose an abortion if she has already had at least one.

Marital status is a key factor in the decision to abort a pregnancy, one that may be independent of parity. If the woman is married, it is much less likely that she is located far to the right on continuum C, where the pregnancy is wholly unwanted or unexpected and represents a major problem.[7] An unmarried noncohabiting woman, by comparison, is more likely to be located toward the right end of that continuum. While many unmarried women may desire and intend the pregnancy, the married woman typically faces lower costs or greater benefits from having the child than does the unmarried women. Thus, the married woman lies closer to the left end of continuum C and is less likely to choose abortion. We might expect the cohabiting woman to be somewhere between the married and the unmarried women in terms of the attractiveness of carrying the pregnancy to term.

A third factor is the age of the woman at conception. If she is quite young, say, under age eighteen, regardless of parity, the pregnancy is less likely to have been planned and is more likely to interfere with her schooling and her further development. So, if the pregnancy occurs at a very young age, I expect the woman to be located toward the right end of continuum C and thus to wish to end the pregnancy.[8] A woman in her twenties or thirties is more likely, all else constant, to desire the pregnancy, to have expected it, and to have the emotional, material, and social resources to provide for the child. Thus, that older woman is less likely to be located far to the right on continuum C. At older ages, say, beyond age forty, it is again increasingly likely that the pregnancy is unplanned or unwanted, and, perhaps more important, it is increasingly likely that the fetus will have some genetic defect that would cause the woman to be located further to the right on continuum C. These arguments imply a U-shaped pattern for the rate of abortion by a woman's age. That is the pattern described in our earlier work with these NHSLS data (see *SOS*, 461) and also reported in several of the studies of abortion described above.

A fourth factor affecting the abortion decision is the opportunity cost of the woman's time. As her time costs rise, the cost of bearing and rearing children rises; all else constant, this implies that a pregnant woman with a higher time cost will be located further to the right on continuum C. There is substantial evidence of a negative association between a woman's time cost and her fertility since caring for children is relatively time intensive (see, e.g., Hotz, Klerman, and Willis 1997). But there is a complication here, and all else is *not* constant. Consequently, there may be no simple relation between the woman's time value and her choice of whether to have an abortion. The complication arises because there is also much evidence to suggest that women whose time is valued more highly or who are more highly educated are more likely to use contraception and to do so more effectively, so the likelihood of a more educated woman having an unwanted pregnancy is much lower (see Michael 1973; Michael and Willis 1976; Rosenzweig and Seiver 1982).

So the argument here is that, if the pregnancy is inadvertent, it is likely that the more educated woman will face higher costs if she bears the child, be located further to the right on continuum C, and be more likely to have an abortion. However, a more educated woman is also less likely to become pregnant inadvertently, so, given that she is pregnant, she is more likely to be located further to the left on continuum C. My hypothesis is that, if the woman is very young, then, of these two factors, the former probably dominates: her pregnancy is likely to be inadvertent, the opportunity cost of her time dominates, and she is located to the right. If so, the more highly educated she is, the more likely it is that she chooses abortion because of the opportunity cost of bearing and rearing the child. At older ages, however, say from the early twenties on, the second of the two factors probably dominates, implying that, the more highly-educated she is, the more likely it is that the pregnancy was intended. The positive relation between education and abortion may wholly disappear at older ages.

With cross-sectional data of the type used here, an additional complication arises when investigating the influence of education. Many women conceive before their education is completed, and it is particularly these younger women for whom a positive relation between planned education and abortion is hypothesized. Indeed, the value of time spent in school is one of the deterrents to having a child. It would be statistically inappropriate to use the 1992 level of schooling to explain an abortion that may have occurred many years before that schooling level was attained. Of course, one might argue that the education level was fully anticipated and, in the sense of rational expectations theory, that her ultimate schooling level affected the abortion decision even before it was in fact obtained. Yet there is also evidence that an unplanned birth affects the prospects for continued education, so the causal direction of effect between abortion at one age and education level at a later age is not clear. To address this statistical problem, I use a proxy variable for the decision maker's education level, one that is not itself altered by the outcome of that pregnancy: the education level of the respondent's parents, measured as the higher grade of schooling attained by either parent if both are recorded. My expectation is that, the higher the parents' schooling level, the higher will be the opportunity cost of the birth and so the greater the likelihood of abortion if the conception occurs at a young age.

For those women who are young, say, under age eighteen, parents' schooling level is, therefore, expected to be positively associated with the probability of abortion. Beyond some age, however, that association may disappear, for either of two reasons. First, when the woman is mature and experienced, it is more likely that any pregnancy is intended or desired. Second, at an older age, after a woman has made her decisions about her own schooling and career, her parents' education level probably becomes a less accurate proxy for her own time value. To the extent that a very young woman's parents directly influence her decision about abortion, that direct influence probably declines over time as she matures and establishes greater independence from her parents. Consequently, the positive association between probability of abortion and parents' education is expected to weaken as the respondent ages. I interact parents' education level with the woman's age at pregnancy in order to test for this difference.

Finally, there is an additional important factor that affects the cost of having an abortion: the procedure's legal status. That status changed dramatically during the time period the NHSLS respondents are reporting about. If the conception occurred before 1973 and *Roe v. Wade*, the cost of having the abortion, in terms of access, risks, and violation of the law in many circumstances, was much higher. So, of course, before 1973, a woman would have been far less likely to choose to have an abortion. (As discussed above, it is unfortunate that the NHSLS cannot also allow us to include the state of residence to control for pre-1973 abortion law differences and differences in state funding of abortions for women on Medicaid.)

The Opinions Affecting the Choice

These few personal attributes of or circumstances faced by the pregnant woman or her partner may help locate the decision maker along continuum C. Consider next the factors that might locate that decision maker along continuum O, the opinion regarding abortion. It seems reasonable that those who are members of particular religious communities would be likely to have well-defined and determining opinions about abortion. Therefore, since no religious faith with which I am familiar promotes abortion and some firmly oppose it, one indicator that may predict opposition to abortion is the frequency with which the decision maker attends any religious services. Additionally, in terms of specific faiths, perhaps Catholics, fundamentalist Protestants, or those who report having been born again, compared to others, may be less likely to consider abortion acceptable or proper.

Similarly, those who grew up in an intact family may have a different opinion about abortion than those who grew up in a family structured in some other way. An intact family may have nurtured traditional family values, and these may have included a resistance to abortion. But one can anticipate an argument on the other side: an intact family many have encouraged self-determination and a commitment to training and to the work ethic, and these things may in turn have encouraged the opinion that having an abortion is a less unattractive option than having a baby that one does not want. I know of no useful theory that can enlighten us on this point, so at this point I explore the relation between family structure in youth and the decision to have an abortion empirically as a useful strategy.

Those whose mother was employed when the respondent was, say, age fourteen may have had greater opportunity to engage in sexual exploration at an early age (because they were not as carefully supervised after school) and may therefore be more likely to face an unwanted pregnancy and choose to have an abortion. It is not so clear that this factor should affect later pregnancies or first pregnancies that occur at older ages.

There may be a wholly different route through which mother's employment has an influence on the abortion decision. It may serve to demonstrate to the daughter the value of preparing for a career, thus affecting her assessment of the cost of giving birth. Of course, this should influence her resolve to avoid conceiving as well as her inclination to have an abortion if she becomes pregnant, so the effect may not be evident in this conditional choice. This argument, too, seems more relevant at an early age for the daughter and probably only for the first of her pregnancies.

Racial and ethnic differences in abortion practices have often been observed in other studies, as described briefly above, and they are expected here as well. To summarize, I expect the decision to have an abortion to be affected by the decision maker's location along two continua, one (continuum C) reflecting the current circumstances of that pregnancy in terms of its attractiveness or its potential costs, the other (continuum O) reflecting the decision maker's opinions or beliefs about the appropriateness of abortion as a means of fertility control. Factors expected to be associated with abortion choice include, for *continuum* C (circumstances, varying from conception to conception), parity (highest likelihood with the first conception), marital status (highest for those not married), age (higher at very young ages, e.g., under eighteen), parents' education level (higher if parents are highly educated, particularly if pregnancy occurs at a very young age), and legal status of abortion (higher after 1973) and, for *continuum* O (opinions, considered constant over the lifetime), religion (higher if less religious or less observant), family structure (perhaps higher if raised in a nonintact family), mother's employment (higher if living with an employed mother when young), and racial and ethnic characteristics (direction unclear). These are the main factors that are explored empirically with the NHSLS data.

There is one final matter to be considered. Unlike most other surveys, the NHSLS questionnaire was designed so that men and women were responding to as comparable a set of questions as was feasible. Men as well as women were asked about pregnancy outcomes. In this case, of course, the man was asked to report on any and all conceptions for which he was responsible. The concept was not difficult, and, for the most part, the men, like the women, appeared to be able and willing to provide answers that seem to be valid and to exhibit internal consistency. In the empirical work reported below, the men's as well as the women's answers are analyzed. Since there are clear differences between the genders in terms of the experience of pregnancy, however, all the analyses are conducted separately by gender. Most of the factors discussed here should, I think, have the same qualitative effect for the men as for the women. One difference is that the men typically have partners who are a few years younger than they themselves are, so, in the age-graded behavior, one would expect to see men of a given age reporting outcomes that are more like those reported by women two to four years younger.

11.3 Empirical Results

Prevalence

To begin the empirical inquiry, consider the prevalence of abortion in the adult population aged eighteen to fifty-nine. Including all observations, and weighting the statistic, 16.1 percent of all the women in this wide age interval report ever having had an abortion, and 11.4 percent of all the men report having had a sex partner who aborted a pregnancy for which they were responsible. Again, since many of these adults had their conceptions prior to 1973, averages by age group are more informative and are shown in table 11.1. The first two columns show the percentages of men and women who reported ever having an abortion, including in the base those who had not ever conceived. Clearly, many fewer of those who were already in their thirties by the time of *Roe v. Wade* report ever having had an abortion, as one would expect. Notice that the proportions do not vary much over the age interval from about twenty-five to forty-four, reflecting the fact that a first abortion is much more likely to occur before age twenty-five and not to occur over the subsequent twenty years, in which much childbearing does occur. For women, who typically report their first birth as having occurred at an earlier age than men do, roughly one in five has had an abortion by the late twenties, and that proportion does not

Table 11.1 Percentage Who Have Ever Had an Abortion or a Miscarriage (Men Reporting on a Partner's Pregnancy), by Age and Gender, and Including and Excluding Those Who Have Never Conceived

Age at Interview and in 1973, Respectively	Abortions				Miscarriages			
			Those with One or More Conceptions				Those with One or More Conceptions	
	All Men	All Women	Men	Women	All Men	All Women	Men	Women
18–24, --5	8	18	31	35	5	13	18	25
25–29, 6–10	14	21	29	28	10	17	20	23
30–34, 11–15	14	20	23	25	13	20	21	25
35–39, 16–20	15	20	19	23	15	24	19	27
40–44, 21–25	13	16	15	18	17	24	20	27
45–49, 26–30	9	15	10	16	16	27	19	30
50–54, 31–35	4	3	4	4	24	27	28	31
55–59, 36–40	6	5	6	6	18	28	19	30
All	11	16	17	20	13	22	21	27
N	1,511	1,921	979	1,533	1,511	1,921	979	1,533

increase thereafter. (This interpretation is only suggestive, however, since I am interpreting the cross-sectional responses as if they reflect the patterns that occur to a cohort over time, and this is not the nature of these data.)

Columns 3 and 4 in table 11.1 show the same statistic excluding those who had never conceived, so these figures are higher and do show a tendency to decline from ages around the mid-twenties on as women whose first pregnancy occurred at later ages are less likely to have an abortion. The pattern of very low abortion rates for the older cohorts, who essentially completed their fertility prior to 1973, is clearly seen.[9]

Before proceeding to a more refined investigation, it is instructive to look as well at the right-hand panel of table 11.1, which shows the reported rates of miscarriage. Columns 5 and 6 include all respondents, even those who had never conceived, so the rates of miscarriage shown there are lower than those in columns 7 and 8, which include only those who had conceived at least once. Two observations seem warranted here. First, there is no apparent age relation in the pattern for those who have conceived: about 20 percent of the men and about 27 percent of the women of each age group report that they have experienced a miscarriage. Both these facts—the absence of an age pattern and the higher rate reported by women than by men—have face validity. There is no reason to expect an abrupt change over time in the rate of miscarriage, as there is to expect a change in the abortion rate before and after 1973.[10] It is reasonable that some men were unaware that a miscarriage had taken place, especially if they were no longer involved with the woman in question by the time the pregnancy was confirmed and/or ended in miscarriage (the same may be so for abortions, of course).

Second, in the political discussion of abortion or the intentional termination of pregnancy, there is little recognition of miscarriage. As discussed above, many conceptions may end quite early in undetected miscarriages, and women may not necessarily recognize or be inclined to acknowledge that a miscarriage has taken place. It does not follow logically that one's concern about abortion should be altered by the fact of miscarriage, but it may be relevant in thinking about abortion to realize that many pregnancies end unintentionally and naturally by miscarriage. To disregard the incidence of miscarriage creates the impression that conception can have only two outcomes. It also overstates the percentage of all pregnancies that end in abortion as well as overstating the percentage that end in a live birth.

Table 11.2 shows the NHSLS pattern of abortion in greater detail. While table 11.1 above showed the lifetime experience of each person up to his or her current age, table 11.2 reports outcomes for each conception. It includes only those conceptions that occurred after 1973 and only the

Table 11.2 Abortion Rates by Conception Number, Age at Conception, and Gender, for Conceptions after 1973 (Cross-Sectional Sample Only, All Figures Based on 30 or More Observations)

Age at Conception	First Conception		Second Conception		Third Conception		Fourth Conception		Fifth or Higher Conception	
	Men	Women	Men	Women	Men	Women	Men	Women	Men	Women
<15		36								
15	40%			23						
16		30	20							
17		29		17						
18	30	19		4		11				
19		21		19						19
20	25	15	20	15	26			9		
21	22	18		13		15				
22	18	12	7	7		17	12		31	
23	19	15	3	7		11				
24	13	16	9	5		6				
25	17	17	8	5	0	18				
26	11	9		2	2	3		9		
27			9	6		0	14	11	6	18
28	10	4		6	4	6		7		
29		21	2		3	3		6		
30	13		6	6		11	0		29	14
31				8	6			19		18
32										
33	3	10	11	12			10			
34									17	5
35					10	6		6		15
36										
37										
38										
39										
40										
41+										

cross-sectional sample from the NHSLS, and it reports by gender and age at the time of the conception. The reported abortion rate is the percentage of all conceptions (including those that miscarry or result in a stillbirth) that end in abortion.

Look first at columns 1 and 2, the rates at which men and women report aborting the first pregnancy.[11] For first conceptions, table 11.2 shows a dramatic decline in the rate of abortion as the age of the respondent rises. For those whose first conception occurred before age eighteen, the abortion rate is 40 percent for men and, on average, 30 percent or more for women. For those whose first conception occurred at ages eighteen or nineteen, the abortion rate is 30 percent for men and about 20 percent for women. (Since men typically have partners who are two to four years younger than they themselves are, these gender-specific reports of abortions actually match up quite well.) For those whose first conception occurred in their mid-twenties, the rate of abortion is about 16 percent, while, for those whose first conception occurred after their mid-twenties, the rate of abortion is generally lower still, although somewhat more erratic in value. (The rate for all those whose first conception is at or over age thirty is only 6 percent for men and 8 percent for women.) In stylized manner, then, we can summarize this pattern of rates of abortion by age and gender for first conceptions as shown in table 11.3. These are dramatic age differences indeed. The argument offered above seems to be borne out by this simple tabulation: those whose first pregnancy occurs at a very young age are far more likely to abort that pregnancy, and this suggests that these first and early conceptions are disproportionately unplanned and undesired.

Columns 3 and 4 of table 11.2 above show the abortion rates for the second conception by gender and age. For men with a second conception by age twenty or twenty-two, the abortion rate remains high—20 percent—but, for those whose second conception occurs at ages twenty-three through the early thirties, the abortion rate is below 10 percent, increasing somewhat after age thirty-two or so. For women, there is also an indication of a decline in the abortion rate by age from the teen years into the

Table 11.3 Summary Rates of Abortion, First Conception (%)

Age	Men	Women
17 or younger	40	30
18 or 19	30	20
20 to 29	16	15
30 or older	6	8

early twenties, and then the rate remains well below 10 percent thereafter. These rates are typically lower than those for the first conception.

With successive pairs of columns, we see the abortion rate by age and gender for the third, fourth, and fifth and higher-order conceptions. For the higher-order conceptions, the rate generally exhibits an increase at older ages. (Since the number of cases declines at higher parities, the age ranges there are much wider in order to capture at least thirty cases in each calculation.)

Taken as a whole, table 11.2 above reveals why the pattern of abortion by age has the U shape reported in chapter 12 of *SOS* and clarifies the pattern reported in several studies that show a negative age effect if the sample is of young women but a positive age effect if the sample is of women over age twenty. At very young ages, these are first conceptions that are being aborted, and, as age at first conception increases, the likelihood of abortion falls. However, it rises again at ages over thirty-five or so, and the pregnancies being aborted here tend to be third or higher-order conceptions. The pattern shown in table 11.1 above is quite similar to that reported by Trent and Powell-Griner (1991) as described above for their two subsamples of women under and over age twenty.

The Conception-by-Conception Logistic Model

The empirical analysis of abortion choice employs a logistic regression of the form

$$P = 1/1 + e^{-X_i B_i}.$$

Each observation is the respondent's parity-specific conception, where P is a dummy variable defined as 1 if that conception ended in abortion and 0 otherwise; it is interpreted as the probability that the respondent chose to abort that conception. The covariates are the X_is, and B_i (variable X_i's coefficient in the logistic) is the estimated parameter. A positive value implies that the probability of an abortion is positively associated with that variable; the easiest way to interpret these coefficients is to convert them into the partial effect of the exogenous variable on the probability, $\delta P/\delta X$, equal to $B_i(P)(1 - P)$, usually expressed at the mean value of P.

I argued above that the circumstances surrounding the conception bear on the abortion decision, and that these circumstances differ from one conception to another for the same individual. The implication of this argument is that statistical analyses should be undertaken separately conception by conception if the interest is in understanding the abortion choice. One indication that the choice is quite different at different parities is that the rate of abortion differs quite dramatically by parity, as seen in

Table 11.4 Abortion Rate by Conception and Gender (Cross-sectional Sample Only; Weighted)

Conception Number	Men		Women	
	Rate	N	Rate	N
First	11.8	901	12.3	1,385
Second	5.7	673	6.2	1,120
Third	5.9	393	6.4	752
Fourth	10.1	212	6.8	430
Fifth or higher order	20.6	253	12.0	489

table 11.4. Many of the factors that may influence the abortion choice may differ by parity. Table 11.5 shows the mean values, by gender and conception number, for the personal characteristics discussed above and used in the multivariate analyses. Marital status, for example, changes across conceptions as many more are married at their second conception than at their first. Other variables do not change for a given individual (i.e., race) but can still have a different average in different conceptions if there is a systematic tendency for those with that characteristic to have more or fewer conceptions than average.

In the analysis reported below, all the observations in the NHSLS cross section are included. In all, 878 men and 1,334 women reported a first conception. Columns 1 and 2 of table 11.5 indicate that about the same proportions (12 percent) of both genders report that that first conception ended in abortion. Of all the first conceptions, about 57 percent occurred after 1973, and the table shows the mean values for all the variables used in the subsequent statistical analyses. As one would expect, there are no major differences between the genders for the first conception except in the proportion who were under age eighteen at the time since women typically have their first child two or three years younger than men.[12] There is also a systematically higher proportion of women than men with affirmative opinions about two of the three issues shown in the table: that religion guides the respondent's sexual behavior and that premarital sex is always wrong. There is not a difference by gender in the proportion who believe that discretionary abortion should be legal.

Columns 3 and 4 of table 11.5 show the means for the second conception reported by these same respondents—655 men and 1077 women. The proportion ending this conception with abortion is much lower—about 6 percent. For the third conception (cols. 5 and 6), an even smaller number of cases, the abortion rate remained at about the same low level (6 percent). From these data, we see that the dummy variable that indicates that the conception occurred after *Roe v. Wade* increases somewhat from con-

Table 11.5 Means of Variables Used in Analysis of Abortions, by Conception Number (Weighted)

Variable	First Conception		Second Conception		Third Conception	
	Men	Women	Men	Women	Men	Women
Abortion	.121	.123	.058	.064	.060	.065
	(.33)	(.33)				
Roe v. Wade (1973)	.573	.571	.609	.618	.643	.634
	(.50)	(.50)				
Parent HS (< 18)	.038	.103	. . .	. . .	. . .	. . .
	(.19)	(.30)				
Parent College (< 18)	.008	.016	. . .	. . .	. . .	. . .
	(.09)	(.13)				
Parent HS	.675	.643	.664	.624	.634	.606
	(.47)	(.48)				
Parent College	.168	.166	.162	.152	.172	.153
	(.37)	(.37)				
Intact at 14	.755	.754	.782	.752	.781	.737
	(.43)	(.43)				
Mom worked at 14	.468	.499	.429	.484	.418	.478
	(.50)	(.50)				
Black	.082	.107	.081	.109	.091	.127
	(.28)	(.31)				
Hispanic	.077	.076	.071	.082	.086	.079
	(.27)	(.26)				
Married at conception	.562	.544	.799	.771	.840	.811
	(.50)	(.50)				
Cohabing at	.085	.067	.077	.078	.072	.089
conception	(.28)	(.25)				
Age < 18	.062	.208	. . .	. . .	. . .	. . .
	(.24)	(.41)				
Religion guides sex	.519	.617	.542	.638	.537	.668
	(.50)	(.49)				
Premarital sex is wrong	.277	.349	.303	.367	.309	.403
	(.45)	(.48)				
Ab should be legal	.462	.476	.436	.459	.450	.448
	(.50)	(.50)				
Attend religious serv	.287	.356	.309	.378	.321	.387
	(.45)	(.48)				
Rural	.167	.174	.179	.190	.164	.197
	(.37)	(.38)				
City	.230	.244	.211	.225	.204	.229
	(.42)	(.43)				
Aborted #1	. . .	. . .	.095	.107	.108	.104
Aborted #2	. . .	. . .	. . .	. . .	.072	.060
N	878	1,334	655	1,077	381	717

Note: Standard deviations are given in parentheses.

ception to conception. There is a slight increase in the proportion who are black in the later conceptions, reflecting the higher fertility rate among blacks. Finally, the rate of marriage is much higher for the second and third conceptions.

First Conception

Table 11.6 shows three statistical models of the decision to abort the first pregnancy, estimated separately by the gender of the respondent. In model 1, all the variables used are unequivocally exogenous to the abortion decision, as is assumed by the statistical model. In this model, we see that those whose conception occurred after *Roe v. Wade* were far more likely to have an abortion, as we would expect. The coefficient is 1.689 for the men and 1.313 for the women. As noted above, the easiest way to interpret these coefficients is to calculate the partial effect of the exogenous variable on the probability $\delta P/\delta X$, which is equal to $B_i(P)(1 - P)$. Using the mean of P ($= 0.12$) as the value at which this derivative is evaluated, $(P)(1 - P) = 0.1056$, implying that the partial derivative of each variable for both genders in table 11.6 is about one-tenth the magnitude of the reported coefficient. That is, the men whose conception occurred after 1973 had a probability of choosing abortion about 17 percentage points higher than that of those men whose conception occurred before 1973; for the women, the increase in the probability is about 13 percentage points.[13]

Those whose parent graduated from high school or college were much more likely to have an abortion than were those whose parent did not finish high school. Model 1 has two parent-education dummy variables and also interacts those two education variables with a dummy indicating that the conception occurred at an age under eighteen, so the interpretation of these four education coefficients warrants some discussion. If the woman's parent was a high school graduate, the likelihood that she had an abortion is 10.4 percentage points higher ($= 0.983 \times 0.1056$) than it is if her parent was not a high school graduate. But, if the pregnancy occurred before the woman was eighteen, then the likelihood that she had an abortion is 21.5 percentage points higher ($= [0.983 + 1.051] \times 0.1056$) if her parent was a high school graduate. The schooling effect is much stronger if that pregnancy occurred before the woman's eighteenth birthday. Similarly, if the woman's parent had a college degree, she is 3.6 percentage points ($= 0.341 \times 0.1056$) more likely to have an abortion than if they did not, assuming that she was over age eighteen at conception. If she was under age eighteen, then, if a parent had a college degree, she is 20.4 percentage points ($= [0.341 + 1.592] \times 0.1056$) more likely to have an abortion than her counterpart whose parents were less well educated.

The education effect was expected to be much stronger for conceptions

Table 11.6 Logistic Regressions on Abortion of First Conception, by Gender (Weighted)

	Men			Women		
	Model 1	Model 2	Model 3	Model 1	Model 2	Model 3
Roe v. Wade (1973)	1.689	1.861	1.842	1.313	1.486	1.449
	(.000)	(.000)	(.000)	(.000)	(.000)	(.000)
Parent HS (< 18)[a]	2.081	.700	.559	1.051	.637	.877
	(.000)	(.461)	(.558)	(.000)	(.287)	(.162)
Parent Coll (< 18)[b]	−.465	−.463	−.630	1.592	1.920	1.646
	(.640)	(.653)	(.552)	(.008)	(.006)	(.040)
Parent HS	.852	.859	.677	.983	1.284	1.052
	(.015)	(.030)	(.094)	(.000)	(.000)	(.003)
Parent College	.711	.816	.848	.341	.347	.297
	(.010)	(.015)	(.014)	(.148)	(.193)	(.292)
Intact family at 14	−.287	.191	.324	−.313	−.074	−.018
	(.277)	(.517)	(.289)	(.143)	(.754)	(.941)
Mom worked at 14	.887	.941	.916	−.035	−.148	−.131
	(.000)	(.001)	(.001)	(.847)	(.463)	(.541)
Black	−.043	−.391	−.340	−1.128	−1.617	−1.589
	(.924)	(.407)	(.482)	(.006)	(.000)	(.000)
Hispanic	1.220	.731	.714	−.038	.125	.146
	(.003)	(.095)	(.118)	(.912)	(.732)	(.707)
Married		−3.857	−3.693		−2.965	−2.815
		(.000)	(.000)		(.000)	(.000)
Cohabitating		−1.071	−1.077		−.627	−.752
		(.004)	(.005)		(.037)	(.020)
Age < 18		.268	.368		−.652	−.801
		(.741)	(.651)		(.221)	(.150)
Religion guides sex			−.470			−.557
			(.108)			(.011)
Abort should be legal			.760			1.722
			(.008)			(.000)
Constant	−4.604	−3.861	−4.074	−3.581	−2.745	−3.484
	(.000)	(.000)	(.000)	(.000)	(.000)	(.000)
χ^2	119.96	239.47	246.19	148.99	310.30	379.82
Prob > χ^2	.000	.000	.000	.000	.000	.000
Pseudo-R^2	.190	.385	.401	.150	.312	.387
N	865	852	839	1,325	1,317	1,289

Note: The two-sided significance level of the coefficient's *t*-statistic is given in parentheses; i.e., values lower than 0.050 are statistically significant at the 95 percent confidence levels.
[a]Respondent with a parent who had a high-school education; had a conception before age 18.
[b]Respondent with a parent who had a college education; had a conception before age 18.

that occurred at younger ages, and, indeed, it is.[14] It is worth stressing that, for a woman whose first conception occurs before age eighteen, the relation between the likelihood of abortion and her parents' education is exceedingly strong: comparing a young woman whose parent is not a high school graduate and one whose parent is a college graduate, the likelihood that the latter aborts her first pregnancy is 41.9 percentage points higher.

According to model 1, living in an intact family at age fourteen has no statistically significant effect on the probability of abortion for either the men or the women. If the mother was employed when the respondent was age fourteen, there is a strong positive effect on the likelihood of abortion for the men (the partial derivative is $0.887 \times 0.1056 = 0.094$, or over 9 percentage points), but the effect is not significant for the women. I suggested above that this variable might reflect less careful supervision and therefore easier access to sex; if that interpretation obtains, then it is the boy's home, not the girl's home, that is the determining factor.

Race/ethnicity has different coefficients for the men and the women: among the men, Hispanics, but not blacks, are more likely to abort the pregnancy than are white men; among the women, blacks, but not Hispanics, are less likely to abort the conception than are whites. (Both these race/ethnicity relations disappear in the subsequent models.)

Model 1 surely suggests that there are systematic patterns between these several background factors and the decision to abort the first pregnancy. Model 1 is, however, stark in that it contains very little of the respondent's life situation at the time the conception occurred. It has the attractive feature that all nine covariates are clearly unaffected by the choice being analyzed here. Model 2 adds three new variables, measuring the marital status and living arrangements of the respondent and his or her age at the time of the conception. These are clearly factors that are expected to influence the abortion decision, but they are also factors that might be affected by the prior knowledge that an abortion would or would not be sought if a conception occurred. Here, I consider them exogenous factors nonetheless. Marital status and living arrangements both have very strong statistical associations with the decision to abort that first conception. Those who are married at the time of the conception are dramatically less likely to choose abortion—the partial derivative implies a -40.7 percentage point difference for men ($= 3.857 \times 0.1056$) and a -31.3 percentage point difference for women ($= 2.965 \times 0.1056$). The relation for those who are cohabiting is smaller but still statistically significant, compared to those who are unmarried and not living with their partner.

The dummy variable indicating that the person was under age eighteen at the time of the conception is interesting. As formulated in model 2, the effect of being young (i.e., under age eighteen) at the time of the conception differs by gender and by parents' education level. For the men whose parents did not complete high school, the effect of a conception at an age under eighteen is the coefficient on "age < 18," 0.268, and is not significant. For the men with a parent who did complete high school, the effect of age under eighteen is the sum of two coefficients, 0.268 + 0.700, but neither is statistically significant; and, for the men whose parent completed college, the effect of age under eighteen is the sum of three coefficients, 0.268 + 0.700 − 0.463, and, again, none of the three have statistical significance. For the women, one of the three coefficients is statistically significant. While, as do other data, the NHSLS raw data show a very strong relation between young age at conception and a high likelihood of abortion, these regressions suggest that this relation does not persist when one analyzes the first conception alone and controls for marital status, parents' education level, and family structure during adolescence.

To explore the effectiveness of model 2 in partitioning the respondents by their likelihood of aborting their first conception, the predicted value of P, the probability of abortion, was calculated for each person on the basis of model 2. The samples of men and women were then partitioned into three groups: those with a predicted probability of abortion less than 5 percent, those with a predicted probability between 5 and 30 percent, and those with a predicted probability above 30 percent. Table 11.7 shows the mean values of the personal characteristics and of the actual abortion rate for each of these three subgroups. (Overall, the simple correlation of the predicted probability based on model 2 and the dummy indicating an

Table 11.7 Means for Subsets of Respondents Defined by Predicted Probability of Abortion of First Conception (Model 2), by Gender

	Men			Women		
	< .05	.05–.30	.30–.99	< .05	.05–.30	.30–.99
Abortion	.012	.190	.465	.027	.117	.496
Roe v. Wade (1973)	.522	.624	.984	.434	.700	.982
Parent HS (< 18)	.004	.038	.228	.039	.114	.329
Parent College (< 18)	0	.010	.047	.001	.013	.088
Parent HS	.616	.657	.961	.520	.660	1.00
Parent College	.153	.081	.394	.052	.326	.298
Intact family at 14	.794	.724	.677	.761	.684	.689
Mom worked at 14	.408	.457	.780	.486	.483	.553
Black	.097	.138	.126	.194	.156	.004
Hispanic	.052	.114	.110	.059	.125	.070
Age < 18	.031	.081	.260	.192	.212	.329
Married at conception	.895	0	0	.808	.310	.004
Cohabing at conception	.023	.276	.071	.010	.106	.215
N	515	210	127	712	377	228

actual abortion was 0.52 for the men and 0.54 for the women.) From table 11.7, we see that the prediction did a good job of partitioning the sample into three groups by the actual abortion rates: those three groups had actual reported rates of 1.2, 19.0, and 46.5 percent, respectively, for the men and 2.7, 11.7, and 49.6 percent, respectively, for the women. From the column-by-column comparisons, we can observe how influential each of the personal characteristics is in partitioning the sample by the probability of having an abortion. For example, while about half the men (52.2 percent) with a low probability of abortion had their conception after 1973, a whopping 98.4 percent of those who had a high probability of abortion had their conception after 1973. Those with a high probability also had more educated parents and were far less likely to be married at the time the conception occurred. Notice, also, how few of the women with a high probability of abortion are black.

Another way to explore the discriminating power of the model is to see how different the estimated probability of abortion is for individuals with different characteristics. Table 11.8 defines four synthetic or constructed individuals. Using model 2 in table 11.6 above to predict the probability of each of these eight individuals having an abortion yields the following results: individual A, 0.00 (man) and 0.00 (woman); individual B, 0.47 (man) and 0.57 (woman); individual C, 0.41 (man) and 0.16 (woman); and individual D, 0.26 (man) and 0.33 (woman). In general, this statistical model does indeed yield substantially different predicted probabilities for these eight hypothetical men and women. Since these four synthetic cases vary more than one attribute or characteristic at once, the analysis cannot reveal the influence of each separately. That is done in Table 11.9 for three important characteristics, marital status, parents' education level, and race.

In table 11.9A, one sees the very strong effect of marital status. The italicized probabilities are those given in the text above, and, reading across the other columns for each row, we see the effect on the estimated probability of the other marital statuses or living arrangements. The effect for woman B, for example, is a tenfold difference: a married woman with woman B's characteristics has an estimated likelihood of aborting her first conception of only 0.06, while the estimate for a single woman who is not cohabiting is 0.57! If the woman is cohabiting, the estimated likelihood lies between these two, at 0.42. Similar differences are seen for the other synthetic cases for women and for the men as well.[15]

In table 11.9B, the strong effect of parents' education is observed, especially for those whose first conception occurs before age eighteen. Look at woman B in this comparison. If neither of her parents had graduated from high school, the predicted probability is 0.12, whereas, if one or both had graduated from high school, that probability rises to 0.48, and, if either

Table 11.8 Characteristics of Four Synthetic Individuals

Individual	Race	Parents' Education	Family Intact at Age 14?	Mother Working at Age 14?	Younger Than 18 at Conception?	Married?	Cohabiting?	After 1973?
A	Black	11	No	No	No	Yes	No	No
B	White	16	Yes	No	No	No	No	Yes
C	Black	12	Yes	No	Yes	No	No	Yes
D	White	12	Yes	No	Yes	No	Yes	Yes

Table 11.9 Predicted Likelihood of Abortion of First Conception, Based on Model 2, Table 11.6, Using the Four Synthetic Individuals (See Table 11.8)

A. Differences by Marital Status and Living Arrangements

	Men			Women		
Person	Married	Cohab	Not Cohab	Married	Cohab	Not Cohab
A	*.00*	.00	.01	*.00*	.01	.01
B	.02	.23	*.47*	.06	.42	*.57*
C	.01	.19	*.41*	.01	.09	*.16*
D	.02	*.26*	.50	.05	*.33*	.48

B. Differences by Parents' Education

	Men			Women		
Person	< High School	High School	College	< High School	High School	College
Conception occurred before age 18						
A	.00	.00	.00	.00	.00	.02
B	.18	.50	.59	.12	.48	.90
C	.13	*.41*	.50	.03	*.16*	.64
D	.07	*.26*	.33	.07	*.33*	.83
Conception occurred on or after age 18						
A.	*.00*	.00	.00	*.00*	.00	.00
B	.14	.28	*.47*	.21	.49	.57
C	.10	.21	.37	.05	.16	.21
D	.05	.12	.23	.12	.34	.42

C. Differences by Race

	Men		Women	
Person	Black	White	Black	White
A	*.00*	.00	*.00*	.00
B	.37	*.47*	.21	*.57*
C	*.41*	.50	*.16*	.48
D	.19	*.26*	.09	*.33*

Note: For definitions of the four synthetic persons, A, B, C, D, see table 11.8 above. *Italicization* indicates probabilities given in the text.

had completed four years of college, that predicted probability is a whopping 0.90. The relation is somewhat weaker if she is over age eighteen when the conception occurs, but it is still quite substantial. The magnitude of the race difference seen in table 11.9C for the unmarried is 7–10 percentage points for the men and 24–36 percentage points for the women, with whites more likely to abort their first conception.

Model 3 in table 11.6 above adds two additional variables reflecting the opinion of the respondent: whether he or she thinks abortion should be legal and whether the statement "religion guides my sexual behavior" accurately reflects his or her behavior. For both these opinions, the direction of the empirical effect is what one would expect: those who believe that abortion should be legal are much more likely to have aborted their first conception, other factors held constant. For the women (men), that opinion is associated with about a 17 (7) percentage point increase in the likelihood of abortion. The assertion that religion guides sexual behavior is not related to abortion behavior as reported by the men but is negatively associated with the likelihood of abortion for the women. Model 3 shows that including these two measures of opinion has little influence on any of the other estimated coefficients in the model.

Several additional variables were also introduced into the logistic regression, but the results are not reported here. Those variables include a dummy for religious preference, in particular, one for Catholicism and one for Protestant fundamentalism. Neither had statistical significance for men or women. The absence of a strong religious affiliation effect mirrors the finding reported by Stevans, Register, and Sessions (1992), although other studies have found that specific religious affiliations do affect the abortion decision (e.g., in her study of young black women, Murry [1995] found a positive effect for belonging to the Baptist church). When the dummy variable that indicates that religion guides sexual behavior was replaced by one measuring church attendance, the latter was significant and negative. The overlap with the former variable, however, was sufficiently strong that, when both were included in the model, multicollinearity resulted in neither showing statistical significance, so these data do not permit the inclusion of both.

Since the attendance variable measures behavior at the time of the survey (1992), and since I contend that the opinion reflects a lifelong attitude, albeit measured in 1992, the opinion, rather than the current behavior, is the preferred variable in model 3 since many of the abortion decisions took place long before 1992. In another model, I also included two dummy variables indicating that the respondent reported having been forced to have sex and had been touched sexually before puberty (see chap. 4 above). Here, these variables did not show statistical significance, but we note that they were not measured in a way that permitted the abuse to be linked to that pregnancy, so this lack of a finding does not conflict with the findings reported elsewhere.

Before turning to an analysis of the second conception, consider a little more closely the linkage between the opinion about the legal status of abortion and abortion behavior. In the literature on abortion opinion, this issue is seldom addressed since few surveys obtain all the relevant information. If one is interested in public opinion about the legal status of abortion, one might think that those who have had an abortion would be much more likely to favor continued legalization. The empirical estimate in model 3 indicates that a woman approving of legalized abortion had, other factors held constant, a 17 percentage point higher likelihood of aborting her first conception.

The NHSLS interview (*SOS,* 668) asked respondents, "Please tell me whether or not you think it should be possible for a pregnant woman to obtain a *legal* abortion if she became pregnant as a result of rape?" and, " . . . if the woman wants it for any reason" (the possible responses were yes, no, do not know, and no response). The variable used in the statistical analysis in table 11.6 above is a dummy variable defined as 1 if the answer to the second of these questions was yes. The overall distributions of both these questions, by gender, is seen in table 11.10. As do other surveys, the NHSLS shows just how evenly divided is the adult population in its opinion about the legalization of abortion when the choice is left to a woman's discretion. In the case of a pregnancy that results from a rape, there is a much stronger sentiment in favor of legal abortion. It is noteworthy that there is no difference by gender; as reported earlier, Rodman (1987) found that men's attitudes were more favorable.

Without asserting any causal ordering, we can investigate whether the women who have ever had an abortion (or the men whose partner has ever had one) hold decidedly different opinions than those who have never had an abortion. Table 11.11 shows this intersection. We can express this intersection in several different ways. Among those women who have ever had an abortion, 83 percent (= 0.15/0.18) hold a favorable opinion, and,

Table 11.10 Percentage Holding the Opinion That Abortion Should Be Legal, Two Circumstances, by Gender

	For Any Reason?		If Rape?	
	Women	Men	Women	Men
Yes	49	49	85	85
No	46	46	11	11
Don't know or no answer	5	4	4	3

Table 11.11 Intersection of Opinion toward Abortion for Any Reason and Experience Ever Having (for Men, Partner Ever Having) an Abortion (%)

	Women	Men
Opposed and no abortion	44	46
Opposed and abortion	3	3
Favor and no abortion	38	43
Favor and abortion	15	8
Total	100	100

Table 11.12 Percentage Who Think Abortion Should Be Legal by Whether They Ever Had an Abortion, by Gender and Age

	Men				Women			
Abortion Status	18–29	30–44	45–59	All	18–29	30–44	45–59	All
Have ever had	69	71	62	69	82	81	85	82
Have never had	49	46	43	46	46	44	42	44

among those who have never had one, 46 percent (= 0.38/0.82) hold a favorable opinion. That is a substantial difference, but it is not the case that all those who report having had an abortion hold a favorable opinion—17 percent of the women who have had an abortion say that they are opposed to a woman having the right to do so for any reason. (Among the men, the proportion of those whose partner has ever had an abortion but who oppose abortion nonetheless is an even higher 27 percent [= 0.03/0.11], but, of course, we do not know the opinion of the partner who in fact had the abortion.) It would be interesting to know (although, given the NHSLS data, we have no way of determining) whether the experience of abortion altered these women's and men's opinion. Alternatively, it would be interesting to know how those who have had an abortion but say that they oppose its general availability for any reason would reconcile the seeming inconsistency between their opinion and their behavior. Perhaps the experience has altered their view; perhaps the pregnancy fell into what they considered to be an exempted category.

Looking at the relation between behavior and opinion by respondent's age (see table 11.12), one sees a consistently higher proportion favoring abortion among those who have experienced an abortion. There is little difference by age in this pattern.

To summarize the linkage between the opinion expressed and behavior regarding abortion, there is a clear pattern of a positive association. However, some few who report that they oppose the legalization of abortion for whatever reason nonetheless report having had an abortion, and of course many who report being in favor of legalized abortion have not themselves had an abortion, nor has their partner.

Second Conception

Table 11.13 shows the logistic regression for the second conception. Of course, fewer men and women have a second conception, so the sample sizes are noticeably smaller here. Also, there are so few whose second conception occurred before age eighteen that the distinction is dropped from the analysis.[16] In all other respects, the models are analogous to those in table 11.6 above for the first conception. Since the rate at which second conceptions are aborted is much lower than that at which first conceptions are aborted, the multiplier by which the estimated coefficient shown in table 11.13 is converted to a partial derivative is also lower (i.e., $P[1 - P]$ is 0.055 for the men and 0.060 for the women throughout the table).

Those whose second conception occurred after 1973 were again more likely to have an abortion, as would be expected. Parents' education is less strongly related to abortion choice with this second conception. Nonetheless, having a parent who graduated from high school was significantly related to abortion choice for men and having a parent who graduated from college for women. Mirroring the results for the first conception, the mother being employed at the time the respondent was age fourteen is again associated with a higher rate of aborting the second conception for the men but not for the women. Unlike the first conception, however, a second conception is substantially less likely to end in abortion if the woman lived in an intact family at age fourteen. Blacks and whites show no differences here, so the strong aversion to abortion evinced by black women in the first conception has disappeared. The higher rate of abortion for Hispanic men, however, continues to be very strong in magnitude and statistical significance.

Model 2 in table 11.13 adds the marital and cohabitation status of the individual at the time of the second conception, and, again, we see a very strong relation with both: those who are married or cohabiting are far less likely to abort the second conception as well as the first. When marital status and living arrangements are controlled, as in model 2, having a college-educated parent is more strongly associated with an increase in the likelihood of an abortion.

The results of estimating the probability of aborting the second conception from model 2 and then partitioning the sample by that estimated probability, as was done for the first conception in table 11.7 above, are shown in table 11.14. Here, again, we see that the model was effective in

Table 11.13 Logistic Regressions on Abortion of Second Conception, by Gender (Weighted)

	Men			Women		
	Model 1	Model 2	Model 3	Model 1	Model 2	Model 3
Roe v. Wade (1973)	1.240	1.631	1.464	1.834	1.663	1.573
	(.016)	(.006)	(.017)	(.000)	(.000)	(.001)
Parent HS	1.090	1.144	.973	-.065	.080	-.261
	(.049)	(.070)	(.129)	(.833)	(.822)	(.493)
Parent College	.687	.841	.650	.974	1.514	1.469
	(.102)	(.087)	(.208)	(.003)	(.000)	(.001)
Intact family at 14	-.255	.524	.521	-.948	-.057	-.029
	(.557)	(.305)	(.324)	(.001)	(.862)	(.930)
Mom worked at 14	.990	.948	.760	.317	.547	.645
	(.013)	(.041)	(.114)	(.233)	(.081)	(.047)
Black	.349	-.527	-.362	.044	-1.026	-.837
	(.625)	(.497)	(.646)	(.918)	(.024)	(.073)
Hispanic	2.359	2.121	2.074	.685	.333	.373
	(.000)	(.000)	(.001)	(.073)	(.460)	(.409)
Married		-3.635	-3.283		-4.044	-3.779
		(.000)	(.000)		(.000)	(.000)
Cohabitating		-1.563	-1.447		-.841	-.916
		(.007)	(.015)		(.024)	(.016)
Aborted #1			1.040			1.079
			(.033)			(.003)
Constant	-5.455	-4.232	-4.236	-3.881	-2.550	-2.695
	(.000)	(.000)	(.000)	(.000)	(.000)	(.000)
χ^2	43.52	104.42	108.80	56.53	190.82	199.64
Prob > χ^2	.000	.000	.000	.000	.000	.000
Pseudo-R^2	.158	.386	.402	.110	.377	.395
N	639	628	628	1,067	1,050	1,050

Note: The significance level is given in parentheses (see table 11.6 above).

Table 11.14 Means for Subsets of Respondents Defined by Predicted Probability of Abortion of Second Conception (Model 2), by Gender

	Men			Women		
	< .05	.05–.30	.30–.99	< .05	.05–.30	.30–.99
Abortion	.008	.162	.541	.008	.146	.423
Roe v. Wade (1973)	.582	.829	.946	.538	.879	.987
Parent HS	.621	.762	.919	.616	.592	.769
Parent College	.109	.305	.405	.121	.233	.346
Intact family at 14	.790	.743	.784	.781	.607	.487
Mom worked at 14	.366	.667	.784	.440	.597	.679
Black	.103	.152	.081	.115	.335	.026
Hispanic	.033	.181	.270	.074	.078	.192
Married at conception	.930	.305	.027	.956	.218	0
Cohabitating at conception	.037	.314	.135	.013	.350	.167
Aborted #1	.056	.210	.459	.060	.184	.436
N	486	105	37	766	206	78

partitioning the samples by their actual probabilities of abortion: the rates for the three groups, respectively, are 0.8, 16.2, and 54.1 percent for the men and 0.8, 14.6, and 42.3 percent for the women. Notice the relatively high rates of parents' college graduation for those with the high estimated probability and the dramatic association with marital status shown again here.

Again, we can investigate the discriminative power of model 2 by estimating the probability that the four synthetic individuals introduced earlier have an abortion. The predicted probabilities are as follows: individual A, 0.00 (man) and 0.00 (woman); individual B, 0.48 (man) and 0.66 (woman); individual C, 0.19 (man) and 0.13 (woman); and individual D, 0.08 (man) and 0.15 (woman). These probabilities are quite similar to those estimated for the first conception for individuals with characteristics A and B but much lower for men with characteristics C and D. The model yields dramatically different estimates of the probability as the characteristics change.

Model 3 in table 11.13 above is not a replica of model 3 in table 11.6 above. Instead, I have added here a new piece of information not available before: the outcome of the previous conception. In particular, the additional variable is a dummy defined as 1 if the first conception ended in abortion. Model 3 in table 11.13 shows that individuals who abort a first conception are much more likely to abort the second: the partial derivative implies an increase of 5.7 percentage points in the likelihood for the men and an increase of 6.5 percentage points for the women, controlling for the other characteristics in the model.

This coefficient should be interpreted with caution, however. It was stressed in chapter 12 of *SOS* that abortion did not appear to be a customary form of fertility control for many people, that instead the rate of abortion was high for the first conception but not so thereafter, until the fifth or higher-order conception. That point is not inconsistent with the strong, positive coefficient reported here.

Consider the following: Of the 134 women who aborted their first pregnancy, 22.3 percent aborted their second, and, of the 1,103 women who did not abort their first pregnancy, 4.8 percent aborted their second. And, of the 75 men whose partners aborted their first pregnancy, 34.7 percent had partners who aborted their second, and, of the 651 men whose partners did not abort their first pregnancy, 4.0 percent had partners who aborted their second.

So, if we are predicting whether the second conception ended in abortion, the outcome of the first is of statistical importance. But the same facts can be expressed this way as well: three-quarters of the women who aborted their first conception did not abort their second. There is a correlation here, but it is not a strong one: the (weighted) simple correlation of the abortion dummies for the first and second conceptions is 0.39 for the men and 0.28 for the women.

Third Conception

Table 11.15 shows the empirical estimation for the third conception. There are fewer characteristics that are systematically related to the choice to abort this third conception, which is the reported outcome of about 6 percent of these conceptions. In model 1 for the men, the *Roe v. Wade* variable no longer has relevance, parents' high school completion is still positively associated with the probability of abortion, and the variable indicating that the man lived in an intact family at age fourteen is, oddly, strongly related to the abortion decision. This is the direction of effect suggested earlier, but it was not in evidence for the first two conceptions, and I have no good explanation why it shows up here. For the women, model 1 is not statistically significant as a whole, judging by the χ^2 statistic. Only the *Roe v. Wade* coefficient for these women is statistically significant.

In model 2, which adds marital status, the overall models are again quite significant for both genders. In this third conception, again, there is a strong association between being married and not having an abortion for both the men and the women. Cohabiting has a smaller effect in the same direction, but it does not have statistical significance. In model 3, we see that having aborted the first conception is strongly positively related to choosing to abort this third conception for both the men and the women. Choosing to abort the second conception does not have so strong a rela-

Table 11.15 Logistic Regressions on Abortion of Third Conception, by Gender (Weighted)

	Men			Women		
	Model 1	Model 2	Model 3	Model 1	Model 2	Model 3
Roe v. Wade (1973)	.006	-.077	-.679	1.051	.951	.825
	(.990)	(.888)	(.278)	(.012)	(.030)	(.081)
Parent HS	1.560	1.190	.996	.292	.605	.106
	(.019)	(.084)	(.177)	(.422)	(.119)	(.796)
Parent College	-.110	.206	-.855	.223	.131	.067
	(.853)	(.746)	(.310)	(.611)	(.784)	(.895)
Intact family at 14	-1.544	-.965	-1.568	-.484	.005	.007
	(.002)	(.075)	(.012)	(.177)	(.989)	(.986)
Mom worked at 14	-.167	-.419	-1.304	.032	.018	.240
	(.736)	(.438)	(.055)	(.922)	(.959)	(.517)
Black	1.173	.729	1.360	.466	-.507	-.203
	(.072)	(.317)	(.100)	(.285)	(.288)	(.690)
Hispanic	-.428	-1.238	-1.826	-.298	-.472	-.737
	(.707)	(.296)	(.177)	(.661)	(.510)	(.323)
Married		-2.465	-1.361		-2.760	-2.410
		(.000)	(.055)		(.000)	(.000)
Cohabitating		-1.123	-.787		-.514	-.477
		(.160)	(.410)		(.267)	(.340)
Aborted #1			2.537			1.720
			(.001)			(.000)
Aborted #2			1.466			.786
			(.065)			(.084)
Constant	-2.926	-.995	-1.251	-3.447	-1.907	-2.353
	(.000)	(.238)	(.166)	(.000)	(.001)	(.000)
χ^2	18.77	35.70	53.79	13.94	61.88	84.39
Prob > χ^2	.009	.000	.000	.052	.000	.000
Pseudo-R^2	.115	.220	.332	.042	.188	.256
N	365	359	359	707	697	697

Note: The significance level is given in parentheses (see table 11.6 above).

tion to choosing to abort the third, however. The marital status effect remains quite strong in model 3, especially for the women.

I have not analyzed the abortion choice in higher-order pregnancies. While the rate of abortion rises in these subsequent pregnancies, as shown earlier, the number of observations declines quite dramatically. One issue that deserves further consideration across the several pregnancies is the finding that fewer black women choose to abort their first pregnancy (there are no other race difference across the three pregnancies). This seems somewhat at odds with the literature reporting that blacks have more abortions than whites, although that finding is not universal. However, these two patterns can be reconciled when it is realized that my analysis was conducted for each of the first three pregnancies separately, whereas, in many other studies, the abortion pattern is studied per person, not per pregnancy. Blacks have more pregnancies, so it is feasible for them to have a lower rate of abortion per pregnancy and also have a higher rate of abortion per woman. That seems to be the case. The number of pregnancies reported by the men and women in the NHSLS is shown in table 11.16. Blacks have a higher mean number of pregnancies (this is not statistically significant owing to the small sample size and the large within-group variation), and a substantially higher proportion has five or more pregnancies. Thus, the opportunity to have had an abortion is greater for black women. The distinction between the rate per pregnancy and the rate per person is affirmed in table 11.17, which shows that, although (unadjusted for any covariates) whites abort the first pregnancy at a higher rate, blacks abort some subsequent pregnancies at higher rates, and, overall, blacks report a slightly higher rate of abortion than do the whites.

Finally, it is of interest to track the subsequent fertility behavior of those who do abort their first conception. Table 11.18 shows that behavior in terms of the total number of pregnancies and the total number of live births that those men and women had. The modal behavior was not to

Table 11.16 Number of Pregnancies, by Race/Ethnicity and Gender

	Whites	Blacks	Hispanics
Mean			
Men	2.2	3.5	2.2
	(7.2)	(11.7)	(2.4)
Women	2.4	3.3	2.8
	(4.8)	(5.6)	(2.3)
% with 5 or more			
Men	6.0	11.5	16.1
Women	11.2	20.3	17.0

Note: Standard deviations are given in parentheses.

Table 11.17 Abortion Rates, Lifetime and by Conception Number, by Gender and Race

	Men			Women		
	Whites	Blacks	Hispanics	Whites	Blacks	Hispanics
Any abortion, whether any conception or not	11.0 (1,167)	13.9 (202)	11.3 (62)	15.4 (1,395)	17.9 (336)	22.2 (99)
Any abortion, if one or more conceptions	17.1 (749)	20.1 (139)	16.7 (42)	19.9 (1,078)	20.3 (296)	26.8 (82)
Conception number:						
First	11.6 (763)	9.9 (142)	9.3 (42)	12.6 (1,097)	6.1 (303)	12.9 (83)
Second	5.4 (569)	7.9 (105)	10.9 (31)	6.3 (874)	6.6 (250)	10.1 (73)
Third	4.5 (322)	15.0 (72)	. . .	5.8 (570)	9.1 (189)	4.7 (46)
Fourth	8.3 (167)	6.0 (45)	. . .	7.0 (319)	7.1 (121)	7.4 (31)
Fifth or higher order	14.4 (174)	12.0 (72)	. . .	10.7 (323)	14.6 (187)	15.8 (45)

Note: The conception number is based on the supplemented sample and is weighted. Numbers in parentheses give number of observations (i.e., cell size) on which percentages are based.

Table 11.18 Subsequent Fertility Behavior by Those Who Aborted Their First Conception, by Gender

Total Number of Conceptions	Men	Women	Total Number of Live Births	Men	Women
1	43 (36)	59 (31)	0	65 (55)	83 (43)
2	29 (24)	48 (25)	1	23 (19)	47 (24)
3	22 (19)	29 (15)	2	21 (18)	38 (20)
4	11 (9)	25 (13)	3	8 (7)	19 (10)
5	7 (6)	18 (9)	4	1 (1)	3 (2)
6–10	4 (3)	11 (6)	5	. . .	1 (1)
11–20	1 (1)	3 (2)	N.A.	. . .	2 (1)
21–30	. . .	. . .	Total	118 (100)	193 (100)
32	1 (1)	. . .			
Total	118 (100)	193 (100)			

Note: Percentages are given in parentheses. N.A. = not available.

conceive again after the first pregnancy, but a majority did in fact go on to have other pregnancies, a few many times. In terms of subsequent births, nearly half the men and over half the women who aborted their first pregnancy did in fact subsequently have a child, with more than one-quarter of the men and more than one-third of the women having two or more children following that initial abortion.

11.4 Discussion

First, let us consider how these empirical results support or modify the theoretical expectations discussed above regarding the personal character-istics that might influence the abortion decision. The factors predicted to be associated with continuum C and expected to lead to a higher probabil-ity of choosing to have an abortion were being single, being young at the time of the pregnancy, having more educated parents (especially if the pregnancy occurred at a young age), it being the first conception, and the conception occurring after the *Roe v. Wade* Supreme Court decision. The factors identified as associated with continuum O, lifetime opinions or beliefs, and expected to be associated with a higher probability of abor-tion were being less religious, having an employed mother at a young age, probably not being raised in a traditional family, and perhaps racial/eth-nic differences.

What these logistic models show is that, indeed, marital status is closely related to the abortion choice: those who are not married are more likely to choose abortion. Those who are cohabiting have a probability of choos-ing abortion that lies between that for those who are single and that for those who are married. The statistical results strongly confirm this hypoth-esis and show that it is quite robust: the systematic pattern persists through each of the first three pregnancies for both the men's reports and the women's. This finding reinforces one of the general themes in our ear-lier books: *marital status is by far the most powerfully influential factor re-garding sexual behavior that is subject to control by the individual.* (The other two major demographic factors that profoundly affect sexual behav-ior are gender and age.) Marital status is also a dominant factor in the abortion decision.

Age per se, measured by the dummy for age under eighteen, is not a strong factor when controlling for the other characteristics in the model and conducting the analysis conception by conception. The often-found effect of age in models of abortion is capturing, I think, an effect of parity, one that is fully controlled here.

Parents' education does have a strong positive relation with choosing to have an abortion, as expected. However, the findings presented here imply that the emphasis is more appropriately placed at the higher end of the educational scale than at the lower: it is those whose parent had a college education who were most likely to choose abortion, and that effect is much stronger if the pregnancy occurred when the respondent was under age eighteen. If the parent had a college education and the respondent was under eighteen, the model for the first pregnancy yielded estimated probabilities of abortion that are twice as high as those that obtain when the parent had only a high school education and nearly ten times as high as those that obtain when neither parent had completed high school. It is not just the relative size that is high: the estimated levels of these estimated probabilities arc in excess of 0.80. The argument made above is that the parents' schooling level proxies the opportunity cost to the respondent of having a baby at a young age. The more educated parents may play a direct role in discouraging parenthood at a young age as well as helping the respondent understand, or anticipate, or act on, the fact that having the baby at a young age imposes an obstacle to plans for schooling, career, and future personal growth.[17] The statistical model does not reveal what the mechanism is, but it certainly does reveal the strong association between parents' schooling level and the respondent's abortion decision.

The timing of the conception, vis-à-vis *Roe v. Wade,* is of critical importance, of course.

The evidence pertaining to continuum O factors is less compelling. There is some indication that those who consider religion an important guide to sexual behavior are in fact less likely to choose abortion, ceteris paribus. The result is stronger for the women, suggesting that perhaps the abortion decision is more closely linked to the woman's opinions, which seems reasonable. Beliefs about whether abortion should be legal are statistically associated with the choice of abortion, in the direction and with a magnitude that also makes sense. Having an employed mother at age fourteen has a positive association, but only for males, and only in the first conception. Black women, but not black men, reported much lower rates of abortion, but only in the first conception.

So, in summary, the empirical results do support most of the expected relations discussed earlier. Moreover, there are large differences in abortion rates by conception number, and the estimated partial relations for many of the variables differed by parity. These differences justify a research strategy that analyzes the abortion decision conception by conception.

Several further reflections on these findings are in order. First, it is evident from these results that the choice to have an abortion is not random or arbitrary; it is clearly systematically related to the individual's personal characteristics and opinions. While, like those regarding so much sexual and sex-related behavior, this choice is probably not among the most rational and strategic of the decisions that adults make, neither is it capricious, unstructured, or unrelated to measurable characteristics. Additionally, most of the factors found to have a partial correlation with the abortion decision for women also partially correlate with the outcomes of conceptions reported by the men.

In my interpretation of these findings, there is a strong negative relation between the individual's economic and social incentives to have a child and the likelihood of choosing to abort the pregnancy. Having a child is costly in terms of both time and money, and a woman who becomes pregnant acts as if she weighs the consequences of having the child when deciding whether to have an abortion. If she is married, she is much more likely to have the child. If she is quite young and has parents who are relatively highly educated, the opportunity costs of having the child are high, and she is much more likely to have an abortion.

Reflecting on this finding, which is also observed in other studies (as suggested in the literature review presented earlier), I think that it suggests how difficult it would be to use legislation or judicial opinion outlawing abortion to eradicate the practice of abortion. The evidence here surely suggests that there are more abortions performed when the procedure is legal, but it also suggests that there is a very strong tendency for young women who become pregnant and have well-educated (and therefore relatively well-off) parents to abort that pregnancy. These are young women who would likely have the financial resources to obtain an abortion even if the procedure were not generally available. Of course, the medical and other risks might in that case be very high, but the motivation evinced here, as interpreted from these coefficients, seems to suggest that generally reducing access to abortion might have a much different (and smaller) effect on those with substantial financial means than on those without. This income or class difference is parallel to the difference imposed on relatively lower-income women compared to middle-class women by a decision to restrict Medicaid financing of abortion.

Comparing model 2 with model 3, it is interesting to note that, while her own opinion about the appropriateness of abortion does, certainly, affect a woman's abortion decision and in the direction one would expect, it has very little effect on the other measured variables that affect that decision. We see in table 11.6 above that almost none of the dozen variables in model 2 are appreciably affected by controlling for the woman's own opinion about abortion! Those economic forces are not overwhelmed by the opinions; both are relevant to the decision. This may suggest that the more effective way of influencing the abortion decision may be, not by attempting to alter opinion about its appropriateness, but by promoting the avoidance of pregnancy through both abstinence and access to and use of contraceptives.

Unfortunately, since the NHSLS does not contain information about respondents' state of residence, about whether they have access to abortion services, or about whether they could receive government support to cover the cost of abortion, I cannot here address some relevant policy-oriented questions. But, as the illustrative cases presented in table 11.9 above reveal, the factors in the models estimated here do have a large effect on the abortion choice.

Returning to the issue of data quality, which was introduced in some detail earlier, one might ask whether there are grounds for thinking that any of the findings presented here are generated by biased responses instead of by causal influence. If there were an across-the-board reluctance to admit to having had an abortion when surveyed, that would not impose a bias on the coefficients in the estimated models. It would affect the overall levels or rates of abortion if, say, one of every four or five abortions was randomly not reported, but that would not affect the estimated relations among the variables. Those relations would be affected and would be biased if that reluctance to report an abortion were systematically associated with any of the factors emphasized in the model. It is certainly logically possible that this is so, but that does not make it so.

Marital status, for example, would be one potential factor affected by a bias: if married women or their partners are more reluctant to admit to having had an abortion than are unmarried adults, this could certainly "explain" the finding presented here that those who are married are much less likely to chose to have an abortion. But I do not know of any evidence that this systematic tendency exists. The bias would go in the opposite direction if single adults were in fact more reluctant to admit having had an abortion. Either is possible; the fact is that I cannot determine whether either bias exists in these data, nor do I know how to do so in survey data in general.

Similarly, it could be that those whose parents were more highly educated are more willing to report having had an abortion, but I do not see any reason to think that this is so. More likely, perhaps, would be a tendency for those who say that religion guides their sexual behavior to consider abortion inappropriate and to be reluctant to admit to having had one.

More problematic, I think, is the fact that blacks underreporting abortion relative to whites could yield the race coefficients found here for women in their first pregnancy. But then that difference is observed only for the women, not for the men, and only for the first conception, not for the second conception or the third. That makes it more difficult to accept the explanation that the finding can be attributed to a reporting bias since that same behavior should be expected in the second and third conceptions and probably also for men as well as for women.

Another explanation might be that, just as sexually transmitted diseases are reported differentially by public and private medical facilities, public health clinics may tend to consider more procedures abortion than do private practitioners. If so, the greater discrepancy for blacks than for whites between the institutionally reported abortion rate and the personally reported abortion rate in surveys may have a different interpretation than the one usually given: it may be the habit or inclination of clinics that service blacks to report as abortions procedures that private practitioners who treat whites report under other names, and this could explain that larger discrepancy between the personal report and the institutional report for blacks than for whites. I have not investigated these reporting practices. But I have seen no convincing evidence that the systematic patterns evinced in survey data such as the NHSLS should be disregarded. They certainly should be interpreted with caution, of course, and much more investigation is warranted.

Turning to a different aspect of data quality, I suggest that the nature of the results reported here illustrates the value of studying abortion behavior from different perspectives, including those provided by administrative records, such as the hospital and clinic reports collected by the Alan Guttmacher Institute, and those provided by survey responses, such as those in the NHSLS and other quality, national surveys. No single data source provides all the relevant information, so it seems to me to be a good research strategy to make use of the several opportunities to learn about this complex decision that women, families, and society face. Medical reports about numbers of abortions performed are of great value, but, since they cannot have associated with them all the relevant details about the woman, her family, and the context in which abortion is chosen, the data that they provide are necessarily limited. One cannot, for example, use these data to investigate how the outcome of previous conceptions influences the abortion decision. Like other clinical data, institutional records or reports provide information only about the cases that are presented in the clinic, so none of the other outcomes that one may wish to compare are captured. Survey data, on the other hand, are rich in contextual details and do include those who choose not to have an abortion, but these data are likely to be incomplete, under- or even misreported. So the use of quite different types of data has considerable value. Triangulating the varied perspectives afforded by different types of data can improve our understanding. It is important that we take advantage of the several, albeit limited, sources of useful information.

This point, made here regarding our understanding of the abortion decision, has relevance to several of the topics addressed in this volume. Information about sexually transmitted diseases, about sexual dysfunctions, about such procedures as infant male circumcision, about the prevalence of HIV/AIDS, as well as about abortions remains incomplete if we look only to one type of data or only to one source. The clinical under-standing of the nature and severity of sexual dysfunction, for example, is limited to the cases of those who choose to present themselves for treat-ment. Surveys add a wholly different perspective on the prevalence, distri-bution, and character of sexual dysfunction. The attributes, correlates, and perspectives of different data sources can help us better understand the topic and should be exploited.

Finally, going somewhat beyond the data reported here, I suggest a link-age between one of the broad puzzles reported here and one of the major puzzles often found in surveys of sexual behavior. That linkage is a system-atic difference in perception, in orientation, and thus in cognition and consequently in survey responses. The puzzle faced by this chapter is why it is that fewer abortions are reported than are implied by national esti-mates (calculated by AGI on the basis of institutional reports of abortion). The related puzzle is the ubiquitous finding that men report having more female sex partners than women report having male sex partners. In chap-ter 5 of *SOS*, we suggested seven logical explanations for this phenome-non; others have also offered explanations (see Smith 1990).

In my judgment, the most promising explanation of this latter puzzle, which I have not substantiated empirically, is this: men tend to count as sex partners women with whom they have very marginal sexual encounters, while women tend to discount men with whom they have had marginal encounters. There are some events that unequivocally constitute a sexual relationship and thus establish a sexual partnership; both the man and the woman in such a relationship would consider, and would report, that part-ner as a sex partner. But there are other events that do not clearly establish a sexual partnership. A brief and incomplete groping or a partial or near sexual experience might or might not fit one's definition of a sex act.

In our survey, we offered respondents our definition of a sex act, but no definition is unambiguous, and there will always be events that are not clearly covered by a given definition. If men are systematically more in-clined to consider marginal or relatively incomplete or inconsequential events as establishing a sexual partnership while women are systematically more inclined to consider these same events as not establishing a sexual partnership, then, when an interviewer asks men and women about their total number of sexual events or sex partners, the two genders will honestly interpret the matter differently. This systematic difference in perception can, and I believe probably does, explain much of the discrepancy in men's and women's responses about number of partners.

Now, it is also the case that there is a margin that differentiates an event that is an abortion and an event that is a miscarriage or an unintended ending of a pregnancy. If a pregnant woman goes to a private practitioner or a medical clinic with vaginal bleeding but with no real intention of seeking an abortion and then loses the baby, it is not unlikely that she considers her experience an unintended ending to the pregnancy, and she might well cognitively and emotionally code that event as closer to a miscarriage than to an abortion; her physician or her clinic, however, might equally justifiably code that event as an abortion. Or, if a fetus is not viable for some medical reason and the pregnancy is ended by a physician, the woman involved may well consider that event a medical necessity and a lost pregnancy, while her physician might consider it an abortion. Neither is reporting an untruth; neither is shading the truth necessarily. The perception differs, and therefore there may not be an unambiguously correct or incorrect answer to the question how that pregnancy ended.

The political overtones of a discussion of abortion tend to dominate this definitional margin, but subtle distinctions may exist and may partly or wholly explain the persistent difference between institutional reports and survey responses. Not every survey avoids response bias, but not every survey of abortion behavior should be discarded, its results remaining unexplored, because it reveals a much lower incidence than potentially biased institutional reports. Both have value; much more research is required before we will be able to reconcile the two sources of information. In this chapter, at a minimum, I hope that I have made a convincing case for the value of that research.

Appendix 11A Quality of Abortion Data: The AGI-CDC Data and the NHSLS Data

NHSLS versus AGI Estimates

A side-by-side comparison indicates that the NHSLS figures are substantially lower than the AGI estimates.

Table 11A.1 shows the AGI-CDC abortion ratio reported by Henshaw, Koonin, and Smith (1991) for several years during the 1980s, overall and by age, race, and marital status. The NHSLS numbers are calculated by identifying the pregnancy outcomes reported for that single year by the women only and showing that same ratio of number of abortions to number of abortions plus live births expressed per one hundred. Thus, the NHSLS figure for 1980, for example, includes all pregnancies that women respondents said ended in a live birth or an abortion in that calendar year. These are then partitioned by the woman's age at that time, her marital status at that time, and her race. Of course, since there are only 1,921 women in the whole NHSLS sample and only a small fraction had a pregnancy that ended in 1980, these comparisons are based on few cases (never fewer than thirty, however; e.g., there were 158 pregnancies that ended in 1980).

That table allows one to see the issue clearly. In 1980, for example, the

Table 11A.1 Comparison of AGI-CDC and NHSLS "Abortion Ratios" for Selected Years and Characteristics

	AGI				NHSLS				1980–89	
	1980	1985	1986	1987	1980	1985	1986	1987	Unweighted	Weighted
Total	30.0	29.7	29.4	28.9	18.7	9.1	16.9	12.0	13.6	13.0
Age										
< 20	41.2	42.1	41.8	41.6	...	...	...	...	28.0	28.9
20–24	30.1	31.5	31.5	31.5	20.4	6.4	20.5	8.8	12.2	11.4
25–29	21.8	22.0	22.0	21.4	15.2	2.3	...	4.3	9.2	8.8
30–34	23.3	21.8	21.5	20.8	...	...	...	...	7.1	6.6
Race										
White	27.4	26.5	25.9	25.2	19.1	7.3	20.7	11.4	14.4	13.8
Other	39.2	39.7	39.8	39.3	17.8	12.8	9.3	13.3	12.1	10.8
Blacks only					21.2	...	...	...	12.1	10.4
Marital status										
Married	9.8	8.8	8.8	8.7	4.9	1.4	5.7	4.7	3.9	3.7
Unmarried	64.9	60.5	58.9	57.1	37.9	19.6	30.0	25.5	27.2	29.2

Source: AGI: Henshaw, Koonin, and Smith (1991, table 1, p. 76); NHSLS: author's calculations.
Note: The abortion ratio is defined as abortions per 100 live births plus abortions.

AGI calculation is that 30.0 percent of all births plus abortions were abortions, whereas the NHSLS proportion is only 18.7 percent. Comparing the two surveys year by year or characteristic by characteristic, the AGI estimate is far higher than the NHSLS estimate. Comparisons of this nature led Jones and Forrest (1992, 113) to conclude, as discussed earlier, that "abortion reporting is found to be highly deficient in all the surveys" (meaning the NSFGs, the NLSY, and the NSYW, which they compared to AGI-CDC figures).

NHSLS versus Vital Statistics Estimates

A comparison of NHSLS figures with vital statistics figures shows a somewhat smaller discrepancy, but the comparison is based on very few cases.

If we compare the NHSLS to the vital statistics figures for the year 1991 reported in *The Statistical Abstract of the United States* (U.S. Bureau of the Census 1995, table 106, 82), shown in table 11A.2, the discrepancy appears to be smaller, although again the comparison is based on very few cases. The *Statistical Abstract* table reports four numbers: pregnancies, live births, induced abortions, and fetal losses for non-Hispanic whites by

Table 11A.2 Comparison of Vital Statistics (VS) and NHSLS Abortion Rates for Whites in 1991, for Selected Age Groups[a]

	20–24		25–29		30–34		35–39	
	VS	NHSLS	VS	NHSLS	VS	NHSLS	VS	NHSLS
Pregnancy	1007	28	1145	38	884	28	367	6
	(100)	(100)	(100)	(100)	(100)	(100)	(100)	
Live birth	637	18	834	30	640	18	235	...
	(63.3)	(64.3)	(72.8)	(79.3)	(72.4)	(64.3)	(64.1)	
Abortion	264	5	163	4	106	4	58	...
	(26.2)	(17.9)	(14.2)	(10.5)	(12.0)	(14.3)	(15.8)	
Fetal loss	107	5	148	4	138	6	76	...
	(10.6)	(17.9)	(12.9)	(10.5)	(15.6)	(21.4)	(20.7)	
Rate per								
1,000 women								
Pregnancy	151.4	153.0	154.7	204.3	107.6	106.9	47.3	29.9
Live birth	95.7	98.4	112.7	161.3	77.9	68.7	30.2	...
Abortion	39.6	27.3	22.0	21.5	12.9	15.3	7.4	...
Fetal loss	16.0	27.3	20.0	21.5	16.8	22.9	9.7	...
N		183		186		262		201

Sources: VS: U.S. Bureau of the Census (1995, table 106, p. 82); NHSLS: author's calculations. [VS numbers expressed in thousands]
Note: Numbers in parentheses are percentages.
[a]There are an insufficient number of blacks in the NHSLS to make this comparison.

age intervals as shown. I have calculated the percentages for each age group. We see, for example, that women aged twenty to twenty-four had slightly over 1 million pregnancies end in 1991, of which 63.3 percent resulted in live births, 26.2 percent ended in abortion, and 10.6 percent ended in fetal loss (miscarriages and stillbirths). The NHSLS data shown are all pregnancies reported by the white women in the survey to have ended in that same year, 1991, by those same age groupings. The table shows that the 183 white women in the age interval twenty to twenty-four had twenty-eight pregnancies end that year; of those, 64.3 percent resulted in live births, 17.9 percent ended in abortion, and 17.9 percent ended in fetal loss.

While the percentage ending in abortion is somewhat lower in the NHSLS than in the *Statistical Abstract* table for the age groups twenty to twenty-four and twenty-five to twenty-nine, the percentage for the age group thirty to thirty-four is actually slightly higher.

Now, the NHSLS numbers reported here are based on very few cases, so they do not have acceptable statistical precision. Moreover, the *Statistical Abstract* figures on induced abortion come from published AGI reports, while the estimates of live births come from vital statistics, and the NSFG is used to obtain the estimates of miscarriages. So, apparently, the three components of total pregnancies were obtained from different sources, although they are then reported as coming from the U.S. National Center for Health Statistics, *Monthly Vital Statistics Report,* vol. 43, no. 12. So the basic source of the data on abortion is AGI. That raises the question why the NHSLS figures are rather more similar to these figures than to the AGI figures shown in table 11A.1 above. Most likely, the discrepancy is explained by the fact that the figures happen to be for a different year and are presented in a different fashion (by age group rather than by total for the year). Thus, I do not suggest that the NHSLS numbers are more similar to the vital statistics numbers than to the AGI numbers, but I do point out that, when organized in a somewhat different manner, these estimates are not so dramatically discrepant, at least for this one year and these age groups, the only year and grouping I have compared. I repeat that the NHSLS numbers reported here are based on too few cases to warrant much attention.

The NHSLS Data

While the NHSLS data on abortion are certainly not flawless and probably somewhat underreported, they have reassuring internal consistency. Moreover, the reported rates of abortion are lower than the reported rates of socially stigmatized or undesirable sexually related behaviors and experiences, suggesting that respondents were not reluctant to report unpleasant, embarrassing, or undesirable events in the context of this survey.

The NHSLS survey is unusual in the detail in which several very private and intimate facets of respondents' sex lives were discussed. In the context of a need to know because of HIV/AIDS and public health policy, the survey instrument was administered to 79 percent of the selected sample of adults. The assessment by the experienced NORC interviewers was that the respondents were eager to share their information, generally knowledgeable, and forthcoming as well as cooperative.

The survey asked about several potentially embarrassing and socially inappropriate behaviors, and the rates of these behaviors as reported by respondents were in many cases surprisingly high. About half the respondents reported having some sexual dysfunction within the past year, about one-sixth reported having had a sexually transmitted infection in their lifetime, and about that same proportion reported some inappropriate sexual encounter or touching before puberty, while even a larger proportion of women said that they had been forced to do something sexual that they did not want to do. The survey included all manner of detailed questions about sexual practices, including oral sex, anal sex, masturbation, and extramarital sex. In that context, the questions about the outcome of all pregnancies the women (or the men's partners) had were not exceptional in their implied request for trust in exposing intimate facts or admitting to behavior that might in other contexts prove to be dangerous or embarrassing or socially unacceptable.

My comparative argument here has generated some dispute, and I do not wish to overstate the claim that I make. There is probably some unknown amount of underreporting of abortion in the NHSLS survey data. There may also be underreporting of other socially proscribed or embarrassing sexual events or behaviors. But the NHSLS has overcome much of people's reluctance to discuss these matters, and the fact that several other topics yield much higher rates of incidence than abortion suggests to me that the rates of abortion may not be too badly underreported. However, I cannot confirm this. Perhaps women are more reluctant to report an abortion that is a politically charged event, or one that may have moral or ethical overtones, or one that may be more under her control, than to report, say, being forced to have sex, or being touched sexually before puberty, or having contracted a sexually transmitted disease. But perhaps not. This topic needs to be further investigated, and I do not claim to have resolved the issue here. I leave it to the reader to judge my argument that the openness and willingness of the sampled adults suggest a commitment to providing truthful and accurate information.

The NHSLS questionnaire obtained information about abortions principally in the face-to-face section of the interview, through a sequence of questions that asked first about the total number of pregnancies the woman had ever had or the total number of pregnancies the man's sex partners had ever had by him. Respondents were then asked about the total number of live births, and, after each baby's date of birth and gender and a few other facts were elicited, in those cases where there had been more pregnancies than live births the respondent was asked which, if any, of the pregnancies had ended in miscarriage, stillbirth, or abortion and the dates of each such event. The self-administered questionnaire (SAQ) also asked about abortion. There, following a series of questions about number of partners, same-gender partners, paid partners, masturbation, and oral, anal, paid-for, and forced sex, was the simple question, "Have you ever had an abortion?" (*SOS*, 674), or, "Have you ever had a sexual partner who become pregnant by you and ended that pregnancy by an abortion?" (*SOS*, 676). Several other questions followed about "what you have done sexually . . . since you reached puberty" with a same-gender partner. In those cases in which respondents answered both questions (self- and interviewer administered) about abortion, 95.9 percent of the men and 97.5 percent of the women gave the same answer both times (for a detailed breakdown, see *SOS*, 457, n. 5).

Given this high rate of internal consistency and the forthcoming responses to questions about what would seem to be proscribed behavior, I conclude that the NHSLS data on abortions are useful and informative and should be analyzed.

The AGI Data

Despite AGI's best efforts, its estimate of the total number of abortions in the United States rests on reports from many sources, sources whose reliability varies. The estimated total number of abortions may be an overestimate. Since there is no way to measure the accuracy of the AGI estimate and neither the AGI survey response rate nor the supplemental information that it provides justifies great confidence, I suggest that the AGI estimate should not be taken, presumptively, to be correct and that it should not be taken as the standard against which all other estimates of the number of abortions in the United States are judged.

For over two decades, the Alan Guttmacher Institute has been collecting data on the number of abortions performed in the United States and publishing and interpreting its findings in a long series of reports in its own publication, *Family Planning Perspectives* (see Henshaw and O'Reilly 1983; Henshaw et al. 1985; Henshaw and Van Vort 1990, 1994; and Henshaw, Koonin, and Smith 1991). As the AGI web page puts it, "Nationally valid data [on abortion] are available from *only* two sources: the federal Centers for Disease Control and Prevention (CDC) and The Alan Guttmacher Institute (AGI)" (my emphasis).[18] Few, if any, private institutions in the country have as exclusive an influence on any population wide statistic as has AGI on information about U.S. abortion behavior.

The manner in which AGI obtains its abortion data is complex, based on now over two decades of canvassing hospitals, clinics, and physicians. That canvassing procedure is publicly documented in the AGI publications, and, from reading the descriptions given there, one has the sense that AGI makes quite a careful, thorough, and scientifically responsible effort to obtain these data and to disseminate them widely and readily. Few methods of data capture or measurement are, however, without some limitation or not subject to some flaw or error, and the AGI abortion statistics are no exception. AGI currently conducts its institutional/physician survey every four years and focuses nearly exclusively on estimating the total number of abortions performed in the United States as a whole and by geographic area (i.e., by state). Many subsequent AGI publications report in detail on how the survey is conducted (see, e.g., Henshaw and Van Vort 1994). The AGI-CDC estimate of the total number of abortions is then arrayed by demographic characteristics in other *Family Planning Perspectives* publications. These papers and results are not derived from AGI's own survey of institutions but instead based on AGI's estimate of the total

Table 11A.3 AGI Survey Response Rates Calculated for Three Lists, 1991–92

	All Known Abortion Providers[a]		AMA Physicians Sample		Hospital Sample	
	N	%	N	%	N	%
Number surveyed	3,156	100	1,125[b]	100	289	100
Completed	1,606	51	600	52	215	74
Partial interview by phone	831	26				
Nonresponse[c]	719	23	525	47	74	26

[a]A complete list of hospitals, clinics, and physicians surveyed by AGI in the previous survey round, 1989, and a list of possible new providers.
[b]Eliminating from this AMA sample those covered by the "known providers" survey and those who "had moved or closed and could not be located" (Henshaw and Van Vort 1994, 101).
[c]AGI "used health department data for 328 providers" and "knowledgeable sources in their communities" for 121 others.

number of abortions that year and the CDC's abortion surveillance system, which has information on certain characteristics of women whose abortions are reported to the CDC system.

As best I can discern, if one takes the 1991–92 AGI survey of hospitals, clinics, and physicians' offices as three distinct lists and calculates the percentage of the list that yields a completed response, the "response rate" would be something like that displayed in table 11A.3. For most other social science data collection efforts, response rates at these levels would be considered no more than barely adequate, if that.

These respondents' reports to AGI are augmented by several types of activities that reflect AGI's effort to obtain a full and accurate estimate. While these efforts reduce the coverage bias, they introduce a measurement bias that may more than counterbalance the improvements in coverage. While AGI performs a very valuable service by conducting its abortion surveys, the data that it produces are not flawless.

Consider the matter of the direction of bias in the response to AGI's survey, which is conducted periodically with the same providers. While the direction of bias in an individual's response to a personal interview about abortion in the context of a household survey conducted by an unknown survey organization is probably discernible, that is not the case with this AGI survey, and this is not necessarily an advantage. The individual respondent in a household survey is not likely to report systematically and erroneously *more* abortions than she in fact has had. Few women would consider an abortion so socially attractive that they would purposely overstate the number that they have had, and few will have had so many that a personal estimate would involve some rounding algorithm that might somehow be upwardly biased. And, surely, some respondents are likely to be inclined to understate the number of abortions that they have had since there is great social and political pressure opposing abortion. The result is that, in the household survey, the direction of bias is downward, although the magnitude of the bias is not clear.

In the case of the AGI survey of clinics, hospitals, and physicians, however, even the direction of bias is not clear. Some may underreport, especially if abortion is not a major component of their business. But other clinics or service delivery facilities either specialize in abortion or consider abortion to be of great value and take pride in delivering this service, and these facilities may be inclined to overstate the number of abortions performed or to define as an abortion a procedure that preempts a pending miscarriage or even a consultation about the procedure. Similar incentives exist in other domains, of course: in measuring the number of homeless, for example, surveys of homeless shelters have been found to overstate the number of daily clients, compared to spot audit counts of occupied beds. And it is common to suppose that an organization will be eager to emphasize the value of its product and the demand for its services—whether it is a Pentagon assessment of a weapon or a university's assessment of its student loan program. An organization that performs abortions and faces political pressure because of that practice is probably inclined to report an upper- rather than a lower-bound estimate in a confidential report to an organization known to favor that practice.

Even though AGI provides a reasonably complete description of its procedures for estimating the number of abortions performed by the large number of service providers sampled who do not respond to the survey, one cannot tell the direction of bias that may be introduced by those procedures. There is, understandably, insufficient detail provided in the published results to provide assurance that the methods by which AGI augments the actual survey data (by means, e.g., of calculations based on "knowledgeable sources in their communities") result in good or reliable or unbiased numbers.

An indication that the AGI numbers may be on the high side is found in Joyce (1988, 627). Joyce notes that the New York City Department of Health reported 96,802 induced abortions for 1984 while AGI, "based on its survey of providers, estimated that 124,570 induced abortions occurred in New York City in that same year." The AGI number is 129 percent of the Health Department number. I am not able to judge the accuracy of either of these numbers. Similarly, Henshaw, Koonin, and Smith (1991, 75) report that, for 1987, the CDC Abortion Surveillance Survey of health departments in forty-three states and the District of Columbia as well as hospitals and other medical facilities in seven states reported 13 percent fewer abortions than did AGI for that same year. The CDC survey is used, as noted above, to apportion the estimated number of abortions among women by age, race, and marital status. Again, I do not know, and do not claim, that the AGI numbers are inferior to these health departments reports. I note the discrepancies between the two and suggest that this should alert analysts to the fact that the AGI numbers are not necessarily accurate and may be overestimates.

So it is not clear what direction of bias may dominate the AGI estimate of number of abortions performed in the United States. I can see no clear ground on which to argue that the number reported by those who do report is higher or lower than the actual number, and there are arguments why it may be too high or too low, as suggested above. The more speculative estimates of the remainder may well be biased upward to an unknown extent since those "knowledgeable sources" are more likely to be advocates than opponents of abortion and AGI is not a neutral or unknown agent in abortion politics. The statement that AGI personnel make, in independent, refereed publications as well as its own, is that "the AGI statistics nevertheless are widely accepted as the best available estimates of the incidence of abortion in the United States (U.S. Bureau of the Census)" (Jones and Forrest 1992, 114). That is not a strong or reassuring statement, even though it is surely an accurate one. I am not persuaded, however, that AGI estimates are of such great accuracy or reliability that they should be used presumptively as the standard against which all other measures of abortion should be judged. Nor should it be assumed that the AGI estimates are not overestimates. This is the current common practice, however.

The AGI-CDC Data

The AGI-CDC estimation of the distribution of abortion by women's characteristics (age, race, etc.) also relies on partial information, so these distributions should also be considered only useful estimates, not necessarily the standard against which all other estimates should be judged.

The distribution of abortion by characteristics of women relies on the CDC Abortion Surveillance Survey. This annual survey, first conducted in 1969, obtains data from fifty states and the District of Columbia—specifically, from central health agencies in forty-seven states, New York City, and the District of Columbia and from hospitals and other medical facilities in five other areas (for 1991) (Koonin, Smith, and Ramick 1995). The reports collected contain information about the age, race, parity, and marital status of the woman, weeks of gestation, and type of procedure used, although not all reporting units (states) report all these characteristics. The report on the 1991 Abortion Surveillance Survey, for example, notes that only thirty-four of the states reported on race (Koonin, Smith, and Ramick 1995, 27).

Some states, apparently, do not make full reports, and others seem to report little, if anything. A footnote reveals that the reported number of abortions for the most populous state, California, which accounted for an estimated 25 percent of the nation's abortions in 1991, is a "CDC estimate" (Koonin, Smith, and Ramick 1995, 29). California is notably absent in the state-by-state tables reporting abortion by age, race, ethnicity, marital status, parity, weeks of gestation, and medical procedure (Koonin, Smith, and Ramick 1995, 34, 42, 43, 44, 46, 38, and 40). It is unclear, therefore, what procedure AGI-CDC uses when applying "the percentage distributions of women obtaining abortions, according to various characteristics, as compiled by the U.S. Centers for Disease Control" (Henshaw and O'Reilly 1983, 5) to the total number of abortions estimated by AGI. If California is excluded from the information base on which a distribution by age or marital status or race or ethnicity is produced, it is not a highly reliable distribution to apply to the United States as a whole; if California is included on some basis other than the CDC survey, it is not clear what that basis is or how accurate it is.

Other Data

Other data on abortion behavior are often not relied on, apparently because they are not similar in level or distribution to the AGI-CDC estimates. In my judgment, despite outstanding efforts to be complete and accurate, the imprecision with which these latter estimates are made does not justify this practice.

There are several household surveys that include questions about abortion behavior. These include the NLSY, the several NSFGs, and the NSYW, among others. This appendix will not review their attributes or the substantive patterns of abortion that they reveal. The 1995 National Survey of Family Growth has a special supplemental section focused on abortion, conducted by audio-CASI in the context of a 103-minute CAPI instrument administered to over ten thousand women aged fifteen to forty-four. I have not yet sought nor seen information about that abortion module, but I note one issue. In the official NCHS publication (Abma et al. 1997), the abortion data are not presented.

Despite sections about such other important complementary behavior as HIV testing, cigarette smoking, sex education, pelvic inflammatory disease, and douching, about the only mention of abortion in that otherwise informative publication is in the definition of a *family planning or medical service*. The tables on contraception or fertility control more broadly do include sterilization and such esoteric birth control methods as the female condom, but abortion is never mentioned. Abortion is not even listed in the glossary of terms, and, when pregnancy outcomes are described, there is a brief explanation that, although the audio-CASI asked about pregnancies ending in abortion, the information from that module is not included:

"Including data from the self-administered (Audio CASI) part of the survey raises the number of abortions reported, but comparisons with other data show that reporting is still incomplete" (Abma et al. 1997, 111).

Surely, it is important not to report inaccurate or misleading data, and the caution evinced in this NCHS report is laudatory since it would be easy just to include the abortion data. Apparently, those who know this survey have appropriately used their best judgment in deciding not to report the abortion data. Nonetheless, I point to this decision as another indication that there is a very strong and pervasive stance today that only the AGI estimate of abortion has merit and that no other estimates from any other source, particularly from household surveys, are useful or reliable.

I do not see any ground for that stance in the public descriptions of the AGI data capture methods, procedures, or products. This is not intended as a criticism of the work done by AGI; rather, my argument is that other data sources have their own strengths and limitations. Survey data are not without flaws and known as well as unknown biases, but it is too extreme, I contend, to continue to take the position that only AGI and only institutional surveys can adequately provide information about abortion in the United States. If surveys understate the number of abortions, this is problematic for model estimation only if that underestimation is not random and is systematic in ways that create bias in estimates of parameters of interest.

Conclusion

My conclusion is that information on abortion contained in survey data should not be disregarded simply because it is not consistent with AGI-CDC estimates, which themselves have evident flaws and may be upwardly biased. The reverse is also true: the AGI-CDC estimates are probably currently our best point estimates of abortion levels and trends in the United States, and they too should not be disregarded.

We can advance our understanding of abortion behavior by exploiting what is of value in several quality data sets, mindful of the limitations of each. If we act as if one method of data capture or one quasi-official estimate that has evident limitations is fully accurate, we will not advance our understanding as effectively as if we acknowledge that no current measure is flawless, that several measures have merit, and that all need to be improved.

Notes

I acknowledge the assistance of Audrey Smolkin, who undertook much of the preliminary statistical analysis and contributed to the focus and structure of the chapter. Useful suggestions by Christine Bachrach, Rebecca Blank, Michael Grossman, Martha Van Haitzma,

Theodore Joyce, Ann Kuta, Edward Laumann, Nancy Michael, Susan Newcomer, Tom Smith, and Niña Trefler are also acknowledged and appreciated. Robin Tepper and Kara Foehrkolb provided useful research assistance.

1. I emphasize here the literature on the determinants of choices. There is also an extensive literature on the psychological effect of the abortion choice (see, e.g., Gilligan 1982; Rind 1991; and Stotland 1992).

2. This reversal in rates across racial groups is not found in a study that uses more states and distinguishes between whites and "all others" instead of whites and blacks. In that *Monthly Vital Statistics Report* (Ventura et al. 1995, table 4, p. 17), the four rates of induced abortion for 1991 are 6.6 percent for married whites, 39.1 percent for unmarried whites, 20.6 percent for married "all other," and 75.8 percent for unmarried "all other." Invariably, the abortion rate is much higher for the unmarried than for those who are married, for both whites and "all others," and that pattern is nearly as strong for 1980 and 1990 as well.

3. It has been suggested to me that, unlike most of these other admissions of unattractive behavior, an admission of abortion may come with a different "emotional loading" since it is more an admission of a mistake than is, say, that of a sexual dysfunction or a disease that is "caught from someone else."

4. Alberman (1992) reports that "data assembled by Kline et al. (1989) show that most retrospective inquiries about previous pregnancy outcome report fetal death rates . . . of between 11% and 16%, while two large studies of rates derived from hospital admissions for spontaneous abortions report rates between 6.8% and 7.2% (Narod and Khazen 1989) and between 7.8% and 10.2% (Lindbohm and Hemminki 1988) respectively" (pp. 11–12).

5. To reconcile the statements about miscarriage and abortion considered in the preceding few pages, consider the following, hypothetical circumstance. Suppose that a sample of women has in fact had one hundred fertilized eggs, of which fifty were lost to spontaneous abortion or miscarriage, and that one-third of these miscarriages were detected by the women and reported when later interviewed about all the pregnancies they had ever had. The sample of women would then report a total of sixty-seven pregnancies (the other thirty-three having ended by miscarriage that was never detected). Suppose, further, that there were fifteen induced abortions and thirty-five live births (thus fifty pregnancies that survived spontaneous abortion). Then the survey would have recorded seventeen miscarriages, fifteen abortions, and thirty-five live births. Here, there would have been about as many abortions as miscarriages reported, even though in fact half of all fertilized eggs spontaneously aborted. If the "abortion ratio" were calculated, it would be 30 percent (= 15 abortions/50 abortions plus live births).

6. Introducing the topic of adolescent sexuality, the U.S. Department of Health and Human Services annual report on children and youth says, "Because sexual intercourse during the teen years, especially first intercourse, is often unplanned, it is also often unprotected by contraception" (Office of the ASPE 1997, 238). The NSFG-1995 shows the "wantedness status of births, and indicates that among live births, not pregnancies, 27% of first births were mistimed, while only 18% of second births were mistimed. Of course, the percentages that were 'unwanted' as distinguished from mistimed, rises with birth order, especially from the second upward—the percent unwanted is 4% of first births, 6% of second births, and 21% of third or higher births" (Abma et al. 1997, table 14, p. 25).

7. Some indication of this fact is seen in the NSFG-1995, which asked the women respondents about the "wantedness status at conception" of each birth in the five years preceding the interview. These births are then characterized as falling into one of three categories: intended, mistimed, or unwanted. The proportions of the births that were intended, by the marital status of the woman at conception, were 80.9 percent for married women, 61.1 percent for formerly married women, and 43.6 percent for never married women. Note that none of these pregnancies were aborted: the survey asked this question only about live births. The NSFG also asked each woman how happy she was to be pregnant (for pregnancies in

the time interval 1991–95). Responses were given in terms of a ten-point scale, ranging from 1, "very unhappy to be pregnant," to 10, "very happy to be pregnant," and, apparently, all pregnancies, not just live births, were included. Among the women who were married, only 10.6 percent of responses were in the range 1–3, whereas, among the unmarried women, 35.4 percent of responses were in the range 1–3. Conversely, among the married women, 74.8 percent of responses and, among the unmarried women, only 35.2 percent of responses were in the range 8–10 (see Abma et al. 1997, table 14, p. 25, and table 17, p. 27).

8. Again, the NSFG-1995 indicates the "wantedness status" of births in the past five years; the proportion "intended," by the woman's age, is 34.3 percent for women age under twenty, 61.1 percent for women twenty to twenty-four, 77.8 percent for women twenty-five to twenty-nine, and 80.1 percent for women thirty to forty-four. Regarding how happy these women were with their pregnancies, 32.7 percent of those fifteen–nineteen, 19.2 percent of those twenty to twenty-nine, and 14.5 percent of those thirty to forty-four responded in the range 1–3, while 36.3 percent of those fifteen to nineteen, 61.4 percent of those twenty to twenty-nine, and 69.4 percent of those thirty–forty-four responded in the range 8–10 (see Abma et al. 1997, table 14, p. 25, and table 16, p. 27).

9. It is noteworthy that the percentage of men in the NHSLS cross-sectional sample who report one of their partners becoming pregnant is only 65 percent while the percentage of women who report becoming pregnant is much higher, 80 percent. That percentage for women is roughly comparable to the percentage of women in the CPS aged fifteen to forty-four who have ever borne a child—82 percent—but a comparable figure for men is not so readily available. Most fertility statistics disregard men. It is possible that men in the NHSLS have understated the rate at which their partners conceived, but the right-hand panel of table 11.1 suggests that, if so, it is in large measure the miscarriages that are underreported. (For the rate cited for childlessness among women, see U.S. Bureau of the Census [1995, table 102, 80]. No comparable table is presented for men.)

10. If abortion averts some miscarriages, then one might expect to see a decline in the report of miscarriage when the rate of abortion rises, and there is some hint of a decline in col. 8, comparing women in their fifties and those under thirty, who report much higher rates of abortion.

11. All rates here are based on thirty or more cases, so the ages have been grouped together where there were fewer than thirty observations at that age; the brackets indicate all the ages that are combined in each number. That is, in col. 1, e.g., 40 percent of men through age seventeen, 30 percent of men age eighteen and nineteen, and 25 percent of men age twenty report that their partner aborted her first pregnancy.

12. The two variables "parent HS (< 18)" and "parent college (< 18)" are interaction terms, multiplying the dummy variable for parents' education by the dummy variable for the respondent being under age eighteen at the time of conception. The point made in the body of the text—that women are typically younger at the first pregnancy than are their partners—is seen in the variable "age < 18," which has a mean of 0.062 for the men and 0.208 for the women, and that is the explanation for the differences in the means of these interaction terms as well.

13. Calculating these partial derivatives for dummy variables should be considered only as illustrative of the effects. A more precise characterization of the key effects is offered in the discussion of table 11.9 below.

14. Chapter 2 above also reports a strong effect using these same data only for women whose first conception occurred before age eighteen. Here, the analysis is not limited to these early conceptions, nor is it limited only to women.

15. Table 11.9A also suggests the interactions among these variables. Notice how little marital status affects man A or woman A. That is primarily because A's conception occurs before 1973, so the illegality of abortion is seen to dominate the marital status effect. One sees the same pattern in tables 11.9B and 11.9C.

16. The number of cases of a second conception occurring before age eighteen was twelve for the men and ninety-six for the women (of these ninety-six, fifty-seven occurred at age seventeen, nineteen at age sixteen, and the remainder at even younger ages). For the third conception before age eighteen, the numbers were one for the men and eighteen for the women. For the fourth conception before age eighteen, the numbers were one for the men and six for the women. No one reported five conceptions occurring before age eighteen.

17. Some caution is warranted regarding this view, however. Hotz, McElroy, and Sanders (1996) compare young mothers with comparable young women who had miscarriages instead and, after looking at their subsequent schooling, earnings, and other behavior, conclude that "it is not the case that teen mothers would fare substantively better in life if they delayed their childbearing" (p. 56).

18. The AGI web page can be found at www.agi-usa.org/pubs/ibl4/ibl4.html: "Issues in Brief—the Limitations of U.S. Statistics on Abortion."

CHAPTER TWELVE

■

Private Sexual Behavior, Public Opinion, and Public Health Policy Related to Sexually Transmitted Diseases: A U.S.-British Comparison

ROBERT T. MICHAEL, JANE WADSWORTH, JOEL A. FEINLEIB, ANNE M. JOHNSON,

EDWARD O. LAUMANN, AND KAYE WELLINGS

The transmission of sexually transmitted diseases (STDs) in populations is determined by the interaction among the biological properties of the infecting organisms, the behavioral characteristics of the population, and the effectiveness of control programs (Hethcote and Yorke 1984). Until recently, little attention has been paid to the distribution of sexual behavior in populations, but, with the emerging HIV epidemic, national studies have been conducted in Europe (Johnson et al. 1994; ACSF Investigators 1993; Spira, Bajos, and Group 1994; Kontula and Haavio-Mannila 1993), the United States (Sonenstein, Pleck, and Ku 1989; Catania et al. 1992; Billy et al. 1993; *SOS;* Catania et al. 1995; Abma et al. 1997) and several developing countries (Cleland and Ferry 1995).

Studies in the developed world have been more remarkable for their findings of similarity rather than differences in sexual behavior (Bajos et al. 1995), yet there are important differences in the epidemiology of STDs, including HIV, among countries with superficially similar sexual behavior patterns. The 1994 U.S. gonorrhea rate per 100,000 population aged fifteen to sixty-four, for example, was 246, while in Britain it was only 33. In Britain, the number of reported cases of chlamydia trachomatis in 1994 was threefold higher than reported cases of gonorrhea, while the United States reported almost equal numbers of chlamydia trachomatis and gonorrhea cases (CDC 1994; *Sexually Transmitted Diseases* 1996). The 1996 incidence of AIDS in Britain was 24 per million population (ECEMA 1997), while in the United States it was 256 per million population (CDC 1996, 1997), despite the fact that HIV was probably introduced into Britain shortly after it was introduced into the United States (Knox, MacArthur, and Simons 1993).

The incidence of HIV is estimated to have peaked in Britain around 1982–84 with an intense epidemic in homosexual men and limited spread to intravenous drug users. Probably owing to behavior change, a declining incidence followed, so the prevalence observed in Britain has never reached the intensity seen in high-risk populations in the United States. In the United States, no such peak occurred early in the epidemic. Regarding the known transmission mechanisms of all AIDS cases by 1996, 50 percent of U.S. and 59 percent of British cases involve transmission between men who have sex with men, 26 percent of U.S. and 10 percent of British cases involve intravenous drug users (with another 6 percent in the United States and another 2 percent in Britain involving both men who have sex with men and intravenous drug users), and 9 percent of U.S. and 20 percent of British cases involve heterosexual contact (CDC 1996, 1997; Report of Expert Group 1996).

Britain operates a national network of free, open-access STD clinics, responsible for STD reporting. These are thought to treat the majority of STDs and are known to be used by all sectors of the population (Johnson et al. 1996). Thus, underreporting in Britain is unlikely to be the explanation for the observed differences in incidence, which probably reflect differences in sexual behavior patterns and in STD control programs. In this chapter, we compare patterns of sexual behavior in the United States and Britain, drawing on data from recent national probability sample surveys. Reflecting on those reported differences in both sexual behavior and reported opinions about what is considered appropriate sexual behavior in the two countries, we suggest that those behavioral differences and opinions may help explain the differences in the rates of STDs between the two countries. They may also help explain the differences in public health policies with regard to HIV/AIDS.

12.1 Methods

Britain

Between May 1990 and December 1991, a sample of 18,876 adults in England, Wales, and Scotland was interviewed. Households were randomly selected from the Post Office Small Users Postcode address file. One member of each household aged between sixteen and fifty-nine was selected; data were collected using face-to-face interviews and self-administered questionnaires. Respondents were not offered financial payment for participating, and the overall response rate was 65 percent. The final sample broadly represented the demographic characteristics of Great Britain's population (see Johnson et al. 1992; Wadsworth et al. 1993; and Johnson et al. 1994).

United States

Between February and August 1992, a sample of 3,432 adults in the United States was interviewed. Households were selected from a stratified, clustered national sample, with random selection of one English-speaking member aged eighteen to fifty-nine. Blacks and Hispanics were over-sampled. The overall response rate was 79 percent. Forty-six percent of respondents were paid a nominal fee of $10.00–$25.00, 41 percent were paid no fee, and the remainder were paid a fee exceeding $25.00; no indication was found of any effect of these payments on the answers provided. The face-to-face interview lasted on average ninety minutes and included several self-administered components and memory aids. The data set is known as the National Health and Social Life Survey (NHSLS) (see *SOS;* and *SIA*).

Comparison

This comparative analysis uses British respondents aged eighteen to fifty-nine and excludes the U.S. oversamples; all tables report weighted statistics adjusted for household size. Although the two surveys were conducted independently, using different protocols, the general character of the information obtained is similar, facilitating cross-national comparisons. There is little evidence in these data or elsewhere of a response bias in sexual behavior surveys (see Johnson et al. 1994; *SOS; SIA;* and Biggar and Melbye 1992). Statistical analysis has been restricted to comparisons of proportions where there are minimal differences in question wording; Mantel Haenzel χ^2 statistics are reported for significance tests of cross-country differences, separately by gender.

The data on STDs are derived differently in the two surveys. In the British survey, respondents were asked whether they had attended an STD clinic, irrespective of a positive diagnosis. In the U.S. study, respondents were asked if they had been diagnosed specifically with any of nine sexually transmitted infections (STIs) (listed in table 12.3 below). The lack of correspondence between the questions used in the two surveys makes direct comparison difficult. Using STD clinic attendance as the indicator rather than diagnosis of an STD may lead to an overestimate of prevalence for Britain compared to the United States, but it may also result in underestimate since some conditions may be treated in other settings in Britain, such as general practice, student health services, or family planning clinics. The comparisons for the two countries are therefore inexact.

12.2 Results

Sexual Behavior

NUMBER OF PARTNERS

Table 12.1 shows the distribution of numbers of opposite-sex partners by age, gender, and country, for the past year (panel A) and over the adult lifetime (panel B). A relatively high proportion of the youngest and oldest age groups report no sex partner in the past year. There is a strong decline in the proportion having two or more sex partners with increasing age in both countries. Consistently fewer women than men, and fewer in Britain than in the United States, report having two or more sex partners (cross-country $\chi^2 = 23.2$, $p < .001$, for men and 16.9, $p < .001$, for women). In all age groups, the British were more likely to have only one partner, and women were more likely than men to report only one partner.

Questions about the number of opposite-sex partners over the lifetime were asked differently in the two surveys: U.S. respondents reported the number of partners since age eighteen, while British respondents reported the number of partners ever. Many of the patterns seen in panel A are also observed in panel B. The number of partners rises with age as partners are accumulated. For both genders in most age groups, larger proportions in the United States had both no partner and more than twenty partners. As found in other studies, men report substantially more partners over the lifetime than do women (Smith 1990; *SOS;* Wadsworth et al. 1996).

SEXUAL PRACTICES

Table 12.2 shows the percentages reporting different sexual behaviors. Panel A shows the percentages of the British and U.S. samples who first had intercourse before age eighteen. In both countries, and in all age groups, men were more likely than women to be sexually active before age eighteen, and younger cohorts were more likely to be sexually active than older ones, especially women. Panel B shows the percentages who reported never having had sexual intercourse before their first marriage. The patterns are again quite similar across the two countries, except at the youngest age group, which is based on a small sample for the United States (all numbers are based on thirty or more cases). In both countries, the percentages who were virgins at marriage have declined across the decades, more steeply in Britain than in the United States, and the rates are typically higher for women.

Panels C and D show the percentages reporting a same-gender sex partner in the past year or over the lifetime (Britain) or since age eighteen (United States). In the past year, the rate of reported homosexual experience is higher in the United States than in Britain ($\chi^2 = 14.3$, $p < .001$,

Table 12.1 Distribution of Heterosexual Partners

Age, Gender, Country	Number of Partners				Base
	0	1	2–4	5+	
A. *Within the past year*					
18–24:					
Men:					
Britain	19.4	51.5	25.2	3.9	1,565
United States	17.7	46.4	27.1	8.7	289
Women:					
Britain	14.3	70.0	14.9	.8	1,747
United States	13.0	59.7	20.7	6.6	302
25–34:					
Men:					
Britain	8.6	76.8	12.7	1.9	2,102
United States	11.4	67.7	17.5	3.4	443
Women:					
Britain	6.7	86.8	6.2	.3	2,798
United States	7.9	85.1	6.0	1.0	490
35–44:					
Men:					
Britain	6.8	84.1	8.3	.8	1,974
United States	6.5	78.7	13.5	1.3	378
Women:					
Britain	7.4	88.4	4.1	.1	2,483
United States	10.4	84.3	4.9	.3	479
45–59:					
Men:					
Britain	10.8	83.9	5.4	.1	2,031
United States	11.1	83.3	5.0	.6	355
Women:					
Britain	19.3	78.8	1.8	.0	2,583
United States	22.8	74.8	2.3	.1	416
All ages:					
Men:					
Britain	11.0	75.4	12.2	1.5	7,673
United States	11.3	70.1	15.4	3.2	1,466
Women:					
Britain	11.7	82.0	6.1	.3	9,611
United States	13.2	77.8	7.4	1.6	1,687

(continued)

for men and 13.2, $p < .001$, for women), and the annual rate is highest in the age category twenty-five to thirty-four for men in both countries and for women in the United States. Over the lifetime, rates differ within a few percentage points between the United States and Britain, for each age and gender group.

Panel E shows similar proportions reporting extramarital sex in the last year in Britain and the United States—overall, about 5 percent of men

Table 12.1 (continued)

Age, Gender, Country	Number of Partners						Base
	0	1	2–4	5–10	11–20	21+	
B. *Over the Lifetime (Britain) or since age 18 (United States)*							
18–24:							
Men:							
Britain	12.0	16.6	32.8	24.2	9.8	4.7	1,562
United States	15.8	21.5	28.5	20.2	8.9	5.1	279
Women:							
Britain	10.7	29.8	37.8	17.9	2.0	.8	1,747
United States	10.3	27.1	40.8	18.1	2.6	1.1	285
25–34:							
Men:							
Britain	3.1	15.0	27.4	29.1	15.0	10.3	2,098
United States	5.7	16.1	23.8	27.4	13.9	13.1	422
Women:							
Britain	2.1	30.8	40.7	20.4	4.6	1.3	2,795
United States	4.6	29.1	37.3	21.4	5.0	2.5	464
35–44:							
Men:							
Britain	1.9	20.5	27.8	26.5	14.4	8.9	1,966
United States	1.2	16.0	20.4	34.4	13.7	14.4	361
Women:							
Britain	.7	40.7	36.2	16.9	3.5	1.9	2,476
United States	3.5	31.0	34.3	22.0	5.8	3.4	450
45–59:							
Men:							
Britain	1.5	30.5	31.5	21.0	9.0	6.5	2,021
United States	2.0	22.2	21.9	24.7	12.1	17.0	312
Women:							
Britain	1.5	57.7	29.6	8.8	1.8	.6	2,576
United States	4.9	41.7	31.1	16.9	3.2	2.2	389
All ages:							
Men:							
Britain	4.2	20.8	29.7	25.3	12.2	7.8	7,673
United States	5.7	18.6	23.4	27.2	12.4	12.7	1,374
Women:							
Britain	3.2	40.4	36.0	15.9	3.3	1.2	9,595
United States	5.4	32.4	35.6	19.9	4.4	2.4	1,587

and 2 percent of women. There are differences among age groups, but these should be interpreted with caution, especially for the youngest U.S. age groups since these are based on relatively few cases.

Panels F and G show rates of oral and anal sex, respectively, excluding from the denominator those who had no sex partner within the year. The

Table 12.2 Sexual Behavior, by Age, Country, and Gender

Gender and Country	Age				All
	18–24	25–34	35–44	45–59	
A. % having sex before age 18					
Men:					
Britain	65.2	60.0	46.9	31.8	
United States	69.2	55.4	53.3	42.9	
Women:					
Britain	63.3	48.0	33.7	15.3	
United States	59.5	52.4	39.2	29.7	
B. % who were virgins at first marriage					
Men:					
Britain	.0	4.1	7.5	15.0	
United States	22.2	11.9	13.0	18.8	
Women:					
Britain	3.9	6.8	14.7	39.2	
United States	17.9	17.0	24.7	44.4	
C. % reporting any same-gender partners within the past year					
Men:					
Britain	1.4	1.5	.8	.7	1.1
United States	2.9	3.9	1.9	.4	2.4
Women:					
Britain	.7	.6	.2	.1	.4
United States	.1	2.4	.8	.4	1.0
D. % reporting any same-gender partners over the lifetime (Britain) since age 18 (United States)					
Men:					
Britain	3.1	3.7	5.0	3.2	3.8
United States	4.4	6.8	2.0	1.7	3.9
Women:					
Britain	1.6	2.0	2.1	1.3	1.8
United States	.2	3.7	3.5	2.8	2.8
E. % reporting extramarital sex in the past year					
Men:					
Britain	3.9	5.1	5.4	3.7	4.7
United States	5.4	4.8	5.0	4.6	4.8
Women:					
Britain	1.5	2.1	2.4	1.1	1.9
United States	8.5	1.2	.8	1.2	1.6

(continued)

Table 12.2 (continued)

Gender and Country	Age				
	18–24	25–34	35–44	45–59	All
F. % reporting oral sex in the past year					
Men:					
Britain	85.8	84.1	73.0	46.5	71.6
United States	73.1	76.2	76.2	58.4	71.3
Women:					
Britain	81.5	78.6	64.0	37.1	65.2
United States	78.8	76.2	68.7	49.8	68.7
G. % reporting anal sex in the past year					
Men:					
Britain	10.0	7.2	6.6	5.6	7.2
United States	7.2	10.5	13.0	5.9	9.4
Women:					
Britain	10.0	7.1	5.2	5.3	6.7
United States	9.3	10.2	8.9	5.3	8.6
H. % using condoms in last heterosexual event					
Men:					
Britain	37.0	24.0	19.6	13.6	22.5
United States	33.1	24.0	10.9	4.8	17.5
Women:					
Britain	22.9	18.9	16.2	12.4	17.1
United States	29.1	16.2	14.0	4.5	15.3

reported rates of oral sex are slightly higher for men than for women and tend to be higher for the British under age thirty-five and for Americans over thirty-five. Overall, the differences are small and significant only for women ($\chi^2 = 0.6$, $p < .50$, for men and 5.5, $p < .025$, for women). The rates are decidedly lower for those over age forty-five for both genders. For anal sex, there is a lower rate at older ages for the British but a more erratic pattern in the United States. There is no clear difference in the reported rate by gender, but there is a higher rate in the United States than in Britain over age twenty-five and a lower rate under age twenty-five ($\chi^2 = 8.2$, $p < .01$, for men and 7.1, $p < .01$, for women).

Panel H shows condom use the last time the respondent had vaginal intercourse. Reported use is significantly higher among British than American men ($\chi^2 = 15.8$, $p < .001$) but not consistently so for women ($\chi^2 = 3.6$, $p < .10$). This country difference is particularly marked for men over age thirty-five. There is a pronounced age difference in both countries, with younger men and women reporting higher rates of condom use. As noted above, these groups also have more partners, so their risks are correspondingly greater.

Disease Risks

Panel A of table 12.3 shows the rates in the past year of visiting an STD clinic in Britain and of having an STD in the United States, by gender and age. The rates are roughly comparable in the two countries and relatively similar for men and women, although we note again that the questions asked on this matter differ substantially. Panel B shows the U.S. rates of STDs and the British rates of attending an STD clinic ever, and there are pronounced differences by country. The U.S. rates are two or three times as high as the British for men and even greater for women, and the differences exist for every age group. Overall, British men have a rate near 8 percent, and, in the United States, the rate is nearly twice as high, 15 percent, while, for women, the overall rate in Britain is near 6 percent and in the United States is 16 percent. The far higher rates for the United States mirror the higher rates reported in official surveillance data, as cited above.

Panels C and D show a clear positive relation between number of sex partners and the likelihood of contracting an STD. This strong relation is seen in both the U.S. and the British data, for both genders, and both in the short term (panel C) and over the lifetime (panel D).

Opinions

Table 12.4 shows that there are great differences between the two countries in opinions about premarital, extramarital, and homosexual sex. The British are much more tolerant of premarital sex, at all age groups, and there is far greater tolerance among younger generations in both nations. There is less tolerance of extramarital sex than of premarital sex in both countries, and there is less difference in opinion about extramarital sex between Britain and the United States; there is little difference by age in opinions about extramarital sex.

The questions about homosexual sex were asked differently in the two surveys. In the United States, no distinction was made between sex between men and sex between women, whereas separate questions were asked in Britain. The results show that both genders at each age are more tolerant of homosexual behavior in Britain than in the United States. In fact, overall, table 12.4 shows remarkable consistency. For all four age groups within each country, the tolerance ranking is the same: premarital sex is most tolerated, homosexual sex is next, and extramarital sex is least tolerated; and, within each of the twenty-four age-gender comparisons, the British exhibit greater tolerance.

Table 12.3 Sexual Transmitted Diseases, by Duration of Time, Age, and Number of Partners (Britain: Visited an STD Clinic; United States: Diagnosed as Having One of Nine STDs)

Gender and Country	Age				
	18–24	25–34	35–44	45–59	All
A. In the past year, by age					
Men:					
Britain	1.5	1.2	.7	.2	.9
United States	3.7	1.2	.3	.4	1.3
Women:					
Britain	1.6	1.3	.1	.1	.7
United States	5.2	1.6	1.1	.3	1.8
B. Ever, by age					
Men:					
Britain	5.2	11.7	10.5	5.3	8.4
United States	9.2	16.3	18.4	14.3	15.0
Women:					
Britain	5.3	8.2	6.4	2.6	5.7
United States	16.3	18.2	17.9	10.8	16.0

	Number of Male or Female Partners in the Last Year				
	0	1	2	3	4+
C. In the past year, by number of partners					
Men:					
Britain	.1	.5	2.0	3.6	8.8
United States	.0	.6	.8	6.5	6.0
Women:					
Britain	.3	.6	2.9	7.4	3.7
United States	.2	1.2	3.4	4.8	17.2

	Number of Male or Female Partners Ever (Britain) or since Age 18 (United States)					
	0	1	2–4	5–10	11–20	21+
D. Ever, by number of partners						
Men:						
Britain	.5	1.1	3.2	8.8	18.7	29.8
United States	.0	3.2	5.4	13.7	27.6	38.2
Women:						
Britain	.3	1.3	4.3	12.3	28.7	47.6
United States	.1	4.7	12.0	31.5	47.6	50.6

Note: The nine STDs separately asked about in the U.S. survey were gonorrhea, syphilis, genital herpes, chlamydia, genital warts, hepatitis B, HIV, pelvic inflammatory disease (women only), and nongonococcal urethritis (men only).

Table 12.4 Opinions about Sexual Behavior (% Agreeing with Statement)

Gender and Country	Age				All
	18–24	25–34	35–44	45–59	
A. Premarital sex is always wrong or almost always wrong					
Men:					
Britain	4.7	5.2	7.6	14.0	8.1
United States	17.8	19.1	25.1	37.5	24.8
Women:					
Britain	4.8	5.9	9.2	21.0	10.7
United States	20.7	28.2	33.4	46.3	32.7
B. Extramarital sex is always wrong or almost always wrong					
Men:					
Britain	79.4	75.2	72.5	79.2	76.4
United States	92.6	89.7	87.5	86.2	88.9
Women:					
Britain	84.3	83.2	78.6	84.6	82.6
United States	95.8	94.3	92.1	92.5	93.5
C. Homosexual sex is always wrong or almost always wrong					
Men:					
Britain					
Between 2 men	66.4	62.1	64.8	75.6	67.4
Between 2 women	59.6	55.8	58.7	69.8	61.1
United States	71.9	70.7	76.3	80.5	74.7
Women:					
Britain:					
Between 2 men	49.6	48.9	52.0	62.7	53.6
Between 2 women	52.0	49.8	52.4	63.8	54.7
United States	65.7	66.8	69.7	74.3	69.3

12.3 Discussion

Because Britain and the United States are similar in social structure, legal system, and language, it is not surprising that there are many similarities between the two nations in terms of their populations' sexual behavior. There are also profound differences between the two countries in geographic dispersion, religious affiliation, and the homogeneity of the populations' race/ethnicity (i.e., in Britain, about 5 percent of the population is nonwhite; in the United States, about 25 percent is nonwhite or Hispanic in origin). Thus, it is also not surprising that sexual behavior is not identical in the two countries.

While many studies report patterns of sexual behavior as seen in tables 12.1 and 12.2 above (e.g., Turner et al. 1989; Hayes 1987; Zelnik and Kantner 1980), few make comparisons across countries (Bajos et al. 1995). We discuss two public health issues resulting from the comparison, one reinforced by the similarities between the two countries, the other emerging from their differences.

Public Health Implications

The first of these two public health implications is clear and compelling. Panels C and D of table 12.3 above present strong evidence that the risk of contracting an STD is closely associated with number of sex partners. For Britain and the United States, this evidence is consistent with the epidemiology of sexually transmitted infections. The magnitude of the risk change is dramatic as the number of sex partners rises. There is suggestive evidence in panel H of table 13.2 above that, in both countries, those at greater risk of disease (younger men and women) are more likely to use condoms.

The second public health issue relates to a greater disjuncture in the United States than in Britain between the need for policy intervention and the social resolve to effect it. Consider the following three differences between the British and the U.S., as seen in the tables: (1) There is greater dispersion in sexual behavior in the United States than in Britain; in particular, larger proportions of the U.S. population are found in *both* tails of the distributions of many sexual behaviors. For example, in most age groups, larger proportions in the United States than in Britain report both having no sex partner and having five or more partners in the last year, and larger proportions in the United States than in Britain report both being virgins at their first marriage and having intercourse before age eighteen. (2) Table 12.4 above shows that, for every gender-age group, a larger proportion of the U.S. population holds unconditional or absolute opinions against extramarital sex, nonmarital sex, and homosexuality. (3) The United States has substantially higher rates of STDs, as evinced in table 12.3 and as described in official surveillance statistics.

We suggest that this third difference is partially explained by the interaction of the first two. The greater dispersion in sexual behavior in the United States would, by itself, make the formulation of effective and efficient public health policy more difficult. A public health effort to address a risk faced by one segment of the population would have little direct value to another segment whose behavior was different and who correctly considered that risk of remote relevance to themselves. As Catania et al. (1995) suggest, perhaps 85 percent of American adults aged eighteen to forty-nine have no risk or very little risk of contracting HIV, while the other 15 percent have varying risks that are, in some cases, quite substantial. Efforts such as the CDC's "prevention marketing initiative" (Ogden and Shepherd, 1996) stress the marketing strategy of segmenting audiences and targeting specific messages. These appropriate marketing techniques encounter resistance, however, when one segment of society holds strong, absolute opinions that the behavior creating the public health risk is itself inappropriate and unacceptable.

So these two facts—the greater diversity of sexual behavior and the greater degree of absolute opinion about improper sexual behavior— make it much more difficult to mount an effective public health effort in the United States than in Britain. The strong, unconditional opinions in the United States about sexual behavior suggest why there is serious resistance to a public health policy that promotes safer sexual behavior: a sizable portion of the population considers much of that behavior unacceptable and inappropriate, not primarily risky. Exacerbating this situation, these strong censorious attitudes may also discourage individuals reluctant to disclose their condition, even to physicians, from seeking health care. Absence of aggressive public health messages and actions may reinforce this reluctance.

One can see this dilemma within almost any population subgroup: for example, compare percentages in tables 12.1 and 12.4 above for U.S. and British young men. The proportion having five or more partners within the past year in the United States is more than twice as high as in Britain, yet the rate at which they consider premarital sex always wrong is nearly four times as high in the United States as in Britain. These are different men; there is simply greater dispersion in both sexual behavior and opinion in the United States. Thus, the dilemma for public health officials is how to address the needs of the distribution at one tail—that is, the young men with many partners—without clashing with the majority of young men, a different subset, who think that this behavior is wrong and should not be accommodated. And these opinions are not casual: analysis of British data indicates that those with premarital, extramarital, or homosexual experience have more tolerant attitudes toward these behaviors than do others, and conversely (Johnson et al. 1994, 245). So the behavior and the opinions are internally consistent, and, consequently, they are probably resistant to change.

This dilemma is greater in the United States than in Britain because extreme views and extreme behaviors are both more prevalent in the United States. This creates public ambivalence in the United States about policies regarding safe sex, and this probably also affects the rate at which health care is sought. This has surely contributed to the "public health tragedy" described by Vermund (1995) in characterizing "our society's failure to encourage and even to permit aggressive, widespread marketing of condoms in the national media" (p. 1488).

That ambivalence is also seen in the public health responses to HIV/ AIDS in the two countries. By the mid-1980s (when the total number of AIDS cases was about five-hundred), Britain conducted a national household leaflet drop about the transmission of HIV, a series of advertising campaigns on prime-time television, and the early introduction of needle-exchange programs, particularly in London. Successive secretaries of state for health maintained a high profile on the public health importance of AIDS. In addition, Britain has a national network of open-access STD clinics for the diagnosis and treatment and a national health service, available free at the time of need and used by all sectors of the population.

The contrast in the United States is sobering. Illustrative of the highly contested character of U.S. public health initiatives is the protracted struggle over the content of Surgeon General Koop's message sent as a public health warning to every household in the country about the threat posed by the AIDS epidemic. The measure was proposed in the mid-1980s (when the total number of AIDS cases exceeded 20,000); a pamphlet was drafted and readied for distribution at a cost of some $25 million, only to require a redraft at the last minute with a stronger statement about sexual abstinence. The message was finally sent out in spring 1988, as the number of AIDS cases approached 100,000.

Although both countries were slow to see the necessity for condom advertising, British HIV/AIDS public education was characterized by early and energetic efforts to raise awareness of the epidemic; in the United States, even circumspect advertising about condoms did not appear on television until 1995. Regarding the spread of AIDS among intravenous drug users, Britain conducted an experiment regarding the efficacy of a needle-exchange program and quickly approved a program. Despite generally positive results in these experiments, implementation of similar programs in the United States is still limited to scattered sites under highly controlled supervision. A ban against the use of federal funds for needle-exchange programs continues in the United States.

The legacy of failure to mount an effective U.S. public health campaign about sex and HIV may well have contributed to the higher rate of that disease in the United States than in Britain. We do not claim to have shown a causal link between the combination of greater dispersion in sexual behavior and unconditional opinions about sexual behavior in the United States, a link that leads to a weaker public health stance. Yet our comparisons are consistent with this linkage, and we suggest that it deserves further investigation. There is great public resistance in the United States to addressing forthrightly the risks of having many sex partners and of engaging in risky sexual practices. That resistance comes in large part from the strong opinions that such behavior is preemptively unacceptable, not that it is risky. American public health may be the high price paid for American public opinion.

Note

Reprinted with permission from the *American Journal of Public Health* (see Michael et al. 1998).

■

Sex and Health

Chapters 7–12 look into yet another important aspect of sexual behavior, its relation to health and medical care. The subject areas in these chapters are diverse, ranging from infant circumcision to abortion, from sexual dysfunction to sexual disease. While the two chapters in part 1 of this volume represented archetypical examples of the (social) institutional and (individual) rational choice perspectives and did not attempt to integrate them, these several chapters on sex and health do, revealing their complementarity.

Consider the topic of chapter 7, for example, the prevalence of infant circumcision. To be sure, there is a choice involved, one made by the parents on behalf of their son. Presumably, the parents reflect on the pros and cons of circumcision. Yet the primary reason it is chosen almost certainly has less to do with the parents' assessment and more to do with the medical community's expectations. If the procedure were not covered by the parents' insurance, cost would influence its use. If that choice were made without the encouragement or expectation of hospitals and physicians in the United States, the prevalence of circumcision among American-born men in the survey probably would not have been over 80 percent higher than that among non-American-born men in the survey! Or the rate in the Northeast would not have been twice as high as that in the South. These differences reflect the various medical and social customs in one location or another, among one subset of the population or another. Call it a cultural norm or a community standard, the circumcision decision reflects the institutional forces that frame that decision and thereby influence the outcome.

Decision makers who may not be disposed to have an infant circumcised may change their minds if the community standard is likely to result in nearly all that young boy's friends being circumcised. This is a case where rational choice is greatly influenced by institutional norms. The chapter argues that it is not easy to find any objective evidence that circumcision does anything particularly useful for the young man, yet it is a common practice, one that, nationally, involves substantial medical costs annually. When the choice is formulated as a medical issue and promoted by the medical establishment, the parent's options are quite circumscribed.

Consider the case of an abortion. Ultimately, only the pregnant woman can chose whether to have an abortion. That fact, however, does not stop supposedly concerned others—whether medical professionals or representatives of various interest groups—from attempting to influence her decision. The institutional perspective and the rational choice perspective inform one another in a case like this one. Some chapters—and the chapter on the abortion choice is one—tend to emphasize the choice elements over the context, the social forces, or the institutional structures that restrict and shape those choices. Others do the opposite. Choice of emphasis may in part reflect the subject matter, but it also reflects the disciplines and styles of the authors.

Another example of the interplay of the two perspectives can be found in chapter 10, which describes the distribution of sexual dysfunction across social categories. The importance of sexual history as a generator of dysfunction implies that, as does any other form of social action, sexual conduct incorporates rules with attendant sanctions and rewards. That conduct, then, is reflected in shared social norms and is also incorporated into social personality. A sanction—shame or guilt, for example—involves the experience of emotional distress that in turn affects sexual function. From this point of view, sexual dysfunction is a social fact. Chapter 10 shows that the experience of sexual dysfunction is associated with many indicators of lessened personal and relationship well-being among men and even more so among women. So sexual dysfunction is a serious psychological phenomenon that is, in large part, socially organized and generated.

The relative obscurity of sexual dysfunction, at least until the firestorm of publicity generated by Viagra, suggests that sexual health may be "discovered" as a social problem. However, the debate surrounding Viagra also suggests that many institutional forces intend to use this impotency drug to promote other issues, not related to sexual health.

Also, if sexual dysfunction is a social fact, then sexual health is not exclusively a medical problem. The distinction between *need* and *enhancement* in determining the medical insurance status of a sexual problem, for example, becomes artificial, and the physician's accustomed role in defining *need* is undermined. If, as chapter 10 indicates, there are sociogenic causes of sexual problems, then sexual health is normatively defined.

Preventing access to an impotency drug, then, represents institutional control of the notion of what is sexually healthy or sexually permissible, as do efforts to prevent access to sexually explicit entertainment, fertility-controlling devices, or abortion. They are efforts to circumscribe various modes of sexual expression. From this institutional perspective, the controversy over drugs like Viagra and RU-486 are as much debates about sexual conduct and propriety as they are debates about health.

The several chapters addressing sexually transmitted disease (STD) show the interplay between the institutional and the rational choice perspectives in yet another light. Here, choosing certain sexual practices as a way of reducing risk is clearly a conscious strategy. And, indeed, chapter 8 documents that many of those who are most at risk of contracting an STD are in fact those who report having altered their sexual behavior to reduce that risk. Analogously, chapter 9 documents that those most at risk are not a random subset of the adult population but have interests, attitudes, and beliefs and exhibit sexual as well as nonsexual behaviors that are internally consistent and expose them to such risks. Their behavior seems purposive and strategic.

Yet the social context in which these adults make their choices is determined in large measure by the institutional forces that influence social policy regarding the availability of information about the risks of STDs, the access to means of risk reduction, and the incentives to adopt measures to reduce these risks. Chapter 12 argues that the very diversity of our population, in terms of both patterns of sexual practices and strongly held opinions about which sexual behaviors are acceptable and which unacceptable or wrong, makes it difficult to mount effective public health efforts to promote risk reduction. Those who contend that the behavior is wrong often oppose efforts to diminish that behavior's adverse effects on the logical grounds that doing so lowers the cost of the behavior and thus promotes behavior that should be discouraged. That is the argument underlying the "abstinence only" campaigns—don't instruct our children about less-risky sexual behavior; just teach them to say no. That same logic can be applied to abortion—if it is made easily available, that fact alone may encourage young couples who would otherwise avoid it—to have sex. Our point is that this argument brings into play the institutional forces that seek to alter the available choices and thereby influence the outcome. People's choices are determined, or at least greatly influenced, by the politicians and policy makers who frame the options and determine their social meanings.

We note one final example of the fact that institutional and collective social forces deeply influence private valuations. Even in a domain as individualistic as one's own assessment of the quality of one's current sexual partnership, chapter 6 showed that those in formal marriages judge their own sexual partnerships to be more emotionally satisfying and physically pleasurable than do those who are in less socially approved relationships! Now, it may be that the associations reported are no more than reflections of statistical censoring, with the longer-lived formal marriages capturing those partnerships that happen to be more successful and the shorter-lived causal partnerships including more unsuccessful pairings that will soon dissolve. But it may instead be a fact that marriages are privately deemed superior because they are socially approved. That is, the overwhelming institutional approval of marriage and the widespread disapproval of non-marital sexual relations may be a key reason for the relative assessments of the quality of these two types of sexual partnerships.

Chapter 7: Circumcision in the United States: Prevalence, Prophylactic Effects, and Sexual Practice

The National Health and Social Life Survey (NHSLS) is one of the first surveys to permit analysis of the incidence of neonatal circumcision across social categories of men in the United States and of the linkages between circumcision and the incidence of sexually transmitted diseases (STDs), sexual dysfunction, and sexual practices and preferences. While over three-fourths of the native-born men in the survey reported that they were circumcised, the rates differ among groups. There are higher rates for those born more recently, for whites, and for those whose mother was more highly educated. The racial/ethnic differences are most striking: adjusted rates for men born in the 1960s are 86 percent for whites, 76 percent for blacks, and 56 percent for Hispanics. Regarding rates of STDs, there is a slight (statistically insignificant) pattern of circumcised men having higher, not lower, rates of disease, persistent across groups and across specific diseases, but, again, this is not a statistically significant difference. As the chapter stresses, however, there is no evidence here of a protective effect of circumcision since the slight pattern goes in the opposite direction.

Regarding the relation of circumcision to sexual dysfunction, the results are again not strong statistically, but there is a mild pattern for the older (age forty-five to fifty-nine) men in the sample: those who were not circumcised have somewhat higher rates of dysfunction, and in particular of premature ejaculation and erectile dysfunction, and higher rates of sexual anxiety compared to those who were. As far as sexual practices are concerned, the data suggest that circumcised men engage in several practices at higher rates than do uncircumcised men; these practices include oral and anal sex and more frequent masturbation. These patterns were found to differ by race/ethnicity, with generally stronger patterns among whites. In comparisons of the appeal of several sexual practices, again there is a systematic and statistically significant pattern: circumcised men expressed a greater preference for every form of sexual behavior except one. For the practice of fellatio, in particular, circumcised men expressed a substantially stronger preference that remained significant after other control variables were included; this effect was also stronger for whites.

Chapter 8: Reported Changes in Sexual Behavior in
Response to AIDS in the United States

This chapter exploits an open-ended question in the NHSLS about what the respondent said he or she did in particular when he or she responded affirmatively to the question, "Have you made any kind of changes in your sexual behavior because of AIDS?" (*SOS,* 664). The chapter details the wide range of changes that are reported, some of which are quite effective in lowering risk and others that are, as best we understand, ineffective. While some 30 percent of all adults in the survey said that they had in fact changed their behavior in some way, there was a wide variety of changes and of systematic patterns of who changed in particular ways.

The good news in this chapter is that, in general, those at risk were those who reported a behavior change and that that change could be considered appropriate, informed, and potentially effective in reducing the risk of contracting a disease through sex. The bad news is that, of those who are most at risk in terms of number of sex partners, about one-quarter of this small group disregard the risks and resist any behavior change. These are primarily young, unmarried men, and they contract and spread disease.

The chapter also makes comparisons between reported behavior change and reported actual sexual behavior in order to see if there is evidence in the actual behavior of the reported change. Here, as well, one finds reasonably good evidence that those who said, for example, that they use condoms more frequently or stick to one partner do in fact report high rates of condom use or relatively high rates of monogamy, thus confirming in their description of their actual sexual behavior the nature of the change that they reported elsewhere in the survey interview.

Chapter 9: Racial/Ethnic Group Differences in the Prevalence of Sexually Transmitted Diseases in the United States: A Network Explanation

Many studies have observed that African Americans have comparatively high rates of selected sexually transmitted diseases, often ten to twenty times higher than whites and other racial/ethnic groups, but no convincing explanation has been proposed. The chapter suggests a solution to the puzzle using a network approach. First, using a logistic regression analysis, it is demonstrated that, even after controlling for all the appropriate individual-level risk factors, African Americans are almost five times more likely to be infected with bacterial diseases than are members of the other racial/ethnic groups. Second, it is shown that African Americans' higher rate of infection with bacterial diseases can be explained by the patterns of sexual networks within and between different racial/ethnic groups. Infections are more widespread in the African American population at large because partner choice is more highly dissortative—meaning that "peripheral" African Americans (those who have had only one partner in the past year) are five times more likely to choose "core" African Americans (those who have had four or more partners in the past year) than peripheral whites are to choose core whites. Moreover, sexually transmitted infections stay within the African American population because their partner choices are more segregated (assortative mating) than are those of the other groups. The likelihood of African Americans having a sexually transmitted infection is 1.3 times greater than it is for whites because of this factor alone. Especially noteworthy in these results regarding intra- and interracial networks is that they would not have been detected in a study of individual risk factors alone but required a concentration on behavior patterns within populations and a focus on both infected and uninfected persons.

Powerful implications for public policy may be drawn from these results. They suggest that public health intervention programs targeted at core groups (who constitute roughly 5 percent of their respective racial/ethnic groups) would have especially potent effects in disrupting the transmission dynamics of sexually transmitted diseases.

Chapter 10: Sexual Dysfunction in the United States: Prevalence and Predictors

Sexual dysfunctions are characterized by disturbances in sexual desire and in the psychophysiological changes associated with the sexual response cycle in men and women. This chapter provides the first population-based assessment of the epidemiology of sexual dysfunction in the half century since Kinsey's work. Sexual dysfunction is more prevalent for women (43 percent) than for men (31 percent) and is associated with various demographic characteristics, including age and educational attainment. Women of different racial groups demonstrate different patterns of sexual dysfunction. Differences among men are not as marked but are generally consistent with those among women. Experience of sexual dysfunction is more likely among women and men in poor physical and emotional health. Moreover, sexual dysfunction is highly associated with negative experiences in sexual relationships and overall well-being. Given the strong association between dysfunction and impaired quality of life, this problem warrants recognition as a significant public health concern.

Chapter 11: Abortion Decisions in the United States

This chapter investigates the correlates of the decision to have an abortion, using the survey responses by both the men and the women in the NHSLS. (The analysis conducted in chap. 2 above was limited to women and to pregnancies before age eighteen.) The percentage who report ever having had an abortion, among those who had at least one conception, was as high as 31–35 percent for the men and women aged eighteen to twenty-four. The rate declined to about 5 percent for those older respondents who had been in their thirties at the time of the *Roe v. Wade* Supreme Court decision legalizing abortion.

The analysis is conducted separately by gender and separately by conception. For the first conception, of which about 12 percent were aborted overall, those for whom the conception occurred after *Roe v. Wade* were about 15 percentage points more likely to have an abortion. Also, those married were dramatically less likely to abort their first conception than were noncohabiting singles, while those cohabiting were more likely to abort than those married but significantly less likely to do so than those not cohabiting. Other factors held constant, those who held the opinion that abortion should be legal were more likely to abort their first pregnancy—8 percent more likely for the men and 17 percent more likely for the women.

Most of the other personal characteristics had different effects for the women and for the men who were reporting on the outcomes of their partners' pregnancies. The men who had more highly educated parents and those whose mother was employed when they were young adolescents were more likely to report that their partner had had an abortion. The man's age at the time his partner got pregnant had no effect on the likelihood of abortion when these other personal characteristics were accounted for. Among the women, those who had their first pregnancy at an early age—under eighteen—and had better-educated parents were much more likely to have an abortion than other women were. Also, black women were much less likely to abort than white women.

The magnitudes of the implied relations are quite large for this first pregnancy. Among the women whose pregnancy occurred before age eighteen, for instance, if neither of their parents had graduated from high school, the predicted probability of abortion was 12 percent, but, if either parent had completed high school, the probability rose to 48 percent, and, if either had completed college, the probability rose to 90 percent.

In the second and third conception as well, there were strong positive effects of both having the pregnancy after the *Roe v. Wade* decision and not being married at the time of the pregnancy. In these subsequent pregnancies for both the men and the women, a prior abortion raised the likelihood of a subsequent abortion. However, well over half of all the women and nearly half the men who reported aborting their first conception went on to have one or more live births.

The study shows how important it is to look at the decision to abort for each conception separately since the circumstances surrounding the conception—the person's age, marital status, prior abortion experience, and so forth—have a big influence on that decision.

The data reveal the interesting fact that, although black women reported far lower rates of abortion for their first conception, they reported higher rates of abortion for their third and higher-order pregnancies. Since blacks also report more pregnancies overall, a higher proportion of black women than white women had an abortion at one time or another.

Chapter 12: Private Sexual Behavior, Public Opinion, and Public Health Policy: A U.S.-British Comparison

In this chapter, the basic patterns of reported sexual behavior in the United States, based on the NHSLS, are compared to the patterns reported in the large British sex survey of 1990–91. The core tables in the chapter compare sexual behavior in the two countries in terms of number of sex partners within the past year and over the adult lifetime and several other behaviors, including the age at first sex, the proportion reporting being virgins at their first marriage, and rates of same-gender, extramarital, and oral and anal sex. Rates of STDs and opinions about certain sexual behaviors are also reported.

The theme of the chapter is based on the comparison of the differences in sexual behavior, sexual opinion, and sexual diseases. The tables show that the dispersion in sexual behavior in the United States is much greater than it is in Britain. In the United States, there are both more virgins at marriage and more people who have had sex before age eighteen; there are also more men and women over twenty-five who have never had a sex partner and more who have had five or more partners within the past year or twenty-one or more in their adult lifetime. While there are many patterns that are similar in the two countries, there is a far greater range in behavior in the United States and much less homogeneity of sexual behavior. There is also a larger proportion who consider premarital sex, extramarital sex, and homosexual sex always wrong or almost always wrong.

The surveys also confirm reports based on official health statistics in the two nations: the rates of sexually transmitted diseases are far higher in the United States than in Britain, while rates of condom use are much lower in the United States for those over age twenty-five.

The chapter suggests that a key reason for the higher rates of STDs, including HIV/AIDS, in the United States is the greater dispersion in sexual behavior and the high rates of strong, categorical opinion opposed to certain sexual behaviors that tend to be relatively risky. These strongly held social opinions make it much more difficult for public health officials in the United States to mount strong programs designed to address the risks of these behaviors. Opposition to the public health messages and programs comes from those who neither engage in those behaviors nor think them socially worthy. There is strong opposition to addressing the risks in ways that might encourage behavior considered wrong to begin with.

Epilogue

CHAPTER THIRTEEN

■

Private Sex and Public Policy

ROBERT T. MICHAEL

This final chapter explores several implications of the fact that sexual behavior is private behavior with public repercussions. While it discusses
several controversial social policy issues, a policy position is taken on only
one topic: the importance of obtaining more social scientific information
about sexual behavior. The chapter does not analyze public policy regarding sexual behavior, nor does it summarize the volume. It is, rather, about
the intricate links between private sex and public policy regarding sex and
about some of the information in the preceding chapters that might inform
public policy decisions.

It may be useful to begin by briefly summarizing some of the points
made below. First, despite the privacy accorded sexual activity, that activity abounds in complexity because it simultaneously involves so many outcomes and actors. This "jointness" of sexual behavior implies that there
are many competing objectives and considerations involved in making sexual choices. Some of the products of sex are delightful, and these motivate
the behavior, but there are also potential outcomes that are decidedly unappealing. Sex typically involves two people whose experience of the activity is not identical, and the consequences of their sexual behavior often
are not restricted to them alone, so many people at times have a stake in
the outcome of private sexual events.

Second, sex involves many choices. Privately, these include choices
about partners and a wide variety of practices and strategies, many of
which are detailed in the various chapters of this book as well as elsewhere.
There are also public or collective choices to be made, and these can be
characterized as decisions about rules governing sexual behavior and decisions about subsidies or costs imposed on certain sexual behaviors or resulting conditions. This chapter will focus on these public choices.

Third, the sexual choices that one makes can have important consequences for both personal and social welfare. Moreover, several of the
difficult social policy issues currently facing our society are related to sexual choice. Thus, this domain is neither frivolous nor inconsequential, although it is often trivialized, exploited, and accorded little respect.

Fourth, information about sex can improve the choices made both privately and collectively, so access to accurate information can be of considerable value to public policy analyses as well as private choice. I suggest below how some of the findings reported in the previous chapters can be used to improve public choices.

Fifth, until recently, efforts to obtain social scientific knowledge about sexual behavior have been thwarted. For decades, despite several fine examples to the contrary, there was a consensus among social scientists that information about sexual behavior could not be obtained through surveys, so social research was considered futile.[1] Furthermore, some who believe that sex research should not be undertaken have successfully influenced government policy and discouraged such research. Consequently, little research has been conducted and little knowledge accumulated about sexual behavior until the past decade. Some of the social and medical problems that we face today (e.g., the spread of HIV) could have been more adequately addressed had such research been conducted.

The Jointness of Sexual Behavior

Sexual activity has at least six "products": physical pleasure, emotional satisfaction, intimate bonding with one's partner that may promote love, reputation or peer judgment, the probability of pregnancy, and the probability of transmission of disease. Generally, people have sex in order to obtain the first two or three of these products, and occasionally the fourth or fifth, but never the sixth. When disease occurs, it is an unfortunate and undesirable outcome of sex, and the risk of disease has a major effect on sexual practices, ranging from the use of condoms for protection, to more careful selection of sex partners, to the choice of mutual monogamy to avoid that risk almost entirely. Pregnancy is also something that most people wish to avoid at least most of the time, and many sexual practices are undertaken to reduce that risk as well.

Even if there were no other complications to sexual behavior than these six products, one would still need to weigh these risks of pregnancy and disease against the anticipated satisfaction when making choices about sexual behavior (practices, partners, protection), which would be complex and challenging if there were no further complications. Yet this is only the tip of the iceberg!

The person with whom one has sexual relations is selected for many and varied reasons. Sexual compatibility, prowess, or attributes per se may be the reasons one selects certain partners when sexual pleasure is the only goal. But, overwhelmingly, sex is shared with someone who becomes a lifetime or long-term social partner. Since a large majority of sexually active adults are married or cohabiting, the vast majority of instances of sexual intercourse in any given time period in the nation will be between married or cohabiting partners. In these cases, the partner has been chosen not exclusively or even primarily for sexual potential. Sex is only one of the relevant factors influencing the choice. The partner is, typically, a resident partner, a financial partner, a social partner, a confidant and friend, and a coparent of one's children as well as a sex partner. The choice of a spouse or long-term partner reflects these several dimensions of the relationship, and sexual compatibility is not the only, or necessarily the most important, consideration. This means that, as we reflect on the positive products of our own sexual experience with our primary partner, the quality of the overall relationship is assessed, not just the quality of the sexual relationship.

Since sex is overwhelmingly an activity involving two people, the sexual practices that are undertaken are jointly experienced, but the two people may have quite different assessments of the practices or may experience the same event in very different ways. In the terms of one recent research tradition, sex occurs in a "nonshared environment," even for the two individuals involved. Both may not experience the same activity; reciprocity does not always pertain. Both may not enjoy the same activity. Both cannot get pregnant. Both may not wish to be engaged in sex at that time and in those circumstances.

Several aspects of sexual behavior are unavoidably public goods, shared generally, whether we like it or not. A public good is a nonexcludable and nonexhaustive good, which means that the good is not easily denied to one person if it is made available to another and that the enjoyment or use of the good by the one person does not limit its availability to another. The best example of a public good is national defense: my use of it does not limit yours, and it would be difficult to keep you from using it if I am going to use it myself. Other examples include public parks or scenic views. In the sexual arena, examples include access to forms of fertility control (including abortion), the right legally to purchase sexual material or sexual favors, and public nudity on stage or at the beach. Several of these involve laws, and, since we insist that laws must apply to all, they are a particular form of public good. They cannot generally and easily allow one individual access to, say, pornography and at the same time ensure that another individual has no contact with it. Such public goods in the sexual arena are a fourth form of jointness, and, like the others, these make choices about sex more complex.

These several joint attributes of sex cannot generally be uncoupled or separated from sexual behavior, although one or another of them can be controlled or even eliminated with effort and expense. The complexities encountered when making choices about private sexual behavior and public policies that encourage or discourage particular sexual behaviors derive mainly from this jointness. For example, none of us would wish to discourage or prevent the pleasure and harmless satisfaction to be derived from sex. Yet, in many circumstances, we—as parents, friends, even as sex partners—engage in all sorts of activities to prevent sex altogether or modify it because we cannot separate it from one or another outcome.

Public Choices Regarding Sexual Behavior

While sex involves many private choices, this chapter focuses on public or collective choices.[2] These public choices constitute our public policies regarding sex. They can be characterized as (a) decisions about rules governing sexual behavior or (b) decisions about subsidies or costs imposed on certain sexual behaviors or resulting conditions. Both reflect our collective decisions to encourage or discourage some particular sexual behavior by regulating it by law or custom or by taxing or subsidizing it or its consequences.

There are only a few distinct, legitimate grounds for creating a public policy regulating some aspect of sex. One justification is whether something is a public good. Some things we must all either have or not have, see or not see, be allowed to do or not be allowed to do, and society decides collectively whether to allow them. The right to an abortion is an example of an aspect of sexual behavior that has become a public good. Having an abortion is either legal or not legal, and, as we know, our nation has had difficulty making that public policy decision. The point here is only that a collective choice cannot be avoided: we are all subject to the same law, we all have the same rights, so we must make a collective decision about such a public good. That is also the case for a long list of sexually related behaviors that have become legal issues, for example, prostitution, the sale of pornographic material, public nudity, certain rights for homosexual couples, and the right to purchase fertility control. In those instances, we must reach some common, collective judgment and have a common, public policy about it.

A second rationale for public policy about sexual behavior involves what are called *externalities*. These are aspects of one person's behavior that affect others. The principle here is very appealing and widely accepted: if something I do affects you, you may have the right to influence my decision to do it. We all think that this is true regarding reckless or drunken driving on public streets. My enjoyment of driving drunk is irrelevant; since my doing so can adversely affect you, you can, collectively, prevent me from doing it. The principle of collective action in instances of externalities applies to the regulation of pollution, to extending patent rights for new inventions, to tax waivers for certain institutions, such as churches, synagogues, and schools, and many other widely diverse circumstances. Of course, simply asserting that an externality exists does not make it so, and there are many notorious cases of arguments that this or that imposes externalities, and thus should be taxed or subsidized, when in fact those things do not.[3]

As far as sexual behavior is concerned, the spread of sexually transmitted disease involves externalities in at least two ways. First, one person's decision to expose himself or herself to infection makes it more likely that others will subsequently confront disease in their sexual activities. That is a case in which that first person's behavior directly imposes risks on future sex partners—a negative externality. Second, the costs of containing the disease and treating those who do get infected are typically paid partly by us all through public health efforts financed by taxes. So, in this manner, the private decision of one person can put others at risk and impose costs on the rest of society. These negative externalities provide a rationale for stepping in collectively to influence private sexual behavior.

In the regulation of sexual behavior, the assertion of externality is common: pornography should be banned since it may encourage bad behavior; prostitution should be illegal since it cheapens our neighborhoods and imposes costs on local homeowners. Even more subtle is the argument of externality in the case of certain sex acts even between consenting adults. Some states outlaw "sodomy" (which includes oral and anal sex), for example, because certain citizens find reprehensible and disgusting the notion that others would do these things, even in private. By outlawing such activities, we eliminate what is technically called a *negative consumption externality!* Or so the argument goes. These arguments illustrate the assertion of an externality that is then used as a rationale for collective action, which usually takes the form of government legislation or regulation.[4]

Externalities can be positive as well as negative. We subsidize home ownership in our country by giving tax advantages to certain expenses (e.g., mortgage interest payments) because we consider home ownership to have important externalities for communities. These include a stake in the well-being of the neighborhood, residential stability, the upkeep of property, and so forth. We encourage the behavior by providing a positive incentive: the government will in effect subsidize all home-owning taxpayers but not renters. The same is true for sex! There is political pressure to change federal tax policy to stop inadvertently discouraging formal marriage through tax disincentives; here, the argument is that marriage as a social institution involves certain positive externalities.

We collectively encourage education about sex in our public schools on the ground that accurate information leads to better informed and wiser private decisions. (Below, I argue that acquiring further information about sexual behavior through social research should be encouraged for just that reason.) Less formally, there is social approval (but not yet much cold cash) given young married parents who spend time raising their baby as a sign of our approval of their having and caring for that baby. There is often a deference to and solicitousness of an appropriately "sexy" person in social interactions. Another illustration of a supposed positive externality to be derived from sexual behavior is when, in discussing a neighbor or friend or coworker, one hears the opinion expressed that what that person needs to improve his or her attitude or outlook or mood is a good lover.

In general, then, externalities may be good or bad, and through our social policies we collectively attempt to encourage the good ones (by offering tax relief, or a subsidy, or sometimes only a public nod of approval) and discourage the bad ones (by imposing costs or creating legal restrictions or regulatory limitations or social pressure).

A third rationale for policy about sex is in areas in which we already have virtually unanimous collective judgment and apply that judgment to sexual behavior as well.[5] One person's behavior that is harmful to and forced on another is an example. Rape fits that description, as does child sexual abuse. Increasingly, this applies to sexual harassment as well, although just what the limits of sexual harassment are have yet to be determined.

The Public Consequences of Sexual Behavior

The private and collective choices that we make about sexual behavior profoundly affect our lives. Unfortunately, most of the consequences that capture our collective attention are the negative ones, although there are surely many positive consequences as well. Nearly all these positive consequences are private, enjoyed by the individual and his or her partner; they can be intense; they can promote well-being; and the memory of them can be long-lasting. These positive private outcomes, after all, motivate nearly all sexual behavior. Yet there are surprisingly few unequivocally positive public outcomes or consequences of sex. One major exception to this point is the long-run effect of sexual behavior on population size and growth. After all, the size, age structure, and growth of the population are of great importance, and growth in particular can be either a positive or a negative externality of sex, depending on whether it is rapid or slow. Historically and internationally, efforts to influence population growth probably constitute the most important sex-related social policy. Until very recently, the concern was about populations growing too rapidly, so even in this regard it has been the negative, not the positive, externalities of sex that have been emphasized. In fact, there are many negative consequences of sexual behavior that are public in nature as well as many negative consequences that are distinctly private.

Perhaps it is this imbalance between the private and the public conse-quences of sex—with most positive results remaining private and many negative results becoming public—that explains why the public discussion of sex is so often couched in negative terms. The joys of sex we keep to ourselves; the woes of sex we proclaim publicly. The joys of sex are private, after all, and we have little need or occasion to know about anyone else's intimate pleasures. We typically become ill at ease when an acquaintance wants to talk about joys of sex in any detail. On the other hand, the ad-verse consequences or negative aspects of sexual behavior often become public and impose costs on us collectively or require that we make collec-tive decisions about them.

Below, I identify twelve issues that arise as alleged negative conse-quences of sexual behavior and that have led to public policy debate and a need for collective decision. Four of these issues occur because of joint outcomes of sex per se. One is disease transmitted by sex; it is an unwanted joint product of sex that imposes costs privately and collectively. Three of the issues (unwanted pregnancy, abortion, and access to and promotion of birth control) result from the joint product of sex and pregnancy. The risk of pregnancy and personal strategies to avoid or end unwanted preg-nancy cause society to confront several public goods, including the right to an abortion, the right to birth control, the promotion of sex education in public schools as a means of preventing unwanted pregnancy, and gen-eral reproductive health and public health messages. These public goods require collective decisions.

There are other adverse consequences of unwanted pregnancies that affect us publicly and are more indirect. These include the costs to society of supporting, training, and caring for children who are not well cared for or adequately nurtured or socialized by their parents. These are logically appropriate costs to consider when assessing public policies encouraging or discouraging certain forms of private behavior. (There may also be the unexpected but logically possible outcome of an unwanted child who nev-ertheless contributes significantly to the common good. This is a positive externality.)

Another three of the dozen issues (rape, child sexual abuse, and sexual harassment or gender discrimination) fall into the third category of anti-social behavior that is sexual in content. Unfortunately, sexual behavior is one of the means by which harm is imposed, one of the manifestations through which bad behavior is evinced, and, in cataloging the adverse outcomes of sex, this domain arises.

The remaining five issues (infidelity, prostitution, pornography, public nudity, and homosexuality) fall into a final category of collective action problems. This involves sexual behavior about which tastes, preferences, and judgments differ. In many instances in which tastes differ about nonsexual issues, an efficient and equitable market solution can be found by the simple mechanism of selling a variety of products to those who wish to buy them. So, to cite a trivial example, the fact that many of us do not like brussels sprouts is not a problem: groceries simply stock and sell fewer pounds of brussels sprouts than of the more popular peas and carrots.

But brussels sprouts are not a public good, and no one I know of has argued that they involve any adverse externality. But, when we come to certain sexual activities, the claim of negative externality leads to a necessity for a collective action involving laws or regulations, and at that point the matter becomes a public good. Once the matter becomes a public good, we must all have the same access or right, so a collective judgment is then required. Notice that it is the claim of an externality that creates the need for a collective judgment. This is a point to which I return below.

Table 13.1 lists these twelve issues that involve public choices about sexual behavior. The table notes the chapters in this volume that address a related issue and indicates its relation to the collective decisions. In the next section, I draw from these chapters, emphasizing the relevance of some of their findings to these public choices.

Table 13.1 Public Policy Topics Related to Sexual Behavior

	Collective Decisions			
	Externality	Public Goods	Antisocial	Tastes
Jointness: disease (chaps. 7–10, 12)				
STDs, including HIV/AIDS	✓			
Jointness: pregnancy (chaps. 1–2, 4, 11)				
Unwanted pregnancy, teen parents	✓			✓
Abortion	✓	✓		
Access to and promotion of birth control	✓	✓		
Antisocial behavior (chap. 4)				
Rape			✓	
Child sexual abuse			✓	
Sexual harassment	✓		✓	✓
Tastes, preferences, and judgments (chaps. 3, 5–6, 12)				
Infidelity	✓			✓
Prostitution	✓	✓		✓
Pornography	✓	✓		✓
Public nudity		✓		✓
Homosexuality		✓		✓

Chapter Summaries and Insights about Public Policy Issues

This section reflects on many of the findings reported in the chapters above, organized around the twelve issues just discussed. As the focus here is on the public policy issues, and as the chapters themselves are not necessarily organized around these issues, this discussion is not a summary of chapters. Instead, it is only one lens through which these chapters can be viewed.

Diseases and Other Health Issues

Several chapters in this volume address issues of public health. Chapter 7 focuses exclusively on a single medical procedure, the circumcision of newborn boys, while chapters 8 and 9 address topics related to STDs and HIV/AIDS in particular. Chapter 10 discusses sexual dysfunction, and chapter 12 argues that there is an important relation between diversity of sexual expression and public health policy. In these chapters, one sees the usefulness of survey data in exploring the context and health consequences of sexual behavior and some of the ways in which the risk of disease affects our sexual behavior.

Chapter 7 exemplifies one of the major points of this final chapter: the importance of adequate and accurate information about sex. Even though over the past half century useful data have become available on most other aspects of social interaction and behavior, there has been an absence of useful survey data about sexual behavior in all its varied forms. The result has been that we know less than we should about sexual behavior and that we have not often explored the correlates and relations among sexual factors.

The practice of neonatal circumcision is one that confronts the parents of every male child born in a hospital or under a doctor's care. Many questions arise in the process: How many children like ours are circumcised? What is the reason for doing this? What are the risks and adverse consequences? What are the repercussions for my son's sex life? etc. Medical advice may adequately indicate the immediate risk of complications arising from the minor operation itself. However, it is doubtful that such advice provides useful information about how circumcision might affect the relationship of the boy to his peers, or how it might affect his later sexual behavior, or the association between circumcision and the risk of disease or sexual dysfunction. The lack of data regarding this practice and of normal social scientific descriptive analysis and exploration of it means that we do not assemble new information about this practice and its correlates, as we do with most other practices that are asked about in surveys and routinely studied. We have become so accustomed to being ill informed about sex that it does not seem odd that the doctor cannot provide much useful information about such sexual issues.

Chapter 7 provides some interesting and suggestive findings about the linkages between circumcision, health, and behavior. There is no indication that this practice helps avoid disease or dysfunction. To the contrary, there is suggestive evidence that it is detrimental to both. This is an instance in which the information obtained may be of greater use to private individuals—the parents who must decide whether to have their son circumcised—than to public policy makers. However, insurance payments for this practice and the medical profession's stance regarding its promotion may also be influenced by the sort of evidence that this chapter provides.

Findings of this kind are a long way from the primary motive of the three of us, John Gagnon, Ed Laumann, and myself, who crafted the NHSLS or those who paid for it. But often the benefits to be derived from a well-designed omnibus survey of a broadly gauged area of behavior lie in the serendipitous findings of analyses undertaken after the primary purposes of the survey have been addressed.

Chapter 8 has implications for public health officials as they plan programs to encourage safer sex and also for clinicians who discuss the risks of certain sexual behaviors with their patients. For the latter, there is the useful and encouraging finding that many adults both already understand the need for risk reduction and have a good sense of what method of risk reduction is appropriate for their circumstances. The chapter suggests that the physician would do well to ascertain the general sexual lifestyle choice of the patient before offering any advice about risk reduction since the survey evidence implies that most adults adjust their behavior at the margin consistent with their lifestyle. Those with many partners do not chose to become monogamous, but they do chose to use a condom more frequently, and they do select their partners with greater care, and they do have sex with fewer partners. All these changes can help reduce risk. On the other hand, the person with two or three partners may find it very difficult or impossible to use a condom if one of his or her partners considers their relationship to be monogamous but may be more receptive to reducing his or her number of partners.

Advice about making changes at the relevant margin of behavior seems most likely to be effective. Advising people, "Just say no!" is neither always silly nor always effective: the efficacy depends on the individual's circumstances. The young, sexually inexperienced, but curious and receptive adolescent may be influenced by a just-say-no program if some other means of sexual exploration is available. By contrast, the teenager who has had sex a few times may be influenced by a peer-led campaign of "second-chance virginity," while the sexually active teen may be receptive only to condom promotions and other risk-reduction schemes. Changes at the margin, not dramatic changes in sexual lifestyle, are the reality reported by respondents in the NHSLS. A better understanding of the demographic characteristics of those who make behavioral responses is useful to those who formulate public health policy.

Complementarity of methods is also found in these reports—condoms and near monogamy, for example, do not mix, while condom use and more careful selection of partners by those with many partners do.

One of the more intriguing results from this study is that about one in eleven adults said that the behavior change was in his or her attitude about sex—a reduced receptivity to a sexual advance, a greater reluctance to allow a friendship to become sexual. While this sort of change may be susceptible to self-delusion or overstatement, the chapter points out that it can be a very effective means of reducing risk and therefore should perhaps be given more attention in public health campaigns and public education efforts.

The small pool of young unmarried men who seem to resist any risk reduction constitute a major public health challenge.

Chapter 9 singles out those who are most at risk of contracting a sexually transmitted infection and characterizes them. In the first instance, this is a descriptive exercise, and the figures and tables convey the message that those who are and are not at considerable risk are systematically, not randomly, distributed through the population. The chapter documents many social and psychological attributes that are dramatically associated with sexual behavior involving high risk of disease. This description itself is potentially very helpful to public policy aimed at educating or persuading people about the risk of disease posed by sex. It helps identify whom to target and with what message. It does not, of course, suggest the mechanism through which the risk is incurred. Thinking frequently about sex is not, per se, a risk-enhancing activity, but it is, apparently, closely associated with the behaviors that are risky (see table 9.5 above). So knowing of that association implies that one can "segment the market" and direct cautionary messages toward those who buy those magazines, attend those events, and frequent those establishments that are themselves associated with frequently thinking about sex! (The reader may find this not very surprising and perhaps even self-evident. Yet the number of intuitions about sexual behavior that the NHSLS data have shown to be faulty implies, I think, that it is useful to nail down with real evidence even those associations that seem obvious.)

The second part of the chapter exploits a contact network analysis that focuses on who has sex with whom. That analysis is used in the chapter to address one of the perplexing issues in the study of sexually transmitted infections: Why it is that some diseases, in particular gonorrhea, seem to be so prevalent among one subgroup of the population, African Americans, compared to its prevalence among other groups such as whites and Hispanics? Understanding why this is so has obvious public health implications. Part of the explanation has been known for some time. It is a fact that there is a substantial difference between the rates of sexual activity occurring within and between racial/ethnic groups. Most people from each distinct group select as sex partners others from within their own group. Chapter 6 of *SOS,* for example, had shown that over 90 percent of sexual partnerships occurred between two people of the same race/ethnicity. Table 6.4 of that chapter (p. 255) showed that this pattern holds not only for married partners but also for those who are cohabiting and even for those who are short-term partners. So one explanation for how a disease can stay within one group and not migrate to another is that some groups—and racial groups are surely an example—remain quite separate from others in terms of their sexual partnerships. So, if a disease is present in one group and not so prevalent in another, it can remain confined since relatively few partnerships bridge the gap between groups.

Chapter 9 of this volume adds a second, key point. It first characterizes individuals in terms of the concepts of *core, adjacent,* and *periphery* partner behavior, indicating the extent to which the person's sexual partnering promotes the transmission of disease. Even if the proportions of the African American and the white populations in these three mutually exclusive categories are similar, the analysis in chapter 9 shows an interesting and important fact: African Americans in the core group are much more likely to have sex with other African Americans who are in the periphery than core whites are to have sex with peripheral whites. While bridging partnerships between African Americans and whites are few, the pattern within the two racial subpopulations is very different. This is not a statement about the number of partners an African American has compared to the number a white person has; it is a statement about what kinds of partnerships African American tend to form, partnerships that bridge subgroups within the African American population. This fact can help explain why a disease as easily transmitted as gonorrhea (where the risk of contraction from heterosexual sex with an infected male partner is about 0.50 and from an infected female partner is 0.20 [see *SOS,* 392]) is effectively spread among a whole racially distinct population and not limited to any one subgroup.

Chapter 10 reports on the evidence of sexual dysfunction among the NHSLS respondents and presents descriptive evidence of the correlates of and associations among various sexual problems. While the descriptions in *SOS* (chap. 10) showed the incidence of seven distinct sexual problems and the simple relation of each with age, marital status, education, race,

religion, and income, this chapter looks more deeply at the topic, statistically collapsing those several problems into three domains that differ somewhat by gender: for women, a lack of sexual desire, difficulty with arousal,
and pain; for men, difficulty achieving orgasm, difficulty achieving an erection, and lack of sexual desire. The statistical analysis explores the association of each of these three, by gender, with measures of health, lifestyle,
and social status and with sexual experience. The widespread prevalence
of these several sexual problems was the primary emphasis of the report
in *SOS,* while this volume's chapter 10 offers a more extensive statistical
analysis that begins to show some of the subtlety that one might hope
to find.

The chapter notes, for example, that the presence of sexual problems
seems to be more common among younger women but older men. The
nature of the problems leads to the conjecture that, for the women, they
may result from inexperience, relatively high numbers of partners, and the
infrequency of sex, while the older men's complaints seem more likely to
be associated with physical changes accompanying the aging process. The
chapter documents that surprisingly few of those reporting a sexual problem seek professional help, especially among older men and minority populations.

Chapter 12 discusses the dilemma of U.S. public health policy. While the
chapter offers a provocative explanation for the higher rates of STDs in
the United States than in Britain, the evidence supporting that explanation
is only suggestive. The argument can be illustrated by the thought experiment of crafting a single public health strategy to combat the transmission
of STDs worldwide while being respectful of and sensitive to the various
cultural differences in attitudes toward sex. Clearly, that would be quite
difficult. It would be far easier to craft such a strategy in a single, homogeneous nation than across all nations and cultures. Similarly, the chapter
argues, it is easier to do so in Britain, where there is greater homogeneity
of both sexual behavior and opinions about sex than there is in the
United States.

By comparing the distributions of behavior outcomes and opinions in
the United States and Britain, chapter 12 reveals how much greater is the
heterogeneity within the U.S. population in terms of what people do and
what their opinions about sex are. No wonder, then, that it is more difficult
to put together an advertising campaign promoting condoms among
singles in the United States than it is in Britain when three times as many
men and women in the United States aged thirty-five to forty-four, for
example, consider premarital sex always or almost always wrong. Or no
wonder it is more difficult to reach agreement about a citywide curriculum
for sex education in lower elementary schools when the adults in those

communities have very different agendas for what children should be taught.

The diversity in our country, often characterized as one of our strengths as a nation, can become an impediment when a common policy must be adopted. A society with widely differing and deeply held views cannot easily come to agreement about such matters as promoting safer sex on television and in publications with a general readership. But, without agreement on these matters, public health messages are inadequate or absent. The consequence, the chapter suggests, is more disease and, as a result, higher costs of medical care, which is no one's preferred outcome.

Pregnancy and Its Attendant Concerns: Teenage Parenting, Abortion, and Birth Control

One of the joint products of sexual activity is pregnancy, at certain times and in certain contexts highly sought and much desired, at other times and in other contexts much feared. Much social policy as well as much private effort is directed toward this joint product of sexual activity. Chapters 1 and 2 focus on teenage sex and childbearing in the United States, one investigating the changes in determinants of early sex before and after the sexual revolution of the 1960s, the other decomposing the risk of childbearing by teenagers into three distinct choices about having sex, getting pregnant, and having an abortion. Additionally, chapter 11 looks in more detail at this latter choice, the decision to have an abortion.

To illustrate the nature of the findings presented in *chapter 1,* let us review the effect of two factors on the likelihood of teenage sexual activity. These two factors are growing up in a single-parent household and having a mother who was employed when the adolescent was age fourteen. The effects of these two variables differ among the four groups studied, blacks and whites, boys and girls. As the paper stresses, the effects differ as well between two periods, the era of relative sexual restrictiveness prior to the late 1960s and that of greater sexual permissiveness following the sexual revolution.

Having a single parent seems to have no effect on whether boys begin having sex by age eighteen, whereas, for girls, both white and black, there is a sizable effect: those who were living with a single parent at age fourteen were about half again as likely to have begun having sex by age eighteen. But the further partitioning of that finding shows that the effect occurred only in the pre–sexual revolution period. That is, there was no effect of living with one parent at age fourteen for those who did so after 1970! So, here, we have a factor that had been important, in terms of a systematic correlation with the onset of sex, before, but seems to have evaporated after, the sexual revolution. Living with only one parent has no discernible correlation with the onset of sex for either racial group or either gender after 1970.

The other factor, having a mother who was employed at the time the respondent was fourteen, also seems to have a complex interaction with calendar year, but a very different one. For this variable, there seems to be no influence for blacks, either boys or girls, but a sizable effect for white girls: those whose mother did work outside the home are more likely to have begun having sex by age eighteen. While the effect is not significant before the 1970s, it becomes highly significant after that date for girls but not boys. The girls who came of age after 1970 and whose mother did work were more than 40 percent more likely to have begun having sex by age eighteen than those whose mother did not work.

Taken at face value, these two findings should have implications for social policy formation. To illustrate, if the latter finding is interpreted to imply that in recent years, young white women have a greater opportunity to have sex if their mother works outside the home, then one might want to pay particular attention to after-school programs in communities in which most mothers are employed. But, like many social scientific findings of this nature, these actually raise as many questions as they settle: Why is the effect strong for white girls but not white boys or blacks? Is the chapter's explanation as to why this effect for white girls is so strong after 1970 but not before convincing, and, if it is, what are the implications? etc.

One would hope that social policy need not be made on evidence as limited as the facts reported in this chapter. In fact, there are other surveys of adolescent boys and girls that can be and have been used successfully to address some of these same issues, and these are cited in chapter 1. However, these facts do add a new dimension to our understanding: they raise concerns about the complex interactions of time and circumstance that make older data less pertinent to current policy decisions, and they serve to remind us of some of the complexities in this decision-making domain.

This chapter raises many new questions for future research. Scientific knowledge is practically always acquired little by little, piece by piece. With the exception of a few notable "paradigm shifts" that, with a single finding or perception, transform the way we see evidence or the way we understand a broad reality, the findings of scientific research accumulate incrementally, leading to a broader, more complete understanding over time, through replication and modification, by further testing and confirmation using better measurements and greater controls. The issue being addressed in this chapter is subtle and complex; it should not be surprising that a single investigation does not yield a clear-cut, simple, and settled conclusion. It would be odd if answers to complex problems came so easily. But this does not imply that the effort to understand these problems is futile or wasted. It means, I think, that some progress has been made and some ideas about the determinants of sex before age eighteen given empirical support and other ideas refuted by these data.

The value of the findings in *chapter 2* comes in comparing and contrasting the influence of a factor on the overall probability of having given birth by age eighteen and on its three constituent components, the probability of a young woman having sex, getting pregnant if she has sex, and having an abortion if she does get pregnant. Some characteristics of the women affect only one of these three components, while others affect two or more. In some cases, these two or three effects reinforce each other; in others, they offset each other.

A case in point is the age at which the person reaches puberty (the mean age at puberty is 12.7 years). The finding reported in table 2.3 is that those who are one year older when they reach puberty are significantly less likely to have given birth by age eighteen: the effect on the odds ratio is 0.88. Translating that effect at the mean implies that, if the woman had reached puberty at ages 11.7 or 12.7 or 13.7, holding the other variables constant, the probability that she would have given birth by her eighteenth birthday is estimated to be 9.6, 11.0, and 11.8 percent, respectively.[6] This is not a very large effect, but it is statistically significant. Now, when we then look at the effect of this factor—the age at which she reached puberty—on those three components, we find that its whole effect comes through an effect on the likelihood of having sex before age eighteen. There is no effect of age at puberty on the probability of conception given that she has sex, and there is no effect on the probability that she has an abortion if she gets pregnant.

Contrast that with the estimated effect of living with both natural parents at age fourteen on the likelihood of having given birth by age eighteen. This is a factor that seems to have offsetting effects: there is not a statistically significant effect of this characteristic on the probability of having given birth by age eighteen, but there is a strong, statistically significant effect lowering the probability of having sex. This is offset, however, by a slight (not significant) effect raising the probability of conceiving if she has sex and a much larger (not statistically significant) effect lowering the probability of having an abortion if she does get pregnant. So, loosely described, the net result of living in an intact family is nil—she is a bit less likely to have sex but a lot less likely to abort a pregnancy if she does get pregnant, and these offset each other, leaving no systematic correlation with the likelihood of having given birth by age eighteen.

Two personal characteristics have effects that are particularly noteworthy. First, the education level of the youth's parents has a profound effect. Here, the three constituents reinforce each other: if the youth has a college-educated parent, she is much less likely to have sex before age eighteen, she is much less likely to get pregnant if she does have sex, and she is dramatically more likely to abort a pregnancy if she conceives before age eighteen. Putting these three components of the decision together implies that the effect on the odds ratio accumulates to an astoundingly low 0.15. Expressed in terms of the probability of giving birth by age eighteen, that probability is lowered from a mean of 11.0 percent to 1.6 percent. If that probability is then applied to, say, 1,000 young women, at the mean 110 of them would be expected to have given birth by age eighteen, whereas, of a comparable 1,000 young women with a college-educated parent, only 16 would be expected to have given birth by age eighteen.

The other effect is that of race. The finding is that blacks are far more likely to have given birth at an early age than are whites: even holding constant all the other variables in the model, the odds of a black woman having given birth before she turns eighteen are 1.73 times as high as those of a white woman. Here, too, the effect on the likelihood of having given birth is an accumulation of the three effects that reinforce each other: the black woman is more likely to have sex (the effect of race on that odds ratio is 1.62), she is more likely to get pregnant if she has sex (the effect of race on that odds ratio is 1.65), and she is less likely (but not statistically so) to have an abortion if she gets pregnant. Putting these together, the black adolescent is far more likely to have given birth than her white counterpart, and that likelihood is the product of all three sequential decisions.

Chapter 11 reports that about half the respondents in the NHSLS held the opinion that abortion should be legal—a proportion that is roughly similar to that found in other recent samples of adults in the United States. About one-third of the respondents who were under thirty-five and had had a pregnancy (or, among the men, whose partner had had a pregnancy) reported having had an abortion. The probability of having an abortion is seen to be highly linked to marital status, with many more unmarried couples choosing to have an abortion.

Of the several personal background characteristics that are systematically related to the choice of abortion, parents' education level is most influential: those with more educated parents, especially college-educated parents, are far more likely to have an abortion if the pregnancy occurs at a young age.

The complexity of and interactions among the several variables that appear to influence the abortion decision make clear how difficult it is to map out a public policy that has the intended effect. Moreover, there are major differences of judgment in our society, of course, regarding what the intended outcome should be. For those who are most concerned about nonmarital fertility among young women, one strategy would be to encourage young black women to adopt the same behavior as young white women, who abort a far larger portion of their first pregnancies. On the other hand, if the objective is to lower the incidence of abortion in the nation, then promotion of more effective contraception would seem to be an effective policy since those who are having the abortions have well-educated parents who probably have the resources to arrange for abortion if the need arises, even if the costs are high or access limited. Another strategy that the empirical evidence suggests would be effective is encouraging pregnancy in the context of marriage since marriage is a highly influential factor inhibiting abortion.

Antisocial Behavior: Rape, Child Sexual Abuse, and Harassment

The NHSLS did not focus on antisocial sexual behaviors. There were, however, a few questions about abuse or force. One set of questions asked, "Did anyone touch you sexually" (*SOS,* 650) before puberty (age twelve or thirteen), while another asked, Did a person ever "force you to do anything sexually that you did not want to do?" (*SOS,* 654). The latter question was analyzed in our previous books, and, in this volume, chapter 4 investigates the issue of childhood sexual abuse.

Chapter 4 concludes that the life-course trajectory is the better model to use in predicting the effects of adult-child sexual experience on later well-being. This, then, is an optimistic finding in terms of public policies meant to diminish the adverse effects on young women and men who have been abused. If these young people can be identified, they can be encouraged to follow a less active and risky sexual lifestyle and can be given the extra attention that may provide them with the skills needed to manage their sex lives adequately. As the chapter suggests, in the absence of this identification, generalized sex education can also provide these skills, and, in some cases, this may involve "sex reeducation."

Tastes, Preferences, and Judgments: The Issues of Infidelity, Prostitution, Pornography, Public Nudity, and Homosexuality

The relevance of *chapter 3* for social policy about sex is inherently the same as that of the explicit discussion in chapter 12. Chapter 3 shows that there are widely varied modes of sexual expression in our nation: for some adults, sex is a major aspect of their life and self-identity, while, for others, it is of only occasional importance. Some engage in sexual behavior (such as using sex toys and sexually explicit materials) that others not only do not engage in but also consider unattractive or even inappropriate. Other activities related to sex but not directly sexual, such as public nudity, also fall into this same category: they are attractive to some in certain conditions but embarrassing and unappealing to others. About half the men and women in the categories featured in this chapter do none of the eight things listed under "seeking erotic stimulation" (including public nudity, paid sex, and buying a sexually explicit magazine or movie), while 80 percent of the men and 40 percent of the women in the other half do buy these items or engage in some of these activities.

Here, then, we see the dilemma when attempting to form social policy or take collective action regarding activities that are partial public goods. Consider the relatively benign issue of nudity at the beach. If half the population enjoys it, say, and half thinks it is inappropriate and wants to avoid confronting it, then what should be our collective decision or our community standard?

Moreover, the evidence presented in chapter 3 suggests that these differences in modes of sexual expression are not random. On the contrary, they are shown to be systematically related to the individual's personal and social circumstances—to prior experiences as a child, to physical health and age, to religious affiliation, education level, marital status, and many other conditions. This implies neither that they are arbitrarily adopted lifestyles nor that they are casually held. The forms of sexual expression in which the population engages are both varied and deeply embedded. They are probably long-term patterns of behavior, not easily altered by argument, information, or government regulation, although this conjecture goes well beyond the empirical evidence presented. The breadth of sexual expression and the deeply held convictions about what is right and wrong make it difficult to reach consensus on these social policy issues.

Chapter 5 again documents in another way the reality of the great discrepancy among adults in our country in terms of sexual behavior, sexual attitudes, and even the appeal of many sexual practices. We are a very varied nation! Consider, for example, attitudes toward homosexuality. The raw data tell us that, while 63 percent of white women think that homosexual activity is wrong, a much larger 85 percent of Mexican American women think that it is wrong; among some racial groups, a larger proportion of men consider it wrong, while, among others, a larger proportion of women consider it wrong. If we are looking for a consensus or plurality of agreement on the matter, of all the broad categories of adults considered here, well over half of each consider homosexual activity wrong. Whatever that means about their own sexual behavior or about their opinion regarding protecting homosexuality legally, it must mean that they would not favor encouraging it. In the analyses, the Mexican Americans exhibit two or three times greater odds of considering homosexuality wrong, conservative Protestants have odds of considering it wrong that are six to nine times as high as those of nonreligious adults, and those with some college education have odds of considering it wrong that are only a third as high as those with less than a high school education.

Imagine that you are a politician faced with formulating a social policy position on the matter of homosexuality, that your objective is simply to anger or alienate the fewest constituents possible, and that you wish to be guided by public opinion polls. Probably you would oppose supporting gay rights given that at least two of three adults in every group shown here consider the activity wrong. Yet your more-educated constituents would be upset. (In reality, not all these adults vote, and not all of them care equally about the matter, so the vocal and active subset who target this single issue may be influential beyond their numbers if your objective really is to have the least adverse effect on your next election, but this line of argument takes us far afield.)

Chapter 6 addresses the intriguing issue of the relation between the individual's assessment of his or her sexual experiences with the current partner and the characteristics of that partnership. The assessments include both the emotional satisfaction and the physical pleasure derived from a partnership as reported by the respondent. As the chapter stresses in its conclusion, a cross-sectional data set such as the NHSLS cannot identify the direction of causation underlying the observed correlations without imposing structure by means of formal modeling. Nonetheless, there are quite interesting patterns of relations reported here, and the chapter offers an interpretation based on the importance to the respondent of the extent of exclusivity of the partnership, the amount of emotional investment expended by the partners, and the time horizon anticipated for the partnerships that were not formal marriages or cohabitations. There are patterned differences for the men and the women. The chapter argues that these patterns support the suggestion, although not the firm conclusion, that commitment from one's partner is more important for women than for men.

The investigation here extends these correlations between partner type (spouse, cohabitant, casual partner) and the assessment of the quality of the partnership that were reported in chapter 10 of *SOS*. It shows the potential of this type of analysis, and, as the chapter emphasizes, panel data with observations on these subtle and judgmental reports at more than one point in time and with measures of changes in circumstances will be required to determine causation.

Reflections on the Reported Findings

Before turning to the final topic of this chapter, I offer two observations based on the findings reviewed here. I have suggested that the jointness of private sexual behavior generates public consequences and that these consequences justify collective action (which may include government regulation, subsidy, and taxation). However, reaching consensus about these collective actions requires agreement about objectives. The evidence from the NHSLS, and from other national data sets as well, is that the adult population in our country evinces a very wide range of sexual interests, attitudes, opinions, and preferences and an equally wide range of actual sexual behavior. So reaching agreement about those policies cannot be an easy matter.

One of the principal findings emphasized in our earlier volumes, *The Social Organization of Sexuality* and *Sex in America,* has been confirmed in chapters 3 and 5: the sexual life of Americans is deeply embedded in social structure, custom, and community. The wide range of sexual practices and opinions observed, therefore, is strongly enforced by social networks. Consequently, it would be difficult to change these attitudes and opinions about what is appropriate sexual behavior. As further evidence of that reality, consider the fact that, despite all the public attention given in recent decades to the pros and cons of abortion and homosexuality, public opinion about the two has changed very little.

Put these two facts together: sex has public consequences necessitating common policy and collective judgments, but sexual behavior and opinion vary widely and are strongly reinforced by family and peers. This diversity makes collective judgment difficult.[7] It is unlikely that we will find consensus on many sexual topics, and the difficulty in doing so is seen in the often-contentious debates about public policy regarding matters sexual.

I suggest two strategies for addressing this dilemma. First, we might back away from collective action by insisting on a higher standard for the level of externality or public good before we agree to seek a common or collective judgment. That is, when I assert that your behavior regarding some sexual issue imposes costs (monetary or psychological) on me and that it therefore warrants government action to protect me, this assertion prompts the debate whether that sexual behavior is or is not harmful, worthy, or proper. Since we as a nation do not agree on what is worthy or proper regarding a wide domain of sexual practices, we should attempt to impose collective action and face the need to reach consensus only if the case for those harmful externalities is compelling. The social cost of attempting to determine a consensus policy is itself very great, both monetarily and in terms of the social fabric. "Back off" may be a useful admonition and a wise social policy. The suggestion, then, is to leave as much choice about sexual issues in private hands as is possible and set a high threshold for permitting an issue to become a matter of social choice, in recognition of the difficulty and cost of doing so.

A second strategy is to avoid framing public policy about sex in moralistic or religious terms and instead to promote and adopt greater respect for the judgment of others. Sexual issues are frequently framed as right or wrong, good or bad. Compromise in discussions about sex is often criticized as situational or relativistic morality. If the efforts to develop effective policy were focused on those principles that do command wide

consensus—principles of equity, fairness, and personal responsibility—
the particulars of public policy regarding sex might not be quite so difficult
to frame. Great diversity of opinion exists in this country about what is
"proper" sexual behavior; that should be accepted and acknowledged, not
resisted. It is not likely to be overcome by strident, all-or-nothing arguments. "Sexual pluralism" is the stance suggested by Reiss (1997), and I
endorse that position.

My other observation also joins two sets of facts and reflects on the relation between them. Again, the first of these facts is the wide diversity of
opinion, practice, and appeal reported in this volume regarding adult sexual behavior. The second fact is that few aspects of human behavior have
been so seldom investigated or reported on by social science. Because of
this, adult sexual behavior is relatively poorly understood. Perhaps these
two facts are mutually causally related.

Perhaps the absence of normal social scientific studies and reports helps
explain why we differ so dramatically in our opinions about sex and our
sexual preferences. Additionally, the fact of these divergent opinions
probably explains at least in part why so little normal research on this
topic has been conducted over the past half century. Perhaps our limited
understanding of sexual behavior has created or encouraged these widely
varied attitudes, preferences, and opinions, which, in turn, make it so
difficult to design successful and broadly acceptable public policies regarding sexual behavior. Perhaps the effort to keep sex out of the normal
channels of inquiry has ironically resulted in it becoming a central obstacle
to creating effective public policy regarding a wide range of issues from
abortion to sex education, from explicit public health messages to sexual
harassment in the workplace. Perhaps a reluctance to study sex, to report
findings about and analytic models of sex, and to talk more matter-of-
factly about sex has made it so difficult to formulate effective public policies.

Research on Sexual Behavior

It is a matter of some curiosity that a topic as salient and fascinating to
so many of us as is sex should be one on which so little social scientific
information is available. There is, to be sure, a lot of media exposure given
sex, but most of that is either pure entertainment, a sales vehicle, or part
of some political agenda. However, for several decades now, a small number of social science researchers have undertaken ordinary, useful scientific research on aspects of sexual behavior. While that work has been
fruitful, it has remained peripheral. Typically, one thinks that an area of
inquiry that does not capture wider interest must offer few insights or be
of little importance, so one is inclined to leave to the competitive forces

of the intellectual marketplace the judgment about the worthiness of a subject. There is a case to be made, however, that research on sexual behavior has for many years been at a distinct disadvantage in that marketplace. If so, some reassessment of its potential is warranted.

That case is this. There has been near consensus among influential researchers that basic data on sexual behavior among the general population *could not* be obtained at any practical expense. There has also been a politically active minority of nonresearchers who have advocated policies based on the judgment that such research *should not* be undertaken and that its conduct and the dissemination of its results would in fact be harmful. We have therefore lacked basic data on sex, data that are similar to those available on most other social phenomena, data that improve in quality over the years. There were no (or very few) data to explore descriptively and to use to test theories and to construct models of relations of interest. So there has not been the opportunity or the stimulus for the creative intellectual activity focused on most areas of human behavior. Accordingly, there has not been much success in winning researchers' attention or major funding.

Usually, cries of "unfair" are simply self-serving, but not always. I think that, in this case, social scientific research on sexual behavior has been treated unfairly—although I should add that my colleagues and I have in fact been gratifyingly successful in obtaining funding and attention, so personally I am not so much aggrieved as pessimistic. I am concerned that the window of opportunity to conduct research afforded by the scourge of HIV/AIDS may soon close—to the detriment of social scientific knowledge.

It was Alfred Kinsey who asserted (without evidence) in 1948 that the ordinary scientific study of sexual behavior, informed by surveys of *randomly* selected samples of the general population, was impossible. That belief has been an article of faith in much of the survey research community until the last few years, despite some evidence to the contrary (e.g., the NORC/Kinsey survey in 1970, based on a quota, not a probability, sample, was conducted with great success). More recently, several good studies in the United States and elsewhere have shown that the general population, both teenagers and adults of all ages and in all locations, will in fact participate in a survey about sexual behavior.[8]

We have described elsewhere (see *SOS*) the political pressure imposed on us and on public funding of surveys asking adults or teenagers about their sexual behavior, surveys initiated by the National Institute of Child Health and Human Development in 1988. That pressure reflects the influence of those who believe that such studies should not be conducted. That in the early 1950s the House Un-American Activities Committee threatened the Rockefeller Foundation's tax-exempt status if it persisted in supporting Alfred Kinsey's research suggests that the political pressure of the late 1980s was not an aberration, representing an opinion held by only one or two out-of-touch senators or congressmen. There seems to be a widespread sentiment that the best strategy for dealing with sexual issues is to ignore them; this view has probably always had its advocates. The adoption of this view—that ignorance is bliss or that public discourse is inappropriate—as public policy is both erroneous and dangerous.

There is an additional, less sinister, reason why sexual behavior has not captured the interest of many practitioners of one useful social science, economics. That is because, like several other public policy issues, sexual behavior suffers from a "money illusion." If the matter is not conveniently measured in monetary units, the matter is frequently overlooked or under-valued in policy discussions. Examples of this money illusion include the productive efforts of homemakers and volunteers, the time spent waiting in line for "cheaper" services, or the assessment of who among us is poor by counting only money income and disregarding the value of the time not spent in the labor market (see Michael 1996). Sex surfaces as a subject of inquiry when it costs money: when medical expenses are incurred, when welfare checks are written to single mothers, when police protection is required in cases of sexual abuse, or when the explicit sale of sex is a focus of a vice squad raid, for example. But all the time and effort that go into the planning and implementation of our various sexual exploits and expe-riences remain relatively unexplored by economists because the resources that are used do not *directly* involve receiving or spending money.

So the argument is that research on sexual behavior has been at a disad-vantage in the competition for research attention, funding, and status. Next, consider why this research should be given high priority, even ur-gency, among social scientists. Put briefly, there are many sexual decisions made, both private and public, about which information is now unavail-able, but such information might be useful to those decision makers. As-suming that greater knowledge and understanding of the costs and conse-quences of any choice would improve that choice, a lack of knowledge about sexual behavior implies that less well-informed decisions regarding sexual behavior will be made than otherwise might be.

There are other reasons why sexual choice may be especially ill in-formed. First, because sex is intimate, we are reluctant to ask for advice about the subject or even to signal to trusted friends or family members that we might in fact need such advice. (It is self-serving, but it may also be true, that *Sex in America,* a trade book, did not sell well partly because many educated middle-class Americans who buy books are reluctant to be seen reading a book with the word *sex* in big red letters on the cover.) The privacy afforded sex means that less information, experience, and knowledge about this domain of life is shared than is shared about most others.

We are not all good cooks, but there is ample opportunity to learn about the principles of good cooking from many sources, formal and informal. Our friends happily share good recipes and secrets. We do not, however, so readily share our knowledge of sex, nor is our knowledge necessarily of interest to our friends and family members since our own experience is partner specific. While there are many "how-to" books, articles, videos, and gurus offering advice about sex, that advice is typically anecdotal, entertainment oriented, focused on the unusual or the bizarre, and usually not very useful.

Second, there is no competitive mechanism that works to improve sexual behavior or to assure that new information or insight is disseminated. While the activity of selecting and attracting a sex partner is arguably highly competitive, the resulting sexual behavior itself is private and not revealed. The selection of a partner involves many considerations, as discussed earlier, and sexual skill figures only partly in that decision. In past decades, when sexual experimentation prior to forming a long-term partnership was less common, often only the prediction of sexual compatibility, not any actual experience, directed partner choice. Since sexual behavior is only part of the reason most of us select our partners, there is no effective competitive force discouraging poor sexual behavior or rewarding exceptionally effective sexual behavior. This characteristic implies that there is no competitive force to replace ignorance with knowledge, ineptness with skill, inhibition and anxiety with healthy pleasure and receptivity.

Because of the reluctance to discuss sexual behavior, there is no competitive mechanism by which the better advice or the more useful information wins out over poorer advice or less useful information. Few of us have ever been directly instructed in sexual behavior by a trusted and caring family member or by a loved one who was not actually a sex partner; few of us have ever observed other couples having sex. The stylized and scripted events of popular films, television shows, and novels certainly do not offer much useful information in this regard.

Third, since there are few areas in which the search for knowledge has been so actively opposed, it is not surprising that sexual behavior has not been openly researched or discussed and, consequently, that there is far less accurate information available on which to base good advice and instruction. The *Joy of Sex* (Comfort 1972) struck a responsive chord in the 1970s, less because of the particular information it conveyed, than because of its unabashed stance of encouraging sexual exploration and experimentation.

So it is no wonder that our decisions about sexual behavior are relatively poorly informed. We are embarrassed or reluctant to seek advice or to show interest in sex, there is little competitive market pressure for new information to drive out bad information, and the production of new knowledge has been systematically inhibited. Thus, on the ground of marginal value added, one would think that the domain of research on sexual behavior is ripe for advancement since it is so unexplored.

Finally, does it really matter that our knowledge about sexual behavior is so limited? Perhaps sex is so instinctive, so primal, that no lessons are needed, no information required. We have, after all, seemed to figure out how to have babies, increase the population, and get on with having pretty good sex lives without academic research to guide us. However, the sexual choices that we make, both privately and collectively, matter a great deal. The effect on one's personal life of one's sexual choices is profound—from a decision that results in a viral disease that cannot be cured to a pregnancy that inadvertently creates a new life with a lifetime bond and mutual obligations between parent and child. Similarly, the effect on the community can be substantial—from decisions about any of the sexual behaviors or practices that involve sexually transmitted diseases, to the problems of teenage childbearing, the dependence on welfare of single teenage mothers, access to and funding of abortion, the promotion of birth control and disease prevention, rape, sexual harassment, pornography, nudity, infidelity, and on and on. These several topics that are intricately related to sexual behavior are among the more explosive and divisive in many of our communities. Better information may not solve these complex problems, but information can improve the sexual choices that we make both privately and collectively.

Notes

I thank Yasuyo Abe, Norman Bradburn, Alex Cavallo, and Ed Laumann for comments on an early draft of this chapter.

1. A few highly successful surveys and analyses were conducted in the 1960s and 1970s, but they did not alter the general perception that this was not a fruitful area of social scientific inquiry. See, e.g., Gagnon and Simon (1973), Reiss (1960, 1967), and the NORC/Kinsey 1970 survey described in Klassen, Williams, and Levitt (1989).

2. Most decisions made about sexual behavior are the private ones made daily by countless couples; this is "private policy," and most attention focuses on it. I focus here instead on the collective decisions that constitute "public policy" regarding sex.

3. A frivolous example is found in the *The Music Man,* where the "trouble right here in River City" is alleged to come from a pool hall. A more contemporary example is the alleged economic value to cities of domed sports stadiums (see Noll and Zimbalist 1997).

4. A closely related rationale, although a very different basis for regulation, is a form of paternalism in which a behavior is considered wrong on ethical or religious grounds. That behavior is then discouraged by making it illegal. Prostitution is an example.

5. There are other good reasons for government or collective action. One that arises in the sexual arena, as elsewhere, is the role of certifying the quality of some vendor whose quality cannot easily be ascertained by a buyer without actually purchasing the product. A license or certification can be justified in some of these cases, although a "seal of approval" or an endorsement given by a reputable private party can often do the same job more efficiently

than can a government-sponsored solution. Another issue involves social concern about distribution. We may collectively have compassion for those with a dysfunction or a limitation and collectively decide to spend resources to help such individuals.

6. Translating this magnitude of the effect of a one-year difference in age at puberty on the probability of giving birth depends on the level at which the comparison is made. Let us take $P = 0.11$ as the probability of giving birth by age eighteen, which is the average across all these women. The odds are $P/1 - P = 0.11/0.89 = 0.12$, so an effect that changes that probability by 0.88 implies that the odds change to 0.1056 ($= 0.88 \times 0.12$), and those odds of 0.1056 mean that the probability is then 0.0955 ($0.1056 = P'/1 - P'$). All this then tells us that, had a woman who reached puberty at, say, the average age of 12.7 and had a probability of giving birth by age eighteen that is equal to 0.11 actually reached puberty one year later, at age 13.7 instead, she would have had a probability of giving birth at age eighteen of 0.0955, and, similarly, that, had she reached puberty a year earlier, at age 11.7, she would have had a probability of giving birth of 0.118 ($P = 0.12 \times 1.12/[1 + 0.12 \times 1.12]$).

7. Reliance on community standards is a useful strategy for creating a more homogeneous social community that is more likely to reach a consensus.

8. I note one indication of how resistant to evidence is the belief that a useful survey of sexual behaviors and attitudes can be conducted, even in the face of quality data measured by all the usual and conventional measures. In a long complaint about the NHSLS, one critic (Lewontin 1995) argued that adults who ostensibly have cooperated in the survey have in fact given misinformation rather than accurate information since they have a deluded sense of their own past behavior and attitudes. The contention was that respondents could not reliably answer questions about their own behaviors and attitudes! There is no evidence, I hasten to note, for this odd contention. Surely, there are those who are delusional, and all of us probably have some self-protective distortion built into our perceptions and memories, but we do successfully communicate with each other in many modes, including structured survey interviews, and the truth content of these communications is usually taken to be sufficient to warrant analysis of the data obtained. I see this argument as a desperate attempt to hold on to the comfortable old myth that these surveys cannot successfully be conducted, a myth that is exposed by our and other's successful surveys of sexual behavior within the past decade.

REFERENCES

■

Abbott, A. 1990. Positivism and interpretation in sociology: Lessons for sociologists from the history of stress research. *Sociological Forum* 5:435–58.

Abma, J., A. Chandra, W. Mosher, L. Peterson, and L. Piccinino. 1997. Fertility, family planning, and women's health: New data from the 1995 National Survey of Family Growth. *Vital and Health Statistics* (National Center for Health Statistics) 23:19.

Abramson, P. R., and S. D. Pinkerton. 1995. *With pleasure: Thoughts on the nature of human sexuality.* New York: Oxford University Press.

ACSF Investigators. 1993. *Les comportements sexuels en France.* Paris: La Documentation Française.

Aggleton, P., K. O'Reilly, G. Slutkin, and P. Davies. 1994. Risking everything? Risk behavior, behavior change, and AIDS. *Science* 265 (July): 341–45.

Ahituv, A., J. Hotz, and T. Philipson. 1993. Condom use and the risk of AIDS: Has protection increased with the spread of the epidemic? Working paper. Chicago: University of Chicago, Population Research Center.

———. 1996. The responsiveness of the demand for condoms to the local prevalence of AIDS. *Journal of Human Resources* 21:809–69.

Akerlof, G. A., J. L. Yellen, and M. L. Katz. 1996. An analysis of out-of-wedlock childbearing in the United States. *Quarterly Journal of Economics* 111 (May): 277–317.

Akers, R. L. 1973. *Deviant behavior: A social learning approach.* Belmont, Calif.: Wadsworth.

Alberman, E. 1992. Spontaneous abortions: Epidemiology. In *Spontaneous abortion: Diagnosis and treatment,* ed. I. Stabile, G. Grudzinskas, and T. Chard. London: Springer.

Alexander, C. S., M. R. Somerfield, M. E. Ensminger, K. E. Johnson, and Y. J. Kim. 1993. Consistency of adolescents' self-report of sexual behavior in a longitudinal study. *Journal of Youth and Adolescence* 22, no. 5:455–71.

American Academy of Pediatrics (AAP). 1999. Report of the Task Force on Circumcision. *Pediatrics* 84, no. 2:388–91.

American Psychiatric Association (APA). 1994. *Diagnostic and statistical manual of mental disorders.* 4th ed. Washington, D.C.

Anderson, E. 1990. *Streetwise: Race, class, and change in an urban community.* Chicago: University of Chicago Press.

———. 1991. Neighborhood effects on teenage pregnancy. In *The urban underclass,* ed. C. Jencks and P. Peterson. Washington, D.C.: Brookings.

———. 1993. Sex codes and family life among poor inner-city youths. In *The ghetto underclass: Social science perspectives,* ed. W. J. Wilson. Newbury Park, Calif.: Sage.

Anderson, J. E., L. McCormick, and R. Fichtner. 1994. Factors associated with self-reported STDs: Data from a national survey. *Sexually Transmitted Diseases* 21:303–8.

Anderson, R. M. 1991. The transmission dynamics of sexually transmitted diseases: The behavioral component. In *Research issues in human behavior and sexually transmitted diseases in the AIDS era,* ed. J. N. Wasserheit, S. O. Aral, K. K. Holmes, and P. J. Hitchcock. Washington, D.C.: American Society for Microbiology.

494   REFERENCES

Anderson, R. M., S. Gupta, and W. Ng. 1990. The significance of sexual partner contact networks for the transmitted dynamics of HIV. *Journal of Acquired Immune Deficiency Syndromes* 3:417–29.

Anderson, R. M., and R. M. May. 1992. Understanding the AIDS pandemic. *Scientific American* 266, no. 5 (May): 59–66.

Anderson, R. M., G. F. Medley, R. M. May, and A. M. Johnson. 1986. A preliminary study of the transmission dynamics of human immunodeficiency virus (HIV), the causative agent of AIDS. *IMA Journal of Mathematics Applied in Medicine and Biology* 3:229–63.

Aquilino, W. S. 1993. Effects of spouse presence during the interview on survey responses concerning marriage. *Public Opinion Quarterly* 57:358–76.

Aral, S. O. 1996. The social context of syphilis persistence in the Southern United States. *Sexually Transmitted Diseases* 23:9–15.

Aral, S. O., R. E. Fullilove, R. A. Countinho, and J. Hoek. 1991. Demographic and societal factors influencing risk behaviors. In *Research issues in human behavior and sexually transmitted diseases in the AIDS era,* ed. J. N. Wasserheit, S. O. Aral, K. K. Holmes, and P. J. Hitchcock. Washington, D.C.: American Society for Microbiology.

Aral, S. O., and M. E. Guinau. 1984. Women and sexually transmitted diseases. In *Transmitted diseases,* ed. K. K. Holmes et al. New York: McGraw-Hill.

Aral, S. O., and K. K. Holmes. 1990. Epidemiology of sexual behavior and sexually transmitted diseases. In *Sexually transmitted diseases,* ed. K. K. Holmes, P. A. Mardh, P. Weisner, J. W. Cates, S. M. Lemon, and W. E. Stamm. New York: McGraw-Hill.

———. 1991. Sexually transmitted diseases in the AIDS era. *Scientific American,* 264, no. 2:62–69.

Arminger, G. 1995. Specification and estimation of mean structures. In *Handbook of statistical modeling for the social and behavioral sciences,* ed. G. Arminger, C. C. Clogg, and M. E. Sobel. New York: Plenum.

Armstrong, L. 1978. *Kiss Daddy goodnight.* New York: Hawthorn.

Bachrach, C. A., and W. Baldwin. 1991. Letter from reader. *Family Planning Perspectives* 23, no. 5 (September/October): 233.

Bajos, N., J. Wadsworth, B. Ducot, A. M. Johnson, F. LePont, K. Wellings, A. Spira, and J. Field. 1995. Sexual behavior and HIV epidemiology: Comparative analysis in France and Britain. *AIDS* 9:735–43.

Bandura, A. 1973. *Aggression: A social learning analysis.* Englewood Cliffs, N.J.: Prentice-Hall.

———. 1977. Self-efficacy: Toward a unifying theory of behavioral change. *Psychological Review* 84:191–215.

Bean, J. A., J. D. Leeper, R. B. Wallace, B. M. Sherman, and H. Jagger. 1979. Variations in the reporting of menstrual histories. *American Journal of Epidemiology* 109, no. 2: 181–85.

Becker, G. S. 1981. *A treatise on the family.* Cambridge, Mass.: Harvard University Press.

———. 1991. *A treatise on the family.* 2d ed. Cambridge, Mass.: Harvard University Press.

Becker, G. S., and N. Tomes. 1986. Human capital and the rise and fall of families. *Journal of Labor Economics* 4:S1–S39.

Becker, M. H., and J. G. Joseph. 1988. AIDS and behavioral change to reduce risk: A review. *American Journal of Public Health* 78, no. 4 (April): 394–410.

Beitchman, J. H., K. J. Zucker, J. E. Hood, and G. A. daCosta. 1991. A review of the short-term effects of child sexual abuse. *Child Abuse and Neglect* 15:537–56.

Belcastro, P. A. 1985. Sexual behavior differences between black and white students. *Journal of Sex Research* 21, no. 1:56–67.

Bellah, R. N., R. Madsen, W. M. Sullivan, A. Swidler, and S. M. Tipton. 1985. *Habits of the heart.* New York: Harper & Row.

Bem, D. J. 1996. Exotic becomes erotic: A developmental theory of sexual orientation. *Psychological Review* 103:320.

Bernard, J. 1972. *The future of marriage.* New Haven, Conn.: Yale University Press.

Biggar, R. J., and M. Melbye. 1992. Responses to anonymous questionnaires concerning sexual behavior: A method to examine potential biases. *American Journal of Public Health* 82, no. 11:1506–12.

Billy, J. O., K. L. Brewster, and W. R. Grady. 1994. Contextual effects on the sexual behavior of adolescent women. *Journal of Marriage and the Family* 56:387–404.

Billy, J. O. G., K. Tanfer, W. R. Grady, and D. H. Kelpiinger. 1993. The sexual behavior of men in the United States. *Family Planning Perspectives* 25:52–60.

Birkelund, G. S., L. A. Goodman, and D. Rose. 1996. The latent structure of job characteristics of men and women. *American Journal of Sociology* 102:80–113.

Blank, R. M., C. C. George, and R. A. London. 1996. State abortion rates: The impact of policies, providers, politics, demographics, and economic environment. *Journal of Health Economics* 15:513–53.

Blau, P., and O. D. Duncan. 1967. *The American occupational structure.* New York: Wilcy.

Blower, S. M., G. J. P. V. Griensven, and E. Kaplan. 1995. An analysis of the process of human immunodeficiency virus sexual risk behavior change. *Epidemiology* 6:238–42.

Blumstein, P., and P. Schwartz. 1983. *American couples: Money, work, sex.* New York: Morrow.

Boolell, M., J. C. Gepi-Attee, and M. J. Allen. 1996. Sildenafil, a novel effective oral therapy for male erectile dysfunction. *British Journal of Urology* 78:257–61.

Bourdieu, P. 1984. *Distinction: A social critique of the judgment of taste.* Cambridge, Mass.: Harvard University Press.

Bowser, B. 1994. African-American male sexuality through the early life course. In *Sexuality across the life course,* ed. A. Rossi. Chicago: University of Chicago Press.

Boyle, M. 1994. Gender, science, and sexual dysfunction. In *Constructing the social,* ed. T. R. Sarbin and J. I. Kitsuse. London: Sage.

Bozon, M., and H. Leridon. 1996. *Sexuality and the social sciences: A French survey on sexual behavior.* Aldershot: Dartmouth.

Bradburn, N. M. 1969. *The structure of psychological well-being.* Chicago: Aldine.

Bradburn, N. M., and S. Sudman. 1974. *Response effects in surveys.* Chicago: Aldine.

Brandt, A. 1987. *No magic bullet.* Oxford: Oxford University Press.

Brewster, K. L. 1994. Race differences in sexual activity among adolescent women: The role of neighborhood characteristics. *American Sociological Review* 59 (June): 408–24.

Brewster, K. L., J. O. G. Billy, and W. A. Grady. 1993. Social context and adolescent behavior: The impact of community on the transition to sexual activity. *Social Forces* 71, no. 3:713–40.

Brewster, K. L., E. C. Cooksey, D. K. Guilkey, and R. R. Rindfuss. 1988. The changing impact of religion on the sexual and contraceptive behavior of adolescent women in the United States. *Journal of Marriage and the Family* 60:493–504.

Briere, J., and J. R. Conte. 1993. Self-reported amnesia for abuse in adults molested as children. *Journal of Traumatic Stress* 6:21–31.

Briggs, L., and P. R. Joyce. 1997. What determines post-traumatic stress disorder symptomatology for survivors of childhood sexual abuse? *Child Abuse and Neglect* 21:575–82.

Bringle, R. G., and B. P. Buunk. 1991. Extradyadic relationships and sexual jealousy. In *Sexuality in close relationships,* ed. K. McKinney and S. Sprecher. Hillsdale, N.J.: Erlbaum.

Brown, M. S., and C. A. Brown. 1987. Circumcision decision: Prominence of social concerns. *Pediatrics* 80:215–19.

Brown, S. L., and A. Booth. 1996. Cohabitation versus marriage: A comparison of relationship quality. *Journal of Marriage and the Family* 58:668–78.

Browne, A., and D. Finkelhor. 1986. The impact of child sexual abuse: A review of the research. *Psychological Bulletin* 99, no. 1:66–77.

Browning, C. R. 1997. *Trauma or transition.* Chicago: University of Chicago Dissertation.

Browning, C., and E. O. Laumann. 1997. Sexual contact between children and adults: Tracking the long-term effects. *American Sociological Review* 62 (August): 540–60.

Bumpass, L. L., J. A. Sweet, and A. Cherlin. 1991. The role of cohabitation in declining rates of marriage. *Journal of Marriage and the Family* 53:913–27.

Burger, R., and T. Guthrie. 1974. Why circumcision? *Pediatrics* 54:362.

Burnett, A. L. 1995. The role of nitric oxide in the physiology of erection. *Biology of Reproduction* 52:485–89.

Buss, D. M. 1994. *The evolution of desire: Strategies of human mating.* New York: Basic.

Butler, J. 1990. *Gender trouble: Feminism and the subversion of identity.* New York: Routledge.

Buunk, B. P., O. Angleitner, and D. M. Buss. 1996. Sexual differences in jealousy in evolutionary and cultural perspective. *Psychological Science* 7:359–63.

Call, V., S. Sprecher, S. Schwartz, and P. Schwartz. 1995. The incidence and frequency of marital sex in a national sample. *Journal of Marriage and the Family* 57:639–52.

Carrier, J. 1995. *De los otros: Intimacy and homosexuality among Mexican men.* New York: Columbia University Press.

Caspi, A. 1987. Personality in the life course. *Journal of Personality and Social Psychology* 53, no. 6:1203–13.

Caspi, A., G. H. Elder Jr., and D. J. Bem. 1987. Moving against the world: Life-course patterns of explosive children. *Developmental Psychology* 23:308–13.

Catania, J. A., D. Binson, M. M. Dolcini, R. Stall, K.-H. Choi, L. M. Pollack, E. S. Hudes, J. Canchola, K. Phillips, J. T. Moskowitz, and T. J. Coates. 1995. Risk factors for HIV and other sexually transmitted diseases and prevention practices among U.S. heterosexual adults: Changes from 1990 to 1992. *American Journal of Public Health* 85, no. 11 (November): 1492–99.

Catania, J. A., T. J. Coates, E. Golden, et al. 1994. Correlates of condom use among black, Hispanic, and white heterosexuals in San Francisco: The Amen Longitudinal Survey. *AIDS Education and Prevention* 6:12–26.

Catania, J. A., T. J. Coates, R. Stall, H. Turner, and J. Peterson. 1992. Prevalence of AIDS-related risk factors and condom use in the United States. *Science* 248, no. 585:1101–6.

Catania, J. A., S. M. Kegels, and T. J. Coates. 1990. Towards an understanding of risk behavior: An AIDS risk reduction model (ARRM). *Health Education Quarterly* 17, no. 1 (spring): 53–72.

Cates, W., and K. M. Stone. 1992a. Family planning, sexually transmitted disease, and contraceptive choice: A literature update—part 1. *Family Planning Perspectives* 85, no. 11 (November): 75–84.

———. 1992b. Family planning, sexually transmitted disease, and contraceptive choice: A literature update—part 2. *Family Planning Perspectives* 24, no. 3 (May): 122–28.

Centers for Disease Control and Prevention (CDC). 1994. *HIV/AIDS surveillance report 6, number 2.* Year-end ed. Atlanta.

———. 1995. *Sexually transmitted disease surveillance.* Atlanta: U.S. Department of Health and Human Services.

———. 1996. *HIV/AIDS surveillance report 2. 8.* Atlanta.

———. 1997. *HIV/AIDS surveillance report 1. 9.* Atlanta.

———. 1998. *Sexually Transmitted Disease Surveillance.* Atlanta.

Central Statistical Office (CSO). 1992. *Social trends 22: 1992 edition.* London: H. M. Stationery Office.

Cherlin, A. J. 1992. *Marriage, divorce, remarriage.* Cambridge, Mass.: Harvard University Press.

Chilman, S. C. 1980. *Adolescent pregnancy and childrearing: Findings from research.* Washington, D.C.: U.S. Government Printing Office.

Chodorow, N. 1978. *The reproduction of mothering: Psychoanalysis and the sociology of gender.* Berkeley and Los Angeles: University of California Press.

Choi, K., and T. J. Coates. 1994. Prevention of HIV infection. *AIDS* 8:1371–89.

Clarkberg, M., R. M. Stolzenberg, and L. J. Waite. 1995. Attitudes, values, and entrance into cohabitational versus marital unions. *Social Forces* 74:609–34.

Clarke, S. C. 1995. Advance report of final marriage statistics, 1989–1990. In *Monthly vital statistics report,* ed. National Center for Health Statistics. Washington, D.C.: U.S. Government Printing Office.

Cleary, P. D. 1987. Why people take precautions against health risks. In *Taking care: Understanding and encouraging self-protective behavior,* ed. N. D. Weinstein. New York: Cambridge University Press.

Cleary, T., and S. Kohl. 1979. Overwhelming infection with group B beta-hemolytic streptococcus associated with circumcision. *Pediatrics* 64:301–3.

Cleland, J., and B. Ferry. 1995. *Sexual behavior and AIDS in the developing world.* London: Taylor Francis.

Clogg, C. C. 1995. Latent class models. In *Handbook of statistical modeling for the social and behavioral sciences,* ed. G. Arminger, C. C. Clogg, and M. E. Sobel. New York: Plenum.

Coleman, J. S. 1961. *The adolescent society.* New York: Free Press.

———. 1966. Female status and premarital sexual codes. *American Journal of Sociology* 72, no. 2:217.

Comfort, A., ed. 1972. *The joy of sex: A Cordon Bleu guide to lovemaking.* New York: Simon & Schuster.

Committee on Fetus and Newborn (CFN). 1975. Report of the ad hoc Task Force on Circumcision. *Pediatrics* 56:610–11.

Connell, R. W. 1995. *Masculinities: Knowledge, power, and social change.* Berkeley and Los Angeles: University of California Press.

Cook, L. S., L. A. Koutsky, and K. K. Holmes. 1994. Circumcision and sexually transmitted diseases. *American Journal of Public Health* 84:197–201.

Cooksey, E. C. 1990. Factors in the resolution of adolescent premarital pregnancies. *Demography* 27, no. 2 (May): 207–18.

Cooksey, E. C., R. R. Rindfuss, and D. K. Guilkey. 1996. The initiation of adolescent sexual and contraceptive behavior during changing times. *Journal of Health and Sexual Behavior* 37:59–74.

Craig, B. H., and D. M. O'Brien. 1993. *Abortion and American Politics.* Chatham, N.J.: Chatham House.

Davis, D. 1991. Understanding AIDS—the national AIDS mailer. *Public Health Reports* 106:656–62.

Davis, K., and F. van den Oever. 1982. Demographic foundations of new sex roles. *Population and Development Review* 8, no. 3:495–511.

Day, R. D. 1992. The transition to first intercourse among racially and culturally diverse youth. *Journal of Marriage and the Family* 54:749–62.

Deblinger, E., S. V. McLeer, M. S. Atkins, D. Ralphe, and E. Foa. 1989. Post-traumatic stress in sexually abused, physically abused, and nonabused children. *Child Abuse and Neglect* 13:403–8.

Des Jarlais, D.C., P. Friedmann, H. Hagen, and S. R. Friedman. 1996. The protective effects of AIDS-related behavioral change among injection drug users: A cross-national study. *American Journal of Public Health* 86:1780–85.

DeLamater, J. 1987. Gender differences in sexual scenarios. In *Females, males, and sexuality,* ed. K. Kelley. Albany, N.Y.: SUNY Press.

———. 1995. The NORC sex survey. *Science* 270:501–3.

DeMaris, A. 1992. *Logit modeling: Practical applications.* Newbury Park, Calif.: Sage.

DiMaggio, P. 1994. Social stratification, life-style, and social cognition. In *Social stratification: Class, race, and gender in sociological perspective,* ed. D. B. Grusky. Boulder, Colo.: Westview.

DiMaggio, P. J., and W. W. Powell. 1991. Introduction. In *The new institutionalism in organizational analysis,* ed. W. W. Powell and P. J. DiMaggio. Chicago: University of Chicago Press.

Division of STI/HIV Prevention (DSHP). 1994. *Sexually transmitted disease surveillance, 1993.* Atlanta: Centers for Disease Control and Prevention.

Donnelly, D. A. 1993. Sexually inactive marriage. *Journal of Sex Research* 30, no. 2:171–79.

Donovan, B., I. Bassett, and N.J. Bodsworth. 1994. Male circumcision and common sexually transmissible diseases in developed nation setting. *Genitourinary Medicine* 70:317–20.

Downs, W. R. 1993. Developmental considerations for the effects of childhood sexual abuse. *Journal of Interpersonal Violence* 8:331–45.

Duncan, G. J., and S. D. Hoffman. 1990. Welfare benefits, economic opportunities, and out-of-wedlock births among black teenage girls. *Demography* 27, no. 4:519–35.

———. 1991. Teenage underclass behavior and subsequent poverty: Have the rules changed? In *The urban underclass,* ed. C. Jencks and P. Peterson. Washington, D.C.: Brookings.

Duneier, M. 1992. *Slim's table: Race, respectability, and masculinity.* Chicago: University of Chicago Press.

Durkheim, E. 1951. *Suicide: A study in sociology.* New York: Free Press.

Eaton, W. W., A. McCutcheon, A. Dryman, and A. Sorenson. 1989. Latent class analysis of anxiety and depression. *Sociological Methods and Research* 18:104–25.

Edwards, J. N., and A. Booth. 1994. Sexuality, marriage, and well-being: The middle years. In *Sexuality across the life course,* ed. A. S. Rossi. Chicago: University of Chicago Press.

Eggert, L. L., and M. R. Parks. 1983. Romantic involvement and social network involvement. *Social Psychology Quarterly* 46:116–31.

Ehrhardt, A. A., and J. N. Wasserheit. 1991. Age, gender, and sexual risk behaviors for sexually transmitted diseases in the United States. In *Research issues in human behavior and sexually transmitted diseases in the AIDS era,* ed. J. N. Wasserheit, S. O. Aral, K. K. Holmes, and P. J. Hitchcock. Washington, D.C.: American Society for Microbiology.

Elder, G. H., Jr. 1974. *Children of the Great Depression.* Chicago: University of Chicago Press.

Elder, G. H. 1985. Perspectives on the life course. In *Trajectories and transitions, 1968–1980,* ed. J. G. H. Elder. Ithaca, N.Y.: Cornell University Press.

Elliott, D. S., D. Huizinga, and S. Ageton. 1985. *Explaining delinquency and drug use.* Beverly Hills, Calif.: Sage.

Elmer-Dewitt, P. 1994. Now for the truth about Americans and sex. *Time,* 17 October, 62–70.

England, P., and G. Farkas. 1986. *Households, employment, and gender: A social, economic, and demographic view.* New York: Aldine DeGruyter.

Epstein, S. 1996. *Impure science: AIDS, activism, and the politics of knowledge.* Berkeley and Los Angeles: University of California Press.

Ericksen, J. A. 1999. *Kiss and tell: Surveying sex in the twentieth century.* Cambridge, Mass.: Harvard University Press.

European Centre for the Epidemiological Monitoring of AIDS (ECEMA). 1997. *HIV/AIDS surveillance in Europe.* Saint-Maurice: World Health Organization.

Falliers, C. 1970. Circumcision. *Journal of the American Medical Association* 212:2194.

Feingold, A. 1992. Gender differences in mate selection preferences: A test of the parental investment model. *Psychological Bulletin* 112:125–39.

Feinleib, J. A., and R. T. Michael. 1998. Reported changes in sexual behavior in response to AIDS in the United States. *Preventive Medicine* 27:400–411.

Feldman, H. A., I. Goldstein, D. G. Hatzichristou, R. J. Krane, and J. B. McKinlay. 1994. Impotence and its medical and psychosocial correlates: Results of the Massachusetts male aging study. *Journal of Urology* 151:54–61.

Feldman, S. S., D. R. Rosenthal, N. L. Brown, and R. D. Canning. 1995. Predicting sexual experience in adolescent boys from peer rejection and acceptance during childhood. *Journal of Research on Adolescence* 5, no. 4:387–411.

Finkel, M. L., and D. J. Finkel. 1981. Sexual and contraceptive knowledge, attitudes, and behavior of male adolescents. In *Teenage sexuality, pregnancy, and childbearing,* ed. J. F. F. Furstenberg, R. Lincoln, and J. Menken. Philadelphia: University of Pennsylvania Press.

Finkelhor, D. 1979. *Sexually victimized children.* New York: Free Press.

———. 1984. *Child sexual abuse: New theory and research.* New York: Free Press.

———. 1985. The traumatic impact of child sexual abuse: A conceptualization. *American Journal of Orthopsychiatry* 55:4.

———. 1988. The trauma of child sexual abuse: Two models. In *Lasting effects of child sexual abuse,* ed. G. E. Wyatt and G. J. Powell. Newbury Park, Calif.: Sage.

Finkelhor, D. 1995. The victimization of children: A developmental perspective. *American Journal of Orthopsychiatry* 65:177–93.

Finkelhor, D., G. Hotaling, I. A. Lewis, and C. Smith. 1990. Sexual abuse in a national survey of adult men and women: Prevalence, characteristics, and risk factors. *Child Abuse and Neglect* 14:19–28.

Finkelhor, D., and K. Kendall-Tackett. 1997. A developmental perspective on the childhood impact of crime, abuse, and violent victimization. In *Developmental perspectives on trauma: Theory, research, and intervention,* ed. D. Cicchetti and S. L. Toth. Rochester, N.Y.: University of Rochester Press.

Fishbein, M., and S. E. Middlestadt. 1989. Using the theory of reasoned action as a framework for understanding and changing AIDS-related behaviors. In *Primary prevention of AIDS: Psychological approaches,* ed. V. M. Mays, G. W. Albee, and S. F. Schneider. Newbury Park, Calif.: Sage.

Fisher, J., and W. A. Fisher. 1992. Changing AIDS risk behavior. *Psychological Bulletin* 111, no. 3:455–74.

Fleming, D. T., G. M. McQuillan, R. E. Johnson, A. J. Nahmias, S. O. Aral, F. K. Lee, and M. C. Louis. 1997. Herpes simplex virus type II in the United States, 1976–1994. *New England Journal of Medicine* 337:1105–11.

Forrest, J. D. 1994. Epidemiology of unintended pregnancy and contraceptive use. *American Journal of Obstetrics and Gynecology* 170, no. 5:1485–89.

Forste, R., and K. Tanfer. 1996. Sexual exclusivity among dating, cohabiting, and married women. *Journal of Marriage and the Family* 58:33–47.

Frank, E., C. Anderson, and D. Rubinstein. 1978. Frequency of sexual dysfunction in "normal" couples. *New England Journal of Medicine* 299:111–15.

Freud, S. [1896] 1955. The etiology of hysteria. In *The standard edition of the complete psychological works of Sigmund Freud,* vol. 3, ed. J. Strachey. London: Hogarth.

Freud, S. 1920. Beyond the pleasure principle. In *The standard edition of the complete psychological works of Sigmund Freud,* vol. 7, ed. J. Strachey. London: Hogarth, 1962.

Freyd, J. 1996. *Betrayal trauma.* Cambridge, Mass.: Harvard University Press.

Fu, H., J. E. Darroch, S. K. Henshaw, and E. Kolb. 1998. Measuring the extent of abortion underreporting in the 1995 National Survey of Family Growth. *Family Planning Perspectives* 30, no. 3 (May/June): 128–33.

Fugl-Meyer, A., G. Lodnert, I.-B. Branholm, and K. S. Fugl-Meyer. 1997. On life satisfaction in male erectile dysfunction. *International Journal of Impotence Research* 9:141–48.

Furstenberg, F. 1976. *Unplanned parenthood: The social consequences of teenage childbearing.* New York: Free Press.

————. 1980. The social consequences of teenage pregnancy. In *Adolescent pregnancy and childbearing: Findings from research.* National Institutes of Health Publication no. 81–2077. Washington, D.C.: U.S. Department of Health and Human Services.

Furstenberg, F., P. Morgan, K. Moore, and J. Peterson. 1987. Race differences in the timing of adolescent intercourse. *American Sociological Review* 52:511–18.

Gagnon, J. H., and R. G. Parker. 1995. Conceiving sexuality. In *Conceiving sexuality: Approaches to sex research in a postmodern world,* ed. J. H. Gagnon and R. G. Parker. New York: Routledge.

Gagnon, J. H., and W. Simon. 1973. *Sexual conduct: The social sources of human sexuality.* Chicago: Aldine.

————. 1987. The sexual scripting of oral genital contacts. *Archives of Sexual Behavior* 16, no. 1:1–25.

Gairdner, D. 1949. The fate of the foreskin. *British Medical Journal* 2:1433–37.

Garnett, G., and R. M. Anderson. 1993. Contact tracing and the estimation of sexual mixing patterns: The epidemiology of gonococcal infections. *Sexually Transmitted Diseases* 20, no. 4:181–91.

Garnett, G. P., R. C. Brunham, and R. M. Anderson. 1992. Gonococcal infection, infertility, and population growth: 2. The influence of heterogeneity in sexual behavior. *IMA Journal of Mathematics Applied in Medicine and Biology* 9:127–44.

Gay, P. 1989. *The Freud reader.* New York: Norton.

Gebhard, P. H., and A. B. Johnson. 1979. *The Kinsey data: Marginal tabulations of the 1938–1963 interviews conducted by the Institute for Sex Research.* Philadelphia: Saunders.

Gelinas, D. J. 1983. The persisting effects of incest. *Psychiatry* 46:312–32.

General Accounting Office (GAO). 1989. *GAO report: AIDS forecasting: Undercount of cases and lack of key data weaken existing estimate.* n. Washington, D.C.

Gilligan, C. 1982. *In a different voice.* Cambridge, Mass.: Harvard University Press.

Gilmore, D. 1990. *Manhood in the making: Cultural concepts of masculinity.* New Haven, Conn.: Yale University Press.

Gilmore, S., J. DeLamater, and D. Wagstaff. 1996. Sexual decision making by inner city black adolescent males: A focus group study. *Journal of Sex Research* 33, no. 4:363–71.

Glenn, N. D. 1975. The contribution of marriage to the psychological well-being of males and females. *Journal of Marriage and the Family* 37:594–600.

————. 1996. Values, attitudes, and the state of American marriage. In *Promises to keep: Decline and renewal of marriage in America,* ed. D. Popoenoe, J. B. Elshtain, and D. Blankenhorn. Lanham, Mass.: Rowman & Littlefield.

Glenn, N. D., and C. N. Wever. 1988. The changing relationship of marital status to reported happiness. *Journal of Marriage and the Family* 50:317–24.

Goldscheider, C., and W. D. Mosher. 1991. Patterns of contraceptive use in the United States: The importance of religious factors. *Studies in Family Planning* 22, no. 2:102–15.

Goldscheider, F. K., and L. J. Waite. 1991. *New families, no families?* Berkeley and Los Angeles: University of California Press.

Gomes-Schwarz, B., J. Horowitz, and A. Cardarelli. 1990. *Child sexual abuse: The initial effects.* Newbury Park, Calif.: Sage.

Goode, W. J. 1960. Illegitimacy in the Caribbean social structure. *American Sociological Review* 25:21–30.

Goodwin, W. 1990. Uncircumcision: A technique for plastic reconstruction of a prepuce after circumcision. *Journal of Urology* 144:1203–5.

Gordon, A., and J. Collin. 1993. Save the normal foreskin. *British Medical Journal* 306:1–2.

Gorner, P. 1994. Sex study shatters kinky assumptions. *Chicago Tribune,* 6 October, 1.

Gottfredson, M., and T. Hirschi. 1986. *A general theory of crime.* Stanford, Calif.: Stanford University Press.

————. 1990. *A general theory of crime.* Stanford, Calif.: Stanford University Press.

Gove, W. R. 1972. The relationship between sex roles, marital status, and mental illness. *Social Forces* 51:34–44.

———. 1973. Sex, marital status, and morality. *American Journal of Sociology* 79:45–67.

Graves, E. J. 1995. Detailed diagnoses and procedures: National Hospital Discharge Survey, 1993: National Center for Health Statistics. *Vital Health Statistics* 13, no. 122:128.

Greeley, A. M. 1990. *The Catholic myth.* New York: Collier.

———. 1993. Religion not dying out around the world. *Origins: CNS Documentary Service* 23 (10 June): 49–58.

———. 1994. *Sex: The Catholic experience.* Allen, Tex.: Tabor.

Green, A. H. 1992. Applications of psychoanalytic theory in the treatment of the victim and the family. In *Sexual abuse of children: Clinical issues,* ed. W. O'Donohue and J. H. Greer. Hillsdale, N.J.: Erlbaum.

———. 1993. Child sexual abuse: Immediate and long-term effects and intervention. *Journal of the American Academy of Child and Adolescent Psychiatry* 32:5.

Grossbard-Shechtman, S. 1993. *On the economics of marriage—a theory of marriage, labor, and divorce.* Boulder, Colo.: Westview.

Gupta, S., R. M. Anderson, and R. M. May. 1989. Networks of sexual contacts: Implications for the pattern of spread of HIV. *AIDS* 3:807–17.

Guttentag, M., and P. Secord. 1983. *Too many women? The sex ratio question.* Beverly Hills, Calif.: Sage.

Hand, E. A. 1949. Circumcision and venereal disease. *Archive of Dermatology and Syphilology* 60:341.

Hand, E. A., and M. C. Nelson. 1951. Circumcision and primary syphilis. *Archive of Dermatology and Syphilology* 63:504.

Hannerz, U. 1969. *Soulside: Inquiries into ghetto culture and community.* New York: Columbia University Press.

Harris, K. M. 1998. The health status and risk behavior of adolescents in immigrant families. In *The health and well-being of children of immigrants,* ed. D. Hernandez and E. Charney. Washington, D.C.: National Academy Press.

Hart, G. 1992. Factors associated with genital chlamydial and gonococcal infection in males. *Genitourinary Medicine* 69:393–96.

Haurin, R. J., and F. L. Mott. 1990. Adolescent sexual activity in the family context: The impact of older siblings. *Demography* 27, no. 4:537–57.

Hayes, C. D., ed. 1987. *Risking the future: Adolescent sexuality, pregnancy, and childbearing.* Washington, D.C.: National Academy Press.

Hearst, N., and S. Hulley. 1988. Preventing the heterosexual spread of AIDS: Are we giving our patients the best advice? *Journal of the American Medical Association* 259, no. 16:22–29.

Heaton, J. P., A. Morales, M. A. Adams, B. Johnston, and R. el-Rashidy. 1995. Recovery of erectile function by the oral administration of apomorphine. *Urology* 45:200–206.

Heckman, J. J., and R. J. Willis. 1975. Estimation of a stochastic model of reproduction: An econometric approach. In *Household production and consumption,* ed. N. E. Terleckyj. New York: Columbia University Press.

Heinen, T. 1996. *Latent class and discrete latent trait models: Similarities and differences.* Thousand Oaks, Calif.: Sage.

Henshaw, S. K. 1989. Teenage abortion, birth, and pregnancy statistics: An update. *Family Planning Perspectives* 21:85–88.

Henshaw, S. K., N.J. Binkin, E. Blaine, and J. C. Smith. 1985. A portrait of American women who obtain abortions. *Family Planning Perspectives* 17, no. 2 (March/April): 90–96.

Henshaw, S. K., L. M. Koonin, and J. C. Smith. 1991. Characteristics of U.S. women having abortions, 1987. *Family Planning Perspectives* 23, no. 2 (March/April): 75–81.

Henshaw, S. K., and K. O'Reilly. 1983. Characteristics of abortion patients in the United States, 1979 and 1980. *Family Planning Perspectives* 15, no. 1 (January/February): 5–16.

Henshaw, S. K., and J. Van Vort. 1989. Teenage abortion, birth, and pregnancy statistics: An update. *Family Planning Perspectives* 21:85–88.

———. 1990. Abortion services in the United States, 1987 and 1988. *Family Planning Perspectives* 22, no. 3 (May/June): 102–8.

———. 1994. Abortion services in the United States, 1991 and 1992. *Family Planning Perspectives* 26, no. 3 (May/June): 100–112.

Herman, J. L., and E. Schatzow. 1987. Recovery and verification of memories of childhood sexual trauma. *Psychoanalytic Psychology* 4:1–14.

Herzog, L. 1989. Urinary tract infections and circumcision: A case control study. *American Journal of Diseases of Childhood* 143:348–50.

Hethcote, H. W. 1996. Modeling heterogeneous mixing in infectious disease dynamics. In *Models for infectious human diseases: Their structure and relation to data,* ed. V. Isham and G. Medley. Cambridge: Cambridge University Press.

Hethcote, H. W., and J. A. V. Ark. 1987. Epidemiological models for heterogeneous populations: Proportionate mixing, parameter estimation, and immunization programs. *Mathematical Biosciences* 84:85–118.

Hethcote, H. W., and J. A. Yorke. 1984. Gonorrhea transmission: Dynamics and control. *Biomathematics* 56:1–105.

Hill, C. A. 1997. The distinctiveness of sexual motives in relation to sexual desire and desirable partner attributes. *Journal of Sex Research* 34, no. 2:139–53.

Hines, P., and E. Culotta. 1998. Frontiers in biology: The evolution of sex. *Science,* 25 September, 1979–2008.

Hirschi, T. 1969. *Causes of delinquency.* Berkeley: University of California Press.

Hirschi, T., and M. R. Gottfredson. 1994. *The generality of deviance.* New Brunswick, N.J.: Transaction.

Hobcraft, J., and K. Kiernan. 1995. Becoming a parent in Europe. Discussion Paper no. 116. London School of Economics, Suntory and Toyota International Centre for Economics and Related Disciplines.

Hofferth, S. 1990. Trends in adolescent sexual activity, contraception, and pregnancy in the U.S. In *Adolescence and puberty,* ed. J. Bancroft and J. M. Reinisch. Oxford: Oxford University Press.

Hofferth, S. L., and C. D. Hayes, eds. 1987. *Risking the future: Adolescent sexuality, pregnancy, and childbearing.* Washington, D.C.: National Academy Press.

Hogan, D. 1987. *Transition and social change: The early lives of American men.* New York: Academic.

Hogan, D. P., D. J. Eggebeen, and C. C. Clogg. 1993. The structure of intergenerational exchanges in American families. *American Journal of Sociology* 98:1428–58.

Hogan, D., and E. Kitagawa. 1985. The impact of social status, family structure, and neighborhood on the fertility of black adolescents. *American Journal of Sociology* 90, no. 4:825–55.

Hoier, T. S., C. R. Shawbuck, and G. M. Pallotta. 1992. The impact of sexual abuse: A cognitive-behavioral model. In *Sexual abuse of children: Clinical issues,* ed. J. H. Geer and W. O'Donohue. Hillsdale, N.J.: Erlbaum.

Hollingshead, A. B. 1949. *Elmtown's youth: The impact of social classes on adolescents.* New Brunswick, N.J.: Rutgers University Press.

Hooks, B. 1990. *Yearning: Race, gender, and cultural politics.* Boston: South End.

Horowitz, M. J. 1976. *Stress response syndromes.* New York: Jason Aronson.

———. 1983. *Honor and the American dream: Culture and identity in a Chicano community.* New Brunswick, N.J.: Rutgers University Press.

Hosmer, D. W., and S. Lemeshow. 1989. *Applied logistic regression.* New York: Wiley.

Hotz, V. J., J. A. Klerman, and R. J. Willis. 1997. The economics of fertility in developed countries: A survey. In *Handbook of population and family economics* (vol. 1A), ed. M. R. Rosenzweig and O. Stark. New York: Elsevier.

Hotz, V. J., S. W. McElroy, and S. G. Sanders. 1996. Costs and consequences of teenage childbearing. *Chicago Policy Review* 1, no. 1 (fall): 55–94.

Hughes, E. C. 1994. *Work and self: On work, race, and the sociological imagination.* Chicago: University of Chicago Press.

Institute of Medicine. 1986. *Confronting AIDS: Directions for Public Health, Health Care, and Research.* Washington, D.C.: National Academy Press.

———. 1997. *Hidden epidemics.* Edited by R. E. Thomas and T. B. William. Washington, D.C.: National Academy Press.

Jaccard, J., and C. K. Wan. 1995. A paradigm for studying the accuracy of self-reports of risk behavior relevant to AIDS: Empirical perspectives on stability, recall bias, and transitory influences. *Journal of Applied Social Psychology* 25:1831–58.

Jacquez, J. A., C. Simon, and J. Koopman. 1995. Core groups and the R_os for subgroups in heterogeneous SIS and SI models. In *Epidemic models: Their structure and relation to data,* ed. D. Mollison. Cambridge: Cambridge University Press.

Jacquez, J. A., C. P. Simon, J. Koopman, L. Sattenpiel, and T. Perry. 1988. Modeling and analyzing HIV transmission: The effect of contact patterns. *Mathematical Biosciences* 92:119–99.

Janoff-Bulman, R. 1985. The aftermath of victimization: Rebuilding shattered assumptions. In *Trauma and its wake: The study and treatment of post-traumatic stress disorders,* ed. C. R. Figley. New York: Brunner/Mazel.

———. 1992. *Shattered assumptions: Towards a new psychology of trauma.* New York: Free Press.

Janz, N. K., and M. H. Becker. 1984. The health belief model: A decade later. *Health Education Quarterly* 11:1–47.

Jaynes, G. D., and Robert M. Williams, ed. 1989. *A common destiny: Blacks and American society.* Washington, D.C.: National Academy Press.

Johnson, A. M., J. Wadsworth, K. Wellings, S. Bradshaw, and J. Field. 1992. Sexual lifestyles and HIV risks. *Nature* 360:410 12.

Johnson, A. M., J. Wadsworth, K. Wellings, and J. Field. 1994. *Sexual attitudes and lifestyles.* Oxford: Blackwell Scientific.

———. 1996. Who goes to sexually transmitted disease clinics? Results from a national population survey. *Genito-Urinary Medicine* 72:197–202.

Johnson, E. 1992. *What you can do to avoid AIDS.* New York: Times Books.

Jones, E. F., and J. D. Forrest. 1992. Underreporting of abortion in surveys of U.S. women, 1979–1988. *Demography* 29, no. 1 (February): 113–26.

Jones, R. B., and J. N. Wasserheit. 1991. Introduction to the biology and natural history of sexually transmitted diseases. In *Research issues in human behavior and sexually transmitted diseases in the AIDS era,* ed. J. N. Wasserheit, S. O. Aral, K. K. Holmes, and P. J. Hitchcock. Washington, D.C.: American Society for Microbiology.

Joyce, T. 1988. The social and economic correlates of pregnancy resolution among adolescents in New York City, by race and ethnicity: A multivariate analysis. *American Journal of Public Health* 78, no. 6 (June): 626–30.

Joyce, T., S. K. Henshaw, and J. D. Skatrud. 1997. The impact of Mississippi's mandatory delay law on abortions and births. *Journal of the American Medical Association* 278, no. 8 (27 August 1997): 653–58.

Joyce, T., and R. Kaestner. 1996. The effect of expansions in Medicaid income eligibility on abortion. *Demography* 33, no. 2 (May): 181–92.

Judson, F. N., and M. E. M. Paalman. 1991. Behavioral interventions in industrialized countries. In *Research issues in human behavior and sexually transmitted diseases in the AIDS era,* ed. J. N. Wasserheit, S. O. Aral, K. K. Holmes, and P. J. Hitchcock. Washington, D.C.: American Society for Microbiology.

Kaeming, K. L., and R. R. Bootzin. 1990. Behavior change strategies for increasing condom use. *Evaluation and Program Planning* 13:47–54.

Kahn, J. R., R. R. Rindfuss, and D. K. Guilkey. 1990. Adolescent contraceptive method choices. *Demography* 27, no. 3:323–35.

Kanouse, D. E., S. H. Berry, E. M. Gorman, E. M. Yano, S. Carson, and A. F. Abrahamse. 1991. *AIDS-related knowledge, attitudes, and beliefs in Los Angeles County.* Santa Monica, Calif.: Rand.

Kaplan, G. 1977. Circumcision—an overview. *Current Problems in Pediatrics* 1:1–33.

Kelly, J. A., D. A. Murphy, K. J. Sikkema, and S. C. Kalichman. 1993. Psychological interventions to prevent HIV infection are urgently needed: New priorities for behavioral research in the second decade of AIDS. *American Psychologist* 48:1023–34.

Kennedy, P. 1985. *A guide to econometrics.* Cambridge, Mass.: MIT Press.

Kinsey, A. C., W. B. Pomeroy, and C. E. Martin. 1948. *Sexual behavior in the human male.* Philadelphia: W. B. Saunders.

Kinsey, A. C., W. B. Pomeroy, C. E. Martin, and P. H. Gebhard. 1953. *Sexual behavior in the human female.* Philadelphia: W. B. Saunders.

Klassen, A. D., C. J. Williams, and E. E. Levitt. 1989. *Sex and morality in the U.S.* Middletown, Conn.: Wesleyan University Press.

Klerman, J. A. 1998. Welfare reform and abortion. In *Welfare, the family, and reproductive behavior: Research perspectives,* ed. R. A. Moffitt. Washington, D.C.: National Academy Press.

Kline, J., Z. Stein, and M. Susser. 1989. *Conception to birth.* New York: Oxford University Press.

Knoth, R., K. Boyd, and B. Singer. 1988. Empirical tests of sexual selection theory. *Journal of Sex Research* 24:73–89.

Knox, E. G., C. MacArthur, and K. J. Simons. 1993. *Sexual behavior and AIDS in Britain.* London: H. M. Stationery Office.

Kohlman, T., and A. K. Formann. 1997. Using latent class models to analyze response patterns in epidemiological mail surveys. In *Applications of latent trait and latent class models in the social sciences,* ed. J. Rost and R. Langeheine. New York: Waxmann Munster.

Kontula, T. O., and J. E. Haavio-Mannila. 1993. *Suomalainen seksi.* Helenski: Werner Soderstrom.

Koonin, L. M., J. C. Smith, and M. Ramick. 1995. Abortion surveillance—United States, 1991. *Morbidity and Mortality Weekly Reports* 44, no. SS-2 (5 May 1995): 23–53.

Kornhauser, R. R. 1978. *Social sources of delinquency.* Chicago: University of Chicago Press.

Kretzschmar, M., and M. Morris. 1996. Measures of concurrency in networks and the spread of infectious disease. *Mathematical Biosciences* 133:165–95.

Ku, L., F. Sonenstein, and J. H. Pleck. 1993. Neighborhood, family, and work: Influences on the premarital behaviors of adolescent males. *Social Forces* 72, no. 2:479–503.

Kuntson, J. F. 1995. Psychological characteristics of maltreated children: Putative risk factors and consequences. *Annual Review of Psychology* 46:401–31.

Lancaster, J. B. 1994. Human sexuality, life histories, and evolutionary ecology. In *Sexuality across the life course,* ed. A. S. Rossi. Chicago: University of Chicago Press.

Laub, J. H., D. S. Nagin, and R. J. Sampson. 1998. Trajectories of change in criminal offending: Good marriages and the desistance process. *American Sociological Review* 62:225–38.

Laub, J. H., and R. J. Sampson. 1993. Turning points in the life course: Why change matters to the study of crime. *Criminology* 31:301–25.

Laumann, E. O. 1999. The circumcision dilemma. *Scientific American Presents* 10, no. 2: 68–72.

————. 2000. Love, sex, and public morality in the United States: Moving to the Right? In *Morality and Public Life: Is America in Moral Decline?* Ithaca, N.Y.: Cornell University Press.

Laumann, E. O., and J. H. Gagnon. 1995. A sociological perspective on sexual action. In *Conceiving sexuality: Approaches to sex research in the postmodern world,* ed. J. H. Gagnon and R. G. Parker. New York: Routledge.

Laumann, E. O., J. H. Gagnon, and R. T. Michael. 1989a. Life course and network considerations in the design of the survey of health and sexual behavior. In *Conference proceedings of the fifth conference on health survey research methods,* ed. F. J. Fowler. Keystone, Colo.: U.S. Department of Health and Human Services, Public Health Service.

Laumann, E. O., J. H. Gagnon, and R. T. Michael. 1989b. *The National Study of Health and Sexual Behavior design report.* Chicago: National Opinion Research Center.

————. 1994. A political history of the National Sex Survey of Adults. *Family Planning Perspectives* 26, no. 1 (January/February): 34–38.

Laumann, E. O., J. H. Gagnon, R. T. Michael, and S. Michaels. 1994. *The social organization of sexuality: Sexual practices in the United States.* Chicago: University of Chicago Press.

Laumann, E. O., J. H. Gagnon, S. Michaels, R. T. Michael, and L. P. Schumm. 1993. Monitoring AIDS and other rare population events: A network approach. *Journal of Health and Social Behavior* 34:7–22.

Laumann, E. O., and D. Knoke. 1987. *The organizational state: Social choice in national policy domains.* Madison: University of Wisconsin Press.

Laumann, E. O., C. M. Masi, and E. W. Zuckerman. 1997. Circumcision in the United States: Prevalence, prophylaxis, and sexual practice. *Journal of the American Medical Association* 278, no. 13: 1052–57.

Laumann, E. O., A. Paik, and R. C. Rosen. 1999. Sexual dysfunction in the United States: Prevalence and predictors. *Journal of the American Medical Association* 281, no. 6: 537–44.

Laumann, E. O., and Y. Youm. 1999. Race ethnic/group differences in the prevalence of sexually transmitted diseases in the United States. *Sexually Transmitted Diseases* 26 (May): 250–61.

Lauritsen, J. L. 1994. Explaining race and gender differences in adolescent sexual behavior. *Social Forces* 72, no. 3:859–84.

Leibowitz, A., M. Eisen, and W. K. Chow. 1986. An economic model of teenage pregnancy decision-making. *Demography* 23, no. 1 (February): 67–77.

Lesthaeghe, R. 1983. A century of demographic and cultural change in Western Europe: An exploration of underlying dimensions. *Population and Development Review* 9, no. 3: 411–35.

Lewin, T. 1994. Sex in America: Faithfulness in marriage thrives after all. *New York Times,* 7 October, 1.

Lewontin, R. C. 1995. Sex, lies, and social science. *New York Review of Books,* 20 April 1995, 24–29.

Liebow, E. 1967. *Tally's corner: A study of Negro streetcorner men.* Boston: Little, Brown.

Lilienfeld, A. M., and S. Graham. 1958. Validity of determining circumcision status by questionnaire as related to epidemiological studies of cancer of the cervix. *Journal of the National Cancer Institute* 21:713–20.

Lillard, L. A., and L. J. Waite. 1995. Til death do us part: Marital disruption and mortality. *American Journal of Sociology* 100:1131–56.

Lin, N., and W. M. Ensel. 1989. Life stressors and health: Stressors and resources. *American Sociological Review* 54:382–99.

Lindbohm, M. L., and K. Hemminki. 1988. National data base on medically diagnosed spontaneous abortions in Finland. *International Journal of Epidemiology* 17:568–73.

Lipset, S. M. 1963. *The first new nation: The United States in historical and comparative perspective.* New York: Basic.

Loftus, E. F., S. Polonsky, and M. T. Fullilove. 1994. Memories of childhood sexual abuse. *Psychology of Women Quarterly* 18:67–84.

Louis, F., and S. O. Aral. 1996. Untangling the persistence of syphilis in the South. *Sexually Transmitted Diseases* 23:1–4.

Luker, K. 1984. *Abortion and the politics of motherhood.* Berkeley and Los Angeles: University of California Press.

———. 1996. *Dubious conceptions.* Cambridge, Mass.: Harvard University Press.

Lundberg, S., and R. D. Plotnick. 1990. Effects of state welfare, abortion, and family planning policies on premarital childbearing among white adolescents. *Family Planning Perspectives* 22:246–75.

Luster, T., and S. A. Small. 1994. Factors associated with sexual risk-taking behaviors among adolescents. *Journal of Marriage and the Family* 56:622–32.

Lynxwiler, J., and D. Gay. 1994. Reconsidering race differences in abortion attitudes. *Social Science Quarterly* 75, no. 1 (March): 67–84.

Lytton, H. 1990. Child and parent effects in boys' conduct disorder: A reinterpretation. *Developmental Psychology* 26:683–97.

Maimonides, M. 1904. *The guide for the perplexed.* New York: Dover.

Malinowski, B. [1927] 1970. *Sex and repression in savage society.* Cleveland: Meridian.

Marín, B. V. 1996. Cultural issues in HIV prevention for Latinos: Should we try to change gender roles? In *Understanding and preventing HIV risk behavior: Safer sex and drug use,* ed. S. Oskamp and S. C. Thompson. Thousand Oaks, Calif.: Sage.

Masi, C. M. 1995. Circumcision: The medical issues. Working paper. University of Chicago, School of Social Services Administration.

Mason, K. O. 1974. *Women's labor force participation and fertility.* Research Triangle Park, N.C.: Research Triangle Institute.

Masson, J. M. 1984. *The assault on truth: Freud's suppression of the seduction of theory.* New York: Farrar Straus Giroux.

Masters, W., and V. Johnson. 1966. *Human sexual response.* Boston: Little, Brown.

Mausert-Mooney, R., P. K. Trickett, and F. W. Putnam. 1995. *Appeal and vulnerability patterns in girl victims of incest.* Washington, D.C.: American Psychological Association. Typescript.

May, R. M., R. M. Anderson, and S. M. Blowe. 1989. The epidemiology and transmission dynamics of HIV-AIDS. *Daedalus* 118, no. 2:163–201.

Mayer, S. 1997. *What money can't buy: Family income and children's life chances.* Cambridge, Mass.: Harvard University Press.

McClelland, D.C. 1975. *Power: The inner experience.* New York: Irvington.

McClelland, G. H., W. D. Schultze, and D. L. Coursey. 1993. Insurance for low probability hazards: A bimodal response to unlikely events. *Journal of Risk and Uncertainty* 7, no. 1:95–116.

McCutcheon, A. L. 1987. *Latent class analysis.* Newbury Park, Calif.: Sage.

McElrath, K., D. D. Chitwood, D. K. Griffen, and M. Comerford. 1994. The consistency of self-reported HIV risk behavior among injection drug users. *American Journal of Public Health* 84:1965–70.

McKinlay, J. B., and H. A. Feldman. 1994. Age-related variation in sexual activity and interest in normal men: Results from the Massachusetts Male Aging Study. In *Sexuality across the life course,* ed. A. S. Rossi. Chicago: University of Chicago Press.

McLanahan, S. 1985. Family structure and the reproduction of poverty. *American Journal of Sociology* 90, no. 4:873–901.

McLeer, S. V., E. Deblinger, M. Atkins, E. Foa, and D. Ralphe. 1988. Post-traumatic stress disorder in sexually abused children. *Journal of the American Academy of Child and Adolescent Psychiatry* 27:650–54.

Medoff, M. H. 1988. An economic analysis of the demand for abortions. *Economic Inquiry* 26 (April): 353–59.

Mellanby, A. R., F. A. Phelps, N.J. Crichton, and H. J. Tripp. 1995. School sex education: An experimental programme with educational and medical benefit. *British Medical Journal* 311:414–17.

Menard, S. 1995. *Applied logistic regression.* Thousand Oaks, Calif.: Sage.

Merton, R. 1938. Social structure and anomie. *American Sociological Review* 3:672–82.

Michael, R. T. 1973. Education and the derived demand for children. *Journal of Political Economy* 81, suppl. (March/April): 128–64.

———. 1988. Why did the U.S. divorce rate double within a decade? *Research in Population Economics* 6:367–99.

———. 1995. Monitoring sexually transmitted disease: A comparative study of five Midwestern cities. University of Chicago, Harris Graduate School of Public Policy Studies. Typescript.

———. 1996. Money illusion: The importance of household time use in social policy making. *Journal of Family and Economic Issues* 17, no. 314 (winter): 245–60.

Michael, R. T., V. R. Fuchs, and S. R. Scott. 1980. Changes in the propensity to live alone, 1950–1976. *Demography* 17, no. 1:39–56.

Michael, R. T., J. H. Gagnon, E. O. Laumann, and G. Kolata. 1994a. *Sex in America.* Boston: Little, Brown.

Michael, R. T., J. H. Gagnon, E. O. Laumann, and G. Kolata. 1994b. Who's doing it? and how? Major U.S. sex survey. *Glamour,* November, 176–79, 249.

Michael, R. T., J. Wadsworth, J. A. Feinleib, A. M. Johnson, E. O. Laumann, and K. Wellings. 1998. Private sexual behavior, public opinion, and public health policy related to sexually transmitted diseases: A. U.S.-British comparison. *American Journal of Public Health* 88, no. 5:749–54.

Michael, R. T., and R. J. Willis. 1976. Contraception and fertility: Household production under uncertainty. In *Household production and consumption,* ed. N. E. Terleckyj. New York: Columbia University Press.

Miller, B. C., and K. A. Moore. 1990. Adolescent sexual behavior, pregnancy, and parenting: Research through the 1980s. *Journal of Marriage and the Family* 52:1025–44.

Miller, H. G., C. F. Turner, and L. E. Moses, eds. 1990. *AIDS: The second decade.* Washington, D.C.: National Academy Press.

Miller, P. 1995. They said it couldn't be done: The National Health and Social Life Survey. *Public Opinion Quarterly* 59:404–19.

Modell, J. 1989. *Into one's own: From youth to adulthood in the United States, 1920–1975.* Berkeley and Los Angeles: University of California Press.

Montague, A. 1973. Circumcision. In *Encyclopedia britannica.* Chicago: William Benton.

Morales, A., J. P. Heaton, B. Johnston, and M. Adams. 1995. Oral and topical treatment of erectile dysfunction: Present and future. *Urological Clinics of North America,* 22:879–86.

Morgan, W. 1967. Penile plunder. *Medical Journal of Australia* 1:1102–3.

Morokoff, P. J., and R. Gillilland. 1993. Stress, sexual functioning, and marital satisfaction. *Journal of Sex Research* 30, no. 1:43–54.

Morris, M. 1993a. Epidemiology and social networks: Modeling structural diffusion. *Sociological Methods and Research* 22, no. 1:99–126.

———. 1993b. Telling tails explain the discrepancy in sexual partner reports. *Nature* 365: 437–40.

Morris, M., and L. Dean. 1994. Effect of sexual behavior change on long-term human immunodeficiency virus prevalence among homosexual men. *American Journal of Epidemiology* 140:217–32.

Morrow, K. B., and G. T. Sorell. 1989. Factors affecting self-esteem, depression, and negative
behaviors in sexually abused female adolescents. *Journal of Marriage and the Family*
51:677–86.

Morrow, R. 1994. The sexological construction of sexual dysfunction. *Australian and New
Zealand Journal of Sociology* 270: 83–90.

Moses, S., F. A. Plummer, J. E. Bradley, et al. 1994. The association between lack of male
circumcision and risk for HIV infection: A review of the epidemiological data. *Sexually
Transmitted Diseases* 4 (July): 201–10.

Mosher, W. D., and C. A. Bachrach. 1987. First premarital contraceptive use: United States,
1960–82. *Studies in Family Planning* 18, no. 2 (March/April): 83–95.

Mosher, W. D., and J. W. McNally. 1991. Contraceptive use at first premarital intercourse:
United States, 1965–88. *Family Planning Perspectives* 23, no. 3 (May/June): 108–16.

Mosher, W. D., and W. F. Pratt. 1993. AIDS-related behavior among women 15–44 years of
age: United States, 1988 and 1990. *Advance Data* (National Center for Health Statistics), no. 239:94–110.

Mott, F. L. 1983. *Fertility-related data in the 1982 National Longitudinal Survey of
Work Experience of Youth: An evaluation of data quality and some preliminary analyt-
ical results.* Columbus: Ohio State University, Center for Human Resource Research.

Murry, V. McB. 1995. An ecological analysis of pregnancy resolution decisions among African American and Hispanic adolescent females. *Youth and Society* 26, no. 3 (March):
325–50.

Musick, J. S. 1993. *Young, poor, and pregnant.* New Haven, Conn.: Yale University Press.

Nagel, J. 1999. Ethnosexual frontiers: Constructing and crossing racial, ethnic, nationalist,
and sexual boundaries. Paper presented at the annual meeting of the American Sociological Association, 9 August.

Nakashima, A. K., R. T. Rolfs, M. L. Flock, P. Kilmarx, and J. R. Greenspan. 1996. Epidemiology of syphilis in the United States, 1941–1993. *Sexually Transmitted Diseases*
23:16–23.

Narod, S. A., and R. Khazen. 1989. Spontaneous abortions in Ontario, 1979–1984. *Cana-
dian Journal of Public Health* 80:209–13.

Nathanson, C. A. 1991. *Dangerous passage: The social control of sexuality in women's adolescence.* Philadelphia: Temple University Press.

Nathanson, C. A., and Y. J. Kim. 1989. Components of change in adolescent fertility, 1971–
1979. *Demography* 26, no. 1:85–98.

Newcomb, M. D. 1986. Sexual behavior of cohabitors: A comparison of three independent
samples. *Journal of Sex Research* 22:492–513.

NIH Consensus Development Panel on Impotence. 1993. Impotence. *Journal of the American Medical Association* 270:83–90.

Nock, S. L. 1995. Commitment and dependency in marriage. *Journal of Marriage and the
Family* 57:503–14.

Noll, R. G., and A. Zimbalist, eds. 1997. *Sports, jobs, and taxes.* Washington, D.C.: Brookings Institution Press.

Office of the Assistant Secretary for Planning and Evaluation (ASPE). 1996. *Trends in the
well-being of America's children and youth: 1996.* Washington, D.C.: U.S. Department
of Health and Human Services.

———. 1997. *Trends in the well-being of America's children and youth.* Washington, D.C.:
U.S. Department of Health and Human Services.

Ogden, L., and M. Shepherd. 1996. *Applying prevention marketing.* Atlanta: Centers for Disease Control/National AIDS Clearinghouse.

Ortner, S. B., and H. Whitehead. 1981. *Sexual meanings: The cultural construction of gender and sexuality.* New York: Cambridge University Press.

Padian, N. S., S. C. Chiboski, and P. Hitchcock. 1991. Risk factors for acquisition of sexually transmitted diseases and development of complications. In *Research issues in human biology and sexually transmitted diseases in the AIDS era,* ed. J. N. Wasserheit, S. O. Aral, K. K. Holmes, and P. J. Hitchcock. Washington, D.C.: American Society for Microbiology.

Park, K., I. Goldstein, C. Andry, M. B. Siroky, R. J. Krane, and K. M. Azadzoi. 1997. Vasculogenic female sexual dysfunction: The hemodynamic basis for vaginal engorgement insufficiency and clitoral erectile insufficiency. *International Journal of Impotence Research* 9:27–37.

Parker, S., A. J. Stewart, M. N. Wren, et al. 1983. Circumcision and sexually transmissible disease. *Medical Journal of Australia* 2:288–90.

Parkin, F. 1979. *Marxism and class theory: A bourgeois critique.* New York: Columbia University Press.

Parks, M. R., and M. B. Adelman. 1983. Communication-networks and the development of romantic relationships: An expansion of uncertainty reduction theory. *Human Communication Research* 10:55–79.

Parsons, T. 1978a. Health and disease: A sociological and action perspective. In *Action theory and the human condition,* ed. T. Parsons. New York: Free Press.

Parsons, T. 1978b. The sick role and the role of the physician reconsidered. In *Action theory and the human condition,* ed. T. Parsons. New York: Free Press.

Perlman, S. D., and P. R. Abramson. 1982. Sexual satisfaction among married and cohabiting individuals. *Journal of Counseling and Clinical Psychology* 50:458–60.

Persky, L. 1974. Comment. *Medical Aspects of Human Sexuality* 8:55.

Philipson, J. T., and R. A. Posner. 1993. *Private choices and public health: The AIDS epidemic in an economic perspective.* Cambridge, Mass.: Harvard University Press.

Pinkerton, S. D., and P. R. Abramson. 1993. Evaluating the risks: A Bernoulli process model of HIV infection and risk reduction. *Evaluation Review* 17:504–28.

Plaut, A., and A. C. Kohn-Speyer. 1947. The carcinogenic action of smegma. *Science* 105:392.

Pleck, J. H., F. L. Sonenstein, and L. C. Ku. 1991. Adolescent males' condom use: Relationships between perceived cost-benefits and consistency. *Journal of Marriage and the Family* 53:733–45.

Posner, R. A. 1992. *Sex and reason.* Cambridge, Mass.: Harvard University Press.

Potterat, J. 1992. Socio-geographic space and sexually transmissible diseases in the 1990s. *Today's Life Science* 16:16–22, 31.

Potterat, J., R. B. Rothenberg, D. E. Woodhouse, J. B. Muth, C. I. Pratts, and J. S. Fogle. 1985. Gonorrhea as a social disease. *Sexually Transmitted Diseases* 12:25–32.

Pratt, W. F., W. D. Mosher, C. A. Bachrach, and M. C. Horn. 1984. Understanding U.S. fertility: Findings from the National Survey of Family Growth, Cycle III. *Population Bulletin* 39, no. 5: 1–42.

Preston, E. 1970. Whither the foreskin? A consideration of routine neonatal circumcision. *Journal of the American Medical Association* 213:1853–58.

Prochaska, J. O., W. F. Velicer, J. S. Rossi, M. G. Goldstein, B. H. Marcus, W. Rakowski, C. Fiore, et al. 1994. Stages of change and decisional balance for 12 problem behaviors. *Health Psychology,* 13:39–46.

Pynoos, R. S., and S. Eth. 1985. *Post-traumatic stress disorders in children.* Washington, D.C.: American Psychiatric Press.

Rajfer, J., W. J. Aronson, P. A. Bush, F. J. Dorey, and L. J. Ignarro. 1992. Nitric oxide as a mediator of relaxation of the corpus cavernosum in response to nonadrenergic, noncholinergic neurotransmission. *New England Journal of Medicine* 326:90–94.

Rao, K. V., and A. DeMaris. 1995. Coital frequency among married and cohabiting couples in the United States. *Journal of Biosocial Science* 27:135–50.

Reiss, I. L. 1960. *Premarital sexual standards in America.* New York: Free Press.

———. 1967. *The social context of premarital sexual permissiveness.* New York: Holt, Rinehart, & Winston.

Reiss, I. L., and H. M. Reiss. 1997. *Solving America's sexual crises.* Amherst, Mass.: Prometheus.

Report of an Expert Group. 1996. The incidence and prevalence of AIDS and prevalence of other severe HIV diseases in England and Wales for 1995 to 1999; projections using data to the end of 1994. *Communicable Disease Report* 6:R1–R24.

Report of the Presidential Commission on the Human Immunodeficiency Virus Epidemic. 1988. Washington, D.C.: U.S. Government Printing Office.

Rind, P. 1991. Depression and anxiety decrease after abortion, regardless of method. *Family Planning Perspective* 23:237–38.

Rindfuss, R. R., and A. VandenHeuvel. 1990. Cohabitation: Precursor to marriage or alternative to being single? *Population and Development Review* 16:703–26.

Rindskopf, D., and W. Rindskopf. 1985. The value of latent class analysis in medical diagnosis. *Statistics in Medicine* 5:21–27.

Robinson, P. 1994. The way we do the things we do: Everything you always wanted to know about the sexual habits of your fellow Americans. *New York Times Book Review,* 30 October, 1–3.

Rodman, H. 1971. *Lower-class families: The culture of poverty in Negro Trinidad.* London: Oxford University Press.

———. 1987. *The Abortion Question.* New York: Columbia University Press.

Roof, W. C. 1993. *A generation of seekers: The spiritual journey of the baby boom generation.* San Francisco: Harper Collins.

———, ed. 1995. *Religion in America today.* Beverly Hills, Calif.: Sage.

Roof, W. C., and W. McKinney. 1987. *American mainline religion: Its changing shape and failure.* New Brunswick, N.J.: Rutgers University Press.

Roosa, M. W. 1997. The relationship of childhood sexual abuse to teenage pregnancy. *Journal of Marriage and the Family* 59:119–30.

Rosen, R. C., and A. K. Ashton. 1993. Prosexual drugs: Empirical status of the "new aphrodisiacs." *Archives of Sexual Behavior* 22:521–43.

Rosen, R. C., J. F. Taylor, S. R. Leiblum, and G. A. Bachmann. 1993. Prevalence of sexual dysfunction in women: Results of a survey study of 329 women in an outpatient gynecological clinic. *Journal of Sex and Marital Therapy* 19:171–88.

Rosenzweig, M., and T. P. Schultz. 1989. Schooling, information, and non-market productivity: Contraceptive use and its effectiveness. *International Economic Review* 27, no. 1: 55–76.

Rosenzweig, M. R., and D. A. Seiver. 1982. Education and contraceptive choice: A conditional demand framework. *International Economic Review* 23, no. 1 (February): 171–98.

Ross, C. E., J. Mirowsky, and K. Goldsteen. 1990. The impact of the family on health: Decade in review. *Journal of Marriage and the Family* 52:1059–78.

Ross, M. 1989. Relation of implicit theories to the construction of personal histories. *Psychological Review* 96:341–57.

Rossi, A. S. 1994a. Eros and caritas: A biopsychosocial approach to human sexuality and reproduction. In *Sexuality across the life course,* ed. A. S. Rossi. Chicago: University of Chicago Press.

————, ed. 1994b. *Sexuality across the life course.* Chicago: University of Chicago Press.

Rothenberg, R. B. 1983. The geography of gonorrhea. *American Journal of Epidemiology* 117, no. 6:688–94.

Rothenberg, R. B., and J. Potterat. 1988. Temporal and social aspects of gonorrhea transmission: The force of infectivity. *Sexually Transmitted Diseases* 15, no. 2:88–92.

Rothenberg, R. B., J. Potterat, and D. E. Woodhouse. 1996. Personal risk taking and the spread of disease: Beyond core groups. *Journal of Infectious Diseases* 174, suppl. 2:S144–S149.

Rowe, D.C., and J. L. Rodgers. 1994. A social contagion model of adolescent sexual behavior. *Social Biology* 41:1–18.

Rubin, L. B. 1976. *Worlds of pain.* New York: Basic.

————. 1983. *Intimate strangers.* New York: Harper & Row.

————. 1990. *Erotic wars: What happened to the sexual revolution?* New York: Harper Perennial.

————. 1994. *Families on the fault line.* New York: Harper Perennial.

Russell, D. 1983. The incidence and prevalence of intrafamilial and extrafamilial sexual abuse of female children. *Child Abuse and Neglect* 7:133–46.

Russell, D. E. H. 1986. *The secret trauma: Incest in the lives of girls and women.* New York: Basic.

Rutter, M. 1988. Longitudinal data in the study of causal processes: Some uses and some pitfalls. In *Studies of psychosocial risk: The power of longitudinal data,* ed. M. Rutter. Cambridge: Cambridge University Press.

Rutter, M., R. Harrington, D. Quinton, and A. Pickles. 1994. Adult outcome of conduct disorder in childhood: Implications for concepts and definitions of patterns of psychopathology. In *Adolescent problem behaviors: Issues and research,* ed. R. D. Ketterlinus and M. E. Lamb. Hillsdale, N.J.: Erlbaum.

Ryder, N. B., and C. F. Westoff. 1971. *Reproduction in the United States, 1965.* Princeton, N.J.: Princeton University Press.

Sabogal, F., B. Faigeles, and J. A. Catania. 1993. Data from the national AIDS behavioral surveys: 2. Multiple sexual partners among Hispanics in high-risk cities. *Family Planning Perspectives* 25, no. 6:257–62.

Saltonstall, D. 1994. Marrieds do it more. *Daily News,* 6 October, 1.

Sampson, R. J., and J. H. Laub. 1993. *Crime in the making: Pathways and turning points through life.* Cambridge, Mass.: Harvard University Press.

Scanzoni, J., K. Polonko, J. Teachman, and L. Thompson. 1989. *The sexual bond: Rethinking families and close relationships.* Newbury Park, Calif.: Sage.

Schlossberger, N. M., R. A. Turner, and C. E. Irwin. 1991. Early adolescent knowledge and attitudes about circumcision: Methods and implications for research. *Journal of Adolescent Health* 12:293–97.

Schmiedeskamp, M. 1999. Anticircumcisionists decry a male's first sacrifice. *Scientific American* 10, no. 2:73.

Schoen, E. J. 1990. The status of circumcision of newborns. *New England Journal of Medicine* 322:1308–11.

Sexually transmitted diseases: England, 1995. 1996. London: Department of Health.

Schrof, J. M. 1994. Sex in America. *U.S. News and World Report,* 17 October, 74–81.

Scott, J. 1988. *Gender and the politics of history.* New York: Columbia University Press.

Segraves, R. T., A. Saran, K. Segraves, and E. Maguire. 1993. Clomipramine versus placebo in the treatment of premature ejaculation: A pilot study. *Journal of Sex and Marital Therapy* 19:198–200.

Shilts, R. 1988. *And the band played on: Politics, people, and the AIDS epidemic.* 2d ed. New York: Viking Penguin.

Siegel, J. S., S. B. Sorenson, J. M. Golding, M. A. Burnam, and J. A. Stein. 1987. The preva-

lence of childhood sexual assault: The Los Angeles epidemiologic catchment area project. *American Journal of Epidemiology* 126:1141–53.

Silverstein, M., and V. L. Bengston. 1997. Intergenerational solidarity and the structure of
adult child–parent relationships in American families. *American Journal of Sociology*
103:429–60.

Simon, W., A. S. Berger, and J. Gagnon. 1972. Beyond anxiety and fantasy: The coital experiences of college youth. *Journal of Youth and Adolescence* 1, no. 3:203–23.

Simon, W., and J. H. Gagnon. 1987a. Sexual scripts: Permanence and change. *Archives of
Sexual Behavior* 15:97–120.

———. 1987b. A sexual scripts approach. In *Theories of human sexuality,* ed. W. T. O'Donohue. New York: Plenum.

Singer, B. 1985. A comparison of evolutionary and environmental theories of erotic response:
1. Structural features. *Journal of Sex Research* 21:229–57.

Skeen, D. 1991. *Different sexual worlds: Contemporary case studies of sexuality.* Lexington,
Mass.: Lexington.

Slovic, P., B. Fischoff, and S. Lichtenstein. 1987. Behavioral decision theory perspectives
on protective behavior. In *Taking care: Understanding and encouraging self-protective
behavior,* ed. N. D. Weinstein. New York: Cambridge University Press.

Smith, G. L., R. Greenup, and E. T. Takafuji. 1987. Circumcision as a risk factor for urethritis in racial groups. *American Journal of Public Health* 77:452–54.

Smith, T. 1990. Discrepancies between men and women in reporting number of sexual partners. GSS Methodological Report no. 68. Chicago: National Opinion Research Center.

———. 1994. Attitudes toward sexual permissiveness: Trends, correlates, and behavioral
connections. In *Sexuality across the life course,* ed. A. S. Rossi. Chicago: University of
Chicago Press.

———. 1995. Pro-choice? Pro-life? No, pro-middle. *GSS News* 9 (August): 2–3.

Snowman, L. 1971. Circumcision. In *Encyclopedia judaica.* Jerusalem: Macmillan.

Sonenstein, F. L., J. H. Pleck, and L. C. Ku. 1989. Sexual activity, condom use, and AIDS
awareness among adolescent males. *Family Planning Perspectives* 21:152–58.

Sparling, P. F., and S. O. Aral. 1991. The importance of an interdisciplinary approach to
the prevention of sexually transmitted diseases. In *Research issues in human behavior and sexually transmitted diseases in the AIDS era,* ed. J. N. Wasserheit, S. O. Aral,
K. K. Holmes, and P. J. Hitchcock. Washington, D.C.: American Society for Microbiology.

Spector, I. P., and M. P. Carey. 1990. Incidence and prevalence of the sexual dysfunctions:
A critical review of the empirical literature. *Archives of Sexual Behavior* 19:389–408.

Speert, H. 1953. Circumcision of the newborn. *American Journal of Obstetrics and Gynecology* 2:166.

Spelman, E. 1988. Gender in the context of race and class. In *Inessential woman: Problems
of exclusion in feminist thought.* Boston: Beacon.

Spira, A., N. Bajos, and A. Group. 1994. *Sexual behavior and AIDS.* Brookfield, Vt.: Ash-
gate.

Spitze, G. D. 1978. Role experiences of young women: A longitudinal test of the role hiatus
hypothesis. *Journal of Marriage and the Family* 40:471–80.

Sprecher, S., and K. McKinney. 1993. *Sexuality.* Newbury Park, Calif.: Sage.

Stanley, S. M., and H. J. Markman. 1992. Assessing commitment in personal relationships.
Journal of Marriage and the Family 54:595–608.

Staples, R. 1972. The sexuality of black women. *Sexual Behavior* 2:4–15.

———. 1978. *The black family: Essays and studies.* Belmont, Calif.: Wadsworth.

———. 1981. *The world of black singles: Changing patterns of male/female relations.* West-
port, Conn.: Greenwood.

Stata. 1997. Version 5. 0. College Station, Tex.: Stata Corp.

Sterk-Elifson, C. 1994. Sexuality among African-American women. In *Sexuality across the life course,* ed. A. S. Rossi. Chicago: University of Chicago Press.

Stevans, L. K., C. A. Register, and D. N. Sessions. 1992. The abortion decision: A qualitative choice approach. *Social Indicators Research* 27:327–44.

Stotland, N. 1992. The myth of the abortion trauma syndrome. *Journal of American Medical Association,* 21 October, 2078–79.

Sweet, J. A., and L. L. Bumpass. 1987. *American families and households.* New York: Russell Sage.

Symons, D. 1979. *The evolution of human sexuality.* Oxford: Oxford University Press.

Tanfer, K., and J. J. Schoori. 1992. Premarital sexual careers and partner change. *Archives of Sexual Behavior* 21:45–68.

Task Force on Circumcision. 1989. Report of the Task Force on Circumcision. *Pediatrics* 84:388–91.

Terr, L. C. 1991. Childhood traumas: An outline and overview. *American Journal of Psychiatry* 148:10–20.

Thomas, J. C., and M. J. Tucker. 1996. The development and use of the concept of a sexually transmitted disease core. *Journal of Infectious Diseases* 174, suppl. 2:S134–S143.

Thomas, R. E., and T. B. William, eds. 1997. *Institute of Medicine: Hidden epidemic.* Washington, D.C.: National Academy Press.

Thomson, E., and U. Colella. 1992. Cohabitation and marital stability: Quality or commitment? *Journal of Marriage and the Family* 54:259–67.

Thornton, A. 1989. Changing attitudes toward family issues in the United States. *Journal of Marriage and the Family* 51:873–93.

———. 1993. Contemporary attitudes and studies of human sexuality and family life. In *Communicating the Catholic vision of life,* ed. R. E. Smith. Braintree, Mass.: Pope John Center.

Thornton, A., and D. Camburn. 1987. The influence of the family on premarital sexual attitudes and behavior. *Demography* 24, no. 3:323–40.

———. 1989. Religious participation and adolescent sexual behavior and attitudes. *Journal of Marriage and the Family* 51 (August): 641–53.

Timberlake, C. A., and W. D. Carpenter. 1990. Sexuality attitudes of African American adults. *Urban League Review* 15:1.

Townsend, J. M. 1995. Sex without emotional involvement: An evolutionary interpretation of sex differences. *Archives of Sexual Behavior* 24:173–206.

Trent, K., and E. Powell-Griner. 1991. Differences in race, marital status, and education among women obtaining abortions. *Social Forces* 69, no. 4:1121–41.

Tribe, L. H. 1990. *Abortion: The clash of absolutes.* New York: Norton.

Trussell, J., J. Menken, B. L. Lindheim, and B. Vaughan. 1980. The impact of restricting Medicaid financing for abortion. *Family Planning Perspectives* 12, no. 3:120–30.

Turner, C. F., L. Ku, S. M. Rogers, L. D. Lindberg, J. H. Pleck, and F. L. Sonenstein. 1998. Adolescent sexual behavior, drug use, and violence: Increased reporting with computer survey technology. *Science* 280, no. 5365:867–73.

Turner, C. F., H. G. Miller, and L. E. Moses, eds. 1989. *AIDS: Sexual behavior and intravenous drug use.* Washington, D.C.: National Academy Press.

Udry, J. R. 1988. Biological predispositions and social control in adolescent sexual behavior. *American Sociological Review* 53:709–22.

———. 1990. Hormonal and social determinants of adolescent sexual initiation. In *Adolescence and puberty,* ed. J. Bancroft and J. M. Reinisch. Oxford: Oxford University Press.

Udry, J. R., and J. Billy. 1987. Initiation of coitus in early adolescence. *American Sociological Review* 52:841–55.

Udry, J. R., and B. C. Campbell. 1994. Getting started on sexual behavior. In *Sexuality across the life course,* ed. A. S. Rossi. Chicago: University of Chicago Press.

Udry, J. R., J. Kovenock, N. M. Morris, and B. J. V. D. Berg. 1995. Childhood precursors of age at first intercourse. *Archives of Sexual Behavior* 24, no. 3: 329–37.

Uebersax, J. S., and W. M. Grove. 1990. Latent class analysis of diagnostic agreement. *Statistics in Medicine* 9:559–72.

Umberson, D. 1987. Family status and health behaviors: Social control as a dimension of social integration. *Journal of Health and Social Behavior* 28:306–19.

Urquiza, A. J., and M. Capra. 1990. The impact of sexual abuse: Initial and long-term effects. In *The sexually abused male,* ed. M. Hunter. Lexington, Mass.: Lexington.

U.S. Bureau of the Census. 1992. *Statistical abstract of the United States.* Washington, D.C.: U.S. Government Printing Office.

———. 1995. *Statistical abstract of the United States.* Washington, D.C.: U.S. Government Printing Office.

U.S. Department of Health and Human Services (DHHS). 1998. *Trends in well-being of America's children and youth.* Washington, D.C.: U.S. Government Printing Office.

Van Howe, R. S. 1999. Does circumcision influence sexually transmitted diseases? A literature review. *British Journal of Urology* 82 (suppl. 1): 52–62.

Ventura, S. J., S. M. Taffel, W. D. Mosher, J. B. Wilson, and S. Henshaw. 1995. Trends in pregnancies and pregnancy rates: Estimates for the United States, 1980–92. *Monthly Vital Statistics Report* 42, no. 11S (25 May): 1–23.

Vermund, S. H. 1995. Editorial: Casual sex and HIV transmission. *American Journal of Public Health* 85, no. 11 (November): 1488–89.

Vincenzi, I. D., and T. Mertens. 1994. Male circumcision: A role in HIV prevention? *AIDS* 8:153–60.

Vinovskis, M. 1988. *An "epidemic" of adolescent pregnancy? Some historical and policy considerations.* New York: Oxford University Press.

Vital Statistics of the United States. 1937–71. Hyattsville, Md.: National Center for Health Statistics.

Vobejda, B. 1994. Survey finds most adults sexually staid: Americans' average is once per week. *Washington Post,* 7 October, 1.

Wadsworth, J., J. Field, A. M. Johnson, S. Bradshaw, and K. Wellings. 1993. Methodology of the National Survey of Sexual Attitudes and Lifestyles. *Journal of the Royal Statistical Society* 156:407–21.

Wadsworth, J., A. M. Johnson, K. Wellings, and J. Field. 1996. What's in a mean? An examination of the inconsistency between men and women in reporting sexual partnerships. *Journal of the Royal Statistical Society* 159:111–23.

Waite, L. J. 1995. Does marriage matter? *Demography* 32:483–507.

Waite, L. J., F. K. Goldscheider, and C. Witsberger. 1986. Nonfamily living and the erosion of traditional family orientations among young adults. *American Sociological Review* 51:541–54.

Wallerstein, E. 1980. *Circumcision: An American health fallacy.* New York: Springer.

Walzer, S. 1994. The role of gender in determining abortion attitudes. *Social Science Quarterly* 75, no. 3 (September): 687–93.

Wasserheit, J. N. 1995. Response [to a letter to the editor]: Core groups by any other name? *Sexually Transmitted Diseases* 2:164–65.

Wasserheit, J. N., and S. O. Aral. 1996. The dynamic topology sexually transmitted disease epidemic: Implications for prevention strategies. *Journal of Infectious Diseases* 174, suppl. 2:S201–S213.

Weinberg, M., I. L. Lottes, and F. M. Shaver. 1985. Swedish or American heterosexual college youth: Who is more permissive? *Archives of Sexual Behaviors* 24, no. 4:409–37.

Weinberg, M., and C. Williams. 1980. Sexual embourgeoisement? Social class and sexual activity, 1938–1970. *American Sociological Review* 45:33–48.

———. 1988. Black sexuality: A test of two theories. *Journal of Sex Research* 25, no. 2:197–218.

Weiss, G. N., and E. B. Weiss. 1994. A perspective on controversies over neonatal circumcision. *Clinical Pediatrics* 33:726–30.

Welch, M. R., D.C. Leege, and J. C. Cavendish. 1995. Attitudes toward abortion among U.S. Catholics: Another case of symbolic politics. *Social Science Quarterly* 76, no. 1 (March): 142–57.

Wellings, K., J. Field, A. M. Johnson, and J. Wadsworth. 1994. *Sexual behavior in Britain: The National Survey of Sexual Attitudes and Lifestyles.* London: Penguin.

Wellings, K., J. Wadsworth, A. M. Johnson, J. Field, L. Whitaker, and B. Field. 1995. Provision of sex education and early sexual experience: The relationship examined. *British Medical Journal* 311:417–20.

Westoff, C. F., and N. B. Ryder. 1977. *The contraceptive revolution.* Princeton, N.J.: Princeton University Press.

Wiederman, M. W. 1997. The truth must be in here somewhere: Examining the gender discrepancy in self-reported lifetime number of sex partners. *Journal of Sex Research* 34:375–86.

Williams, L. 1994. Recall of childhood trauma: A prospective study of women's memories of child sexual abuse. *Journal of Consulting and Clinical Psychology* 62:1167–76.

Wilson, W. J. 1978. *The declining significance of race.* Chicago: University of Chicago Press.

———, ed. 1987. *The truly disadvantaged: The inner city, the underclass, and public policy.* Chicago: University of Chicago Press.

Wilson, W. J., and K. Neckerman. 1987. Poverty and family structure: The widening gap between evidence and public policy issues. In *The truly disadvantaged,* ed. W. J. Wilson. Chicago: University of Chicago Press.

Wincze, J. P., and M. P. Carey. 1991. *Sexual dysfunction: A guide for assessment and treatment.* New York: Guilford.

Wingood, G. M., and R. J. DiClemente. 1996. HIV sexual risk reduction interventions for women: A review. *Journal of Preventive Medicine* 12:209–17.

Wirth, J. 1978. Statistics on circumcision in Canada and Australia. *American Journal of Obstetrics and Gynecology* 130:236–39.

Wiswell, T., F. R. Smith, and J. W. Bass. 1985. Decreased incidence of urinary tract infection in circumcised male infants. *Pediatrics* 75:901–3.

Wolpin, K. I. 1984. An estimable dynamic stochastic model of fertility and child mortality. *Journal of Political Economy* 92, no. 5:852–74.

Wood, P. B., W. R. Gove, J. A. Wilson, and J. K. Cochran. 1997. Nonsocial reinforcement and habitual criminal conduct: An extension of learning theory. *Criminology* 35: 335–66.

Wu, L. L., and B. C. Martinson. 1993. Family structure and the risk of a premarital birth. *American Sociological Review* 58:210–32.

Wyatt, G. E. 1985. The sexual abuse of Afro-American and white-American women in childhood. *Child Abuse and Neglect* 9:507–19.

———. 1990. Changing influences on adolescent sexuality over the past forty years. In *Adolescence and puberty,* ed. J. Bancroft and J. M. Reinisch. Oxford: Oxford University Press.

Wyatt, G. E., M. D. Newcomb, and M. H. Riederle. 1993. *Sexual abuse and consensual sex: Women's developmental patterns and outcomes.* Newbury Park, Calif.: Sage.

Wyatt, G. E., and G. J. Powell, eds. 1988. *Lasting effects of child sexual abuse.* Newbury Park, Calif.: Sage.

Yamaguchi, K. 1990. Homophily and social distance in the choice of multiple friends. *Journal of the American Statistical Association* 85, no. 410:356–66.

————. 1998. Multinomial logit latent-class regression models: An analysis of the predictors of gender-role attitudes among Japanese women. University of Chicago. Typescript.

Yelsma, P. 1986. Marriage vs. cohabitation: Couples' communication practices and satisfaction. *Journal of Communication* 36:94–107.

Yorke, J. A., H. W. Hethcote, and A. Nold. 1978. Dynamics and control of transmission of gonorrhea. *Sexually Transmitted Diseases* 5:51–56.

Young, M. A. 1983. Evaluating diagnostic criteria: A latent class paradigm. *Journal of Psychiatric Research* 17:285–96.

Young, M. A., M. A. Tanner, and H. Y. Meltzer. 1982. Operational definitions of schizophrenia: What do they identify? *Journal of Nervous and Mental Disease* 170:443–47.

Zabin, L. S., E. A. Smith, M. B. Hirsch, and J. B. Hardy. 1986. Ages of physical maturation and first intercourse in black teenage males and females. *Demography* 23:595–605.

Zelnik, M., and J. F. Kantner. 1980. Sexual activity, contraceptive use, and pregnancy among metropolitan-area teenagers, 1971–1979. *Family Planning Perspectives* 12:230–37.

Zelnik, M., J. Kantner, and K. Ford. 1981. *Sex and pregnancy in adolescence.* Beverly Hills, Calif.: Sage.

CONTRIBUTORS

■

Christopher R. Browning is an assistant professor in the Department of Sociology at Ohio State University.

Joel A. Feinleib holds an M. A. from the Harris Graduate School of Public Policy Studies at the University of Chicago.

Anne M. Johnson is a professor of epidemiology in the Department of Sexually Transmitted Diseases at the Royal Free and University College Medical School, London.

Kara Joyner is an assistant professor in the Department of Policy Analysis and Management at Cornell University.

Edward O. Laumann is the George Herbert Mead Distinguished Service Professor of Sociology in the Department of Sociology and in the College at the University of Chicago.

Jenna Mahay is a research assistant in the Department of Sociology at the University of Chicago.

Christopher M. Masi is a physician specializing in adolescent pediatrics and a doctoral candidate in the School of Social Service Administration at the University of Chicago.

Robert T. Michael is the dean of and the Eliakim Hastings Moore Distinguished Service Professor in the Harris Graduate School of Public Policy Studies and in the College at the University of Chicago.

Stuart Michaels is a postdoctoral fellow at the Institut National de la Santé et de la Recherche Médicale, Paris.

Anthony Paik is a research assistant in the Department of Sociology at the University of Chicago.

Raymond C. Rosen is a clinical psychologist at and codirector of the Center for Sex Therapy and a professor of psychiatry at the Robert Wood Johnson Medical School.

The late Jane Wadsworth was a senior researcher in statistics at the Imperial College School of Medicine at St. Mary's, London.

Linda J. Waite is a professor in the Department of Sociology and in the College at the University of Chicago.

Kaye Wellings is head of the Sexual Health Programme in the Department of Public Health and Policy at the London School of Hygiene and Tropical Medicine.

Yoosik Youm is a research assistant in the Department of Sociology at the University of Chicago.

Ezra W. Zuckerman is an assistant professor in the Graduate School of Business at Stanford University.

Author Index

■

Abbott, A., 353
Abma, J., 434–35, 439
Abramson, P. R., 110, 303
Adelman, M. B., 9
Ageton, S., 149, 155
Aggleton, P., 321
Ahituv, A., 303, 317–18
Akerlof, G. A., 74
Akers, R. L., 149, 155
Alberman, E., 386–87
Allen, M. J., 354
Anderson, C., 354
Anderson, E., 42, 200, 201, 204, 224
Anderson, J. E., 341–43
Anderson, R. M., 328, 330, 334, 345
Angleitner, O., 240, 241
Aquilino, W. S., 246
Aral, S. O., 327, 329, 331, 333, 343, 345
Arminger, G., 249
Ashton, A. K., 354

Bachrach, C. A., 77, 384
Bajos, N., 439, 450
Baldwin, W., 384
Bandura, A., 149, 155, 302
Bass, J. W., 280
Becker, G. S., 47
Becker, M. H., 302
Beitchman, J. H., 156
Belcastro, P. A., 110
Bellah, R. N., 47
Bem, D. J., 158–59
Bengston, V. L., 356
Berger, A. S., 43
Bernard, J., 242
Biggar, R. J., 441
Billy, J., 41
Billy, J. O., 42, 46
Billy, J. O. G., 42, 46, 76, 302, 439

Birkelund, G. S., 356, 371
Blank, R. M., 380
Blau, P., 44
Blow, S. M., 330
Blower, S. M., 303
Blumstein, P., 197, 202
Boolell, M., 354
Booth, A., 244
Bootzin, R. R., 303
Bourdieu, P., 206
Bowser, B., 200, 201, 203, 224
Boyd, K., 241
Boyle, M., 352
Bradburn, N. M., 2
Brandt, A., 11
Brewster, K. L., 41–42, 42, 46, 76, 200, 201
Briggs, L., 149, 152
Brown, C. A., 296
Brown, M. S., 296
Browne, A., 41, 153
Browning, C., 356, 368
Browning, C. R., 156, 157, 161
Bumpass, L. L., 44, 53, 242
Burger, R., 280
Burnett, A. L., 354
Buss, D. M., 240, 241, 257
Butler, J., 197–98
Buunk, B. P., 240, 241

Call, V., 246
Campbell, B. C., 7, 112
Capra, M., 152, 156
Cardarelli, A., 157
Carey, M. P., 165, 354
Carpenter, W. D., 201
Carrier, J., 219
Caspi, A., 149, 158–59
Catania, J. A., 302, 303, 317–18, 321, 327, 439, 451

Cavendish, J. C., 379
Cherlin, A., 242
Cherlin, A. J., 239
Choi, K., 302
Chow, W. K., 42, 380
Cleary, P. D., 321
Cleary, T., 280
Cleland, J., 439
Clogg, C. C., 356, 357, 369, 370
Coates, T. J., 302, 303, 321
Colella, U., 243
Coleman, J. S., 41, 42, 43, 44, 203
Collin, J., 278
Comfort, A., 489
Connell, R. W., 197–98
Cooksey, E. C., 41–42
Culotta, E., 7

Davis, D., 303
Davis, K., 43, 47
Day, R. D., 46, 66
Dean, L., 303
Deblinger, E., 149
DeLamater, J., 2, 201, 241
DeMaris, A., 53, 249
Des Jarlais, D. C., 304
DiClemente, R. J., 302–3
DiMaggio, P., 206
DiMaggio, P. J., 11
Donnelly, D. A., 110
Duncan, G. J., 42, 200, 205
Duncan, O. D., 44
Duneier, M., 197, 200, 201
Durkheim, E., 352

Eaton, W. W., 356, 370
Edwards, J. N., 244
Eggebeen, D. J., 356
Eggert, L. L., 9
Eisen, M., 42, 380
Elder, G. H., 149
Elder, G. H., Jr., 158–59
Elliott, D. S., 149, 155
Elmer-Dewitt, P., 1
England, P., 241, 242
Epstein, S., 11
Ericksen, J. A., 4, 12
Eth, S., 152

Faigeles, B., 327
Farkas, G., 241, 242
Feingold, A., 240

Feldman, H. A., 112, 354, 367
Feldman, S. S., 110
Ferry, B., 439
Fichtner, R., 341–43
Finkel, D. J., 200
Finkel, M. L., 200
Finkelhor, D., 41, 149, 153, 156, 157
Fishbein, M., 302
Fisher, J., 302
Fisher, W. A., 302
Fleming, D. T., 343
Ford, K., 77, 91, 200
Formann, A. K., 356, 370
Forrest, J. D., 383, 384, 426, 433
Forste, R., 243
Frank, E., 354
Freud, S., 152, 161
Freyd, J., 148, 153, 161
Fu, H., 385
Fuchs, V. R., 46
Fugl-Meyer, A., 354
Furstenberg, F., 42, 200, 201, 205

Gagnon, J. H., 1, 3, 4, 6, 8, 17–19, 21, 22,
    23, 24–25, 43, 50, 110, 113, 114, 141,
    156, 157, 158, 163, 164, 198, 199, 207,
    210, 211, 212, 213, 224, 230, 239, 241,
    242, 243, 244, 245, 258, 265, 283, 292,
    293, 299, 302, 304, 322, 327, 329, 331,
    333, 336, 352, 355, 356, 368, 372, 380,
    388, 391, 410, 429, 439, 441, 442, 476,
    482, 487
Gairdner, D., 279
Garnett, G., 328, 330, 334, 345
Gay, D., 379
Gay, P., 149–50
Gebhard, P. H., 369
Gelinas, D. J., 152
George, C. C., 380
Gepi-Attee, J. C., 354
Gillilland, R., 354
Gilmore, S., 201
Goldscheider, C., 48
Goldscheider, F. K., 46, 47
Goldsteen, K., 158–59
Gomes-Schwartz, B., 157, 158
Goodman, L. A., 356, 371
Goodwin, W., 280
Gordon, A., 278
Gottfredson, M., 155–56, 192
Gove, W. R., 158
Grady, W. A., 42, 46, 76

Grady, W. R., 42, 46
Graham, S., 297
Greeley, A. M., 44, 48, 91, 93
Green, A. H., 152
Griensven, G. J. P. V., 303
Grossbard-Shechtman, S., 47
Group, A., 439
Grove, W. M., 356, 370
Guilkey, D. K., 41–42
Guinau, M. E., 333
Guthrie, T., 280
Guttentag, M., 47

Haavio-Mannila, J. E., 439
Hand, E. A., 279
Hannerz, U., 224
Harris, K. M., 63
Hayes, C. D., 41, 45, 46, 53, 450
Hearst, N., 321–22
Heaton, J. P., 354
Henshaw, S. K., 380–81, 425, 426, 430, 431, 434
Herzog, L., 280, 284
Hethcote, H. W., 330, 334, 439
Hill, C. A., 110, 112
Hines, P., 7
Hirschi, T., 149, 155–56, 192
Hofferth, S. L., 41, 45, 46, 53
Hoffman, S. D., 42
Hogan, D., 41, 42, 43, 44, 48, 200, 201, 203, 204, 206
Hogan, D. P., 356
Hoier, T. S., 149, 152–53
Hollingshead, A. B., 203
Holmes, K. K., 327, 329, 331, 333, 343
Hooks, B., 197–98
Horowitz, J., 157
Horowitz, M. J., 152, 202, 223, 237
Hotz, J., 303, 317–18
Hotz, V. J., 391
Hughes, E. C., 352
Huizinga, D., 149, 155
Hulley, S., 321–22

Irwin, C. E., 297

Jaccard, J., 304
Jacquez, J. A., 334, 345
Janoff-Bulman, R., 152
Janz, N. K., 302
Jaynes, G. D., 199–200
Johnson, A. B., 369

Johnson, A. M., 317, 439, 440, 441, 451
Johnson, E., 303
Johnson, V., 280
Jones, E. F., 383, 384, 426, 433
Jones, R. B., 344
Joseph, J. G., 302
Joyce, P. R., 149, 152
Joyce, T., 380–81, 381, 432

Kaeming, K. L., 303
Kaestner, R., 381
Kanouse, D. E., 303, 317
Kantner, J., 77, 91, 200
Kantner, J. F., 41, 450
Kaplan, E., 303
Kaplan, G., 277, 278
Katz, M. L., 74
Kegels, S. M., 302, 303, 321
Kelly, J. A., 302
Kendall-Tackett, K., 157
Kennedy, P., 53
Kim, Y. K., 74
Kinsey, A. C., 4, 203, 369
Kitagawa, E., 41, 43, 44, 48, 200, 201, 203, 204, 206
Klassen, A. D., 47, 201
Klerman, J. A., 381, 391
Knoke, D., 10
Knoth, R., 241
Knox, E. G., 439
Knutson, J. F., 156
Kohlman, T., 356, 370
Kohn-Speyer, A. C., 279
Kolata, G., 1, 17–18, 21, 23, 24–25, 322, 441
Kontula, T. O., 439
Koonin, L. M., 425, 426, 430, 432, 433, 434
Koopman, J., 334, 345
Kornhauser, R. R., 155
Ku, L., 46, 201
Ku, L. C., 77, 91, 200, 439

Lancaster, J. B., 112
Laub, J. H., 149, 155–56, 158–59, 188
Laumann, E. O., 1, 3, 4, 5, 8, 10, 14, 17–18, 17–19, 21, 22, 23, 24–25, 50, 113, 114, 141, 157, 158, 163, 164, 199, 207, 210, 211, 212, 213, 230, 239, 241, 242, 243, 244, 245, 258, 265, 283, 292, 293, 299, 302, 304, 322, 327, 329, 331, 333, 336, 352, 355, 356, 368, 372, 380, 388, 391, 410, 429, 439, 441, 442, 476, 482, 487

Lauritsen, J. L., 46, 200
Leege, D. C., 379
Leibowitz, A., 42, 380
Lesthaeghe, R., 46–47
Levitt, E. E., 47, 201
Lewin, T., 1
Lewontin, R. C., 2, 491
Lilienfeld, A. M., 297
London, R. A., 380
Louis, F., 327
Luker, K., 47
Lundberg, S., 74
Luster, T., 46
Lynxwiler, J., 379
Lytton, H., 158

MacArthur, C., 439
Maimonides, M., 278
Malinowski, B., 141
Marin, B. V., 201
Martin, C. E., 4, 203, 369
Martinson, B. C., 45, 63
Masi, C. M., 281
Mason, K. O., 46
Masson, J. M., 150
Masters, W., 280
May, R. M., 330
Mayer, S., 206
McClelland, D.C., 110
McCormick, L., 341–43
McCutcheon, A. L., 356, 369, 370, 371
McElrath, K., 304
McKinlay, J. B., 112
McKinney, K., 244
McKinney, W., 53
McLanahan, S., 45
McLeer, S. V., 149
Medoff, M. H., 380
Melbye, M., 441
Meltzer, H. Y., 356
Menard, S., 335, 338
Merton, R., 151–52
Michael, R. T., 1, 3, 4, 8, 17–19, 21, 22, 23,
    24–25, 46, 50, 113, 114, 141, 156, 158,
    163, 164, 199, 207, 210, 211, 212, 213,
    230, 239, 241, 242, 243, 244, 245, 258,
    265, 283, 292, 293, 299, 302, 304, 322,
    327, 329, 331, 333, 336, 352, 355, 356,
    368, 372, 380, 388, 391, 410, 429, 439,
    441, 442, 476, 482, 487, 488
Michaels, S., 1, 3, 17–19, 21, 22, 23, 24–25,
    50, 113, 114, 141, 157, 158, 163, 164, 199,

207, 210, 211, 212, 213, 230, 239, 241,
    242, 243, 244, 245, 258, 265, 283, 292,
    293, 299, 302, 304, 322, 327, 329, 331,
    333, 336, 352, 355, 356, 368, 372, 380,
    388, 391, 410, 429, 439, 441, 442, 476,
    482, 487
Middlestadt, S. E., 302
Miller, B. C., 45–46, 78
Miller, P., 304
Mirowsky, J., 158–59
Modell, J., 43, 44, 48
Montague, A., 277
Moore, K. A., 45–46, 78
Morales, A., 354
Morgan, W., 280
Morokoff, P. J., 354
Morris, M., 4, 303, 336
Morrow, K. B., 66
Morrow, R., 352
Mosher, W. D., 48, 77, 303, 317
Mott, F. L., 384
Murry. V. McB., 383, 409
Musick, J. S., 45

Nagel, J., 197–98
Nagin, D. S., 188
Nakashima, A. K., 327
Nathanson, C. A., 10–11, 43, 44–45, 74
Neckerman, K., 44
Nelson, M. C., 279
Newcomb, M. D., 156
Nold, A., 330, 334

Ogden, L., 451
O'Reilly, K., 430, 434
Ortner, S. B., 7

Pallotta, G. M., 149
Park, K., 354
Parker, R. G., 141
Parker, S., 280
Parkin, F., 45
Parks, M. R., 9
Parsons, T., 353
Philipson, J. T., 327, 343
Philipson, T., 303, 317–18
Pinkerton, S. D., 110, 303
Plaut, A., 279
Pleck, J. H., 46, 77, 91, 200, 201, 439
Plotnick, R. D., 74
Pomeroy, W. B., 4, 203, 369
Posner, A. R., 327, 343

Posner, R. A., 110, 241, 243
Potterat, J., 330, 345
Powell, W. W., 11
Powell-Griner, E., 382, 399
Pratt, W. F., 303, 317
Preston, E., 280
Prochaska, J. O., 302, 321
Pynoos, R. S., 152

Rajfer, J., 354
Ramick, M., 433, 434
Register, C. A., 382, 409
Reiss, I. L., 42, 43, 44, 47–48, 48, 62–63, 486
Riederle, M. H., 156
Rindfuss, R. R., 41–42
Rindskopf, D., 370
Rindskopf, W., 370
Robinson, P., 2
Rodman, H., 201, 379, 410
Roff, W. C., 53
Roosa, M. W., 157
Rose, D., 356, 371
Rosen, R. C., 354
Rosenzweig, M. R., 391
Ross, C. E., 158–59
Ross, M., 304
Rossi, A. S., 110, 112
Rothenberg, R. B., 328, 330, 334, 345
Rubin, L. B., 43–44, 46, 109
Rubinstein, D., 354
Rutter, M., 150–51, 157
Ryder, N. B., 46, 48, 91, 93

Sabogal, F., 327
Saltonstall, D., 1
Sampson, R. J., 149, 155–56, 158–59, 188
Scanzoni, J., 239
Schlossberger, N. M., 297
Schmiedeskamp, M., 280
Schoen, E. J., 279
Schrof, J. M., 1
Schwartz, P., 197
Scott, J., 197–98
Scott, S. R., 46
Secord, P., 47
Segraves, R. T., 354
Seiver, D. A., 391
Sessions, D. N., 382, 409
Shawbuck, C. R., 149
Shepherd, M., 451
Shilts, R., 11

Silverstein, M., 356
Simon, C., 334, 345
Simon, W., 6, 43, 198, 199, 224
Simons, K. J., 439
Singer, B., 241
Skatrud, J. D., 380–81
Skeen, D., 109
Small, S. A., 46
Smith, F. R., 280
Smith, J. C., 425, 426, 430, 432, 433, 434
Smith, T., 201, 239, 379, 424, 442
Snowman, L., 278
Sonenstein, F., 46, 201
Sonenstein, F. L., 77, 91, 200, 439
Sorell, G. T., 66
Spector, I. P., 354
Spelman, E., 197–98, 200
Spira, A., 439
Spitze, G. D., 46
Sprecher, S., 244
Staples, R., 197, 201
Sterk-Elifson, C., 200, 201, 203
Stevans, L. K., 382, 409
Sudman, S., 2
Sweet, J. A., 44, 53, 242
Symons, D., 240

Tanfer, K., 243
Tanner, M. A., 356
Terr, L. C., 149, 153
Thomas, J. C., 330
Thomson, E., 243
Thornton, A., 41, 44, 48, 239
Timberlake, C. A., 201
Townsend, J. M., 240, 241, 267
Trent, K., 382, 399
Tribe, L. H., 378
Trussell, J., 380
Tucker, M. J., 330
Turner, C. F., 3, 450
Turner, R. A., 297

Udry, J. R., 7, 41, 45, 47, 75–76, 78, 112, 200
Uebersax, J. S., 356, 370
Umberson, D, 158–59
Urquiza, A. J., 152, 156

van den Oever, F., 43
Van Howe, R. S., 297
Van Vort, J., 430, 431
Vermund, S. H., 452

Vinovskis, M., 77
Vobejda, B., 1

Wadsworth, J., 440, 442
Wagstaff, D., 201
Waite, L. J., 46, 47, 239
Wallerstein, E., 278, 279
Walzer, S., 379
Wasserheit, J. N., 330, 344, 345
Weinberg, M., 200, 203, 204, 205, 206
Weiss, E. B., 277
Weiss, G. N., 277
Welch, M. R., 379
Westoff, C. F., 46, 48, 91, 93
Whitehead, H., 7
Wiederman, M. W., 4
Williams, C., 200, 203, 204
Williams, C. J., 47, 201
Williams, L., 161
Williams, R. M., 199–200

Willis, R. J., 391
Wilson, W. J., 44, 204, 205
Wincze, J. P., 165
Wingood, G. M., 302–3
Wirth, J., 278
Wiswell, T., 280
Witsberger, C., 46
Wood, P. B., 155
Woodhouse, D. E., 345
Wu, L. L., 45, 63
Wyatt, G. E., 46, 156

Yamaguchi, K., 371
Yellen, J. L., 74
York, J. A., 439
Yorke, J. A., 330, 334
Young, M. A., 356, 370

Zelnik, M., 41, 77, 91, 200, 450

SUBJECT INDEX

■

abortion: adolescents and, 78, *86,* 87, 99, 104n. 28; AGI-CDC data on, 385–86, 430–31, 434–35; circumstances affecting choice of, 389–93, 394, 419–20, 481; conception by conception model, 33–34, *397,* 398–400, *400, 401,* 402, 420; data quality and, 383–86, 422–24, 435; definition of, 424–25; demographic characteristics and, 381–83; determinants of, 377–78, 380–83, 388–89, 419–25, 459–61; first conception and, 402, *403,* 404–6, *405, 407, 408,* 409–12, *410, 411;* Medicaid and, 380, 381, 421–22; NHSLS compared to AGI data, 384, 425–26, *426,* 428; NHSLS compared to vital statistics data, 426–28, *427;* NHSLS data on, 384, 425–30, *426, 427;* opinions affecting choice of, 393–94, *403,* 409, *410,* 410–12, *411,* 420; prevalence of, *395,* 395–96, *397, 398,* 398–99; previously reported results, 388; as public good, 468; public opinion about, 378, 379; *Roe v. Wade* and, 3, 46; second conception and, 412, *413, 414,* 414–15; spontaneous vs. induced, 386–87, 424–25; subsequent fertility behavior and, 417, *418,* 419; third conception and, 415, *416,* 417, *417, 418,* 419; waiting period for, 380–81. *See also* Alan Guttmacher Institute (AGI) data

abstinence, 474–75

adjacents, 334, 476

adolescents: abortion and, 78, *86,* 87, 99, 104n. 28; birth control and, 77–78, 93–95, *96,* 97, *98;* delinquency theories and, 155–56; deviant behavior in, 175, 187, 193

adolescent sexual experience: analysis of, 50–51; Catholicism and, 48; childhood sexual contact and, 49; class and, 47–48; cost and rewards of, 42–45; descriptive statistics on, 51, *52,* 53; determinants of, 42; education of parents and, 57, *58,* 60; estimates of, *68–70;* family structure and, 48–49; females and, 57, *58–60,* 60; as forced, 102n. 19; frequency of activity, 77, 91, 94–95, *96,* 97, *98;* males, 53, *54–56,* 56–57, 61–64; models of, 53, *54–56,* 56–57, *58–60,* 60–61; outcomes of, 41; overview of, 105–6; personal biography and, 45, 67; pubertal development and, 45, 49, 65; race and, 48; research on, 41–42, 200; sample and data on, 49; sexual revolution and, 46; sibling sexual behavior and, 102–3n. 21; social controls on, 47; substantive variables in, 50. *See also* teenage childbearing; teenage pregnancy

adult-child sexual experience: description of, 151, 163, 272; men and, *177,* 187–89, 192; peer contact and, 196n. 17; sexual dysfunction and, 365; trauma concept and, 152–53, 193; withdrawal from sexual activity and, 189–90; women and, *176,* 183, 186–87, 191–92. *See also* childhood sexual experience; psychogenic perspective

"Aetiology of Hysteria, The" (Freud), 149–50

affairs: Britain compared to U.S., 443–44, *445;* emotional satisfaction and, 257–58; physical pleasure and, 263–64; reverse causality and, 267–68

African Americans. *See* black individuals

age: abortion and, 391, *397, 398,* 398–99; 419; abortion at first conception and, *403,* 404–5; circumcision, sexual dysfunction, and, 289, *290,* 298–99; as master status, 7–8; sexual behavior and, 16; sexual expression and, *124,* 126; sexual scripts and, 210

AIDS: appropriateness of behavior change due to, 317–18, 320; behavior change due to, 26–27, 302–3, 316–17, 458, 474–75; Britain compared to U.S., 439–40, 452–53; demographics of behavior change due to, 306, *307, 308, 309–10,* 311–13, *312;* inconsistencies in behavior change due to, 318; measures of behavior change due to, 303–4; NHSLS and, 4–5; number of cases of, 13; prevalence of behavior change due to, 316–17, 322–23; prevention efforts for, 27, 302, 303, 317–18, 319–20; purposiveness of behavior change due to, 319; risk of, 26; sex practices and behavior change, 313–16, *314;* spread of, 13, 26–27; types of behavior change due to, 304–6, *305*

Alan Guttmacher Institute (AGI) data: accuracy of, 385, 424; description of, 383, 430–33, *431;* NHSLS data compared to, 384, 425–26, *426,* 428; Web page for, 438n. 18

Alan Guttmacher Institute (AGI)[nd]Centers for Disease Control (CDC) data, 385–86, 430–31, 434–35

anal sex, 446, *446*

antisocial behavior, 471, *472,* 482

anxiety during sexual activity, 188, 189

autoerotic activity: as category, 114; circumcision and, *291,* 292, 299; emotional satisfaction and, 257, 267–68; frequency of, 116; men and, 118; partnered sexual activity and, 245–46; women and, 121

autoerotic single category of women, *120,* 120–21, *122, 123*

baby boom era, adolescent sexual behavior in, 43–45

backward stepwise selection method, 335

Baltimore, David, 13

behavior change: advice giving and, 319–20, 474; AIDS and, *25,* 26–27, 302–3, 458; appropriateness of, 317–18, 320; attitude change compared to, 318, 321; choice compared to institutional model and, 11–12; demographics of, 306, *307, 308, 309–10,* 311–13, *312;* inconsistencies in, 318; at margins, 474–75; measures of, 303–4; number of sex partners and, *307, 308, 310,* 311–13, *312;* prevalence of, 316–17, 322–23; purposiveness of, 319;

self-report measures of, 323; sex practices, AIDS, and, 313–16, *314,* 318; types reported, 304–6, *305;* verbatim responses about, 323–25. *See also* risk-reduction behavior

biological data, 7

birth control: adolescents and, 77–78, 93–95, *96,* 97, *98;* Catholic Church and, 44; choice and outcome of, 73; contraceptive revolution, 46; marital status and, 103–4n. 27; methods of, 103n. 23; women and, 47. *See also* abortion; condoms

black individuals: adolescent interpersonal scripts, 223–24; adolescent sexual behavior in, 44; adult interpersonal scripts, 225, *226–29,* 230; class and sex practices of, 204–5; description of category of, 208; likelihood of early sex and, 62, 64, 65; sex practices of, 200, 201, 203; sexual attitudes of, 214, *215, 216–17,* 218, 235–36; sexual expression and, *125,* 126, 142; STD risk factors for, 338, *339,* 344–47, 351n. 1; STDs in, *342;* teen childbearing and, 81, 86, 87

Britain: number of partners in, 442, *443–44;* opinions about sex practices in, 447, *449;* public policy in, 477; sex practices in, 442–44, *445–46,* 446–47, 461; STDs in, 439–40, 447, *448;* U.S. compared to, 441

Browning, Christopher, viii

cancer and circumcision, 279, 281

Catholic Church and birth control, 44

Catholicism and adolescent sexual experience: likelihood of before age 18, 85–86; men and, 62; teachings on, 48; women and, 64, 65, 91, *92,* 93

Centers for Disease Control and Prevention (CDC): abortion data of, 385–86, 430–31, 432–33, 434–35; AIDS data of, 13; bias in statistics of, 32; prevention marketing initiative of, 451

Cheit, Ross, 148

Chicago Health and Social Life Survey project, viii–ix

Chicago Tribune, 1

childhood sexual experience: background variables, 165–66, *167, 168;* contact variables, 163–64; delinquency theories and, 155–56; dependent measures of, 164–

65; dose-response hypothesis, 176, *178;* effects of, 30–31, 156–58, 482; likelihood of early sex and, 64–65; modeling and, 175–76, *176, 177,* 190–91; nonresponse as source of error and, 160–61; outcome measures and, 166–68, *169–70,* 170, *171–72,* 172, 176–77, *179–83,* 183, *184–85,* 186; outcomes of, 41, 45, 46, 49, 148–49, 192; overview of, 271–72; peer contact in, 163–64, 170, 173, *174,* 177, 191, 192; prevalence data and self-report of, 161–62; psychogenic perspective on, 150–51; rates of, 3; reinforcement in, 156, 190–91; response to, 172–73, *174,* 175; seduction hypothesis, 149–50; sexual dysfunction and, 365, 368–69; sexual expression and, 141–42; social control implications of, 158–59. *See also* adult-child sexual experience

chlamydia trachomatis, 439

choice model: description of, 10, 11–12; institutional model and, 454–57; sexual satisfaction and, 241

choices about sex, 465

circumcision: age at, 301n. 3; analysis of, 282–83; appeal of sex practices and, 292–93, *294–95,* 296, 299–300; community standards and, 454–55; data on, 473–74; debate on, 280–82; in English-speaking countries, 278, 279–80; frequency of, 31, 277, 280, *281;* historical practice of, 277–78; measures of, 283–84; overview of, 457; prevalence of, 284–85, *285,* 296–97; rates of, 285, *286,* 287; sex practices and, 289, *291,* 292, 299; sexual dysfunction and, 289, *290,* 298–99; STDs and, 278, 279, 280, 281, 287, *288,* 289, 297–98; in U.S., 278–80

class: abortion and, 421; adolescent sexual experience and, 47–48; circumcision rates and, 296–97; definition and measurement of, 206; sex practices and, 203–6; sexual attitudes and, 214, *215, 216–17,* 218–20; STD reporting and, 298. *See also* social status

cohabitation: abortion at first conception and, *403,* 404, 406, *408;* commitment and, 243; description of, 239; marriage and dating compared to, 242; sexual expression and, 142–43

cohort effect, 8

collective action problems, 471–72

comfortable monogamist category: of men, 116–17, *117, 119;* of women, 120, *120, 123*

condoms: advertising about, 452; Britain compared to U.S., *446,* 446–47; increase in use of, 101n. 7, 317–18; number of sex partners and use of, 26, *314,* 314–15; race and, 344, *344;* STD risk and use of, 450

confidentiality of data, 380

Confronting AIDS, 13

constructivist approach to sexual dysfunction, 352–53

contact matrix for STDs: construction of, *347,* 347–48, *349;* data on, 333–34, *334, 337,* 343; discussion of, 475–76. *See also* sexual network

contraception. *See* birth control

contraceptive revolution, 46

coping response model, 154

core group concept: analysis of, 330–31; demographic factors and, 335–36, 476; description of, 330, 334; interracial network effect, *342,* 345–46; intraracial network effect, 344–45

cultural scenarios in sexual scripts: description of, 198; measures of, 210–11; race, gender, and class in, 214, *215, 216–17,* 218–20; sex practices and, 220, 223

cunnilingus, appeal of, *231,* 232, *235*

dating: baby boom era and, 43–45; changes in, 62–63; definition of, 244; heterogeneity of, 243; marriage and cohabitation compared to, 242; time horizon, satisfaction, and pleasure, 264–65

delinquency, theories of, 155–56

desire, disorders of, 165

dose-response hypothesis, 150–51, 152–53, 176, *178*

double standard in baby boom era, 43, 44

economic choice framework for abortion, 380

education: abortion and, 391–92, 419–20; abortion at first conception and, 402, *403,* 404, 406, *408,* 409; abortion at second conception and, 412, *413,* 414, *414;* circumcision rates and, *286,* 287; decision of teen to have sex and, 57, *58–60,* 60–61, 63, 65, 80, 86, 87, 480–81; effect of on sex practices, 203–5; sexual atti-

education (*continued*)
    tudes and, *215, 216–17,* 218–20; sexual
    dysfunction and, *358, 360,* 361; sexual ex-
    pression and, *124,* 127. *See also* class
education of parents: abortion and, 87;
    abortion at first conception and, 402,
    403, 404, 406, *408,* 409; abortion at sec-
    ond conception and, 412, *413,* 414, *414;*
    female sexual behavior and, 57, *58,* 60–
    61, 65; likelihood of early sex and, 86,
    87; male sexual behavior and, 63; teen
    childbearing and, 80, 86, *86,* 87, 480–81
emotional investment: description of,
    242–43; emotional satisfaction and, *251–*
    52, 253–54, 255–56; measures of, 245;
    men and, 265–66, *269;* physical pleasure
    and, 263
emotional problems and stress, 129, 131,
    132–33
employment status of mother: teen
    childbearing and, 100; teen sexual activ-
    ity and, 479
England: circumcision in, 278, 279. *See*
    also Britain
enthusiastic cohabitor category of women,
    120, 121, *123*
enthusiastic polygamist category of men,
    117, 118–19, *119*
erectile dysfunction: circumcision and, 289,
    290; as public health problem, 354, 369;
    quality-of-life and, 366
erotic activity, 116, 146n. 4
ethnicity. *See* race
event history model, 71n. 6
evolutionary biology perspective, 240–41,
    243, 257, 263, 267
excitement, disorders of, 165
exclusivity: emotional satisfaction and,
    251–52, 253–54, 256–58; measures of,
    245–46; physical pleasure and, 263–64
externalities: collective judgment and, 471–
    72, 485; social behavior and, 468–70, *472*

family structure: abortion and, 393–94,
    403, 404; adolescent sexual experience
    and, 48–49; at age fourteen, 50; likeli-
    hood of early sex and, 63, 86, *92,* 93; step-
    parent and, 63, 66–67; teen childbearing
    and, 79–80, 100. *See also* single-parent
    family
fantasy, assumptions about, 112
Feinleib, Joel, ix

fellatio: appeal of, *231,* 232, *235;* circumci-
    sion and, 292–93, *294–95,* 296
fertility control. *See* birth control
foreign birth: adolescent sexual behavior
    and, 63, 66, 67; likelihood of early sex
    and, 86; teen childbearing and, 80
Freud, Sigmund, 149–50

Gagnon, John H., vii, 1, 14
gender: abortion and, *397, 398,* 398–99;
    abortion rate by conception and, 399–
    400, *400, 401,* 402; adolescent sexual ac-
    tivity and, 51; blacks, sexual attitudes,
    and, 218; division of roles by, 43–44;
    early sexual activity and, 224–25, *226–29;*
    evolutionary biology perspective and,
    240–41, 243, 257, 263, 267; as master sta-
    tus, 6, 7; monogamous classes and, 121;
    opinions on abortion and, *403,* 409, *410,*
    410–12, *411;* rational choice model and,
    241; reports of pregnancies and, 394;
    satisfaction and, 131, 250; sex practice
    based on, 201–3; sexual attitudes and,
    215, 216–17, 218; sexual behavior and,
    16, *17–18;* sexual content and, 128–29,
    130; sexual dysfunction and, 362, 367;
    sexual expression and, 123, *124–25,* 126–
    28; sexual network and, 122; sexual scripts
    and, 199, 238; STDs and, 333, *333*
Glamour, 1
gonorrhea, 439, 475–76
Gorner, Peter, 1
group membership: adolescent sexual be-
    havior and, 42–43, 64; dating and, 43–45;
    research on, 67; statistics on, 51, *52, 53*

hazard model, 101n. 11
health-illness complex, 352–53
Helms, Jesse, 12
Hispanic individuals: description of cate-
    gory of, 208; likelihood of early sex in,
    63; sex practices of, 201–2; sexual expres-
    sion and, *125,* 126, 142; STDs in, *342;*
    teen pregnancy and, 86. *See also* Mexi-
    can American individuals
HIV/AIDS. *See* AIDS
homosexuality: attitudes toward, 219, 483–
    84. *See also* same-gender sexual scripts;
    same-sex activity
human sexuality: comprehensive approach
    to, 14–15; expressions of, 109–11; view
    of, 4, 5, 20, 22–23

impulse control and childhood sexual experience, 156
individualism, increase in, 46–47
individual-level risk factor, 329
individual preference and sexual expression, 112
infidelity. *See* affairs
institutional model: description of, 10–12; rational choice model and, 454–57; sexual expression and, 455–56
intercourse: pain during, 165. *See also* vaginal intercourse
interpersonal scripts: adolescent type, 223–25; adult type, 225, *226–29*, 230; analysis of, 209; blacks and, 235–36; description of, 198; measures of, 212–13; Mexican Americans and, 236; race, class, and gender in, 220, *221–22*, 223; whites and, 233–34
intrapsychic scripts: analysis of, 209–10; description of, 198; measures of, 213; race, class, and gender in, 230, *231*, 232–33

jointness of sexual behavior, 465, 466–68, 471, *472*, 478–82
Joyner, Kara, viii
Joy of Sex (Comfort), 489

Kinsey, Alfred, 14, 487–88
Kinsey Reports, 4, 13–14
Kolata, Gina, 1

latent class analysis (LCA): comparison of fit of, *145;* description of, 146n. 5, 195n. 6; latent class model, 370; for men, 116–19, *117, 119;* overview of, 111; of sexual dysfunction, 356, 362, *363–64, 366,* 369–72, *371, 372;* stages and results of, 370–72, *371, 372;* for women, *120,* 120–22, *123*
latent class model, 370
Latinos. *See* Hispanic individuals; Mexican American individuals
Laumann, Edward O., 1, 14
legitimacy of relationship, 9
Lewontin, Richard C., 2, 491n. 8
life-course perspective: adult-child sex and, 156–59, 173, *174,* 175; childhood sexual experience and, 30, 482; delinquency theories and, 155–56; description of, 7–8, 149; hypotheses of, 159, 160; modeling and, 175–76, *176, 177,* 190–91; outcome measures and, 176–77, *179–83,* 183, *184–*

85; psychogenic perspective compared to, 154–55; sexual expression and, 144
logistic, 35, *35*
logistic analysis, 35–37
log-linear analysis, 336
log-odds ratio, 37

Mahay, Jenna, viii–ix
marital-specific capital, 242
marital status: abortion and, 382–83, 390, 419; abortion at first conception and, *403,* 404, 406, *408;* abortion at second conception and, 412, *413;* abortion at third conception and, 415, *416,* 417; baby boom era and, 44; emotional investment and, 256; pregnancy and, 436–37n. 7; satisfaction and, 255, 258, 265–68, *268, 269,* 456–57; sexual behavior and, 16; sexual dysfunction and, *358, 359,* 361, 367–68; sexual expression and, *124,* 127, *128;* teen childbearing and, 100, 103n. 26, 103–4n. 27. *See also* cohabitation; dating; marriage
marriage: dating and cohabitation compared to, 242; institution of, 242–44, 267; postponement of, 46; sexual satisfaction and, 243–44
Masi, Christopher, ix
master relationships: "coupleness" and, 31; description of, 8; motivations of participants in, 9–10; social visibility of, 8–9
master statuses: adult interpersonal scripts and, 225, *226–29,* 230; effects of, 7–8; empirical properties of, 6–7; ethnicity and, 207–9; as heterogeneous, 6–7; list of, 6; sexual expression and, 123, *124–25,* 126–28, 237; sexual scripts and, 210
mastery impulse, 150
masturbation. *See* autoerotic activity
matching pattern simulation, 348–50
Medicaid and abortion, 380, 381, 421–22
men: adult-child sex and, *177,* 187–89, 192; childhood sexual experience and, *168,* 170, *171–72,* 172, *178, 181–82, 184–85,* 192; comfortable monogamist category of, 116–17, *117, 119;* emotional satisfaction of, 250, *251–52,* 255; enthusiastic polygamist category of, *117,* 118–19, *119;* fertility rates of, 437n. 9; health issues and, 195n. 9; likelihood of early sex in, 53, *54–56,* 56–57, 61–64, *68–69;* moderate polygamist category of, 117, *117, 119;*

men (*continued*)
  physical pleasure and, 258, *259–60;* same-
    gender sexual scripts and, 158, 188; satis-
    faction of, 129, 131, *132,* 265–66, *269;*
    sexual dysfunction in, 188–89, 357, *359–
    60,* 361; sexual expression in, 116–19,
    135–37; sexual network pattern among,
    145; stability of relationships and, 188;
    venturesome cohabitor category of, 117,
    117, 119, 122, *122. See also* circumcision
menarche, modal age of, 53
Mexican American individuals: adolescent
    interpersonal scripts, 223; adult interper-
    sonal scripts, 225, *226–29,* 230; descrip-
    tion of category of, 208; sex practices of,
    202; sexual attitudes of, 214, *215, 216–
    17,* 236–37, 483. *See also* Hispanic indi-
    viduals
Michael, Robert T., 1, 14
Michaels, Stuart, viii, 1
miscarriage, 386–87, *395,* 396, 424–25
moderate polygamist category: of men, 117,
    117, 119; of women, *120,* 121, *123*
modes of sexual expression, definition of, 29
money illusion, 488
monogamy. *See* exclusivity; mutually mo-
    nogamous relationship
motivations of participants in relationships,
    9–10
mutually monogamous relationship, 114–
    15, *115, 128,* 143–44
mutually polygamous relationship, 114–15,
    115, 118–19, *128*

National Center for Health Statistics
    (NCHS) data, 434–35
National Health and Social Life Survey
    (NHSLS): approach of, 14–15; books
    based on, 5–6; critique of, 2, 491n. 8; de-
    scription of, 13, 441; features of, 15; fund-
    ing for, 12–13; measurement error and,
    160–61, 162; news stories about, 1–2, 4;
    objectives for, 13; political history of,
    4–5, 12, 14; sample size and, 14; team
    for, vii, 14
National Institutes of Health (NIH), 4–5
National Longitudinal Survey of Youth
    (NLSY), 102–3n. 21, 382, 384, 434
National Opinion Research Center
    (NORC), 13
National Survey of Family Growth
    (NSFG), 76, 77, 80, 383, 434

National Survey of Young Women
    (NSYW), 383–84, 434
neonatal circumcision. *See* circumcision
network. *See* sexual network; social
    network
network-oriented models of epidemiology,
    32–33
New York Daily News, 1
New Yorker, The, 1
New York Review of Books, 2
New York Times, 1, 4
NHSLS. *See* National Health and Social
    Life Survey (NHSLS)
norms and adolescent sexual behavior, 42,
    43–45

odds ratio, 36
opinions about sex practices, Britain com-
    pared to U.S., 447, *449,* 450–51
opportunity cost: abortion and, 391–93,
    421; sexual activity and, 76, 80
oral sex: appeal of, 16, *18,* 19, *231,* 232,
    235; Britain compared to U.S., 444, 446,
    446; childhood sexual experiences and,
    190; circumcision and, *291,* 292–93, *294–
    95,* 296; sexual content and, 128, *130*
ordered logit model, 195n. 12
orgasm and emotional satisfaction, *251,
    253,* 255
orgasmic disorder, 165

Paik, Anthony, viii–ix
pain during intercourse, 165
parents: decision of teen to have sex and,
    76, 102n. 13; education level and abor-
    tion at first conception, 402, *403,* 404,
    406, *408,* 409; education level and abor-
    tion at second conception, 412, *413,* 414,
    414; education level and abortion deci-
    sion, 419–20; education level and deci-
    sion of teen to have sex, 57, *58–60,* 60–
    61, 63, 65, 80, 86, 87, 480–81; mother's
    employment and teen childbearing, 100;
    mother's employment and teen sexual ac-
    tivity, 479; as role models, 45
parity and abortion, 390. *See also* abortion:
    conception by conception model
Parsons, Talcott, 353
partnered sexual activity: autoerotic activ-
    ity and, 118, 121; as category, 114; fre-
    quency of, 115, *144*
peer sexual experience in childhood: adult-

child sexual experience and, 196n. 17; men and, 170, 187; number of sex partners and, 173; overview of, 272; variable for, 163–64, *174;* well-being and, 191, 192; women and, 177

peripherals, 334, 476

physical health and sexual expression, 112, 142

physical pleasure: circumcision and, 299–300; emotional investment and, 263; exclusivity and, 263–64; measures of, 249; satisfaction and, 258, *259–60, 261–62,* 262; time horizon and, 264–65

polarized response to trauma: psychogenic vs. life-course perspective, 159, 172–73, *174,* 175; PTSD framework and, 152, 153, 154

politicization of sexual health, 353, 487–88

population: growth of, 470; segmentation of, 27

posttraumatic stress disorder (PTSD) model, 149, 152–53, 190

pregnancy: marital status and, 436–37n. 7; miscarriage, 386–87, *395,* 396, 424–25; parity and abortion, 390; probability of with early sex, 74, 83, *83,* 86, *86,* 93–99, *96, 98;* spontaneous abortion, 386–87; stigma of, 44. *See also* abortion; teenage childbearing; teenage pregnancy

premature ejaculation, 366, 369

primarily monogamous relationship, 114–15, *115,* 121, *128*

primarily polygamous relationship, 114–15, *115,* 118, 122, 127, *128*

probability: of abortion, *83,* 83–84, *86,* 87, 99; of event, 36; of having early sex, 73, 84–86, *86,* 90–93; hazard rate, 101n. 2; of live birth before age 18, 74, *83,* 83–84, *86,* 87–90, *88;* of pregnancy with early sex, 74, 83, *83,* 86, *86,* 93–99, *96, 98*

probability sample for survey, 13

Protestant, Type I and Type II, *125,* 126, 147n. 12

psychogenic perspective: assumptions of, 150–51; conceptions of trauma, 152–53; description of, 30, 149; hypotheses of, 159, 160; modeling and, 175–76, *176, 177;* response to adult-child sex and, 173, *174;* shortcomings of, 153–55

pubertal development: decision to have sex and, 75; determination of, 71n. 2, 71n. 5;

likelihood of early sex and, 85–86, 91, *92;* menarche, modal age of, 53; sexual activity and, 45, 49, 65; teen childbearing and, 78–79, 480

public good, 467, 468, 472

public nudity, 482–83

public policy: antisocial behavior and, 482; Britain compared to U.S., 450–53, 477–78; choice approach to, 10, 11–12; choices regarding sexual behavior and, 468–70; collective judgment and, 484–86; consequences of sexual behavior and, 470–72, *472;* disease and other health issues, 471, *472,* 473–78; funding of research, 4–5; institutional approach to, 10–12; jointness of sexual behavior and, 465, 466–68, 471, *472,* 478–82; sexual behavior of young people and, 41; sexual choices and, 465–66; sexual data and, 22; STDs and, 456, 459, 461–62; tastes, preferences, and judgments and, 482–84

quality-of-life concomitants of sexual dysfunction, *366,* 366–67, 376

race: abortion and, 382–83, 417, *417, 418,* 422–23; abortion at first conception and, *408,* 409; adolescent interpersonal scripts and, 223–24; adolescent sexual experience and, 44, 48; behavior change due to AIDS and, *309,* 311; categories of, 206–7; circumcision rates and, 285, *286,* 287, 296–97; interpersonal scripts and, 220, *221–22,* 223; intrapsychic scripts and, 230, *231,* 232–33; likelihood of early sex and, 62, 63, 64, 65; oral sex, circumcision, and, 293, *294–95,* 296; sex partnership and, 198–99, 237, 476; sex practices, circumcision, and, *291,* 292; sex practices based on, 199–201, 205; sexual attitudes and, 214, *215, 216–17,* 218; sexual dysfunction and, *359, 360,* 361; sexual expression and, *125,* 126, 142; sexual scripts and, 233, 237–38; STD and interracial effect, 337–38, 341, *342,* 348–50; STD and intraracial effect, 336–37, *337, 340,* 340–41; STD rates and, 327–31, *328,* 458–59; STD risk factors and, 344–45; STD type and, 343–44; teen childbearing and, 81, *98,* 99, 481; teen pregnancy and, 86, 87. *See also* black individuals; Hispanic individuals; white individuals rational choice model. *See* choice model

recreational view of sex: attitudes toward, 219; blacks and, 235; description of, 22–23, 211

relational view of sex: description of, 22–23, 211; whites and, 233–34

relationship: legitimacy of, 9; men and stability of, 188; motivations of participants in, 9–10; social visibility of, 8–9; status of and satisfaction, 265–68, *268, 269. See also specific type of relationship,* e.g. mutually monogamous relationship

religious affiliation: abortion and, 393, *403,* 409; adolescent sexual behavior and, 66; birth control and, 44; circumcision and, 277–78, 285, *286,* 296; fundamentalism, 102n. 20; interpersonal scripts and, 233–34, 236; as latent characteristic, 6; Protestant, *125,* 126, 147n. 12; sexual expression and, *125,* 126; teen childbearing and, 79. *See also* Catholicism and adolescent sexual experience

represssion, 160–61

reproductive view of sex, 22

research on sexual behavior: diversity of opinion, practice, and appeal of and, 486; funding of, 4–5; interactions of time and circumstance on results of, 479–80; overview of, 486–90; views on, 466. *See also* self-report measures

reverse causality, 267–68

risk-reduction behavior: advice about, 319–20, 474; appropriateness of, 317–18, 320; choice of, 318–19, 474–75; complexity of, 321; demographics and, *312,* 313; effectiveness of, 321–22; precursors to, 306, 318, 321; sex practices and, *314,* 315

Roe v. Wade: abortion at first conception and, 402, *403;* description of, 3, 46; public opinion since, 379

Rosen, Raymond C., ix

same-gender sexual scripts, 158, 188, 190–91

same-sex activity: Britain compared to U.S., 442–43, *445;* legality of, 469; opinions about, Britain compared to U.S., 447, *449;* sexual dysfunction and, 365, 368; variable for, 375

satisfaction: adult-child sex, men, and, 187–88; adult-child sex, women, and,

186; analysis of, 246, *247–48,* 249; circumcision and, 280; emotional investment and, *251–52, 253–54,* 255–56; emotional type, 250, *251–52, 253–54,* 255; exclusivity and, *251–52, 253–54,* 256–58; frequency of sex and, *144;* hypotheses of, 243–44; marital status and, 456–57; measures of, 244–46, 249; men and, 265–66, *269;* models of, 246, 248; overview of, *18,* 19–20, 273–74; physical pleasure and, 258, *259–60, 261–62,* 262; relationship status and, 265–68, *268, 269;* sexual dysfunction and, *366,* 366–67; sexual expression and, 129, 131, *132–33,* 134; theories on, 240–41; time horizon and, 264–65; well-being and, 164, 170; women and, 266, *268*

seduction hypothesis, 149–50

self-control and childhood sexual activity, 192

self-report measures: of abortion prevalence, 384, 422, 428–30, 431–32, 436n. 3; of behavior change, 323; of childhood sexual experience, 161–62; overview of, 2–4; of sexual behaviors and attitudes, 491n. 8; of sexual dysfuntion, 355–56; of STDs, 298, 341, 343

Sex in America (Michael, Gagnon, Laumann, and Kolata): criticism of, 488; main findings of, 16–27; publication of, vii; purpose of, 5; release date of, 1

sex partnership: Britain compared to U.S., 442, *443–44;* as category, 114; choices in, 466–67; dimensions of, 114–15; early sex experience and, 157–58; expectations about and behaviors within, 242–44; number of, 3–4, *17,* 351n. 2, 424; number of and AIDS, *307,* 308, *310,* 311–13, *312;* number of and STDs, *24–25, 314,* 315–16, 331, 333, *333;* race and, 198–99, 237, 476; selection in, 321–22; social characteristics and, 20–23, *21;* STDs and, *24–25,* 287, *288,* 289, 322–23, 329–30, 447, *448,* 450; types of, 239–40. *See also* cohabitation; dating; marriage

sexual abuse. *See* adult-child sexual experience; childhood sexual experience

sexual activity: AIDS and, 313–16, *314,* 318; anxiety during, 188, 189; appeal of types of, *18;* Britain compared to U.S., 442–44, *445–46,* 446–47, 449–50, 461; circumcision and, 289, *291,* 292–93, *294–95,* 296, 299–300; as conventional, 16, *17–19,* 19–20; cultural scenarios and, 220, 223; decision to initiate, 75–77; definition of, 15; as form of social action, 352, 353; frequency of, *17,* 77; jointness of, 465, 466–68, 478–82; markers or indicators for, 113; public choices regarding, 468–70; public consequences of, 470–72, *472;* satisfaction and, 244–45. *See also* autoerotic activity; erotic activity; partnered sexual activity

sexual behavior. *See* sexual activity

sexual dysfunction: adult-child sex, men, and, 188–89, 192; adult-child sex, women, and, 186–87; analysis of, 283, 284, 356–57, 476–77; childhood sexual experience and, 165, 168, 170, 172, 365, 368–69; circumcision and, 289, *290,* 298–99; demographic factors and, 367–68; DSM-IV classification of, 354, 355, 362; frequency of, 19; help-seeking behavior and, 367; latent class analysis and, 356, 362, *363–64, 366,* 369–72, *371;* measures of, 355–56; need vs. enhancement in, 455; performance vs. deviance problems, 376n. 3; prevalence of, 3, 33, 357, *358–60,* 361, 459; quality-of-life concomitants of, *366,* 366–67, 376; risk factors for, 362, *363–64,* 365, 368–69; sexual expression and, 131, *132–33;* social epidemiological approach to, 353–55; as subject of study, 352–53; variables for, 372–76

sexual expression: description of, 110; determinants of, 111–13, *135–40,* 483; dimensions of, 111; master statuses and, 123, *124–25,* 126–28; in men, 116–19, *117, 119, 135–37, 145;* overview of, 270–71; satisfaction and, 129, 131, *132–33,* 134; sexual content and, 128–29, *130;* in women, *120,* 120–22, *123, 138–40, 145*

sexuality. *See* human sexuality

sexualized behavior, 154, 156, 157, 158–59, 193

sexually transmitted disease (STD): analysis of, 284, 330–31; bias in statistics on, 32, 327–29; Britain compared to U.S., 34, 439–40, 441, 447, *448,* 461; chlamydia trachomatis, 439; circumcision, number of partners, and, 287, *288,* 289; circumci-

sion and, 278, 279, 280, 281, 297–98; demographic factors and, 335–36, 475; enthusiastic polygamist and, 118; externalities and, 469; gonorrhea, 439, 475–76; interracial effect, 337–38, 341, *342,* 345–46, 348–50; intraracial effect, 336–37, *337, 340,* 340–41, 344–45; lifetime risk of, 338, *339;* network aspects of, 329–30; number of partners and, *314,* 315–16; partner selection and, 321–22; prevalence of, 23, *24–25,* 26, 331, 333, *333;* public policy and, 459, 461–62; race and, 458–59; rates of, 19, 327–31, *328;* rational choice vs. institutional model in, 456; risk factors for, 23, *24–25,* 26, 322–23, 343; self-report measures of, 298, 341, 343; types of, 313; variable measures of, 331, *332;* viral vs. bacterial, 343. *See also* AIDS

sexual network: contact matrix analysis, 333–34, *334, 337,* 343; forms of, 114–15, *115;* men and, 118, *145;* satisfaction and, *144;* sexual expression and, *145;* STDs and, 329–30; STDs and interracial effect, 337–38, 341, *342,* 345–46, 348–50; STDs and intraracial effect, 336–37, *337, 340,* 340–41, 344–45; women and, 122, *122, 145*

sexual pluralism, 485–86

sexual practice. *See* sexual activity

sexual revolution: adolescent sexual behavior and, 46, 51, *52,* 53, 85; dates of, 28; females and, 64–67; males and, 61–64; sex practices and, 239

sexual scripts: analysis of, 209–10; overview of, 197–98, 272–73; race and, 233, 237–38; theories of variations in, 198–99; variables in analysis of, 210–13. *See also* interpersonal scripts; intrapsychic scripts

single-parent family: adolescent sexual activity and, 45, 48–49, 63, 478–79; likelihood of early sex and, 65; stigma of pregnancy and, 44

social class. *See* class

social competence and sexual expression, 112–13, 143

social control: adolescent sexual experience, 47, 75; theory of, 155–56, 158–59

social embeddedness of sex lives, 20–23, *21*

socialization, definition of, 155

social learning theory, 155, 158

social network and sex partnership, 115
social opportunity and sexual expression,
    113
Social Organization of Sexuality, The (Lau-
    mann, Gagnon, Michael, and Michaels):
    authors of, viii; main findings of, 16–27;
    publication of, vii; purpose of, 5; race
    and sex partnership, 198–99; release date
    of, 1; sexual expression dimensions, 113–
    16; truthfulness of respondents and, 2–3
social policy. *See* public policy
social status: early sexual activity and, 224;
    sexual dysfunction and, 365, 368. *See
    also* class
social visibility of relationship, 8–9
"sodomy," 469
sources for information about sex, 16
spontaneous abortion, 386–87
stakeholders and institutional model, 10–
    11, 12
*Statistical Abstract of the United States,
    The*, 426–28, *427*
status groups, 6
STD. *See* sexually transmitted disease
    (STD)
stepparent, 63, 66–67
stress: sexual dysfunction and, 368–69;
    trauma and, 152–53; variable for, 374
survey data: advantages of, 423–24; con-
    cerns about responses to, 2–4; contribu-
    tion of, 4. *See also* self-report measures

teenage childbearing: abortion and, 78, *83,*
    83–84, 86, 87, 99; age and, *92, 98;* anal-
    ysis of, 84–88, *85, 86;* birth control and,
    77–78, 93–95, *96,* 97, *98;* blacks, class,
    and, 204–5; decision to have sex and, 75–
    77, 84–86, *86,* 90–93, 102n. 13; decompo-
    sition of risk of, 73–75, 82–84, *83;* family
    structure and, 79–80, 86, *92,* 93; fertility
    rates and, 102n. 15; foreign birth and, 80,
    86; marriage and, 100, 103n. 26, 103–4n.
    27; mother's employment and, 100; op-
    portunity cost and, 80; overview of, 72,
    106; parent education and, 80, 86, *86,* 87,
    480–81; probability of pregnancy and,
    83, *83,* 86, *86,* 93–99, *96,* 97, *98;* probabil-
    ity predictions and, *88,* 88–90; pubertal
    development and, 78–79, 85–86, 91, *92,*
    480; race and, 81, 86, 87, *98,* 99, 481; reli-
    gious beliefs and, 79, 85–86, 91, *92,* 93;

statistics on, 81–84; time differences and,
    87, 89
teenage pregnancy: abortion and, 383;
    NHSLS data on, 438n. 16; race and, 86,
    87; timing of, 436n. 6
teleonymy, 353, 376n. 2
Time, 1
time horizon, emotional satisfaction, and
    physical pleasure, 246, 258, 264–65
traditional view of sex: description of, 211;
    Mexican Americans and, 214, *215, 216–
    17,* 236
trauma: conceptions of, 149, 152–53, 190,
    193; description of, 150; effects of, *151,*
    151–52; polarized response to, 152, 153,
    154, 159, 172–73, *174,* 175; represssion
    and, 160–61; sexual dysfunction and,
    365, 368–69
traumagenic dynamics model, 149, 153
Trauma or Transition (Browning), 156, 157
truthfulness of respondents to survey. *See*
    self-report measures
"20/20," 1
typological trauma theory, 149, 153

United States: ambivalence in, 451–52; di-
    versity of opinions and practices in, 450–
    51, 477–78, 482–83, 484–85
urinary tract infection and circumcision,
    280, 281
U.S. News and World Report, 1

vaginal intercourse, 230, *231,* 232, 233,
    234
venturesome cohabitor category of men,
    117, *117, 119,* 122, *122*
Viagra, 353, 455–56

Wadsworth, Jane, ix
Waite, Linda, ix
waiting period for abortion, 380–81
Washington Post, 1
well-being, measures of, 164
white individuals: adolescent interpersonal
    scripts, 223; adult interpersonal scripts,
    225, *226–29,* 230; circumcision and, 299–
    300; description of category of, 207–8;
    ethnicity and religious affiliation of, 207;
    oral sex, circumcision, and, 293, *294–95,*
    296; sex practices, circumcision, and,
    291, 292; sex practices of, 202, 203; sex-

ual attitudes and, 214, *215, 216–17,* 233–34; STDs in, 338, *339, 342*

women: adolescent sexual behavior of, 47; adult-child sex and, *176,* 183, 186–87, 191–92; autoerotic single category of, *120,* 120–21, *122, 123;* childhood sexual experience of, *167,* 168, *169–70,* 170, *178, 179–80, 183,* 191–92; comfortable monogamist category of, 120, *120, 123;* courtship autonomy and, 62–63; education of parents and, 57, *58,* 60–61; emotional satisfaction of, 250, *253–54,* 255; enthusiastic cohabitor category of, *120,* 121, *123;* likelihood of early sex in, 51, 57, *58–60,* 60, 64–67; marital status, satisfaction,

and, 258; moderate polygamist category of, *120,* 121, *123;* number of sex partners, STDs, and, 333, *333;* physical pleasure and, 258, *261–62;* predictions of early sex in, *69–70;* satisfaction of, 131, *133,* 134, 266, *268;* sexual dysfunction in, 186–87, 357, *358–59;* sexual expression in, *138–40;* sexual network pattern among, *145. See also* teenage childbearing

Youm, Yoosik, viii–ix

Zuckerman, Ezra, viii